Plant Lives:
Borderline Beings in Indian Traditions

Plant Lives:

Borderline Beings in Indian Traditions

ELLISON BANKS FINDLY

MOTILAL BANARSIDASS PUBLISHERS
PRIVATE LIMITED • DELHI

First Edition: Delhi, 2008

ISBN: 978-81-208-3292-3

MOTILAL BANARSIDASS
41 U.A. Bungalow Road, Jawahar Nagar, Delhi 110 007
8 Mahalaxmi Chamber, 22 Bhulabhai Desai Road, Mumbai 400 026
120 Royapettah High Road, Mylapore, Chennai 600 004
236, 9th Main III Block, Jayanagar, Bangalore 560 011
Sanas Plaza, 1302 Baji Rao Road, Pune 411 002
8 Camac Street, Kolkata 700 017
Ashok Rajpath, Patna 800 004
Chowk, Varanasi 221 001

Printed in India
BY JAINENDRA PRAKASH JAIN AT SHRI JAINENDRA PRESS,
A-45 NARAINA, PHASE-I, NEW DELHI 110 028
AND PUBLISHED BY NARENDRA PRAKASH JAIN FOR
MOTILAL BANARSIDASS PUBLISHERS PRIVATE LIMITED,
BUNGALOW ROAD, DELHI 110 007

for Fred

as *gurudakṣiṇā*

ye keci pāṇabhūt atthi
tasā vā thāvarā vā anavasesā...
sabbesattā bhavantu sukhitattā.
Sn 146-147

Whatever living creatures there are,
moving or still, without exception...
May all those creatures live happily.

Contents

Acknowledgements

We moved often when I was young, and at every stop I took refuge in the company of a tree. In Norfolk, I ate from a neighbor's fig tree, my fingers wet with sticky juice. In Stonington, I sat under the tails of a willow, making crowns with buttercups. In Rothesay, in the woods of Ascog House, I sat in the arms of ancient rhododendrons, swinging high above my brother. Again in Norfolk, touching mimosa leaves, I watched the sky through fuzzy pink clouds. In Key West, I ate around pungent tamarind seeds and raced my brother up bending palms. In Charleston, I first fell in love under sand-rooted yellow pines. In Hillsdale, I sat with my sister on a rock and spied out scrub trees in her fields. And today, in Hartford, I watch a precious Mongolian cherry grow into its shiny rust-colored bark.

These trees, and their many plant companions, have provided sanctuary for me in a world filled with familial comings and goings and they have, thus, nurtured a private life of great fulfillment and satisfaction. But I have taken for them for granted. I have cut down live branches because they obstructed my view; I have picked and crushed leaves to feel the pleasure of their crisp breaks and geometric juicy pieces; I have rooted out dandelions with vigor and have dreamed lustily of their deaths; and I have poisoned crabgrass with a vengeance reserved for no other objects. This study, then, is by way of confession, a request for absolution, and an expression of gratitude – these beings have given me much and I have abused their gifts. I hope to be more mindful now but know, all the while, that we humans are prone to dangerous self-assertion.

Some of my previous work has focused on the "disenfranchised" in Indian traditions. An early article on B. R. Ambedkar describes the Buddhist ethics of this untouchable leader in twentieth century Maharashtrian political life. Other pieces describe the contributions of women such as the Upaniṣadic philosopher Gārgī, the Mughal empress Nūr Jahān, the Buddhist nun Paṭācārā, and women donors to the early Buddhist Saṅgha. Noticing now the raw deal that plants seem to get in Indian traditions, I am drawn to speak out on their behalf – not to over-idealize them, but to highlight a common, positive reading of threads about them that are found in Hinduism, Jainism, and Buddhism. Such a reading might then show that the raw deal for plants can be reread in an entirely other, and reverential, way. In perhaps the highest expression of the *sattva* temperament, plant beings are compassionate and provide selfless service to others. In that the *sattva* temperament can be attributed to plants – as I argue here and as suggested by traditional texts – the gifts of service on the part of plants are one half of a reciprocal relationship. Thus we note this passage, following Manu 8.15: "A tree protects as it is protected" (*vṛkṣo rakṣati rakṣataḥ*).

* * * * *

As always, I wish to thank Trinity College for its generous support, material and otherwise, in giving me time and resources to work on this project. I benefited, in particular, from a Faculty Research Grant extending from 2003-2005 that helped expand my library. Moreover, on a number of occasions, my colleagues at Trinity, both faculty and students, have listened to various versions of the arguments made here, and to all of them I extend warm thanks for listening so carefully and for giving me such helpful feedback. In particular, I would like to thank my student Alicia Flynn for her work on plants and environmental rights. Her paper, "Environmental Ecology and the Language of 'Rights' in Religion and Law," was written as a part of a faculty-student reading group on nature and environmental ethics undertaken in the spring of 2002. I would also like to thank Michael Williams for his unstinting patience in giving me technical support in the late stages of this project.

I also thank all those who agreed to be interviewed as part of my interest in contemporary views on plants among people involved in environmental activism. I begin with that energetic and inspiring group, Trees for Life, and am most grateful to Balbir and Treva Mathur and to all of their diligent and committed coworkers. I thank as well Shyama and Satish B. and Kumeshwar from the Karunamayi group, Narad and June from the Auroville community, Satish Kumar from Resurgence, and Santikaro Bhikkhu, Phra Paisal Visalo, and Phra Noah Yuttadhammo of the Thai forest tradition. Santikaro Bhikkhu was especially helpful on the history of the tradition, and I am most appreciative of his wonderfully candid remarks and thoughtful analyses.

Several have helped with the gathering of illustrations. David Kimble and Jeffrey Faus provided me with images taken by volunteers for Trees for Life in Orissa. And Susan Stem, a fellow Lao-Tai textile lover, provided me with photo documentation of a tree ordination that took place outside Chiang Mai, Thailand in August of 2005.

A number of encounters have proved fortuitous for this project. Sulak Sivaraksa visited Trinity on a speaking tour in February of 2003, and helped with bibliographic resources. Mrs. Lim Tay Poh of Kuala Lumpur, Malayasia guided me towards a new printing of Ajahn Chah's collection of similes, "A Tree in a Forest," that is dedicated to my father, William Ross Banks. Ranchor Prime, Rani Iyer, Cassia Berman, Maurice Wade, and many others have all steered me in productive directions when I got stuck, and I thank them immensely. Others, like May Oo, Zarni, Holly Fisher, and Nicole Reichenbach, have helped me in thinking about the Buddhism of Southeast Asia.

Finally, I thank my children, those mainstays of my life, who have always shored me up with their good cheer, their energy, and their staying power.

And I thank Fred, whom we lost as this went to press. Along with everything else, he has been my spiritual teacher. A model of right attitude and right practice, Fred was fully present for everyone he encountered, and his deep listening and thoughtful returns made life ever more precious for me.

January 2006
Hartford, Connecticut

Abbreviations

A	Aṅguttara Nikāya
AĀ	Aitareya Āraṇyaka
AB	Aitareya Brāhmaṇa
ĀBh	Acārāṅga Bhāṣyam
AP	Agni Purāṇa
ĀpDS	Āpastamba Dharma Sūtra
ĀpŚS	Āpastamba Śrauta Sūtra
Artha	Arthaśāstra
ĀrU	Āruṇi Upaniṣad
ĀS	Ācārāṅga Sūtra
ĀśGS	Āśvalāyana Gṛhya Sūtra
ĀśSs	Aśvalāyana Śrauta Sūtra
ĀśU	Āśrama Upaniṣad
AU	Aitareya Upaniṣad
AV	Atharva Veda
BAU	Bṛhad-Avadhūta Upaniṣad
BĀU	Bṛhad-āraṇyaka Upaniṣad
BŚS	Baudhāyana Śrauta Sūtra
BCA	Bodhicaryāvatāra
BDS	Baudhāyana Dharma Sūtra
BhŚS	Bhāradvāja Śrauta Sūtra

BhU	Bhikṣuka Upaniṣad
BS	Bṛhat Saṁhitā
BSU	Bṛhat-Saṁnyāsa Upaniṣad
BU	Brahma Upaniṣad
ChūlU	Chūlikā Upaniṣad
Cnid	Cullaniddesa
CP	Cariyā Piṭaka
CS	Caraka Saṁhitā
CU	Chāndogya Upaniṣad
D	Dīgha Nikāya
Dh	Dhammapada
Dhs	Dhammasaṅgaṇi
GDS	Gautama Dharma Sūtra
GGS	Gobila Gṛhya Sūtra
Gītā	Bhagavad Gītā
GU	Gāruḍa Upaniṣad
Hem	Hemacandra
HGS	Hiraṇyakeśin Gṛhya Sūtra
Iti	Itivuttaka
Īśa	Īśa Upaniṣad
J	Jātaka
JU	Jābāla Upaniṣad
Kalpa	Kalpa Sūtra
KB	Kauṣītaki Brāhmaṇa
KBU	Kauṣītaki Brāhmaṇa Upaniṣad
Kh	Khuddaka Pāṭha
KhGS	Khādira Gṛhya Sūtra
KS	Kāṭhaka Saṁhitā
KŚS	Kātyāyana Śrauta Sūtra

KśU	Kaṭhaśruti Upaniṣad
KU	Kaṭha Upaniṣad
KV	Kathāvatthu
LŚS	Lāṭyāyana Śrauta Sūtra
LSU	Laghu-Saṁnyāsa Upaniṣad
M	Majjhima Nikāya
Manu	Manusmṛti
Mbh	Mahābhārata
Mil	Milindapañha
Mnid	Mahāniddesa
MS	Maitrāyaṇī Saṁhitā
MU	Maitrī Upaniṣad
MuṇU	Muṇḍaka Upaniṣad
Nett	Nettipakaraṇa
NpU	Nāradaparivrājaka Upaniṣad
NU	Nirvāṇa Upaniṣad
P.	Pali
PaiU	Paiṅgala Upaniṣad
Para	Parāśara
PGS	Pāraskara Gṛhya Sūtra
PhU	Paramahaṁsa Upaniṣad
PpU	Paramahaṁsaparivrājaka Upaniṣad
Ps	Paṭisambhidāmagga
PU	Praśna Upaniṣad
Pv	Petavatthu
Rām	Rāmāyaṇa
RU	Rāmottaratāpanī Upaniṣad
RV	Ṛg Veda
S	Saṁyutta Nikāya

Śak	Śakuntalā
ŚB	Śatapatha Brāhmaṇa
ŚGS	Śāṅkhāyana Gṛhya Sūtra
SK	Sūtrakṛtāṅga
Skt.	Sanskrit
ŚU	Śāṭyāyanīya Upaniṣad
Sur	Surapāla
SuU	Subāla Upaniṣad
ŚveU	Śvetāśvatara Upaniṣad
TĀ	Taittirīya Āraṇyaka
TAS	Tattvārtha Sūtra
TaU	Turīyātītāvadhūta Upaniṣad
TB	Taittirīya Brāhmaṇa
Thera	Theragāthā
Therī	Therīgāthā
TS	Taittirīya Saṁhitā
TU	Taittirīya Upaniṣad
Ud	Udāna
UD	Uttarādhyayana
Vbh	Vibhaṅga
VDS	Vasiṣṭha Dharma Sūtra
Vin	Vinaya
Vism	Visuddhimagga
VP	Viṣṇudharmottara Purāṇa
VS	Vājasaneyi Saṁhitā
VŚS	Vaikhānasa Śrauta Sūtra
VU	Vāsudeva Upaniṣad
Vv	Vimānavatthu

Introduction

The opening of *The Secret Life of Plants* recounts the views of a Viennese biologist writing at the beginning of the twentieth century. Raoul Francé proposed the then "shocking" idea that plants move their bodies as "freely, easily, and gracefully" as humans, though much more slowly. They swing in circles, reach their tendrils out to test their surroundings, and grow into the ground as if by gravity. At the same time, they shoot up in the air as if in defiance of gravity, search for moisture during dry times, and inch toward the nearest support so as to be propped up as they grow. In short, he argued, no plant "is without movement; all growth is a series of movements; plants are constantly preoccupied with bending, turning and quivering." Moreover, he continued, plants "are capable of intent," and are "able to perceive and to react to what is happening in their environment at a level of sophistication far surpassing that of humans." They have "some means of communicating with the outer world, something comparable or superior to our senses," such that there is "some intelligence directing the plant, either from within, or from without."[1] These are not new ideas, he concluded, but have been around "long before the birth of Christ," among people who had a special awareness of plants, like the Celts and "other sensitives," *and like the Hindu sages.* His suggestion of Hindu sages was based on references to the "devas,"[2] probably as beings who inhabited plants. Little did Francé know then that such views about plants in India were less about the *devas in the plants* than about *the very plants themselves.*

The plant lore of India is rich and varied and, at its core, it credits plants with extraordinary contributions of service without which humans would not survive. Plants, for example, are an essential component in the food we eat for nourishment and in the medicines we use for good health. Plants provide fuel to warm us and a variety of materials to protect our bodies – fibers for clothing, thatch and wood for lodging, and lumber for carts and wagons. And plants provide materials to make tools for work, fences for pasture, and beautiful objects for pleasure and contemplation.[3] As the Hindu Bhāgavata Purāṇa says of trees:

> ... these great blessed souls...live only for the welfare of others, suffering stormy winds, heavy rains, heat and frost, saving us from these.
> The birth of trees is truly the most blessed in the world, for it contributes to the well being of all creatures. Just as no one needy returns disappointed from generous persons, so also one who approaches trees for shelter.
> They meet the needs of others with their leaves, flowers, fruits, shade, roots, bark, wood, fragrance, sap, ashes, and coal.[4]

Likewise, in the Jain Ācārāṅga Sūtra, monks and nuns are instructed to speak of the large trees they see in parks, on the side of hills, and in woods in the following way:

> These (trees) are fit for palaces, gates, houses, benches, bolts, boats, buckets, stools, trays, ploughs...machines, poles, the nave of a wheel...seats, beds, cars, sheds.[5]

Because of their centrality in human lives, plants are often the objects of sacred attention and in India, as Lutgendorf notes, trees are "cherished by sages...evocative of high emotion...(and are locations) of transcendence."[6] In this way plants come to play important roles in religious practice, as fuel for the sacred fire, as wood for ritual implements, and as food for priests and gods. They are also the objects of worship themselves, as in the Vṛkṣotsava or Hindu tree festival where the decoration and veneration of the tree, separate from any deity residing in it, is thought to save petitioners from hell.[7]

Moreover, the very matrix of sentient life itself is interwoven with plants, and the arts and texts of India make clear that this flourishing world of experience is a world brimming with the vitality of organic growth. The Dīgha Nikāya of early Buddhism, for example, describes Gotama Buddha and his disciples touring the countryside in "a place teeming with life, with much grassland and woodland and water and corn,"[8] and stone reliefs from Bharhut repeatedly show lush trees, grasses, and shrubs present everywhere in the moments of human life and as the key to a rich experience for spiritual adepts.[9] Again, the Hindu Gītagovinda describes the libidinous bloom of springtime plants that provoke and mirror the intimate play of god and his devotees in this way:

> Tamāla trees' fresh leaves absorb strong scents of deer musk.
> Flame-tree petals, shining nails of Love, tear at young hearts....
> Gleaming saffron flower pistils are golden scepters of Love.
> Trumpet flowers like wanton bees are arrows in Love's quiver....
> Tender buds bloom into laughter as creatures abandon modesty.
> Cactus spikes pierce the sky to wound deserted lovers....
> Scents of twining creepers mingle with perfumes of fresh garlands....
> Budding mango trees tremble from the embrace of rising vines.
> Brindaban forest is washed by meandering Jumna river waters.[10]

With plants as a central resource in the survival of human life, a common presence in the religious practice of devotees, and a consistent and intimate part of every day experience – that is, with the profligate proximity of plants in so much of Indian culture – we ask whether the human intimates of plants ever wonder about the biological and philosophical status of these vegetal things that share so much of their lives. In other words, what do the Hindu, Jain, and Buddhist traditions of India understand about the nature and place of plants in the larger scheme of meaning that they, as humans, project onto their experience? When Francé mentioned the Hindu sages' awareness of plants, was he hinting at something more than just the belief that local deities were thought to live in trees?

Since we must begin somewhere, and since we are interested in common threads about plants in all three of the traditions of Hinduism, Jainism, and Buddhism, we will begin in the middle of a discussion about Buddhist environmentalism as cast by Donald Swearer. He notes: "Out of a concern for the total living environment, Buddhist environmentalists extend loving-kindness and compassion beyond people and animals to include plants and the earth itself."[11] This understanding – that connection among all the parts of our experience is interdependent, holistic, and even sacred – is shared by many strands of Indian traditions, and is corroborated amply in texts ancient, medieval, and modern. We choose this statement from a discussion about Buddhism because it is in the early Pali Buddhist attempt to situate plants somewhere suitable in the human world where the problem of plants is most clearly expressed.

Posing the Dilemma

Lambert Schmithausen's foundational work helps immensely in the untangling of early Buddhist views on plants. His central focus is an analysis of whether plants are considered to be living and sentient beings, and this issue is brought to the fore by Pali teachings on non-violence, where plants are one of the clear objects of the ethics of *ahiṁsā*. In discussions of the Pāṭimokkha, for example, the Vinaya prohibits monks and nuns from cutting down trees *(rukkha)* in the course of repairing their lodgings, from cutting palmyra leaves off palms to wear as shoes, and from walking amongst alms donors during the rainy season because, in doing any of these things, renunciants will injure one-facultied living beings, i.e., plants.[12]

Using Schmithausen's work as a starting point, the following argument can be made. If plants and seeds – including grasses, creepers, bushes, and trees – are, as one of the objects of the ethic of non-violence, not to be injured, then they must be included among those designated as living, sentient beings. And if they are designated as living, sentient beings, then they must be a part of the world of *saṁsāra* and therefore subject to the laws of *kamma*. While the texts of the early Pali canon selectively include plants as the object of the *ahiṁsā* ethic they are, however, as Schmithausen has shown, relatively silent about the place of plants in the overall scheme of life in rebirth. While later Buddhist texts, like the Milindapañha, are clear about plants *not* being counted as sentient beings, earlier texts have "no explicit statement *declaring* plants or even earth and water to be living, sentient beings," nor do they seem to have "an explicit...statement *denying* them the status of sentient beings." Thus, he concludes, plants in earliest Buddhism are "a kind of borderline case."[13]

The reason for the discrepancy between the early and later Pali treatments of plants, argues Schmithausen, is due more to prevailing views in society at different times than to changing notions among the renunciants themselves. The code of non-violence as developed in early Buddhism, he argues, "is *not* concerned with *spiritual* practice *nor* even with *morality* proper (though some of the precepts do coincide with moral commandments), but, mainly, with regulating how monks and nuns had to behave *in society.*"[14] He notes that many local householders of the early period still retain their old Vedic and pre-Vedic beliefs that plants are sentient beings and, although they themselves cannot fully practice an impractical daily standard of full *ahiṁsā*, especially with regard to plants, they think it unfit for ascetics of the time to practice anything but *ahiṁsā* towards plants.

> In the morality of renouncers and ascetics, abstention from killing animals (and even plants) was firmly rooted as the heritage of an earlier cultural stratum – a stratum in which killing animals (and even plants, earth and water) was, in a sense at least, as serious as killing people.[15]

Thus, the Pāṭimokkha proscription on killing plants is not "an element of moral, or ethically motivated, conduct in the strict sense but...rather a matter of *ascetic decorum*,"[16] or as Paul Harvey notes, "the motive of the (Buddhist) rule seems to be to avoid offending popular sensibilities."[17] And, although Schmithausen doesn't make much of the significance of not wanting to run roughshod over householder sentiments, I've argued elsewhere that a clear reason for not wanting to irritate householders and for wanting to generate their good will is precisely because these same householders are the sources of the Saṅgha's material support – that is, they are *donors* to the early Buddhist community. Moreover, these householders are known for openly expressing any critical views of monastic behavior, and for noting when alms seekers don't fit pre-existing views about ascetic behavior. Such a encounter often results in complaints made to the Buddha, and in the Buddha's ruling on the donors' behalf.[18]

Schmithausen then suggests two trends at work as Buddhism matures, and as lay etiquette for donors changes with developments in lay ethics. The first concerns the early period in which ascetic decorum may not be the only influence governing the inclusion of plants in the ethic of non-violence. "It cannot be excluded *a priori,*" he argues,

> that the Suttavibhaṅga has reduced to a mere rule of decorum what originally had (at least also) an ethical dimension; for, the Pāṭi-mokkha-sutta itself would make equally good sense if originally also the monks themselves, and even the Buddha, still somehow held the view that plants and seeds were living beings.[19]

Positing such an early belief by the renunciants themselves in the living and sentient nature of plants, then, makes the ensuing developments even more striking, for Schmithausen goes on to describe a second trend in which Buddhism, as it evolves, narrows down the range of living, sentient beings who are the object of the ethic of non-violence – resulting in the considerable weakening of the prohibition against harming plants. Thus, the offense involved in killing or injuring plants gets less and less, so that at some point, "*ahiṁsā* towards plants" becomes an obsolete practice if not also an obsolete view.

Because, however, the "shifting emphasis from the *ahiṁsā* aspect towards matters of ascetic decorum" is already evident in the discussion of the Pāṭimokkha rule,[20] the eventual standard exclusion of plants from the *ahiṁsā* rule becomes easily explained.

Under rulers like King Aśoka, Buddhism increasingly embraces laicizing tendencies and encourages lay practice in areas particularly of donation and non-violence. For the lay to practice Buddhist *ahiṁsā*, however, the objects of the non-violent ethic have to exclude plants, as lay lives would be impossible without recourse to organic, i.e., vegetable, materials for food, clothing, lodging, and vehicles. Thus, unlike some of the stricter ethical prescriptions available in this general period, Buddhist practice of non-violence is influenced by renunciant desire to please donors – early on, by practicing *ahiṁsā* towards plants themselves and, later on, by declaring plants to be non-living and thus excluded from the protections of *ahiṁsā*. This later situation allows donors to practice non-violence themselves and at the same time to freely use plants and plant products in their own daily lives.[21]

As for Schmithausen's own views, my "personal feeling," he says, is that plants

> are certainly not sentient in the same way as men or so-called higher animals. But they may not be entirely insentient either, and they are certainly alive. We simply do not know what it means for a plant itself to live or to be injured or killed.[22]

Thus, Schmithausen sets the stage for the explorations undertaken here, and briefly taken up in print already.[23] First, he notes that we don't really know what the early Buddhist tradition means when it says that a being is alive as a plant, for all indications are, that one way or another plant life really is a "borderline" case. Because of the difficulty in providing a clear conclusion to the matter, then, Harvey finds, in his summary of Schmithausen's work, that "there was no real interest," presumably in early Buddhist texts, "in resolving the matter as a theoretical issue."[24] Second, Schmithausen points us in a certain direction by suggesting that there is an "old view that plants and seeds are sentient beings"[25] still present among early Buddhist renunciants. This suggestion will now direct us to ferret out those threads in Indian traditions that support the notion that plants are alive and sentient partakers of pleasure and pain, and thus due to be objects of human responsibility. Finally, Schmithausen's own work is not meant to be of academic interest only for, in 1990, he said: "the main motive for this lecture is the contemporary problem of environmental destruction and pollution...(for which we might) expect help from an old tradition for which that problem did not yet exist and by which it was therefore not expressly addressed."[26] Although this excerpt betrays a more complex context, it nevertheless tips our hat to the recognition that answers to problems posed in earlier times might be applicable today.

Scope of the Book

The questions raised in this study fall into two general areas, as they pertain to theory and to practice. Questions of theory are taken up in the first section, and concern the nature of plant life itself as understood in the traditions of Hinduism, Jainism, and Buddhism. I am interested in whether plants are considered "living" and, if so, what being alive as a plant means and how it is experienced; whether plants are thought to have "senses," and if so which ones; whether there is anything remarkable about the designation of plants as sessile or "immobile;" whether the particular status of sentience is related to understandings of consciousness and whether we can talk about "plant consciousness" as a viable process; whether plants can be considered among the "*guṇa* categories" of *tamas, rajas*, and *sattva*; whether plant bodies can serve as mounts for consciousness of any sort, and whether the answers to this question have consequences for the participation of plants as beings in the stream of "*karma* and rebirth;" whether there are different types of *karma* endowment, and whether the accumulation of *karma* seeds can be separated from their expenditure; and, finally, whether understandings of plant life would acknowledge their participation in spiritual advancement and practice.

To address such issues, I rely on a variety of sources – historical, religious, philosophical, political, biological, medical, literary, and artistic. The information in these materials appears to be based on *human observation* of "plant behavior," that is, on observations about changes in plant color, size, temperature, orientation, and movement, as plants are noticed to respond to varied conditions of weather, nutriment, handling, and injury. This is not a scientific study, however, first, because I am interested primarily in what Indian traditions have to say about these issues (not what actually may be "true" of plants) and, second, because these traditions contain only third person observations – with a few apocryphal exceptions, there are no "first person" reports from the plants themselves. Furthermore, the material in Hindu, Jain, and Buddhist sources is not comprehensive and, while there are numerous descriptions of plant behavior, the doctrinal statements are relatively few, but at the same time highly suggestive. For this reason, the discussion is sometimes speculative.

In the second part of the book, I turn to two areas where Indian traditions portray relationships between plants and humans: folkloric stories about plant-human interaction, and questions of plant rights and human duties. In Indian literature about plants and humans a number of themes are addressed: the difference between trees and the deities who may inhabit them, as well as the kinds of deities who are likely to take up residence there; homologies between plants and humans, including those between plants and women's bodies; stories of transformations of humans into plants and trees; stories of conversations with and marriages to trees; and practices of divination using trees and plants. Many of these materials belong to popular and local traditions, and it is often just a matter of luck if they are preserved for us today. Issues of plant rights and human duties moves us into ethical realms and here, with help from such non-Indian thinkers as Paul W. Taylor, James A. Nash, Christopher D. Stone, and Peter Singer, we examine whether the dynamics of human conduct toward the plant world in India derives from plants having rights in and of themselves, or from socially prescribed duties and obligations humans have developed towards them. While there is a recognition that all thought systems are human-centered, the question is most often whether "right behavior" towards plants is based on the "benefits" plants can give humans, either now or in the future, or on plants' inherent worth.

Questions of environmental practice are taken up in the third section of the book, and use the results from the first two sections of the nature of plant life, and on plants' relations with humans, to focus on specific issues of contemporary times. In thinking through a contemporary environmental ethic in South Asia, we propose that it is helpful to return to traditional Indian materials to find old and enduring themes that authentically incorporate plants into them, and that are compatible with contemporary ethical thinking. To this end, the discussion is divided into contemporary environmental movements and activists in Hinduism, Jainism, and Pali Buddhism.

In Hinduism, the discussion includes the Chipko movement, Vandana Shiva, the Vrindavan Forest Revival Project, the Trees for Life project, the Auroville community, and the teachings of two female saints, Karunamayi and Ammachi. In Jainism, we focus primarily on Satish Kumar and on those who had considerable influence on him such as Mohandas K. Gandhi, Vinoba Bhave, and Acharya Tulsi. In Pali Buddhism, the best example is the forest meditation tradition in Thailand, parts of which are associated with environmental activism, and here we turn to Ajahn Chah, Buddhadasa Bhikkhu, and Phra Prayudh Payutto, as well as to practices like tree ordination. Many of these activist movements and people are engaged in large scale efforts at reforestation and tree protection, domestic tree planting, sharing and saving of diverse collections of seeds, and developing ways of practicing the judicious use of plants in human life. The work of many is grounded in traditional philosophic and religious views about the nature of plant life as understood in inherited perspectives, and often uses inherited practices that express veneration and gratitude towards plants for their continued role in human lives.

As will become clear very quickly, the three traditions drawn upon here have different, and often conflicting, views on plants. The Hindu tradition has the greatest variety of relevant material. The Vedic texts honor plants with hymns, see plants as intricate to the cycle of life, use plants in homologies with humans, and include plants in the sacred system of order known as *ṛta*. Dharmaśāstra literature brings to light "plant positive" views on plants and *karma*, plants and consciousness, and plants and pleasure and pain, and is also clear about requiring human care and protection towards plants. Āyurveda literature (for humans) makes reference to plants and the *guṇas*, and to plants and consciousness, and Vṛkṣāyurveda literature, on medical practices especially for plants, expands much further on all manner of plant nature and care. Moreover, throughout Hindu literature there are myriad observations made about plants that support particular attributions to plants as they are living and sentient; and Hindu folklore provides many stories about conversations, marriages, and transformations between the plant and human worlds.

In several standard *sūtras*, the Jain tradition places plants in a complex schema of living beings bound by *karma*, that classifies these beings according their senses, their mobility, and the quality of their consciousness. It is a clear and consistently applied schema, and is the basis out of which the doctrine of *ahiṁsā* or non-violence is practiced. The Buddhist tradition is, as we have already seen, the most inconsistent. Early texts reflect that plants were objects of *ahiṁsā*. Here, donors, who themselves may not have adhered to the ethic, nevertheless expected renunciants they gave to to practice a certain ascetic decorum by not killing plants. This changed later, as donors themselves took up *ahiṁsā* practice, but could not do so if plants were included – hence plants' eventual exclusion from the category of the living. But, oddly, it is in Buddhism where the *sattva* quality of plants emerges early on, for as in Hinduism and Jainism, not only does Buddhism understand forests to be an optimal place for spiritual practice and advancement, but early Buddhism also understands trees to provide the model of ascetic attitude and behavior.

In this study, I hope to show that many of the things that are on our minds today about plants were also on the minds of traditional thinkers in early and medieval India, in ways that had clarity and precision then and that can be appreciated as such now. Moreover, the doctrines about plants developed in traditional religious and philosophical circles in India continue to provide formative and grounding material for activist work there undertaken by individuals and groups today. It is in this spirit, then, that we offer the following contemporary quotes:

From *City of Joy*, 1992, directed by Roland Joffe, spoken by Ram Chander, a rickshawala:

> At my wedding, I was so frightened my brother gave me something to drink. I went out to piss under a tree and fell asleep. And when I woke up, I thought I married the tree. I still love that tree.

From *Earth*, 1999, directed by Deepa Mehta, from a conversation in a garden:

> "It's a sin to cut flowers after sunset, they're sleeping!"
> "Imagine their pain, if they're awake."

From *Desirable Daughters*, 2002, written by Bharati Mukherjee, from the story of Tara Lata, the Tree Bride (p. 16):

> Tara Lata straightens her bowed head, and raises her gaze slowly...Her bridegroom is brave and steadfast. He has waited for her all night in the perilous wilderness...unflinching, though deadly snakes slither out of flooded holes at his feet, and leeches crawl across his toes, and crabs scuttle up his shins and predatory beasts gouge his solid stomach. The bridal gaze angles up his strong, slender torso as tall as a ship's mast, and scales up, up, to where the tip of his head disappears in the night-black of the winter skies. She feels his arms, as strong as tree branches, brush against her, enfold her...And she now recognizes her bridegroom.

Endnotes :

1. Tompkins and Bird, *The Secret Life of Plants*, pp. ix-xiv. Tompkins' and Bird's italics.
2. Tompkins and Bird, *The Secret Life of Plants*, p. xiv.
3. Rajan, "Ancient Indian Approaches Towards Plants," pp. 80-82; Gopal, pp. 7-8; Kane 2.2.893-895.
4. Sullivan, "Paradise Polluted: Religious Dimensions of the *Vrindāvana:* Ecology Movement," p. 565.
5. ĀS 2.4.2.11; Jacobi, *Jaina Sūtras* 1.154.

6 Lutgendorf, "City, Forest, and Cosmos," pp. 279-280.

7 Kane 5.1.415-416.

8 T. W. Rhys Davids, *Dialogues of the Buddha* 1.144.

9 Randhawa, *Cult of Trees*, pp. 13-25.

10 Miller, *Gītagovinda*, pp. 74-75.

11 Swearer, "Buddhism and Ecology: Challenge and Promise, " p. 2.

12 See, for example: First, *kathañ hi nāma samaṇā Sakyaputtiyā rukkhaṁ chindissanti pi chedāpessanti pi. Ekindriyaṁ samaṇā Sakyaputtiyā jīvaṁ viheṭhentīti;* Pācittiya XI, Vin 4.34. See also Vin 3.155-156, and compare Pācittiya X, Vin 4.32. Second, *kathaṁ hi nāma samaṇā Sakyaputtiyā tālataruṇe chedāpetvā tālapattapādukāyo dhāressanti, tāni tālataruṇāni chinnāni milāyanti. Ekindriyaṁ samaṇā Sakyaputtiyā jīvaṁ viheṭhentīti;* Vin 1.189. Third, *kathaṁ hi nāma samaṇā Sakyaputtiyā hemantam pi gimham pi vassam pi cārikaṁ carissanti haritāni tiṇāni sammaddantā ekindriyaṁ jīvaṁ viheṭhentā bahū khuddake pāṇe saṁghātaṁ āpādentā;* Vin 1.137, 138. *Kathaṁ hi nāma bhikkhuniyo...carissanti haritāni tiṇāni sammaddantā ekindriyaṁ jīvaṁ viheṭhentā bahū khuddake pāṇe saṁghātaṁ āpādentā 'ti;* Pācittiya XXXIX, Vin 4.296. While the other three passages noted in this paragraph can be fairly clearly interpreted to support the view that the one-facultied beings not to be injured are the plants themselves, the last two passages concerning the alms tour are ambiguous in that the one-facultied beings may not be the plants themselves at all, but instead the beings who reside in the plants. See also, so *bījagāmabhūtagāmasamārambhā paṭivirato ahosiṁ;* M 3.34.

13 Schmithausen, *Buddhism and Nature*, pp. 5-6; Schmithausen, *Problem of the Sentience of Plants*, p. 21n. My italics.

14 Schmithausen, *Plants as Sentient Beings*, p.10. Schmithausen's italics.

15 Schmithausen, *Buddhism and Nature*, pp. 38-39.

16 Schmithausen, *Problem of the Sentience of Plants*, p. 16; see pp. 23, 26. My italics. This interpretation appears earlier in Hanns Peter Schmidt's discussion of the origin of *ahiṁsā* where he notes, in addressing the phenomenon of vegetarianism based on *ahiṁsā* ideals: "The gist of the whole is not so much a condemnation of the Vedic ritual and its animal sacrifices but rather the propagation of *a renouncer-like conduct.*" (my italics.) Schmidt, "Origin of *Ahiṁsā*," p. 628.

[17] Harvey, *Introduction to Buddhist Ethics*, p. 175.

[18] See Findly, *Dāna*, pp. 337-367.

[19] Schmithausen, *Problem of the Sentience of Plants*, p. 17.

[20] Schmithausen, *Problem of the Sentience of Plants*, p. 43; see also pp. 39-43.

[21] Schmithausen points out as well that the exclusion of plants from the *ahiṁsā* rule occurs as agriculture extends more fully across the Gaṅgā Valley (*Problem of the Sentience of Plants*, p. 77), thus putting plants and vegetation near the center of local material life.

[22] Schmithausen, *Buddhism and Nature*, p. 26.

[23] Findly, " Borderline Beings: Plant Possibilities in Early Buddhism," pp. 252-263.

[24] Harvey, *Introduction to Buddhist Ethics*, p. 175. Harvey continues his summary of Schmithausen's argument by saying that the "*Abhidhamma*, though, lacks reference to 'one-facultied life' in its very detailed analysis of phenomena. In practice, however, plants were still included within the ambit of non-violence for monks,"

[25] Schmithausen, *Plants as Sentient Beings*, p. 11.

[26] Schmithausen, *Buddhism and Nature*, p. 2.

A.
THE NATURE OF PLANT LIFE

1

Raising the Issue of Plant Life : Five Domains

From the double-edged understanding of plant life suggested in Pali Buddhist texts, the problem posed is what a normative traditional Indian view of plants might be and whether such a view can be identified. We begin by examining several areas of Indian religious and cultural life that have plants at their center. Heinrich Zimmer notes that according to "Hindu cosmology and science, it is characteristic of the living principle that, being endowed with an unlimited power of self-transformation, it manifests itself in the innumerable forms of matter, be they minerals, vegetables, or animals."[1] The ascription of a living principle to vegetation, regardless of the philosophical position behind it, is an understanding of plant nature that underlies, we argue, the development of several domains: e.g., Vedic ritual, early Hindu philosophy, medicinal use of plants for humans, Hindu, Jain, and Buddhist ethics of non-violence, and the therapeutic cultivation and care of plants for their own well being. It is the very presence of fields like these in the Indian traditions, and the assumptions about plants behind them, that suggest a thoughtful and complex approach to the issue of whether, and how, plants are alive.

1.1 Ritualized Generativity Through Plants in Vedic Life

In the world, the whole of nature is seen as integrated. All parts of the cosmos have a particular place and contribution based on the operating power of *ṛta,* the "cosmic order or law prevailing in nature...(in) the 'course' of things."[2] *Ṛta* is the truth belonging to each natural element that identifies it and defines its ordered and regular place within the larger sacralized world. The sun's *ṛta,* for example, is to give light and warmth and to mark divisions of time and space; the river's *ṛta* is to flow water; the cow's *ṛta* is to give milk; the fire's *ṛta* is to burn brightly from the kindling sticks, cooking food and carrying offerings to the gods; the gods' *ṛta* is to provide prosperity and blessings; and the *ṛta* of humans is to make sure that the *ṛtas* of all other elements remain truthful and in place.[3] The natural elements imbued with *ṛta* include, of course, plants, and Vedic practice is replete with the presence of plants and plant material, in venues ranging from plants as the objects of worship to plants as the tools humans use to make that worship effective.

Deities

There are, first, a number of hymns in Vedic literature that are dedicated to plants and trees. Hermann Oldenberg notes that it "can be easily understood that very little is said about the Tree and Forest-deities in the *Ṛgveda* as a whole; for the great sacrifices, these minor creatures recede...into the background before the hero Indra and the world-encompassing figure of Varuṇa."[4] Nevertheless, plants and trees are "divinely animated."[5] One hymn, for example, Ṛg Veda 10.97, is devoted to praising annual herbaceous plants *(oṣadhi)* and, in particular, their healing powers.

> 2. Mothers, you have a hundred forms and a thousand sprouts. You who have a hundred ways of working, make this man healthy for me.
> 14. Let one of you help the other; let one stand by the other. All of you (herbs) working together, help this speech of mine to succeed.
> 20. Do not harm the man who digs you up, nor him for whom I dig you up; let all our two-footed and four-footed creatures be without sickness.
> 21. You growing plants who hear this, and those who have gone far away, all coming together unite your power in this plant.[6]

Healing plant deities are also found in the Atharva Veda. Arundhatī, a goddess representing *lākṣā* or lac, is "the queen of all plants," a life-giving material who has the gods as her siblings, the night as her mother, and the clouds as her father. Like Arundhatī, the aromatic plant god Kuṣṭha is a healer thought to be "the medicine for all diseases and the choicest among the herbs." His mythology ties him to Soma, as both are brought from the Himalayan mountains for domestic and ritual use.[7]

The most well known Vedic plant deity is Soma to whom one whole book of hymns in the Ṛg Veda is dedicated. Soma is a herb used in a hallucinogenic drink taken by poet-priests who seek blessings and transcendent visions to inspire their prayers.

> 4. When we have drunk you, O drop of Soma, be good to our heart, kind as a father to his son, thoughtful as a friend to a friend. Far-famed Soma, stretch out our life-span so that we may live.
> 5. The glorious drops that I have drunk set me free in wide space. You have bound me together in my limbs as thongs bind a chariot. Let the drops protect me from the foot that stumbles and keep lameness away from me.[8]

Large trees, known as *vanaspatis* or "lords of the forest," are also addressed as deities[9] and the spirits (Gandharvas and Apsarās) living in them are asked to bestow prosperity on the bride and safety on the bridal car, as wedding processions pass them by.[10] Animation is ascribed to the whole forest that is addressed by the name Araṇyānī, "lady of the woods." RV 10.146 is dedicated to her, and describes the worshipper's experience of her as hearing "the sounds of...the forest whose mystery and horror surround the stray wanderer."[11]

> 4. Whoever stays in the forest at evening imagines: Someone is calling his cow; someone is cutting wood; someone is crying out.
> 5. The spirit of the forest does not kill – not if no one else approaches. She eats sweet fruit and lies down wherever she pleases.
> 6. Mother of wild beasts, untilled by a plough but full of food, sweet-smelling of perfume and balm – to her, the spirit of the forest, I offer my praise.[12]

The Atharva Veda contains a long hymn dedicated to the Earth (12.1), described by Dwivedi as integrating "much of the thoughts of Hindu seers concerning our existence on Earth....Mother Earth is seen as an abode of a large and extended family *(Kuṭumbakam)* of all beings....Every entity and organism is a part of one large... system which is presided over by the eternal Mother Earth."[13]

> 19. The Earth is full of energy, and the same energy flows through its herbs and other medicinal plants, the clouds carry energy in the form of thunder, also there is energy inside stones, and the same energy is prevalent among people and animals in the form of hunger. May that energy sustain us.
> 27. O Mother Earth! You are the sustainer and preserver of all vegetation including medicinal plants as well as all living beings. May you nourish us as long as we live.[14]

Verse 19 describes a world system enlivened throughout by the energy *(agni)* of fire and, in verse 27, the Earth as deity holds the key, through vegetation, to human survival *(dhayasam)*. In an early Vedic world, all parts are animated, ordered, and connected–including shrubs, herbs, and trees. Although plants take their place alongside such things as water, wind, light, and minerals, it is plants, not inanimate materials, who are seen as having vital, life-giving, nourishing, and healing properties essential to the maintenance of the viable world.

Rituals

The Agnicayana rite, or the rite of the piling of the fire altars, is the "most philosophic" moment of the Taittirīya Saṁhitā "for in it finds expression the chief doctrine of the sacrificial ritual, the sacrifice as a cosmic power of the highest potency."[15] Among those materials used is RV 10.97, recited in the section of the Agnicayana for the preparation of the ground before building the fire layers out of brick, describing and honoring the plants of the ground where the altar will stand. In this passage, plants are venerated as goddesses, asked to free the ritual space of defiling and obstructive elements, and beseeched for health and healing:

> The plants born / Three generations before the gods, Of the brown ones I celebrate / The seven and a hundred abodes.
> A hundred, O mother, are your abodes, / A thousand too your shoots, Therefore do ye, with a hundred powers, / Make him whole for me.
> With flowers, with shoots, / Fruit-bearing and without fruit, Like steeds victorious / The plants are strong to help.
> 'Plants,' O ye mothers, / I hail you, O goddesses; Go bearing away defilement, / Defilement destroying.[16]

Other rituals have plants at their center and, like the Agnicayana, they focus on prosperity, well-being, and life transformation and transition but, unlike the Agnicayana, they are less for cosmic than for individual benefit. The Āgrayaṇeṣṭi, or offering *(iṣṭi)*[17] of first fruits *(āgrayaṇa)*, is the first seasonal offering made with grains – rice, barley, or millet – and is performed on a *parvan,* or change of moon (lunar node) day. The performance of this offering of the first freshly harvested grains allows the worshipper to make other offerings using such grains, for he is not allowed to eat new grains until he has offered them first in the Āgrayaṇa ritual. The first-fruit-offering with rice takes place during autumn when the rice grains have become ripe, that with ripened barley grains takes place in the spring, and that with ripened millet grains takes place during the rains.[18] "The sacrificer need not perform a sacrifice of first fruits of *other* grains and vegetables and may consume them at will, because the season of their ripening is not fixed."[19] Later texts note that this Vedic ritual for the honoring of these grains continues as the tradition develops. In the Arthaśāstra, for example, those learned in the Vedas, and those in the process of doing penance, are allowed to use ripe flowers and fruits from the field in their worship of the gods, and those engaged in the Āgrayaṇa ritual, performed at the beginning of the harvest season, may continue to gather grains for their *iṣṭi.*

> Grains and other crops shall be collected as often as they are harvested. No wise man shall leave anything in the fields, not even chaff. Crops, when reaped, shall be heaped up in high piles or in the form of turrets.[20]

Plants are also central in death rituals. One of the hymns to Agni as the cremation fire is RV 10.16, that ends with an invocation to the fire to allow new plants to grow out of the ashes of the body burned during cremation:

> 13. Now, Agni, quench and revive the very one you have burnt up.
> Let Kiyāmba, Pākadūrvā and Vyalkaśa plants grow in this place.[21]

It is in relation to this hope for success in ritual "life renewal" at the cremation site that the Āśvalāyana Gṛhya Sūtra requires that the site be fertile with herbs, but free of plants with thorns.[22]

In the Śānti or peace-making rite, performed by some after the collection of the charred bones of a dead person, flowers, wood, butter, and grass are used by survivors of the deceased to renew their lives after they return home.[23] Mortuary mounds for the deceased's bones are created with the sweeping of the site using special ritual branches (Palāśa), plowing the ground mindful of the deities of the different directions, and then sowing "seeds of all kinds of herbs" – before pouring out the jar of bones and arranging the bones of the dead person limb by limb. Over the top of the mound, once fully prepared, the worshipper sows barley grain in the hopes of warding off sin from himself, and then covers the mound with Avakā plants for moisture and Darbha grass for softness.[24]

Although many offerings of cooked grains and vegetables are used throughout the death rituals, one particular instance exemplifies the role of plants at ritual moments of life transition. In the time following the funeral rituals for the deceased, rites known as Śrāddha are performed in which offerings are made for the ultimate benefit of the *pitṛs,* the immediate generations of the worshipper's ancestors, i.e., the father, the paternal grandfather, and the paternal great grandfather. Part of these rituals is the Sapiṇḍīkaraṇa, the ritual that effects the receiving of the deceased into the community of ancestral fathers accompanied by worship using *piṇḍas* or balls of rice. Just after the death, the worshipper takes a *piṇḍa,* representing the *preta* or spirit of his father "endowed only with its briefest, subtlest body,"[25] and worships with it using incense, flowers, ghee, white threads for clothing, and a cup of water with sesame seeds. This the worshipper does for ten days, increasing the number of cups by one each day.

> ...each day of the rites results in a new portion of the preta's intermediate body, the head being created on the first day, then in succession the neck and shoulders, the heart and torso, the back, the stomach, the thighs and bowels, the lower legs and skin, the knees and hair, the genitals, and, on the tenth day of the offerings, the preta receives digestive powers so that the sufferings of hunger and thirst now experienced by the "body of nourishment" duly created may be allayed by continued offerings of piṇḍas and water from the living.[26]

The use of rice balls to ritually create the new body of the deceased father for life in the community of ancestors, and eventually for rebirth himself among the world of living humans,[27] places plants at the center of this ritual's transformative process.

> Nothing can be more sublime than the formula which one has to repeat at the time of offering *piṇḍas* and water (with sesame) at Gayā 'may those of my ancestors that are in the form of *pretas* be all satiated by means of the (balls made) of barley flour mixed with sesame and may everything, whether moving or immovable from Brahmā up to the blades of grass, derive satisfaction from the water offered by me.'[28]

A third example of the ritual use of plants is in the Atharva Veda where they are known to provide medical benefit and personal transformation. Stalks of reed, for example, are used against injury and disease, particularly the obstruction of the urinary tract;[29] healing herbs are used against leprosy[30] and fever,[31] and to cure many other diseases that tear away at the body;[32] and plants are used to combat the mischief of curses and the ill feelings of the cursers,[33] to gain victory in disputations,[34] to be successful against a rival wife,[35] to recover one's virility,[36] to heal wounds,[37] to discover and counter witches and other enemies,[38] to practice exorcism,[39] and to win and maintain a man's love.[40]

The power of plants is certainly due to the actual physiological processes of healing, but equally, it seems, to ritual principles of similarity, i.e., to "sympathetic" transformations, wherein the appearance, location, or other natural properties of the plant are directly related to the medical problem at hand. Thus,

> We know the reed's father...with that I will make health...for your body; onto the earth let your outflowing be, out of you, with a splash! (Cure of urinary obstruction) (AV 1.3.1)
>
> You, O dusky, black, dark herb *(oṣadhi)*, are born at night. O you colorer, color him who has skin spots and is pale. (Cure of leukoderma) (AV 1.23.1)
> Up, the energies...of herbs *(oṣadhi)*, the essences...of bulls; the virility...of men...do you put together in him, O Indra, ...I make your member taut, like a bowstring on a bow; mount...as it were a stag a doe, unrelaxing always. (Cure of impotence) (AV 4.4.4, 7)
>
> Grower *(rohaṇī)* are you, grower; healer of the severed bone; make this (limb) grow, O *arundhatī*. (Cure of broken bone) (AV 4.12.1)
>
> Tree after tree you climb *(vṛkṣaṁvṛkṣamā rohasi)*, like a lustful girl; conquering, steadfast, and delivering by name are you. (Cure using *arundhatī)* (AV 5.5.3)
>
> An eagle...discovered you; a hog dug you with his snout; you, O herb *(oṣadhi)*, seek to injure him who seeks to injure; smite down the witchcraft-maker. (Cure against witchcraft) (AV 5.14.1)[41]

Although many animal and non-organic elements also have beneficial uses, the presence of plants in rituals of well being in the Atharva Veda is understood as all-purpose. "You, mistress of remedies, O conquering one...we take hold of; *I have made you a ring of thousand-fold energy...for every one, O herb*. The truly-conquering, the curse-repelling, the overcoming...*all the herbs have I called together, saying 'may they save us from this.*'"[42] Statements such as these express what seems to be the general consensus that plants plays a central role in the ritual mechanics that effect successful life transition and transformation.

The Ritual Site

Ritual efficacy begins with the site itself for, as we saw in the case of the death rites, the initial choice of where to hold the ritual is crucial. As the Āśvalāyana Gṛhya Sūtra notes, for example, the presence of fertile plants at the spot chosen for the cremation is important for the homology ensuring fertility and rebirth of the deceased to work. Moreover, as a general rule, texts of the Vedic *śrauta* system require that ritual grass or *barhis* be strewn as a necessary part of preparing the sacrificial ground. Here a layer of Kuśa grass is spread over the sacred field and, in particular, over the central altar or *vedi,* to provide a surface for the presentation of offerings to the gods and as a seat for the divine and human participants. Besides the practical effects of providing a clean and pleasant surface, the grass stre\w ensures that the vitality of plants is present to help promote prosperity in the ritual.

Many of the Gṛhya Sūtras note that site preparation for building a new house is done very carefully with regard to plants. In choosing a site, the worshipper makes sure that the ground is even throughout, not saline or dry, and not on a flood plain, where there could be inundation. Moreover, it is to be covered with grass, but not with plants that have milky juice, thorns, or bitterness. Sites that have Darbha grass growing on them should be chosen by those with religious goals, those with big grasses by those desiring strength, and those with tender grasses by those desiring cattle.[43] Herbs and trees are called on in the preparation of the site to provide vigor to the dwelling place,[44] and the placement of planted trees should be done with particular care. Thus, the worshipper should *avoid* planting the following:

> an Aśvattha tree on the east side of the house, for there it will bring danger from fire;
> a Plakṣa tree on the south side, for there it will bring early death to those in the house;
> a Nyagrodha tree on the west side, for there it will bring oppression through weapons;
> an Uḍumbara tree on the north side, for there it will bring eye disease.

These trees – Aśvattha, sacred to the sun; Plakṣa, sacred to Yama; Nyagrodha, sacred to Varuṇa, and Uḍumbara, sacred to Prajāpati – should all be planted in other places appropriate to their sacred designations.[45]

Ritual Fuel and Implements

The ritual fire, of course, needs fuel and given that the fuel must be organic, it needs to come from something living or once living. Although several materials given into the fire, to be carried as offerings to the gods, do act as fuel and make the fire burn even more brightly – e.g., cooked food, butter *(ghī),* and animal flesh – the standard fuel in the Vedic ritual is kindling wood. The Taittirīya Saṁhitā, for example, notes that kindling wood is normally taken from the Aśvattha, Plakṣa, Nyagrodha, and Uḍumbara trees, the four special sacrificial trees, that happen also to be the homes of the Gandharvas, male spirits governed by Varuṇa, and the Apsarases, female water spirits governed by Soma. By making offerings into the fire, the worshipper honors these spirits in their own homes.[46] These four trees, in their ritual use, are embued with special powers:

> Nyagrodha is the lordly power of the trees.
> Uḍumbara is the paramount rule of the trees.
> Aśvattha is the overlordship of the trees.
> Plakṣa is the self rule and sovereignty of the trees.[47]

Other passages in the *śrauta* literature specify the kinds of woods to be used in fueling the sacred fire, often duplicating the four mentioned above and expanding on the many possible combinations and variations of wood and vine types that can be used. These descriptions make eminently clear that, whatever the fuel, it must be something derived from the vegetable kingdom and often must have some evidence of life or growth attributable to it.[48] Here is an example of such instructions from the Bhāradvāja Śrauta Sūtra:

> A sacrificer desirous of setting up the sacred fires should, before doing so, get two kindling woods prepared of the wood of an *aśvattha* tree, whose roots have penetrated into the earth (through the stem of a *śamī* tree) and which has grown

> upon a *śamī* tree. According to some teachers, the roots may not have penetrated into the earth. While fetching the kindling woods he should recite the verse....(and with) the verses...he should collect the materials mentioned in the *Brāhmaṇa,* namely the seven substances derived from the earth[49] ...and seven substances derived from the vegetable kingdom (= wood of *aśvattha,* of *uḍumbara,* of *palāśa,* of *śamī,* of *vikaṅkata,* of a tree struck by lightning, and a lotus leaf).[50]

If the desirable type of Aśvattha wood is not available, then the worshipper may use ordinary Aśvattha wood so long as it has white sprouts, has not been struck down by lightning or burnt by forest fire or been cut by people of low birth, has only a few birds' nests, and is not dried up or old.[51]

Implements used in the ritual are made of wood as well, and the most important of these is the sacrificial post or *yūpa,* celebrated as *vanaspati,* 'the lord of the forest,' in RV 3.8. Here the post's erect position in the earth, pointing upwards towards heaven, is honored in the hope that this once living "axis mundi" might bring prosperity to the worshippers. Says Oldenberg of the *yūpa* as part of "the Tree-cult...the post represents the tree contained in it, i.e. a divine being:"[52]

> 6. May those splendid timber trees which the God-loving forest-dwellers have firmly planted on the standing posts which their axes have trimmed, bestow upon us wealth and progeny.
> 7. May those timber posts which have been cut down upon the earth, and which have been fabricated by the craftsmen be helpful in accomplishing benevolent works, and bear our precious gifts to divine powers.[53]

This *yūpa* is normally made of Khadira wood and is, moreover, the ritual post animals are fastened to for sacrifice.

Other implements used include vessels, ladles, and bowls and, again, *śrauta* literature notes the woods they are to be made from and the ways they must be made.[54] The Bṛhadāraṇyaka Upaniṣad, for example, describes four things that are to come from the Uḍumbara tree – the spoon, the bowl, the fuel, and the two churning rods (for making the fire)[55] – suggesting, again, the "similarity" principle by which fertile things used in the ritual make the ritual fertile. The stick used to drive the cows is of special import also, and is to be cut only from the Palāśa tree and only from the Lomaśaka type of Palāśa tree. Long descriptions are given about which twig on the tree to use, the direction it must be pointing before it is cut, and the point at which the cut can be made – one, for example, "should not cut off a twig beyond the height up to which a cow can pull at (the leaves), (for) a twig beyond that (height) is not propitious to cattle."[56]

The Atharva Veda notes that some of the amulets used to ward off unwanted things are made out of plants. In a charm bestowing longevity, for example, a decorated wooden amulet is used that is made from ten different kinds of trees:

> I speak to the herbs who spread forth, who are clumpy, who have a single bud [and] who are bushy; for you I summon fibrous, segmented [and] branched plants who [are] related to the All Gods, who are powerful [and] who bring life to humans.[57]

Likewise, the Bṛhat Saṁhitā is concerned about the kinds of materials religious images are made out of – the accepted ones being wood, stone, metal, clay, and gemstones. When an image is made out of wood, many trees are rejected as inappropriate: those growing in "cemeteries, roads, temples, ant hills, gardens, penance-groves, sacred spots...[and at] the confluences of river." Moreover, trees that are stunted, withered, burnt by fire, connected to others, infested with creepers, injured because of lightning, and broken by elephants, and that contain bee hives, have been grown from hand-watering, or have fallen by themselves are not to be used either, as they are inauspicious.[58]

Ritual Foods

The Śatapatha Brāhmaṇa says clearly that plants are necessary for the sacrifice, and they are most often necessary to make food for the priests and gods to eat, the latter eating when ritual food is sent to them by the ritual fire:

> If there were no rice and barley, wherewith wouldst thou sacrifice?... If there were no other herbs, wherewith wouldst

> thou sacrifice?... If there were no forest herbs, wherewith wouldst thou sacrifice?...If there were no fruit of trees, wherewith wouldst thou sacrifice?[59]

The Bṛhadāraṇyaka Upaniṣad specifies the ten cultivated grains that are used in the ritual: rice, barley, sesamum, beans, millet, panic seeds, wheat, lentils, pulse, and vetches. When used for sacrificial purposes, these grains need to be ground up and soaked in curds, honey, and *ghī* before being offered up as part of an oblation.[60] Cakes made of different grains are offered in different directions. In the Āpastamba Śrauta Sūtra, for example, rice and barley cakes are to be wrapped up in leaves from the Uḍumbara tree, and the rice cake is to be placed to the east of where the *brahmaudanika* fire is to be set up, and the barley cake to its west.[61] Moreover, different grains are associated with different ritual powers:

> Rice is the lordly power of the plants.
> Large rice is the overlordship of the plants.
> Panic seeds are the paramount rule of the plants.
> Barley is the leadership of the plants.[62]

Even trees themselves are worshipped with ritual plant foods, and the Bṛhat Saṁhitā notes that images should be installed according to specified directions of trees. Any such tree should then be worshipped at night with a variety of offerings, including milk porridge, sweets, rice, curds, sesamum seeds, and "eatables of various kinds." The food offerings are accompanied by prayers such as the following:

> Oh tree, thou hast been selected for the worship (through an image) of the particular Deity. Salutation to thee! This worship offered by me in accordance with the scriptural rules may kindly be accepted by thee. May all those beings that dwell in this tree accept the offerings made according to the rules, and then depart to another tree for residing. May they pardon us now! We bow to them.[63]

This worship is followed, at least according to the Bṛhat Saṁhitā, with the ritual cutting down of the tree and the consequent divination according to the direction in which the tree fell to the ground.

1.2 Plants in the Cycle of Life and Death

The cycle of rebirth or *saṁsāra* includes humans and animals, but does not, in all traditions, include plants.[64] As early textual materials explore ideas about what may happen to a person after death, however, plants are brought into the process. Some of these understandings of the process classify plants among the non-animate elements, such as the sun, moon and water; others classify plants among clearly living or life-giving items, such as animals and humans or food. One early understanding of the life-cycle process is through "the redistribution of cosmic elements...(or the) well-known ritual circulation of elements,"[65] and here plants feature as a destination or way station for parts of the dead person on his journey. The verse RV 10.16.3, for example, is from a hymn spoken to Agni as the cremation fire, but here the hearer is the dead man himself:

> May your eye go to the sun, your life's breath to the wind. Go to the sky or to earth, as is your nature; or go to the waters, if that is your fate. Take root in the plants with your limbs.[66]

sūryaṁ cakṣur gachatu vātam ātmā
dyām ca gacha pṛthivīṁ ca dharmaṇā
apo vā gacha yadi tatra te hitam
oṣadhīṣu prati tiṣṭhā śarīraiḥ

With this verse, the dead man is "projected back into the three-leveled world according to the cosmic law *(dharman)*...an obvious reversal of the cosmogonic process outlined in the *puruṣasūkta* *(Ṛg Veda* 10.90.13), where the sun is born from the eye of the sacrificial god, Puruṣa, the wind from his breath *(prāṇa)*, the moon from his mind."[67] Filliozat suggests in hymn sixteen the early presence of the five elements,[68] the *mahābhūtas:* the eye is the flash of fire, the life's breath is air, the sky is ether, the earth earth, and the waters water.

RV 10.16.3's ritual dismissal of the dead man's components from the funeral pyre to parts of the cosmos[69] gives early suggestion not only of some kind of rebirth process, but also of plants having a place in that process as mounts either for the person after death or for the person in future new life. We note that this verse is not a description of what is thought to happen but rather a performative utterance or speech act, using the imperative tense, thought to actually bring about the desired results as the official speaks it properly in an appropriate context. Such performative speech action is found again in a Taittirīya Saṁhitā version of a similar sentiment:

> The ancient wise ones grasp
> The breath as it speedeth from the limbs;
> Go to heaven by the paths that lead to the gods;
> Be among the plants with thy members.[70]

In the Upaniṣads, the notion that plants have a place on the dead person's journey is continued. In the Bṛhadāraṇyaka Upaniṣad, Jāratkārava Ārtabhāga asks Yājñavalkya what happens to the person after his parts are distributed as follows: speech of the dead person into the fire, breath into the air, eye to the sun, mind to the moon, hearing to the quarters, self to the ether, hairs of the body to the herbs *(oṣadhi)*, hairs on the head to the trees *(vanaspati)*, and blood and semen into the water. Although Yājñavalkya's answer focuses on *karma*,[71] there is little doubt that the view that a person is recycled back into the world at death, and that that world clearly includes plants, is a powerful and prevailing one. Important to remember here – as in RV 10.16.3 – is that the world the dead person goes to is primarily an inanimate world, and that plants are seen as part of a world of the five elements, but separate from those elements as they make up the world of animals and humans. Nevertheless, that plants in Vedic texts are an intricate part of the recycling process for persons after death is a significant cornerstone for emergent arguments about their vitality and sentience.

Plants are again associated with hairs on a person in the Aitareya Upaniṣad's description of the creation of the cosmic person *(puruṣa):* once the skin is separated out, it gives rise to the hairs, and from the hairs come plants and trees *(oṣadhi-vanaspatayaḥ)*.[72] Describing the reverse process – of powers entering into the cosmic person *(puruṣa)* – the Aitareya notes: "Plants and trees *(oṣadhi-vanaspatayo)*, becoming hairs, entered the skin."[73] Again, plants growing from earth are homologized to hair growing out of the head in the Muṇḍaka Upaniṣad's description of how the world arises from the imperishable: "As a spider sends forth and draws in (its thread), as herbs *(oṣadhi)* grow on the earth, as the hair (grows) on the head and the body of a living person, so from the Imperishable arises here the universe," and from "him (proceeds) fire whose fuel is the sun; from the moon, the rain; herbs *(oṣadhi)* on the earth."[74] Finally, in the Subāla Upaniṣad, as the person *(puruṣa)* came into being, there sprang forth: "from the hairs herbs and trees of the forest *(oṣadhi-vanaspatayo).*"[75] Speaking to all of these passages, N. Ross Reat has tabulated the first Aitareya Upaniṣad's passage on evolutionary correspondences as follows:

Bodily Part	First Evolute	Second Evolute
mouth	speech	fire
nose	in-breath	wind
eye	sight	sun
ear	hearing	quarters
skin	*hair*	*plants*
heart	mind	moon
navel	out-breath	death
penis	semen	water[76]

Here, plants are seen to belong to the process of the evolution of life in the world as we know it but, in that, are classed in a category made up of non-animate elements, i.e., under the second evolute. Note the association of plants and skin, as it will appear again in the discussion of plants and touch.

Sāṁkhya philosophy,[77] prefigured in these Upaniṣadic passages, presents three kinds of evolutionary enumerations: (a) those relating to basic principles, (b) those relating to fundamental predispositions, and (c) those relating to the phenomenal, empirical world of ordinary life. Plants appear in at least two of these three categories. In the first (a), the final basic principle is those "collocations of gross elements that generate one-time-only gross bodies that are womb-born, egg-born, *seed-born,* and moisture-born," placing plants squarely in basic Sāṁkhya evolution spawned by the conjunction of nature *(prakṛti)* and the soul *(puruṣa).* And in the second (c), among the enumerations concerning the phenomenal, empirical world of ordinary life, is the set of five *mukhyasrotas,* or "first or initial streams," being defined as "plant and other simple life forms."[78] This clearly suggests that, with the codification of Sāṁkhya ideas, plants are classified within the evolution of life forms, albeit as an initial or base form.

The Upaniṣadic view of the great person cycling through the cosmos and emerging from plants as food for those on earth is reflected in a passage from the Mahābhārata. Dhaumya, searching for the course rightly supported by law or *dharma,* says the following to Yudhiṣṭhira:

> When the creatures were first created, they suffered great hunger, and in his compassion for them the Sun acted like a father. Going his northern course he absorbed with his rays the saps of heat; then, on returning to his southern course, the Sun impregnated the earth. Thereupon, when he had become the fields, the Lord of the Herbs collected the heat from heaven, and, with the water, engendered the herbs. Thus the Sun, having gone unto earth, and ejaculated by the fervors of the moon, is born as the herbs of the six flowers, which are sacrificial, and thus is he born as the food of the living ones on earth.[79]

Suggestive of the course of the gods *(devāyana)* and the course of the fathers *(pitṛyāna)* – when the sun is in his northern course *(uttarāyana)* and when the sun *(dakṣiṇāyana)* is in his southern course, respectively[80] – this epic passage confirms not only the power of this view of the intercycling of worldly elements, but the continued place of plants in it.

Connected here is the other version of Upaniṣadic cycle followed by the dead. BĀU 6.2.15 and 16 describe a deceased's journey to the world of the gods *(devaloka)* and the world of the fathers *(pitṛloka)*[81] – the former is attained by those who live a life of the mind in forest meditation, and the latter is attained by those who practice sacrificial offerings, charity, and austerities. Those who have passed through the world of the fathers (following the sun's southern course), after having gone from the smoke of the cremation fire into the night, into the half-month of the waning moon, and into the six months when the sun travels southward, then move on from the world of the fathers into the moon where they become food *(anna)*. As food, they are fed upon by the gods, and then pass from them into space; they then pass sequentially into air, rain, and earth, where they become food again to be eaten by human beings. This progression is amplified in CU 5.10.5-6 where the dead pass from space into air and then smoke; moving from smoke, they pass into mist, then clouds, then rain, and are born on earth "as rice and barley, herbs and trees, as sesamum plants and beans."[82]

The interconnection between the food of the earth and plants is given further in BĀU 6.4.1: "The earth, verily, is the essence of all these beings; of earth (the essence is) water; of water (the essence is) plants *(oṣadhi);* of plants (the essence is) flowers; of flowers (the essence is) fruits; of fruits (the essence is) the man *(puruṣa);* of man (the essence is) semen."[83] Here plants are no longer just a part of a cycle of inanimate, elemental interconnections, but now also a part of a cycle that is vital and life enhancing. The missing, but obvious, connection here is food; in that humans eat food, they eat plants, and without this food they cannot live. Plants, hence, become the essence of the person.

The context from which this last passage comes is a ritual setting designed to encourage procreation and generativity as the sacrifice proceeds, and this includes a discussion of the hourglass-shaped sacrificial altar, or *vedi,* which resembles a woman's torso and which homologizes female fecundity. The grass that represents the (pubic) hairs of the *vedi* is *barhis*, a strew of Kuśa grass:

> Her lower part is the (sacrificial) alter *[vedi]*: (her) hairs the (sacrificial) grass *[barhis]*, her skin the *soma*-press. The two labia of the vulva are the fire in the middle...(he) knowing this, practices sexual intercourse; he turns the good deeds of the woman to himself but he, who without knowing this, practices sexual intercourse, his good deeds women turn into themselves.[84]

Verse five of this section continues the use of plants as vehicles for generativity in the ritual – once again in sexual terms. Of semen spilled while awake or asleep, he "should touch it or (without touching) recite: 'Whatever semen of mine has spilt on earth, whatever has flowed to the plants *(oṣadhi)*, whatever to water, I reclaim this very semen, let vigour come to me again, let luster (come to me) again; let glow (come to me) again.'"[85] Note here the homology of water and semen in the AU 1.1.4 tabulation, as well as that of plants and (pubic) hair.

Finally, we return to that part of the Vedic death rites known as the Sapiṇḍīkaraṇa, where through ritual action involving rice balls, there is the "blending of the deceased with his forefathers...(and the) transforming (of) the vulnerable, disembodied spirit *(preta)* of this world into the secure pitṛ of that other world."[86] In order to move from the danger of being a disembodied spirit here to the security of being *pitṛ* among the other *pitaraḥ* of his own kind, the deceased needs the right body, or series of bodies, as well as proper nourishment. This comes about by worshipfully honoring the grain *piṇḍa,* which represents the *preta's* original very subtle body, over a period of ten days at the end of which the *preta* not only has a new and proper body, but is endowed with digestive powers so that he may no longer be hungry.[87] In this way, plant grain is central to the ritual mechanics that cycle the deceased into his next existence.

1.3 Medicinal Uses of Plants

That plants may be living and invigorating beings is suggested as well in their use to treat human sickness. Plants are known not only to have nutritive value and to provide long life,[88] but to be important allies in the curing of ailments,[89] and as antidotes for poisons.[90] As Rajan notes, from "the ancient Indian point of view there is no herb which does not possess medicinal property"[91] and, as previously observed by Zimmer, "there are strictly speaking, no herbs whatsoever that are destitute of healing power."[92] Early on, Vedic texts celebrate plants as healing to the body and restorative to the spirit. In a hymn asking for relief from bleeding wounds, AV 2.3.6 calls on plants for aid: "Weal be to us the waters, (and) propitious (be) the herbs."[93] Again, the long passage in TS 4.2.6, noted above as using material from RV 10.97, repeatedly calls on plants for help with illness.

> In that in strength I seize / These plants in my hand,
> The soul of the disease perisheth, / As before one that taketh alive.
> When plants come together...
> (they are the) overpowerer of diseases.
> Beyond all obstacles, / Like the thief the pen, they have strode,
> The plants have shaken away / Every defilement in the body.
> Rich in steeds, rich in Soma, / Full of strength, full of power,
> I have found all the plants / For his safety.
> The plants whose king is Soma, / And which have entered the earth, Of them thou art the highest, / Impel us to long life.
> Falling from the sky / The plants said,
> 'He, whom we reach while in life, / Shall not come to ill.'[94]

Passages dealing with the Agnicayana also appear in the Śatapatha Brāhmaṇa and there, again, they extol the medicinal powers of plants. Just before the Śatapatha text calls for use of the Taittirīya Saṁhitā material on plants quoted above, it turns to the question of the gods' need to put Agni Prajāpati together on the ground. To put him together, he must be healed with healing medicine: "It is (seed) of all herbs: all herbs is the same as all (kinds of) medicine: by all (kinds of) healing medicine he thus heals him."[95] As a passage spoken for the preparation of the ground, it echoes the sentiment of AV 12.1.17 and 19 that understand that there is a connection between earth and plants, and that to propitiate the former the ritualist must attend as well to the latter: the "all-producing...mother of herbs, the fixed earth...Agni is in the earth...in the herbs."[96]

The medical practices of the Indus Valley Culture are little known to us, but seals showing plants and trees indicate that they are almost certainly significant in religious practice and most likely important in medical practice as well.[97] The Ṛg Veda is familiar with the *bhiṣaj,* or physician, who is generally a healer of human diseases, and specifically one who knows how to heal with herbs.[98] Disease in this period is thought "to be largely due to the visitation of punishing gods or to the evil work of demons,"[99] and several gods, including Varuṇa and the twin Aśvins, are associated with combating illness – Rudra, especially, is thought to promote the use of healing herbs.[100] The most important early hymn to the healing plants, RV 10.97, notes that herbal medicine is commonly used to treat consumption (or tuberculosis; *yakṣma)* as well as a number of other illnesses. Although one of the great healing plants of the Ṛg Veda is Soma, the divine king of plants,[101] there is, in general, an absence of references to "an elaborate medical botany in the hymns of the *Ṛgveda.*" And this "points to the presence of a tradition of professionals specializing in magic and medicine, particular to the *Atharvaveda.*"[102]

The great medical text of the Vedic period, then, is the Atharva Veda. The use of healing plants is associated here with the work of the Atharvan and Aṅgirasa priests,[103] though these priests are not necessarily associated with all the healing uses that can be made of plants. While many things are used for healing besides plants, particularly in the making of amulets – out of water, fire, wood, and metals and minerals – plants are certainly the single most important item in the Atharvan pharmacy, suggesting that this text represents "an indigenous tradition already possessing knowledge of the surrounding flora and its usefulness to mankind."[104] Plants are used to treat specific diseases – for example, leprosy,[105] joint problems,[106] impotence,[107] wounds,[108] fevers,[109] thinning hair,[110] and general restoration to health.[111] Note, for instance, the following passages from AV 8.7, a hymn to healing plants for rejuvenating a person to good health:

4. I speak to the herbs *(oṣadhi)* who spread forth, who are clumpy, who have a single bud [and] who are bushy; for you I summon fibrous, segmented [and] branched plants who [are] related to the All Gods, who are powerful [and] who bring life to humans *(puruṣajīvana)*.
6. In order that this [man] may be unharmed, I invoke here the vigorous, harmless life-giving herb *(jīvantīmoṣadhīm)*, the saving honey-sweet flower, Arundhatī.
13. However many herbs *(oṣadhi)* [there] are on the earth, let those with a thousand leaves release me from death [and] from distress.
19. Let all [those] herbs *(oṣadhi)* heed my words, so that we may rescue this man from difficulty.[112]

Plants are also used to treat issues of sociological and cultural nature, such as winning an argument,[113] winning a man,[114] victory over a rival wife,[115] acquiring a son,[116] turning away evil and witchcraft,[117] and exorcism.[118] That plants, and other products in the Atharvan pharmacy, are used for healing over such a broad spectrum of human afflictions indicates that the Indian physician is beginning to develop "away from the witch-doctor, thaumaturge, and magician, and...(is) in the process of becoming a true physician."[119]

The use of plants for healing reaches systematic maturity in the practice of Āyurveda, the science of long life. This tradition is "linked with sacred lore as an *upāṅga* or secondary science associated with the *Atharva Veda*,"[120] and it provides the foundation for classical Indian medicine. Although much about a current human life is given by past *karma*, efforts to maximize good health and longevity can make a difference. According to Āyurveda, bodily health is based on proper balance of the three natural *doṣas* or humors, *vāta/vāyu* or wind, *pitta* or bile, and *kapha* or phlegm,[121] while mental health is related to the activities of the *guṇas* or strands: *sattva* or goodness, *rajas* or passion, and *tamas* or dullness. Full health in the person depends upon the holistic interweaving of therapies that will bring about a restoration of balance in the humors – a process greatly facilitated by the careful use of plant medicines[122] – and a movement from *tamas* to *sattva* in mental quality.[123]

Āyurveda uses plants not only for curing and preventing specific illness, but also for maintaining a healthy balance in the person, physically and spiritually – thus, Indian medicine is both "invigorative and disease-destroying."[124] There are two types of medicines, the material and the non-material. Non-material treatments include fasting; exposing oneself to winds, sunlight or shade; using incantations and consolatory measures; giving gifts; and subjecting the patient to fear, torment, agitation, delight, hilarity, chiding, sleep, wakefulness, and massage.[125] Material treatments include various kinds of drugs to be used internally and externally and, according to the Caraka Saṁhitā, "the earliest surviving Sanskrit medical manual,"[126] these drugs come from three sources: animal,[127] earth,[128] and plant. The plants used for making drugs belong to four types: 1. *vanaspati,* that bear only fruits, without passing through the flower stage; 2. *vānaspatya,* that bear both flowers and fruits; 3. *oṣadhi,* that perish after they bear fruit, that is, herbaceous annual plants; and 4. *vīrudh,* that are climbers and spreaders, known by their tendrils and vines. The parts of plants that are used in medicinal treatment include root, bark, heartwood, secretions, stalk, alkali, latex, fruit, flower, ash, oil, thorn, leaves, leaf-buds, tubers, and sprouts.[129] According to the Agni Purāṇa, the kinds of medicines made from plants fall into five groups: *rasa* or liquid that is made by crushing plants or plant parts; *śṛta* or liquid made by boiling plants; *phāṇṭa* or newly made *śṛta; kalka* or husk retrieved from the winnowing of flowers, fruits, and seeds; and *śīta* or secretion from plants that occurs during the night.[130] Unlike drugs made from minerals, drugs made from plants require little prior or elaborate treatment before they are used and plant preparations, therefore – decoctions, infusions, pastes, powders – "are comparatively easy, simple and quick."

> Further, the patient's life or health is not endangered by an excessive dosage of the plant-drugs, and therefore are safer to use. Above all, the raw-materials for plant drugs are easily available in the country. These are some of the reasons why Indian medicine employs plant-drugs almost exclusively.[131]

When collecting natural or wild plant materials to be used in making drugs, much attention is paid to the conditions in which the plants are growing. The Suśruta Saṁhitā, another canonical Āyurvedic text, advises not to pick plants growing in soil that has holes, chasms, fissures, or is otherwise uneven; that has gravel, stones, and ant-hills; or that is saline or dry. Instead, one should look for soil that sustains much vegetation, that is soft, pliant, and firm (i.e., not sandy), and that may be black, red, or white in color. Because certain soils are especially beneficial to the curative properties of certain plants, care needs to be taken to make sure that healing plants are picked from their proper types of soils and in their proper regions. The plants themselves should not be afflicted with worms, have fumes, be marked by cuts or injuries, be damaged by too much sun, wind, burning, or water, and should be well-nourished, deep-rooted, and growing, preferably, in the eastern direction. In addition, the overall quality of soil and climate has an affect on the efficacy of plants that heal: mild drugs should be picked only from mild soils and severe ones only from severe soils; likewise, mild drugs should be picked only in mild seasons and severe ones only in severe seasons.[132] Āyurvedic practice then correlates the soil and climatic background of the plants used in healing to the specific conditions of the patient who is to be treated – including the kind of environment the patient has come from – so that the plant medication is individually tailored to be as beneficial as possible to the particular patient in need.[133] In this way, Āyurvedic plant treatments can be regionally specific, as a guide published by the Nepal Ayurveda Association attests at the beginning of the text:

> Nearly five hundred kinds of medicinal plants including nutritional fruits and vegetables have been used in Ayurvedic texts. These plants grow in different climates (alpine, sub-alpine, temperate, tropical and sub-tropical) of Nepal, India and other countries.[134]

Medical use of plants is attested in the early Buddhist context as well and, like Āyurveda, Buddhist medicine may well have derived some of its treatments "from ancient Indian culinary traditions."[135] In addition to the five basic medicines used in Buddhist healing – *ghī,* fresh butter, oil, honey, and molasses – the Pali canon gives evidence that plant materials are added as part of a larger pharmacy for the early Saṅgha. These include roots, tree extracts, leaves, fruits, gums and resins. In general, the root is considered to be "the most medicinal part of the plant," with lists of what falls into each of the five categories differing somewhat between Buddhist and Āyurvedic sources.[136] Buddhist texts also know of plants that are poisonous, and the Jātakas have numerous references to poisonous fruits and trees, whose real, unhealthful nature is known only to the experts.[137] The Girnār Rock Edict I, found near Junagadh, says:

> Medicinal herbs *(oṣadhi)*, suitable for men and animals, have been imported and planted wherever they were not previously available. Also, where roots *(mūla)* and fruits *(phala)* are lacking, they have been imported and planted.[138]

Thus, it is clear from this description of botanical practice by King Aśoka that Buddhist institutions continued to be involved in procuring and using plants for medicine.

1.4 Plants and Ethics of Non-Violence

The attribution of life to plants is further raised by the ethic of non-violence. According to this argument, if *ahiṁsā* has as its object not only humans and animals, but plants as well, then the fact that plants can be killed indicates that they must have life. The doctrine of *ahiṁsā* arises out of the Vedic period in the context of the Upaniṣads, Jainism, and Buddhism and, although there are strong strains of it in many Indian traditions, the quest to live non-violently with regard to plants is complex.

Vedic and Early Hindu Views

Ethics of non-violence are more or less absent in the early Vedic tradition that has, as a central myth, the story of the god Indra's slaying of the serpent Vṛtra, and a ritual practice that includes the sacrifice of animals. Hymns like RV 1.32, for example, dramatically describe the cosmogonic slaying of the serpent by Indra in order to free life-giving light and water for human beings. Almost every verse of the hymn notes that Indra kills *(han),* fights *(yudh)*, and obstructs *(pari sthā)* his enemy Vṛtra, and notes that he does so with the murderous weapon, the *vajra,* or thunderbolt. Slain, the hymn goes on to say in verses 8 and 5, Vṛtra lies flattened on the ground like "a broken reed" and "a tree whose branches have been lopped off by an axe."[139] Although the story celebrates Indra's release of life-giving resources to human communities, the violence of his act does not go unnoticed for, by the end of the hymn, the avenging of Vṛtra's death and the flight of Indra have become issues. It is not unimportant also that, in these verses, the dead Vṛtra is compared to violated plants, suggesting, perhaps, that the latter, like Vṛtra, have once been alive and are now dead.

A later example of ritualized violence is the Vedic animal sacrifice, which occurs either as an independent offering, the

Nirūḍhapaśubandha, or as part of the Soma ritual in which a goat is offered to Agni and Soma. The Nirūḍhapaśubandha is performed every six months or every year by the petitioner who sets up the fires before he eats meat. Following the form of the new moon ritual, the animal victim takes the place of the milk oblation; here the victim is a goat, but in other forms of the ritual, other animals are used – oxen, sheep, doves, owls, hares, black dogs, and asses – while animals such as certain dogs, boars, and rams are excluded from use. After ritual prayers are spoken to the tree – prefiguring later systematic attention to care for plant life – the sacrificial post or *yūpa* is cut.

> ...The tree is solemnly cut down with protestations that it is not being injured, and, when a splinter is struck out of it in the cutting, that (splinter) is kept and placed ultimately in the pit in which the post is inserted. The stump is treated with respect, and receives a libation, accompanied by a prayer that it shall spring up with a hundred shoots.[140]

The animal is then bathed, dedicated to the principle divinity, and tied to the post. After the animal is immolated by fire, the sacrificer's wife pours water over its limbs. Cut open, the body of the animal is dissected and parts, including the omentum and various organs, are cooked further, offered up to the prevailing divinities, and eventually tasted by the priests. As a part of the concluding activities, the worshipper again prays to the sacrificial *yūpa*.[141] Thus, even in two places where violence is ritualized, the Vedic tradition interweaves clear sentiments concerning plants as living entities deserving nurturance, protection, and veneration.

In addition to incorporating ritualized violence (here to animals) into Vedic practice, another approach is found as well: the brushing aside of the possibility that injury is taking place. In the case noted above, for example, when the tree is cut down to be used as the ritual post, a blade of grass is put over the place where the axe will hit the tree and the axe is ordered not to harm the tree. Examining these directives, Keith notes that

> the prescription is precisely the same as that adopted in the domestic ritual when the hair is cut, and in the ordinary cult

> when the victim is slain: *the aim is clearly to avoid injury to the life in the tree by pretending that it is not being injured.*[142]

Another example of what we might call "avoidance of the issue" occurs in the domestic prescriptions for clearing the land before building a house. Given that these rules are addressed in the Gṛhya Sūtras – signifying a clear sanctity and ritual oversight to many of the activities that take place outside the solemn ritual of the *śrauta* sphere and outside the rite of passage arenas of the *saṁskāras* – the ground clearing rules offer what might be considered an authoritative view. In clearing the ground, then, further rules deem certain plants as unpropitious to the well-being of the new home (e.g., those with thorns and milky juice, and those designated as *apāmārga,* potherbs, *tilvaka,* and *parivyādha*), and these plants must be dug up, roots and all, and removed.[143] There is no mention here of possible violence to these plants, only the indirect suggestion that they may be injurious to those newly established in the dwelling.[144] In the Vasiṣṭha Dharma Sūtra, for example, this sentiment is echoed when the king's duties in this regard are described: "He should not damage trees that produce flowers and fruits, but may cut them down to facilitate cultivation or for household needs."[145] Again, the sentiment here seems to be less about nonviolence towards plants, and more about how useful some plants may be in the long term for human benefit.

Suggestions of a view that plants are alive, and not to be injured, do, however, appear sporadically in Vedic passages. In RV 10.146, a hymn to the forest as Araṇyānī, two verses raise the issue:

> 4. Here is a man who calls his cow; here is another one...(who) cuts down the timber; and another one, tarrying in the forest, seems to have heard some one screaming.
> 5. But the Queen of wild life injures none unless some one assails the creatures; men feeding upon the sweet fruit, are free to take with them the fruits, as much as they wish.[146]

Although it is a stretch, yet plausible, to interpret verse four as suggesting that the some one who is screaming is the tree being cut down, verse five provides a protective deity for the living creatures of the forest who seem to include the flora of the forest as well. Moreover, plant products are then enjoyed as food by humans, suggestive of a cycle in which the living support the living. Again, in a Taittirīya Saṁhitā passage from the animal sacrifice of the Soma ritual, it is said that: "They kill the Soma in that they press it."[147] Here we note that although this is not a prescription of non-violence for Soma, the 'killing' of Soma does tell us something about plant life: if Soma is killed then Soma must be alive; and since Soma is the king of plants (TS 6.1.9), then all plants must be able to be killed, and hence must also all be alive. Again, in a Śatapatha Brāhmaṇa passage from the fire preparations of the Soma ritual, a note is made about the Uḍumbara wood used as firewood:

> ...the Uḍumbara is food and sap: with food and sap he thus regales him. They are fresh (green), for that part of trees which is fresh is uninjured and living; he thus regales him with what is uninjured and living in trees.[148]

Finally, a clear inclusion of plants within an ethic of non-violence appears as a hallmark of Vedic and Hindu *dharma* tradition in the Manu Smṛti, a *dharma* text based on the Manava Dharma Śāstra. In a section on lawful and forbidden food where non-injury is discussed, it is said that: "Herbs, trees, cattle, birds, and (other) animals that have been destroyed for sacrifices, receive (being reborn) [in] higher existences *(ucchritīḥ punaḥ)*."[149] Not only are plants *(oṣadhi)* and trees *(vṛkṣa)* here classed with the other beings who are accepted as living, and subject to rules about injury and violence, but they are also included in the cycle of rebirth driven forward by the processes of *karma.* Manu, importantly, goes on to state that, as with moving creatures *(cara)*, those creatures who do not move *(acara)*, i.e., plants, can be injured, though in some cases where this happens the actions are not to be considered injurious, for in these cases "the sacred law shone forth from the Veda."[150]

In other texts, as well, plants are understood to be alive because their lives can be taken, often through murderous means. In the epic tradition of the Rāmāyaṇa, for example, the horror of killing trees is reflected in the description of slain demons: the demons fall down "deformed and deprived of their lives, (lying) on the ground like trees whose roots have been severed." And, again in the Rāmāyaṇa, "they fell down to the earth like mighty trees of many boughs,"[151] while in Jātaka 493, the Bodhisattva teaches that the "tree that gives you pleasant shade, to sit or lie at need, You should not tear...down, [as it is] a cruel [and] wanton deed."[152]

By way of interpretation, Hanns-Peter Schmidt has important views about the origin of *ahiṁsā.* Although in modern India, he argues, *ahiṁsā* "is inseparably connected with vegetarianism... originally ahiṁsā had nothing to do with vegetarianism."[153] Rather, *ahiṁsā* begins "not so much (as) a condemnation of the Vedic ritual and its animal sacrifices, but rather the propagation of a renouncer-like conduct."[154] In this way, the ethic of non-violence arises out of a desire to market for public consumption a certain view about how renunciants should act. Arguing from passages in Dharma literature, Schmidt finds that a *brāhmaṇa* is defined by the fact that he does not cause injury, or only small injury, to living beings by, for example, abstaining from agricultural work: "(for) the wooden (implement) with iron point injures the earth and the (creatures) living in the earth."[155] By a vow of *ahiṁsā,* a *brāhmaṇa* can attain heaven, supernatural powers, and higher bliss, and in this way *ahiṁsā* belongs among those vows that are specifically "not expected of the common man."[156] Schmidt notes, moreover, that the *saṁnyāsin* or wandering renunciant ascetic must follow rigid rules of non-violence and cites Manu 6.46 where the ascetic must be extremely careful about where he puts his foot, for fear of injuring tiny creatures, and about drinking water that has been strained with a cloth to free it of small living beings.[157]

The Vedic renunciant vow of *ahiṁsā* allows those under it to accept only food that has been acquired, that is, killed, by others.[158] While this is more easily done in the case of meat, much discussion around this issue focuses on plant materials. Again, Dharma literature notes that "the ascetic shall not take any limb of plants and trees if it is not (already) separated and that he shall avoid the destruction of seeds," and an Īśa Upaniṣad passage argues that "the sannyāsin must live only on food that is abandoned voluntarily and spontaneously."[159] Again, the Pāraskara Gṛhya Sūtra prescribes that a Vedic student must gather fire wood in the forest without injuring trees, that is, wood that has fallen to the ground by natural course.[160] The inclusion of plants under the ethic of *ahiṁsā* receives early notice in Manu 5.40 where, among the beings that are reborn in higher existences, are plants *(oṣadhi)* and trees *(vṛkṣa)*, and 5.44 where injury to unmoving beings *(acara,* i.e., plants) is discussed as if it were a known and common idea.[161]

Where, however, does the idea of *ahiṁsā* come from? Returning to Schmidt's argument, we find that he locates it in ritual and magical ideas of the *śrauta* practice that focus on the consequences of injuring animate beings, beginning in particular with meat. Again, it is in Manu where a pivotal verse is found:

> 'Me he (māṁ saḥ)' will devour in the next (world), whose flesh I eat in this (life); the wise declare this (to be) the real meaning of the word 'flesh' (māṁsaḥ).[162]

The "pseudo-etymology of the world *māṁsa* 'meat,'" as Schmidt describes it, reflects most importantly "the popular belief that the eater of the meat of an animal will be eaten by this animal in the next world."[163] A more generalized version of this ritual theory is found in a Śatapatha Brāhmaṇa passage: "whatever food a man consumes in this world, that (food), in return, consumes him in yonder world."[164] This view is repeated and amplified in both the Śatapatha and Jaiminīya Brāhmaṇas, in which various legends involving the "yonder world as an inverted world" are recorded: a woodcutter who once cut a tree is now a tree being cut by a woodcutter who was once the first tree being cut; an animal-slaughterer who killed an animal is now an animal being killed by animal-slaughterer who was once the first animal being killed; and a man who once ate a plant is now a plant being eaten by a man who once was the first plant being eaten.[165] Thus, as Schmithausen notes:

> Non-injury *(ahiṁsā)* appears to have started, in the Brāhmaṇa period, as a way of protecting oneself from the vengeance of injured animals (and plants) in the yonder world, and probably also from the vengeance of their congeners in this very life.[166]

In order to eliminate the untoward consequences of injuring animate beings, ritualized behavior, such as mantric invocations addressed to the beings involved in the sacrifice, are designed. But since ritual redress is not generally available to the growing number of renunciants – *brahmacārins, saṁnyāsins,* etc.–the practice of *ahiṁsā* comes into use. "The student who did not yet sacrifice and did not yet know how to eliminate by magical means the evil consequences of injuring animate beings had to practise ahiṁsā."[167] Thus, argues Schmidt,

> ...the idea of ahiṁsā (that) originated among the world-renouncers, was gradually adopted by the Brāhmaṇas and was finally considered to be a rule for the whole society whose values were determined by the precedent of the Brāhmaṇas....Ahiṁsā was one of the most prominent values established by the meta-ritualists, and it was adopted as a general rule of conduct for the Brāhmaṇa.[168]

Schmidt's theory about the origin of *ahiṁsā* argues that there is special significance for *ahiṁsā* of some of the rituals noted in Vedic texts. These practices focus on a variety of objects, and especially important here are those rituals of appeasement that are particularly directed towards plants. "Those who utilize trees for firewood," says Brian K. Smith, "or for the construction of wooden objects must perform a rite in order to avoid karmic retribution at the hand of trees in the next world."[169] RV 10.27.20 is an early example of a request for the collected plant not to injure him who is using the plant for healing: "Do not harm the man who digs you up, nor him for whom I dig you up."[170] In later examples, however, the specific ritual focus is to protect the plant itself as it is being cut for sacrificial use – in both cases, though, the prayers may have as their ultimate function the protection of human beings as they cut plants from their roots for human benefit. In the animal sacrifice, for example, when a tree is being cut down to be used as the sacrificial post or *yūpa:*

> ...precautionary measures are taken to prevent it from being injured: "'O plant, protect it,' he (the adhvaryu) says in order to protect it. 'O axe, do not injure it' – with these words he

> puts this (blade of darbha-grass) between it (the tree) and the thunderbolt – the axe is, in truth, a thunderbolt – so that there be no injury."[171]

The Śatapatha Brāhmaṇa includes the recitation of a similar verse when the altar for the New and Full Moon Sacrifice is being prepared. As the officiant cuts the grasses to put on the ritual ground as the "armour of the earth," he says:

> 'O earth, that affordest the place for making offerings to the gods! May I not injure the root of thy plant!' He thereby makes her, as it were, with roots remaining in her. Whilst he takes up (the earth dug up by the sword), he thus addresses her: 'May I not injure the roots of thy plants!'[172]

Moreover, Manu requires that whenever one cuts fruit trees, shrubs, creepers, or flowering plants, one hundred verses must be recited in penance[173] and, in a number of Purāṇas, the felling of a tree without permission counts as a penal offense.[174] The Bṛhat Saṁhitā notes that when worshipping a tree a *brāhmaṇa* should say the following: "O great tree, hail to thee! The king elects thee for (making) the banner of the Lord of Gods. Kindly accept this worship," or "Oh Tree, thou hast been selected for the worship (through an image) of the particular Deity. Salutation to thee! This worship offered by me in accordance with the scriptural rules may kindly be accepted by thee."[175] In Kauṭilya's Arthaśāstra, it is prescribed that, whenever sowing seeds, those to be laid down first should be bathed in water and, with a piece of gold, sown with this verse: "Salutation to God Prajāpati Kaśyapa. Agriculture may always flourish and the goddess (may reside) in seeds and wealth."[176]

As an ethic of non-violence evolves in the Vedic and Hindu traditions, and as plants come to have a place as objects of that ethic, a hierarchy of objects subject to *ahiṁsā* develops as well. David Kinsley says of the cycle of rebirth that "there is a general tendency for life to evolve into higher forms; in the animal and plant realms, life naturally becomes more complex with the passage of time." That plants are normally thought to be at the bottom of the evolutionary hierarchy of beings translates into a hierarchy that is observed when eating: less violence is done when one eats from the lower realms of living beings than when one eats from the higher. Concerning vegetarianism, he says, "the aim is to keep to a minimum the amount of violence one performs in the course of daily life. Restricting one's diet to vegetables minimizes the amount of violence one inflicts on sentient creatures."[177] In folklore such as the Hitopadeśa, for example, plants are continually in evidence as part of the ubiquitous food chain and, in that chain, they are consistently at the bottom, to be eaten by all above: serpents feed on sandalwood trees and on other roots, alligators on the lotuses growing in the water, bees on the flowers they fly among, monkeys on the branches they run in, and bears on the fruits and berries of their surroundings. Thus, the maxim arises that higher living beings feed on lower ones and plants normally occupy the place of lowest life form.[178]

Within the range of plant life, however, some plants are higher and some are lower. Says Smith, while "all trees are to be respected, some are valued more than others...trees, like animals and humans, are subdivided into those that are fit for participation in the sacrifice and those that are not." One trait some trees have and others don't, then, is a sacrificial quality.[179] The Śatapatha Brāhmaṇa lists those trees that can be used to provide sticks to enclose the sacrificial fire in descending auspicious order: Palāśa, Vikankata, Kārṣmarya, wood apple, cutch, or Uḍumbara.[180] Sacrificially valued trees are also assigned to each caste or *varṇa: brahman* trees include the Palāśa (or Parṇa), wood apple, and Plakṣa; *kṣatriya* trees include the Nyagrodha (banyan), Kārṣmarya, clutch, and occasionally the Pippala (peepal); and *vaiśya* trees include the Pippala and Uḍumbara.[181] Thus:

> Pictured as the "hair" of the earth or of the creator god, trees were regarded as close kin to humans. Together with plants, animals, water, the trees were among the inhabitants with whom humans shared the earth...the social world was projected into the natural world in such a way as to break down any perception of difference between the two realms. The world of trees and the social world of humans became two mutually reflecting versions of the same order of things; nature and society melded into one gigantic scheme organized by *varna*.[182]

While the material above paints a broad picture supporting a Vedic-based worldview in which plants are understood to be alive and to be clear objects of *ahiṁsā* – enough so as to warrant substantial effort to appease plants with ritualized prayers that are delivered to them at moments of their injury or death[183] – this picture is not the only one in the tradition. Taking one text as an example, the Manu Smṛti, we find that there are, in fact, two voices. One voice, often discussing animals, but sometimes plants, clearly rules against violence to beings lower than humans on the developmental scale; this voice says that while eating meat is all right and a natural human thing to do, abstention from it brings greater spiritual rewards.[184] Another voice, however, rules that killing plants and animals, if it is for sacrificial purposes, will result in special spiritual rewards for the victim as well as for the worshipper.[185] Other more prosaic reasons for injuring or killing plants and trees, of course, prevail in Hindu life – food, clothing, lodging, tools, utensils, and traveling vehicles, for example – but rulings either against such injury by humans, or mitigation of such injury through ritual means,[186] continue to be present in Dharma and ritual literature, and continue to be present as influences in the lives of practicing Hindus.

Early Jain Views

Certainly one of the most important Indian traditions in which plants are the objects of a non-violent ethic is that of the Jains, for whom *ahiṁsā* is "the most central (ethical) concept,"[187] and for whom there is a "sensitivity toward living things...[and] a recognition of the interconnectedness of life-forms."[188]

> ...the ahiṁsā ideal is of paramount importance to every Jaina, and...Jainas as a group have traditionally been identified by Indians of all faiths with the doctrine of nonviolence...the history of their fortunes can be clearly understood as following directly from...the Jina's greatest teaching, that of ahiṁsā.[189]

Tatia notes that, concerning the environmental problems faced in the world today, "we do not recognize our own interdependence with the physical world, nor take responsibility for the violence we inflict upon it." In response to this, the Jains have consistently held the view that "souls render service to one another" and recognize "that all things are both autonomous and interdependent" with each one, especially humans, having a "joint responsibility for the common environment we create and share." In terms of *ahiṁsā,* he continues, the "insistence on life" is much more important than the "insistence on truth," because "the nature of truth varies from thinker to thinker but life is an invariable constant that is dear to all."[190]

Although it is in Bṛhadāraṇyaka Upaniṣad 3.2.10.13 where we have one of the earliest mentions "of the ethical importance of karma in the Hindu context" – in Yājñavalkya's statement that good action makes one good and bad action makes one bad – it is in the early documents of Jains, in particular the Ācārāṅga Sūtra, "the oldest extant Jain canonical work,"[191] where we begin to see good action associated with non-violence, that is, the "strict observance of ethical precepts rooted in *ahiṁsā*."[192]

Some, such as Thomas McEvilley, have suggested that the Jain tradition may have originated in the Indus Valley Culture where images have been found pointing to a proto-yoga tradition like that of Jainism – including a figure in the *mūlabandhāsana,* "a sitting yogic pose wherein one's heels are pressed against the perineum with knees pressed firmly to the ground." This figure is often associated with an array of animals, suggesting the presence of traditional *ahiṁsā*-like ideals at work as early as Harappan culture.[193] The particular move by Jainism toward *ahiṁsā* may have stemmed from a reaction against Vedic sacrifice, since for "years, Buddhists and Jainas lobbied against all animal sacrifice, using the argument that such activities violated the first and most important ethical principle: nonviolence."[194]

In Jain canonical texts, *ahiṁsā* is the key to right action, for Jain cosmology postulates that there are countless life souls *(jīva),* individual, independent, and inviolate,[195] who "reincarnate repeatedly until the rare attainment of spiritual liberation."[196] Here, the *whole world* is animated – "not only animals and plants but also the elements earth, fire, water, and air consist in atomic individual souls."[197] According to the Tattvārtha Sūtra ("Treatise on the Reals") of Umāsvāmi / Umāsvāti – "the first and most important sacred text in aphorismic" Sanskrit, thought to be "an authentic and systematic compendium of the essence of Jainism as taught and settled by Lord Mahāvīra" and respected by all denominations of Jainism with an authority that is "definitive and undisputed"[198] – there are a total of 8,400,000 varieties of birth place. These range from "beings destined to be sub-microscopic vegetation eternally" at one extreme, for whom there are 700,000 (or, alternatively, 1,000,000) birthplaces, to humans at the other, for whom there are 1,400,000.[199]

Liberation *(mokṣa)* comes about when, through active *ahiṁsā*, the *karmas* that keep an individual soul in bondage disperse.

> If souls *(jīva)* are ubiquitous, then it is clearly very difficult to do any action at all without harming them. Such harming action *(hiṁsā)* is believed to result in karmic bondage that is to say, the soul is invaded and weighted down by subtle matter which ensures that at death the *jīva* is reborn in this or another world *(saṁsāra)*, rather than rising to a state of liberation and omniscience at the top of the universe. Consequently, the more harm one does, the heavier the bondage and the worse the rebirth.[200]

Thus, "Jains adhere to the vows of nonviolence to purify their *karma* and [to] advance toward the higher states of spiritual attainment *(guṇasthāna)*."[201] The doctrine of *ahiṁsā* then becomes broadly established in the Jain tradition where they consider all matter to have life *(jīva)*.[202]

> That is to say, all acts which harmed any of the six types of living beings, whether *trasa* (mobile) or *sthāvara* (immobile), were considered to be equally binding. (To be clear about his, the ethical attitude is not so much that a man is as worthless as a mango or a louse, but that a mango or a louse is as important as a man, all *jīvas* having equal value.)[203]

In this way, plants are definitively marked as living beings and, in Jain texts, live vegetal materials – in the form of still vital mildew, seeds, and sprouts – are conspicuously avoided by renunciants on their alms rounds.[204] In practicing non-violence, by eschewing "any action accompanied by the giving of pain or the rise of passions,"[205] a mendicant is aware that "killing...is reprehensible not only for the suffering produced in the victims, but even more so because it involves intense passions on the part of the killer, passions that bind him more firmly in the grip of saṁsāra."[206] This is true even when the objects are plants and, as the first great vow shows, plants as living are incorporated into Jain understandings of *ahiṁsā*.[207]

> I renounce all killing of living beings, whether subtile or gross, whether movable or *immovable*. Nor shall I myself kill living beings (nor cause others to do it, nor consent to it).[208]

Again,

> I shall not do (acts relating to *plants)* after having entered the order...For one destroys this (body of a *plant)* by bad and injurious doings, and many other beings, besides, which he hurts by means of *plants,* through his doing acts relating to *plants (vaṇassai)* ...Knowing them, a wise man should not act sinfully towards *plants,* nor cause others to act so, nor allow others to act so. He who knows these causes of sin relating to *plants,* is called a reward-knowing sage.[209]
> All sorts of living beings should not be slain, nor treated with violence, nor abused, nor tormented, nor driven away.[210]

Again, a passage discussed in the Ācārāṅga Bhāṣyam reiterates the protective role Jain ascetics have toward the safe livelihood of all sentient beings: "The monk who does not offend others should not preach anything that is conducive to violence to living beings. Such a great monk is a shelter like an unflooded island to all animates, living beings, souls, and sentient entities."[211]

A Jain monk *(sādhu)* or nun *(sādhvī)* may not walk on pilgrimage during "the rain [that he or she] (...might injure) living beings, mildew, seeds, grass, water, mud."[212] Mendicants may not go to a special occasion "if on their way there, there are many living beings, many seeds, many sprouts," but may go to such an occasion only if "there are few living beings, few seeds."[213]

> A monk or a nun should not ease nature in a place where the householders or their sons have, do, or will put by bulbs, roots, etc....(or) where the householders or their sons have sown, sow, or will sow rice, beans, sesamum, pulse, or barley.[214]

When a Jain monk or nun enters a household, for example, he or she must examine his or her alms bowl and take out any living beings and then wipe the dust off – "The Kevalin says: This is the reason: Living beings, seeds or dust might fall into his bowl."[215]

> A monk or a nun on a begging-tour should not accept such-like raw substances as seeds or sprouts, growing on the top or the root or the stem or the knots (of a plant), likewise the pulp or blossoms of the plantain, cocoa-nut, wild date, and palmyra trees.[216]

A monk or a nun may not accept as food "flattened grains, grains containing much chaff, etc., *which a layman, for the sake of the mendicant, has ground,* grinds, or will grind, has winnowed, winnows, or will winnow."[217] This last rule thus modifies eating habits for mendicants by allowing them to accept only such food as has been specifically prepared by and for somebody else. "He is to accept only food which has been prepared, i.e., killed, by others, including water which must be boiled. Only in this way he is safeguarded against any complicity in depriving an animate being of its life."[218] Such a ruling allows the mendicant to eat without any entanglement in an intention to kill, thus freeing him or her, as noted above, from inflicting suffering on a victim or from harboring passion with regard to the victim.

The Jain Tattvārtha Sūtra confirms the prohibition on a monk's or a nun's eating of animate *(sacitta)* food, or eating anything that has come in contact with animate food, and says as well that a renunciant may not place alms food on, or cover alms food with, animate *(sacitta)* objects.[219] And in the Ācārāṅga Bhāṣyam, a renunciant should spread his straw for resting not on green grass, but only on ground that is free of living beings *(appapāṇaṁ).*[220]

Again, the Jain monk or nun

> ...should not build a house, nor cause others to erect one; for many living beings both movable and immovable, both subtle and gross, are seen to be killed when a house is being built; therefore a monk should abstain from building a house.[221]

And he or she may not accept a robe in which might be hidden other "living beings or seeds or grass."[222] Jain texts specify, as well, the kinds of weapons traditionally used to commit violence against plants. "But they indulge in violent actions to the plant-world with various weapons, which involve destruction of various other classes of beings."[223] These weapons traditionally include such things as scissors, axe, sickle-like heavy knife, spade, chisel, and hatchet; hand, feet, and mouth; weapons made of wood; weapons made of stone or fire; weapons made of mixtures of such materials; and psychic weapons of non-restraint. (Weapons made of wood are considered "homogeneous weapons" in relation to plants as potential objects of violence, and weapons made of stone or fire are considered "heterogeneous" with regard to plants.)[224] Thus the Jain ascetic is enjoined to practice *ahiṁsā* towards plants: "Comprehending this, as intelligent ascetic should not indulge in violence to the plant-world, nor should he instigate others to do so, nor should he approve of such violence committed by others."[225]

It is interesting, moreover, to note the distinction in the Ācārāṅga Bhāṣyam passages above among four words, all of which are used for living beings, and all of which are considered to be the objects of non-violence: *prāṇas, bhūtas, jīvas,* and *sattvas*. They are distinguished as follows:

(1) "The *prāṇas* (animates) are so called because they breathe in, breathe out, inhale or exhale." (Support for plants as among the *prāṇas* comes from texts like ĀBh1.101 where plants are included among the others of this class *(aṇṇe...pāṇe)* and from Akalaṅka's Tattvārtha Rājavārtika where plants are associated with respiration.[226] Others suggest that plants are not included among the class of those who breathe.)[227]

(2) "The *bhūtas* (living beings) are so called because they existed in the past, do exist in the present and will continue to exist in the future." (That plants are included here among those who grow over time is evident from passages such as Sūtrakṛtāṅga 1.9.13.)

(3) "The *jīvas* (souls) are so called because they live and subsist according to their life-span karma." (All beings in Jainism, including plants, have *jīva.*)[228]

(4) "The *sattvas* (living entities) are so called because they are possessed of good and bad deeds."[229] (That plants belong

> here is evident from the many instances of texts like the ĀBh referring to the *vaṇassai-satthaṁ*, e. g., 1.101, 104, 109, 116, 117.)[230]

Although, in the course of our discussion the membership of plants in each of these groups plants will be explored, it is important to note now that, first, all of these groups of beings are the objects of the Jain ethic of non-violence and, second, that plants are among those specifically included as objects of *ahiṁsā.*

When a vow of *ahiṁsā* is taken by a Jain layperson, it is somewhat modified. He or she is allowed to injure or kill plants (who have only one sense), but not those beings who are higher on the developmental scale (those with two senses or more) – in this way minimizing the violence in which he or she engages.[231] Thus the layperson vows:

> I will desist from the knowing or intentional destruction of all great lives [trasa, *souls embodied with two or more senses].* As long as I live, I will neither kill nor cause others to kill. I shall strive to refrain from all such activities, whether of body, speech, or mind.[232]

In this way, a non-violent layperson is able to prepare vegetable dishes for Jain monks and nuns without any violation to the non-violent ethic.

Early Buddhist Views

Early Buddhism, like Jainism, reacts against the violence of the Vedic sacrifice in which a number of animals – such as "bulls, steers, goats, [and] rams" – end "their lives under the priestly blade."[233] They do this, likewise, by focusing on the ethic of *ahiṁsā,* where violence is understood as the cutting off of the faculty of life, destroying it, and harming its duration,[234] and as increasing and intensifying the suffering experienced by sentient beings.[235] Under this ethic, violence is subject to amelioration primarily by empathetic mindfulness that then gives rise to right action.

Plants, at least early on in the Buddhist tradition, are counted among living beings. As an expression of plants' inclusion among the living, and of the special concern given them by human agents, Chatsumarn Kabilsingh notes the following passage from the Sutta Nipāta:

> Know ye the grasses and the trees...Then know ye the worms, and the moths, and the different sorts of ants...Know ye also the four-footed animals small and great, the serpents, the fish which range in the water, the birds that are borne along on wings and move through the air...Know ye the marks that constitute [their] species...and their species are manifold.[236]

As living things, plants are among the objects of Buddhist *ahiṁsā* and, in that the early Buddhist obligation to preserve the sanctity of life includes plants, Padmasiri de Silva argues that the "rules for monks prohibiting cutting down trees, destroying plants, digging in the soil, and so forth may be considered as a warning that very minute forms of life may be destroyed by such action."[237] As noted in the introduction, however, the view that plants are viable objects of *ahiṁsā,* and therefore are to be counted among the living, is not a uniform view over the course of Buddhism's development. But it is a view, as Schmithausen argues, that, at least in early Pali materials, holds some significant sway.

As we will see, there are four words in Pali for sentient beings that come into play as the ethic of non-violence concerns plants: *bhūta, jīva, satta,* and *pāṇa.* When combined with *gāma, bhūta* or "growing being" refers to the vegetal kingdom and, under its rubric, plants are without doubt included as objects of non-violence. *Jīva* or 'enlivened or quickened being' can normally be applied to plants as living beings, where it is modified by *ekindriya* or "one-facultied" – an attribute often used of plants in early Pali texts and suggesting, as we will see, close ties to the contemporary Jain tradition. That *satta* is used to designate plants is evident from a Dīgha Nikāya passage describing a place on the Buddha's tour as "teeming with *satta,* (that is,) with much grassland and woodland and water and corn."[238] And, finally, is the term *pāṇa* that is least conclusive as to its inclusion of plants "breathing beings." Although usually reserved for humans and animals, there is some evidence, at least early on, that it might have included plants.

In the case of *bhūtagāma*, for example, the prescription to act non-violently ordinarily includes plants as its object, for when a monk or nun destroys vegetable growth *(bhūtagāma),* it is said to constitute a Pācittiya offense, or an offense to be confessed and expiated.[239] The Buddha himself models the practice, for in discussing the first in a list of renunciant abstentions, the Dīgha Nikāya notes that "Gotama...holds himself aloof from causing injury to seed or plants."[240] Moreover, that a monk or nun should take the vow of *ahiṁsā* seriously and be mindful of it at every moment is echoed in texts like the Majjhima Nikāya where a virtuous monk reflects on his continued practice of restraint from destroying seed- and vegetable-growth.[241] Things do not always go smoothly in adhering to *ahiṁsā* toward plants, however, for there are many people watching the behavior in the Buddhist community. One story in the Majjhima Nikāya notes that the wanderer Māgandiya goes by the house of a Bhāradvāja brahman one day and sees that the brahman has spread grass down as a bed for the Buddha to lie on when he comes by. This elicits charges from Māgandiya that the Buddha is a killer of plants:

> "Indeed, good Bhāradvāja," he says to the host, "we are seeing a poor sight in seeing the sleeping place of the good Gotama, the destroyer of growth *(bhūnahuno).*"[242]

With the use of the term *jīva* in the non-violent ethic toward plants, monks and nuns are cautioned against trampling down crops and grasses as they walk among alms donors during the rainy season, for fear they may injure one-facultied living beings *(ekindriya jīva).*[243] They are further cautioned to be mindful whenever they are walking – no matter what the season – because they may, at any time, injure plant life embedded in the dirt or growing out of the soil. When violations occur, laypeople are said to ask in the Mahāvagga:

> How can these recluses, sons of the Sakyans, walk on tour during the cold weather and the hot weather and the rains, trampling down the crops and grasses, injuring life that is one-facultied and bringing many small creatures to destruction?[244]

Again in the Mahāvagga, monks and nuns are asked not to cut down young palmyra palms to wear as shoes because they will harm one-facultied living beings.[245] And they are not to cut down trees *(rukkha)* in the course of repairing their lodgings, because in so doing they will cause injury to one-facultied living beings.[246] In describing this kind of offense, a story is told about clearing a site to be used for building a *vihāra.* In making the ground ready, it goes, the monk Channa cuts down a tree that serves as a shrine for the local people of the surrounding area. The local folk become upset and criticize Channa for not only spoiling a religious spot but for depriving a tree of its life as well. They then report the offense to the Buddha who rules against the *hiṁsā* or violence that has taken place, as a Saṅghādisesa offense – an offense that requires a formal meeting of the Saṅgha and that might result in a suspension or a temporary exclusion from the community.[247]

The term *satta* appears in several Nikāyas, as well as the Vinaya, and is used in the sense of "living being." In a number of cases, especially in passages such as A 1.35 and following, it refers to the great variety of living beings in their various births – including, perhaps, birth even in plant body. For the most part, however, it appears to refer to birth in higher states among those who can use mind and who can engage in mental cultivation[248] – that is, *satta* as "a sentient and rational being, a person."[249] Moreover, *satta* occasionally appears with these other three terms, as in D 1.53, *sabbe sattā, sabbe pāṇā, sabbe bhūtā, sabbe jīvā,* translated by T. W. Rhys Davids as: "All animals, all creatures (with one, two, or more senses), all beings (produced from eggs or in a womb), all souls (in plants)." His footnote explaining his translation is as follows:

> Buddhaghosa gives details of these four classes of living beings, showing how they are meant to include all that has life, on this earth, from men down to plants. The explanation is very confused, and makes the terms by no means mutually exclusive. They are frequently used in the same order in the Jaina-Sūtras, and Professor Jacobi renders them accordingly 'Every sentient being, every insect, every living thing, whether animal or vegetable.' Jaina Sūtras, II, xxv. This is much

> better; but we have, in our version, to give the sense in which the Buddhists supposed Gosāla to have taken the words.[250]

In whatever way we assess the T. W. Rhys Davids' discussion, however, it seems that *satta* does not normally have plants among its referents.

In the case of *pāṇa*, the precepts regarding plants are usually general, as in the Mahāvagga section of the Vinaya, where the Buddha gives ten rules for training *(dasa sikkhāpadāni),* the first of which is restraint from injuring or killing creatures *(pāṇātipātā veramaṇī),*[251] an important ruling, but one that does not specifically include plants. A particular mention of plants under the category of *pāṇa* can be found, however, in the early Sutta Nipāta in verses 146-147: "Whatever living creatures there are, moving or still, without exception...let all creatures be happy-minded."[252] Here plants are included in their common identification as those sentient beings who are "still and unmoving" or *thāvarā.*

Echoing these views of early Theravāda texts that often include plants as objects of non-violence, the Mahāsāṅghika Vinaya for nuns declares that using some kinds of grass *(tūla)* as a stuffing for a bed is a Pācattika, or confession-bound offense,[253] presumably because, as above, it involves the killing of plants. This text also prohibits a nun from defecating or urinating on living plants – and doing so is a Pācattika offense for her.

> If she urinates, defecates, spits or drivels on it, her act constitutes a pācattika offense. If the ground is covered with living grass during the rainy season, she takes care of her needs in a barren spot. If there is no barren spot, she should (take care of her needs) on a brick, tile, dried grass and wood, the excrement of cows and horses, or on a path where people pass. If (she can not find such a place), she should at least take care of her needs on a piece of branch and then drop them on some branches and finally drop them on the grass. If there is grass in the place where she walks in circles (while meditating), she should set a spittoon at the end of the area.[254]

Schmithausen's analysis of the early Buddhist material is important for showing the complexity of forces at work in the development of doctrine of *ahiṁsā* towards plants.[255] Although texts like Pācittiya 11[256] in the Pāṭimokkha, that prohibit the destruction of vegetable growth, may seem to support a pro-life plant position in the early canon, Schmithausen argues that the proscription not to injure or kill plants refers, most likely, to prevailing social views rather than to those of the renunciants themselves.[257] He notes that many local householders of the time still retain their old belief in plants as sentient beings and, although they themselves cannot consistently practice an impractical standard like *ahiṁsā,* especially with regard to plants, they think it unfit for ascetics of the time to practice anything but plant *ahiṁsā.*[258] Thus, as noted in the introduction, the Pāṭimokkha proscription on killing plants is not "an element of moral, or ethically motivated, conduct in the strict sense but...rather a matter of *ascetic decorum.*"[259] Or, as Harvey notes, "the motive of the rule seems to be to avoid offending popular sensibilities."[260]

Schmithausen further suggests the confluence of two trends:

> ...it cannot be excluded *a priori* that the Suttavibhaṅga has reduced to a mere rule of decorum what originally had (at least also) an ethical dimension; for, the Pāṭimokkhasutta itself would make equally good sense if originally also the monks themselves, and even the Buddha, still somehow held the view that plants and seeds were living beings.[261]

There was, he offers, a process in which the offense involved in killing or injuring plants gets less and less, so that at some point, plant *ahiṁsā* becomes an obsolete practice if not also an obsolete view. This "shifting emphasis from the *ahiṁsā* aspect towards matters of ascetic decorum is already evident in discussion of the Pāṭimokkha rule[262] and the exclusion of plants from the *ahiṁsā* rule then becomes, more or less, standard practice. Thus, unlike some of the stricter ethical prescriptions at the time, Buddhist practice is influenced, on the one hand, by renunciant desire to please donors (by practicing plant *ahiṁsā* themselves) and, on the other, by allowing householder donors free use of plants and plant products in their daily lives (by, at first, being silent about plants as living things and, later, actively excluding them as objects of a non-violent ethic) and thus making life easier for them in another way.

The increasing prominence of lay Buddhist practice on this issue is later reflected in the edicts of King Aśoka. The first really great Buddhist king, Aśoka shifts the dynamics of the tradition by bringing ethics (especially that of donation *(dāna)* and non-violence) into prominence, by elevating the importance of lay participation in training and discipline, and by politicizing the proselytizing mission of Buddhism. With regard specifically to the processes of ethicizing and laicizing the tradition are the many edicts that advocate non-violence as the highest ethical ideal.[263] Indeed, as Ryan notes, "the Seventh Pillar Edict states that abstention from injuring and slaying living beings is the characteristic way in which devotion to the Dhamma is demonstrated by Aśoka's subjects."[264] Over and over, Aśoka urges the "abstention from killing animals and from cruelty to living beings" *(anaraṁbho praṇa(naṁ) avihisa bhutanaṁ)*,[265] and the "abstention from the slaughter of animals" or the "abstention from killing living creatures" *(pānānaṁ anālaṁbhe)*;[266] he declares that no "living creature shall be slaughtered here" *(na kiṁ-ci jīvaṁ ārabhitpā)*;[267] and he says that he has granted life to living creatures, "two-footed and four-footed *(dupadacatupada)* as well as [to] birds and aquatic animals."[268] Moreover, he urges the importation and planting of medicinal herbs *(osuḍhāni)* that can be used for animals and humans as well as of roots and fruits[269] – suggesting that plants have life-giving properties.

One could argue that the use of *bhūta* in Rock Edict IV and of *jīva* in Rock Edict I reflect an inclusion of plants in the *ahiṁsā* ethic (note the use of *avihisa* in the former), for, as noted above, plants fall under the term *bhūta* in such Pali canon phrases as *bhūtagāma* that refer to the vegetable kingdom,[270] and renunciants are urged in Pali Vinaya texts as well not to injure one-facultied life *(ekindriya jīva),* that is, plants.[271] But there are no specific references in the Aśokan inscriptions to plants as living beings or to plants as objects of the ethic of non-violence. In addition, the other word normally used for living beings, *prāṇa/pāṇa*, refers to living beings as "breathing beings" and rarely includes plants when used in the Pali canon.[272] Thus, we may say that again, in Aśoka, plants fall on the border, and that full commitment to their place as objects of non-violence is wanting, for as Buddhism increasing caters to lay practitioners (and, thus, lay donors) there come to be few prescriptions directly urging abstention from violence to plants.

Remnants of the earlier sentiment of concern expressed whenever plants are purposely or inadvertently injured, however, can be found in later texts such as Aśvaghoṣa's Buddhacarita:

> (Siddhārtha) saw the earth, ploughed up, changed with tracks like waves of water. Seeing that earth in such a state, its young grass torn up and scattered by ploughs, and covered with small insects, worms and killed other creatures, he mourned deeply as if at the death of his own people.[273]

In spite of such views, however, that may well be directed as much to non-Buddhist audiences, the general development in Buddhism is away from listing plants as objects of *ahiṁsā* and thus away from their designation as sentient beings.

1.5 Care and Treatment of Plants

The possibility that Indian traditions understand plants to be living beings is raised, finally, in botanical sciences, where significant attention is given to gardening and to treating plant diseases. We know that the science of caring for plants is already well-developed in early India from texts like the Arthaśāstra, Kāmasūtra, Vasudevahiṇḍī, Bṛhat Saṁhitā, and the Viṣṇudharmottara and Agni Purāṇas, and that some of these texts contain specific sections on Vṛkṣāyurveda, or the science of treating and healing trees, a term that first occurs in the Arthaśāstra.[274] Vṛkṣāyurveda is

> a science result(ing)... from the application of *Āyurveda* to the phenomenon of plant. But the *Āyurveda* of human life could not totally cover all aspects of plant life. The Principle of three humors *(doṣas)* was applied to describe the character of the plants, the nature of their diseases and their treatment. But, mostly it was a case of analogy and not total application.[275]

That the science of plant care and health is called an *Āyurveda* is suggestive for, when applied to human health care, *āyur* as "life" focuses on the body, senses, mind, and soul.[276] The systems of *Āyurveda* help insure good health, and good health *(ārogya)* is a means of securing, among other things, religious merit *(dharma)* and final liberation *(mokṣa)*.[277] The Bhela Saṁhitā notes that the pursuit of *dharma,* material affairs *(artha),* and pleasure *(kāma)* "are indeed obtainable only by life (i.e., only if a person first possesses life)."[278] With some stretch, then, we may assume that the use of the term *Āyurveda* in its application to trees (and to all the other forms of plants) suggests that plants are alive, that they can be healthy and unhealthy[279] and, perhaps less clearly, that they are involved in the process of religious transformation.

We know from Vṛkṣāyurveda texts that gardening plays an important role in Indian civic life and "is closely connected with town-planning, house-building and construction of tanks."[280] The classical formulation of Vṛkṣāyurveda is by Surapāla, a scholar at the court of Bhimapala,[281] who glorifies the use of trees in public and private spaces and who "refers to the merit of planting trees on the side of a road, in a field, and in a pleasure-garden."[282] "What is the use of several trees grown in the forest," Surapāla asks, when a "single tree by the wayside is far better where under people can rest."[283] Plants and trees continue to be central features of public gardens and of overall town planning, for many Puraṇas, such as the Brahma Vaivarta, have substantial sections prescribing roadside plantings, pool-filled flower gardens, thick palisades of trees around cities for purpose of protection, and the use of plants and plant materials in the decoration of the streets, buildings, and public monuments.[284]

The planting of trees is, moreover, immensely helpful on the path to salvation:

> Knowing this truth one should undertake planting of trees since trees yield the means of attaining *dharma, artha, kama,* and *moksha* (the four aims of life).[285]
> Trees alone on the earth give happiness both here and hereafter. Since they "save" from abject poverty they are named "*taravah*" (the saviors).
> Therefore, the trees should be carefully nurtured as through their shade, flowers, and fruits they help immensely in the pursuit of *dharma, artha,* and *kama.*[286]

It is thought, based on verses like these, that Surapāla's text, like others, "was written to help conserve plant biodiversity of selected tree species," and ultimately simply "to persuade people to plant trees." As Nalini Sadhale argues, Surapāla's Vṛkṣāyurveda intends to instill the view that "trees have an important place...for an holistic development of mankind and (for) its welfare in all its spheres."[287]

In order to encourage the proper treatment of trees in public spaces, Kauṭilya's Arthaśāstra prescribes the special office of a "superintendent of forest produce." This person's job is to collect timber and other forest materials through the auspices of forest guards who monitor wooded areas that have resources useful for human life. The superintendent of forest produce is responsible not only for initiating forest works, but also for fixing fines and other compensations that are charged to any person causing damage to forests under his watch –damage incurred during natural disasters, of course, is excluded.[288] The existence of such an office is significant in that it suggests that forests, and the trees and other plants in them, can be injured or damaged – and if plants and trees can be injured, then they must be alive to suffer that injury.

Where and how to plant trees are issues that concern most writers on tree science and, along with Surapāla, the Agni and Viṣṇudharmottara Purāṇas note that trees must be planted in a certain order, in certain directions, and with certain distance between them. Surapāla adds that trees should not be planted in the front of a house when doing domestic landscaping because the shade of a tree should not fall on a human habitation.[289] It is most auspicious when the Plākṣa tree is planted to the north of a building, the Vaṭa tree to the east, the Uḍumbara tree to the south and the Aśvattha tree to the west. The trees with thorns are to be avoided, and it is inauspicious to have a garden on the left side of a residential house.[290] Following this, a multiplicity of trees is to be planted, so long as they are auspicious varieties and are planted in a certain order.[291] If a pool is installed, there should be trees hanging down along its banks so that their reflections may appear in the water – in fact, any body of water on a domesticated property is to have trees planted close by, if only for irrigation purposes.[292]

Proper soil locations for planting specific herbs, shrubs, and trees is important and Kauṭilya notes that creeper fruits grow well on banks near water; long peppers, grapes, and sugarcane on the outskirts of overflows; vegetables and roots on the borders of wells; large grasses on the banks of lakes; and plants reaped by cutting (e.g., perfume and medicinal plants) on ridges. The rule seems to be that gardeners need to know what plants do well in dry regions and what plants in wet, and to place them accordingly.[293] Soft soil is best for planting most things, and is often prepared by planting sesamum on the softest surface; when it blossoms, the sesamum plant is crushed and mixed in with the rest of the soil as a kind of fertilizer before other planting takes place.[294] Surapāla notes that there are three types of soil – barren, moist, and ordinary – and the type at the site should be noted before planting. Moreover, soil can be categorized by color (black, pale, blue, red, white, and yellow) and by taste (sweet, acid, salty, sour, bitter, and pungent), each category being appropriate for different kinds of plants. As with previous authors on Vṛkṣāyurveda, Surapāla says that the best land for plants, herbs, and trees is that which is even, has water nearby, and has a proven record of fertility, i.e., is already "full of green trees and sprouts of grass."[295]

The propagation of a plant depends on its type, and Surapāla notes four kinds – large trees *(vanaspati)* that bear fruit without flowers, other trees *(druma)* that bear fruit with flowers, creepers *(latā)* that spread by growing tendrils, and shrubs *(gulma)* that spread by growing many stems. Some of these are best propagated by sowing seeds, others by planting a section or joint of a mother plant in the ground, and others by planting a bulbous root.[296] Preparing seeds for planting involves detailed work, and Kauṭilya notes that seeds of grains need to be soaked in dew by night and dried in the heat by day for seven days, and for five nights and three days in the case of seeds of pulses. When stalks are serving as seeds they are smeared with honey, *ghī*, and pig's fat mixed with cow dung; bulbous roots smeared with honey and *ghī*; and stone-like seeds smeared with cow dung. When plants sprout, they are to be fed with fish parts and the milk of the *snuhi* plant.[297] Says Surapāla, "All kinds of seeds treated well in the process narrated above become excellent."[298] To encourage the growth of fruits and flowers, the Agni Purāṇa suggests irrigation with *ghī* and cold milk, and with powder made from goat and sheep dung mixed with barley powder and sesamum.[299]

The method of planting is discussed in great detail, and in early texts the concern is with the proper ritual formulations that accompany the plowing and the sowing. The Śatapatha Brāhmaṇa, for example, encourages plowing before sowing, saying that in each case there is healing: with sowing on unplowed ground there is healing only of vital airs, but on plowed ground there is healing both of vital airs and of other parts of the body. All of these practices are preceded by reverence of Agni who represents the season of twelve months in the agricultural calendar. Moreover, water in fifteen jars is ritually poured out, accompanied by fifteen verses combined with the water to represent the thirty syllables of Virāj meter, a referent to the wholeness of food coming from the planting process. This is followed by paeans to the powers of the plants, their stalks, and their fruits that will pierce upwards as the season progresses.[300]

The more scientific texts begin their discussions of planting with a focus on the distance between seeds and between plants, and the depth of the trench for herbs and of the pit for trees. For those seeds that must be sprouted ahead of time, Surapāla's text provides the optimal time when the sprouts can be planted in their permanent growing spots and, for all plants, the text notes the optimal fertilizers to be used and the optimal directions and times of day and season for the planting to take place.[301] When plants such as trees are to be transplanted, the Arthaśāstra prescribes different seasons for transplanting different kinds of trees – those not yet with branches in the cold season, for example, and those with grown branches in the snowy season.[302] And the Bṛhat Saṁhitā prescribes that trees to be transplanted must be smeared from root to stem with such things as *ghī*, sesamum, honey, milk, and cow dung.[303] When planting takes place in the public spaces, the Arthaśāstra provides for a "superintendent of agriculture" whose job it is to oversee the collecting of "seeds of all kinds of grains, flowers, fruits, vegetables, bulbous roots, roots, fiber producing plants, and cotton," and to employ workers to sow the seeds and roots on crown lands that have been properly plowed.[304]

Watering plants and trees is one of the ways gardeners can provide for the well being of their charges – others being protecting their vegetation from too much dew, strong winds, smoke, fire, and insects.[305] Water is known from the time of the Vedas to be a necessary element in any plant's growth, and how often and how much water to give is, in Vṛkṣāyurveda, based on the requirements of the different seasons, the locations of the gardens or fields, and the type of plants involved. A general rule is that trees that are firmly rooted or long grown should be watered both in the morning and evening in the summer, on alternate days in the winter, and in the rainy season only when the soil is dry.[306]

In addition, much attention is given to fertilizers, with young plants and trees attracting particular attention. According to Surapāla, young trees should be protected from undue heat, and should be given specially cooked mixtures of fish, animal flesh, and sesamum on a regular basis. More mature plants should be nourished with water mixed with such things as juices extracted from medicinal plants and fruits, wine, milk, animal dung, fat and flesh, honey, and *ghī*. Another way to nourish and protect trees is fumigation that can be done with specially prepared mixtures of flowers, leaves, tumeric, fish and animal flesh; this helps prevent defects and encourages good fruiting. Trees can also be smeared with mixtures of animal fat, honey, *ghī*, and leaf juice, again to encourage good flowering and fruiting. Moreover, trees do especially well when weeds are taken out of the ground areas around them, and when gardeners loosen the soil around their roots to allow for air and to free the space from other competing root systems. Creepers and vines should be fed with mixtures that may include fat from snakes, pigs, and rats, sting fluids from scorpions, cock stools, *ghī*, and fish and animal flesh. And fruit trees – palm, coconut, date, pomegranate, for example – do well when fertilized with various mixtures that may include honey, *ghī*, animal, bird, and fish flesh and fat, wine, sesamum, barley, rice, milk, sugar, salt, white mustard, various other spices, and juices from fruits.[307]

Finally, there are some unusual methods in Surapāla's text to encourage the flowering and fruiting of trees, one of which involves young women:

> The mango, scratched even by the tip of the nail of a (young) woman, hard like the point of an axe, is thrilled with joy in the form of bearing blossoms.[308]

Again, when an Aśoka tree is kicked hard but lovingly by a young woman, it puts forth an abundance of blossoms. When the Kurabaka tree is closely and playfully clasped by a beautiful woman within her creeper-like arms, it bursts forth in flowers. And when the Tilaka tree merely feels the glance of a beautiful young woman it glows with new blooms.[309] In addition to amorous attention from maidens (producing a kind of contagious magic), plants are thought to respond to sacred incantations planted in the soil. When one is written in lac on a plantain leaf in honor of Hanumān, for example, and planted in the middle or the corner of a field, it will protect crops planted there from such things as rat, locust, moth, worm, and grasshopper infestations.[310]

Preventing and treating plant diseases is a central focus of Vṛkṣāyurveda texts.[311] Plant diseases are thought to arise from sources that are either internal or external to the plant body. Those that arise internally come, as in humans, from imbalances of the three humors *(doṣas),* that is, from disorders of wind *(vāyu* or *vāta)*, phlegm *(kapha)*, and bile *(pitta)*, while those that arise externally come from environmental hazards such as infestations of animals and insects, and extremes of weather. Too much or too little water, wind, sun, heat, cold, fire, and lightning, for example, are problematic for plants and trees, as are some humanly controlled applications like too much or too little fertilizer and chopping a plant's trunk, branches, and roots with an axe. Surapāla's section on the knowledge of plant diseases *(rogajñāna)* makes clear that gardeners of the time watch carefully for the unnatural shriveling, distortion, swelling, drying, paleness, yellowing, and spotting of leaves, flowers, and fruits, and are keenly aware of the appearance of tumors, unusual smells and tastes, roughness, animal and insect infestation, and any unusual blossoming and fructification, that might be, for example, either too early or too late, too scanty or too abundant. Once noticed:

> A person of superior intelligence having diagnosed the various diseases, with the help of their respective symptoms described (here), should administer to the trees the medical treatment with zealous effort.[312]

Treating plant diseases normally follows patterns analogous to traditional Āyurvedic treatment of humans,[313] that is, plant diseases caused by wind disorders are treated with "wind"-related cures: watering the diseased plant with mixtures of flesh, lymph, fat, and *ghī,* for example, and gently fumigating it with mixtures of oils, cow's horn, horse's hair, *ghī,* and pig lymph. Moreover,

> A wise man, for curing the disease of (trees) affected with (disorders of) wind, having dug out the earth near their roots, places there fresh dry earth.[314]

Gardeners respond to plant diseases caused by phlegm disorders with mixtures of astringent, bitter, and pungent materials that include roots from five trees, jasmine water, white mustard, and sesamum. Gardeners treat plant diseases caused by bile disorders with materials that are sweet and have a cool effect; these include waterings made from milk, honey, *ghī,* licorice, and fruits of the ever-healing myrobalan tree, as well as waterings with cold water over the course of several days. In addition, Surapāla describes elaborate mixtures that can be used for insect and worm infestations – including such now commonly noted materials as medicinal plants, cow urine, dung, horn, and flesh, bird flesh, *ghī,* milk, white mustard, and sesamum. Trees that have suffered from frost should be covered around the outside and given waterings of special water and milk; broken branches should be plastered with pastes that include honey, wine, milk, and *ghī,* and splinted with straw and rope; fire-burned trees should have their burns scraped and treated with milk, water, and plant and animal materials. Surapāla also prescribes treatments for lightning burns, jaundice, infertility, problems with the fluxing of sap, shriveling caused by sterile soils, miscellaneous tree wounds, and 'indigestion' caused by water logging. Finally, if all else fails, "plants which are not cured by any one of the various above-stated remedies should be transplanted at other special sites."[315]

Thus texts on Vṛkṣāyurveda like that of Surapāla are deeply and commitedly aware that plants arise, grow to maturity, and die and that, in that process, they go through immense transformations of flowering and fruiting. Note, for example, the following verses from Parāśara:

> The seed when moistened swells and becomes soft, leading to the initiation of the root. (7) The root develops into a seedling that, in turn, bears leaves which nourish the stem. Then the branches come out from the stem. Thus, in the course of time, the plant bears flowers and fruits. Seeds, in due course, pierce upwards through the soil.(8)[316]
> Just as an injury to the heart of an animal causes its eventual death, similarly when the root of a plant is damaged the plant dies and its trunks, branches, leaves, flowers dry up eventually.[317]

The gardeners whose knowledge helps to form such texts testify eloquently to changes in size, shape, color, fragrance, and health of the plants – grasses, herbs, shrubs, and trees – that are under their care. And they testify as well not only to the myriad ways known to Indian scientists to maintain the health and prevent disease in plants, but also how to treat sick plants and bring them back to health. These texts assume that, like humans, plants can get sick and that, also like humans, these sicknesses can be treated so that the cycle of birth, maturity, and death can naturally proceed for these beings that must, like humans, be alive.

Endnotes :

1 Zimmer, p.l, lxi.
2 Macdonell, p. 11; see Keith, *Religion and Philosophy* 1.33, 35, 83.
3 Keith, *Religion and Philosophy* 1.83-84. Divine guardianship over *ṛta* originally lay in the hands of gods like Varuṇa.
4 Oldenberg, *Religion of the Veda*, pp. 129-130.
5 Oldenberg, *Religion of the Veda*, p. 128.

[6] *śataṁ vo amba dhāmāni sahasram uta vo ruhaḥ / adhā śatakratvo yūyam imam me agadaṁ kṛta (2) anyā vo anyām avatv anyānyasyā upāvata / tāḥ sarvāḥ saṁvidānā idam me prāvatā vacaḥ (14) mā vo riṣat khanitā yasmai cāhaṁ khanāmi vaḥ / dvipac catuṣpad asmākaṁ sarvam astv anāturam (20) yāś cedam upaśṛṇvanti yāś ca dūram parāgataḥ / sarvāḥ saṁgatya vīrudho 'syai saṁ datta vīryam;* RV 10.97; O'Flaherty, *Rig Veda*, pp. 285-286; Zysk, *Religious Medicine*, pp. 99-100. See also Keith, *Religion and Philosophy* 1.184-185.

[7] Zysk, *Asceticism and Healing*, pp. 18-19.

[8] *Śaṁ no bhava hṛda ā pīta indo piteva soma sūnave suśevaḥ / sakheva sakhya uruśaṁsa dhīraḥ pra ṇa āyur jīvase soma tārīh (4) ime mā pītā yaśasa uruṣyavo rathaṁ na gāvaḥ sam anāha parvasu / te mā rakṣantu visrasaś carītrād uta mā srāmād yavayantv indavaḥ* (5); RV 8.48; O'Flaherty, *Rig Veda*, p. 135.

[9] RV 1.90.8; 7.34.23; 10.64.8. See also Keith, *Religion and Philosophy* 1.184-185.

[10] AV 14.2.9.

[11] Oldenberg, *Religion of the Veda*, p. 129.

[12] *Gām aṅgaiṣa ā hvayati dārv aṅgaiṣo apāvadhīt / vasann araṇyānyaṁ sāyam akrukṣad iti manyate (4) na vā araṇyānir hanty anyaś cen nābhigachati / svādoḥ phalasya jagdhvāya yathākāmaṁ ni padyate (5) āñjanagandhiṁ surabhiṁ bahvannām akṛṣīvalām / prāham mṛgāṇām mātaram araṇyānim aśaṁsiṣam;* RV 10. 146; O'Flaherty, *Rig Veda*, p. 242. Antonio T. De Nicolás (p. 232) translates these verses as follows:

4. Here a voice calls a cow, there a man
Felled a tree: When the evening falls,
The dweller in the forest imagines
Someone else's scream.
5. The goddess never kills, even if
A murderous enemy approached.
Man eats of her sweet fruit, and then,
At will rests in her womb.
6. This is my song to the goddess of the forest:
The sweet- smelling, fragrant mother
Of a world of green. She does not till,
Yet, stores the food for us all.

[13] Dwivedi, "Vedic Heritage", pp. 29-30.

[14] *Agnir bhūmyāmoṣadhīṣvagnimāpo bibhratyagniraśmasu / agnirantaḥ puruṣeṣu goṣvaśveṣvagnayaḥ (19); yasyāṁ vṛkṣā*

vānaspatyā dhruvāstiṣṭhanti viśvahā / pṛthivīṁ viśvadhāyasaṁ dhṛtāmachāvadāmasi (27). AV 12.1; Dwivedi, "Vedic Heritage" pp. 30, 31.

15 Keith, *Taittirīya Saṃhitā* 1.cxxv.

16 TS 4.2.6: *Yā jātā oṣadhiyo devebhyastriyugaṁ purā / mandāmi babhrūṇāmahaṁ śataṁ dhāmāni sapta ca // śataṁ vo amba dhāmāni sahasramuta vo rūhaḥ / athā śatakratvo yūyamimaṁ me agadaṁ kṛta // puṣpāvatīḥ prasūvatīḥ phalinīraphalā uta /aśvā iva sajitvarīrvīrūdhaḥ pārayiṣṇavaḥ // oṣadhīritì mātarastadvo devīrūpa bruve / rapāṁsi vighnatīrita rupaścātayamānāḥ;/* Keith, *Taittiriya Sanhita* 2.316. O'Flaherty's translation of these verses in RV 10.97.1-4 *(Rig Veda*, p. 285; using Zysk, *Religious Medicine*, p. 99) is as follows:

1. The tawny plants were born in the ancient times, three ages before the gods; now I will meditate upon their hundred and seven forms.
2. Mothers, you have a hundred forms and a thousand sprouts. You who have a hundred ways of working, make this man healthy for me.
3. Be joyful, you plants that bear flowers and those that bear fruit. Like mares that win the race together, the growing plants will carry us across.
4. You mothers who are called plants, I say to you who are goddesses: let me win a horse, a cow, a robe — and your very life, O man.

17 An offering or oblation of butter, fruits, and vegetables, distinct from an animal sacrifice or a Soma offering.

18 *Śrautakoṣa* 1.1.502; Kane 2.2.1106-1107.

19 *Śrautakoṣa* 1.1.502. My italics.

20 Artha 2.24.118; Shamasastry, *Kauṭilya's Arthaśāstra*, p. 130.

21 RV 10.16.13: *Yaṁ tvam agne samadahas tam u nir vāpayā punaḥ / kiyāmbu atra rohatu pākadūrvā vyalkaśā (13);* O'Flaherty, *Rig Veda*, p. 50. See also Oldenberg, *Religion of the Veda*, p. 328.

22 ĀGS 4.1.13, 14.

23 Kane 4.244-245, based, in part, on material in the Āśvalāyana Gṛhya Sūtra.

24 Kane 4. 249-250, based, in part, on material from the Vājasaneyi Saṁhita. See also Oldenberg, *Religion of the Veda*, pp. 328-330.

25 Knipe, "Sapiṇḍīkaraṇa" p. 115.

26 Knipe, "Sapiṇḍīkaraṇa" p. 115.

27 See Kane 4.412-430, 520-551.

28 Kane 4.550.

29 AV 1.2, 3.

30 AV 1.23.

31 AV 5.4.

32 AV 2.8, 25; 5.5.

33 AV 2.7.

34 AV 2.27.

35 AV 3.18.

36 AV 4.4.

37 AV 4.12.

38 AV 4.18, 19, 20; 5.14.

39 AV 5.15.

40 AV 7.38.

41 AV 1.3.1; 1.23.1; 4.4.4, 7; 4.12.1; 5.5.3; 5.14.1; Whitney, *Atharva Veda* 1.4, 24, 150-151, 166, 229, 244; Zysk, *Religious Medicine*, pp. 71, 82, 74. 75. In many of Whitney's translations, I have changed "thee" and "thou" to "you," and "thine" to "yours."

42 AV 4.17.1, 2; Whitney, *Atharva Veda* 1.179. My italics.

43 KGS 4.2.6, 8-11; GGS 4.7.2, 4, 9-11.

44 PGS 3.4.8.

45 GGS 4.7.22-25.

46 TS 3.4.8.4-5.

47 *Kṣatraṁ vā etad vanaspatīnāṁ yan nyagrodho...bhaujyaṁ vā etad vanaspatīnāṁ yad udumbaro...sāmrājyaṁ vā etad vanaspatīnāṁ yad aśvattho...svārājyaṁ ca ha vā etad vairājyaṁ ca vanaspatīnāṁ yat plakṣo;* AB 8.16; from Keith, *Rigveda Brahmanas*, p. 332 .

48 *Śrautakoṣa* 1.1.5, 18, 33, 34, 302; see, for example, BŚS 2.12; 1; 3; 4; 6-7; 13-14; 20.16; 24.12-16; 14.22.

49 I.e., "sand, saline soil, earth dug out by a rat, earth from an ant hill, mud from a pond, earth dug by a hog, and gold or gravel;" *Śrautakoṣa* 1.19.

50 BhŚS 5.1-3; *Śrautakoṣa* 1.18-19.

51 VŚS1.1-6; *Śrautakoṣa* 1.22.

52 Oldenberg, *Religion of the Veda*, p. 129.

53 *Yān vo naro devayanto nimimyur vanaspate svadhitir vā tatakṣa / te devāsaḥ svaravas tasthivāṁsaḥ prajāvad asme didhiṣantu ratnam (6) ye vṛkṇāso adhi kṣami nimitāso yatasrucaḥ / te no vyantu vāryaṁ devatrā kṣetrasādhasaḥ* (7); RV 3.8.6, 7; Sarasvati and Vidyalankar, *Ṛgveda Samhitā* 4.1097.

54 *Śrautakoṣa* 1.6, 26, 27, 101-102, 201, 256, for example.

55 BĀU 6.3.13. Other woods may be used for these items as well; see *Śrautakoṣa* 1.949-950, 955. In fact, according to "Āśmarathya, for those utensils, in connection with the preparation of which the wood of no specific tree is prescribed, one should use the wood of any tree (which is considered to be) fit for sacrificial purpose" BhŚS 1.16.5 - 17.3; *Śrautakoṣa* 1.955.

56 BŚS 1.1; 17.50; 20.1-2; 24.23; *Śrautakoṣa* 1.227.

57 AV 8:7.4: *Prastṛṇatī stambinīrekaśuṅgāḥ pratanvatīroṣadhīrā vadāmi / aṁśumatīḥ kāṇḍinīryā viśākhā vhayāmi te vīrudho vaiśvadevīr ugrāḥ puruṣajīvanīh;* Zimmer, *Hindu Medicine*, p. 11; Zysk, *Religious Medicine*, p. 101.

58 BS 59.2-6; Bhat, *Bṛhat Saṁhitā* 2.564.

59 ŚB 11.3.1.3.

60 BĀU 6.3.13.

61 ĀPŚS 5.1-6; *Śrautakoṣa* 1.21.

62 *Kṣatraṁ vā etad oṣadhīnāṁ yad vrīhayo...sāmrājyaṁ vā etad oṣadhīnāṁ yad mahāvrīhayo... bhaujyaṁ vā etad oṣadhīnāṁ yad priyaṁgavo...saināṇyaṁ vā etad oṣadhīnaṁ yad yavā;* AB 8.16; from Keith, *Rigveda Brahmanas*, p. 332.

63 BS 49; Bhat, *Bṛhat Saṁhitā* 2.565-567.

64 For example, Dwivedi, "Vedic Heritage," p. 33.

65 Knipe, "*Sapiṇḍīkaraṇa,*" p. 113.

66 RV 10.16.3; O'Flaherty, *Rig Veda*, p. 49.

67 Knipe, "*Sapiṇḍīkaraṇa,*" p. 113. Alternately, of this hymn Christopher Key Chapple says: "In this passage, an identity is proclaimed between the external world and the individual human person, indicating an intimate relationship between human beings and their environment...(where the) body finds its roots in the earth;" *Nonviolence*, pp. 50-51.

68 Filliozat, *Classical Doctrine of Indian Medicine*, p. 63. "One may also see in this passage, as it has already been pointed out by Anna Moreshwar Kunte, a type of the announcement of the concept, later become classical, of the organism as formed of five elements *(pañcabhautika)*, if at least it is admitted that here the sky is a prefiguration of space *(ākāśa)* recognised in the classical doctrine."

69 Knipe,"*Sapiṇḍīkaraṇa,*" p. 113.

70 TS 3.1.4: *Prajānantaḥ prati gṛhṇanti pūrve prāṇamaṅgebhyaḥ paryācarantam / suvargaṁ yāhi pathibhir devayānair oṣadhīṣu prati tiṣṭhā śarīraiḥ;* Keith, *Taittiriya Sanhita* 1.226.

71 BĀU 3.2.13.

[72] AU 1.1.4.

[73] AU 1.2.4.

[74] MU 1.1.7; 2.1.5.

[75] SU 2.1; Radhakrishnan, *Principal Upaniṣads*, pp. 516, 517, 673, 681, 864.

[76] Reat, *Origins of Indian Psychology*, p. 217, using AU 1.1.4.

[77] *Sāṁkhya* as a term means number, calculation or, more commonly, "enumeration." As the name of the philosophical system, it refers to "the intellectual or reasoning method" of understanding the evolution of experience as we know it from the coming together of material nature *(prakṛti)* and the eternal self or consciousness *(puruṣa)*. The relation of the twenty-five evolutes are ordinarily understood through charts like the following:

(1) consciousness *(puruṣa)*	(2) primordial materiality *(prakṛti)*
(3) intellect *(buddhi* or *mahat)*	(4) egoity *(ahaṁkāra)*
(5) mind *(manas)*	(6) hearing *(śrotra)*
(7) touching *(tvac)*	(8) seeing *(cakṣus)*
(9) tasting *(rasana)*	(10) smelling *(ghrāṇa)*
(11) speaking *(vāc)*	(12) grasping *(pāṇi)*
(13) walking *(pāda)*	(14) excreting *(pāyu)*
(15) procreating *(upastha)*	(16) sound *(śabda)*
(17) touch *(sparśa)*	(18) form *(rūpa)*
(19) taste *(rasa)*	(20) smell *(gandha)*
(21) space *(ākāśa)*	(22) wind *(vāyu)*
(23) fire *(tejas)*	(24) water *(ap)*
(25) earth *(pṛthvī)*	

(the 11-fold capacities: sensing, motor functioning, and mind *buddhīndriyas, karmendriyas,* and *manas)*	(the 5 subtle elements *tanmātra)*	(the 5 gross elements; *mahābhūtas)*

Sāṁkhya is associated with methods of spiritual discipline *(yoga)* which focus on posture, breathing, concentration, and ascetic practices; Larson & Bhattacharya, *Sāṁkhya*, pp. 3-14; 49, 52.

[78] Larson and Bhattacharya, *Encyclopedia of Indian Philosophies* 2.62-63.

[79] Mbh 3.3.5-8: *purā sṛṣṭāni bhūtāni pīḍyante kṣudhayā bhṛśam /tato 'nukampayā teṣāṁ savitā svapitā iva // gatvottarāyaṇāṁ tejorasānuddhṛtya raśmibhiḥ / dakṣiṇāyanamāvṛtto mahīṁ niviśate raviḥ // kṣetrabhūte tatastasminnoṣadhīroṣadhīpatiḥ / divastejaḥ samuddhṛtya janayāmāsa vāriṇā // niṣiktaścandratejobhiḥ sūyate bhūgato raviḥ / oṣadhyaḥ ṣāḍrasā medhyāstadannaṁ prāṇināṁ bhuvi;* Van Buitenan, *Mahābhārata* 2-3.227.

[80] Keith, *Religion and Philosophy* 1.14-15, 160.

[81] For a description, see Keith, *Religion and Philosophy* 2.575-576.

[82] *Ta iha vrīhi-yavā oṣadhi vanaspatayas tila-māṣā iti jāyante;* Radhakrishnan, *Principal Upaniṣads,* p. 433. The passage goes on to say that "whoever eats the food and sows the seed he becomes like unto him," that is, presumably, the eater becomes like the eaten. See Collins, *Selfless Persons,* pp. 49-51.

[83] Radhakrishnan, *Principal Upaniṣads,* p. 321. CU 1.1.2 says: "The essence of these beings is the earth; the essence of the earth is water. The essence of water is plants *(oṣadhi);* the essence of plants is a person *(puruṣa).* The essence of a person is speech." The passage continues, then, with the cycle moving into speech homologies; Radhakrishnan, *Principal Upaniṣads,* p. 337. See the discussion in Brereton, "Upanishads," pp. 120-121, 132.

[84] Radhakrishnan, *Principal Upaniṣads,* p. 321.

[85] Radhakrishnan, *Principal Upaniṣads,* p. 322.

[86] Knipe, "*Sapiṇḍīkaraṇa,*" p. 111.

[87] Knipe, "*Sapiṇḍīkaraṇa,*" pp.114-115.

[88] The Vāmana Purāṇa, for example, "states that one can survive by consuming *tila, piṇyāka* and vegetables...or by drinking the fruit juice of *āmalakī,*" and similar claims are made for the benefits of consuming many other kinds of fruit and fruit juice in the Kurma Purāṇa. In the Vāyu Purāṇa, "regular consumption" of the fruit juice of the Kālāmra tree "makes the youth of a man constant...and extends the longevity up to 10,000 years," and similar claims are made for the Nyāgrodha, the Lakuca, and the Jambu trees. Moreover, the Agni Purāṇa has a long section on the use of plants to improve longevity with a variety of plant mixtures and of intakes — including intake through the nose. The Kurma Purāṇa also notes the benefits of using the young branches of the "*kṣīri vṛkṣa, mālatī, apāmārga, vilva* and *karavīra,* for brushing the teeth;" Sensarma, *Plants in Indian Purāṇas,* pp. 13, 23-24, 33, 77.

[89] Sensarma, *Plants in Indian Purāṇas,* p. 13.

[90] The Matsya Purāṇa notes the many uses of plants and plant materials to combat the presence of poison in the body. The power of these plant materials is often enhanced when used, as directed, with the spleen of mongoose, horn utensils, gold, salt, and cow urine; Sensarma, *Plants in Indian Purāṇas,* pp. 46-48; Banwari, *Pañcavaṭī: Indian Approach to Environment,* pp. 172-177.

[91] Rajan, p. 83.

[92] Zimmer, *Hindu Medicine*, p. 16.

[93] Whitney, *Atharva Veda* 1.41; Zysk, *Religious Medicine*, pp. 75 78.

[94] TS 4.2.6: *Yadahaṁ vājayannimā oṣadhīr hasta ādadhe / ātmā yakṣmasya naśyati purā jīvagṛbho yathā / yad oṣadhayaḥ saṅgacchante...amīvacātanaḥ...ati viśvāḥ pariṣṭhāḥ stena iva vrajamakramuḥ / oṣadhayaḥ prācucyavuryat kiṁ ca tanuvāṁ rapaḥ // aśvāvatīṁ somavatīmūrjayantīmudojasam / ā vitsi sarvā oṣadhīr asmā ariṣṭātaye // ...yā oṣadhayaḥ somarājñīḥ praviṣṭāḥ pṛthivīmanu/ tāsāṁ tvamasyuttamā pra ṇo jīvātave suva// avapatantīravadan diva oṣadhayaḥ pari / yaṁ jīvamaśnavāmahai na sa riṣyāti pūruṣaḥ;* Keith, *Taittiriya Sanhita* 2.317-318.

[95] ŚB 7.2.4.20; Eggeling, *Śatapatha Brāhmaṇa* 3.338-339.

[96] Whitney, *Atharva Veda* 2.664.

[97] Parpola, *Indus Script*, pp. 9, 251; Wheeler, *Civilizations of the Indus Valley*, p. 38.

[98] RV 10.97.4, 6.

[99] Basham, "Medicine in Ancient and Medieval India," p. 18.

[100] RV 2.33.4, 13.

[101] RV 6.74.

[102] Zysk, *Asceticism and Healing in Ancient India*, p. 19.

[103] E.g., AV 8.7.17, 24. See also Zimmer, *Hindu Medicine*, p. 18.

[104] Zysk, *Asceticism and Healing in Ancient India*, p.19.

[105] *Kilāsa*. AV 1.24.1.

[106] AV 2.9.1.

[107] AV 4.4.1.

[108] AV 4.12.1, 5.

[109] *Takman*. AV 5.4.1.

[110] AV 6.30.2, 3; 6.136.1, 3; 6.137.1, 2, 3.

[111] AV 7.65, 67; 8.7.3, 4, 5, etc.

[112] Zysk, *Religious Medicine*, pp. 101-102; see Whitney, *Atharva Veda* 2.498-499.

[113] AV 2.27.1.

[114] AV 7.38.1.

[115] AV 3.18.1; 7.113, 118.

[116] AV 3.18.1; 7.113, 118.

[117] AV 4.17, 18, 19, 20, 37; 5.14; 10.1.4, 11, 17; 11.10.24.

[118] AV 5.15.

[119] Basham, "Medicine in Ancient and Medieval India," p. 19. This use of many plants to cure many afflictions is reflected in a later Śaivite verse by Mahādevīyakka who cries out: "Every tree in the forest is

the All-Giving Tree, every bush the life-reviving herb;" Ramanujan, *Speaking of Śiva*, p. 133.

[120] Basham, "Medicine in Ancient and Medieval India," p. 20.

[121] Plant medicines are then carefully chosen and prepared to treat illnesses related to each *doṣa*. Moreover, eating certain plants can give rise to illness related to each *doṣa*, as noted in the Brahma Vaivarta Purāṇa; Sensarma, *Plants in Indian Purāṇas*, p. 62.

[122] See Sensarma's detailed description of plant medicines for human use found in the Agni Purāṇa, as well as the ways plants can be used to treat illnesses in elephants, horses, and cows; *Plant in Indian Purāṇas*, pp. 78-87, 88-90.

[123] Rukmani, "Literary Foundations for Ecological Aesthetic," pp. 104-106; Obeyesekere, "Impact of Āyurvedic Ideas," p. 201.

[124] Krishnamurthy, *Source Book of Indian Medicine*, p. 392.

[125] Krishnamurthy, *Source Book of Indian Medicine*, pp. 392, 398.

[126] Basham, "Medicine in Ancient and Medieval India," p. 20.

[127] Animal products include honey, milk, bile, muscle, fat, marrow, blood, flesh, feces, urine, skin, semen, bone, ligament, horn, nail, hoof, hairs, and bile; Sharma, *Caraka Saṁhitā* 1.9.

[128] Drugs obtained from the earth include gold, silver, copper, iron, lead, tin, silica, calcites, realgar, orpiment, gems, salt, ochre, and galena; Sharma, *Caraka Saṁhitā* 1.9.

[129] Sharma, *Caraka Saṁhitā* 1.9-11; Krishnamurthy, *Source Book of Indian Medicine*, pp. 406-407; Ramachandra Rao, *Encyclopedia of Indian Medicine* 2.142-146, 151-152.

[130] Sensarma, *Plants in Indian Purāṇas*, pp. 76-77.

[131] Ramachandra Rao, *Encyclopedia of Indian Medicine* 2.151-152.

[132] Krishnamurthy, *Source Book of Indian Medicine*, pp. 400-402.

[133] Krishnamurthy, *Source Book of Indian Medicine*, pp. 407-412; Sharma, *Caraka Saṁhitā* 1.317, 324; 2.30.

[134] Bajracharya, *Ayurvedic Medicinal Plants*, p.1.

[135] Zysk, *Asceticism and Healing in Ancient India*, p. 73.

[136] Zysk, *Asceticism and Healing in Ancient India*, pp. 77-81.

[137] See Jātakas 54, 85, 149, and 367.

[138] This section, from the Girnār [Rock] Edict II, is as follows: *osuḍhāni ca yāni manusopagāni ca pasopagāni ca yata yata nāsti sarvata hārāpitāni ca ropāpitāni ca mūlāni ca phalāni ca yata yata nāsti sarvata hārāpitāni ca ropāpitāni ca;* Nikam and McKeon, *Edicts of Aśoka*, p. 64; Woolner, *Aśoka Text and Glossary*, pp. 3-4. See Sircar, *Inscriptions of Aśoka*, pp. 19, 32-33; Narayanan, "One Tree Is Equal to Ten Sons," p. 305.

[139] O'Flaherty, *Rig Veda*, p. 150.
[140] Keith, *Religion and Philosophy* 2.324-325.
[141] *Śrautakoṣa* 1.770-773.
[142] Keith, *Religion and Philosophy* 1.185. My italics.
[143] ĀŚGS 2.7.1-6.
[144] ĀŚGS 2.7.9.
[145] VDS 19.11-12; Olivelle, *Dharmasūtras*, p. 300 ; see also Kane 2.2.895.
[146] Sarasvati and Vidyalankar, *Ṛgveda Samhita* 13.4675. See also de Nicolás, *Meditations through the Ṛg Veda*, p. 232.
[147] TS 6.6.7; Keith, *Taittiriya Sanhita* 2.552 .
[148] ŚB 9.2.2.3; Eggeling, *Śatapatha Brāhmaṇa* 4.189
[149] Manu 5.40; Bühler, *Laws of Manu*, p. 175.
[150] Manu 5.44; Bühler, *Laws of Manu*, p.175-176.
[151] M. N. Dutt, *Rāmāyaṇa* 2.552, 565-566.
[152] J 493; Rouse, *Jātaka* 4.222.
[153] Schmidt, "Origin," p. 625.
[154] Schmidt, "Origin," p. 628.
[155] Schmidt, "Origin, " p. 632.
[156] Schmidt, "Origin," pp. 633-634.
[157] Schmidt, "Origin," p. 636.
[158] Schmidt, "Origin," p. 635.
[159] ĪŚU1; Schmidt, "Origin," p. 638.
[160] PGS 2.5.9; 2.2.21; Schmidt, "Origin," pp. 639, 649.
[161] Schmidt, "Origin," p. 631.
[162] Manu 5.55; Bühler, *Laws of Manu*, p. 177. See also Manu 5.33.
[163] Schmidt, "Origin," pp. 629, 643.
[164] ŚB 12.9.1.1; Eggeling, *Śatapatha Brāhmaṇa* 5.260.
[165] Schmidt, "Origin," p. 645.
[166] Schmithausen, "Ecological Ethics," p. 6.
[167] Schmidt, "Origin," p. 649.
[168] Schmidt, "Origin," pp. 642, 654-655.
[169] Smith, *Classifying the Universe*, p. 213.
[170] O'Flaherty, *Rig Veda*, p. 286.
[171] MS 3.9.3; Schmidt, "Origin," p. 647. See *Śrautakoṣa* 1.774, 776; Keith, *Religion and Philosophy* 1.185:

The belief in the life of the tree is very clearly seen in the treatment of the tree from which the sacrificial post is to be taken...the aim is clearly to avoid injury to the life in the tree by pretending that it is not being injured.

[172] ŚB 1.2.4.16; Eggeling, *Śatapatha Brāhmaṇa* 1.56. See also ŚB 1.2.5.11.

[173] Manu 11.143.

[174] Sensarma, *Plants in Indian Purāṇas,* pp. 29, 41, 52, 56, 71. The Matsya Purāṇa states, for example, that cutting down a tree full of fruit results in paying a penalty in gold, the amount to be determined by the king and paid to the owner of the tree, with an additional fine paid into the king's treasury. If one fells such a tree near a reservoir, by the side of a public road, or near a boundary, then the penalty amount is doubled. Smaller penalties in gold are levied for the destruction of shrubs and creepers, and of herbs if they are destroyed for no particular reason; Sensarma, pp. 41-42. For a discussion of the practice of *ahiṁsā* towards animals in such texts as the Rāmāyaṇa, see Wilhelm, "Hunting and the Concept of Dharma," pp. 9-15.

[175] Bhat, *Bṛhat Saṁhitā* 1.346; 2.566.

[176] Shamasastry, *Kauṭilya's Arthaśāstra,* p. 130

[177] Kinsley, *Ecology and Religion,* p. 65.

[178] Kale, *Hitopadeśa,* pp. 67, 113.

[179] Smith, *Classifying the Universe,* p. 213.

[180] ŚB 1.3.3.19-20.

[181] Smith, *Classifying the Universe,* pp. 217-230.

[182] Smith, *Classifying the Universe,* p. 230.

[183] Manu 11.143.

[184] Manu 5.48-56.

[185] Manu 5.40, 42, 44.

[186] E. g., VDS 19.11-12: see Kane 2.2.895; 3.516.

[187] Jaini, *Jaina Path of Purification,* p. 170.

[188] Chapple, *Jainism and Ecology,* p. xxxiii.

[189] Jaini, *Jaina Path of Purification,* p. 312.

[190] Tatia, *Tattvārtha Sūtra: That Which Is,* pp. xix, xx, xxi.

[191] Tobias, *Life Force,* p. 55.

[192] Chapple, *Nonviolence,* p. 3.

[193] Chapple, *Nonviolence,* pp. 5-9.

[194] Chapple, *Nonviolence,* pp. 42-43.

[195] Tobias, *Life Force,* p. 29.

[196] Chapple, *Jainism and Ecology,* p. xxxiv. "The *jīva* is entangled in this network of [its] *karmas* and wanders about under their influence in all sorts of life conditions in the world, experiencing pleasure and pain;" B. Kumar, "Transmigration and *Karma,*" p. 30. A good discussion of "the nature of the force which brings about the

interlocking between the soul and matter" can be found in B. Kumar, "*Astikāyas,*" pp. 22-25. For Jains, the universe is eternal, with no beginning or end. Cosmic cycles succeed themselves endlessly, each having an upswing called *utsarpaṇa* and a downswing called *avasarpaṇa.* Towards the end of each downswing, the Jain religion loses hold among people because of the decline in living conditions; Titze, *Jainism,* p. 5.

197 Schmidt, "Origin," p. 625. My italics.

198 Jain, N. L., *Biology in Jaina Treatise on Reals,* pp. 7, 35; Jain, N. L, *Jaina Karmology,* p. 8. According to Tatia, the

> Tattvārtha Sūtra is by common consent the book of books in the Jaina tradition. Acclaimed as an authentic and systematic compendium of the essence of Jainism as taught and settled by Lord Mahāvīra, and faithfully rooted in the Jaina heritage, it commands the allegiance of the different denominations within the Jaina fold and its authority is definitive and undisputed.

Tatia, *Tattvārtha Sūtra: That Which Is,* p. xi. According to K. K. Dixit, the "*Tattvārthasūtra* of Umāswāti is a compendium of the theoretical positions related to several branches of learning and adopted by the Jainas...(extant -up to) the author's time which could have been c. 3rd—4th centuries" (or, according to others, as early as the 2nd or as late as the 5th centuries) C.E. A number of commentaries are available, and we will be using N. Tatia's translation of the aphorisms with commentaries by Umāsvāti / Umāsvāmā, Pūjyapāda, and Siddhasenagaṇi, pp. 6, 7; N. L. Jain's translation of the aphorisms with *Tattvārtha-Rājavārtika of Akalaṅka,* of Tattvārtha Sūtra chapter two *(Biology in Jaina Treatise on Reals),* chapter five *(The Jaina World of Non-Living),* and chapter eight *(Jaina Karmology);* and a modern commentary by Sukhlalji, translated by K. K. Dixit. There is also available a Hindi translation of the Tattvārtha-Vṛtti of Śrī Śrutasāgara Sūri, another commentary on the Tattvārtha Sūtra. A full discussion of the Tattvārtha Sūtra texts and its commentarial material can be found in Dixit, *Tattvārtha Sūtra,* pp. 7-118.

199 Tatia, *Tattvārtha Suūtra: That Which Is,* p. 53.

200 Johnson, *Harmless Souls,* 1; see also p. 303. Vows of non-violence can be found in Tattvārtha Sūtra aphorisms nos. 7.1, 7.5, 7.6, 7.8, and 7.30.

201 Chapple, *Jainism and Ecology,* p. xxxiv.

202 According to Chapple, Jainism "provides one of India's most thorough attempts to encapsulate a comprehensive worldview...that

integrates the place of the human person within the continuum of the universe;" "Living Earth of Jainism," p. 121.

203 Johnson, *Harmless Souls*, p. 25. He continues by saying,

> Such a distinction between the binding effects of doing harm to *trasa* beings on the one hand, and *sthāvara* beings on the other, only emerged in later Jaina speculation, where the concept of the 'pious householder' is defined as 'one who abstains from all violence to the *trasa* beings,' that done to *sthāvara* ones being tolerated.

204 ĀS 1.8.1.11-12; 2.1.1.1-5; 2.1.11.5-6; SK 2.1.23.

205 Jaini, *Jaina Path of Purification*, p. 170.

206 Jaini, *Jaina Path of Purification*, p. 167.

207 ĀS 1.1.5.4-7; 1.8.1.11-12; 2.3.1.7,12; 2.15.i.1; UD 17.6; 26.30; SK 2.2.10-11.

208 *Paccakkhāmi savvaṁ pāṇāivāyaṁ, se suhumaṁ vā bāyaraṁ vā tasaṁ vā thāvaraṁ vā, n'eva sayaṁ pāṇātivāyaṁ karejjā.* ĀS 2.15.1.1; Jacobi, *Jaina Sūtras* 1.202. My italics, as the category of "immovable" beings normally refers to plants.

209 ĀS 1.1.5.1-7; Jacobi, *Jaina Sūtras* 1.9-11. My italics.

210 *Savve pāṇā savve bhūyā savve jīvā savve sattā na haṁtavvā na ajjāveyavvā na parighettavā na paritāvehavvā na uddaveyavvā;* ĀS 1.4.1.1 - 1.4.2.5; Jacobi, *Jaina Sūtras* 1.39, 36.

211 ĀBh 6.105: *se aṇāsādae aṇāsādamāṇe vujjhamāṇāṇaṁ pāṇāṇaṁ bhūyāṇaṁ jīvāṇaṁ sattāṇaṁ, jahā se dīve asaṁdīṇe, evaṁ se bhavai saraṇaṁ mahāmuṇī;* Tulsi, *Acharanga Bhasyam*, p. 418. The Ācārāṅga Bhāṣyam is a modern Sanskrit commentary on the Āyāro or Ācārāṅga Sūtra, conceived by Ganadhipati Tulsi and executed by *na uddaveyavvā;* ĀS 1.4.1.1 - 1.4.2.5; Jacobi, *Jaina Sūtras* 1.39, 36. Acharya Mahaprajna, with English renderings by Dr. Nathmal Tatia, Muni Dulaharaj, and Muni Mahendra Kumar. It was first published in 2001.

212 ĀS 2.3.1.12; Jacobi, *Jaina Sūtras* 1.138-139.

213 ĀS 2.1.4.1-2; Jacobi, *Jaina Sūtras* 1.97.

214 ĀS 2.10.9-10; Jacobi, *Jaina Sūtras* 1.181.

215 ĀS 2.6.2.1; Jacobi, *Jaina Sūtras* 1.169.

216 ĀS 2.1.8.11; Jacobi, *Jaina Sūtras* 1.110.

217 ĀS 2.1.6.8; Jacobi, *Jaina Sūtras* 1.104. My italics.

218 Schmidt, "Origin," pp. 625-626. This rule adheres in early Buddhism as well for, as D. Seyfort Ruegg notes, a Buddhist "monk must never knowingly eat the flesh of an animal killed for him." More definitively, in the view of the Vinaya, there are

> basically two factors, one factual and the other mental...to be considered as decisive: whether the meat of an already butchered animal was available to the donor and whether the monk has knowingly and intentionally eaten the meat of an animal butchered for him. If neither of these two conditions is violated, there is no offence.

Ruegg, "Ahiṁsā and Vegetarianism in the History of Buddhism," pp. 234-235.

219 Tatia, *Tattvārtha Sūtra: That Which Is*, p. 82.

220 Ṭulsi, *Acharanga Bhasyam*, pp. 489, 492.

221 UD 35.8-9: *Na sayaṁ gihāiṁ kuvvijjā ṇeva annehiṁ kārae / gihakammasamārambhe bhūyāṇāṁ dissae vaho // tasāṇaṁ thāvarāṇaṁ ca suhumāṇaṁ bādarāṇa ya / tamhā gihasamārambhaṁ saṁjao parivajjae;* Jacobi, *Jaina Sūtras* 2.204.

222 ĀS 2.5.1.14; Jacobi, *Jaina Sūtras* 1.161.

223 ĀBh 1.101: *jamiṇāṁ virūvarūveiṁ satthehiṁ vaṇassai-kamma-samāraṁ bheṇaṁ vaṇassai-satthaṁ samāraṁbhamāṇe aṇṇe vaṇegarūve pāṇe vihiṁ sati;* Tulsi, *Acharanga Bhasyam*, p. 70.

224 Tulsi, *Acharanga Bhasyam*, p. 71.

225 ĀBh 1.116: *ta pariṇṇāya mehāvī ṇeva sayaṁ vaṇassai-satthaṁ samāraṁbhejjā, ṇevaṇṇehiṁ vaṇassai-satthaṁ samāraṁbhāvejjā ṇevaṇṇe vaṇassai-satthaṁ samārambhate samaṇujāṇejjā;* Tulsi, *Acharanga Bhasyam*, pp. 74-75. See also Quarnström, *The Yogaśāstra of Hemacandra*, pp. 24, 35 (1.20; 2.21), etc., a twelfth century handbook on Śvetāmbara Jainism.

226 Tulsi, *Acharanga Bhasyam*, pp. 70-71; Jain, *Biology in Jaina Treatise on Reals*, pp. 100, 75.

227 See discussion in Schmithausen, *Problem of Sentience of Plants*, pp. 35n, 36n, 47n, 54, 58, 78n.

228 Tobias, *Life Force*, p. 29.

229 Tulsi, *Acharanga Bhasyam*, pp. 245-246.

230 Tulsi, *Acharanga Bhasyam*, pp. 70-75.

231 Bernhardt, "Pearly Gates," p. 47.

232 Note that the word used for "moving beings" here is *trasa*. As quoted by Jaini, *Jaina Path of Purification*, p. 173. My italics.

233 Ryan, *Buddhism and the Natural World*, p. 42.

234 *Jīvitā voropeyyā 'ti jīvitindriyaṁ upacchindati uparodheti santatiṁ vikopeti;* Vin 3.73. See the discussion in Vin 5.41 on intentionally depriving living things of life *(pāṇaṁ jīvitā)*.

235 See Kinsley, *Ecology and Religion*, pp. 84-85.

[236] Kabilsingh, "Early Buddhist Views on Nature," p. 9. This selection is from the Vāseṭṭha Sutta of the Sutta Nipāta; Sn pp. 117-118. K. R. Norman's translation is as follows:" [Consider grass and trees. Although they do not profess] (any difference), their distinguishing mark arises from their species; manifold indeed are their species," and so forth through the ranks of beetles, moths, ants, termites, quadrupeds, snakes, fish, etc.; Norman, *Group of Discourses*, p.104.

[237] Padmasiri de Silva, "Environmental Ethics in Buddhism," p. 62.

[238] D 1.111, 114, 127.

[239] Vin 5.38. This is true for the nuns of the Mahāsāṅghika tradition as well, where destroying seeds constitutes a Pācattika offense. See Hirakawa, p. 232.

[240] *Bījagāma-bhūtagāma-samārambhā paṭivrato Samaṇo Gotamo*; D 1.5; T. W. Rhys Davids, *Dialogues of the Buddha* 1.5.

[241] *So bījagāmabhūtagāmasamārambhā paṭivirato ahosiṁ;* M 3.34. See also A 5.205.

[242] M 1.502; Horner, *Middle Length Sayings* 2.181.

[243] *Kathaṁ hi nāma samaṇā Sakyaputtiyā hemantam pi gimham pi vassam pi cārikaṁ carissanti haritāni tiṇāni sammaddantā ekindriyaṁ jīvaṁ viheṭhentā bahū khuddake pāṇe saṁghātaṁ āpādentā;* Vin 1.137, 138. *Kathaṁ hi nāma bhikkhuniyo...carissanti haritāni tiṇāni sammaddantā ekindriyaṁ jīvaṁ viheṭhentā bahū khuddake pāṇe saṁghātaṁ āpādentā 'ti;* Pācittiya XXXIX, Vin 4.296. While the other three passages noted in this paragraph can be fairly clearly interpreted to support the view that the one-facultied beings not to be injured are the plants themselves, these particular passages concerning the alms tour are ambiguous in that one could interpret the one-facultied.

[244] *Kathaṁ hi nāma samaṇā Sakyaputtiyā hemantam pi gimham pi vassam pi cārikaṁ carissanti haritāni tiṇāni sammaddantā ekindriyaṁ jīvaṁ viheṭhentā bahū khuddake pāṇe saṁghātaṁ āpādentā;* Horner, *Book of the Discipline* 4.183.

[245] *Kathaṁ hi nāma samaṇā Sakyaputtiyā tālataruṇe chedāpetvā tālapattapādukāyo dhāressanti, tāni tālataruṇāni chinnāni milāyanti. Ekindriyaṁ samaṇā Sakyaputtiyā jīvaṁ viheṭhentīti;* Vin 1.189.

[246] *Kathañ hi nāma samaṇā Sakyaputtiyā rukkhaṁ chindissanti pi chedāpessanti pi. ekindriyaṁ samaṇā Sakyaputtiyā jīvaṁ viheṭhentīti;* Pācittiya XI, Vin 4.34. Compare Pācittiya X and XI, Vin 4.32, 34-35; see also 3.151.

[247] Vin 3.155-157; see Horner, *Book of the Discipline*1.xxix-xxxii.

[248] E.g., D 1.17, 34, 53, 82; 2.68; A 1.35ff., 55ff.; S 1.135; 5.41; Vin 1.5.

[249] T. W. Rhys Davids and Stede, *Pali-English Dictionary*, p. 673.

[250] T. W. Rhys Davids, *Dialogues of the Buddha* 1.71, 71n.

[251] Vin 1.83; see also, for example, Vin 4.125; 5.22-23; D 1.52, 146. "Putting away the killing of living things, Gotama the recluse holds aloof from the destruction of life...he dwells compassionate and kind to all creatures that have life;" Rhys Davids, *Dialogues of the Buddha* 1.3-4. *Pāṇātipātaṁ pahāya pāṇātipātā paṭivirato Samaṇo Gotamo...sabba-pāṇa-bhūta hitānukampī viharatīti;* D 1.4.

[252] Norman, *Group of Discourses*, p. 24; *ye keci pāṇabhūt atthi /tasā vā thāvarā vā ... Sabbe sattā bhavantu sukhitattā;* Sn 25-26.

[253] Hirakawa, p. 246.

[254] Hirakawa, pp. 366-367.

[255] His analysis centers on Pāṭimokkha texts of the Vinaya, as well as other Vinaya, Suttanipāta, and Nikāya passages. Such texts include, for example, Vin 1.137; 4.34-35, 296; D.1.5, 64 (Schmithausen, *Plants as Sentient Beings*, pp. 9, 11, 12); and Vin 1.157, 189; 4.34-35 or Pācittiya 11; 4.124-125 or Pācittiya 61; Sn 600ff.; D 1.141; M 1.13 (Schmithausen, *Problem of the Sentience of Plants*, pp. 30ff., 23ff., 5ff., 17ff., 25, 11, 18ff., 64ff., 58, 30).

[256] See Schmithausen, *Problem of the Sentience of Plants*, p. 21n.

[257] He argues: "This code is *not* concerned with *spiritual* practice *nor* even with *morality* proper (though some of the precepts do coincide with moral commandments), but, mainly, with regulating how monks and nuns had to behave *in society;*" Schmithausen, *Plants as Sentient Beings*, p.10 (his italics).

[258] Schmithausen, *Buddhism and Nature*, pp. 38-39:

> In the morality of renouncers and ascetics, abstention from killing animals (and even plants) was firmly rooted as the heritage of an earlier cultural stratum — a stratum in which killing animals (and even plants, earth and water) was, in a sense at least, as serious as killing people.

[259] Schmithausen, *Problem of the Sentience of Plants*, p. 16; see pp. 23, 26. My italics.

[260] Harvey, *Introduction to Buddhist Ethics*, p. 175. Although Schmithausen does not make much of the significance of not wanting to run roughshod over householder sentiments, I have argued elsewhere (Findly, "Borderline Beings," pp. 252-263) that a clear reason for not wanting to irritate householders and for wanting to generate their good will is precisely because these same household-

ers are the sources of the Saṅgha's material support, that is, they are the Saṅgha's donors.

261 Schmithausen, *Problem of the Sentience of Plants,* p. 17.

262 Schmithausen, *Problem of the Sentience of Plants,* p. 43; see also pp. 39-43.

263 See the discussion in Wilhelm, "Hunting and the Concept of Dharma," pp. 8-9.

264 Ryan, *Buddhism and the Natural World,* p. 91.

265 Nikam and McKeon, *Edicts of Asoka,* p. 31; Woolner, *Asoka Text and Glossary,* p. 6 (Śāhbāzgarhī [Rock] Edict IV). On the verb *rabh,* see Schmithausen, *Problem of the Sentience of Plants,* pp. 19-20.

266 Nikam and McKeon, *Edicts of Asoka,* pp. 45, 58; Woolner, *Asoka Text and Glossary,* pp. 21, 5 (Kālsī [Rock] Edict XI, Kālsī [Rock] Edict III).

267 Nikam and McKeon, *Edicts of Asoka,* p. 55; Woolner, *Asoka Text and Glossary,* p. 2 (Girnār [Rock] Edict I).

268 Nikam and McKeon, *Edicts of Asoka,* p. 41; Woolner, *Asoka Text and Glossary,* p. 40 (Pillar Edict II).

269 Nikam and McKeon, *Edicts of Asoka,* p. 64; Woolner, *Asoka Text and Glossary,* p. 4 (Girnār [Rock] Edict II).

270 Note, for example, Vin 4.34; see the discussion in Schmithausen, *Problem of the Sentience of Plants,* pp. 12-14.

271 See the discussion in Schmithausen, *Problem of the Sentience of Plants,* pp. 14-15, 19, 23-28.

272 See the discussion in Schmithausen, *Problem of the Sentience in Plants,* pp. 18-22. Except see p. 15 where Schmithausen discusses the use of *ekindriya-pāṇin* to describe plants.

273 Schotsman, *Buddhacarita,* p. 76.

274 Gopal, p. 11. The form *gulmavṛkṣāyurveda* or the science of plant life "is based on the reading of a passage in the *Arthaśāstra* of Kauṭilya as originally suggested by Shamashastry;" Gopal, p. 3.

275 Gopal, p. 4.

276 As noted in Dalhana's commentary on the Suśruta Saṁhitā, a classic Āyurveda text; Krishnamurthy, *Source Book of Indian Medicine,* p. 3.

277 From the Nandī Purāṇa, as quoted in Krishnamurthy, *Source Book of Indian Medicine,* p. 17.

278 As quoted by Krishnamurthy, *Source Book of Indian Medicine,* p. 70.

[279] Barrenness in trees is a blight known in a number of texts; see Jātaka 333, for example.

[280] Bhat, *Bṛhat Saṁhitā* 1.527.

[281] The date of the tree scholar Surapāla is difficult to ascertain, but Sadhale argues for assigning him to the tenth century CE. In conclusion, it might be said that "the science of Vṛkṣāyurveda was well developed in ancient India, that Vṛkṣāyurveda was also the name of an authentic text of that science, and that its author was Surapāla;" Sadhale, p. 39.

[282] Gopal, p. 54.

[283] Sur 1.4; Sadhale, p. 43; Gopal, p. 119.

[284] Sensarma, *Plants in the Indian Purāṇas*, pp. 58-59.

[285] *Etat satyaṁ parijñāya vṛkṣāropaṁ samārabhet / dharmārthakāmamokṣāṇāṁ drumebhyaḥ sādhanaṁ yataḥ;* Sur 1.8; Sadhale, p. 43; Gopal, p. 119.

[286] *Bhūtale pādapā eva paratreha ca śarmaṇe / yasmādananta dāridrāt tāraṇāstaravo 'pyamī / ato dharmārthakāmānāṁ chāyāpuṣpaphalādibhiḥ / prasādhakatamā vṛkṣāḥ pālanīyāḥ prayatnataḥ;* Sur 6.97-98; Sadhale, p. 48; Gopal, p. 153.

[287] Sadhale, p. 76. The material in the text is not necessarily knowledge that Surapāla himself gained through scientific work, but the work of sages that he compiled.

[288] Shamasastry, *Kauṭilya's Arthaśāstra*, p. 107.

[289] Sur 2.28; Gopal, p. 54; Sadhale, pp. 43-44. AP 282.8-9; Gopal, p. 115.

[290] VP 2.300.1-2; Gopal, p. 103. See also AP 282.1-3; Gopal, p. 113.

[291] VP 2.300.7-11; Sur 1.9-23; 2.24-34; Gopal, pp. 119-127.

[292] Sur 11.293-300; Sadhale, p. 60; Gopal, pp. 219-221. Note the Purāṇic prescriptions regarding plants in the planning, building, and landscaping of a home as discussed in Sensarma, *Plants in the Indian Purāṇas*, pp. 45-46, 60, 73; Banwari, *Pañcavaṭī: Indian Approach to Environment*, pp. 162-163.

[293] Gopal, pp. 12, 89.

[294] BS 54.2; Gopal, p. 95.

[295] Sur 3.35-39; Gopal, p. 129. Note the reference to plowing the land as important for the abundant growth of crops in TS 6.1.3.7.

[296] Sur 4.45-47; Gopal, p. 133.

[297] Artha 22.24.22-26; BS 55.15-31; Sur 4. 52-61; Gopal, pp. 12, 89, 93, 137.

[298] *Evaṁ vidhena vidhenā parisaṁsthitāni / bījāni santi sakalānyapi śobhanāni*; Sur 4.58; Gopal, p. 137.

[299] AP 282.11-12; Gopal, p. 115. It is noteworthy that sesamum is part of the Vṛkṣāyurvedic collection of plant and seed fertilizers for — apart from sesamum's actual beneficial properties for plant growth— an interesting parallel can be found in the use of sesame seeds in the water poured over the rice ball *(piṇḍa)* to grow the *preta's* intermediate body in the *sapiṇḍīkāraṇa* rite; Knipe, "*Sapiṇḍīkāraṇa,*" p. 115. Other Purāṇic descriptions of the care and preparation of seeds, the preparation of the soil, and of the process of sowing and planting can be found in discussions in Sensarma, *Plants in the Indian Purāṇas,* pp. 11, 40-41, 52, 71, 72, 98, and in Banwari, *Pañcavaṭī: Indian Approach to Environment,* pp. 163-167.

[300] ŚB 7.2.4.22-30.

[301] Sur 5.63-96; Gopal, pp. 141-151.

[302] Kāśyapasaṁhitā, quoted by Bhaṭṭotpala on Bṛhat Saṁhitā, vs.4; Gopal, p. 91.

[303] BS 54.5-7; Gopal, pp. 13, 91, 95-96.

[304] Shamasastry, *Kauṭilya's Arthaśāstra,* p. 127.

[305] Sur 6.99-105; Gopal, pp. 153-155.

[306] BS 54.9; VP 2.300.14-15; AP 282.7-8; Gopal, pp. 97, 107, 115.

[307] Sur 6.97 - 7.164; Gopal, pp. 153-175.

[308] *Nakhāgreṇaiva kāminyā kuṭhārāgreṇa lekhitaḥ / bibharti mukula vyājān mākandaḥ pulakeñjatam;* Sur 7.148; Gopal, p. 169.

[309] Sur 7.149-150; Gopal. p. 171.

[310] Sur 7.160, 163; Gopal, pp. 173, 175.

[311] See the discussion on the therapeutic care of trees in Banwari, *Pañcavaṭī: Indian Approach to Environment,* pp. 167-181.

[312] *Iti vividhagadān avekṣya nityaṁ / nijanijakīrtita lakṣaṇairamībhiḥ/ varatara mitarullasat - prayatno / dharaṇiruheṣu cikitsitaṁ vidadhyāt;* Sur 8.183; Gopal, p. 181.

[313] See Sur 9.184-222; Gopal, pp. 183-193.

[314] Sur 9.189; Gopal, p. 183.

[315] *Iti - vividhavidhiprayuktayogai - rapi na hi śāntimupaiti yasya rogaḥ / tam aparasuviśiṣṭabhūmideśe / dharaṇiruhaṁ pratiropavenmanīṣo;* Sur 9.222; Gopal, p. 193.

[316] *Tathā vyaktāni bījāni saṁsiktānyambhasā punaḥ / ucchṛjatvaṁ mṛdutvaṁ ca mūlabhāvaṁ prayāti ca / tanmūlādaṁkurotpattiraṁkurāt parṇasambhavaḥ / parṇātmakaṁ tataḥ kāṇḍaḥ kāṇḍācca prasaraṁ punaḥ / atha kālaprakarṣeṇa*

puṣpaṁ phalaṁ samanvitam / bījamtu kālaparyāyād udbhittvā pṛthivīṁ nayet; Para 1.7-8; Sircar and Sarkar, *Parāśara*, p. 4.

317 *Yathā prāṇināṁ marmacchinne nipātitā bhavanti tathā vanaspatermūle chinne skandhaśākhāpatrapuṣpaphalādīni praśoṣamāpadayante;* Para 7.3; Sircar and Sarkar, *Parāśara,* p. 89.

2

Plants and Life

We have seen that the possibility of plant life is raised, and assumed, in several domains of Indian culture: first, in the way vital generativity is ritualized through the understanding and use of plants in Vedic practice; second, in the role that plants are thought to play in the cycles of life, death, and rebirth; third, in the medical uses of plants to prevent and cure human illnesses; fourth, in the place that plants have as objects of non-violent ethics; and, finally, in the care and medical treatment that plants themselves receive to maintain their own well-being, and to cure them of injury and disease whenever their bodies are compromised. Given that these venues raise the issue of plant life by assuming that plants are in some way alive, we now turn to questions about the nature of plant life itself. If plants are thought to be alive, *how* are they thought to be alive and what does it mean *to be alive as a plant?* If alive, do plants have senses and, if so, which ones? What kind of behavior exhibited by plants counts as evidence of plant sentience? Does plant sentience suggest anything about the possibility of plant consciousness? Can plants experience pleasure and pain? And do plants, as sentient beings, have the capacity for interior cultivation? These questions are taken up in various Indian textual traditions, some more fully than others and some at odds with one another. If we hope to discern the understanding of plants in contemporary Indian environmental ethics at the end of our study, then identifying a common range of views about plant life in traditional materials is important.

2.1 Are Plants Alive?

Several contemporary Indian scholars of nature and the environment formulate the view, as common, that plants are alive. Speaking for a general audience, Arunkumar Misra, for example, says:

> We consider both plants and animals as living. We call all animals conscious, but hesitate to label consciousness in plants. Life can not be realized without consciousness. Everybody feels consciousness in plants, but hesitates to admit so because physical manifestations of consciousness, through movement of organs and production of sound in animals has no parallel in plants. But all do agree that plants possess sensitivity.[1]

O. P. Dwivedi, in his survey of Vedic materials that contribute to an Indian ethic of environmental stewardship, notes that in Vedic times trees are "considered as being animate and (capable of) feeling happiness and sorrow"[2] and this view – that all plants, not just trees, are alive – permeates his writing on environmental ethics in India.

Plants among the Inanimate

That plants are alive in a way analogous to animals and humans is not a uniform view of Indian traditions, howe\ er. In early Vedic texts, for example, while plants are considered to be part of the cycle of life, death, and rebirth, they are located with other elements that, at least in some Indian traditions, are thought to be of decidedly inanimate quality. Consider RV 10.16.3, for example, where, at his death, a person's eye goes to the sun, his breath to the wind, his body to the sky, earth, or water, and his limbs to the plants. While Jain thought might consider this to be a list of animate things, Vedic thought might not, or at least might have no opinion about whether the list covers animate or inanimate things. Similarly, RV 10.58, also a funeral hymn, is addressed to a spirit who is departing, and speculates about where the spirit might be going – to the sky, earth, ocean, streams, plants, sun, or mountains – again listing plants among other elements not normally considered to be animate. Expanding the kinds of categories included in such lists, AV 1.30 calls upon all the gods for protection and, in verse three, calls upon those gods who are in the heavens, atmosphere, earth, plants, cows, and water. Here the list includes both animate and inanimate, with no clear indication of there being a division between the two, and no indication which division, if there are divisions, might be the natural home of plants. Likewise, AV 5.24 calls upon various gods by name and specifies the area ruled over by each. As above, the list of those ruled over includes humans, plants (ruled over by Soma; *somo vīrudhām adhipatiḥ)*, trees (ruled over by Agni; *agnir vanaspatīnām adhipatiḥ*), creatures (ruled over by Death; *mṛtyuḥ prajānām adhipatiḥ),* waters, rain, mountains, the atmosphere, and heavenly bodies. Again, there is no clear distinction between animate and inanimate subjects and no indication, should there be a distinction, in which of these two groups plants might be found.

Again, in a Taittirīya Saṁhitā hymn used in the cutting of the animal for sacrifice, the petitioner hails the waters, plants, earth, night, and day, and then asks the plants (in the form of grass on top of the victim through which the cut will be made), as well as the axe, not to harm the victim.[3] And, TU 1.7.1, in dividing the world into material existence *(adhibhūta)* and the self *(adhyātma),* lists plants *(oṣadhi)* and trees *(vanaspati)* as well as fire, air, sun, moon, stars, water, ether, and body among those items constitutive of material existence, and breath, sight, hearing, mind, speech, touch, skin, flesh, muscle, bone, and marrow among those items constitutive of the self. In neither passage is it fully clear that plants are only in the category of inanimate things.

Ambiguity in the classifying of plants is found in Buddhism as well.[4] As Schmithausen points out, the early Pali canon clearly includes plants as objects of the non-violent ethic, but in later Indian Buddhism, plants are no longer seen as alive and sentient. His argument for the latter is based on sources such as Jātaka 307 and the Milindapañho, where plants are called *acetana,* incognizant[5] – a sentiment consonant with Aśoka's Pillar Edict V. Here the king declares that many living beings are not to be harmed *(imāni pi jātāni avadhyāni),* and lists specifically all those living beings covered by the edict, including animals, birds, fish, and insects, but not including plants. Later in the edict he notes that husks that "contain living creatures must not be burned," and that forests "must not be burned without reason or in order to kill living creatures," clearly delineating his non-violent concern for *the living creatures that inhabit plants*, but not necessarily for *the plants themselves*.[6] As noted above, Schmithausen suggests that, in the early Pali phase, lay followers of the tradition want renunciants to follow certain ideals of "ascetic decorum,"[7] thus requiring Buddhist monks and nuns to follow non-violence in the extreme. This includes not injuring plants in any way, and eating only what someone else has killed, and killed, moreover, for some person other than the renunciant who is receiving the food. But when non-violence becomes a practice that lay followers are interested in practicing themselves, killing plants (for food, clothing, lodging, etc.) produces no demerit because plants are now considered to be non-living:

> As for *lay* people, their life is kept practicable by confining non-injury, by and large, to *animals*, whereas plants may be utilized more or less freely, and there is a tendency to ignore and, later on, even (to) deny their sentience.[8]

Plants among the Animate

More dominant in Indians traditions, however, is the view that plants have sentience and life – though, as living beings, are found at the lower end of the life scale. Keith notes that, for the Vedic tradition, "the conception of the life of the tree is clear,"[9] and writers like Seshagiri Rao note that the view that plants are alive is assumed by the Hindu tradition: "Human life, animal life, and plant life are all interlinked...(and) I invite you to look at the life of a tree:"

> It gives its leaves to animals; it shares its flowers with bees. It gives its fruits to peoples. It provides shelter to birds and insects. It takes carbon dioxide and gives oxygen to the living world. Finally, it sacrifices itself to be used as construction material or fuel. It lives and dies for the service of others.[10]

We find these views present in the Vedic tradition, of course, where, in passages such as AV 8.8.14, plants are included in the grouping of those natural objects that have life and, in this verse, are included among those sent to slay enemies:

> The forest trees, them of the forest trees, the herbs and the plants, what is biped, what is quadruped I dispatch, that they may slay yonder army.[11]

Here there is no early evidence that plants have any special hierarchical place among other living things; nor is there such evidence in a passage from Taittirīya Saṁhitā describing the propagation of the earth. This process includes plants, and groups them with others that have life.

> This (earth) was hungry. It saw this Virāj, and placing it within itself it won food, plants, trees, offspring, cattle. Thereby it grew, it attained victoriousness and greatness.[12]

Again, a passage in the Aitareya Brāhmaṇa enumerates the life forms entering the earth, and includes such things as snakes, bulls, and birds – and plants *(oṣadhi)*;[13] and Manu, in 5.40, includes herbs *(oṣadhi)* and trees *(vṛkṣa)* among the other animate things (cattle, birds, and other animals) that are destroyed for the purpose of sacrifice and that, as a result of their role in the sacrifice, will be reborn in a higher life form.

In the Rāmāyaṇa, the Pañcavaṭa forest, where Rāma and his immediate family live in exile, is marked by the presence of bountiful (and clearly living) trees: "over there is the mighty wood of Madhukas. Directing your course to the asylum of Nyagrodha trees, go by the north of this Madhuka wood. There arriving at a spot hard by a hill, (you will) come upon the celebrated Panchavati, crowned with blossoming woods."[14] Again, the forests where they live are "scattered with trees bearing fruits and flowers of various kinds by thousands...graced with woods of plantain, beauteous with cocoa-nuts, and blossoming *sāla* and palmyra and *tamāla* trees." These regions have "thousands of woods of sandal exuding gum at their roots, and of choice *aguru*, grateful unto the sense of smell;

and woods and groves of excellent and odorous *takkola* fruits; blossoms of the Tamāla, and thickets of black pepper."[15] Sometimes the forests are "ghastly, impenetrable forests, covered on all sides with groves, trees and creepers...dreary forest(s)...covered with diverse trees and dense groves," but sometimes the forests give pleasure, as when there comes "within the compass of their vision many trees, grown on the summits of the mountains, blossoming with flowers and abounding in fruits tasting sweet like unto honey."[16]

Jain texts concur with the attribution of vitality to plants. The Sūtrakṛtāṅga, for example, says that:

> *All living beings,* all things, the whole world consists of nothing but these (five elements). They are the primary cause of the world, even down to *a blade of grass.*[17]

The Acārāṅga Sūtra then lays out a scheme in which life can be found in even the smallest elements, including earth-bodies, water-bodies, fire-bodies, and wind-bodies; this list is followed by lichens, seeds, and sprouts that, "if narrowly inspected," will be found to be "imbued with life."[18] When a Jain monk or nun who is on alms tour is offered food, he or she has to make sure that it contains no living matter, and must inspect the food that's put in the bowl for mildew, seeds, sprouts, beans, and grains that might still have some vitality.[19] Likewise, Jain renunciants must not accept water from which they themselves have not strained out living plants and animals, and must not accept food from someone who comes to the door drying her hands and arms, for fear that the water used for such washing hasn't yet been strained.[20]

The Jain Tattvārtha Sūtra has a substantial section on biology and uses the term *jīva* "for all types of living beings."[21] It argues that: "Every living being is physically characterized by vitalities" and plants, as beings with only one sense, have four out of ten possible vitalities,[22] these four being the sense organ of touch, bodily strength, respiration, and life-span. The Tattvārtha Sūtra notes that plants "are born living in the first instant" and that the "livingness of the plants is also agreed (on) by the Vedantins." This livingness of plants, moreover, can be experimented upon, unlike the livingness of the other beings at the low end of the scale: "No such experiments have been reported for earth, water, fire and air-bodied beings. Hence, their livingness is under dark for the scientists."[23]

Early Buddhism is also likely to place plants and trees among the living and notes, throughout its texts, that landscapes are abundantly filled with vital beings. Says the Dīgha Nikāya of one of the Buddha's tour to Campā: it is "a place teeming with life *(satta)*, with much grassland and woodland and water and corn."[24] Profusely present in such literature are descriptions of food, medicines, and fuels that depend on vegetable matter from plants and trees for their warming and enlivening powers – or, better, food, medicines, and fuels that depend on the organic living nature of plants to invigorate and give life to other organic beings. In the Majjhima Nikāya, renunciants are instructed on how to dispose of their meal scraps: "if he does not desire to do so (eat them), he throws them out where there are no crops, or he drops them into water where there are no living creatures."[25] We can conclude from this that if places with no crops are places with no living creatures, then plants must be among the living.

Attribution of Life : Sap

There are three properties that early traditions often associate with living things: 1) sap or fluid, 2) growth through birth, maturity, and death, and 3) breath or respiration. Francis Zimmermann locates the first property, that of sap or "unctuosity," in "that fundamental polarity the Indians call the 'Agni-Soma-ness' of the world," in which all "things are necessarily of either *dry* or *unctuous* quality," either hot or cold, depletive or nutritive. The unctuous quality links "*rasa* (organic juice) and *soma* (principle or symbol of unctuosity)" and in human bodies may be associated, in part, with things that come out of the orifices of the body: "the cloudy or clear liquids which form the serums, mucus, humors, excretions, and secretions [that] provide the most favored basis for a dialectic between the pure and the impure."[26] In its application to humans (and animals), the sap quality is also expressed in the circulatory system, where blood moves through the body cleansing and nourishing it; in fact, in the classification of human diseases, blood is a central and defining category.[27] The Suśruta Saṁhitā talks about *rasa* in its chapter on blood, and associates this term for sap or fluid with the lymph cycle as a "substance (marked by)...its continually flowing through and permeating every vital principle of an animated organism."[28]

Thus, Smith notes, "the principal inhabitants of the natural world" are arranged "in hierarchical order, as humans, animals, trees, and plants," and all "share a common essence or life force" that is identified in a number of ways, one of which is a sap *(rasa)* that flows through all things that are living. Thus, without this sap, "there would be no juice *(payas)* in the plants, no ghee in the milk, no fat in the flesh, no hair on the skin, and no leaves on the trees...Sap is the life force that...(is) the mother of all things."[29] In support of this, he quotes the Kauṣītaki Brāhmaṇa:

> [The gods] pushed upward the sap of the waters; it became the plants and the trees. They pushed upward the sap of the plants and the trees; it became fruit. They pushed upward the sap of fruit; it became food. They pushed upward the sap of food; it became seed. They pushed upward the sap of seed; it became man.[30]

Of the sap that circulates in plants, the most common observation in Indian texts is that plants need water to survive and that it is water that produces plants. Bidwell argues that one of the consequences of plants being "architectural" rather than "mechanical" is that "they have no pumps and no closed circulation system." Because plants can become quite massive and grow very tall, "they must transport food" and "enormous qualities of water, often to great heights," as well as regulate materials within, and eliminate wastes from, their bodies.

> Lacking mechanical pumps, plants have a variety of chemical and physical-chemical devices for moving fluids, and an elaborate system of plumbing in the form of specialized tissues that permit the directed movement of their nutritional traffic.[31]

We find this observation early in Vedic literature, and Oldenberg, for example, notes a passage in the Yajur Veda where corn is addressed as follows: "'you have grown through rains;' whenever he (the worshipper) put the corn in the sacrificial meal, he would say to the corn, 'may it embrace you who have grown in the rain.'" And when the worshipper pours water over the flour in the preparation of the ritual meal, "he would say: 'The waters have become one with the plants, the plants with the juice.'"[32] Oldenberg further notes that the connection of water and plants is already a common theme in the Indo-Iranian period and that, in the Vedic period, the connection gets tied to the fire god Agni – a reminder of Zimmermann's "Agni-Soma-ness of the world:"

> 'When he (Agni) is brought from the highest father, he climbs...up the plants in his abode.' The water comes down from the 'highest father,' the heaven; the plants suck their food from the rain and from the water of the earth. This water is in its nature similar to the rain. The plants are indeed the 'first-born essence of waters,' 'water is their nature.'[33]

The invigorating role that sap or fluid has in the natural cycle of life – and of plants – is suggested in the early depictions of the "unctuosity" of a person's life cycle. In the Chāndogya Upaniṣad version of this cycle, for example, when the dead body is burned on the cremation pyre, smoke envigorated with the steam from the body and from the plant-fuel rises into the air and passes into mist. This mist then passes into clouds and into rain, from where it falls back to earth "as rice and barley, herbs and trees, as sesamum plants and beans," to be eaten by animals and humans.[34] Steven Collins sees in this an example of the "water-doctrine" where the

> transformation of water in the life-cycle is explained sequentially as rain vivifying plants; men's consuming their sap, and drinking water, producing 'sap' in them (a sap which is both the physical water of the body and the enlivening of the 'vital airs'); this sap as semen producing a new body. If we add to this the notion...of the cremation of the corpse and its humidity rising to the sky as smoke, the cycle is complete.[35]

This notion of sap flowing through the life continuum is clearly associated with food and with organisms eating organisms, as described in the following Śatapatha Brāhmaṇa passage using the 'rootless/rooted' distinction to differentiate between animals and plants.

> Now cattle are rootless and plants are rooted. From the rootless cattle eating the rooted plants and drinking water, that juice is produced.[36]

The Hindu medical tradition says of plants that they "drink water from the earth, and their sap moves up" *(ūrdhva-retas)*,[37] and the suggestion that plants have circulatory systems is clear from the tree-medicine (Vṛkṣāyurveda) tradition, particularly that of Parāśara. Here there is a category of study called *tvakgaṇasūtrīya,* or the "vascular system of the plants," whereby plant specialists observe the transport of fluids *(rasa)*

> from the earth with the help of root. Thus the plant receives nourishment, and grows. Through Sirā the fluid circulates both in the inward and outward direction...(and) it is presumed...that from the ability of having general functional capacity...and also of the healing of injuries, a plant, necessarily, has the presence of 'Vāyu'...Sirā circulates air ('Vāyu' or 'Vāta'); and Synadanī carries watery fluid or sap.[38]

Note here the designation of important components of the circulatory system for sap: *sirā* that refers to the tubular vessels or channels through which narrow streams of water (and/or air) can move, and *syandanī* that refers to the circulation process through which fluids flow and move quickly:

> the root draws the aqueous fluid from the soil...and supplies it right up to the leaf through the 'Syandanī' (cf. vascular system). And here in the leaf...(the *rasa)* gets digested in [the] presence of the colouring matter...In this process some sort of warm waste material (possibly gaseous) comes out...The sap which is now a finer product nourishes the entire parts of the seedling. Consequently a seedling becomes a full-fledged plant in due course.[39]

These passages are important in that, first, they attribute the internal movement of sap to plants, thus bringing plants clearly within the grouping of "sap-filled" *living* beings. The *rasa* that they suggest is "perceptibly present...in...plant life has its origin in water....[and it] nourishes the plant organs with all the derivatives of [the] five...elementary matters," that is, with aspects of the five *mahābhūtas,* ether, air, water, fire, and earth.[40] Second, they describe the materials moved not only as sap or water but also as wind and, as we will see later, plants are thought to have a special connection with wind through their one sense-faculty of touch. This connection with wind, as part of the circulatory systems of plants, supports the discussion below – that plants are living, as well, because they have a system of air transport and transpiration, that is, a system of the movement of *breath.* Third, they describe a process that is *internal* and again, as we will see later, the limited consciousness that is sometimes ascribed to plants is one that is said to be internal.

Jain texts concur and also find sap to be an essential attribute of plant life. Of vegetables, the Ācārāṅga Sūtra says: "They are grown up, they are fully grown, they are strong, they are excellent, they are run to seed, they have spread their seed, they are full of sap."[41] Moreover, the Sūtrakṛtāṅga observes that "beings (that are) born in trees, originated by trees, sprung from trees...these beings feed on the sap of the trees originated in earth,"[42] and that these "creatures feed on the sap of the trees, creepers, grass, herbs, plants...(and) of their roots."[43]

Attribution of Life : Growth

Contemporary texts on biology often begin their discussion of the nature of living things by describing the characteristic of growth as "one of the properties of life."[44] A "living organism (i.e., an individual plant or animal)" has both a specific form that is manifested in a distinctive external appearance and a unique structure that is manifested in the arrangement of its parts within a three-dimensional space. It also has a capacity for development that is expressed in "its ability to change its form and structure through its lifetime."[45] The growth of plants differs from the growth of animals, however. According to Bidwell, while animals are built like machines – are mobile, can seek out their food over a wide geographical range, and must fit into a narrow set of size limits – plants are built architecturally. They are stationary, manufacturing their own food that must be acquired within the limits of their immediate environment but, being stationary, they

> are not limited by size or mechanical considerations – they are built like houses; new rooms can be added continuously (within the confines of structural strength) without problems arising. The plant can grow and develop throughout its life, parts can be abandoned and left to die, new parts can be added here and there as required.[46]

Moreover, the process of development in animals and plants is quite different.

> Animals do most of their developing in a highly coordinated way during a brief part of their life span and, having developed, achieve a more or less fixed steady state that may last for a long time. Plants continue to develop throughout their lifetime, and the various parts develop, mature, and die to a considerable extent independently of each other.[47]

This observation that plants are changing, developing organisms over the course of their entire lifetime can be found in many Indian texts. In the Pali canon, for example, one of the most consistent, and observable, attributes of plants is that they grow – that, given the right conditions, seeds will produce plants that will get larger, more dense, and more complex, and that these plants will, in time and in regular, predictable fashion, wither, decay, and die,[48] following the cycle of commonly identified living beings. One of the clearest indications that this body of authoritative Buddhist texts sees plants as growing is the use of the term *bhūta*. The components for the general term for plants or vegetation, *bhūtagāma*, suggest life and growth in a Buddhist world that is perceived to be continually arising and decaying. In Pali use, *bhūta* is normally used for animate objects such animals, ghosts, and the creating, growing world that includes plants. *Gāma* as a general term refers to a grouping, but in Pali usage most often refers to a social grouping of people, as in a village or town. Together these two suggest an object that is more alive than not and that belongs not with inanimate things but with animate.[49] In the Suttavibhaṅga of the Vinaya, for example, vegetable growth *(bhūtagāma)* takes place according to five methods of propagation: through roots, stems, joints, cuttings, and seeds *(mūlabīja, khandhabīja, phaḷubīja, aggabīja, bījabīja)*,[50] while, early in the canon, the certainty of death in plants is presupposed by the renunciant application of *ahiṁsā* towards them.

In the Hindu Suśruta Saṁhitā, "plants and vegetables (auṣadhis) that grow or sprout during the rainy season, are matured in course of time and ripen in their virtues and potency in the season of Hemanta."[51] And in the Vṛkṣāyurveda of Surapāla, it is said that "a seed is the cause of...perpetuating the continuity of (the) plant kingdom. The inherent nature of a seed is to pierce upwards and sprout."[52] Again, by way of summary of plant growth, Gopal notes:

> A seed germinates into a sprout striking a root into the soil. The root bears leaves from which the stem develops; branches arise from the stem and bear flowers; flowers develop into fruits producing seeds...Thus the (text)...states as to how the germination of a seed maintains the natural process of continuation of plant life.[53]

That, for Hindus, plants "grow" as part of the life process is found in observations that plants transform by maturing, withering, and dying. Here Surapāla notes that, just as animals can die from injury or disease, so can plants whose roots can succumb to damage bringing death and whose trunks, branches, leaves, and flowers can shrivel and dry up.[54]

Of a passage in the Jain Ācārāṅga Sūtra, Jacobi says:

> The plants know the seasons, for they sprout at the proper time, the Aśoka buds and blooms when touched by the foot of a well-attired girl, and the Vakula when watered with wine; the seed grows always upwards: all this would not happen if the plants had no knowledge of the circumstances about them. Such is the reasoning of the commentators.[55]

We have seen that the Ācārāṅga Bhāṣyam enumerates four normative terms used in Jain texts to describe living beings, all of whom are not be injured, that is, all of whom are objects of *ahiṁsā:* the *prāṇas* who breath in and out, the *bhūtas* who exist over time past, present, and future, the *jīvas*, or souls, who live according to the working out of karma, and the *sattvas* who are characterized by good and bad deeds. One of these groups, the *bhūtas*, suggests living beings in the process of their becoming and, insofar as the *bhūta* category includes plants, it confirms for plants the process of growth.[56] We see this demonstrated earlier in the Sūtrakṛtaṅga, where Jain monks and nuns are very careful about not harming plants because, as living beings, they are homologous to humans: "As our body is born, plants are born. As we grow, so plants grow. As we have consciousness, so plants have consciousness. As our body is damaged when cut, so a plant is damaged when cut."[57] Of this teaching, the Ācārāṅga Bhāṣyam says, "the comparison of the human body with plant body is possible in all respects. The characteristics of birth, growth, nutrition, metabolism, death, disease, the states of childhood, adulthood...and consciousness...are the most obvious items of description."[58] In the Tattvārtha Sūtra, plants are part of the large-scale Jain systematization of living beings. Here the text notices and documents the natural movement of plants through life processes: "The fading and growth of plants depends upon their intakes," and it is partly because they have intakes, i.e., food, that they are classified as living.[59] Jains postulate that plants are living from the very first, but that "their livingness is lost when they are weapon-operated or treated in some (injurious) way." Those actions that can injure or bring death to plants include ripening, heating or burning by fire, cutting or operating on with a weapon, mixing two plants or more, cooking, drying, and mixing with water.[60] It should be noted that this list of death possibilities for plants is part of a broader set of lists that describe the various weapons that can kill what Jains designate as the other elementary bodies: e.g., earth-bodies, water-bodies, fire-bodies, and air-bodies. The fifth in this set of lists are the weapons that can kill plant-bodies. As noted earlier, then, to be deemed subject to death implies attributes of birth and growth, of becoming.

Attribution of Life : Breath

The Śāṅkhāyana Āraṇyaka says that "life is breath; breath is life, for as long as breath dwells in the body, so long does life."[61] The question of whether plants are alive because they have breath might focus on whether they have inhalation and exhalation, or whether transpiration of some kind occurs across boundaries within their bodies, and from their bodies to the outside world. Bidwell, for example, notes that plants are like animals in that they rely on gas exchange in order to live for "major nutritional activity, photosynthesis, and respiration."

> An automatic consequence of efficient gas exchange is the loss of water vapor. Plants need sunlight to live. The sun, by heating them, increases water loss by evaporation. Elaborate compromises have evolved in plants that enable them to conserve water and at the same time carry on efficient gas exchange of oxygen and carbon dioxide.[62]

While, in Indian traditions, plants are included among the living by reason of their participation in the cycle of sap flow, and by reason of their attribute of growth – birth, maturation, and death – there is less unanimity on whether plants are included among those who have breath. Speaking to the issue of breath in plants, Smith quotes a long passage from what Keith calls "the most philosophic part of" the Aitareya Āraṇyaka, due to its "determined effort to explain the different stages of conscious life:"[63]

> There are plants *[oṣadhi]* and trees *[vanaspati]* and whatever life there is which is supported by breath *[prāṇabhūt]*...In plants and trees only life sap *(rasa)* is observable; in life which is supported by breath *[prāṇabhūt]*, there is also consciousness *(citta)*. In life that is supported by breath the self becomes more manifest, for in those beings life sap *[rasa]* is also observable, while in the others [i.e., plants and trees] there is no consciousness. In the human the self becomes more manifest, for he is most perfected with intelligence *(prajñānena saṁpannatamo)*. He articulates what he knows *(vijñātam vadati)*; he observes what he knows *(vijñātam paśyati)*; he knows [that there is] the future; he knows [the difference between] what is in the world and what is otherworldly. He desires the obtainment of the immortal through the mortal —

> thus [is his] perfection. Now among the other animals, they perceive only hunger and thirst. They do not articulate what they know; they do not observe what they know; they do not know [that there is] a future; they do not know [the difference between] what is in the world and what is otherworldly. They become only so much, according to their intelligence and capacity.[64]

This passages states very succinctly certain late Vedic views about the ways in which plants are alive and not alive, views that become clear as the tradition develops up through the Upaniṣads. To begin with, says the Aitareya Āraṇyaka, all living beings have life-sap or *rasa,* and this includes plants. Another way to be alive, however, is to be supported by breath *(prāṇa),* and to be supported by breath is to be supported by consciousness: plants and trees, says this text, are not supported by breath and so have no consciousness. Animals and humans are both supported by breath and so have consciousness, but animals are aware only of their hunger and thirst, while humans are conscious of much higher things – such as that they know and that they observe that they know, that there is a future, that there is a difference between worldly and other-worldly, and that perfection resides in the quest for the transcendent. Smith sees here the "familiar bifurcation between animate ('those supported by breath') and inanimate nature ('plants and trees')," and while "all of the earth's inhabitants have 'life sap,' inanimate nature is devoid of (breath and therefore of) consciousness."[65]

A list of elements in the Caraka Saṁhitā gives signs of the self that "are found only in living beings and not in dead ones." These signs begin with "inspiration and expiration (respiration)" or *prāṇāpānau,* and proceed through reflexes, "biological functions, psychic movements, *shifting from one sense organ to another,* impulsion and restraint (of mind)," and a number of other aspects of mental and psychic life.[66] Taken in conjunction with the Aitareya Āraṇyaka passage above, the Caraka passage supports the view that plants are not alive when having life is based upon having breath, and therefore being conscious – this we can argue because of the "trans-traditional" view that plants have only *one* sense. Consistent with the Aitareya Āraṇyaka and Caraka, the Jain Tattvārtha

Sūtra tradition notes that "all living beings do not have (at least physical) mind and 1-4-sensed and some 5-sensed beings are said to have no mental activities worth name,"[67] suggesting, at least for plants, that if their livingness is not based on their having active consciousness, it is not based on their having breath.

This view, however, is inconsistent with an early Vedic view of the unity of cosmic elements based on their infusion with *prāṇa.* In assessing the place of the life-breath *(prāṇa-tattva)* in general view of the Atharva Veda, Tiwari suggests the following:

> This life-breath *(prāṇa)* is supreme. The life-breath *(prāṇa)* pervades through the earth, the atmosphere and the heaven. The life-breath *(prāṇa)* of the heaven covers the earth through the sun-rays, the life-breath *(prāṇa)* of the atmosphere reaches the earth through the rains and on the earth the life prevails in the form of life-breath *(prāṇa).* All beings (have) life upon the (earth in the form of) life-breath *(prāṇa).*[68]

Moreover, it is a popular Hindu view that trees purify the air,[69] a view that implies transpiration, that is, inhaling and exhaling, of air by plants. In his Vṛkṣāyurveda, for example, the Hindu tree doctor Surapāla argues that "(p)lants (do) have consciousness,"[70] and suggests that breathing is observed in plants through the "transpiration" of water: plants breathe insofar as they move water around inside their bodies and as they "inhale" and "exhale" water from their environment; and because of this, they are to be protected from too much heat that will desiccate them and dry them out.[71] This notion can be supported by Parāśara's attribution to plants of *sirā,* or channels within plant bodies that circulate both water and air.[72] In fact, the ability of plants to circulate air *(vāyu* or *vāta)* through the *sirā* channels, both inwardly and outwardly, is presumed because of plants' general functionality and because of their ability to be healed from injuries.[73]

The Jain Tattvārtha Sūtra materials further complicate the discussion by attributing the first four vitalities to one-sensed-beings, one category of which is plants. One of these vitalities, significantly, is *respiration.*[74] The text makes clear that respiration is not the same as *intake,* however – as in the "fading and growth of plants depends upon their intakes (of food and water)"[75] – although having intakes does suggest having minimal consciousness, or consciousness "at the lowest level...The one-sensed beings have functional consciousness because they have tendency for intakes (food) etc. like other living beings."[76] Important here is that the word in the text for vitalities – of which plants have four – is *prāṇīs*,[77] suggesting some association of plants with the possession of breath. We remember as well that the Ācārāṅga Bhāṣyam, for example, gives four terms for living beings in Jainism, all of whom are not to be injured: *prāṇas, bhūtas, jīvas,* and *sattvas.*[78] Of these, plants might be said to belong to all four groups, given Schmithausen's discussion noted below.

Early Buddhism, likewise, presents us with an ambiguous situation on whether plants are thought to have breath. Schmithausen's exhaustive work on plant sentience in early Pali sources raises this question in detail. In Pali sources, the same four words are used for "being" as are used in Jain texts, *bhūta* growing being, *jīva* living being, *satt(v)a* sentient being, and *p(r)āṇa* breathing being,[79] though the inclusion of plants in these four categories is more promising earlier in the tradition rather than later on. While *bhūta,* as in *bhūtagāma,* has "plant" as a specialized meaning in early Buddhism ("sprouted or fully developed green, fresh, uncut and uneradicated, 'living'" plant),[80] *satta* is documented as a general term for living beings that includes plants, and *jīva* is more technically applied to plants in their "one-facultied" *(ekindriya)* quality, the canon as a whole is not consistent about whether *pāṇa* uniformly refers to plants.

Ordinarily, Schmithausen notes, *pāṇa* in Vedic, Jain, and Buddhist[81] texts can often only refer to animals and humans.[82] Schmithausen's argument, however, suggests stages in the development of the canon's view on this issue, with the first being that, in the earliest Buddhist material, the term *pāṇa* refers to plants as living, animate (and breathing) beings.[83] In the Sutta Nipāta passage verses 600 and following, for example, the division of species of living beings *(pāṇānaṁ)* is given, and the list begins with grasses and trees *(tiṇarukkha)*. Of this, Schmithausen argues, it is here taken "for granted that plants form a group among animate beings *(pāṇa)*."[84] Again in the Sutta Nipāta, a passage begins with: "Whatever living creatures there are, moving or stationary, without exception..." may they be happy.[85] Here, once more, plants, as stationary beings *(thāvara),* are included among those living beings called *pāṇa,* animate or breathing beings, for "the term 'stationary animate beings' *(thāvarā pāṇā)* cannot but refer to non-animal life, i.e., perhaps, the elements, especially earth and water, but certainly and primarily to (seeds and) plants."[86]

The second stage in the development of the early Buddhist view might be expressed in the rules against killing or injuring living beings – in which plants would be living beings, but not *pāṇa* or breathing beings. In the rule covering non-violence towards plants, Pācittiya 11,[87] for example, the Pali term describing plant life is *bhūtagāma* or "multitude of living beings" in the statement of the rule, and *ekindriyaṁ...jīvaṁ* or "one-sense-facultied living being" in the text leading up to the rule – both of which are common phrases in the canon for plants. In a more general rule covering non-violence for living beings, Pācittiya 61,[88] however, the Pali term describing living being is *pāṇa* and is glossed as *pāṇo nāma tiracchānagatapāṇo vuccati* or *"living thing* means: it is called a living thing that is an animal."[89] As Schmithausen notes, "one could argue (from this) that seeds and plants were obviously not regarded as living beings by the Buddhist monks or even the Buddha himself since killing an animate being *(pāṇa)* is prohibited in a...rule"[90] separate from the rule prohibiting killing plants – that is, plants and seeds fall under the category of *jīva* (Pāc. 11) but not under the category of *pāṇa* (Pāc. 61). On the other hand, continues Schmithausen, there are "no passages...that expressly deny plants sentience...in the earlier parts of the canon"[91] and, since the two precepts (Pācs. 11 and 61) belong to different series of "a larger literary unit which...appears to be composed of components some of which originally may well have had an independent existence," it is possible that the rules are added to the code in the way or order that they come into the tradition. And it may be that "the prohibition to destroy plants (and seeds) precedes the prohibition to kill animals because violence against plants (or seeds) was more probable or had occurred earlier." This would mean, finally, "that Pāc. 61 may...be a kind of *a fortiori* extension of Pāc. 11, and...that

Pāc. 61 does not intend...an exclusion of plants (and seeds) from the sphere of the *pāṇa,* let alone of living beings,"[92] but only intends now to include animals under the ethic.

One of the other suggestions of Schmithausen is interesting here. He notes that a number of the terms for beings in Buddhism and Jainism are used in a way that suggests comprehensiveness – "all *sattas, pāṇas, bhūtas*" and *jīvas* in Buddhism, for example, and "all *pāṇas, bhūtas, jīvas, sattas*" in Jainism. "There is no reason," argues Schmithausen,

> to accept the differentiating interpretations of later commentators. It is much more probable that originally in these phrases the terms are used as quasi-synonyms, with a tendency towards co-extensiveness, or at least no stress on specific delimitations.[93]

Because there is little cohesive evidence of *pāṇa* as a comprehensive term that includes plants in the early canon, however, Schmithausen is left with two possible conclusions for early Buddhism: either to take those canonical passages stating that plants are living beings to be "the actual belief of earliest Buddhism," or to take the ambiguities of the passages as a collection to "not really mean...what they say." Since there are problems with both of these options, he chooses a third option, that in which plants represent "borderline" beings. The "scantiness and evasiveness of the evidence the earliest Buddhist sources yield with regard to the question of whether plants were regarded as living, sentient beings or not is due to the fact that...(plants) were felt to be a kind of *border-line case.*" Either earliest Buddhism is "not sufficiently interested in a clear-cut and explicit theoretical determination of their status, or...more or less deliberately refrained from it."[94] The development of the Buddhist view is not finished, however, for what might be a third or final stage is found in later Buddhist material where arguments appear against sentience for plants altogether. Here plants are thought to lack, for example, the capacity for autonomous motion, bodily heat, signs of tiredness, and, of course, respiration *(prāṇa)*.[95]

Regardless of whether plants are considered *pāṇa* "breathing beings" or not, and in spite of their inclusion under certain auspices of *ahiṁsā*, "the life or sentience of plants was felt to be...significantly inferior to, or less intense than, that of animals, to a degree justifying, even for monks and nuns, a conspicuous difference of behavior in connection with their use."[96] Reflecting a number of the traditions discussed here, a Nyāya-Vaiśeṣika philosopher Praśastapāda "distinguishes bodies into two main sorts, wombborn and non-wombborn. Among the latter kind are to be classed...the bodies of very low forms of life – insects...(and) plants."[97] This view, for the present, will be reflected in the some of the typologies enumerated below.

2.2 Classifying Plants

In the classifying world of ancient India, plants figure in many typologies.[98] The broadest and most general is one we've already met: the distinction between beings that are "movable/ mobile," *jaṅgana/trasa,* and those that are "immovable/stationary," *sthāvara.* This distinction, codified in texts like the Aitareya Upaniṣad[99] and Manu,[100] appears in a number of early contexts and has generally agreed upon referents: plants as the immovable or stationary beings, and all others as the movable or mobile beings.[101] Another general typology divides creatures according to the number of their feet: in the Atharva Veda, for example, there are forest trees, herbs and plants (the footless beings), and the bipeds and the quadrupeds;[102] while in the Aṅguttara Nikāya there are the footless, the two-footed, the four-footed, and the many-footed beings.[103] The *apada* or footless beings here could refer to such things as worms and snakes, but the appearance of the Sanskrit *apada-ruhā* or *apada-rohiṇī* as the parasitical plant, Epidendron Tesselloides, suggests that the term could (also, or only) refer to plants.

A classic division of living beings is made according to their type of birth. One of the earliest examples is in the Chāndogya Upaniṣad where three types of birth are listed: egg-born *(aṇḍaja),* live-being-born *(jīvaja),* and sprout-born *(udbhijja).*[104] This is altered and amplified in the Aitareya Upaniṣad where the list includes egg-born, womb- or embryonic-skin-born *(jāruja/jarāyuja)*, sweat-born *(svedaja)*, and sprout-born.[105] This same list appears in Manu, who notes that egg-born beings include birds, snakes, crocodiles, fish, and tortoises; womb-born beings include cattle, deer, carnivorous beasts, and humans; hot-moisture-born beings include stinging and biting insects, lice, flies, and bugs; and sprout-born beings include all plants – annual and perennial.[106] Note that both of these lists include plants, as does a list of eight possible births found in the Jain Ācārāṅga Sūtra that also includes plants as the sprout-born.[107]

Another list, similar but not equivalent, is found in early Buddhism, but it does not include any possibilities for plants: egg-born *(aṇḍaja)*, womb- or embryonic-skin-born *(jalābuja)*, moisture-born *(saṁsedaja*, as in beings arising from the fluids of rotting materials), and spontaneously-born or born-without-parents *(opapātika*, as in devas).[108] Moreover, a scheme that focuses on the various realms of rebirths, that of the five Buddhist *gatis*, or destinies after death – hell realm *(niraya)*, animal birth *(tiracchāna)*, hungry ghost birth *(pittivisaya)*, human birth *(manussa)*, deity birth *(deva)*[109] – does not include plant rebirth as a possibility among its destinies. This is different from what we find in the Jain tradition where the *gatis* include being born among the gods, humans, hell beings *(nāraki)*, and animals and plants *(tiryañca)* – with the first three of these destinies having "a corresponding realm or 'habitation level' in the vertically-tiered Jaina universe: thus gods, humans and hell beings occupy the higher (heavenly), middle (earthly), and lower (hellish) realms, respectively."[110] We might presume that, in this scheme, animals and plants – the group not associated with a specific habitation level – are born either throughout these three realms as companions (and food) for the inhabitants, or only in the middle or earthly realm as part of the human world.

In a somewhat later Pali tradition we find a different way of thinking about birth categories, one that includes plants, but one that excludes them from the interactive karmic cycle of conscious beings. This scheme is found in a passage from the Milindapañho and it distinguishes among 1.) those things born of *kamma (kammaja)*, 2.) those things born of cause *(hetuja)*, and 3.) those things born of physical change *(utuja)*. *Kamma* beings are those who are cognizant; caused beings are fire and everything born of seeds;[111] and beings born of physical change are earth, the mountains, water, and wind. Plants, in this scheme, are thus excluded from the *kamma/saṁsāra* cycle. Assessing the early Buddhist evidence noted above as a whole, then, Schmithausen's thesis – that plants in this tradition represent a borderline case – seems confirmed.

In the Jain tradition a clear distinction is made between those beings born with *manas* or "mind" and those born without. The Tattvārtha Sūtra (2.11.12) declares that, among the worldly beings *(saṁsāriṇaḥ),* there are those with mind *(samanaska)* and those without mind *(amanaska)*.[112] And Akalaṅka's Rājavārtika on the Sūtra suggests that those without mind include all one, two, three, four, and five-sensed beings (thus including plants), while those with mind are only certain five-sensed beings.[113] Pressed for further explanation, commentaries on the Tattvārtha note that *manas* has two aspects, the physical and the psychical. The physical *(dravya-manas)* is the physical matter or brain of living beings, while the psychical *(bhāva-manas)* is of finer more subtle constituency, that is, "biological information energy," which supports and gives rise to the physical brain. It happens that beings who are declared to be devoid of *manas*, are actually only devoid of *dravya-manas* or the physical brain, but not of *bhāva-manas* or the potential for and creator of the full mental process.[114] Thus, plants are distinguished from humans, for example, by not having a physical brain but not from all sentient beings in that all have the capacity and support for mental activity.

Other typologies are made for plants that seem to presume at least some aspect of "livingness" – to use N.L. Jain's term from the *Biology in Jaina Treatise on Reals* – to be associated with them. Plants are included, for example, among the types of beings for whom food is produced by the earth: e.g., animals, humans, and trees.[115] In the Kauṣītaki Brāhmaṇa, plants are listed among the six-fold kinds of food that are available for human consumption: "wild animals, domesticated animals, plants, trees, that which goes in the waters and that which swims."[116] The Mahābhārata notes that there are four kinds of food that can be prepared for humans in the kitchen, e.g., fruit, roots, viands, and greens.[117] Food, or domesticated, plants fall into seven categories, sesamum, beans, paddy, barley, *priyaṅgu, aṇu,* and wheat – as do plants of the jungle, that is, of the wild, *śyāmāka, nīvāra, jartila, gavīdhuka, gārmuta, vāstva,* and *veṇuyava.*[118] Jain monks and nuns, moreover, are given instructions for their alms tours about what categories there are for small mildews, small seeds, small sprouts, and small flowers that may appear in the food put into their bowls, and that are thus to be avoided. Small mildews, seeds, sprouts, and flowers, the teaching says, may each be found in the five categories of black, blue, red, yellow, and white and, when at rest and not moving, may be very hard to see by renunciants.[119]

Not only are plants included among those foods that are fit for humans, but they are also an important class of materials used in medicines. The Atharva Veda divides medicinal plants into groups "on the basis of their morphological and other properties: *prastṛnati* (spreading), *stambiṇī* (bushy), *ekaśuṅgā* (having a single calyx), *pratanvati* (extending), *aṁśumati* (having many shoots), *kāṇḍint* (having many joints), *viśākhā* (with spreading branches), *jīvalā* (liṿely), *naghāriṣā* (harmless), and *madhumat* (richly sweet)."[120] The Caraka Samhitā notes that medicines are normally made from three kinds of things – animals,[121] plants, or earth (mineral)[122] – and that the plants that can be used for medicines fall into four categories: 1. *vanaspati,* plants whose flowers remain hidden *(apuṣpavanta)* but whose fruits are known; 2. *vānaspatya,* plants whose flowers and fruits are both visible; 3. *oṣadhi*, plants who die immediately after the ripening of their fruits, that is, annual herbaceous plants; and 4. *vīrudh,* plants who are known by their diffuseness, or, as in Parāśara, plants that are creepers having tendrils *(pratāna)*.[123] Ramachandra Rao describes these four categories as follows:

> Plants are broadly classified into four groups: (1) tall trees, which generally grow in forests and are distinguished by fruits but no visible flowers (...for example, the ficus group); (2) medium-sized trees, which are distinguished by fruits as well as flowers (...mango, etc.); (3) shrubs and weak plants, which have a tendency to grow in clusters, spread on the ground, or

climb on trees...like grass; (4) herbs, which are annuals or periodicals (viz., die as soon as they yield fruit or mature).[124]

Such distinctions are actually already known by the time of the Ṛg Veda where plants are divided into those that bear fruit *(phalinī)* and those that are not fruit-bearing *(aphalā),* and those that bear flowers *(puṣpiṇī, puṣpavati, prasūvarī)* and those that don't bear flowers *(apuṣpa).*[125]

In the Caraka, those plant parts that are used for human medicines include roots, bark, heartwood, secretions, stalks, expressed juices, tender leaves, alkali, latex, fruits, flowers, ashes, oil, thorns, leaves, leaf-buds, tubers, and sprouts.[126] And, those plant parts that are known because of the science of plant medicine and plant care include *patra* (leaf), *puṣpa* (flower), *phala* (fruit), *mūla* (root), *kāṇḍa* (stem), *sāra* (heart-wood), *svarasa* (sap), *niryāsa* (exudation), *kaṇṭaka* (spine and prickle), *bīja* (seed) and *praroha* (seedling).[127] For ritual offerings, the Taittirīya Saṁhitā divides plants into these parts: *mūla* (root), *tūla* (panicle), *kaṇḍa* (stem), *valasa* (twig), *puṣpa* (flower), *phala* (fruit), *skandha* (corona), *śākhā* (branch), and *parṇa* (leaves).[128] For similar purposes, the Śatapatha Brāhmaṇa notes the divisions of *parṇa* (leaf), *puṣpa* (flower), *kośī, samudra, dhānā* (grain), *aṣṭhīlta,* and *mūla* (root), while the Bṛhadāraṇyaka Upaniṣad homologizes tree parts to parts of the human body as follows: *parṇa* (leaves and hair), *bahirutpāṭikā* (ectoderm), *niryasa* (latex), *śakara* (mesoderm), *kināṭa* (endoderm), *ābhyantarakāṣṭha* (heart wood), and *majjā (pīha).*[129]

In the Pali canon, there are said to be five ways of propagating vegetable growth, viz., from roots, stems, joints, cuttings, and seeds,[130] and in the Dīgha Nikāya list of these methods of propagation, the text notes that "Gotama the recluse holds aloof from such injury (through propagation) to seedlings and growing plants."[131] Moreover, trees in their normal maturation are said to grow in three ways: in their branches, leaves and foliage; in their bark and shoots; and in their soft-wood and pith.[132]

There is, from early in the tradition, a special interest in large trees *(vanaspati),* and a separate section of Parāśara's Vṛkṣāyurveda is dedicated to their classification.[133] This interest reaches back to the Vedic period and, as Smith notes, its classification allocates certain trees to each of the twice-born *varṇas:* among the *brahmin* trees are the Palāśa or Parṇa, the wood apple, and the Plakṣa; among *kṣatriya* trees are the Nyagrodha or banyan, the Kārṣmarya, the cutch, and the peepal; and among the *vaiśya* trees are the peepal, the Uḍumbara and, again, the wood apple.[134] Especially large trees are also noted in the Pali canon. They "are mighty trees...grown from tiny seeds, of mighty bulk, which overspread (other) trees...(these) trees (like others) overspread, break up, break down, fall to the ground and so lie."[135] These trees include the bo tree, the banyan, the wave-leafed fig, the bunched fig, the cedar, and the wood-apple.[136] The Aṅguttara Nikāya goes on to specify that the rose-apple tree is chief over all, the coral tree chief of the *devas,* the trumpet-flower tree chief of the *asuras,* and the silk-cotton tree chief of the Garuda Birds.[137]

It is in three primary contexts, then – the ritual, the medicinal, and the agricultural – where early Indian traditions develop a precise botanical science for the plants of their environment. Massive details are collected in texts like the Vṛkṣāyurveda of Parāśara where the classification of plants, for example, as well as studies of plant and forest ecology, indicate extensive observation and analysis.[138] The focus in Vṛkṣāyurveda texts like Parāśara on the morphology and physiology of plants, the structure, workings and sexual behaviors of flowers, the morphology and gustatory classification of fruits, and the reproductive structures and propagation of all types of vegetable life suggest a sustained interest and highly developed skills in plant science from a very early period onward.[139] Much work is certainly involved in such study for, as the Tattvārtha Sūtra suggests, "plants have... body-shapes of infinite varieties."[140] Given the broad range of Indian thought focused on the life attributes of flowing sap, growth, and breath to plants, and the scientific examination of types of plants, ways of propagation, and varieties of diseases and treatment, for example, it seems clear that the evidence of Indian traditions strongly favors counting plants among living beings.

Endnotes :

[1] A. Misra, "Consciousness in Plants," p. 179.

[2] Dwivedi, "Vedic Heritage," p. 34; Dwivedi, "*Satyagraha*," p. 156.

[3] TS 1.3.9.

[4] See the following comment by Garry Bernhardt, "Pearly Gates," p. 46:

> Although all life is considered sacred to Buddhists, a distinction is made between sentient and lower life forms. Much consideration is given to the laws of karma and reincarnation, but plant and lower animal forms fall outside these laws.

[5] J 3.24; Mil 172-174.

[6] Nikam and McKeon, *Edicts of Asoka*, pp. 55-56; Woolner, *Asoka Text and Glossary*, pp. 46-49.

[7] See Schmithausen, *Problem of the Sentience of Plants*, pp. 20, 41, 43.

[8] Schmithausen, "Ecological Ethics," p. 9. Schmithausen's italics.

[9] Keith, *Religion and Philosophy* 1.185.

[10] Seshagiri Rao, "Five Great Elements," pp. 29, 36-37.

[11] AV 8.8.14: *Vanaspatīnvānaspatyānoṣadhīruta vīrudhaḥ / dvipāccatuṣpādiṣṇāmi yathā senāmamūṁ hanan*; Whitney, *Atharva Veda* 2.504.

[12] TS 7.4.3: *iyaṁ vā a'. ːdhyat saitāṁ virājamapaśyat tāmātman dhitvā 'nnādyamavārūndhauṣadhīr vanaspatīn prajāṁ paśūn tenāvardhata sā jemānaṁ mahimānamagacchadya*; Keith, *Taittiriya Sanhita* 2.602.

[13] AB 5.23.

[14] After M. N. Dutt, *Rāmāyaṇa* 2.536.

[15] M. N. Dutt, *Rāmāyaṇa* 2.586, 587.

[16] M. N. Dutt, *Rāmāyaṇa* 2.670, 684. Long lists of plant types are also found in Rāmāyaṇa descriptions of forests, such as of the forest where Rāma's immediate family lives in exile and the forest where Sītā goes after final exile from Rāma's court in Ayodhya; M. N. Dutt, *Rāmāyaṇa* 2.540; 4.1715.

[17] SK 2.1.23. My italics.

[18] ĀS 1.8.11-12.

[19] ĀS 2.1.1-5.

[20] ĀS 2.1.6-7.

[21] Jain, *Biology in Jaina Treatise on Reals*, p. 29.

[22] Jain, *Biology in Jaina Treatise on Reals*, p. 32.

[23] Jain, *Biology in Jaina Treatise on Reals*, pp. 100, 102.

[24] *Sattussadaṁ satiṇakaṭṭhodakaṁ sadhaññaṁ;* D 1.111, 114, 127.

[25] *No ce ākaṅkhati, appaharite vā chaḍḍeti appāṇake vā udake opilāpeti;* M 3.157.

[26] Zimmermann, *Jungle & the Aroma of Meats*, pp. 218, 220, 222.

[27] Meulenbeld, "Position of Blood in Indian Medicine," pp. 91-106.

[28] Bhishagratna, *Suśruta Saṁhitā* 1.104; see also 1.116.

[29] PB 24.18.3; Smith, *Classifying the Universe*, pp. 209-210.

[30] KB 2.7; Smith, *Classifying the Universe*, p. 210.

[31] Bidwell, *Plant Physiology*, p. 4.

[32] Oldenberg, *Religion of the Veda*, p. 7.

[33] Oldenberg, *Religion of the Veda*, p. 65.

[34] CU 5.10.5-6; Radhakrishnan, *Principal Upaniṣads*, p. 433.

[35] Collins, *Selfless Persons*, p. 49.

[36] ŚB 2.3.1.12; Eggeling, *Śatapatha Brāhmaṇa* 1.329.

[37] Ramachandra Rao, *Encyclopedia of Indian Medicine* 2.151.

[38] Sircar and Sarkar, *Parāśara*, pp. 91-93.

[39] Sircar and Sarkar, *Parāśara*, p. 106.

[40] Sircar and Sarkar, *Parāśara*, pp. 95-96.

[41] ĀS 2.4.2.16; Jacobi, *Jaina Sūtras*, p. 155.

[42] SK 2.3.3, 5; Jacobi, *Jaina Sūtras*, p. 390.

[43] SK 2.3.20; Jacobi, *Jaina Sūtras*, p. 392.

[44] Noggle and Fritz, *Introductory Plant Physiology*, p. 6.

[45] Noggle and Fritz, *Introductory Plant Physiology*, p.6.

[46] Bidwell, *Plant Physiology*, p. 3.

[47] Bidwell, *Plant Physiology*, p. 4.

[48] D 1.87, 111; 3.44; S 3.137; 5.46; A 3.19, 200, 360; KV 343; Vism 583, 625; Mil 33; J 5.46.

[49] Ryan, *Buddhism and the Natural World*, pp. 17, 52.

[50] Vin 4.34.

[51] Bhishagratna, *Suśruta Saṁhitā* 1.47.

[52] *Iha khalu bījantu vṛkṣāṇāṁ sambhavakāraṇam bhavati / viśeṣato bījānāṁ svabhāva udbhedañca / yasmāt prarohaḥ sambhavati tacca bījam*; Sur 8.2. Gopal, p. 103.

[53] Gopal, p. 108.

[54] Sur 7.3.

[55] ĀS 1.1.5.6; Jacobi, *Jaina Sūtras* 1.10n.

[56] See the use of *bhūta*, for example, in the Jain *Yogaśāstra of Hemacandra*, Quarnström, pp, 39, 40, etc.

[57] The Ācārāṅga Bhāṣyam notes this passage as it lays out the homology of plants to humans on the issue of growth:

> This (human body) is subject to birth *(jāidhammayaṁ)*, so too the plant body.
> This (human body) is subject to growth *(buddhi/vuddhidhammayaṁ)*, so too the plant body.
> This (human body) is endowed with consciousness *(cittamaṁtayaṁ)*, so too the plant body.
> This (human body) withers *(chinnaṁ milāi)*, so too the plant body.
> This (human body) needs nutrition *(āhāragaṁ)*, so too the plant body.

Tulsi, *Acharanga, Bhasyam*, p. 73.

58 Tulsi, *Acharanga, Bhasyam*, p. 73.

59 Jain, *Biology in Jaina Treatise on Reals*, pp. 98, 101.

60 Jain, *Biology in Jaina Treatise on Reals*, pp. 102-103.

61 ŚĀ 5.2; Keith, *Śāṅkhāyana Āraṇyaka*, p. 31.

62 Bidwell, *Plant Physiology*, p. 4.

63 Keith, *Aitareya Āraṇyaka*, p. 216n.

64 AĀ 2.3.2, as quoted by Smith, *Classifying the Universe*, p. 211. I have added what's in brackets [ ]. Keith translates this same passage as follows:

> There are plants and trees and animals, and he knows the self more and more clearly (in them). For in plants and trees sap only is seen, in animals' consciousness. In animals the self becomes more and more clear, because in them sap also is seen, while thought is not seen in others. The self is more and more clear in man. For he is most endowed with intelligence, he says what he has known, he sees what he has known, he knows to-morrow, he knows the world and what is not the world. By the mortal he desires the immortal, being thus endowed. As for the others, animals, hunger and thirst comprise their power of knowledge. They say not what they have known, they see not what they have known. They know not to-morrow, they know not the world and what is not the world. They go so far, for their experiences are according to the measure of the intelligence.

Keith, *Aitareya Āraṇyaka*, pp. 216-217.

65 Smith, *Classifying the Universe*, pp. 211-212.

66 Sharma, *Caraka Saṁhitā* 1.403-404. My italics.

67 Jain, *Biology in Jaina Treatise on Reals*, p. 31. A discussion of the difference between the physical mind *(dravya-manas)* and the psychical mind *(bhāva-manas)* appears later in this chapter.

68 Tiwari, "Element of Life-Breath in the Atharvaveda," pp. 48, 50.

69 Prime, *Hinduism and Ecology*, p. 11.

70 *Vṛkṣaḥ sajño bhavedantaḥ;* Sircar and Sarkar, *Parāśara*, pp. 2, 4.

71 Sur 7.108; 8.167, 168. Gopal, pp. 157, 177.

72 See notes 37-39 and 36. See Roy (*Mahābhārata* 9.238), whose translations of the properties of wind, the element associated with touch, include the "breaths inhaled and exhaled, life..and birth (including death)," suggesting that touch capacities, such as those in plants, include transpiration from interior to exterior and vice versa.

73 Sircar and Sarkar, *Parāśara*, pp. 91-93.

74 Jain, *Biology in Jaina Treatise on Reals*, p. 100.

75 Jain, *Biology in Jaina Treatise on Reals*, p. 98.

76 Jain, *Biology in Jaina Treatise on Reals*, p. 101.

77 Jain, *Biology in Jaina Treatise on Reals*, p. 103. Schmithausen notes that the terms *p(r)āṇātipāta* and *p(r)āṇa* have in Buddhist and Jain texts the same meaning as *p(r)āṇin*.
Schmithausen, *Problem of the Sentience of Plants*, p. 1n.

78 Tulsi, *Acharanga Bhasyam*, pp. 245-246.

79 Schmithausen, *Problem of the Sentience of Plants*, pp. 1n-2n.

80 Schmithausen, *Problem of the Sentience of Plants*, p. 5.

81 Schmithausen, *Problem of the Sentience of Plants*, p. 5.

82 Schmithausen, *Problem of the Sentience of Plants*, pp. 35n, 36n, 47n, 54, 58, 78n.

83 Schmithausen, *Problem of the Sentience of Plants*, p. 67.

84 Sn 600-601. See Schmithausen, *Problem of the Sentience of Plants*, pp. 64-65.

85 *Ye keci pāṇabhūt' atthi / tasā vā thāvarā vā anavasesā*; Sn 146 147. See Vism 310.

86 See Schmithausen, *Problem of the Sentience of Plants*, pp. 61-64.

87 Vin 4.34: *bhūtagāmapātabyatāya pācittiyan;* "For the destruction of vegetable growth there is an offence of expiation;" Horner, *Book of the Discipline* 2.226.

88 Vin 4.124: *yo pana bhikkhu sañcicca pāṇaṁ jīvitā voropeyya, pācittiyan;* "Whatever monk should intentionally deprive a living thing of life, there is an offence of expiation;" Horner, *Book of the Discipline* 3.1.

89 Vin 4.124; Horner, *Book of the Discipline* 3.2. See also, Sn nos. 117, 157, 242, 247, 394; Vin 1.83, 85, 193; D 3.48, 63, 68, 70, 82, 133, 149, 182, 235; M 3.22, 23; S 1.209; 2.167; A 2.176, 192; It 63.

90 Schmithausen, *Problem of the Sentience of Plants*, p. 18.

[91] Schmithausen, *Problem of the Sentience of Plants*, p. 67.
[92] Schmithausen, *Problem of the Sentience of Plants*, p. 21, 21n.
[93] Schmithausen, *Problem of the Sentience of Plants*, p. 21, 21n.
[94] Schmithausen, *Problem of the Sentience of Plants*, p. 69.
[95] Schmithausen, *Problem of the Sentience of Plants*, pp. 92-93.
[96] Schmithausen, *Problem of the Sentience of Plants*, p. 72.
[97] Potter, *Encyclopedia of Indian Philosophies* 2.88.
[98] This title best describes the material that follows. In using it, I have following the title of Brian K. Smith's excellent and very useful book, *Classifying the Universe: The Ancient Indian Varṇa System and the Origins of Caste*. The reference is made with the greatest appreciation for his work, and all misuses of the term are mine. For many other types of plant classifications, see Zimmermann, *Jungle & the Aroma of Meats*, pp. 74-80, 92-95, 198-202.
[99] AU 3.1.3.
[100] AU 3.1.3.
[101] Schmithausen, *Problem of the Sentience of Plants*, pp. 59-61. Another view of this distinction, put forward by Schmithausen, will become important later in our argument: that *t(r)asa* beings are not really mobile, but full of fear and desire, and that *(s)thāvara* beings are not really stationary but free from fear and desire in that they are spiritually and emotionally stable; *Problem of the Sentience of Plants*, pp. 61-64.

This two part typology is mirrored in Buddhaghosa's report of the Ājīvika tradition, which makes a division of beings into unconscious *(asaññi)* and conscious *(saññi)* — those born into an unconscious birth *(asaññigabbhā)* include, suggests Basham, seven categories of plant beings such as rice, barley, and wheat, while those born into a conscious birth *(saññigabbā)* include seven categories of other beings, that is, humans, mammals, birds, reptiles, fish, insects, and worms. A third category *(nigaṇṭhigabbhā)* is given and understood by Buddhaghosa as referring to plants born from knots, such as sugar-cane, bamboo, and reeds, but is re-interpreted by Basham as referring to "those not bound," that is, those "beings not so closely tied to gross matter as are mortals," and might include seven types of demigods such as *yakṣas* and *apsaras*. While Buddhaghosa's interpretation in the Pali would clearly confirm a division into plants beings and other beings, similar to the mobile-stationary division, Basham reports that the Ājīvika Bhagavatī Sūtra "list makes no mention of the *asaññigabbhā* of the Pali." Basham, *History and Doctrines of the Ājīvikas*, pp. 248-250.

102 AV 8.8.14.

103 *Sattā apadā vā dvipadā va catuppadā va bahuppadā vā*; A 3. 35.

104 CU 6.3.1.

105 AU 3.1.3; see also Bhishagratna, *Suśruta Saṁhitā* 1.8-9. Praśastapāda of the Nyāya-Vaiśeṣikas

> distinguishes bodies into two main sorts, wombborn and non-wombborn. Among the latter kind are to be classed both the bodies of very low forms of life — insects, plants — and also the bodies of the gods and semidivinities recognized in Hindu lore. Such bodies may be made of any of the 4 substances. The lower forms of life have earthy bodies, but the gods may have watery, fiery, or airy bodies depending on the part of the universe in which they reside. As for wombborn bodies, they are of two types: viviparous and oviparous. Udayana thinks that plants should be included as a third sort, while Praśastapāda relegates plants to a place among the lower forms.

Potter, *Encyclopedia of Indian Philosophies* 2.88.

106 Manu 1.43-46.

107 ĀS 1.1.6.1.

108 D 3.230; M 1.73; S 3.247. See Schmithausen, *Problem of the Sentience of Plants*, pp. 79-80.

109 D 3.234; M 1.73; A 4.459.

110 Jaini, *Jaina Path of Purification*, p. 108; see the diagram in Titze, *Jainism*, p. 238.

111 *Aggi ca sabbāni ca bījajātāni hetujāni*, Mil 271.

112 Commentary on TAS 1.14 says: "There are beings without mind such as plants, trees and some lower animals whose knowledge is necessarily through their senses alone. Plants and trees have only one sense, the tactile sense, and so their perception is produced by touch alone." Tatia, *Tattvārtha Sūtra: That Which Is*, p. 14.

113 Jain, *Biology in Jaina Treatise on Reals*, pp. 94-97.

114 Jain, *Biology in Jaina Treatise on Reals*, p. 96; see Tatia, *Tattvārtha Sūtra: That Which Is*, pp. 40-41; Dixit, *Sukhlalji's Commentary on Tattvārtha Sūtra*, pp. 85-86. Sukhlalji's commentary notes further that *manas* "is present wherever there is breath;" p. 93.

115 "The Upayāma indeed is this (earth), since it is this (earth) that bears (upa-yam) food here for cattle and men and trees;" ŚB 4.1.2.8; Eggeling, *Śatapatha Brāhmaṇa* 2.260.

116 KB 20.1, as quoted by Smith, *Classifying the Universe*, p. 210.

117 Van Buitenan 2-3.229.

[118] Smith, *Classifying the Universe*, p. 212. It is not clear how many, if any, of the plants grown on jungle *(jaṅgala)* land are edible, but Surapāla notes that jungle land is not auspicious for growing plants — only on *sādhāraṇa* land do all kinds of trees grow. Jungle land, moreover, is considered to be barren, though Surapāla does prescribe a watering cycle for those trees that do grow on it. Sur 3.40; 7.109; Gopal, pp. 131, 157.

[119] Kalpa rules for Yatis no. 16; Jacobi, *Jaina Sūtras* 1.304-305.

[120] Gopal, p. 8; AV 8.7.4.

[121] Those medicinal materials that are of animal origin include honey, milk, bile, muscle, fat, marrow, blood, flesh, feces, urine, skin, semen, bone, ligament, horn, nail, hoof, hairs, and bile; Sharma, *Caraka Saṁhitā* 1.9.

[122] Those medicines that are of earth origin include gold, silver, copper, iron, lead, tin, silica, calcites, realgar, orpiment, gems, salt, ochre, and galena; Sharma, *Caraka Saṁhitā* 1.9.

[123] Sharma, *Caraka Saṁhitā* 1.9; this grouping appears for perhaps the first time in AV 8.8.14; 11.9.24; 15.6.2. A slightly different version is found in the Suśruta Saṁhitā (Bhishagratna 1.10; see also 1.46 on *oṣadhis):*

> Those trees which bear fruit without blossoming are called the Vanaspatis (such as, the Plakṣa and the Audumbuṛa). Those that bear both fruits and flowers are called the Vṛkṣas. Shrubs and creepers that trail on the ground are called Vīrudhas, whereas those plants which die with the ripening of their fruits, are called Oṣadhis proper (such as cereals).

For a full discussion, see Sircar and Sarkar, *Parāśara*, pp. xxviii-xxx, 4-5.

[124] Ramachandra Rao, *Encyclopedia of Indian Medicine* 2.152. For a full description of all types of plants, as understood in the Vṛkṣāyurveda tradition, see Sircar and Sarkar, *Parāśara*, pp. 109, 157.

[125] See RV 10.97.3 and AV 8.7.26.

[126] Sharma, *Caraka Saṁhitā* 1.9; see Manu 1.47-48.

[127] Sircar and Sarkar, *Parāśara*, pp. 5, 25.

[128] TS 7.4.19-20.

[129] Gopal, p. 9.

[130] *Mūlabīja, khandhabīja, phaḷubīja, aggabīja, bījabīja*, Vin 4.34; D 1.5; 3.44; S 3.54; see Manu 1.48.

[131] T. W. Rhys Davids, *Dialogues of the Buddha* 1.6-7; *bījagāma bhūtagāma-samārambhā paṭivirato Samaṇo Gotamo;* D 1.5.

[132] *Sākhāpattapalāsena vaḍḍhanti tacapapaṭikāya vaḍḍhanti pheggusārena vaḍḍhanti;* A 1.152. The same list is given in A 3.44, except that the growths are named as five: *sākhāpattapalāsena...tacena...papaṭikāya... pheggunā...sārena:* 1. branches, leaves and foliage; 2. bark; 3. shoots; 4. pith; and 5. heart.

[133] Sircar and Sarkar, *Parāśara,* Vanaspati Kāṇḍa, chs. 1-3.

[134] Smith, *Classifying the Universe,* pp. 217-230; see Kane 2.2.894.

[135] Woodward, *Kindred Sayings* 5.80.

[136] S 5.96.

[137] S 5.237-239.

[138] Sircar and Sarkar, *Parāśara,* chs. 1-3.

[139] Sircar and Sarkar, *Parāśara,* chs. 4-8.

[140] Jain, *Biology in Jaina Treatise on Reals,* p. 103.

3
Plant Sentience: Touch

As others often do, Thomas Hobbes begins his discussion of the human person with the physical senses because, of all the body parts, the "Originall of them all, is that which we call Sense (For there is no conception in a man's mind which hath not...been begotten upon the organs of Sense). The rest are derived from that originall."[1] The importance of deriving mental functions from the workings of the senses, and of locating sense activity in the physical world, is foundational in Indian traditions as well. The empirical approach of early Buddhism is a good example for, when the Buddha asks about the nature of our experience, the answer is that it derives only from the eye and the objects of sight, the ear and the objects of hearing, the nose and the objects of smell, the tongue and the objects of tasting, and the body and the objects of touch. In this way, any discussion of the world using information from sources outside of the sense-faculties, then, is just empty words, because whoever is talking is talking about something outside of possible knowledge.

3.1 Plants and Sentience

Sensory functioning is a critical element in several Indian views of how living beings come into the world. In the Sāṁkhya tradition, for example, the five sense organs, the *pañcendriya,* appear early in the process of evolution, as the sixth through tenth elements, just after the individualizing agent *(ahaṁkāra)* and the perceiving mind *(manas)*.[2] The senses' foundational importance is apparent, again, in the Buddhist twelve-fold chain of dependent origination, the *pratītyasamutpāda,* in which the physical body, the *nāmarūpa,* is the immediate antecedent of the five senses which are then the necessary bodily attributes that allow experience of the world to take place.[3] And the recognition that there are such things as senses, and that there are five of them, is found as early as the Atharva Veda[4] with repeated mention made in such early Hindu sources as the Upaniṣads,[5] the Manu Smṛti,[6] the Caraka Saṁhitā,[7] the Mahābhārata,[8] and the Bhagavad Gītā,[9] as well as in the Jain Tattvārtha Sūtra tradition where there is full discussion of the five senses, their functioning, and their relation to the mind.[10] Although all of these examples represent views (and therefore theories) about the world, all, nevertheless, understand the senses as bringing in reliable information about the world, and as leading to empirically reliable knowledge of our physical environment – commensurable, of course, with what each believes is the worldview of its own texts.

The Five Senses

In the Vedic tradition, before there are five senses proper, there are other groupings of what might be called bodily functions, which include at least one of what we later refer to as sense-faculties. For example, in the Śāṅkhyāna Āraṇyaka, there are ritual-based passages which explore issues of psychology and the development of personhood, and that name bodily functions. One passage names speech, breath, *eye*, and mind,[11] expressing functions of the body that make the person viable but also allow homology with ritual referents. Other passages name breath, *eye, ear,* mind, and speech;[12] two other passages name groups that include three sense-faculties, one group including *eye, ear, savor of food,* and the other containing *smell, sight, hearing.*[13] And one section includes all five sense-faculties speech, *smell, sight, hearing, tongue, hand,* and *body.*[14] This last passage is of interest because there are two referents for the organ of touch (normally given as the hand, but more often as the body) and each is given here for different purposes. The hand is included because it is the function/organ of "action," while the body is included as the function/organ of "pleasure and pain."

The traditional term for sense-faculty or organ is *indriya,* which is derived from the name of the ennabling Vedic god Indra and, in the Ṛg Veda, refers to the power of Indra's acts.[15] It becomes, in the Atharva Veda and in later texts, a referent to bodily powers and thus to the location of the body's power as expressed through the sense organs. The *indriyas,* then, are the body's "controlling powers" or sense faculties and, in this way, are the body's "instruments of transaction with the outside world."[16] The five sense capacities are known throughout texts like the Mahābhārata and, in the Sāṁkhya tradition, for example, these *buddhīndriyas* are designated as hearing *(śrota),* touching *(tvac),* seeing *(cakṣus),* tasting *(rasana),* and smelling *(ghrāṇa)* and the five subtle elements *(tanmātras),* those that are taken in by the sense organ, are sound *(śabda),* contact *(sparśa),* form *(rūpa),* taste *(rasa),* and smell *(gandha).*[17] The gross or physical organs of sense, then, are the ear (Skt. *śrotra* / P. *sota);* the hand (Skt. / P. *pāṇi),*[18] the skin *(tvac / taca),*[19] or the body *(kāya);* the eye *(cakṣu / cakkhu)*, the tongue *(jivhā)*, and the nose *(ghrāṇa / ghāna).*[20]

These aspects of the sensing process – the capacity to sense, the sense organ, and the sensory information taken in – are thought to be intrinsically connected for, according to Āyurvedic sources, "man secures the objects of the different senses by the organs of the senses concerned. This is so possible because the senses and the sense organs are born from a similar cause (in every case)."[21] And according to the Gītā: "Ear, eye, touch, taste, and smell he turns to due account – so too the mind; [with these] he moves along the objects of the sense."[22]

A detailed account of the sensing process can be derived from early Buddhist sources where the process of perception begins with the senses and is based on *āyatanas* or "spheres" associated with each of the faculties. Each sphere has two aspects, an inner or subjective one *(ajjhattika)* and an outer or objective one *(bahiddhā, bāhira).* The interior aspect designates the organ itself, i.e., eye, ear, nose, tongue, and body, and the exterior aspect designates the objects, i.e., the visible, the audible, the olfactory, the gustatory, and the tactile, with which the organ comes in contact.[23] When there is contact *(phassa)* between an organ and an object, there is sensing and knowing.[24] For example, in the case of touch, the body *(kāya)*[25] comes in contact with a tangible *(phoṭṭhabba)* and there is touching *(phusitvā)*[26] as well as the sensory knowledge that is brought about by touching, or the consciousness gained by means of touch *(kāyaviññāṇa).*[27] Moreover, because through touch the tangible is known, that which is to be perceived by touch, *phoṭṭhabba,* is known as the *kāyaviññeyya.*[28] The sense faculties are then known as the *ñāṇindriya*[29] in later Buddhist discussion, because they belong to the processes leading to knowledge.

Often, texts will add a sixth sense to the list, that of mind, but in traditions like that of the Jain Tattvārtha Sūtra, the mind is excluded from the grouping of the five senses. "There are five senses *(pañcendriyāṇi),*" says the text, and the "five senses are skin, tongue, nose, eye and ear *(sparśana-rasana-ghrāṇa-cakṣuḥ-ṣrotrāṇi);*" moreover, "the objects of the five senses are, respectively, touch, taste, smell, colour and sound *(sparśa-rasa-gandha-varṇa-ṣabdās teśām arthāḥ).*[30] That the "mind is not a sense" is due, first, to the view that the "mind...has no fixed position in the body like the senses of sight, etc.," and, second, to the view that the mind is thought to function before the senses – color can be seen, for example, only when the "man, who wishes to see the colour...first thinks about to see such colour."[31] In the Caraka Saṁhitā,

> there are five sense faculties, five sense materials, five sense organs, five sense objects and five sense perceptions. The mind however is superior to these senses...The sense organs become capable of cognising the meaning of their sense objects (only) when they are led by the mind (and not other wise).[32]

In the classical Sāṁkhya scheme, the five subtle elements or *tanmātras*

> are emergents or evolutes of the *ahaṁkāra,* and are placed parallel with the emergence of *manas,* the five senses, and the five organs of action. The subtle elements function somewhat like the *manas* in that they represent a kind of bridge between the internal and external or between the individual and the

> world. They are products of self-awareness, and yet they in turn come in contact with or generate the external world.[33]

As an aspect of the physical body of sentient creatures, each of the five senses is associated with one of the five gross or physical elements. According to the Caraka, the "five sense organs are composed of the five mahābhūtas...with predominance of one in each."[34] Thus, "sight, hearing, smell, taste and touch are the five sense faculties. Sky (ether), air, light, water and earth are the five sense materials."[35] Using the Sāṁkhya enumeration, we derive the following:

hearing/sound/ear	=	space/ether *(ākāśa)*
touching/contact/body	=	*wind/air (vāyu)*
seeing/form/eye	=	fire *(tejas)*
tasting/taste/tongue	=	water *(ap)*
smelling/smell/ nose	=	earth *(pṛthivī)*[36]

Dwivedi says of these five cosmic elements, the *mahābhūtas,* that they "create, nurture and sustain all forms of life," and absorb what they created earlier as living beings decay and die. Not only, then, are these "all pervasive and omnipresent" elements significant as powerful materials of creation, but they also "play an important role in preserving and sustaining the environment."[37]

Senses and Sentient Beings

It is in the Jain tradition where we find the most developed system of classifying sentient beings based on the attribution of these senses to them. In Jainism, the

> careful cataloguing of species on the basis of sensory complexity, reproductive methods and possession of a brain...are in tune with the logic of modern biological taxonomy. The concept of a universe teeming with microscopic living bodies...and of infinitesimal units of matter that make up the basic building blocks of the cosmos...reveal an intuitive grasp of the physical world.[38]

Jainism divides reality into the living *(jīva)* and the non-living, with the former including matter that otherwise might be thought inert, such as earth, fire, water, and air. Each *jīva* is "said to contain consciousness, energy, and bliss" and to be colored by *karma*; and each *jīva* is also said to be defined by the characteristic of "sentience," or *upayoga*.[39] The quality of one's *karma,* as in Hinduism and Buddhism, is responsible for the nature of one's successive embodiment and, in Jainism, negative *karma* acts as a restraint sending the soul down to lower rebirths, while positive *karma* "releases the negative, binding qualities of *karma* and allows for an ascent to higher realms." In contrast with other traditions, however, the Jain tradition posits that *karmas* are "fine mattergic particles" that have the qualities of touch, taste, color, and smell, and that manifest themselves in the 'form' of the living beings, e.g., their class, position, wealth, knowledge, feelings, passions, and activities. *Karmas* make up a system of cause and effect, they cause pain and pleasure, and they veil the non-mattergic soul or *jīva.* "It is the karmas which lead one to the cycle of transmigrations," and it is the *karmas* whose elimination will give rise to liberation.[40]

Ultimately, the purifying path of Jainism results in the liberation *(kevala)* of the soul from sense-bound worldly life. As the Tattvārtha Sūtra says (10.5, 6):

> When all karmic bondage is eliminated, the soul soars upwards to the border of cosmic space (5). The soul soars up by virtue of the antecedent impetus, separation from karmic particles, severance of the karmic bondage and its innate mode of upward flight (6).[41]

Towards this end, the Jain ascetic moves to a practice of physical attrition where, unable to carry out his regular duties, he gradually reduces his food, thins out his passions, and works towards the abandonment of his body and realization of equanimity. In preparing for attrition, the ascetic, traditionally, begs for straw and retires to a secluded spot and, examining the ground to make sure that there are "no eggs, nor living beings, nor seeds, nor sprouts, not dew, nor water, nor anthills, nor mildew, nor mud, nor cobwebs," he spreads out his straw and lays down prepared to fast unto death.[42] The ensuing state of ecstasy is like "a plank of wood chiseled on both sides"[43] and, moving towards liberation, the karmic body is consumed and dried out:

> Even as fire consumes the worn out wood, exactly so the ascetic, engrossed in meditation and unafflicted by passions, shakes, thins and desiccates the karmic body.[44]

At liberation, the soul is then released "from all *karma* and dwell(s) in a state of eternal consciousness, energy, omniscience, and bliss."[45]

Jain tradition divides the rebirth destinies *(gatis)* into four categories – gods *(devas),* humans *(manuṣya),* hell beings *(nāraki),* and animals and plants *(tiryañca)*[46] – with the notion that, in the course of *saṁsāra,* any rebirth is possible and beings from any one destiny can be reborn into any of the others, whatever their course in the rebirth cycle.[47] There are, according to the Tattvārtha tradition's calculations, 8,400,000 varieties of birth places, ranging from the "lowest," that is, "beings destined to be sub-microscopic vegetation eternally" (with 700,000 or, alternately, 1,000,000 varieties) to the "highest," that is, humans (with 1,400,000 varieties).[48] The general division of senses over this schema begins with the one-sensed beings, beings with the single sense of touch, and including earth-bodied, water-bodied, air-bodied, fire-bodied and plant-bodied beings, and continues with the two-to-five sensed beings who are arrayed as follows:

* worms, leeches, *mollusca, curculionidae, vermes* 2 senses – touch, taste
* ants, fleas, plant-lice, cotton-seed insects, termites, centipedes 3 senses – touch, taste, smell
* bees, wasps, flies, gnats, mosquitoes, butterflies, moths, scorpions 4 senses – touch, taste, smell, sight
* larger animals such as fish, birds, and quadrupeds, humans, infernals and gods 5 senses – touch, taste, smell, sight, hearing[49]

The first, lowest, or least complex *gati* category – that of animals and plants *(tiryañca)* – constitutes, according to Jain tradition, a special case. This "lowest of possible destinies (is) characterized by extremely gross sensory activity and pervasive ignorance." Among the beings of this group are several sub-groups who are divided according to sense faculty, "that is, the number of modalities through which members of each group are able to experience the world." At the bottom of this category are the *nigodas,* the lowest form of life who possess only the sense of touch – a category sometimes called "the store-house of unevolved *jivas.*"[50] *Nigodas,* says Tatia, are "microscopic single-sensed beings which inhabit almost every corner of the universe and are especially prevalent in sweet or fermented substances."[51] In this category are, first, beings that are "so tiny and undifferentiated that they lack even individual bodies; large clusters of them are born together as colonies which die a fraction of a second later." Such colonies of tiny, undifferentiated beings are found in every part of the universe and, in earthly realms, they inhabit such places as the tissues of plant, animal, and human hosts, and are said to contract and expand, "as the requirement may be, to fit in with the corporeal frames." Moreover, they take "on...different stages of...migratory existence in order to enjoy pleasures or suffer from pains."[52]

> The whole universe is full of minute beings called *nigodas;* they are groups of infinite number of souls forming very small clusters, having respiration and nutrition in common and experiencing extreme pains. The whole space of the world is closely packed with them like a box filled with powder.[53]

Jain cosmology, as given in texts like the Tattvārtha Sūtra (5.7, 8, 9), posits units *(dharmas)* of soul *(jīva)* and units of space *(ākāśa),* both of which are innumerable *(ananta)* in number. Soul units differ from space units (or "the units of a cluster of matter"), however, in that the soul is indivisible and its units are "non-detachable." "A soul can occupy space that is one innumerablth part, or more, of cosmic space," and "like the light of a lamp, the soul assumes the size of the body it happens to occupy on account of the contraction and expansion of its space units" (5.15, 16).[54] The size and quality of *saṁsāra* bodies depends upon *karma,* and it is said that the *nigodas* "occupy the least number of occupied spacepoints."[55]

"Just above the *nigoda* is another group of single-sense organisms whose members take the very elements – the subtlest possible units of matter – as their bodies." These are the

earth-bodies	=	*pṛthivī- kāyika*	=	body like lentil grain	=	injured by digging, heating, mixing, liquids, plowing, woods and grasses, feces and urine, poultices[56]
water-bodies	=	*āpo-kāyika*	=	body like water drop	=	injured by filtration, drawing from well, washing, transportation, heating, mixing with soil, making salty or sweet, poultices[57]
fire-bodies	=	*tejo-kāyika*	=	body like needle	=	injured by earth, sand, blankets, water, wet vegetables, mobile beings, mutual fires[58]
air-bodies[59]	=	*vāyu-kāyika*	=	body like flag or kite	=	injured by heating, mixing with other airs, blowing by fan, water-bubbling, fires, cooling and chilling[60]

These element-bodies, likewise, are found throughout the universe, but unlike the *nigoda,* they do not use the bodies of other beings as hosts. The element-bodies are known to come in a finite number of varieties, each with a minimum and maximum number of forms per class, as follows:

	minimum/maximum
earth-bodied	20-40
water-bodied	5-19
air-bodied	6-19
fire-bodied	6-12[61]

The final two groups in the *tiryañca* category are plants and animals proper, and they live only within the earthly realms.[62] Plant-bodies in the Jain tradition are known as *vanaspati-kāya* and may, within the cycle of rebirth, take an individual *(pratyeka)* form or, more commonly, collective *(sādhāraṇa)* forms.[63] Those plants in which each soul has its own body include trees, shrubby plants, shrubs, big plants such as lotus, creeping plants such as gourds, grass, palms, plants of knotty stems or stalks such as sugar-cane, mushrooms, water-plants, annual plants such as rice, and herbs. Those plants in which many souls have one body include such things as ginger, onion, garlic, plantain-tree, and tumeric.[64]

> Plants in which only one soul is embodied are always gross; they exist in the habitable part of the world only. But those plants of which each is a colony of plant lives may also bc subtle and invisible, and in that case they are distributed all over the world.[65]

Unlike the element-bodies noted above, however, plant-bodies are found in an infinite variety of shapes. Plants resemble the lower *tiryañca* in that they possess only the sense-faculty of touch, but they are different from those lower in this group because they have a longer lifespan and more complex physical structures.[66]

The remaining members of the *tiryañca* group are the animals who can possess anywhere from two to five senses and who are thought to have even more complex physical structures than plants. Those animals who have five senses are further broken down into the lower animals who are totally instinctive and without reason or mind *(asaṁjñī/amanaska)*[67] – like beings with one, two, three, or four senses – and the higher animals or beings who are able to reason by virtue of having reason or mind (*saṁjñī/samanaska*).[68]

3.2 Plants and Touch

If our goal is to discern whether plants are alive, how they are alive, and whether they are sentient, then the first clear answer given by some traditions is that plants are *ekindriya* or one-facultied beings, with that one sense-faculty being touch *(sparśa)* and the sense-organ being the body *(kāya)* or skin *(tvac)*. Before turning to the two traditions that are clearest about this attribution of plants, Jainism and Buddhism, we begin with how the plant question gets asked in the Mahābhārata – the answer to which will ascribe all five sense faculties to plants. Bharadvāja's questions to the priest Bhṛgu, for example, about whether plants are composed of the five *mahābhūtas* and have the five *indriyas,* are as follows:

> If all mobile *(jaṅgama* = animals) and immobile *(sthāvara* = plants) objects are composed of the five elements, why is it that in all immobile objects (plants) these elements are not visible?
> Trees do not appear to have any heat. They do not seem to have any motion. They are again made up of dense particles. The five elements are not noticeable in them.
> Trees do not hear; they do not see; they are not capable of the perceptions of smell or taste. They do not have the perception of touch. How then can they be regarded as composed of the five elements?
> It seems to me that in consequence of the absence of any liquid material in them, of any heat, of any earth, of any wind, and of any empty space, trees cannot be regarded as compounds of the five elements.[69]

Bhṛgu then responds with this teaching on the sentience of plants:

10. Without doubt, though possessed of density, trees have space within them. Because of this, the putting forth of flowers and fruits is always taking place in them.
11. They have heat within them in consequence of which leaf, bark, fruit, and flower, are seen to droop. They sicken and dry up. That shows they have the perception of 'touch.'
12. Through sound of wind and fire and thunder, their fruits and flowers drop down. Sound is perceived through the ear. Trees have, therefore, ears and do 'hear.'
13. A creeper winds round a tree and goes about all its sides. A blind thing cannot find its way. For this reason it is evident that trees have 'vision.'
14. Then again trees recover vigor and put forth flowers in consequence of odors good and bad, of the sacred perfume of diverse kinds of *dhupas.* It is plain that trees have 'smell.'
15. They drink water by their roots. They catch diseases of diverse kinds. Those diseases again are cured by different operations. From this it is evident that trees have perceptions of 'taste.'
16. As one can suck up water through a bent lotus-stalk, trees also, with the aid of the wind, drink through their roots.

17. They are susceptible to pleasure and pain, and grow when cut or lopped off. From these circumstances I see that trees have life. They are not inanimate.
18. Fire and wind cause the water thus sucked up to be digested. According, again to the quantity of the water taken up, the tree advances in growth and becomes turgid.[70]

This passage belongs to a special dialogue in the Sānti Parvan between Bharadvāja and Bhṛgu that covers an account of the universe and posits a primeval being named Manasa/Brahman from whom all creations come as a result of the interaction between the five elements.[71] Concerning this passage's views on plants, the attribution of all five senses to them is unusual for Indian traditions, and must be taken as an anomaly, for the usual bio-medical description of plants is that "they are sensitive [only] to pressure or touch which is felt inward" *(antaḥ-sparśa).*"[72] The passage may be important for scholars such as A. Misra, however, who use the passage for more general purposes: i.e., to confirm that the idea of plants as living entities is a central one in Vedic tradition. While hesitating to ascribe consciousness to plants, Misra uses the passage to underscore the tradition's agreement "that plants possess sensitivity" and that plants are "capable of feeling the touch of others."[73]

Plants as One-Sensed Beings : Touch

The tradition that most clearly states that plants are one-facultied beings with the sense of touch is Jainism. The Ācārāṇga Sūtra gives an early Jain classification of the eight kinds of births of animate beings: 1) from eggs, such as birds; 2) from a fetus, such as elephants; 3) from a fetus with an enveloping membrane, such as cows and buffaloes; 4) from fluids, such as worms; 5) from sweat, such as bugs and lice; 6) by coagulation, such as locusts and ants; 7) from sprouts, such as butterflies and wagtails; and 8) by regeneration, such as men, gods, and hell-beings. According to the early Jains, this classification accounts for the births of all types of beings – including plants, who would fall into the sprout-born category. The Ācārāṅga passage continues as follows:

> ...all beings, those with two, three, four senses, plants, those with five senses, and the rest of creation, (experience) individually pleasure or displeasure, pain, great terror, and unhappiness.[74]

This passage enumerates beings according to the sense-faculties that they have; beings with two, three, four, and five are designated, and the only other item in the list is plants; we infer that, because we are missing a designation of the one-sensed beings, and because plants are included without a sense-designation, plants must be the stand-in for one-sensed beings, and that this fact is so well known that the text does not need to say so explicitly.

Again, in the Uttarādhyayana, an early rendition of the various birth bodies available for souls is given, beginning with earth-bodies, water-bodies, fire-bodies, wind-bodies, and vegetable- or plant-bodies.[75] Once the recitation of plant-bodies has passed, UD 10.10 notes that the text is now talking about two-sense facultied beings *(dvīndriya),* three-sense facultied beings *(trīndriya),* four-sense facultied beings *(caturindriya)* and, finally, five-sense facultied beings *(pañcendriya)* – the last category, which is very hard to achieve, includes hell-beings, gods, and humans.[76] This signifies that before the text begins to talk about two-sensed beings, it must be talking about one-sensed beings, and this would suggest that the element- and plant-bodies are designated in this text as one-sensed. The Uttarādhyayana goes on to give, in lecture thirty-six, a full and detailed account of the schema of living beings as known in early Jainism.

Later, the Jain Tattvārtha Sūtra (2.23) consistently identifies those beings with earth-bodies, water-bodies, fire-bodies, air-bodies, and plant-bodies as having one sense-faculty, and that the sense-faculty that they have is touch.[77] According to Akalaṅka's commentary:

> The embodied earth, water, fire, air and plants have one sense of touch only...The earth-bodied (etc.)...and plant-bodied are 1-sensed living beings...There is (only) one (physical) sense in the living beings up to plants...The word 'one' means the first one. And the first one is the sense of touch...it is undoubtedly clear that the senses increase one by one beginning from the first sense of touch onwards.[78]

The evidence is clear, as well, that early Buddhists also consider plants to be one-facultied living beings. Most of the early designations of plants as *ekindriya* occur in passages where the lay donors are criticizing Buddhist renunciants who, in the course of their normal lives, appear to be injuring one-facultied living beings:

> "How can these recluses, sons of the Sakyans, have a tree cut down that is used as a shrine revered by a village...revered by the kingdom? The recluses, sons of the Sakyans, are depriving a *one-facultied thing of life.*"[79]
> "How can these recluses, sons of the Sakyans, having had young palmyra palms cut, wear shoes of palmyra palm leaves? These young palmyra palms which were cut, are withering. These recluses, sons of the Sakyans, are harming *life that is one-facultied.*"[80]
> "How can these recluses, sons of the Sakyans, cut down trees and have them cut down? These recluses, sons of the Sakyans, are harming *life that is one-facultied.*"[81]
> "How can these nuns walk on almstour during the rains, trampling down the crops and grasses, injuring *life that is one-facultied*, bringing many small creatures to destruction?"[82]

In each instance, when the case of harming plants is brought before the Buddha, he responds with a ruling in favor of practicing *ahiṁsā* towards one-facultied living beings, that is, towards plants. It is only somewhat more circumstantially that early Buddhist texts openly identify plants as being endowed with "touch." Although I. B. Horner gives us this information in a footnote to her Vinaya translation,[83] we would actually only know that plants are endowed with touch from the *descriptions of plant behavior* in the Pali canon, as discussed below. The certainty that it is the sense faculty of touch that is being referred to by the designation "one-sense faculty" *(ekindriya)* in the Pali texts is most likely based on the considerable contact, attested in the canon, between early Buddhist and Jain communities during this period. If both communities are talking about one-sense facultied beings, and the Jains are identifying this sense as that of touch, then the Buddhists, even in their silence, are probably making that same identification as well.

To Be Endowed With Touch

What does it mean to be endowed with touch? In the human somatic sensory system, there are, according to Eric Kandel and Thomas Jessell, four major modalities:

> ...*discriminative touch,* (required to recognize the size, shape and texture of objects and their movement across the skin), *proprioception* (the sense of static position and movement of limbs and body), *nociception* (the signaling of tissue damage, often perceived as pain), and *temperature sense* (warmth and cold).[84]

Such sensations are among those noted by texts in early Indian traditions beginning with the Aitareya Upaniṣad's understanding that touch happens when the skin comes in contact with some kind of object: "touching is through the skin...if [the person] had taken hold of it [food] by the skin (i.e., by touching food) one would have had the satisfaction of food."[85] And in the Bṛhat-Saṁnyāsa Upaniṣad touch "comes into being by the grace of consciousness and...is grasped by no other means than the skin that soon perishes."[86]

The sense of touch *(kāyendriya)* is the faculty associated with *wind* or *air* alone: "Vāta is the predominant (element) in the sense of touch and the sense of touch resides in the skin."[87] Manu notes that "from ether *(ākāśa)*, modifying itself, springs the pure, powerful *wind (vāyu);* the vehicle of all perfumes; that is held to possess the quality of *touch (sparśaguṇa).*"[88] In the Vedic order, "the role of the motor and of the regulator of the Heavenly bodies...(is) ascribed to the wind by the astronomy of classical India,"[89] and in the Bṛhadāraṇyaka Upaniṣad wind is the breath of the sacrificial horse interpreted cosmically in rituals of creation.[90] According to the Āyurveda, wind is the most active of the bodily elements and, with fire and water, signifies "the motor *par excellence.*"[91] For the Caraka Saṁhitā, wind consists of front breath *(prāṇa),* upward breath *(udāna),* concentrated breath *(samāna),* diffused breath *(vyāna),* and low breath *(apāna)* – that is, those forces that keep the living being living – and it promotes movements of all types. Among other things, wind or breath conveys the objects of all the faculties, it distributes all the elements of the organism, it brings about coherence in the body, and it makes embryos.[92] Wind is also associated with "respiration, twinkling of eye, contraction and relaxation, movement, propulsion and retention along with touch and tactile sense."[93] For the Suśruta Saṁhitā, wind in the body acts promptly and circulates constantly: when it is not excited, wind ensures the equilibrium of bodily impurities and of the organic elements in the body. "The wind...goes everywhere (in the body and) covers successively the constitutive elements of the hands, the feet, (and) the head."[94] In this way, the medical texts describe the nature and role of wind/breath in the body as foundational and as effecting matters throughout – as *vāyu* or wind is especially associated with mobility.[95]

When the full layout of the five *mahābhūtas* – earth, water, fire, air, and ether – is listed in the order of creation, or of coming into being, it corresponds to list of the five sense-faculties as follows:

> sound/ear *(śabda)* <—> ether *(ākāśa):* the "properties of space are sound, extension, capacity of being enclosed, absence of refuge for resting upon...status of being unmanifest, capacity for modification, incapacity for producing resistance, material cause for producing the sense of hearing, and the unoccupied portions of the human body."
> *touch/skin (sparśa) <—> air (vāyu):* the "properties of the wind are touch that is neither hot nor cool, capacity to assist the organ of speech, independence (in respect of motion), strength, celerity, power to assist all kinds of emission or discharge, power to raise other objects, breaths inhaled and exhaled, life (as the attribute of chit), and birth (including death)."
> vision/eye *(rūpa* as form or *varṇa* as color) <—> fire *(agni):* the "properties of fire are irresistible energy, inflammability, heat, capacity to soften, light, sorrow, disease, speed, fury, and invariably upward motion."
> taste/tongue *(rasa)* <—> water *(ap):* the "properties of water are coolness, taste, moisture, liquidity, softness, agreeableness...fluidity, capacity to be congealed, and power to melt many earthly products."
> smell/nose *(gandha)* <—> earth *(pṛthivī):* the "properties possessed by earth are immobility, weight, hardness, productiveness, scent, density, capacity to absorb scents of

> all kinds, cohesion, habitableness...and that attribute of the mind which is called patience or the capacity to bear."[96]

Here it's important to note some of the properties attributed to wind as the primary element of touch by the Mahābhārata: temperature, motion, movement of objects, breathing, and the extremities of life in birth and death. From the creation point of view, however, the development of the elements, means the accumulation of sense faculties:

ether — has sound[97]
air — has touch and sound
fire — has color, touch, and sound
water — has taste, color, touch, and sound
earth — has smell, taste, color, touch, and sound

As Dasgupta notes of the second chart, touch can involve the elements of earth, water, fire, and air in terms of the kinds of qualities perceived as a result of "touch contact," and these qualities can be named as distinctive of touch:

> The sense of touch...has for its object the four elements and the qualities of smoothness, roughness, lightness, heaviness, cold, hunger and thirst. These qualities represent the feelings generated in sentient beings by the objects of touch, hunger, thirst, etc., and are also counted under it, as they are the organic effects produced by a touch which excites the physical frame at a time when the energy of wind becomes active in our body and predominates over other energies.[98]

Thus, in the Chāndogya Upaniṣad, one perceives warmth through the sense of touch,[99] in the Bhagavad Gītā contact brings sensations of hot/cold, pleasure/pain,[100] and in the Caraka Saṁhitā, touch produces sensations of hot/cold, rough/smooth, and heavy/ light; it is also associated with such qualities as mobility, impulsion, liquidity, and non-interruption.[101] This list can also be found in the Jain Uttarādhyayana, and includes a fourth pair of hard/soft: hard/soft, heavy/light, cold/hot, and smooth/rough.[102] In later Buddhist texts, other details are available. In the Dhammasaṅgaṇi, for example, tangibles include things that are solid, heat producing, gaseous, hard/ soft, smooth/rough, pleasant/painful, and heavy/light.[103] In the

Vibhaṅga, the tangible base includes elements of extension, heat, motion, hard/soft, smooth/rough, pleasure/pain, and heavy/light.[104] And in the Visuddhimagga – reminiscent of the ubiquitous presence of the wind and of the Caraka's attribution of liquidity – the "body [sensitivity] is to be found everywhere, like a liquid that soaks a layer of cotton."[105] Given these attributes of touch, it's possible to suggest an understanding of plants consonant with knowledge of the properties of touch in various traditions and, therefore, further support the notion that plants are one-facultied, with touch alone.

3.3 Touch Behavior in Plants

Contemporary studies of plant behavior are often studies of plant movements that, as "Darwin recognized...can (often) be interpreted as adaptations (of plants) to their environments." Most plant movements fall into two categories, those that are *tropisms,* "in which the direction of the environmental stimulus determines the direction of the movement" and those that are *nastic movements* "which are triggered by an external stimulus...but in which the stimulus direction *does not* determine the direction of the movement." Examples of tropisms are stems growing away from gravity and growing toward a light source, and examples of nastic movements are daily leaf movements and transpirational openings and closings.[106] Nastic movements are of several types: *hyponasty* is the "upward bending of an organ" while *epinasty* is its downward bending. *Nyctinasty* is the rotation of leaves "from nearly horizontal during the day to nearly vertical at night," and is an example of "rhythmic processes controlled by interactions between the environment and the biological clock," sometimes noted as "sleep movements."[107]

Hydronasty or *hygronasty* "involves a folding or rolling up of leaves...in response to water stress instead of light" (as is the case in *nyctinasty)*. And *thigmonasty* refers to nastic movements that come from touch – such as in the mimosa plant, whose leaves fold up when "touched, shaken, heated, rapidly cooled, or treated with an electrical stimulus."[108] There are also "developmental responses to mechanical stress (called) *thigmomorphogenesis*" that are responses to rubbing, resulting in "slower stem elongation and increased stem diameter...(i.e.) short, stocky plants." Finally, *seismomorphogenesis* describes plant responses to shaking, where "the bending effects of wind influence plant development," and plants that are "grown outside (and) hardened by wind and bright sunlight, show little further response to mechanical stress."[109]

With this in mind, we now examine what Indian traditions observe about plants: if plants are *ekindriya* and if their one sense is that of touch, what attributes of touch consonant with Indian traditions can be found in the traditions' descriptions of plants? And, what are the implications of these attributes of "touch in plants" as understood by the larger traditional systems of thought?

Touch: Plants Exhibit Behavior of Growth

One of the most consistently observed attributes of plants is that they *grow*. In RV 7.101.2, for example, the rain-cloud Parjanya is beseeched to send water that plant life may grow abundantly;[110] and, in RV 10.97, healing plants are addressed as "you growing plants" who "have a hundred forms and a thousand growths...(and) bear flowers and...fruit."[111] In AV 8.7, plants are called spreading, extending, stretching over the earth, and growing on mountains and on plains,[112] and AV 8.10.18 notes that "what is cut of the forest trees grows over in a year."[113] In the Taittirīya Saṁhitā, the ritualist calls out "O tree, grow with a hundred shoots; may we grow with a thousand shoots," hoping that the ritual power of homology will bring him many sons.[114] And in the Agnicayana, during the laying of the bricks for the fire-hearth, plants are placed on the earth, "for on this earth those (plants) spring up, and along her they grow."[115] The plucking of harvest grains comes due for the Āgrayaṇa festival and, in connection with that, the Kauṣītaki Brāhmaṇa notes that when "spring has come and the bamboo seeds are ripe, he gives orders to pluck" them.[116] The Chāndogya Upaniṣad says that growing life *(jīva)* is present in all parts of a mighty tree, for

> if someone should strike at the root it would bleed but still live: if someone should strike at the middle, it would bleed but still live. If someone should strike at the top, it would bleed but still live.[117]

In the tree-medicine tradition, Surapāla says that "a seed is the cause of...perpetuating the continuity of (the) plant kingdom...(and that the) inherent nature of a seed is to pierce upwards and sprout." Moreover, all "kinds of seeds treated well...become excellent. Trees that grow from them (are) rich in excellent sprouts (and) very soon bear abundant flowers and fruits."[118] Life is known, likewise, when it is on the wane and, as Parāśara notes,

> Just as an injury to the heart of an animal causes its eventual death, similarly when the root of a plant is damaged the plant dies and its trunks, branches, leaves, flowers dry up eventually.[119]

And the Jain Ācārāṅga Sūtra observes that just as

> ...the nature of this (i.e. men) is to be born and to grow old, so is the nature of that (i.e. plants) to be born and to grow old; as this has reason, so that has reason; as this falls sick when cut, so that falls sick when cut; as this needs food, so that needs food; as this will decay, so that will decay; as this is not eternal, so that is not eternal...as this is changing, so that is changing.[120]

In the Uttarādhyayana, in a lecture called "The Leaf of the Tree," philosophers observe that just as "the fallow leaf of the tree falls to the ground, when its days are gone, even so the life of men (will come to its close)."[121] And in studies on the Tattvārtha Sūtra, much discussion is given to the "growth (and) fading...of plants," for "they grow with the help of all the earth, water, etc." and the livingness that is observed in plants is found "in the very first (and the very last) instant."[122] Hemachandra observes that in "that country, when the crop has been cut on time and harvested by the farmers, it immediately grows again, like grass."[123]

Again, in the early Buddhist canon, it is clear that, given the right conditions, seeds will produce plants that will get larger, denser, and more complex, and that these plants will, in time and in regular, predictable, fashion, wither, decay, and die.[124] Large trees are especially significant for early Buddhists for these "mighty trees...(are) grown from tiny seeds (and are) of mighty bulk...(for they) overspread (other) trees...(and then) break up, break down, fall to the ground and so lie."[125] The Jātaka tales describe throughout the profuse growth of plants, abundant with flowering and fruiting, and frequently note a specific plant to be either young or old. From the Tittira-Jātaka comes the following debate among animals using the growth of a tree to establish who is the oldest:

> Said the elephant, "When I was a baby, this banyan was a mere bush, over which I used to walk; and as I stood astride of it, its top most branches used just to reach up to my belly. I've known the tree since it was a mere bush."
> (The monkey) replied, "My friends, when I was a youngling, I had only to stretch out my neck as I sat on the ground, and I could eat the topmost sprouts of this banyan. So I've known this banyan since it was very tiny."
> Then the partridge...said, "Friends, of old there was a great banyan-tree at such and such a spot; I ate its seeds, and voided them here; that was the origin of this tree. Therefore, I have knowledge of this tree from before it was born, and am older than the pair of you."[126]

Finally, the Sarabha-Miga-Jātaka describes a "miracle" performed when the Buddha gave a mango seed to his disciple Ānanda and said,

> "Ānanda, give the gardener this *stone* to plant here on the spot; this shall be the knot-mango tree." The Elder did so. The gardener dug a hole in the earth, and planted it. On the instant the stone burst, roots sprouted forth, up sprang a red shoot tall as a plough-pole; even as the crowd stared it grew into a mango tree of a hundred cubits, with a trunk fifty cubits and branches of fifty cubits in height; at the same time flowers bloomed, fruit ripened; the tree stood filling the sky, covered with bees, laden with golden fruit; when the wind blew on it, sweet fruits fell.[127]

Touch: Plants Respond to Hot and Cold

Indian traditions also observe that plants need temperatures that are moderately *hot* and moderately *cold* in order for their growth cycles to function properly. In Parāśara, moderate heat is beneficial for it "is necessary for the total thermal and colouring phenomena involved in the process of sprouting of a seed and thereafter for the growth of the plant."[128] Excessive heat, however, is not beneficial, for in the cremation hymn, Ṛg Veda 10.16, after the ritual fire has burned out, Agni is asked to "quench and revive the very one you have burnt up. Let...(the) plants grow in this place."[129] Again, the Bṛhat Saṁhitā records that one of the kinds of harm that can come to plants is for them to wither from excess heat or to burn up from contact with fire.[130] And it quotes other texts attesting to the plant diseases that can be caused by excessively cold and hot weather, as well as the special watering schedules that have to be followed for plants to do well in the hot summer and cold winter.[131] Surapāla observes that some plants grow well out of ground that has been scorched hot by fire, but that newly planted young trees are to be kept away from excessive heat – in fact, he observes, many trees can be "afflicted by excessive heat" or by fire and lightning and, as a result, suffer from "drying up, yellowness of leaves, and much paleness of their sprouts."[132] To treat a tree that has been burnt by fire or lightning, Surapāla recommends scrapping away the burnt material and irrigating it with special fluid mixtures, smearings with special pastes, and fumigation with animal parts.[133] Extreme cold is noxious for plants as well, and Vidyāpati is aware of what happens to plants under harsh winter conditions when he says that the "new leaves (are) bitten by frost."[134]

Trees and groups of plants, moreover, can create an environment of cool beneath the heat of the sun, and the Hitopadeśa "mentions that the trees provide shade and fruits even to those who have come to fell them."[135] In Śakuntalā, "a tree endures burning heat to give shade from the summer sun,"[136] and in Hemachandra a couple rests "again and again under the thick shade of the trees, taking pleasure in the touch of the cool leaves of the banana trees."[137] The Uttarādhyayana speaks lovingly of the sacred Manorama tree "full of leaves, flowers, and fruits, which sheds a cool shadow,"[138] while Campantar speaks of the "cool wooded marshes"[139] and Aiyūr Muṭavaṉ of "the cool dense shade of a flowering grove of the black *punnai.*"[140] Early Buddhist renunciants are encouraged not to go out in the especially cold or hot seasons for fear of injuring vulnerable one-facultied beings, i.e., plants.[141] And the Pali canon goes on to note that being subject to growth for plants means, first, that they prosper and flourish in response to the warmth and heat of the sun and, second, that they wither and die in response to the cold of winter.[142]

Plants are also known to develop an "internal heat" when they grow and the Mahābhārata says, "the fire that occurs in all embodied creatures" is constituted, among other things, of "internal heat and that other heat which digest the food that is taken" in. While beneficial in moderation, however, internal temperatures can be harmful in the extreme, as seen in the Mahābhārata that says that trees "have heat within them in consequence of which leaf, bark, fruit, and flower, are seen to droop."[143]

Touch: Plants Respond to Light and Dark

That plants are sensitive to the cyclical movement of the day's progress throughout periods of *light* and *dark* is readily observable for, ordinarily, trees need the light and warmth of the sun to grow properly. The tree-medicine text of Surapāla, for example, observes that trees can be destroyed if kept constantly in a shady spot without experiencing the warmth of the sun.[144] Other kinds of observations, however, focus on plant responses to night-time light, for the "*oṣadhis* or medicinal plants respond to the light of the moon."[145] In the Atharva Veda, for example, a healing herb that is used against leprosy is called "night-born;"[146] in Śakuntalā, the "moon...makes lotuses open, the sun's light awakens lilies,"[147] and in Miḷaipperuṅ Kantaṉ "the *mullai* begins to bloom in the dusk."[148]

Touch: Plants Respond to Wet and Dry

Indian traditions describe plants as flourishing when the air and soil around them is *moist* and *wet,* and as not flourishing when the air and soil around them is *desiccated* and *dry.* The Taittirīya Saṁhitā, for example, notes that the ritual strew on which the gods are invited to sit during the new- and full-moon sacrifices are "made to grow by the rains;" that the "water divine" that comes down "to avert diseases for men" creates wet space and "from their place...arise plants with fair leaves;" and that "where there are waters, there plants take root."[149] In the Śatapatha Brāhmaṇa, the winnowing basket is addressed with "'Rain-grown art thou!' For rain-grown it is indeed, whether it be made of reeds or of cane or of rushes, since it is the rain that makes these grow." Again, the ritual strew *(barhis)* is called autumn "inasmuch as these plants which shrink during the summer and winter grow by the rains, and in autumn lie spread open after the fashion of barhis." Moreover, the "swell of the waters is the plants, for wherever the waters keep swelling, there plants grow," and the Agnicayana continues to be enlivened by mantras like "Make the waters swell! Quicken the plants!..Draw thou the rain from the sky!" which is followed by a ritual sprinkling of water.[150]

In the Mahābhārata, trees "drink water by their roots," for "as one can suck up water through a bent lotus-stalk, trees also, with the aid of wind, drink through their roots...and fire and water (then) cause the water that has been sucked up to be digested. According...to the quantity of the water taken up, the tree advances in growth and becomes turgid."[151] Again, the Hindu Vṛkṣāyurveda is careful to point out that

> organic life originate(s)...when water (is) transformed into a jelly like substance...it was eventually formed (into) a dense organic mass...Then by a regulated process, it attained the nature of a germ cell....(and) went through metabolic changes induced by contact with water and by heat released from the soil...The seed when moistened swells and becomes soft, leading to the initiation of the root.[152]

The centrality of water in Vṛkṣāyurveda texts appears in observations that, while some plants do well in especially dry regions and some in especially wet regions,[153] most do best in moderate climates. Moreover, several texts give detailed schedules of watering both for newly planted grasses, shrubs, and trees as well as for those plants who have been in the ground for some time[154] and, with these schedules in mind, Surapāla cautions against underwatering and overwatering (or water-logging) plants.[155] The Arthaśāstra recommends the soaking of some seeds in water before planting, and the Viṣṇudharmottara Purāṇa encourages checking on the purity of the water used for plants as well as the deep depths to which wells should be dug before setting up a garden.[156] Irrigation techniques are known from a fairly early time, and the Agni Purāṇa describes the digging of water channels into gardens and of reservoirs that are to be used for storing garden waters.[157] Plants must always be placed in regions that have water sources close-by, and a mantra spoken during the transplanting of a tree makes this issue clear: "O tree, I shall transfer thee from this place to a better place and shall provide thee watering so that thou shall obtain satisfaction."[158]

The importance of water to plants is clear in Hindu devotional poetry as well. Vidyāpati says of a woman that her "flowing tears made (such) pools at her feet...(that the) lotus that grew on the land now floats on water."[159] Basavaṇṇa notes that "the root is the mouth of the tree: pour water there at the bottom and, look, it sprouts green at the top,"[160] and Appar describes Śiva as blazing up in many places of human experience "as the places where life stirs, as grain, as the earth in which it grows, as the water that gives it life."[161] Orēruṛavaṉār describes land that is "all wet and ready for seed," Varumulaiyāritti notes that when rainstorms pour down on distant lands they become green, and Okkūr Mācātti says that rains bring a "new leaf upon the fields," the shooting up of grass spears, and the budding of the jasmine creeper.[162] Moreover, Kōvatattaṉ describes the gullibility of the "fat *koṉrai* trees" who mistake untimely rains by putting "out their long arrangements of flowers on the twigs as if for a proper monsoon," and Kōkkuḷamuṟṟaṉ notes that the rain flowers of "the sponge gourd...grow...lush with leaves among the tall wet grasses on our farm."[163]

These observations are found among Jains and Buddhists as well. The Ācārāṅga Sūtra notes that plants need food and water[164] and a story, attributed to Mahāvīra by the Bhagavatī Sūtra about his Ājīvika rival, Gosāla, focuses on the tremendous reinvorating powers of water on plants. According to the story, the two religious come upon a sesamum plant and Gosāla asks Mahāvīra what will happen to the plant in the future. Mahāvīra replies that it will continue to grow, flower, and fruit. Gosāla, displeased and determined to show Mahāvīra a liar, pulls the sesamum plant up by the roots. At this point, "a shower of rain fell, the plant took root again...the flowers ripened and seven sesamum pods were produced in one cluster, just as Mahāvīra had prophesied." A return trip to the spot confirms that the plant has indeed been "reanimated by the shower and...(is) once more living."[165] Finally, Hemacandra observes that in "that country, the earth is everywhere fertile, since the clouds produce rain in the proper season," that "the water scoops showering water onto the sugar cane groves, like a new kind of rain cloud," and that by "the rim of the well grew a fig-tree; one of its long roots hung down into the middle of the (water in the) well."[166]

Passages in the Pali canon frequently note that plants respond vigorously to contact with water and poorly to its absence.[167] In the Majjhima Nikāya, for example, some monks tell Gotama, "there may be faltering and vicisitudes for young seeds if they do not get water" and, in the Saṁyutta Nikāya, the Buddha says: "Just as...a dark blue lotus or a white lotus, born in the water, come to full growth in the water, rises to the surface and stands unspotted by the water,"[168] so the Tathāgatha comes and goes through the world unspotted. Again, fertile seeds can come to growth only when "there is both soil and water," and "seeds come to growth, increase, abundance...(only) if the sky rains down steadily."[169] The Jātakas describe healthy plants that are pulled from the mud as dripping with water, and characters make observations like this: "This grass...can only have grown up here thanks to the presence of water underneath."[170] A funny story appears at least twice about a gardener who leaves the watering of the plants in the hands of a group of monkeys. The king of the monkeys doesn't want to waste water and decides that the monkeys should give water only according to the size of the roots. Thus, he instructs his cohorts, "as you water, first pull each young tree up and look at the size of its roots. Then give plenty of water to those whose roots strike deep, but only a little to those with tiny roots." This becomes, as we might imagine, the story of "the ape that killed the garden trees."[171] In the Mahāyāna tradition, texts like "The Parable of the Medicinal Herbs" in the Saddharmapuṇḍarīka use the watering of plants as an allegory for the teaching of Buddhist doctrine.

The rain falls everywhere,
coming down on all four sides.
Its flow and saturation are measureless,
reaching to every area of the earth,
to the ravines and valleys of the mountains and streams,
to the remote and secluded places where grow
plants, bushes, medicinal herbs,
trees large and small,
a hundred grains, rice seedlings,
sugar cane, grape vines.
The rain moistens them all,
none fails to receive its full share.
The parched ground is everywhere watered,
herbs and trees alike grow lush.
What falls from the cloud
is water of a single flavor,
but the plants and trees, thickets and groves,
each accept the moisture that is appropriate to its portion.
All the various trees,
whether superior, middling or inferior,
take what is fitting for large or small
and each is enabled to sprout and grow.
Root, stem, limb, leaf,
the glow and hue of flower and fruit –
one rain extends to them
and all are able to become fresh and glossy,
the moistening they receive is one,
but each grows and flourishes in its own way.[172]

Touch: Plants Respond to Heavy and Light

That plants "feel" the qualities of *heavy* and *light* is evident throughout the traditions, for when trees are weighed down by their fruit their branches bend close to the ground, and when their fruit is picked or dropped, that is, when there is a lightening of weight on the branch, the branches rise up again. Surapāla observes that the pomegranate tree "becomes bent under the weight of very large fruits containing seeds rich in sweet and abundant juice" as does the Nāriṇgaka tree when proper care brings fruit whose weight bends the branches down.[173] In the Rāmāyaṇa for example, as Rāma and his party begin their search for Sītā, they pass through many forests:

> There stand beautifully many a tree lowered down with the burden of fruits, containing towering branches, dense as a collection of clouds or a mountain. Ascending those trees and lowering them, Lakshmana shall offer thee, fruits like unto ambrosia.[174]

In Śakuntalā, Kālidāsa "observes that trees laden with fruits bend down, indicating that good men should be humble even when they are prosperous,"[175] and again

> Boughs bend, heavy with ripened fruit,
> clouds descend with fresh rain,
> noble men are gracious with wealth –
> that is the nature of bountiful things.[176]

Ālaṅṭi Vaṅkaṉār watches "the mangoes as they fall, ripe from the trees on the edge of the field,"[177] Campantar knows of a "great hill where the leafy bamboo, bent and let go by the elephant, springs back with such force as to pierce the dark clouds,"[178] and Kollaṉ Aṛici sees near him "the tender branches of the flower-clustered tree...let fall their blue-sapphire flowers."[179] The Jain elder Hemacandra calls on us to "look at these citron trees stooping down with the burden of their fruit" and to see a man, as a prostitute does, who "has come here because he is oppressed by the burden of his vows, as the trunk of a plantain tree is by its fruit."[180] The Amba-Jātaka tells the story of a sage who has a charm by which he strikes a mango tree with water and leaves immediately sprout forth, flowers bloom and fall, and "mango fruits swell out." In one moment, however, the mangoes "are ripe, they are sweet and luscious, they grow like fruit divine, (and) they drop from the tree"[181] with a "thud." Other Jātakas describe trees laden with fruit bending over under their weight and, with reverence, note that "this is the tree whose branch you see droop, bend, but never break."[182] Moreover, tall trees become sorrowful when they see children, and bow "down their branches to their hands" so that the young might pick their fill.[183]

Touch: Plants Exhibit Behavior of Extension

Plants also show *extension* when they grow, as in RV 10.97.12 where plants "creep limb by limb, joint by joint."[184] In AV 5.5.3, the poet addresses a creeper by saying "Tree after tree thou climbest, like a lustful girl,"[185] and in AV 8.7.4 the poet calls healing plants "the spreading, the bushy...the extending herbs...(with) spreading branches."[186] The Śatapatha Brāhmaṇa observes that the ritual *barhis* is spread in a certain way because the ritualist knows how the roots will extend into the earth: "He spreads it (the *barhis)* with the roots below (the tops); for it is with their roots below that those plants are firmly established in this earth: for this reason he spreads it with the roots below."[187] The Mahābhārata says that a "creeper winds round a tree and goes about all its sides,"[188] and in Parāśara, when "a seed comes in contact with the soil, it softens and swells. Next it manifests itself by striking a root into the soil. Thus it completes the sprouting process...Once the sprouting takes place, the seedling draws its nourishment."[189] In Jayadeva's Gītagovinda, "cactus spikes pierce the sky,"[190] and Appar describes a place "where the arecca tree with broad fronds grows tall" and where "cool fragrant honey flow(s) out of blossoming flowers."[191]

The Ācārāṅga Sūtra observes that when monks and nuns see a big tree in they park, they are likely to notice that these "trees are noble, high and round, big; they have many branches, extended branches, they are very magnificent."[192] They will also notice the extension displayed by "a creeper encircl(ing) a tree growing in the forest."[193] Moreover, Hemacandra observes that when a farmer diligently sows grain seeds at the right time of the year, shoots of grain will spring up in the field, looking "like masses of thick hair tied in braids."[194]

In the Pali canon, it is often observed that plants grow by stretching out their trunks, branches, and roots, and are thus responsive to spans of earth, water, and air.[195] In fact, as they exhibit behavior of extension, plants move out into a world where they encounter smoothness and roughness, openness and blockage, and flatness and undulation. The Aṅguttara Nikāya describes what happens when seeds and roots come in contact with such conditions as they are unfavorable to growth: in "the field that is undulating, rocky and pebbly, saltish, without depth of tilth...seed sown in a field so conditioned is not very fruitful."[196] The Dadhi-Vāhana-Jātaka shows what happens when the conditions are favorable:

> (The farmer) planted limbs and creepers about the choice mango tree. By and by the limbs sprouted up. Above and below, root with root, and branch with branch, these were entangled with the mango tree...Round about the trunk entwining, branch with branch, and root with root, see the bitter creeper climbing.[197]

Extension, then, brings another kind of touch experience for plants in that, as roots shoot through the ground, they encounter coarse and smooth textures of soil and must move around stones in their path while, in extending out in the air, branches encounter objects like other trees and cliff sides, and must respond accordingly.

Touch: Plants Respond to Forces of Motion

Plants are also affected by forces of *motion,* such as the agitation of wind, rain, and human handling. Under such forces, trunks and branches bend and shake, and leaves are torn loose from their holds – and, in turn, these motions influence patterns of growth and adaptation. In the Ṛg Veda, the Maruts or storm gods bring such terrifying winds that forests bend down to get out of their way, and their driving wind spreads fire through the forests causing their hair to be sheared off the earth.[198] In the Atharva Veda, witchcraft is thought to crush down its victim, like wind racing through trees:

> As the wind breaks with force the trees, the forest-trees, so do thou break my rivals...
> As both wind and fire devour the trees, the forest-trees, so do thou devour my rivals...
> As, destroyed by the wind, the trees lie prostrate, so do thou destroy, prostrate my rivals...[199]

Again, Surapāla observes that by "the velocity of gale (the trees) are broken, or uprooted or are bent down," and that such broken trees can be restored to health by adding fertile soil and watering quickly with diluted buffalo milk.[200]

In the Mahābhārata, "a fierce gale shakes a tree"[201] and through the "sound of wind and fire and thunder...(a tree's) fruits and flowers drop down."[202] In Bilhaṇa's Caurapañcāśikā, a beloved is described as "wanton like a creeper shaken by the wind"[203] and Jayadeva's description of nature's springtime effulgence is one of plant motion:

> Tender buds bloom into laughter as creatures abandon modesty....
> Budding mango trees tremble from the embrace of rising vines....
> Wind perfumes the forests with fine pollen
> Shaken loose from newly blossomed jasmine
> As it blows Love's cactus-fragrant breath
> To torture every heart it touches here.[204]

This motion can be seen in the work of Perumpatumaṉār where "in these places the winds beat upon the *vākai* trees and make the white seedpods rattle like drums for acrobats dancing on the tight-ropes," of Uruttiraṉ where "the bandit...climbs high places on the look-out for passers-by" and in so doing the fruits "of the *ukāy* tree...are shaken down,"[205] and of Campantar where the "darkness..(is) banished by sparks rising from bamboos brushing against each other." Moreover, Campantar says, there is a place "where coconuts full of sweet water knock down clusters of *kamuku* fruit, which crush to pulp ripe plantains fallen in the paddyfields."[206] Such effects of wind, rain, and human handling on plants are also observed in Jain texts – "as the trees do not leave their place (though shaken by storms)."[207] Hemacandra reports that the parents of a young man desiring to become a monk tell him not to do it "without reason (for he will) become a wind uprooting the tendrils of our hopes," and that Cāṇakya wants to uproot the king Nanda and his forces "like a hurricane uprooting a tree."[208] The Jātakas often note the way that a strong wind will blow trees over to touch the ground and, in doing so, will break off branches:[209]

> Like sāl-trees prostrate in a storm, their branches broken, roots uptorn...
> There shrubs, and creeper, horsear, sāl and many another tree
> Sway in the wind like drunken men for anyone to see.[210]

And in Aśvaghoṣa's Buddhacarita, the "rose apple tree...had beautiful waving leaves on all sides...(and the) golden plantain trees...(had) waving leaves."[211] Like Campantar above, the author of the Sakuṇa-Jātaka notes the sparks that can go forth from two boughs rubbing up against each other in a gusty wind: "If these two boughs go on grinding against one another like this, they will produce fire,"[212] and such sparks will certainly set the whole tree aflame, causing suffering for the people below.

In these ways, Indian authors record their observations about various aspects of plant behavior: among them, that plants grow, that they respond to hot and cold temperatures, that they respond to the presence and absence of light, that they respond to the presence and absence of water, that they respond to the weight of heavy things and their absence, that they extend their roots and branches into soil, air, and along hard and soft surfaces, and that they respond to forces of motion. Thus, we see examples of *tropism* (turning toward the light, growing away from gravity, extending tendrils along surfaces, bending down under the weight of fruit, and bending down before the wind, for example) and of *nastic movements* (responding to hot and cold, and to wet and dry, for example). Again, we see the recognition of size, shape, and texture of objects, as well as movement in space, as plants extend themselves through soil, air, and water, over and around rocks and up or down embankments – as well as their responsiveness to the presence and absence of natural and human compulsions. Using traditional Indian categories, moreover, plant behaviors are keenly observed to fall within the boundaries of the sense of touch: hot/cold, rough/smooth, heavy/light, motion/stability, and hunger/thirst. One category often given for touch but, here, left unexamined is that of pleasure/pain, and this discussion will be taken up in a following section.

3.4 Touch as the Foundational Sense

The *saṁsāra* possibilities for sentient beings endowed with touch, like plants, include more than just the kinds of sensations that touch can bring to their experience. These possibilities can also include those unique characteristics of touch that *distinguish* it from the other four sense faculties. The two most important things that distinguish touch – that it is present at the beginning and ending of a life, and that it is the foundation of the other four senses – show why it is not a coincidence that beings identified as having *only one sense faculty* are also those very same beings who are said to have only *touch.*[213]

Touch, first, is identified as the only sense faculty that survives the scattering of faculties at death to then reappear at the beginning of the process of rebirth. In support of this is the rather fixed way in which some lists of sense faculties are given. In the Upaniṣads, touch is either the *first* in the list[214] or the *last* in the list,[215] and in Jain texts[216] and in the Pali canon it is normally the *last* in the list. This suggests that touch is observed to be either the first of the sense faculties to be expressed in the newborn and/or the last faculty observed to be present at death, that is, that sense-faculty associated with the beginning and ending of lives, and also with the connections made between lives. The birth connection is suggested in the Tattvārtha Sūtra when it notes that "the first one is the sense of touch...(and) the word 'one' means the 'first one' in the order." Thus, when this text asks the question of how the sense of touch originates, the answer is given that the "manifestation of the first sense of touch...(is) due to many concurrent karmic causes,"[217] karmic causes being those that converge at the very first moment in the womb.

The death connection, that is, that touch appears as the last functioning sense of the dying, is described in the Ācārāṅga Sūtra:

> For when with the deterioration of the perceptions of the ear, eye, organs of smelling, tasting, (and) touching, a man becomes aware of the decline of life, they (the failing perceptions) after a time produce dotage.[218]

The Caraka Saṁhitā concurs when it notes that if a person, when dying, perceives the touch sensations of such things as hot/cold, coarse/smooth and/or soft/hard, then that person is about to die. Likewise, someone who is attending a dying person can best determine "the remaining span of (the) life of a patient mainly by touch" and can palpate the entire body of the dying with his or her hand.

> While palpating the body he should know about the following entities such as – loss of pulsation in body parts having constant pulsation, presence of coldness in those which are always hot. Similarly hardness of the soft ones, coarseness of the smooth ones, absence of the existent ones, looseness, dislocation or falling down of the joints, loss of flesh and blood, hardness, excessive perspiration, or stiffness....[219]

This suggests either that touch is both the most under-developed and the most fully-developed of the faculties, *or* that it is the most fundamental to the whole process of sense perception and therefore the one most present when others have yet to appear or when others have already disappeared. In this way, it would be the sole sense-faculty remaining unbroken in the cycle of *saṁsāra*. Such is suggested in the Kathāvatthu, where the continuity of touch, "alone among the sense-organs," is thought to be unbroken from one birth to the other, while the "remaining four organs (eye and ear mechanism, smell and taste mechanism)," having scattered, "take seventy-seven days to come to birth."[220]

Second, touch may be the base sense serving as the foundation for the other four. In some Buddhist texts, the five sense faculties are thought to be mutually exclusive.[221] In the Nikāyas, for example, the sense faculties are portrayed as distinct in range and "pasture" from one another and, generally, as not reacting to the range and "pasture" of one another. That is, each sense does only what it does and does not cross over into the function of another.[222] In other settings, like the Hindu philosophical system of Nyāya-Vaiśeṣika, however, each of the five elements (air, ether, fire, water, and earth) is said to have touch as a foundational component,[223] and the Caraka Saṁhitā notes that, of all the senses, "the tactile sense alone pervades all the sense organs."[224] For the Jain Tattvārtha Sūtra, the simpler bodies – the earth-bodies, water-bodies, fire-bodies, air-bodies, and plant bodies – have only one sense, that of touch, and this "sense senses all the functions (of other senses) in them." As Akalaṅka's commentary on Tattvārtha Sūtra 5.23 notes, the

> Property of touch has been mentioned first because it is most predominantly experienced in objects. All objects have predominant touch. It is manifested first among all contactile sense organs. Moreover, this property is also comprehended by all worldly living beings.[225]

In the Jain list of ten vitalities, the first four of which are attributed to plants, the very first one given is the sense organ of touch.[226] Again in lists such as those mentioned above, the "sense of touch has been placed first...as it is pervasive of the whole body of the individual," and, not only that, "it is found in all the worldly beings. Hence, it is pervasive in all the living beings."[227] The rationale for this in Jain philosophy has to do with the size of the sense organ:

> The description of the size of the sense organ with respect to the approximate number of space points contained in them is a good visual observation — (i) the eye has the least size...(ii) the ear has larger than eye size...(iii) the nose has somewhat larger than the eye size...(iv) the tongue is larger in size than nose...and (v) the skin has the largest or infinite times the size of the other senses.[228]

Hence, touch is the most pervasive sense because of the size of its agentive medium – the skin is infinitely larger than the size of any of the other sense organs.

This view is the most prominent in Buddhism as well, for touch is said to be the one sense faculty that pervades all others. As the sense that underlies all others, the only sense organ at base, then, is that of the skin. Turning first to the doctrine of the *khandhas* or aggregates of the 'self,' Aloysius Pieris describes the first aggregate, that of form *(nāmarūpa),* as that aggregate which identifies experience as originating in the body as sense organ. Here he notes that

> *kāya* may also refer to the whole 'body' of psycho-physical factors generally known as the Five Aggregates...In other words, the *kāya* which is the locus of *citta* may not denote merely the fifth *khandha* as it often does, but the whole pentad of aggregates, including the *citta.*[229]

Again, as Herbert Guenther comments:

> If it were not for the fact that we are tactilely programmed, we would not only not feel anything, we would also not be able to set up a subjective relationship with the outside world and explore not only the near-infinite spectrum of flavors the external world holds for us, but also the immense wealth of our inner world.[230]

The Dīgha Nikāya points out what is clearly known from another doctrine where touch plays a role, the *paṭiccasamuppāda,* by saying that the process of touch is the paradigm for all sensory input: for there can be sensation *(vedanā,* item seven) only when there is contact *(phassa,* item six), and there can be contact only when there are the sense-faculties *(saḷāyatana,* item five), the one corresponding to 'contact' *phassa* being 'touch' *kāya.*[231] Again, using the language of the *paṭiccasamuppāda* to look at the process of touch, *phassa* or contact "is generalized to include all *receptive* experience, sensory as well as ideational, and to represent the essential antecedent and condition of all feeling (or sensation)," that is, *vedanā.*[232] So, while touch – *phusati,* s/he touches; *phoṭṭhabba,* the tangible – is "specialized to express the activity of one of the senses,"[233] the same stem is used to describe *all contact* between sense organs and objects and, thus, all reception of data contributing to the perception of the 'self.'

Moreover, according to the Visuddhimagga, touch or "body [sensitivity] is to be found everywhere, like a liquid that soaks a layer of cotton."[234] Here touch *(kāya)* "is diffused over the whole bodily form just as oil pervades an entire cotton rag" or, alternately as above, bodily sensitivity is to be found everywhere like a liquid thoroughly soaking through a piece of cloth.[235] Says C. A. F. Rhys Davids of touch as discussed in the Dhammasaṅgiṇi: "...the Buddhists regarded Touch as giving us knowledge of things 'without' in a more fundamental way than the other senses could."[236] She quotes the proverb, "Seeing is believing, but Touch is the real thing," and says of the Dhammasaṅgiṇi:

> It likens the four senses, excluding touch, to the striking of the four balls of cotton-wool on anvils by other lumps of cotton. But in touch, as it were, a hammer smites through the wool getting at the bare anvil.[237]

It appears, then, that while the sense faculties operate distinctly one from the other, i.e, are functionally mutually exclusive, they are at the same time connected one to the other by a foundation in the faculty of touch.

3.5 Plants and the Implications of Having Touch

One conclusion from this, then, is that if plants are in fact endowed with touch (that is, if they are only, or at least, *ekindrīya*, of one-sense faculty), and if touch or contact is the foundation of all reception of sense data, then plant experience must be seen as belonging to the Buddhist scheme of the *paṭiccasamuppāda* and plants must be subject, as are all participants in this process of moral dependent origination, to ignorance, desire, and attachment. By implication from this scheme, and from the data offered by Hinduism and Jainism that also place plants right in the middle of the cycle of rebirth, plants might be considered to have some kind of consciousness, to experience pleasure and pain, and to participate in the process of self-cultivation – all components of the experience of *saṁsāra.*

Being Conscious

Contemporary plant physiologists are clear about whether plants have consciousness in the ordinary understanding of the term, for a final difference between plants and animals is that plants have "no nervous system."

> Animals, operating mechanically, need nerves for constant precise control of movement. This...has permitted the evolution of a brain. Plants have no need for nerves. Their behavior is largely expressed in their patterns of growth and development, processes that are controlled by biochemical and physi-

> ological integration rather than by the integration of nerves and thought.[238]

While ad hoc statements about plant consciousness appear in popular literature – e.g., "all plants are conscious beings with distinct personalities"[239] and "plants respond to our emotions and intents"[240] – the issue of whether plants, in fact, do or do not have consciousness as understood in Indian traditions is one of some discussion. Misra notes, for example,

> We consider both plants and animals as living. We call all animals conscious, but hesitate to label consciousness in plants. Life cannot be realized without consciousness. Everybody feels consciousness in plants, but hesitates to admit so because physical manifestations of consciousness, through movement of organs and production of sound in animals have no parallel in plants. But all do agree that plants possess sensitivity.[241]

This issue – of plants having or not having consciousness – receives support on both sides in early Indian texts, and the debate centers on three terms: *manas, citta,* and *saṁjñā.*

(1) ***Manas***. The first term *manas,* mind, can sometimes be used as a criterion by which to divide the broad range of living beings into the thinking and the non-thinking. As one of the terms used in traditional Jainism, for example, the capacity for actualized *manas* is not found in such beings as plants, for non-human sentient beings, including touch-only sentient beings, do not have the active power of thought. The text of Tattvārtha Sūtra 2.11 states that "worldly souls *(saṁsāriṇas)* fall into two groups, souls that possess a mind and souls that do not *(samanaska-amanaska)*.[242] Accordingly, this divides beings with one through four senses, and some with five senses (e.g., those who are *amanaska)*, from those remaining beings with five senses (e.g., those who are *samanaska)*. Thus, those who are *amanaska* – *saṁsāra* beings of one to four senses and some of five senses – have "no mental activities" or "functional consciousness," and "are postulated to be non-mind-

possessing because they do not possess activities characteristic of mind."[243]

The larger teaching explains that all souls have the psychic mind *(bhāva-manas)*, but only some have, as well, the physical mind *(dravya-manas)*. While the physical mind is the actual brain itself, and is created by the psychic mind, the psychic mind is the "capacity and activity of the brain...(that is the living being's) *potential for thought.*" And while the physical mind is "the result of actively arising karma," being made up of material particles and having size and location, the psychic mind is associated with the partial elimination and suppression of both the mind-covering and the energy-obstructing *karma* and, therefore, says Tatia, it "finds expression as consciousness, awareness, sensation, attention and so on."[244] Further clarifying the Jain position, then, plants as one of "the one-sensed beings have only dormant mental functionings," for the senses may perform their functions, but the beings "have no capacity to think."[245] According to Sukhlalji's commentary on this issue plants, though "declared to be devoid of *manas,*" are really devoid only of physical mind, possessing "*manas*...of the *bhāva* type." And being without physical mind is just like being

> an extremely old man, even if possessed of legs and of the capacity to move about, (who) cannot move about without the assistance of a stick, similarly *bhāva-manas* cannot undertake clear reflection without the assistance of *dravya-manas.*[246]

The presence of the psychic mind *(bhāva-manas)* in one- to four-sensed and some five-sensed beings is significant for plants for Jaini notes that "Jainas believe that in every...state, no matter how low or simple, there will always be some residue of qualities that define the soul: perception, knowledge, energy, bliss, and so on."[247] Of the Jain position on plant consciousness, Paul Dundas says the following:

> Of all the lowest categories of life, it is plants alone which are deemed to share certain characteristics with human beings. It is obvious that plants develop and decay like all higher forms of life but, more specifically, they are also regarded by Jainism

> as *possessing a form of consciousness and awareness of their surroundings* in common with those of animals and humans.

Jains believe this to be true, he continues, because plants can be seen to germinate at regular times of the year.[248] Such an interpretation, in fact, is supported by a passage from the Ācārāṅga Sūtra, about which Jacobi says:

> The plants know the seasons, for they sprout at the proper time, the Aśoka buds and blooms when touched by the foot of a well-attired girl, and the Vakula when watered with wine; the seed grows always upwards: all this would not happen if the plants had no knowledge of the circumstances about them. Such is the reasoning of the commentators.[249]

The term *manas,* however, can be associated with plants in an indirect way – through the sense-faculty of touch. In the Hindu Caraka Saṁhitā, we have verses that say: "the location of sensations *(vedanā)* is mind *(manas)* (and) the body equipped with sense organs *(indriyaḥ),*" and "contact with the tactile sense organ *(sparśanendriyasaṁsparśa)* and that with the mind *(sparśomānasa)* – this twofold contact gives rise to pleasant and painful sensations *(sukhaduḥkha vedanā).*"[250] If plants are thought to have the single sense-faculty of touch and if, as we will see, they are thought to experience pleasure and pain (through that sense-faculty of touch), then it may be possible to argue that plants also have to have a *manas,* to act, as Pieris argues, as their "noetic 'opening'...to the outside world."[251]

(2) ***Citta***. A second word used for the thinking process is *citta.* Under its rubric, there are several moments where texts specifically deny that plants have consciousness. The Aitareya Āraṇyaka, for example, notes that "in plants and trees *(oṣadhi-vanaspati)* only sap *(rasa)* is seen, (while) in animals *(prāṇabhṛt)*, (there is) consciousness *(citta)*" as well.[252] Moreover, the later Pali tradition in Buddhism describes plants as being *acetana* "without consciousness/intention," and Jātaka 307 quotes a verse in which a wise *(jāna)* brahman is asked why he is addressing "this unconscious, unhearing, unknowing Palāśa tree" *(acetanaṁ...assuṇantaṁ...ajānantam imaṁ palāsaṁ)*[253] – a verse quoted also in the Milindapañha.[254]

Nevertheless, the association of a *citta*-derivative, *cetas* or consciousness, with plants can be argued – once again via the sense-faculty of touch, and, once again using a passage from the Caraka Saṁhitā. For example,

> Out of all the senses the tactile sense *[sparśa]* alone pervades all the sense organs and is also associated inherently with mind *[cetas] so due to pervading of tactile sense, mind also pervades.* So the condition of all the sense organs (is) produced by the overall tactile sensation.[255]

Here the observation is made that touch *(sparśa)* pervades all the other senses, and this pervasion by touch then accounts for the pervasion of all the senses by the mind *(cetaś).*

Another supporting argument can be drawn from Buddhism for, as noted above, touch is the paradigmatic sense of reference in the doctrines both of the *khandhas,* which supports the early Buddhist view of a "person," and of the *paṭiccasamuppāda.* As Buddhaghoṣa explains the process of Buddhist psychology, "consciousness *(citta)* first comes into touch *(phassa)* with its object *(ārammaṇa)* and thereafter feeling, conception *(saññā)* and volition *(cetanā)* come in."[256] This suggests that touch leads naturally to conception and volition and, conversely, that conception and volition cannot occur without the preceding appearance of touch.

(3) ***Saṁjñā.*** The attribution of the third word *saṁjñā/saññā,* discernment or intelligence to plants is denied, according to Buddhaghoṣa, by the Ājīvikas. This group places sentient beings in various classes, the first two being of special interest here: *saññi-gabbha,* a category including sentient beings such as camels and oxen, and *asaññi-gabbha,* a category including rice, barley, and wheat.[257]

For others, however, plants are said to have a basic process of perception and response, that is, to have a *saṁjñā* that is interior. This is a hallmark of Hindu medical texts, for Ramachandra Rao notes that plants

> are described as composed of the five primary forms of matter and *possessed of internal consciousness (antaḥsaṁjñā),* as distinguished from animals which, although similarly con-

> stituted, possess consciousness both internally and externally *(bhair-antaścetanā)*.[258]

In this way, the Vṛkṣāyurveda of Parāśara uses the term *saṁjñā* for plants – "plants have *saṁjñā*," says Parāśara, for example, *vṛkṣaḥ sajño bhavedantaḥ*[259] – suggesting an ability in plants to identify and distinguish an incoming sensation and to respond to it appropriately. And Manu, in the Hindu *dharmaśāstra* tradition, notes that plants "possess internal consciousness *(antaḥsaṁjñā)*," that then accounts for their being able to experience pleasure and pain *(sukhaduḥkhasamanvita)*.[260]

Jain sources like the Tattvārtha Sūtra (2.24), however, equate *saṁjñā* with *manas* – *saṁjñinaḥ samanaskāḥ* – and thus, the "possessors of *saṁjñā* are those who are the possessors of *manas*."[261] This then leads to a breakdown of *saṁjñā* into two categories, for commentators note that being *saṁjñinaḥ* means that those with physical mind have intelligence, which gives them "the capacity to remember the past and ponder the future." They also differentiate between intelligence as "thoughtful knowledge" and intelligence as "subconsciously motivated behavior," that is, between the thoughtful evaluation and assessment of objects and situations, and the instinct for survival that concerns things such as finding food, responding to threats, and reproducing.[262] Sukhlalji's commentary on Tattvārtha 2.24 reiterates the distinction between the *dravya-manas* type (physically manifest) and the *bhāva-manas* type (internally potential) as follows – with plants belonging in the 'insect' category:

> In the case of the insects etc. too *manas* of an extremely subtle type does exist. And it is on account of it that they manage to move towards what is beneficial and to move away from what is undesirable. But this *manas* of theirs is of use for a bare maintenance of body – not for any thing else. In the present context, on the other hand, by *manas* is understood such an advanced type of it as enables one, when suitable means are available, to undertake reflection that goes beyond the question of a bare maintenance of body – that is, such as enables one even to recall one's past birth.[263]

Fully operating *saṁjñā* appears to be like fully operating *manas:*

> In the present context *saṁjñā* means not ordinary behavior but a specific type of it. This specific type of behaviour is of the form of that reflection over the merits and demerits of things which enables one to attain what is beneficial and avoid what is harmful...This form of *saṁjñā* is the function of *manas* and is such as is clearly found to be exhibited only in the case of heavenly beings, the hellish beings, the human beings born of a womb, the animals born of a womb. That is why they alone are considered to be possessed of *manas*.[264]

In crossing traditions, then, we suggest that the *bhāva* type of operation of *manas* and of *saṁjñā* (i.e., the type that is internally potential, supportive, and creative of the physically manifest *dravya* type) may have a parallel in the *antaḥsaṁjñā* that is attributed to plants in the Hindu bio-medical and *dharmaśāstra* traditions. This might mean that for these Hindu passages "plant consciousness" is an interior intelligence that pertains to a plant's ability to detect, to identify, and to respond in contexts of basic survival – e. g., food, safety, and reproduction.

The understanding of plants as having *saṁjñā* is also suggested in the early Buddhist Suttavibhaṅga. Schmithausen tells a canonical story of a time when monks chop down a tree, and the action is disapproved of by the local (lay/donor) people because it constitutes an act of injuring. This disapproval is based on the people's "regard (of) trees as living beings *(jīvasaññino... rukkhasmiṁ)*,"[265] a belief that sees trees as living beings who have perception, discernment or cognition, with cognition *(saññā)* being, for Keown, "to understand and discriminate correctly."[266] This notion fits well with the doctrine of the five *khandhas* – through which the "selfing process" takes place. Sensory data is initially received through the sense organs as *rūpa* or form, and is then processed through more complex functions: *rūpa* ("form"), *vedanā* ("sensation"), *saññā* ("perception"), *sankhārā* ("concrete mental syntheses"), and *viññāṇa* ("consciousness") – thus giving rise to the idea of "self" that is perceived and experienced as the individual. Here, one might argue, any organ (such as the skin) that receives sensory data (such as what is touchable) is necessarily connected to mental processes that begin with perception or cognition. This would be true because there are no caveats with regard to the *khandha* doctrine that all senses have to be present to ensure its viability.

As for the issue of interiority, a distinction made in the Dhammasaṅgaṇi may be helpful. It teaches that there are two kinds of states: those that are "inward" or "interior" *(ajjhatta)* and those that are "outward" or "external" *(bahiddha)*. According to this text, the *ajjhatta* or interior modes are ones "which, for this or that being, are of the self, self-referable, one's own, individual," while the *bahiddha* or exterior modes are ones "which, for this or that *other* being, for *other* individuals, are of the self, self-referable, their own, individual."[267] When applied to plants in the context of their having an interior consciousness, this passage might suggest that plants are conscious only in a self-referential way, while those with an (interior and) exterior consciousness might be conscious as well in an other-referential way, i.e., conscious that own self and other selves are all conscious self-referentially. Diane Ackerman notes, however, that of all the senses, it is touch that in fact mediates between the interior and the exterior for, of the senses, touch

> is the oldest sense, and the most urgent... In fetuses, touch is the first sense to develop, and in newborns it's automatic before the eyes open or the baby begins to make sense of the world...Among other things, touch teaches us the difference between *I* and *other,* that there can be someone outside of ourselves, (for example,) the mother.[268]

On the whole, however, the traditions examined here are inconsistent and at odds over the attribution of mental faculties to plants. While some, such as the Caraka Saṁhitā, may be more open to it than others, such as the Tattvārtha Sūtra, it is not clear that there is any clarity or uniformity in the meaning of terms used to describe the various conscious processes, much less exactly what and how plants may be dealing with sensations, should they have them, as they are incoming into the body.

Experiencing Pleasure and Pain

When raised, the question of plants having consciousness often comes up at the same time as a question of whether plants experience pleasure and pain, and some traditional materials see the experience of pleasure and pain (or the experience of suffering) as an implication of having the sense-faculty of touch. John Martin and Thomas Jessell note that somatic sensibilities "are called the *skin senses* or *body senses*" and that among these there "are four distinct somatic modalities:"

1. *Touch,* elicited by mechanical stimulation of the body surface.
2. *Proprioceptive sensations,* elicited by mechanical displacements of the muscles and joints.
3. *Pain,* elicited by noxious (tissue damaging) stimuli.
4. *Thermal sensations,* elicited by cool and warm stimuli.[269]

This layout of somatic modalities identifies touch, mechanical displacement (in plants, for example, of branches, tendrils, flowers, and fruits), and temperature sensitivity as being among the "skin senses," three "modalities" that Indian traditions, as we have seen, observe in plant behavior. It also introduces another, the responsiveness to pain, that turns out to be an additional attribute of plant sentience in Indian traditions, for that particular sensation that skin can bring to bodily experience "corresponds with...pleasure and pain."[270]

Jessell and Dennis Kelly go on to say that pain "is the *perception* of an aversive or unpleasant sensation that originates from a specific region of the body," and that it can, "like other sensations...[be] modulated by a wide range of behavioral experiences." That pain is a perception means that, like all "perceptions[, it] involves an abstraction and elaboration of sensory input"[271] – an understanding we have seen reflected before, for example, in the early Buddhist layout of the five aggregates or *khandhas,* where sensory input leads to perception, which leads to more complex mental functions.

That pain involves, first, a noxious stimulus and an aversive sensation and, second, the possibility of actual damage or harm to the body is important. In the first case, if a noxious stimulus and aversive sensation can be shown to be present in plants, it strengthens the attribution of touch to them. And, in the second case, the possibility of actual harm to the plant body supports a non-violent policy towards plants based on their capacity for suffering.[272] Schmithausen makes this connection for early Buddhism, in fact, and at the same time he suggests that there may be a gradation among sentient beings based upon the amount of suffering experienced, and perhaps a consequent complexity of demerit. "The early Buddhist concept of non-injury may admit of a gradation in terms of the intensity of suffering caused by killing or injuring different kinds of animals."[273] Does this suggest that plants are those beings who suffer least under *hiṁsā* acts (as they are already of a dark nature), and that their injuries bring the perpetrator less demerit than other objects of violent acts? So far, there is only some textual support for the last of these views.

The suggestion that plants feel pain is found as early as the Ṛg Veda. In RV 10.146.4, a hymn to the forest Araṇyānī, for example, one interpretation is that the imagined scream in the forest belongs to the tree who has just been felled:

> Here a voice calls a cow, there a man
> Felled a tree: When the evening falls,
> The dweller in the forest imagines
> Someone else's scream.[274]

Dwivedi states that during the period of the Hindu epics and Purāṇas, "trees were considered as being animate and feeling happiness and sorrow."[275] This is a view corroborated in the Mahābhārata, where "imminent grief...(is known to have) insuperable impact...upon the five senses,"[276] and the Bhṛgu passage cited above states clearly that plants are "susceptible to pleasure and pain" *(sukha-duḥkha).*[277] Another story in the Mahābhārata describes the Aśoka tree as a tree that can free people from their sorrows. A young heroine, Damayantī, for example, is grieving for her lost husband,

> ...her eyes filled with tears...Then she saw an *aśoka* tree. She approached that *aśoka*, best of trees, which stood in full

> bloom, bending under the weight of its shoots...'Ah, woe on me, here stands this beautiful tree in the deep of the forest...Rid me swiftly of my grief, beautiful *aśoka*: Have you chanced to see the king, free from sorrow and fear and torment?...Make it come about, *aśoka* tree, that I find without sorrow my hero...make it come about that I find him come to this forest! Be true to your name, *aśoka,* by dispelling my sorrow!'[278]

The Aśoka tree, whose name means "without sorrow" and "is believed to be a remover of sorrow," is one of those trees of the subcontinent who has been "treated like human beings, endowed with a soul, a heart that weeps with grief and laughs with joy." It is sacred to Hindus, particularly to devotees of Śiva and Kāmadeva, and is associated with women for, as *vṛkṣikās* or forest maidens, women are often depicted "in sculpture, standing against the trunk of a *Ashoka* tree." The Aśoka is also sacred to Jains, as Mahāvīra is said to have attained omniscience under one, and to Buddhists, as Śakyamuni is said to have been born under one.

Manu states clearly that plants can "experience pleasure and pain *(sukhaduḥkhasamanvita)*,"[279] and the Caraka Saṁhitā provides the foundation for plants experiencing pain in its general description of the experiencing process: "contact *(sparśa)* with the tactile sense organ *(saṁsparśa)* and that with mind *(manas)* – this twofold contact gives rise to pleasant and painful sensations *(sukhaduḥkhānāṁ vedanānāṁ)*."[280] More definitively, the Caraka Saṁhitā states that

> The many varieties of trees and bushes and so also the diverse kinds of grasses...these (do) have a sense of internal perception *(antaḥ saṁjñā)* and are endowed with (a feeling of) happiness and unhappiness *(sukha duḥkha samanvita)*.[281]

Gopal, in his introduction to his anthology of tree-medicine texts, notes that early Vedic texts attribute to plants the capability "to suffer pain from axes," and Surapāla, the standard Vṛkṣāyurveda author, prescribes what to do for trees who are "suffering from indigestion."[282] Later, the tree-medicine author Parāśara says that plants *(vṛkṣa)* "have consciousness *(saṁjñā)* and are capable of feeling the sense of pleasure and pain *(sukha-duḥkha-*

samanvita).[283] In fact, the treatment of plant diseases, which is a large part of the Vṛkṣāyurveda, presupposes what is posited at the beginning, first, that plants can feel noxious stimuli and have aversive sensations and, second, that plants can suffer injury and harm – thus conjoining the attribution of some kind of consciousness in plants with the ability to experience pleasure and pain. These texts argue further that disease is anything that brings sadness and grief to a being[284] such that, if disease is presumed in a being, then sadness and grief must be presumed as well. In the Purāṇas, for example, the "leaves of Tulasi are never plucked on Tuesdays and Sundays or ever boiled as that torments the soul of the plant,"[285] and Śāṅkara identifies plants as belonging to the group lowest in the cycle of *saṁsāra* and, as such, the group that is highest in "extreme misery." It is because of very bad *karma*, then, that "souls are born as plants, which endure suffering when they are harvested, cooked, and eaten."[286]

For Jains, the experience of pleasure and pain is intrinsic to the experience of the soul in its association with matter: the "production of pleasure, pain, life and death is also due to matter."[287] "Pleasure and pain," says a commentary, "are due to the internal condition of pleasure-giving and pain-giving karmas coming to fruition, and to the appropriate external objects and conditions."[288] Of plants in this regard, the early and formative Ācārāṅga Sūtra states the Jain position clearly:

> ...all beings, those with two, three, four senses, plants, those with five senses, and the rest of creation (experience) individually pleasure or displeasure, pain, great terror, and unhappiness.[289]

and the Uttarādhyayana confirms this view by recounting the story of the prince Mṛgāputra who tells his parents of his many painful rebirths: "an infinite number of times have I suffered dreadful pains of body and mind, repeatedly misery and dangers." Among these painful rebirths are as a hell-being, as an antelope, as a fish, as a bird, and as a tree, and the verse about his tree-rebirth is as follows:

> As a tree I have been felled, slit, sawn into planks,
> and stripped of the bark by carpenters with axes, hatches...
> an infinite number of times.[290]

These passages are important for several reasons. They are canonical evidence, first, that Jains believe there can be rebirth as a tree; second, that as a tree one has the ability to be self-conscious of one's own experiences and can express something about them; and third, that as a tree one has the capacity to feel the pain, through touch, associated with injury inflicted externally. Such a story is supported by the Jain doctrine that the term *jīva* refers to all living beings, including plants. Plants as *jīvas,* then, have karmic effects – the four primary ones being happiness, sorrow, fear, and anger – because, they point out, these experiences "are the resultant effects of the evergoing karmic accumulation... associated with the embodied soul."[291] These "karmas pertain...to feelings, which produce the ever-changing experiences of happiness *(sātā)* and unhappiness *(asātā)* that characterize mental life...(for the) karma theory indicates the...resultant effects of earlier earned or current feeling producing (pleasure, pain)."[292] Thus, as we shall see, this story is also important because being self-conscious of one's experience and having experiences of pain are traditionally tied to a doctrine in which feeling pain is the result of *karma.*

In Buddhism, as in Hinduism and Jainism,[293] some of the plant behaviors that indicate a sense-faculty of touch – i.e., of prospering and flourishing in response to warmth and the heat of the sun, and of withering and dying in response to the cold – suggest experiences of *pleasure* and *pain.* That is, because plants are observed to flourish, or to experience well being, in the heat and warmth and not to flourish in the cold, we may attribute pleasure with the experience of heat and warmth and pain with the experience of cold. Schmithausen surmises, in fact, that, to "be sure, existence as an animal (and perhaps even as a plant) is, even in open nature, doubtless not a paradisic one; there is stress and frustration, ghastly pain and agony."[294] We see the early Buddhist attribution of this capacity to experience pain in the important Vinaya passage1.189, where renunciants are prohibited from cutting young palmyra palms to wear as shoes because they will be harming one-facultied living beings. The specifically horrific evidence for this prohibition is that when cut, i.e., when injury is inflicted, the young palmyra palms wither up – suggesting that they are feeling pain and are expressing their painful response to the outside world.

Cultivation of the Self

While there are several scholars who deny the possibility of mental or spiritual cultivation for plants,[295] it is important to raise some of the issues that might be suggestive of just such processes. We now ask do plants have needs, desires, and longings? Do plants develop, and is such development associated with "progress" or any kind of valuation? And, finally, are plants ranked among those who are salvable, and can they take in and respond to any kind of teachings? The sources available provide only limited guidance in proposing answers.

As for *needs, desire, and longings in plants*, the Vṛkṣāyurveda tradition is clear, for example, that plants have special yearnings, and in particular "pregnancy yearnings" *(dohada).* These are found in trees, they argue, and can be responded to by gardeners with special prescriptions for promoting the growth of flowers and fruit. Thus, from the Viṣṇudharmottara:

> I speak chiefly of the pregnancy cravings *(dohada)* of the trees. The irrigating of mango (trees) is desired with cold water (washing) of fish.
> Viḍaṅga covered with rice (tandula) and the meat of fish is considered to fulfil the frequency-longings of all the trees without exception.[296]

A clue as to what "pregnancy-longings" might be comes from the Jain text by Hemacandra where women have "pregnancy-longings" that "conform to the nature of the children they are carrying" and that can be very strong and unusual, but that can ultimately be satisfied and fulfilled.[297] We might see these, then, as none other than the special cravings (usually for food) that visit pregnant women, to be found in plants as well who need appropriate or conforming nutriment to encourage the growth of the seeds they are carrying.

More broadly, the Caraka Saṁhitā suggests that the experience of sensations of pleasure and pain *(sukhaduḥkha)* give rise to allurement *(tṛṣṇā)* in the guise of desire and aversion *(icchādveṣa)*.[298] Of the Jain position on plants, Dundas notes that plants are thought to have "a desire for nourishment...and sexual reproduction and a sense of both fear and possession...They are even capable of the expression of morally negative feelings."[299] This suggests, using the Buddhist *paṭiccasamuppāda* as a model, that a sense organ naturally gives rise to contact, that contact naturally gives rise to sensation (of pleasure or pain), and that sensation naturally gives rise to response to sensation (e.g., desire or aversion). Alternately, there cannot be desire or aversion without the sensation of pleasure or pain, and there cannot be the sensation of pleasure or pain without contact, and there cannot be contact without a sense organ. Thus, if plants have a sense organ, that of touch, then there is a natural causal process that moves from that sense organ to sensation, and from that sensation to a response to that sensation. Thus, it is part of the natural causal process that having a sense organ, e.g., will give rise to desire or aversion.

In terms of early Buddhist evidence, for example, we can argue that the Pali canon's description of plants' search for water, sunlight, and space in the soil and air to grow represent expressions of needs and desires.[300] Most certainly, the canon is aware of plants having needs that, if met, will encourage their flourishing growth and prosperity. And the needs most particularly noted are that seeds need to be well cared for (e.g., not split open prior to planting), that they need to be properly planted in a fertile field, and that there needs to be good and continuous supplies of water and nourishment.[301] In these instances, it is the touch property of "extension" that perhaps best expresses a plant's behavioral adaptation to the meeting of its needs.

Having needs, desires, and longings posits a direction and goal for a living being, but it is the *capacity to develop* that will enable the living being to so direct its movement in a way that will ensure the meeting of its goal. Here, most importantly, we note previous discussions about plants and growth – Hinduism, Jainism, and Buddhism all record many observations of plants sprouting from seed, growing to maturity, and dying. The shooting up of stalks, the reaching out of branches, the unfolding and withering of leaves, the opening up of buds into flowers, and the ripening and falling of fruit are all images that fill the traditional texts, and that confirm that plants are able to change and develop in the regular span of their lives.

An important feature of the regular pattern of growth is that as a being develops, its senses develop with it. Thus, to take early Buddhism as an example, the *indriyas* are seen to play a critical role in the "becoming" process of the person. In the Pali canon, the sense faculties are acquired as a part of a group of processes involved in birth, and they change and mature as the person does, for their development is intricately involved in the ripening of a person to adulthood.[302] With age, the sense faculties decay and fade and, at death, they dissipate and scatter and[303] – with the exception only of the sense of touch – they are regrouped again during rebirth. Just as people are uniquely composed due to past *kamma,* so the sense faculties are individually expressed with each person.[304]

Just as sentient beings express needs, desires, and longings, and just as they show capacity for development, so also there are suggestions that this capacity for development can bring them to *spiritual transformation*. Manu suggests that members of the animal kingdom, including smaller and perhaps simpler forms, have the capacity to perform austerities: "Insects, snakes, moths, bees, birds and *beings bereft of motion (sthāvarāṇi bhūtāni),* reach heaven by the power of austerities *(tapas).*"[305] The inclusion of beings "bereft of motion," a usual term for plants, in this list states a *dharmaśāstra* view that, in a plant body, one can perform actions of self-cultivation leading to salvation.

That "Jainism accepted the real possibility of the spiritual perfectibility of plants," is expressed in a story about Mahāvīra who predicts that a tree and two of its branches traumatized by heat, drought, and fire will "first be reborn at a slightly more advanced level as sacred trees and subsequently progress to human birth and enlightenment."[306] In Jainism, moreover, there is some

> residue of qualities that define the soul: perception, knowledge, energy, bliss, and so on. Thus, even the huge mass of karmic matter which oppresses the very lowest being will not keep its soul at such a level forever; the potential for spiritual growth (progress to higher states) is never eliminated completely.[307]

More specifically, it is a central doctrine of Jainism, that the term *jīva* refers to all living beings and excludes "all other reals or realities," and that *karma* effects are found only among the living,[308] a category that includes plants. These *karma* effects

> are the uncommon characteristics of the living reals only...They are the intrinsic properties of the living just as the eight different parts (feet, hands, head, breast, back, and buttocks) of the body or five components (stem, branch, leaves, flower and fruits) of the trees are intrinsic parts of the corresponding entities.[309]

The fifth *karma* effect is due to "the inherent or natural transformation capacity of the living," and thus the living *jīva*

> is permanently in the midst of transformations. It has different modes – some subtle like knowledge, pleasure, pain, etc. And some visible like embodiment etc. under different conditions. All of them are intrinsic or extrinsic qualities of the living.[310]

Thus, the Jain position is that, because plants are *jīvas,* they are not only capable of experiencing (rather, obliged to experience) pleasure and pain, but also of undergoing transformation that will lead to salvation. Whether participation in the transformative process is a self-conscious process in plants, given that they fall into the non-rational and non-mind-possessing category of *jīva,* is less likely, however.

In the Gītā, the cultivation of the senses is necessary for spiritual transformation and, in particular, the withdrawal of sense organs from sense objects, such that desire and attachment to the fruit of action will abate.[311] This is also true in Buddhist practice, where sense-faculties are central to *dhamma* training. Here cultivation *(bhāvanā)* can only happen when these faculties are guarded and checked in the fostering of mindfulness. Thus, a wise renunciant has learned to control his or her sense faculties, watching carefully over them and taking caution not to be misled by them,[312] while a spiritually lazy or distracted adept lives with senses unguarded and uncontrolled.[313] Renunciants who have, thus, cultivated their sense faculties are calm, clear, serene, and tranquil.[314] Again, in Aśvaghoṣa's Buddhacarita, just as the senses urge us on to survival, so also they and their objects are "the means for the remedy of suffering," for their presence allows practitioners to meet needs in a basic way and, through cultivation, to eschew the fulfillment of desires in the extreme.

> For water is sought for suppression of thirst,
> and food to eliminate hunger; likewise
> a dress for protection against the cold, and
> a house to protect against wind, heat, water.[315]

"Cultivation" is a word we have used to describe the development of the senses in such a way that the cultivator is then able to live in the world without possessing it, to be "in" but not "of" the world. Cultivation may also be seen as a (self-conscious) process engaged in by some one to bring about his or her own wellbeing. As such, this kind of cultivation is observed among plants – as they adapt to the soil and weather conditions of new environments with the result of flourishing, or as they find ways to use the space available to them in an optimal fashion. Such plant behaviors, for example, are based on the faculty of touch – responses to hot/cold, dark/light, heavy/light, hard/soft, smooth/coarse, and applied motion – and suggest the possibilities of "directed plant conduct" engaged in by a plant to find the most beneficial living conditions for itself. A good example of this would be the behavior of "extension" noted by so many Indian observers. We might even suggest here that plant conduct is intended, has intent, or *cetanā,* and note that one of the words used by Indian medical traditions to describe the interior consciousness of plants is *antaḥ cetanā,* where *cetanā* is a common word used for "intention," the *karma*-bearing component of any thought, speech, or action.[316] The intention of such cultivation "for self-well-being," then, may be for individual and group improvement, as well as for finding a better, more compatible, way for all to fit together in an interrelated world of other beings, and here such 'intentions' are again suggested by many of the plant behaviors of touch.

Thus, we have argued that, insofar as plants are considered to be one-sense-facultied living beings, their one sense is touch. This is made evident not only by doctrinal statements to that effect, but also by the conformation of observed plant behavior to categories of touch as determined, and as demonstrated, by the various Indian traditions themselves. To be endowed with touch, then suggests that plants may reside at the beginning and/or end of the continuum of life, that the sense-faculty they possess (touch) is the foundational faculty of all the senses, and that having a sense faculty may position plants to belong in a process of spiritual transformation.

Endnotes :

1 Tuck, *Hobbes' Leviathan*, p. 13.

2 In Sāṁkhya, the senses are known as the five *buddhīndriyas*. See Larson, *Classical Sāṁkhya*, pp. 203-204; Larson and Bhattacharya, *Encyclopedia of Indian Philosophies* 4.49-73, 279 281, 295-297, etc.

3 Early Pali texts frequently mention the five or six (with the mind) *indriyas* either alone, or as the first section of longer lists. When a sixth *indriya* is named it is *manas*, mind. See, for example, Sn nos. 214, 340, 516; Vin 1.183, 294; 2.240,120; 3.156; D 2.120; 3.107, 239; M 1.9, 295, 437, 453; 2.11, 106; 3.296; S 1.26, 48, 61, 138, 203, 204; 2.2, 42, 218, 231, 271, 275; 3.2, 46, 93, 96, 153, 207, 225, 226, 235; 4.36, 40, 103, 112, 140, 168, 175, 176, 294, 365; 5.74, 204, 205, 207ff., 211, 216ff., 230, 269, 301; A 1.70, 75, 94, 113, 181, 236; 2.6, 16, 38, 39; 3.70, 99, 138, 163, 173, 199, 380, 387, 441, 449; 4.25, 166, 264; 5.134, 203, 204, 348; Therī no.196; It 23, 24; Cnid 252, 475; Mnid 14; Vbh 14, 70-73, 248, 415; Ps 1.190; Vism 350, 447; Mil 259. There is a list of twenty-two senses, for example, in which the six sense *indriyas* followed by *itthi*, femininity; *purisa*, masculinity; *jīvita*, vitality; *sukkha*, happiness; *dukkha*, sadness, suffering; *somanassa*, mental ease; *domanassa*, mental dis-ease; *upekhā*, equanimity; *saddhā*, confidence; *viriya*, energy; *sati*, mindfulness;

samādhi, concentration; *paññā*, wisdom; *anaññātaññassāmīti*, "I am knowing the unknown;" *añña*, knowing; and *aññātāvī*, one who knows completely (Vbh 122). See D 3.239; S 5.193ff., 216ff.; A 4.125ff., 203, 225; 5.56, 175; It 53; Dhs nos. 121, 528, 556, 560, 644, 661, 709-717, 736, 971-973; Ps 1.16, 21, 88, 115, 137, 180; 2.1-34, 49, 51, 84, 86, 119, 132, 143, 145, 166, 223; Nett 69; Vbh 13, 15,122-134, 341, 384, 415; Mnid 14, 45, 171, 341 ; Cnid 628; KV 589.

4 AV 19.9.5.

5 E.g., BĀU 4.3.23-31; 4.4.2; 4.5.12, 15; CU 1.2.1-6; 3.13.8; 3.14.4; 5.1.1-15; AU 1.1.4; 1.2.4; 1.3.3-10; KBU 3.6; MU 6.7; 6.10, 11; KU 1.3.15; 2.1.3; 2.3.6; PU 4.8, 9; MunU 2.1.3; SuU 9.1-5; PaiU 2.4, 6. On the development of the faculties as a system, see Reat, *Origins of Indian Psychology*, pp. 211-231.

6 Manu 12.98.

7 Sharma, *Caraka Saṁhitā* 1.7, 326, 362, 398, 457. See Krishnamurthy, *Source Book of Indian Medicine*, pp. 77, 194.

8 E.g., van Buitenan, 2-3.226, 241.

9 Gītā 15.9. For a discussion of the *indriyas* in various early Indian traditions, see Reat, *Origins of Indian Psychology*, pp. 214-231.

10 Jain, *Biology in Jaina Treatise on Reals*, pp. 106-120.

11 ŚĀ 1.8; Keith, *Śāṅkhāyana Āraṇyaka*, p. 6.

12 ŚĀ 4.1-3; 4.13; 6.20; 8.1, 5; 9.3-7; 10.1; 11.2; Keith, *Śāṅkhāyana Āraṇyaka*, pp. 21-22, 27-28, 40, 51, 5, 57, 59, 61.

13 ŚĀ 4.15; 5.4; Keith, *Śāṅkhāyana Āraṇyaka*, pp. 29, 32.

14 ŚĀ 5.5; Keith, *Śāṅkhāyana Āraṇyaka*, p. 33.

15 See RV 1.107.2; AV 19.27.1.

16 Ramachandra Rao, *Encyclopedia of Indian Medicine* 1.115.

17 Larson, *Classical Sāṁkhya*, pp. 203-205; Larson and Bhattacharya, *Encyclopedia of Indian Philosophies* 4.49.

18 Sharma, *Caraka Saṁhitā* 1.326-327.

19 See BĀU 4.5.12.

20 Again, for a full discussion of this in the Upaniṣads, see Reat, *Origins of Indian Physchology*, pp. 211-231.

21 Sharma, *Source Book of Indian Medicine*, p, 81.

22 Gītā 15.9; *śrotraṁ cakṣuḥ sparśanaṁ ca rasanaṁ ghrāṇam eva ca adhiṣṭhāya manaś c'āyaṁ viṣayān upasevate;* Zaehner, *Gītā*, pp. 365. See *Gītā* 5.8.

23 Padmal de Silva, "Buddhist Psychology," pp. 60-61.

24 See the discussion in C. A. F. Rhys Davids, *Dhamma-Saṅgaṇi*, pp. lxi, 5n.

[25] *Kāyāyatana* "sense of touch," D 3. 243, 280, 290; Dhs nos. 613-616, 653; *kāyindriya* "sense of touch," D 3.239; Dhs nos. 613-616, 971-973.

[26] D 1.245; 3.102, 226, 239, 250, 269; M 1.33; 2.42; S 4.104, 112; A 5.11; Dhs 613-616, 971-973.

[27] D 3.243; Dhs 556, 585, 651, 685, 790; Mil 59; Vbh 180.

[28] *Kāyaviññeyya*, "perceived through the sense of touch," D. 1.245; 2.281; 3.234; M 1.85; Dhs 967, 1095; Vbh 14; KV 210; Mil 270. On this, see the discussion in C. A. F. Rhys Davids, *Buddhist Psychology*, p. 68.

[29] Dhs157.

[30] TAS 2.15; 2.20; 2.21; Tatia, *Tattvārtha Sūtra: That Which Is*, pp. 43, 44.

[31] Jain, *Biology in Jaina Treatise on Reals*, p. 106. Again (p. 107): "The mind cannot be called a sense because (i) it has no definite location in the body like the other senses and (ii) it functions before the senses function."

[32] Krishnamurthy, *Source Book of Indian Medicine*, p.193.

[33] Larson, *Classical Sāṁkhya*, pp. 205-206; see also Bhishagratna, *Suśruta Saṁhitā* 2.131-136.

[34] Sharma, *Caraka Saṁhitā* 1.399.

[35] Krishnamurthy, *Source Book of Indian Medicine*, p.194.

[36] Larson and Bhattacharya, *Encyclopedia of Indian Philosophies* 4.49; Dwivedi, "Vedic Heritage for Environmental Stewardship," p. 27; Bhishagratna, *Suśruta Saṁhitā* 1.364; 2.139.

[37] Dwivedi, "Vedic Heritage for Environmental Stewardship," p. 27.

[38] Tatia, *Tattvārtha Sūtra: That Which Is*, pp. xxi-xxii.

[39] TAS 2.8 Tatia, *Tattvārtha Sūtra: That Which Is*, p. 39; see also Dixit, *Sukhlalji's Commentary on Tattvārtha Sūtra*, pp. 79-84.

[40] Jain, *Jaina Karmology*, pp. 70-72.

[41] TAS 10.5, 6: *tadanantaram ūrdhvaṁ gacchaty ā lokāntāt; pūrvaprayogād asaṅgatvād bandhacchedāt tathāgatipariṇāmāc ca tadgatiḥ;* Tatia, *Tattvārtha Sūtra: That Which Is*, p. 255.

[42] Tulsi, *Acharanga Bhasyam*, p. 477.

[43] Tulsi, *Acharanga Bhasyam*, p. 475.

[44] ĀBh 4.33; *jahā juṇṇāiṁ kaṭṭhāiṁ, havvavāho pamatthati, evaṁ attasamāhie aṇihe;* Tulsi, *Acharanga Bhasyam*, p. 265.

[45] Chapple, "Living Earth of Jainism and the New Story," p. 123.

[46] Jaini, *Jaina Path of Purification*, p. 108; Chapple, "Living Earth of Jainism and the New Story," pp. 127-130.

[47] E.g., stationary beings can become mobile, and mobile beings can become stationary, though there will never be a time when only stationary or only mobile beings will exist. ĀS 1.8.1.13; SK 2.7.11, 12, 26-35.

[48] Tatia, *Tattvārtha Sūtra: That Which Is*, p. 53.

[49] Jain, *Biology in Jaina Treatise on Reals*, pp.122-125; Tatia, *Tattvārtha Sūtra: That Which Is*, pp. 45, 46; see Potter, *Encyclopedia of Indian Philosophies* 2.214, 277-278. This order of the correspondence of senses to the beings is found in the Mahābhārata; Roy, *Mahābhārata* 9.77.

[50] B. Kumar, "*Astikāyas,*" p. 23.

[51] Tatia, *Tattvārtha Sūtra That Which Is*, p. xxix.

[52] Nahar and Ghosh, *Jainism* 1.4.

[53] Dasgupta, *History of Indian Philosophy*, p. 190.

[54] TAS 5.15, 16: *asaṅkhyeyabhāgādiṣu jīvānām (15); pradeśasaṁhāra-visargābhyāṁ (visarpābhyām) pradīpavat;* Tatia, *Tattvārtha Sūtra: That Which Is*, p. 127.

[55] Jain, *Jaina World of Non-Living*, pp. 136-143.

[56] A list of all the substances that fall under "earth lives" is found in the Uttarādhyana; there are thirty-six kinds of "rough earth" and one kind of "subtile earth" and time limits are given for various conditions of earth life. The earth-body is considered an immovable being; UD 36.70-84.

[57] Again, the Uttarādhyayana notes that there are five kinds of "gross life" for water-bodies (considered an immovable being): pure water, dew, exudations, fog, and ice, with only one kind of "subtile life;" UD 36.85-92.

[58] The Uttarādhyayana that the "gross lives" of fire-bodies (considered a movable being without an organic body) include coal, burning chaff, fire, flame, meteors, and lightning, while the "subtle life" is of one kind; UD 36.108-117.

[59] Jain, *Biology in Jaina Treatise on Reals*, p. 103. In the Jain text, the Uttarādhyayana, *saṁsāra* beings are divided into the mobile and the stationary, with the stationary beings subdivided into earth lives, water lives, and plant lives (UD 10.5-13). Much is said about the first two groups, and of plants as well for these latter are of two kinds, subtle and gross (UD 36.69-92). Under plants, the text notes that subtle plants are of one kind with no variety, but that gross, fully developed plants can be of two types: either many may have one body in common, or each may have its own body, the former category including ginger, onion, garlic and the plantain tree, with the

latter category including trees, shrubs, big plants, creepers, and grass (UD 36.93-106). Stationary beings are followed by mobile beings, a category divided into fire lives, wind lives, and lives with organic bodies. The rationale for these categories is the number of sense faculties that are operative and, while stationary beings, and beings of fire and wind bodies, are one-facultied, mobile beings with organic bodies are divided into those with two sense faculties (e.g., shells and leeches), three faculties (e.g., ants), four faculties (e.g., flies, mosquitoes, bees, moths, scorpions, crickets), and five faculties (e.g., inhabitants of hell, animals, humans, and gods) (UD 36.108 156). It is a rare thing to be born into a five-facultied body; UD 10.13-20.

60 The Uttarādhyayana notes that the "gross lives" of wind-bodies (considered a movable being without an organic body) includes squalls, whirlwinds, thick winds, high winds, and low winds, while the "subtle life" is of one kind; UD 36.118-126; Jain, *Biology in Jaina Treatise on Reals,* pp.102-103.

61 Jain, *Biology in Jaina Treatise on Reals*, pp. 103-104.

62 Jaini, *Jaina Path of Purification*, pp. 108-109.

63 UD 36.93-94.

64 UD 36.95-100; Jaini, *Jaina Path of Purification*, pp. 109-110; Jain, *Biology in Jaina Treatise on Reals*, p. 103.

65 Dasgupta, *History of Indian Philosophy*, p. 190.

66 Dasgupta, *History of Indian Philosophy*, p. 190.

67 TAS 2.11: *samanaskā-manaskāḥ;* "The worldly souls fall into two groups, souls that possess a mind and souls that do not;" Tatia, *Tattvārtha Sūtra: That Which Is*, p. 40.

68 TAS 2.25: *saṁjñinaḥ samanaskāḥ;* Tatia, *Tattvārtha Sūtra: That Which Is*, p. 46.

> This sutra explains the unique quality of those who have a physical mind. Intelligence or rationality means the capacity to remember the past and ponder the future. Only the five-sensed beings who have a mind have this capacity.

See also Jaini, *Jaina Path of Purification*, p. 110; Dasgupta, *History of Indian Philosophy*, p. 189.

69 Roy, *Mahābhārata* 9.28, with some emendations. See also A. Misra, "Consciousness in Plants," p. 180.

70 *Bhṛguruvāca:*

> *ghanānāmapi vṛkṣāṇāmākāśo 'sti na saṁśayaḥ teśāṁ*
> *puṣpaphale vyaktirnityaṁ samupalabhyate (10)*
> *ūṣmato glānaparṇānāṁ tvakpphalaṁ puṣpameva ca*

mlāyate caiva śītena sparśastenātra vidyate (11)
vāyvagnyaśaninispeṣaiḥ phalapuṣpaṁ viśīryate
śrotreṇa gṛhyate śabdastasmācchṛṇvanti pādapaḥ (12)
vallī veṣṭayate vṛkṣaṁ sarvataścaiva gacchatina hyadṛṣṭeśca
mārgo 'sti tasmātpaśyanti pādapāḥ (13)
puṇyāpuṇyaistathā gandhairdhūpaiśca vividhairapi
arogāḥ puṣpitāḥ santi tasmājjighranti pādapāḥ (14)
pādaiḥ salilapānaṁ ca vyādhīnāmapi darśanam
vyādhipratikriyatvācca vidyate rasanaṁ drume (15)
vaktreṇotpalanālena yathordhve jalamādadet
tathā pavanasaṁyuktaḥ pādaiḥ pibati pādapaḥ (16)
grahaṇātsukhaduḥkhasya chinnasya ca virohaṇāt
jīvaṁ paśyāmi vṛkṣāṇāmacaitanyaṁ na vidyate (17)
tena tajjalamādattaṁ jarayatyagnimārutau
āhārapariṇāmācca sneho vṛddhiśca jāyate (18)

Mbh 12.177.10-18. Roy, *Mahābhārata* 9.28-29.

According to Madhu Khanna ("Ritual Capsule of Durgā Pūjā," p. 478):

> Bhṛgu's most important contribution lay in creating a link between plant life and the process of sense perception experienced by humans. The natural process of human sensory experience is applied to plants. Plants respond to sound, touch, taste, and smell in the same way that humans respond to their senses. Plants are endowed with great sensitivity to touch, heat, and thunder. They can, as it were, see, hear, smell, taste, share joy and sorrow, and repair and rejuvenate their damaged parts. The skin of the tree has tactual perception; it is affected by thunderous sound and is said to possess auditory powers. Plants are known to be affected by smell. They seek sap from the earth, so they have the power of taste.

71 V. S. Sukthankar notes that the Bhṛgu class of priests helped shape the Mahābhārata by taking a hypothetical epic nucleus that had been compiled by *kṣatriya* bards and reworking it: they "swallowed up the epic nucleus such as it was, and digested it completely...it would be a hazardous venture now to reconstruct the lost Kṣatriya ballad of love and war." The contribution of the Bhṛgu priests has much to do with the religious and philosophical material intertwined in the various narratives, and much to do, especially, with the narrative of Kṛṣṇa; Sukthankar, *Meaning of the Mahābhārata*, pp. 39, 110.

72 Ramachandra Rao, *Encyclopedia of Indian Medicine* 2.151.

73 A. Misra, "Consciousness in Plants," pp. 179-180.

74 ĀS 1.1.6.1-2.

[75] UD 10.5-9.

[76] UD 10.10-18.

[77] TAS 2.23: *vāyvantānām ekam;* "the classes of beings, up to the air-bodied ones, have only the sense of touch;" variant: *vanaspatyantānām ekam;* "the classes of beings, up to the plant-bodied ones, have only the sense of touch;" Tatia, *Tattvārtha Sūtra: That Which Is,* p. 45; Jain, *Biology in Jaina Treatise on Reals,* pp. 32, 76, 99, 102, 108, 122, 123.

[78] Jain, *Biology in Jaina Treatise on Reals,* pp. 32, 123, 122, 124. This idea is popular knowledge about Jains, viz.: "Every living thing, from the greatest to the tiniest, is considered a *jiva,* an independent, eternal living soul. To minimize violence, Jainists restrict their diets to creatures with only one sense: plants, whose sense is touch." Bernhardt, "Dreading Those Pearly Gates," p. 47.

[79] *Kathaṁ hi nāma samaṇā Sakyaputtiyā cetiyarukkhaṁ chedāpessanti gāmapūjitaṁ...raṭṭhapūjitaṁ. Ekindriyaṁ samaṇā Sakyaputtiyā jīvaṁ viheṭhenti*; Vin 3.155-156; Horner, *Book of the Discipline* 1.266. My italics.

[80] *Kathaṁ hi nāma samaṇā Sakyaputtiyā tālataruṇe chedāpetvā tālapattapādukāyo dhāressanti, tāni tālataruṇāni chinnāni milāyanti. Ekindriyaṁ samaṇā Sakyaputtiyā jīvaṁ viheṭhenti;* Vin 1.189; Horner, *Book of the Discipline* 4.251. My italics. Padmasiri De Silva ("Environmental Ethics: Buddhist Perspective," p. 179) notes the following:

> (Buddhist) sensitivity was extended to the minutest creatures. The rules for monks that prohibit cutting down trees, destroying plants, digging in the soil, and so forth may be interpreted as a warning that the minute forms of life may be destroyed by these actions. According to the Indian ways of thinking, as expressed in the Pāli canon, a certain form of life called "one-facultied" *(ekindriya jiva),* inhabits trees, plants and the soil, and even water may have creatures or "breathers"*(sappanaka udaka)* in it.

This last sentiment is more reminiscent of the Jain tradition than that of the early Buddhists.

[81] *Kathañ hi nāma samaṇā Sakyaputtiyā rukkhaṁ chindissanti pi chedāpessanti pi. Ekindriyaṁ samaṇa Sakyaputtiyā jīvaṁ viheṭhenti*; Vin 4.34; Horner, *Book of the Discipline* 2.226. My italics.

[82] *Kathaṁ hi nāma bhikkuniyo...carissanti haritāni tiṇāni sammaddantā ekindriyaṁ jīvaṁ viheṭhentā bahū khuddake pāṇe saṁghātaṁ āpādentā;* Vin 4.296; Horner, *Book of the Discipline* 3.320. My italics.

83 See Horner, *Book of the Discipline* 1.266n; Jacobi, *Jaina Sūtras* 2.42n.

84 Kandel and Jessell, "Touch," p. 367.

85 *Tvacā spṛṣṭam;* AU 1.3.11, 7.

86 BSU 256; taken from the Yogavāsiṣṭha 5.34.12, as quoted in Olivelle, *Saṁnyāsa Upaniṣads*, p. 246.

87 CS 5.87-89, as quoted in Krishnamurthy, *Source Book of Indian Medicine*, p. 240.

88 Manu 1.76; Bühler, *Laws of Manu*, p. 21.

89 Filliozat, *Classical Doctrine of Indian Medicine*, p. 63.

90 *Vātaḥ prāṇaḥ*; BĀU 1.1.1.

91 Filliozat, *Classical Doctrine of Indian Medicine*, p. 61. Filliozat's italics.

92 Filliozat, *Classical Doctrine of Indian Medicine*, pp. 199-200.

93 Sharma, *Caraka Saṁhitā* 1.460.

94 Filliozat, *Classical Doctrine of Indian Medicine*, pp. 209, 210, 212; see Bhishagratna, *Suśruta Saṁhitā* 2.1-8.

95 Sharma, *Caraka Saṁhitā* 1.399; see Padmasiri De Silva, "Environmental Ethics: Buddhist Perspective," p. 176. This creates an interesting issue for those in the tradition who would argue that plants don't breath. If plants are one-facultied, and if that one faculty is touch, and if touch is especially associated with wind or air, and if air is especially associated with mobility, then touch in plants must be associated with the movement of air (here we insert *prāṇa)* inside the body. Unfortunately, this argument shifts slightly the understanding of how movement is used in this context. When Bhṛgu (Roy, *Mahābhārata* 9.30) says, for example, "the living creature is, in every respect, caused by *Prana* to move about and exert," he is not saying that air or the *prāṇas* are moving about inside the body, but that they are causing the body they are in to move about the world. Thus, we have to begin with movement and work backwards: in this way, if a body moves, it must be breathing; or to the point here, if a body does not move (i.e., is a plant), then it is not breathing, and is not a *prāṇin*.

96 Mbh 12.147.3-7; Roy, *Mahābhārata* 9.237-238; CS 1.399, 403.

97 Sharma, *Caraka Saṁhitā* 1.399, 403, where the order of appearance in creation is given as ether/sound, air/touch, fire/vision, water/taste, and earth/ smell; see also Krishnamurthy, *Source Book of Indian Medicine*, p. 135; Ramachandra Rao, *Encyclopedia of Medicine* 2.138-141; Roy, *Mahābhārata* 9.49, 96, 170. The chart in the

Vaiśeṣika view, as represented in the Tattvārtha Sūtra, uses only four elements, leaving out ether/sound, and thus showing air and therefore touch as the first as the basic sense; Jain, *Biology in Jaina Treatise on Reals*, p. 117. The Nyāya-Vaiśeṣikas, likewise, note that air's "peculiar quality is tangibility;" Potter, *Encyclopedia of Indian Philosophies* 2.87.

98 Dasgupta, *History of Indian Philosophy*, p. 123.

99 CU 3.13.8.

100 Gītā 2.14.

101 Sharma, *Caraka Saṁhitā* 1.55, 75-76,185, 399, 430, 460.

102 UD 36.20.

103 Dhs 613-616, 636, 647-651.

104 Vbh 71-72.

105 Ñāṇamoli, *Path of Purification*, pp. 444, 446.

106 Salisbury and Ross, "Power of Movement in Plants," *Plant Physiology*, p. 408. Salisbury and Ross's italics.

107 Salisbury and Ross, "Power of Movement in Plants," *Plant Physiology*, p. 409.

108 Salisbury and Ross, "Power of Movement in Plants," *Plant Physiology*, p. 411.

109 Salisbury and Ross, "Power of Movement in Plants," *Plant Physiology*, pp. 414-415.

110 O'Flaherty, *Rig Veda*, pp. 174-175. See Macdonell, *Vedic Mythology*, p. 84 where as "the shedder of rain Parjanya...quickens the earth with his seed, (and) the plants spring up...he is the fructifier and increaser of plants...reeds and grass are produced by his action."

111 RV 10.27.21, 2, 12, 3; O'Flaherty, *Rig Veda*, pp. 285-286.

112 AV 8.7.4, 16, 17.

113 AV 8.10.18: *Tasmād vanaspatīnāṁ saṁvatsare vṛkṇam api rohati.* Whitney, *Atharva Veda* 2.513.

114 TS 1.3.5: *vanaspate śatavalśo vi roha, sahasravalśā vi vayaṁ ruhema.* Keith, *Taittiriya Sanhita* 1.40.

115 *Hyevaitā jāyanta 'imām (bhūvīm) anu prarohanti.* ŚB 7.4.2.13; Eggeling, *Śatapatha Brāhmaṇa* 3.380-381.

116 KB 4.13; Keith, *Rigveda Brahmanas*, p. 369.

117 CU 6.11.1; Radhakrishnan, *Principal Upaniṣads*, p. 461.

118 *Iha khalu bījantu vṛkṣāṇāṁ sambhavakāraṇaṁ bhavati / viśeṣato bījānāṁ svabhāva udbhedanañca / yasmāt prarohaḥ sambhavati tacca bījam;* Sircar and Sarkar, *Parāśara*, pp. 99, 103. *Evaṁ vidhena vidhinā parisaṁsthitāni / bījāni santi sakalānyapi śobhanāni /*

tajjāśca nūnam acirāt taravo bahanti / puṣpaṁ phalaṁ pracuram uttam pallavāṭhayāḥ; Sur 4.58; Gopal, p. 137.

119 Sircar and Sarkar, *Parāśara*, p. 89.

120 ĀS 1.1.5.6; Jacobi, *Jaina Sūtras* 1.10

121 UD 10.l; Jacobi, *Jaina Sūtras* 2.41-42.

122 Jain, *Biology in Jaina Treatise on Reals*, pp. 98, 100, 102.

123 Hem 1.9; Fynes, *Hemacandra*, p. 6.

124 D 1.87, 111; 3.44; S 3.137; 5.46; A 3.19, 200, 360; KV 343; Vism 583, 625; Mil 33; J 5.46. Of AS 1.1.5.6, Jacobi (1.10n) says:

> The plants know the seasons, for they sprout at the proper time, the Aśoka buds and blooms when touched by the foot of a well-attired girl, and the Vakula when watered with wine; the seed grows always upwards: all this would not happen if the plants had no knowledge of the circumstances about them. Such is the reasoning of the commentators.

125 Woodward, *Kindred Sayings* 5.80.

126 J 37; Chalmers, *Jātaka* 1.93-94.

127 J 483; Rouse, *Jātaka* 4. 167-168. My italics.

128 Sircar and Sarkar, *Parāśara*, p. 107.

129 O'Flaherty, *Rig Veda*, p. 50.

130 BS 59.2-6; *Bṛhat Saṁhitā* 2.564 .

131 The Kāśyapa Saṁhitā and Varāhamihira as quoted in BS; see Gopal, pp. 93, 97. See also Sur 7.112; Gopal 157, on watering plants not being advised in rainy or cold seasons.

132 Sur 5.68; 7.108; 8.173, 175; Gopal, pp. 143, 157, 179.

133 Sur 9.204, 205, 206, 207; Gopal, pp. 187, 189.

134 Bhattacharya and Archer, *Vidyāpati*, p. 73.

135 Rajan, "Ancient Indian Approach towards Plants," p. 84.

136 Śak 5.7; Miller in Thapar, *Śakuntalā*, p. 131.

137 Hem 2.31; Fynes, *Hemachandra*, p. 41.

138 UD 9.9; Jacobi, *Jaina Sūtras* 2.36.

139 Peterson, *Poems to Śiva*, p. 108.

140 Ramanujan, *Interior Landscape*, p. 55.

141 Vin 1.137.

142 A 1.137; Vism 74-75, 554, 625.

143 Mbh 12.177.11, 21; Roy, *Mahābhārata* 9.28, 29.

144 Sur 8.182; Gopal, p. 181.

145 Shakti Gupta, *Plant Myths and Traditions in India*, p. ix.

146 AV 1.23.1; Whitney, *Atharva Veda* 1.24.

147 Śak 5.28; Miller in Thapar, *Śakuntalā*, p. 138.

148 Ramanujan, *Interior Landscape*, p. 74.

[149] TS 1.1.2; 4.1.2; 5.1.3; Keith, *Taittiriya Sanhita* 1.2; 2.292, 393.

[150] ŚB 1.1.4.19-20; 1.5.3.12; 7.5.2.47; 8.2.3.6; Eggeling, *Śatapatha Brāhmaṇa* 1.30-31, 147; 3.415; 4.35. The beneficial liquid may be water-like, for in the Bṛhadāraṇyaka Upaniṣad, a certain knowledge is passed down from teacher to pupil, and that knowledge is: "If one should sprinkle this (melted butter) even on a dry stump, branches would grow and leaves spring forth." BĀU 6.3. 7-12; Radhakrishnan, *Principal Upaniṣads*, p. 319.

[151] Mbh 12.177.15, 16, 18; Roy, *Mahābhārata* 9.28-29. With some emendations.

[152] Sircar and Sarkar, *Parāśara*, p. 4.

[153] Gopal, pp. 12, 89.

[154] BS 54.9; VP 2.300.14-15; AP 282.7-8; Sur 6.99-105, 110-112; Gopal, pp. 97, 107, 115, 153-155, 157.

[155] Sur 8.167, 178; 9.209, 219; Gopal, pp. 177, 179, 189, 191.

[156] Artha 2.24; VP 2.300. 7-8; Gopal, pp. 89, 105.

[157] AP 282.4-5; Gopal, p. 113.

[158] Sur 3.39; Gopal, p. 129. *He vṛkṣa tvām itaḥ sthānānneṣyāmyanyad guṇontaram / tathā sekaṁ pradāsyāmi nirvṛttiṁ yena yāsyasi;* Sur 5.85; Gopal, p. 147.

[159] Bhattacharya and Archer, *Vidyāpati*, p. 73.

[160] Ramanujan, *Speaking of Śiva*, p. 80.

[161] Peterson, *Poems to Śiva*, p. 113.

[162] Ramanujan, *Interior Landscape*, pp. 59, 66, 67.

[163] Ramanujan, *Interior Landscape*, pp. 44, 51.

[164] ĀS 1.1.5.6; Jacobi, *Jaina Sūtras* 1.10.

[165] Basham, *History of the Ājīvikas*, pp. 47-48.

[166] Hem 1.12; 2.27, 200; Fynes, *Hemacandra*, pp. 7, 41, 53.

[167] Sn no. 77; M 1.457; S 1.134, 172; 3.54, 91; A 1.32, 135, 229, 239; 3.404; 4.237; 5.213.Vism 688; J 1.108.

[168] M1.457; Horner, *Middle Length Sayings* 2.130; S 3.137; Woodward, *Kindred Sayings* 3.118.

[169] S 3.54; Woodward, *Kindred Sayings* 3.46-47; A 1.135; Woodward, *Gradual Sayings* 1.118.

[170] J 2 (Vaṇṇupatha-Jātaka); Chalmers, *Jātaka* 1.11.

[171] J 46 (Ārāmadūsaka-Jātaka); Chalmers, *Jātaka* 1.119. See J 268 (Ārāma-Dūsa-Jātaka); Rouse, *Jātaka* 2.238-239.

[172] Watson, *Lotus Sutra*, p. 101.

[173] Sur 7.128, 129, 131, 132, 142; Gopal, pp. 163, 165, 167.

[174] M. N. Dutt, *Rāmāyāṇa* 2.681.

[175] Rajan, "Ancient Indian Approach Towards Plants," p. 84.

[176] Śak 5.12; Miller in Thapar, *Śakuntalā,* p. 132; see also Ryder, *Shakuntala,* p. 55 for alternate translation.

[177] Ramanujan, *Interior Landscape,* p. 22.

[178] Peterson, *Poems to Śiva,* p. 167.

[179] Ramanujan, *Interior Landscape,* p. 61.

[180] Hem 2.35; 8.120; Fynes, *Hemacandra,* pp. 42, 165.

[181] J 474; Rouse, *Jātaka* 4.124-127.

[182] J. 475 (Phandana-Jātaka); Rouse, *Jātaka* 4. 130.

[183] J. 547 (Vessantara-Jātaka); Cowell and Rouse, *Jātaka* 6. 266.

[184] O'Flaherty, *Rig Veda,* p. 286.

[185] Whitney, *Atharva Veda* 1.229.

[186] Whitney, *Atharva Veda* 2.499.

[187] ŚB 1.3.3.10; Eggeling, *Śatapatha Brāhmaṇa* 1.86-87.

[188] Mbh 12.177.13; Roy, *Mahābhārata* 9.28.

[189] Sircar and Sarkar, *Parāśara,* p. 105.

[190] Miller, *Gītagovinda,* p. 75.

[191] Peterson, *Poems to Śiva,* pp. 120, 123.

[192] ĀS 2.4.2.12; Jacobi, *Jaina Sūtras* 1.154-155.

[193] SK 1.3.2.10; Jacobi, *Jaina Sūtras* 2.264.

[194] Hem 2.358; Fynes, *Hemacandra,* p. 63.

[195] D 87, 111; M 1.457; S 3.137; A 4.99, 336; J 1.108; Vism 688

[196] A 4.237; Hare, *Gradual Sayings* 4.161-162.

[197] J 186; Rouse, *Jātaka* 2.73.

[198] RV 5.57.3; 5.60.2; 1.65.8.

[199] AV 10.1.17; 10.3.13-15; Whitney, *Atharva Veda* 2.565, 574.

[200] *Pracaṇḍapavanodvegairbhaṅgonmūlanamoṭanam;* Sur 8.174; Gopal, p. 179. Sur 9.201; Gopal, p. 187.

[201] Van Buitenan, *Mahābhārata* 2-3.243.

[202] Mbh 12.177.12; Roy, *Mahābhārata* 9.28.

[203] Miller, *Caurapañcāśikā,* p. 91.

[204] Miller, *Gītagovinda,* p. 75.

[205] Ramanujan, *Interior Landscapes,* pp. 21, 81.

[206] Peterson, *Poems to Śiva,* pp. 173, 265. Surapāla is always aware of the damage that can be done to plants when friction to or between trees is present; Sur 8.182; Gopal, p. 181.

[207] ĀS 1.6.1.2; Jacobi, *Jaina Sūtras* 1.53.

[208] Hem 2.115; 8.225; Fynes, *Hemacandra,* pp. 47, 172.

[209] As in J 4 (Cullaka-Seṭṭhi-Jātaka), J 475 (Phandana-Jātaka), and J 547 (Vessantara-Jātaka).

210 J 543 (Bhūridatta-Jātaka), J 547 (Vessantara-Jātaka); Cowell and Rouse, *Jātaka* 6.100, 275.

211 Schotsman, *Buddhacarita*, pp. 76, 132

212 J 36; Cowell, *Jātaka* 1.91.

213 There are two lists involving the senses and they are somewhat at odds with one another. The first is the list of sense-faculties as they are associated with increasingly complex sentient beings:

> one-sensed beings have touch
> two-sensed beings have touch and taste
> three-sensed beings have touch, taste, and smell
> four-sensed beings have touch, taste, smell, and sight
> five-sensed beings have touch, taste, smell, sight, and hearing

This gives us an order of *touch, taste, smell, sight, and hearing*, as compared to *hearing, touch, sight, taste, smell*, such as we find in Jain texts like studies on the Tattvārtha Sūtra (e.g., Jain, *Biology in Jaina Treatise on Reals*, p. 113). The other list is based on the creation order of elements as they are associated with corresponding sense-faculties: ether - hearing; air - touch; fire - sight; water - taste; and earth - smell, such as we find in the Caraka Saṁhitā (CS 1.399, 403). We are using the first order in this section because it reflects the sense-based hierarchy of living things, one of which is plants, rather than material evolution of the elements ranging from subtle to increasingly gross.

214 See, for example, BĀU4.5.12; CU 3.13.8.

215 See, for example, BĀU 4.4.2; 4.5.15; CU 7.8.1; 7.9.1; AU 1.1.4; KU 2.1.3.

216 ĀS 1.2.1.2, 5; UD 16.10; 29.63-66; 32.22-99; SK 2.1.36, 42, 51.

217 Jain, *Biology in Jaina Treatise on Reals*, pp. 122-123.

218 ĀS 1.1.2; Jacobi, *Jaina Sūtras* 1.15-16.

219 Sharma, *Caraka Saṁhitā* 1.498, 502.

220 KV 14.2; Aung and C. A. F. Rhys Davids, *Points of Controversy*, pp. 283-284.

221 Dhs 1095.

222 M 1.295; S 5.217; KV 125. See C. A. F. Rhys Davids, *Buddhist Manual of Psychological Ethics*, p. lxxxvii.

223 Potter, *Encyclopedia of Indian Philosophies* 2.119; see 2.230, 259.

224 Sharma, *Caraka Saṁhitā* 1.76.

225 Jain, *Jaina World of Non-Living*, p. 201.

226 See Tatia, *Tattvārtha Sūtra: That Which Is*, pp. 42-43; Jain, *Biology in Jaina Treatise on Reals*, p. 100.

[227] Jain, *Biology in Jaina Treatise on Reals*, pp. 32, 113.

[228] Jain, *Biology in Jaina Treatise on Reals*, p. 116..

[229] Pieris, "Notions of Citta, Attā and Attabhāva," pp. 213, 214, 220. Here Pieris is arguing that *citta* and *viññāṇa*, the fifth *khandha*, are functionally equivalent: *citta, mano,* and *viññāṇa* are *"different* (though, at times, partially overlapping) dimensions of the *same* general complex of consciousness," with *mano* being "the most precise" and *viññāṇa* being "the most elastic and elusive...*Citta* is *mano*-centred *viññāṇa*," with *viññāṇa* referring to subliminal consciousness and *mano* referring to the awakening door providing access.

[230] Guenther, "Basic Features of Buddhist Psychology," p. 79.

[231] D 1.41-45. "As the seat of feeling, *kāya* is the fifth in the enumeration of the senses *(āyatanāni)*. It is *ajjhattika* as sense (i.e. subjective) and its object is the tangible *(phoṭṭhabba)*. The contact between subject and object consists either in touching *(phusitvā)* or in sensing *(viññeyya)*." T. W. Rhys Davids and Stede, *Pali-English Dictionary*, p. 207. My italics.

[232] C. A. F. Rhys Davids, *Buddhist Manual of Psychological Ethics*, p. lxiii. C. A. F. Rhys David's italics. See also Pickering, "Selfhood is a Process," pp. 159, 164-165.

[233] C. A. F. Rhys Davids, *Buddhist Manual of Psychologial Ethics*, p. lxiii.

[234] Vism 447; Ñāṇamoli, *Path of Purification*, p. 446.

[235] Dhs 613-616; C. A. F. Rhys Davids, *Buddhist Manual of Psychological Ethics*, p. 166n; Vism 447.

[236] C. A. F. Rhys Davids, *Buddhist Manual of Psychological Ethics*, p. lxiii. In addition, she says, "it is only through Touch that a knowledge of the *underived elements* of the world of sense could be obtained, the fluid or moist element along excepted." Her italics. Concerning *rūpa*, she continues, three of the four elements (i.e., earth, fire, and air) are thus considered underived and tangible, so that the sense organs and their objects are derived from the tangible and from the fluid (p. lxiv).

[237] C. A. F. Rhys Davids, *Buddhist Manual of Psychological Ethics*, p. lxiv; see C. A. F. Rhys Davids, *Buddhist Psychology*, pp. 145, 186.

[238] Bidwell, *Plant Physiology*, p. 4.

[239] "Sacred Trees," http://www.indianculture online.com/Mystica/html/sacred_trees.htm.

[240] Jensen, "Plants Respond: Cleve Backster," p. 4.

241 A. Misra, "Consciousness in Plants," p. 179.
242 Tatia, *Tattvārtha Sūtra: That Which Is*, p. 40.
243 Jain, *Biology in Jaina Treatise on Reals*, pp. 31, 30, 95.
244 Tatia, *Tattvārtha Sūtra: That Which Is*, p. 41. My italics.
245 Jain, *Biology in Jaina Treatise on Reals*, p. 97.
246 Dixit, *Sukhlalji's Commentary on Tattvārtha Sūtra*, p. 86.
247 Jaini, *Jaina Path or Purification*, p. 111.
248 Dundas, *The Jains*, p. 90. My italics.
249 ĀS 1.1.5.6; Jacobi, *Jaina Sūtras* 1.10n.
250 CS Śārīrasthānam 136, 133; Sharma, *Caraka Saṁhitā* 1.409.
251 Pieris, "Notions of Citta, Attā and Attabhāva," p. 213.
252 AĀ 2.3.2; Keith, *Aitareya Āraṇyaka*, p. 216; see Smith, *Classifying the Universe*, p. 211. Notable here is that the Aitareya uses *citta* "consciousness" and not *prajñā* "wisdom, intelligence" or *saṁjñā* "perception" as other traditions do in connection with plants.
253 J 3.24.
254 Mil 172.
255 Sharma, *Caraka Saṁhitā* 1.76. My italics.
256 Dasgupta, *History of Indian Philosophy*, p. 96.
257 Basham, *History and Doctrine of the Ājīvikas*, p. 248.
258 Ramachandra Rao, *Encyclopedia of Indian Medicine* 2.151. My italics.
259 Sircar and Sarkar, *Parāśara*, pp. 2, 4.
260 Manu 1.49.
261 Dixit, *Sukhlalji's Commentary on Tattvārtha Sūtra*, p. 94.
262 TAS 2.25: *saṁjñinaḥ samanaskāḥ;* "those that have mind are intelligent beings;" Tatia, *Tattvārtha Sūtra: That Which Is*, p. 46. Jain, *Biology in Jaina Treatise on Reals*, pp. 126-127. This view is noted earlier in our discussion of the animal members of the Jain *tiryañca* group who can possess anywhere from two to five senses. Those animals who have five senses are broken down into the lower animals who are totally instinctive and without consciousness and mind *(asaṁjñī/amanaska)* and the higher animals — human beings, hell-beings, and gods — who are able to reason by virtue of being conscious or having a mind *(saṁjñī/samanaska)*.
263 Dixit, *Sukhlalji's Commentary on Tattvārtha Sūtra*, p. 96.
264 Dixit, *Sukhlalji's Commentary on Tattvārtha Sūtra*, p. 96.
265 Schmithausen, *Problem of the Sentience of Plants*, p. 14.
266 Keown, *Buddhist Ethics*, p. 67. As Keown (pp. 69-70) notes,

> Cognition *(saṁjñā)* consists in the apprehension of characteristics. The apprehension of different natures – noticing that it

> is blue, yellow, long, short, man, woman, friend, enemy, pleasant, or unpleasant, etc.

Thus, he argues, *saññā* and *vedanā*, "operate closely in conjunction.".

267 Dhs 1044-1046; C. A. F. Rhys Davids, *Buddhist Manual of Psychological Ethics*, p.250. My italics.

268 Ackerman, *Natural History of the Senses*, pp. 80, 79.

269 Martin and Jessell, "Modality Coding in the Somatic Sensory System," p. 341. Martin and Jessell's italics.

270 ŚĀ 5.5; Keith, *Śāṅkhyāna Āraṇyaka*, p. 33.

271 Jessell and Kelly, "Pain and Analgesia," p. 385. Jessell and Kelley's italics.

272 Note Jaini's remark about the Jain tradition, that "*hiṁsā* refers to any action accompanied by the giving of pain or the rise of passions;" Jaini, *Jaina Path of Purification*, p. 170. My italics. This argument, based on the work of Peter Singer in *Animal Liberation*, comes in the discussion of the human attribution of "rights" to plants based on their capacity for suffering. While Singer documents a persuasive argument for the suffering of animals, he goes on to say that "the belief that plants feel pain appears to be quite unjustified." Singer, *Animal Liberation*, pp. 219-220, 225, 235-236.

273 Schmithausen, "Ecological Ethics," p. 9.

274 De Nicolás, *Meditations through the Ṛg Veda*, p. 232.

275 Dwivedi, "*Satyagraha* for Conservation: Awakening the Spirit of Hinduism," p. 156; see also Dwivedi, "Vedic Heritage," p. 34.

276 Van Buitenan, *Mahābhārata* 2-3.241.

277 Mbh 12.177.17; Roy, *Mahābhārata* 9.28.

278 Van Buitenan, *Mahābhārata* 2-3.340. Note Hem 1.31, where an Aśoka tree is described: "its branches were wafted upwards by the breeze, it seemed to be issuing an invitation to all living creatures." Fynes, *Hemacandra*, p. 8.

279 Manu 1.49; Bühler, *Laws of Manu*, p. 16.

280 Sharma, *Caraka Saṁhitā* 1.409. It should be noted also that the next verse makes clear what the consequences are of being able to experience pleasure and pain:

> Happiness and misery give rise to allurement in the guise of desire and aversion, the allurement, in turn, acts as cause of happiness and misery. It collects the entities which offer resort to sensations. If there be no collection of entities, there cannot be contact and without contact the sensations cannot be felt (Sharma 1.409).

Thus, to be subject to the experience of pleasure and pain, as a result of being sentient, signifies the further possibility of having the capacity for desire and aversion.

281 Krishnamurthy, *Source Book of Indian Medicine*, p. 195.

282 Gopal, pp. 9, 191.

283 Sircar and Sarkar, *Parāśara*, p. 4; see Ramachandra Rao, *Encyclopedia of Indian Medicine* 2.151, who draws on this passage when he says that "being internally conscious, they (plants) are capable of experiencing pleasure and pain."

284 Krishnamurthy, *Source Book of Indian Medicine*, p. 275.

285 Gupta, *Plant Myths and Traditions in India*, p. 71.

286 Nelson, "Dualism of Nondualism," p. 67.

287 5.20: *sukha-duḥkha-jīvita-maraṇopagrahaś ca.* Tatia, *Tattvārtha Sūtra: That Which Is*, p. 131.

288 Tatia, *Tattvārtha Sūtra: That Which Is*, p. 131.

289 ĀS 1.1.6.1-2; Jacobi, *Jaina Sūtras* 1.11.

290 UD 19.45, 66; Jacobi, *Jaina Sūtras* 2.93, 96.

291 Jain, *Biology in Jaina Treatise on Reals*, pp. 40, 42, 44.

292 Jaini, *Jaina Path of Purification*, p. 113. My italics. Jain, *Biology in Jaina Treatise on Reals*, p. 44.

293 In addition, the view of Makkhali Gosāla, the leader of the sect of Ājīvikas, on this is given by the Dīgha Nikāya and attributed to Pūraṇa Kassapa. All beings — *sabbe sattā, sabbe pāṇā, sabbe bhūtā, sabbe jīvā* — including all the souls of plants, "are without force and power and energy of their own."

> They are bent this way and that by their fate, by the necessary conditions of the class to which they belong, by their individual nature: and it is according to their position in one or other of the six classes that they experience ease or pain *(sukha-dukkhaṁ paṭisaṁvedenti).*

D 1.53-54; T. W. Rhys Davids, *Dialogues of the Buddha* 1.71, 71n.

294 Schmithausen, *Buddhism and Nature*, p. 37.

295 James McDermott says of animals that they "as such are not considered to be capable of growth in the *dhamma* and the *vinaya;*" McDermott, "Animals and Humans in Early Buddhism," p. 270.

296 Gopal, pp. 84, 109, 111 (VD 2.300.23, 32); Banwari, *Pañcavaṭī: Indian Approach to Environment*, p. 142.

297 Hem 1.394, 396; 2.61, 62; 8.231, 233, 239; Fynes, *Hemacandra*, pp. 32, 43, 172.

298 Sharma, *Caraka Saṁhitā* 1.409.

299 Dundas, *The Jains*, pp. 90-91, quoting the Sūtrakṛtāṅgasūtram (2.3), the Tattvārthavārttika (on 2.24 and Shilanka on the Ācārāṅga Sūtra 1.1.5.6-7).

300 For a good discussion on views in later texts, see Schmithausen, *Problem of the Sentience of Plants*, pp. 87n-88n.

301 Sn 77; S 1.21, 227; 3. 54; 4.315; 5.46; A 1.135, 229, 239; 3.404; 4. 237; 5.213; Vism 688; Mil 33.

302 S 2.2, 42; A 5.203; Cnid 252.

303 S 3.207; 4.294; Vism 350; Vbh 137.

304 M 1.437, 453.

305 Manu 11.240; Bühler, *Laws of Manu*, p. 478 (in translation, numbered as verse 241). My italics.

306 Dundas, *The Jains*, p. 91.

307 Jaini, *Jaina Path of Purification*, p. 111.

308 Jain, *Biology in Jaina Treatise on Reals*, pp. 40, 42.

309 Jain, *Biology in Jaina Treatise on Reals*, p. 43.

310 Jain, *Biology in Jaina Treatise on Reals*, pp. 37, 42.

311 Gītā 2.58, 64.

312 Sn 214, 340; D 3.107; M 1.9; 2.22, 106; 3.296; S 1.26, 138; 2.218, 231, 271; 4.103, 112, 175; A 1.25, 94, 113, 236; 2.6, 16, 38, 39; 3.70, 99, 138, 163,173, 387, 441, 449; 4.25, 166, 264; 5.134, 348; Therī 196; It 23, 24; Mnid 14.

313 S 1.61, 203, 204; 3.93; 5.269; A 1.70; 3.199.

314 Sn 516; S 1.48; 2.275; 3.2, 235; 4.140, 294; 5.301; A 1.181; 3.380.

315 Schotsman, *Buddhacarita*, p. 186.

316 Collins notes that Buddhism's contribution to the discussion of *karma* is to make the crucial focus a mental one, such that the presence of *cetanā* in the agent would have the significance of karmic force; Collins, *Selfless Persons*, p. 201. Thus, intention or *cetanā* is understood in the Dhammasaṅgaṇi as the "volition, purpose, purposefulness, which is born of contact with the appropriate element of representative intellection — this is the volition that there then is;" C. A. F. Rhys Davids, *Buddhist Manual of Psychological Ethics*, p. 8.

4
Plant Behavior: Stability

To the degree that there is consensus among those Indian traditions who talk about plants, there emerges a reasonably common view: that plants are *ekindriya* "one sense-facultied" and that the sense faculty at work is that of *sparśa* "touch," with the *kāya* "body" or *tvac* "skin" acting as the major sense organ. This conclusion arises from canonical statements asserting so, and from textual observations about plants that can be used to match their behavior to traditional characteristics of touch. Discussions about plants as sentient, however, though positive in their attribution, also adhere to notions of a hierarchy among sentient beings and, in particular, place plants at the lower end of that hierarchy – as the attribution of only one sense, as opposed to two or more senses, confirms. We now raise these questions: Is there a scale of living beings and, if so, where on that scale do plants fall? Moreover, what is it about plant nature that consigns them to one place on the scale and not to another?

4.1 Living Beings : The Stationary and the Mobile

Generally, Indian traditions divide living beings into two main categories: the unmoving *(sthāvara)* and the moving *(jaṅgama)*,[1] or in an alternate phrase and order, the moving *(cara)* and the unmoving *(acara)*.[2] This kind of division goes back to the Saṁhitā and Brāhmanṇa periods, with such phrases as *carācarebhyaḥ avāhā*, "Hail to moving and unmoving creatures!" found in the Vājasaneyi,

Taittirīya, Maitrāyaṇī, and Kāṭhaka Saṁhitās,[3] and *sthāvara* found in several Taittirīya texts, including a conjunction with *jaṅgama* in the Taittirīya Āraṇyaka.[4] A division between "rooted" and "rootless" beings is found among food groups several times in the Śatapatha Brāhmaṇa. And in concluding offerings for the New and Full-Moon sacrifices, for example, the priest says, the "spotted cow...is this (earth): whatever rooted and rootless food is here on this (earth), by that this (earth) is a spotted cow."[5] Again, the text notes that that "which affords (means of) subsistence is of two kinds; namely, either rooted or rootless."[6] Another kind of division is the one we've seen in the Aitareya Āraṇyaka – that between plants and trees as bearers of sap *(rasa)* alone, and animals as bearers of sap and of consciousness *(citta)*.[7]

The Dharmaśāstra manual of Manu uses the terms movable *(jaṅgama/cara)* and immovable *(sthāvara/acara)* in several contexts. "Thus...this whole (creation)," says Manu, is "both the immovable *(sthāvara)* and the movable *(jaṅgama)*,"[8] and surveillance over the moving and unmoving creatures *(carācara)* is one of the things that fruit- and root-eating (i.e., vegetarian) sages spend their time doing.[9] Moreover, in promoting violence for certain ritual purposes as acts of piety, he continues, practitioners should "know that the injury to moving creatures and to those destitute of motion *(carācara)*...is no injury at all."[10] Passages in the Mahābhārata use a variety of terms for "moving/mobile" and "unmoving/immobile," including *jaṅgama-ajaṅgama, jaṅgama-sthāvara, cara-acara, sthāvara-jaṅgama, jaṅgama-dhruva, sthāvara-cara,* and *jaṅgama-agama,*[11] all suggesting an inclusive description of the variety of beings in the world.

In the Bhagavad Gītā, Kṛṣṇa tells Arjuna that there is no existence of all beings *(sarva-bhūtānāṁ),* whether moving or unmoving *(carācaram)*, that is separate from him as divine ground, for this whole universe *(jagat kṛtsnaṁ),* containing moving and unmoving things *(sacarācaram),* is Kṛṣṇa. Arjuna responds by telling his charioteer, "You are the father of the world of moving and unmoving things *(carācara),*" and is then himself told that "whatever being *(sattva)* comes to be, be it motionless or moving *(sthāvara-jaṅgama),*" comes from the union of the field and the knower of the field.[12] Again, in the Rāmāyaṇa, Rāma bewails his fortune after Sītā's kidnapping and says, "in all this world of things that move and do not move *(carācara)*, there exists no one more luckless than I, no one entangled in a net of disaster so vast as mine."[13] And, in the Caraka Saṁhitā, poison is said to have been placed by Brahmā in two sources, the mobile and the immobile *(jaṅgamasthāvara),* while one's diet can be taken from the two food groups, mobile and immobile *(sthāvarajaṅgama)*.[14] Thus, both variants – *cara-acara* and *sthāvara-jaṅgama* – among others, are used normatively for moving and unmoving, stationary and mobile, in Vedic and Hindu texts.

Jain tradition, as well, divides sentient beings into the movable and the unmovable. In the Ācārāṅga Sūtra, for example, these beings are the object of the ethic of non-violence – "I renounce all killing of living beings...whether movable or immovable"[15] – and the non-injury of the movable and immovable is part of the ethic of the liberated, of someone who is a true *brāhmaṇa,* and someone no longer acquiring gross *karma.*[16] The Sūtrakṛtāṅga describes the kind of passage back and forth that can happen between these two modes of being:

> ...though they be (now) immovable beings, they will (some time) become movable ones, or though they be (now) movable beings, they will become immovable ones; when they leave the bodies of immovable beings, they will be born in bodies of movable ones, and when they leave the bodies of movable beings, they will be born in bodies of immovable ones.[17]

This is rendered in the Ācārāṅga Bhāṣyam as follows:

> The mobile beings are re-born as immobiles and also the immobiles as mobiles. The living beings could be re-born in any species whatsoever. The ignorants are re-born in different species due to their respective karma.[18]

According to the Sūtrakṛtāṅga, there will never be a time, however, when "all movable beings will die out and become immovable ones...(or when) all immovable beings die out and become movable ones;"[19] karmic quality will remain various and differentiations will continue throughout the course of *saṁsāra*. And in the Ācārāṅga Bhāṣyam:

> Like the birds dwelling on the trees in the night and dispersing in different directions in the morning, everyday people migrating from different species of life live together for sometime and at the end migrate to different forms of life. In other words, they are involved in the cycle of birth and death in different species of life such as one-sensed beings (plants) and the like.[20]

The large schema of living beings given in the Uttarādhyayana divides living beings still belonging to *saṁsāra* into the movable and immovable, and says of the immovable that there are three kinds: earth-lives, water-lives, and plant-lives. In the course of UD 36.70-107, the subdivisions of these categories are enumerated, with their subtle and gross aspects, as well as their aspects as still undeveloped (i.e., still within the "continuous flow") or now fully developed. Verses 108-247 then describe all the movable beings, including those beings with fire-lives and wind-lives,[21] those with organic bodies having two through five senses, those who are inhabitants of the various *gatis* or destinies (e.g, hell-beings, animals, humans, devas), and those who are perfected.

The Tattvārtha Sūtra confirms "mobility" as a category of living beings and places it in a more refined overall structure:

I. Worldly wanderers *(saṁsāriṇaḥ)* : karmically bonded beings earning and/or enjoying their karmic fruits; it is only as a worldly wanderer that one can attain salvation.
   A. Mind-possessing : having a physical brain as well as psychical volitions; the mind works for all the senses and has a capacity for desire and aversion; includes some 5-sensed *moving* beings.
   B. Non-mind-possessing : having only psychical volitions; includes *unmoving* 1-sensed beings (earth-bodies, water-bodies, and plants), *moving* 1-sensed beings (fire-bodies and wind-bodies), *moving* 2-4-sensed beings, and some *moving* 5-sensed beings.

II. Salvated ones *(muktāḥ)*: beings free of karmic bonds.[22]

The Tattvārtha Sūtra says that there are two kinds of worldly beings, those who move *(trasa)* and those who are stationary *(sthāvara)*.[23] Belonging to each of these groups is the result of having *karma* that specifically codes for whatever group one is in. Moreover, this text, unlike the Uttarādhyayana, says that there are actually five bodies that are unmoving, not three; these five are earth-bodies, water-bodies, fire-bodies, air-bodies, and plants.[24] Each of these appears in four varieties. Using earth as an example, the varieties are:

> Earth: "an entity devoid of consciousness, undergoing natural transformations," having properties, but having no realization of physicalizing *karma*.
> Dead embodied earth: "an entity abandoned by the living unit present in it," like a dead body of a person.
> Living embodied earth: "the living (soul) entity which is embodied by earth and subjugated with its conjunction."
> Would-be living earth: "the entity which has acquired" the physicalizing *karma* "of earth body and is in transit with its karmic body but...has not yet acquired the earth as its embodiment."[25]

The other unmoving beings – water, fire, air, and plants – can be substituted for earth in each of the four varieties. In each case of substitution, "the first two are non-living varieties, while the last two are living varieties." Moreover, the last three varieties "are defined on the basis of (their) internal and external" physicalizing karmic causes, for it is only in the "embodied" varieties that these beings have the one sense of touch.[26] Thus, the category of unmoving or immobile beings becomes significantly complex in the hands of Jain theorists.

The Pali canon uses this division as well, distinguishing, like the Jain tradition, between the mobile *(tasa)* and the stationary *(thāvara)*,[27] and both groups together, argues Schmithausen, represent the totality of living, breathing, animate beings who are not to be injured.[28] The Sutta Nipāta, for example, notes that

> Whatever living creatures there are, moving or still *(tasā vā thāvarā)* without exception, whichever are long or large, or

> middle-sized or short, small or great, whichever are seen or unseen, whichever live far or near, whether they already exist or are going to be, let all creatures be happy-minded.[29]

Again, this early text describes the ethic of *ahiṁsā* as laying aside "violence in respect of all beings, moving or still *(bhūtesu tasesu thāvaresu ca).*"[30] The Saṁyutta Nikāya, likewise, uses the term *tasa-thāvara* "the moving and unmoving" to describe the objects of non-violence, warning "backsliders with their...pride...o'ercome by wrath, exceeding violent" not to injure the moving and the unmoving *(tasa-thāvara).*[31] The noble disciple *(ariyasāvaka)* abstains from the taking of life *(pāṇātipāta),* and in so doing does not oppress the moving or the still *(tasaṁ vā thāvaraṁ vā).*[32] The Theragāthā, again, uses the prescription of non-violence as a context for mentioning the moving and unmoving *(tasa-thāvara),*[33] and Jātaka 527 describes the inhabitants of the earth as the *tasa* and the *thāvara.*[34]

It is interesting that the Pali does not use a form of *jaṅgama* to describe the moving, but *tasa* instead. This term comes from the Skt. *trasa* "trembling, quivering, moving" and is the form used, as we saw, with *sthāvara* in the Jain Tattvārtha Sūtra. Why *tasa* becomes the norm in Pali and not some other word for moving, such as *jaṅgama* or *cara,* remains unclear. There appear, however, to be a variety of "lineages" for terms describing the moving and unmoving, and it could be that the Pali tradition draws on the same lineage used by the Jain Tattvārtha Sūtra. This suggests that early Buddhism is influenced heavily by its Jain neighbors for various aspects of the *ahiṁsā* doctrine including, probably, the use of *ekindriya* "one-sense-facultied" for plant sentient beings, and of *trasa/tasa* "moving" for non-plant sentient beings.

Schmithausen discusses an alternate etymology for *tasa* as suggested in the Pali commentaries, that of understanding *tasa* as

> those animate beings who are still under the sway of Thirst or Desire *(tasiṇā, taṇhā)* and of fear *(bhayabherava),* i.e., ordinary beings, whereas the *thāvara,* the stationary ones, are those who are free from thirst and fear, i.e., the saints.

In this interpretation, *tasa* would be taken from either *tṛṣ* "to be thirsty" or *tras* "to tremble," as with fear,[35] and is, in fact, an etymology used in John Ross Carter and Mahinda Palihawadana's translation of a verse from the Dhammapada:

> Having laid down the rod
> With regard to beings, the frightful *(tasa)* and
> the firm *(sthāvara)*,
> Who neither slays nor causes to slay –
> That one I call a *brāhmaṇa*.[36]

Here *bhūtesu tasesu thāvaresu* is taken as "beings frightful and firm," with *tasa* specifically signifying "'those in fright' with fright of craving,"[37] making use, as Schmithausen notes above, of the Pali commentaries for guidance. While this has some appeal, as we will see, the traditional origin from *trasa,* "moving," remains workable in drawing the analogy between *jaṅgama-sthāvara* and *tasa-thāvara.*

Questions about this etymology come up as well in studies on the Tattvārtha Sūtra. The text is very clear about the terms it uses for moving and unmoving. A questioner, for example, puts forward the possibility that the "root *'trasa'* has a meaning of agitation or movement out of fear. Thus," he argues, "the mobiles should be defined as those who move (out of fear)." The text's reply, however, is that this "derivative meaning is not correct," for this would suggest that non-movers would be able to live in the womb, under incubation, when asleep, and when fainted, i.e., in situations where fear is not observed, and therefore not likely to be present.[38] Though the alternate etymology is refuted, the words used for moving *(trasa)* and stationary *(sthāvara)* do indicate that the Tattvārtha Sūtra is in the "classifying lineage" of the Pali texts above.

Plants As Immobile

Contemporary biologists describe certain differences between plant and animal life. Bidwell, for example, notes that animals have a machine-like structure and are determinate in growth and life. This means that animals are more mobile, have to seek out their food, and have to fit into a set of narrow size limits "in order to operate successfully." Plants, on the other hand, are stationary, manufacture their own food by working with what they can retrieve from their own immediate environment, and "are not limited by size or mechanical considerations." He suggests that plants, then, are built architecturally, like houses, with new rooms beings added continuously, though under some strength constraints. Older parts of their bodies can fall away, having been "abandoned and left to die, (while) new parts can be added here and there as required." While, "the animal must maintain it mechanical integrity; the plant is under no such constraint."[39]

While it would seem obvious that plants fall under the 'unmoving' or 'rooted' category of the standard Indian classification of *sthāvara-jaṅgama,* it is important that texts actually make that designation. The Śatapatha Brāhmaṇa, for example, after noting that there are rooted and rootless kinds of foods, goes on to say – "now cattle are rootless *(amūla)* and plants are rooted *(mūlin).* From the rootless cattle eating the rooted plants and drinking water, that juice *(rasa)* is produced."[40] Manu suggests several times that plants are those who are unmoving. "What is destitute of motion *(acara)* is the food of those endowed with locomotion *(cara),*"[41] and so forth up the food chain, suggesting that plants are at this lowest station. Again, when he notes that "insects, snakes, moths, bees, birds and beings bereft of motion *(sthāvara)*, reach heaven by the power of austerities *(tapas),*"[42] he observes that among this non-human, non-mammal group of beings there is a group other than the flying and the crawling – leaving plants as the likely referent of those "beings bereft of motion." This is confirmed with another verse that says "herbs *(oṣadhi)*, trees, cattle, birds, and (other) animals that have been destroyed for sacrifices, receive (being reborn) higher existences,"[43] that makes clear that plants are among those beings who can attain spiritual rewards. Finally, Parāśara makes a decided identification as he opens his text: "Brahmā...in his desire to bring diverse kinds of animates created first the immobile *(sthāvara)* forms – trees, shrubs *(vṛkṣā-vīrudha).*"[44]

For early Buddhism, Schmithausen persuasively shows that the category of immobile, stationary beings specifically signifies plants: "...in all probability, the...expression *'tasa-thāvarā-pāṇā'*...(is) in earliest Buddhism, understood as 'mobile and stationary animate beings', the stationary animate beings being the plants."[45] In time, however, "the notion of stationary animate beings...(is) found to be at variance with the Buddhist doctrine" and, as plants come to be no longer considered animate beings, the concept of mobile and stationary is reinterpretated in commentarial texts.[46]

Again, clear identification is given in the Jain Tattvārtha Sūtra 2.13 where, as we have seen, plants *(vanaspatayaḥ)* are ordinarily included among those kinds of bodies that are non-mobile *(sthāvara),* the other named non-mobiles being earth-bodies, water-bodies, fire-bodies, and air-bodies.[47] The generally named distinction of the Jains is one between the animal kingdom (mobiles) and the plant kingdom (non-mobiles), this latter also including earth, water, fire, and air lives. Moreover, the text says, "plants are placed at the end," presumably meaning the beginning extremity, "because they grow with the help of all the earth, water, etc....(and) are infinite times the number in comparison to all the others." And here at the beginning extremity, plants are the holders of consciousness "in the lowest form because it has a specific nature of gradual decrease...from infiniteness in space up to atoms."[48]

An interesting inconsistency needs to be mentioned here. We saw in the previous chapter that plants are one sense-facultied and that that faculty is touch; we also saw that touch is associated with the element *(mahābhūta)* of air or wind *(vāyu)* – that is, "wind (is expressed) in the (faculty of) touch."[49] Moreover, we saw that touch belongs with wind because of the latter's capacity for movement or mobility, that is, it is movement across the surface of objects, like that of wind, that allows touch to give rise to sensations of hot/cold, wet/dry, heavy/light, smooth/rough, extension, and motion. While it would appear that there is a problem with an immobile being (plant) of only one sense (touch) being associated with the element known for its movement (wind), it is significant here that the association of plants with wind is not direct, but mediated by touch – and it is on this point that the connection makes sense. Descriptions of "wind" in the Caraka Saṁhitā say that *vāyu* is the "bearer of the mechanism and the machinery (of the body)" because of its expression in the five *prāṇas* or breaths moving throughout. Thus, wind effects the body's activities as "the controller and the leader" of the body, and because it employs the mind and all the sense organs as "the carrier of the meaning of all the sense-organs, (as) the systematiser of the constituents of the whole body, and (as) the unifyer of the body."[50] In this way, *vāyu* and touch are connected because of their common unifying, ubiquitous, and foundational nature in the body, as well as their common operation of movement across the surface of objects. Touch and plants are then connected because their experience of sensations comes about from full-body contact (think of plant "skin"), and because plants' full-body contact is with the surface of "touched" objects (air, water, soil, and other plants) creating behaviors in plants expressive of the touch experience. Thus, to repeat, it is plants' contact along (or movement across) the surface of objects that allows their "touch" to express the specific sensations attributed to them.

4.2 The *Guṇas* and the *Guṇa* of *Tamas*

What does it mean for plants to be immobile or stationary, *sthāvara, acara,* or *ajaṅgama?* To answer this we need to consult those passages that describe plants in as fulsome a manner as traditional texts are willing to do. We take for example a creation passage from Manu that begins with a discussion of mobile and immobile beings (1.40-41), proceeds to the kinds of births various beings can have including seed- or sprout-born (1.43-46), continues with the kinds of plants there are (1.46-48), and ends with 1.49:

> These (plants) that are surrounded by multiform Darkness *(tamas)*, the result of their acts *(karmahetu,* in former existences), possess internal consciousness and experience pleasure and pain.[51]

This verse is clarified in 1.50 as being about a continuum that is expressed as *saṁsāra* and that has as its highest state the, presumably most perfected, mode of Brahman and as its lowest the, presumably most unperfected, mode of immobile beings just described in the immediately previous verse.

With the word "darkness," the Manu passage suggests another system that is useful in discussing the status of plants as living beings, that is, that they belong to the Hindu classification system of the *guṇas.* The word for darkness used is *tamas,* one of the *guṇas* or strands that compose living beings and that reflect the qualities of *karma* any given being has at the moment. The use of this term for plants in Manu, as well as in other places, opens up the discussion to the role that *guṇas* might play in characterizing plant life and in endowing plants with properties of *karma.*

Important in classical Sāṁkhya and *dharmaśāstra* literature, and in popularly available texts like the Bhagavad Gītā, the *guṇas* are described as distinctive strands or threads making up personalities, uniquely shaped by past *karma* and determinative of present life. The three *guṇas* – *tamas, rajas,* and *sattva* – characterize what are thought to be the three main qualifying elements in the tendencies of living beings, having arisen from the products of their past experiences and creating a continuum from the most unperfected of beings to the most perfected.

Tamas or "darkness" is the quality (1) of heaviness, coarseness, opaqueness, envelopment, impenetrability, indiscernibility, and obstruction; (2) of idleness, inertia, lethargy, sleepiness, slothfulness, procrastination, inattention, despondency, impotence, latency, timidity, and stagnation; (3) of ignorance, lack of intelligence, dullness, stupidity, foolishness, dissoluteness, confusion, and delusion; and (4) of indulgence, infatuation, attachment, craving, and covetousness – and, thus, it is an attribute of being resulting from demeritorious *karma* in the past.[52] While *tama* is a concept known to the Pali canon, its normal usage is to describe a condition of ignorance to be dispelled by the experience of the truth of Buddhist teaching;[53] it is not used to characterize the *kamma* composition of sentient beings. The *guṇa* of *tamas,* then, born of ignorance and causing delusion, is negative and inactive, and is most associated with the properties of water and earth.[54] It clings to one effect of creation without thought to any other, cares not for consequence, and brings delusion *(moha).*[55]

Rajas or "passion" is the quality (1) of energy, initiative, leadership, work, movement, activity, physical exertion, and change;

(2) of unsteadiness, instability, agitation, excitement, fierceness, violence, and domination; (3) of egoism, conceit, pride, arrogance, intolerance, stinginess, aggravation, anger, vengeance, mercilessness, and cruelty; and (4) of lust, attachment, gluttony, and addiction to food, meat, and women.[56] The *guṇa* of *rajas*, then, born of attachment, is positive and overactive, and is most associated with the properties of air and fire.[57] It sees all beings as separate and distinct one from the other, especially the own self, and brings sorrow *(duḥkha)*.[58]

Sattva or "goodness" is the quality (1) of illumination, lightness, cleanliness, self-control, mental vigor, intelligence, learning, studiousness, consciousness, understanding, lack of confusion, and foresight; (2) of equanimity, serenity, contentment, constancy, restraint, forbearance, resoluteness, piety, truth-speaking, vow-taking, devotion to virtue, and practice of non-violence; (3) of attention to right conduct and right speech, humility, non-attachment, and lack of doubt, passion, spite, anger, greed, conceit, envy, and intolerance; and (4) of delight, cheerfulness, compassion, generosity, hospitality, agreeableness, and patience.[59] The *guṇa* of *sattva*, then, characterized by the luminous and pure, is positive and passive, and is most associated with the properties of space, fire, and water.[60] It is marked by renunciation of fruit *(tyaktvā phalaṁ)* and of pleasure and pain, is non-self-centered and sees all beings as undivided one from the other, and brings happiness *(sukha)*.[61] It is, therefore, the *guṇa* associated with compassionate service to others.

These three *guṇas* pervade all living beings, clinging to everything that has been created, and change in proportion over time as the living being's *karma* make-up changes, resulting in a change of body or mount for its *karma*. Thus the proportion of one *guṇa* to the others reflects "the particular nature of the acts and of the knowledge"[62] of the living being.

> Thus (the result) of the threefold action, the whole system of transmigration which (consists) of three classes, (each) with three subdivisions, and which includes all created beings, has been fully pointed out.[63]

In the Sāṁkhya system, specifically, the three *guṇas* are the most important characteristics of primodial nature *(mūlaprakṛti)* "for they pervade the entire manifest world from *buddhi* down to the gross elements." Again, the *guṇas* are distinguished as follows:

> *sattva* – characterized by pleasure *(prīti)* and illumination *(prakāśa)*; it is buoyant *(laghu)* and shining *(prakāśaka)*.
>
> *rajas* – characterized by pain *(aprīti)* and actuation *(pravṛtti)*; it is stimulating *(upaṣṭambhaka)* and moving *(cala)*.
>
> *tamas* – characterized by indifference *(viṣāda)* and restraint *(niyama)*; it is heavy *(guru)* and enveloping *(varṇaka)*.[64]

Over and against "that which is made up of the three *guṇas*...over (and) against the entire manifest and unmanifest world" are the souls or *puruṣas.* The *puruṣas* add nothing to *mūlaprakṛti,* but instead are present in the world as witnesses to its modifications.[65] These modifications of nature begin with *buddhi* (intellect), *ahaṁkāra* (egoity), and *manas* (mind), and move through the five *buddhindriyas* (sense faculties), the five *karmendriyas* (action capacities), the five *tanmātras* (subtle elements), and the five *mahābhūtas* (gross elements).[66] And all these modifications of nature are thoroughly, and throughout, permeated with transmutations of *sattva, rajas,* and *tamas*

Plants As Tamas Beings

Ludo Rocher notes that *tamas* is important in the Dharmśāstras for describing the traditional placement of plants. Plants are among those born into the *tamas* realm of darkness, and as "immovable beings," they are born into the lowest part of this *tamas* realm.[67] This is described in Manu who gives a short list of the beings classed in each of the three categories *(trividha)* that depend upon the three *guṇas*. Among the *tamoguṇin* group are (1) those of the lowest *tamas* state *(tāmasīgati)*, that is, immovable beings *(sthāvara;* plants), insects, fish, snakes, tortoises, cattle, and wild animal; (2) those of the middling *tamas* state, that is, elephants, horses, lions, tigers, boars, and *śūdras* and barbarous peoples; and (3) those of the highest *tamas* state, that is, *cāraṇas, suparṇas, rākṣasas, piśācas,* and hypocrites. Among the *rajoguṇin* group are, among the lowest, people who live by despicable livelihoods and those addicted to drinking and gambling; among the middling, kings and *kṣatriyas;* and among the highest, *gandharvas, apsarases, guhyakas*, and the servants of the gods. And among the *sattvaguṇin* group are, among the lowest, hermits, ascetics, *brāhmaṇas,* and certain deities; among the middling, sacrificers, sages, and the gods; and among the highest, Brahmā, the creators of the universe, and the indiscernible one.[68]

In addition to having the actual attribution of plants as *tamoguṇin* in Manu 1.49 and 12.42, the text describes creation as a process whereby the soul first enters darkness and is there endowed with sense organs but without their functioning. In time, as material development takes place, the first bodies to emerge are those of plants, and then animals:

> 55. When this (soul) has entered *the darkness (tamas),* it remains for a long time united with the organs (of sensation, *indriya),* but performs not its functions.
> 56. When, being clothed with minute particles (only), *it enters into vegetable or animal seed (bījaṁ sthāsnucariṣṇu)*, it then assumes, united (with the fine body), a (new) corporeal frame.
> 57. Thus he, the imperishable one, by (alternately) waking and slumbering, incessantly revivifies and destroys this whole *movable and immovable (carācara)* (creation).[69]

Thus, the appearance of plant-bodies occurs at the beginning of the creation of the world, and their occurrence is in the first emergence from the darkness. Says Parāśara, for example, "Brahmā...in his desire to bring diverse kinds of animates created first the immobile forms – trees (and) shrubs."[70] The suggestion that creation comes out of, and is imbued at the beginning with, darkness is supported by a passage in the Mahābhārata:

> That Intelligence which transcends the three qualities exist in the mind in a pure state of (unmodified) existence alone. The quality of Darkness *(tamo-guṇa),* however, that impels to action, soon pursues it. At that time the Intelligence sets all the senses to action.[71]

Again, in the creation section of the first chapter, Manu states that "plants are surrounded by multiform Darkness *(tamas)*,"[72] a view referring, perhaps, both to the arising of plants out of the darkness at the beginning of a world cycle, and to the cloaking of plants in the *guṇa* of darkness *(tamas)* as a description of their present nature. The view is corroborated in the Caraka Saṁhitā that describes the "many varieties of trees and bushes and so also the diverse kinds of grasses...[as] beclouded...by *tamas* and non-*dharma*."[73] Confirming that this is the normative medical view about plants, Ramachandra Rao declares that plants "are dominated by tamas, and...[because of this] they do not move about."[74]

Lance Nelson notes that the Advaita view on plants as *tamoguṇin* is similar, but not the same, as in other Hindu traditions. When there is mention "of nonhuman species in Advaita literature, they are not...valued as fellow embodiments of spirit...(but instead) are held before us as symbols of the sufferings experienced in *saṁsāra.*" Although bound together within the same cosmic system, the beings in this system are "not a community, but a hierarchy" in which the gods experience great happiness and animals experience great misery.

> As the result of evil *karma,* souls are born as plants, which endure suffering when they are harvested, cooked, and eaten...Trees and other plants...serve as bodies in which the results of sins may be experienced through reincarnation.[75]

Thus, bound in darkness *(tamas)* as a result of past bad deeds, plants and lower animals suffer tremendously more than those beings above them in the hierarchy, for they are "driven into terrible darkness from which it is difficult to escape, as if into a bottomless sea without any raft, without hope of crossing it."[76] This view of plants and suffering is quite different from that suggested by Schmithausen, in the previous chapter, who raises the possibility that, of all beings, plants suffer the least under acts of *hiṁsā* – due presumably to their already dark nature – and that injuring them brings the perpetrator less demerit than injuring other kinds of beings.

Actual descriptions of plant behavior as stationary *(sthāvara)* or immobile make clear the argument that plants may be seen to have most in common with *tamoguṇin* life. The Ācārāṅga Sūtra, for example, says that trees do not leave their places,[77] and the Sūtrakṛtaṅga adds that a tree growing in the forest is so still that a creeper can encircle it.[78] Thus, the *tamas* attributes of idleness, inertia, lethargy, sleepiness, slothfulness, stagnation, inattention, impotence, and laziness appear as apt characterizations of plants' behavior, for they are beings who are rooted to the ground, and who do not move around like active, energetic animals and humans do. This corresponds with Zimmermann's description of the *guṇa* doctrine: "The scale of beings is thus founded on the moral principles of 'error' in the plants, 'incapacity' in the animals, 'contentment' in gods, and 'accomplishment' and 'realization' in men," giving thus a "curve of creation...(rising up) from the plants and animals up to the gods and then...(descending) again to man."[79]

Tamas Beings and Consciousness

The darkness of *tamas* beings is expressed not only in the lack of activity and inertia that plants are observed to exhibit, but also in a darkness of mind that is imputed to them. We noted above that *tamas* is marked, first, by mental qualities of being opaque, enveloped, impenetrable, and indiscernible to others who cannot get to know "what's going on inside" a plant, and, second, by behavior that seems to observers to be dull, stupid, and devoid of intelligence, moral persuasion, and the ability or capacity to make choices. Ramachandra Rao, for example, notes that plants "are dominated by tamas, and (that) therefore they do not move about, nor do they actively cognize the external world."[80]

This understanding of darkness as *tama* as mentally obscured, and obscuring, is reflected in several early Buddhist texts. The Sutta Nipāta, for example, notes that there "is darkness *(tama)* for those who are enveloped (in ignorance); (there is) blackness for those who do not see. But for the good, who see, it is uncovered like a light."[81] Moreover, he alone attains to joy *(rati)* who has "dispelled the darkness *(tama)* (of ignorance)."[82] Again from the Sutta Nipāta, "[Arrived at downfall], (going) from womb to womb, from darkness to darkness *(tamā tamaṁ)*, that (one)... being of such a kind goes to misery, when he has passed away;"[83] and "if no man were ever to disperse defilements *(kilesa)*...the whole world, enveloped, would be darkness *(tama)* indeed."[84] Moreover, that the goal of early Buddhism is to get rid of the darkness of ignorance and to arise into the light of knowledge is reflected in the title the Buddha has as the "thruster-away of darkness" *(tamonuda)*.[85] This then leads to various Buddhist categories of beings: 1) those who live in darkness and are bound for darkness; 2) those who live in darkness and are bound for light; 3) those who live in light and are bound for darkness; and 4) those who live in light and are bound for light.[86]

While the above descriptions of those living in darkness *(tama)* normally apply to human beings in early Buddhist texts, we do have some evidence that the tradition identifies plants and trees as beings who are not self-conscious or conscious of self-differentiation. Again, in the Sutta Nipāta, for example, we are asked to "[Consider grass and trees *(tiṇarukkha)*. Although they do not profess] (any difference) *(na cāpi paṭijānare)*, their distinguishing mark *(liṅga)* arises from their species"[87] – a suggestion that plants themselves do not have discriminating faculties that would allow them to differentiate among themselves, and that observation of the differences among plants is noticed only by other beings who are able to see plants' distinguishing marks. Another passage, this from the Visuddhimagga, suggests that plants and grasses are not conscious of self. Here the analogy is made between grasses growing out of anthills and hairs growing out of the head, or between grasses growing in the squares of empty villages and hairs growing out of skin. Just as the hairs growing out of the head or growing out of the skin do not know "we grow on...skin that envelops the skull" (or) "we grow on...skin that envelops the body," so grasses growing on ant hills or on squares of empty villages do not know "we are growing on the top of an ant-hill (or) we grow on the square in an empty village." In this way hairs, and therefore plants, are "without thought, [morally] indeterminate, void, and not a living being."[88]

We see here, then, some consensus for a claim that plant behavior does not exhibit external and observable marks of conscious or self-conscious activity, due, as text suggests, to that aspect of *tamoguṇin* endowment that is reflected in dullness, stupidity, denseness, obtuseness, stolidness, and absence of mental activity. With this in mind, we remember what has been attributed above to plants and trees in terms of consciousness and find that, primarily in the *dharmaśāstra* and medical texts, there is a claim that plants have an inner or interior consciousness *(antaḥ-saṁjñā)* and a hidden or unmanifest intelligence *(avyakta-cetanā)*. This claim has been made by Ramachandra Rao, and is found in such texts as Manu[89] and Parāśara.[90]

One way of understanding the claim for an interior consciousness in plants can be found in discussions of the Jain Tattvārtha Sūtra's two categories of living beings, based on the positing of two types of mind: the physical *(dravya-manas)* and the psychical *(bhāva-manas)*. The physical mind, it is thought, "could be equated with the brain of the living beings which is a material mass of complex nature due to specific karmic causes including the physique (body)-making karma of limbs and minor limbs." The psychical mind, on the other hand, though being of a material nature because of its support by the material brain, has much more subtle and "much finer constituents in the form of energy. It is biological information energy" related to the "destruction-cum-subsidence" qualities of specific *karma* – that is, "to the partial elimination and partial suppression of the karma which obscures articulate knowledge" – and "allows the physical mind to function in the desired direction."[91] Of the major division of living beings relating to minds, the first category, those possessing both physical *(dravya)* and psychical *(bhāva)* minds, thus "mind-possessing," covers only some five-sensed beings, while the second category, those possessing only the psychical *(bhāva)* mind, thus "non-mind-possessing," covers the rest of the five-sensed beings, and all the one- to four-sensed beings, including plants and trees.

This would account, first, for the belief that plants as *tamas* beings do not exhibit *overt signs* of consciousness, such as some five-sensed beings do, but that they do carry some, as Jaini says, "residue of qualities that define the soul: perception, knowledge, energy, bliss, and so on."[92] Or as Dundas notes, "plants...are also regarded by Jainism as possessing a form of consciousness and awareness of their surroundings in common with those of animals and humans."[93] To have (only) psychical mind abilities, as plants have according to the Tattvārtha Sūtra, means then that the being has "the resultant effects of the evergoing karmic accumulation and dripping processes associated with the embodied soul."

> The karma theory indicates the volitions to be the resultant effects of earlier earned or current feeling producing (pleasure, pain) and deluding (passions and instincts) karmas. In addition, it also adds that all these volitions cause the influx of newer karmas for carry-over results.[94]

While we make no claim that this view about plants and inner consciousness and volitions is in any way a common one in Indian traditions, it does allow us, first, to put together some fragmented claims made about plants, *tamas,* and consciousness and, second, to lead naturally into a discussion of plants and *karma*.

Endnotes :

1 See AU 5.3; ChūḷU 17; GU 2; VU 3; RU 5; Gītā 13.26.

2 See ŚveU 3.18 *(sthāvara/cara).*

3 VS 22.29; TS 1.8.13.3; MS 3.12.10; 163.12; KS 15.3.

4 See TS 7.4.13.1; TB 3.12.7.2; TĀ 1.11.4.

5 ŚB 1.8.3.15; Eggeling, *Śatapatha Brāhmaṇa* 1.242, quoting Vājasaneyi Saṁhitā 2.16 and following. See also ŚB 5.1.3.3.

6 ŚB 2.3.1.10; Eggeling, *Śatapatha Brāhmaṇa* 1.329.

7 AĀ 2.3.2.

8 Manu 1.41; Bühler, *Laws of Manu,* p. 15.

9 Manu 11.236; Bühler, *Laws of Manu,* p. 478 (verse no. 237 in translation).

10 Manu 5.44; Bühler, *Laws of Manu,* p. 175; see Schmidt, "Origin of *Ahiṁsā,*" p. 631.

11 E.g., Mbh 12.9.16; 12.15.22; 12.100.15; 12.169.23; 12.177.6; 12.225.1, 2; 12.231.32; 12.290.102; 12.326.66; 12.328.52; 12.336.30; Roy, *Mahābhārata* 8.14, 25, 226; 9.7, 28, 188, 192; 10.417, 555, 573, 311.

12 Gītā 10.39; 11.7, 43; 13.26.

[13] Rām (Araṇyakāṇḍa) 3.63.23; Pollock, *Rāmāyaṇa* 3.226.

[14] CS Chikitsāsthānam, vs. 6; Sūtrasthāna, vs.36; Sharma, *Caraka Saṁhitā* 2.365; 1.166-167.

[15] *Paccakkhāmi savvaṁ pāṇāivāyaṁ, se suhumaṁ vā bāyaraṁ vā tasaṁ vā thāvaraṁ vā.* ĀS 2.15.1.1; Jacobi, *Jaina Sūtras* 1.202; see the discussion of comparable materials in the Ācārāṅga Bhāṣyam: 9.1.12: *puḍhaviṁ ca āukāyaṁ, teukāyaṁ ca vāukāyaṁ ca. paṇagāiṁ bīya-hariyāiṁ, tasakāyaṁ ca savvaso ṇaccā.* Bhāṣyam Verse 12: "In the first chapter, the order of the six classes of living beings was somewhat differently described. Lichens, seeds and sprouts are the varieties of vegetation." Tulsi, *Acharanga Bhasyam*, p. 511.

[16] *Tasathāvarāduhī.* ĀS 2.16.4; see also UD 25.23; SK 2.1.52; 2.2.5.

[17] SK 2.7.6; Jacobi, *Jaina Sūtras* 2.421-422. See SK 2.7.6-14, for the full discussion on birth in either of these two modes.

[18] 9.1.14: *adu thāvarā tasattāe, tasajīvā ya thāvarattāe. adu savvajoṇiyā sattā, kammuṇā kappiyā puḍho bālā.* Tulsi, *Acharanga Bhasyam*, p. 512.

[19] SK 2.7.35; Jacobi, *Jaina Sūtras* 2.433.

[20] Tulsi, *Acharanga Bhasyam*, p. 251.

[21] See discussions in the Ācārāṅga Bhāṣyam, Tulsi, *Acharanga Bhasyam*, p. 249. Studies in the Tattvārtha Sūtra note that the "Śvetāmbara canons mention air and fire (water also) to be mobiles. It seems this is a pre-karmic theory concept;" Jain, *Biology in Jaina Treatise on Reals*, p. 99.

[22] Taken from Jain, *Biology in Jaina Treatise on Reals*, p. 31; see also passages in Quarnstrom, *Yogaśāstra of Hemacandra*, pp. 24, 35, 95 (1.20; 2.21; 4.107) that uses *trasa-sthāvara* for the mobile-immobile distinction.

[23] TAS 2.12: *saṁsāriṇas trasa-sthāvaraḥ;* "the worldly souls are further classified as mobile and immobile beings;" Tatia, *Tattvārtha Sūtra*, p. 41; see also Jaini, *Jaina Path of Purification*, p. 173.

[24] TAS 2.13: *pṛthivy-ambu-vanaspatayaḥ sthāvarāḥ;* "the earth bodied, water-bodied and plant-bodied souls are immobile beings;" variant: *pṛthivy-ap-tejo-vāyu-vanaspatayaḥ sthāvarāḥ;* "the earth-bodied, water-bodied, fire-bodied, air-bodied and plant-bodied souls are immobile beings;" Tatia, *Tattvārtha Sūtra*, p. 41. Although note TAS 2.14: *tejo-vāyū dvīndriyādayaś ca trasāḥ;* "fire and air, as well as those with two or more senses, are mobile beings;" and its variant: *dvīndriyādayas trasāḥ;* "those with two or more senses are mobile beings;" Tatia, *Tattvārtha Sūtra*, p. 42. Using studies on the Tattvārtha

Sūtra, Tatia (p. 42) notes that only "beings with at least two senses are genuinely mobile creatures...the fire-bodied and air-bodied do not move of their own accord and as such, truly speaking, do not belong to the class of mobile creatures."

25 Taken from Jain, *Biology in Jaina Treatise on Reals*, pp. 99-100.

26 Taken from Jain, *Biology in Jaina Treatise on Reals*, pp. 32, 100, 101.

27 Buddhist tradition: e.g., Sn 146, 629; S 1.141; 4.117, 351; 5.393. Jain tradition: e.g., UD 35.8-9: *Na sayaṁ gihāiṁ kuvvijjā ṇeva annehiṁ kārae / gihakammasamārambhe bhūyāṇaṁ dissae vaho // tasāṇaṁ thāvarāṇaṁ ca suhumāṇaṁ bādarāṇa ya / tamhā gihasamārambhaṁ saṁjao parivajjae /* Jacobi, *Jaina Sūtras* 2.204.

28 Schmithausen, *Problem of the Sentience of Plants*, pp. 60-61, 76n, 99n.

29 *Ye keci pāṇabhūt' atthi / tasā vā thāvarā anavasesā / dīghā vā ye mahantā vā / majjhimā rassakā aṇukathūlā / diṭṭhā vā ye vā addiṭṭhā, / ye ca dūre vasanti avidūre, / bhūtā vā sambhavesī vā — / sabbe sattā bhavantu sukhitattā;* Sn 146-147; Norman, *Group of Discourses*, p. 24.

30 Sn 629; Norman, *Group of Discourses*, p. 106.

31 *Nikkhittadaṇḍo tasathāvaresu.* S 1.141. Says C. A. F. Rhys Davids in a note to the translation: "Even if he use a staff *(daṇḍa*...staff...used symbolically for force), he has no will to injure with it." Rhys Davids' translation is: "All force renouncing toward both weak and strong." *Kindred Saying* 1.178, 178n. S 4.117; Woodward, *Kindred Sayings* 4.74.

32 S 4.350-351; Woodward, *Kindred Sayings* 4.252-253. See also S 5.393.

33 Thera 876.

34 J 5.221.

35 Schmithausen, *Problem of the Sentience of Plants*, pp. 61-62.

36 Dh 405; Carter and Palihawadana, *Dhammapada*, pp. 404-405.

37 Ross and Palihawadana, *Dhammapada*, p.405.

38 Jain, *Biology in Jaina Treatise on Reals*, p. 97.

39 Bidwell, *Plant Physiology*, p. 3.

40 *Paśavo mūlā oṣadhayo mūlinyaste paśavo mūlā oṣadhīrmūlinorjagdhvāpaḥ pītvā tata eṣa rasaḥ sambhavati.* ŚB 2.3.1.10; Eggeling, *Śatapatha Brāhmaṇa* 1.329.

41 Manu 5.29; Bühler, *Laws of Manu*, p. 173.

[42] Manu 11.240; Bühler, *Laws of Manu*, p. 478 (verse no. 241 in translation).

[43] Manu 5.40; Bühler, *Laws of Manu*, p. 175.

[44] Para 1.2; Sircar and Sarkar, *Parāśara*, p. 3.

[45] Schmithausen, *Problem of the Sentience of Plants*, p. 65. See also, pp. 75-76; *Plants as Sentient Beings*, p. 21.

[46] Schmithausen, *Problem of the Sentience of Plants*, p. 63.

[47] Jain, *Biology in Jaina Treatise on Reals*, pp. 31-32; see TAS 2.12, 13, 14 and their variants in Tatia, *Tattvārtha Sūtra: That Which Is*, pp. 41-42. Fire and air-bodies can be classified, alternately, among the mobile beings.

[48] Jain, *Biology in Jaina Treatise on Reals*, pp. 99, 100, 101.

[49] Krishnamurthy, *Source Book of Indian Medicine*, p. 195.

[50] Krishnamurthy, *Source Book of Indian Medicine*, p. 135.

[51] Manu 1.49; Bühler, *Laws of Manu*, p. 16.

[52] Mbh 12.239.22, 25; Manu 12.26-51, 95; CS Śārīrasthānam 39; Sharma, *Caraka Saṁhitā* 1.438; Sharma, *Source Book of Indian Medicine*, pp. 75, 111, 152, 193, 491. Included among philosophies founded on *tamas*, for example, are all "those traditions...and all those despiccable systems of philosophy, which are not based on the Veda, (and) produce no reward after death." Manu 12.95; Bühler, *Laws of Manu*, p. 505.

[53] Sn 278, 348, 763, 956, 1133, 1135; D. 3.233; S 1.93; A 2.85; It 32, 108; Mil 1, 21; Vbh 367.

[54] Sharma, *Source Book of Indian Medicine*, pp. 151, 153, 501.

[55] Mbh 12.187.25; Gītā 18.7, 22, 25, 32, 35, 39.

[56] Mbh 12.239.21, 24; CS Śārīrasthānam 38; Sharma, *Caraka Saṁhitā* 1.437-438; Sharma, *Source Book of Indian Medicine*, pp. 75, 111, 152, 193, 491.

[57] Sharma, *Source Book of Indian Medicine*, pp. 151, 153, 501.

[58] Mbh 12.187.29; Gītā 18.8, 21, 24, 27, 31, 34, 38.

[59] Mbh 12.239.20, 23; Gītā 18.9-10; CS Śārīrasthānam 37; Sharma, *Caraka Saṁhitā* 1.436-437; Sharma, *Source Book of Indian Medicine*, pp. 75, 111, 152, 193, 491.

[60] Sharma, *Source Book of Indian Medicine*, pp. 151, 153, 501.

[61] Mbh 12.187.29; Gītā 18.9, 20, 23, 26, 30, 33, 37.

[62] Manu 12.41; Bühler, *Laws of Manu*, p. 493.

[63] Manu 12.51; Bühler, *Laws of Manu*, p. 495.

[64] Larson, *Classical Sāṁkhya*, p. 175.

[65] Larson, *Classical Sāṁkhya*, p. 183.
[66] Larson, *Classical Sāṁkhya*, p. 183.
[67] Rocher, "Karma and Rebirth in the Dharmaśāstras," p. 66. This low section of *tamoguṇin* life includes immovable beings, worms and insects, fish, snakes, tortoises, domestic beasts, and wild beasts.
[68] Manu 12.42-50; Bühler, *Laws of Manu*, pp. 493-495. See the tabulation in Rocher, "Karma and Rebirth in the Dharmaśāstras," p. 66.
[69] Manu 1.55-57; Bühler, *Laws of Manu*, pp. 17-18. My italics.
[70] *Brahmā...sisṛkṣu vividha prajāḥ / agre sasaṁja stāvarātmāno vṛkṣavīrudhaḥ*; Sircar and Sarkar, *Parāśara*, p. 3.
[71] Mbh 12.187.28ff.; Roy, *Mahābhārata* 9.51.
[72] Manu 1.49; Bühler, *Laws of Manu*, p. 16.
[73] Sharma, *Source Book of Indian Medicine*, p. 195.
[74] Ramachandra Rao, *Encyclopedia of Indian Medicine* 2.151
[75] Nelson, "Dualism of Nondualism," p. 67, quoting the Brahma Sūtra with Śāṅkara's Bhāṣya 2.1.34; 3.1.24.
[76] Nelson, "Dualism of Nondualism," p. 68, quoting the Chāndogya Upaniṣad with Śāṅkara's Bhāṣya.
[77] AS 1.6.1.1.
[78] KS 1.3.2.10.
[79] Zimmermann, *Jungle & the Aroma of Meats*, p. 212.
[80] Ramachandra Rao, *Encyclopedia of Indian Medicine* 2.151.
[81] Sn 763; Norman, *Group of Discourses*, p. 127.
[82] Sn 956; Norman, *Group of Discourses*, p. 156.
[83] Sn 278; Norman, *Group of Discourses*, p. 48.
[84] Sn 348; Norman, *Group of Discourses*, p. 58.
[85] Sn 1133, 1136; It 32, 108, Mil 1, 21.
[86] D 3.233; A 2.85; S 1.93. These passages describes these categories as they are applied to different groups of human beings.
[87] Sn 601; Norman, *Group of Discourses*, p. 104.
[88] Vism 353; Ñāṇamoli, *Path of Purification*, p. 349.
[89] Manu 1.49.
[90] Sircar and Sarkar, *Parāśaṛa*, pp. 2, 4.
[91] Tatia, *Tattvārtha Sūtra: That Which Is*, p. 41; Dixit, *Sukhlalji's Commentary on the Tattvārtha Sūtra*, pp. 85-87. Jain, *Biology in Jaina Treatise on Reals*, p. 96. Or, the distinction between the physical and psychical mind are described as, in the first case, the "perceptible attribute of potential and functional consciousness," and in the second the "five psychical volitions based on manifestable forms of different karmas." While mind-possessing beings have both of these

categories -- psychical volitions and functional consciousness (physical brain) — non-mind-possessing beings have only one, psychical volitions; Jain, *Biology in Jaina Treatise on Reals*, p. 30.

92 Jaini, *Jaina Path of Purification*, p. 111.

93 Dundas, *The Jains*, p. 90.

94 Jain, *Biology in Jaina Treatise on Reals*, p. 44.

5

Plant *Karma*: Borderline Beings

Harold Coward has suggested that "a helpful and ethically responsible answer as to how humans ought to interact with the environment can be generated from *karma* theory." This might be useful, be argues, because *karma* theory rejects the dualism between nature and humans, finding "no radical separation between humans and other forms of beings" and, instead, "binds humans into (a) continuity with natural processes."[1] With this in mind, we note that, in traditions like Buddhism, a number of ways are given to describe natural relationships and causal patterns, one of which deals with *karma.* Such laws cover a variety of "different realms: physical or seasonal laws *(utu-niyāma)*, biological or seed laws *(bīja-niyāma)*, moral laws *(kamma-niyāma)*, psychological laws *(citta-niyāma)*, and liberational laws *(dhamma-niyāma)*."[2] The possibility that plants might be governed by more than just physical and/or biological laws is of significance in developing an overall ecological theory, for if plants are governed, in addition, by laws of *karma*, this would lay the foundation for their governance by the laws next in sequence, that is, by psychological and then by spiritual laws. Understanding the full parameters of the *karma* network for environmental purposes becomes important, then, not just for humans to see their *karma* relationship to, and therefore responsibility for, the plant world, but for plants to be understood as *karma* beings in their relation to the world of human beings.

To raise the issue of *karma* with regard to plants, however, is to raise questions about whether plant bodies are physically equipped to be mounts of *karma*, whether there is "individuality" or "selfhood" in plants, whether they are conscious, whether they can be ignorant, whether they can have desires and attachments, and whether they can have a religious practice. We won't have final answers for these questions, but to raise them, at least, is to have them in mind as we make our way through materials from the three traditions that might be helpful in understanding the complexity of Indian views on plants.

As Eliot Deutsch has noted,[3] *karma* is a "convenient fiction," through which we observe causes and effects in our experience and project them onto a moral sphere. Because we note that actions produce results, we assume that we can produce a certain result by choosing a certain action; when results differ, we account for these differences by noting that the antecedent actions chosen are different. Thus, differences among people, animals, and presumably plants, can be accounted for by different choices made by the "agents" at some earlier time, that is, by differences in their *karmas*.[4]

To make best use of Coward's suggestion, then, we need to consider the degree to which plants, belonging as they do to the same ecological network as human beings, are included within the same systems of laws. If the possibility of plants being subject to laws of *karma* can be entertained, we must note, first, that (1) *karma* posits a system of cause and effect, within which: (2) there are lives that are embodied,[5] (3) there are differences among living bodies, (4) there are changes observed in the life patterns of bodies over time, (5) there are behaviors that suggest choices are being made according to recognizable rules, and (6) there are consequences of these choices that are observable in embodied lives. From the materials recorded earlier that describe plant behavior, we need to make a case, second, for these elements being present in plant lives. And, third, we can see what happens when we "project" a pattern of *karma* onto plant lives, as we do onto human lives, and thus, project the notion (1) that an individual life stream extends over multiple embodied lives, (2) that these embodied lives are connected and have recognizable rationales for the ways in which they appear, and (3) that this rationale is based on knowledge of specific choices that are made in relation to recognized valuations of these choices. Proving the presence of such a scheme in human life is a task indeed; but doing so for plants is even greater. Nevertheless, some Indian traditions do posit *karma* as operative for plants. The rule of the subsequent laws in plant lives, however – those of the mind and of spiritual cultivation – are much more tenuous.

5.1 Plants in Systems of Rebirth

We now turn to specific systems of rebirth, many of which allow for the possibility of rebirth in a plant body. First, however, we must note that there are some systems, particularly Buddhist, that declare quite explicitly that plants are not included in *karma* and rebirth. As Padmasiri de Silva says of Buddhism, "plants have not been integrated into the doctrine of *kamma* and rebirth,"[6] and Harvey notes that early "Buddhist texts...do not say that it is possible to be reborn as a plant, or for a plant to be reborn, and later texts explicitly deny this."[7] In the Dīgha and Majjhima Nikāyas, for example, there are four categories of birth *(yoni):* egg-born *(aṇḍaja)*, womb-born *(jalāja)*, moisture-born *(saṁsedaja)*, and spontaneously arisen *(opapātika)*.[8] And while the first two categories clearly omit plants up front, the second two might work. Moisture-born beings, however, include those arising out of rotting rice, fish, corpses or out of dirty pools of water, and spontaneously-arisen beings include devas, hell-beings, some humans, and some despondent beings. Thus, by gloss, the last two categories specifically exclude plants as well.

Again, in all four Nikāyas, there is a system of destinies *(gatis)* that enumerate five realms where, presumably, *karma* beings can be reborn: hell realm *(niraya)*, animal realm *(tiracchāna-yoni)*, ancestral realm *(pettivisaya)*, human realm *(manussa)*, and divine realm *(deva)*.[9] The only possible place for plant rebirth would be in the animal realm, but glossing passages, again, say nothing about the possibility of anything other than animals being included in this category.[10]

Lastly, in the Milindapañho, there are three kinds of origin, birth through *karma (kammajā)*, birth through cause *(hetujā)*, and birth through physical change *(utujā)*. Only those beings who are considered to be conscious *(sacetana)* are placed in the *karma*-born category, while fire *(aggi)* and all seed-born *(bījajāta)* beings, i.e., plants, are born of cause, and earth, mountains, wind, and water are said to be born of physical change.[11]

Turning to other traditions, particularly Hinduism and Jainism, however, we find that there is more openness in them to the inclusion of plants within the system of *karma*. We have already seen that, in the Vedic period, plants are often included in the cycle traversed by the dead, or parts of the dead person's body, as they move through the natural world to be reborn on earth once again. An important passage here is RV 10.16.3 where, during the cremation ritual, the dead person hears the priest intone: "May your eye go to the sun, your life's breath to the wind. Go to the sky or to earth, as is your nature; or go to the waters, if that is your fate. Take root in the plants with your limbs."[12] Again, in the Taittirīya Saṁhitā, as breath leaves the dead person's body, he is encouraged to "go to heaven by the paths which lead to the gods; be among the plants with thy members."[13] In both of these, and in other cases, then, plants accept parts of the dead into their own bodies in a continuing cycle of death giving rise to new life.

Another theme in the Vedic period involving plants and rebirth centers on the idea of action-bearing-corresponding-fruit that Schmidt argues, is one of the earliest appearances of plants in a proto-*karma* network. This idea occurs in the ritual context, where we find the "belief that the animal whose meat is eaten in this world will eat, in return, the eater in the next world,"[14] for, as Manu notes: "Me he...will devour in the next (world), whose flesh I eat in this (life)."[15] Thus, the act of ritually consuming some food in this world will result in being consumed by that very same being in the next world – a causal process that works even in the case of vegetable matter, for "a plant which was eaten (then)...is now eating the eater."[16] Although the context is the *śrauta* ritual, and not specifically the *karma* network, there is agency attributed here to plants (as the present eater of the former eater), and there is participation attributed to plant "action" within the interchange of cause and effect.

In a different version of the types of births that beings can have, the Chāndogya Upaniṣad proposes three categories: the egg-born *(aṇḍaja)*, the live-born *(jīvaja)*, and the sprout-born *(udbhijja)*,[17] and in its wake, the Aitareya Upaniṣad proposes four categories. The passage in the latter describes a world with divine powers, the five elements, and beings that are moving *(jaṅgama)*, flying *(patatrin)*, and stationary *(sthāvara)*. It also names four types of origins for these beings: the egg-born *(aṇḍaja)*, the womb-born *(jarāuja or Jāruja)*, the sweat-born *(svedaja)*, and the sprout-born *(udbhijja)*. This list corresponds in three parts to the Buddhist list – egg-born, live- or womb-born, and moisture/sweat-born – but instead of spontaneously-arisen *(opapātika)*, the Upaniṣads use sprout-born, clearly a definitive inclusion of the plant kingdom among possible destinies in the process of (re)birth.[18] Keith says of passages such as this that the "idea is seen frequently...where animals, insects, vegetables and gods appear as subject to transmigration."[19] The Aitareya list then becomes somewhat normative, for it is found in other later texts such as the Caraka Saṁhitā.[20]

By the time of the *dharmaśāstra* manuals, plants are indisputably described as bound up in the *karma* system. In the first chapter of Manu, for example:

> 40. Small and large worms and beetles, moths, lice, flies, bugs, all stinging and biting insects and the several kinds of immovable things *(sthāvara)*.
> 41. Thus was this whole (creation), both the immovable and the movable *(sthāvarajaṅgama)*, produced by those high-minded ones by means of austerities *(tapas)* and at my command, (each being) according to (the results of) its actions *(karma)*.
> 42. But whatever act *(karma)* is stated (to belong) to (each of) those creatures *(bhūta)* here below, that I will truly declare to you, as well as their order in respect to birth *(janman)*.[21]

These verses are then followed by three verses describing the womb-born (43), the egg-born (44), and the hot moisture-born (45), and are then followed by four verses focusing on plants *(oṣadhi)* – three of these (46-48) differentiate among kinds of plants, and the fourth (49) gives the important canonical view about the nature of plants:

> 49. These (plants) which are surrounded by multiform Darkness *(tamas)*, the result of their acts *(karmahetu;* in former

> existences), possess internal consciousness *(antaḥsaṁjñā)* and experience pleasure and pain *(sukhaduḥkhasamanvita)*.[22]

We then progress a few more verses into Manu's narrative of creation, and find the following description of what happens at the beginning of the world:

> 55. When this (soul) has entered darkness *(tamas)*, it remains for a long time united with the organs (of sensation; *indriya)*, but performs not its functions; it then leaves the corporeal frame.
> 56. When, being clothed with minute particles (only), it enters into vegetable or animal seed *(bījaṁ sthāsnucariṣṇu)*, it then assumes, united (with the fine body), a (new) corporeal frame.
> 57. Thus he, the imperishable one, by (alternately) waking and slumbering, incessantly revivifies and destroys this whole movable and immovable *(carācara;* creation).[23]

Thus, this section of Manu's first chapter places plants without any doubt right in the middle of the system of *karma.* First, plant bodies are embedded with full and equal place in a grouping that consists of all the other animate bodies known in nature, and are allocated to one of the normative classification systems of this grouping that assigns bodies to different birth types. Second, plants belong to whatever causal network there is that imbues the context of these bodies with life, such that the shapes of their present lives are the results of actions in the past. Third, plants are part of the hierarchy resulting from the arrangement of present bodies arising out of past actions and, in this hierarchy, plants occupy a low place but a place in which they can and do exhibit great variety of form. Fourth, as a result of past actions, plants are now encased in "multiform darkness" in which they, like other bodies, experience pleasure and pain, but, unlike other bodies, have only internal consciousness. And, fifth, the darkness that plants are encased in is homologous to the darkness present just as a new creation cycle is to begin, when the imperishable one is "sleeping," and when the sense faculties are present but not functioning. And it is out of this darkness, in the imperishable one's awakening, that fine and gross bodies emerge, beginning with vegetable and (then) animal bodies, and revivifying the whole world of immobile and mobile beings. With this account, there is no question that, in this tradition at least, plants belong to the traditional Hindu system of *karma*.

Like the Hindu tradition, the Jain tradition provides a place for plants in the system of rebirth: the category that plants are in is the "one-sensed non-mobiles" and these "non-mobiles (1-sensed) [are what they are] due to the fruition of the karma of non-mobiles."[24] According to the Sūtrakṛtāṅga:

> Immovable beings are called so, when they get this character through the taking effect of the Karman relating to immovable beings. But when their duration of life as an immovable being comes to its close, the (soul), embodied in an immovable being, leaves its life as such and takes again a new form of existence... Beings belong to the Circle of Births, though they be (now) immovable beings, they will (some time) become movable ones, and though they be movable beings, they will become immovable ones.[25]

Moreover, as commentaries on Tattvārtha Sūtra 8.2 note, all "life-spanned" entities intake *karma* while non-life-spanned entities do not bind *karma;* a life-spanned entity is a *jīva* and the word *jīva*, "'living'...refers to all the varieties of the living world beginning from observable one-sensed to five-sensed ones."[26] And in the Yogaśāstra of Hemacandra the inclusion of plants in the rebirth cycle is made eminently clear: "Medicinal herbs *(oṣadhi),* beasts, trees *(vṛkṣa),* [other] animals and birds, which are killed for the sake of sacrifice, later on become reborn in high [birthplaces] *(prāptāḥ prāpnuvanty ucchritiṁ punaḥ).* "[27]

One way the Jain system includes plants as *karma*-bound is, in the system of destinies *(gati),* by reinterpreting the *tiryañca* category as not just animals, but as animals and plants. The Jain system of *gatis,* then, is four-fold – gods *(devas),* humans *(manuṣya),* hell beings *(nāraki),* and plants and animals *(tiryañca)* – a system symbolized in the four-pronged *svastika* design representing the well being of the whole creation.[28] In this four-fold classification, the *tiryañca* category represents "the lowest of possible destinies, characterized by extremely gross sensory activity and pervasive ignorance,"[29] and is said to be the result of past deceitfulness.[30] As noted previously, in the Jain view, plant-beings *(vanaspati-kāya),* in the *tiryañca* category, may appear in one of two types of embodiment: either in an individual embodiment *(pratyeka)* or in a collective embodiment *(sādhāraṇa),* and Jaini gives, as an example of collective embodiment, the possibility that a particular tree may be made up of, not one, but many souls.[31]

A second view of the place of plants in Jainism is as one of the three types of birth processes: "by agglutination of material particles, by the womb and by descent" *(sammūrchana-garbho-papātā janma).*[32] Plants belong in the first category, for those born by agglutination of material particles include all those beings with one through four senses, and some five-sensed beings.[33] In birth through the "agglutination of material particles," it is thought that the soul takes on material particles that are located at its place of birth and, through *karma,* converts them into an agglutinated body.[34]

The Tattvārtha Sūtra states that there are five types of bodies:

1. the gross – the visible physical body made from clusters of material
2. the protean – "made of clusters of matter with various supernatural powers"
3. the conveyance – "made from clusters of matter that are auspicious, white and pure," and normally used by an ascetic in the course of spiritual practices
4. the fiery – "made of fiery particles...(and) a permanent possession of the worldly soul," and normally used for digestion of food
5. the karmic – "made from suitable clusters of matter...(and) the 'basket' that holds all the karmic particles of the soul.. (as well as) the seed from which all bodies are grown by the soul."[35]

In Jainism, *karma* "is itself actual *matter,*"[36] "an aggregate of extremely fine matter which is imperceptible to the senses."[37] Tattvārtha commentaries note that the *karma* body "is a mattergic entity causing the living being to wander in the world," with death being the "fruition of current life-span karma"[38] and birth being the realization of new life-span *karma.* Such bodies are made up of *karmas* or "very fine material particles having (a) 4-touch (hot, cold, positive, negative) character," and large numbers of *karmas,* aggregating together, form an entity "capable of homolocation and mutual contact with the soul," and whose association with the soul allows for transmigration. The five bodies, from one to five, become progressively denser in clusters of matter, so that the *karma* body is the densest, with the most material clusters. While, in the case of plants, the gross body would be the body formed by agglutination, the fiery and *karma* bodies are subtle bodies and, co-existing one with the other, are associated with the soul from the beginning.[39]

> The association of the fiery and karmic bodies with the soul has no beginning in the sense that they are never absent from the soul during its worldly existence. However...(they) are changing from moment to moment and so do have a beginning in the sense that they are constantly becoming something new. Each continues to exist in a sequence of mutual cause and effect, just as a tree follows seed and seed follows tree in an ongoing cycle.[40]

Moreover, the "karmically embodied soul enters the womb at the precise instant of fertilisation," and its component *karmas,* though not equated with genes, have functions that are "very much akin."[41]

The discussion of any particular *saṁsāra* or worldly body – in this case, plants – begins, in Jainism, with views about the bondage *(bandha)* of the soul *(jīva)* through *karma.* According to the Tattvārtha Sūtra 8.2, "bondage is defined as the acquirement of the fine mattergic particles capable of being transformed into karmas due to the association of passions with the living (soul) one."[42] The physical activities of living beings attract particles of *karma* to them and bind the beings to these particles, such that "good actions cause the inflow of beneficial karma" and "evil actions cause the inflow of harmful karma."[43] Thus, bound to particles of *karma*, there is pleasure and pain.[44] There are five causes of bondage by *karma* (wrong view, non-abstinence, laxness, passions, and activity of body, speech, and mind),[45] and four aspects of bondage by *karma* (type or species, duration, fruitional intensity, and "mass of material particles assimilated").[46] Of the aspect of *karma* bondage known as "type or species," there are eights categories: "knowledge-covering, intuition-covering, sensation, deluding, lifespan, body, status, and obstructive."[47] Inhibiting or stopping the inflows *(āsravas)* of *karma* "has two aspects, psychic *(bhāva)* and physical *(dravya)*. Psychic inhibition is when the mind disengages from worldly action. Physical inhibition is when the inflow of *karma* actually ceases because of this mental detachment."[48] Stopping the *karma* inflow of *āsravas* results from various types of careful movement, overcoming hardships, and practicing good conduct, while the unbinding or wearing off of *karmas* comes from their ripening or maturation, from austerities (like fasting),[49] and from the practice of *ahiṁsā,* for non-violence is the greatest and most powerful way that "souls render service to one another."[50] With regard to *ahiṁsā*, "'insistence on life' is a superior moral value to 'insistence on truth' because the nature of truth varies from thinker to thinker but life is an invariable constant that is dear to all."[51]

Within this Jain system, plants can be most specifically understood by looking at two of the eight categories of "type or species" bondage by *karma*, that is, "body *(nāma)*-making *karma*" and "life-span *(āyuḥ)*-making *karma.*" The most prominent here is body-making *karma* for among its forty-two sub-species are such things as non-mobile bodies and various senses – both of which are involved in the placement of plants within the system as a whole.[52] Thus,

> The physique [body] -making karmic sub-species of individual body is defined as that whose realization results in enjoying an individual body formed due to the karma of body by a single living being. This species refers to a single body for the single self.
> The physique [body] -making karmic sub-species of non-mobiles is defined as that whose realization results in the birth as one-sensed living beings with embodiments of earth, water, fire, air and plants.[53]

If plants, then, as one-sensed beings, are non-mobile because of the fruition of the *karma* of non-mobiles, then all "five kinds of non-mobile beings (are) due to the fruition of specific physique making karmas." In this way, particular flowers, for example, arise from "specific karmic realisation of physique-making karma of [a] plant body."[54] Thus, birth location, or the "specific birth of...

living beings has...karmic origin," and, mobileness or immobileness, consequently, depends solely on the realisation of specific *karma*.[55]

Turning to the second pertinent type or species bondage by *karma*, that is, life-span making *karma*, we find commentators on the Tattvārtha Sūtra noting the following:

> Aliveness is defined as non-cessation or continuance of the characteristics of respiration in the living beings due to the operation of longevity-determining karma causing worldly existence. The cessation of aliveness or extirpation of respirations is known as death.[56]

Being *karma*-bearing, then, means being alive – and vice versa – and, for the Tattvārtha, all of the five non-mobiles have four vitalities or attributes that indicate that they are living: (1) the sense-faculty of touch, (2) bodily strength, (3) respiration, and (4) life-span. These four indicate the "livingness" of non-mobiles as do the fact that they intake food and have some form of consciousness, even if it is the lowest form possible among those counted as living. That *karmas* are characterized by having four "touch" attributes, and that touch is one of the attributes of being alive, then, decisively supports the inclusion of touch-possessing plants in the Jain system of *karma*. Moreover, commentaries on the Tattvārtha Sūtra actually give the high end in years of the possible lifespan of plants: "maximum lifespan...of the vegetation-bodied...[is] 10,000 years."[57]

How, then, does this work with plants? The plant seed is a modification of the soul, because becoming embodied in a seed is the fruition of specific body-making *karma* (that is, of one-sensed beings) and specific life-span-making *karma* (that is, of subhuman beings). The living being in the seed becomes a sprout according to the specifics of its body-making and life-span-making *karmas*, and in accord with these takes in food and water from the soil and changes them "into useful components due to energy produced" as a result of specific *karmas* and such things as solar heat. Thus, gradually, the sprout grows.[58]

There is one last point. In its classification of beings into mind-possessing *(samanaskāḥ)* and non-mind-possessing *(amanaskāḥ)*, the Tattvārtha Sūtra locates plants in the latter, characterizing them as not having a physical brain *(dravya-manas)* but as having psychical volitions *(bhāva-manas)*. These psychical volitions, appearing only in the living, are "the resultant effects of the evergoing karmic accumulation...of earlier earned or current feeling producing (pleasure, pain) and deluding (passions and instincts) karmas." It is the goal of Jainism to reduce the volition-caused miseries experienced by beings, by controlling these *karma*-caused volitions.[59] This can be done by destroying the various types of *karma* that have brought the being, whether plant or human, into its present state; thus, liberation occurs when all bondage by *karma* is eliminated.[60]

With these theoretical affirmations of the possibility of plant inclusion in the *karma* system, what can these same traditions tell us about actual rebirth as a plant? There is an early report of rebirth as a plant in the Atharva Veda, that tells of an *asurī* or demoness who takes the shape of a forest tree in order to make a remedy for leprosy.[61] Shakti Gupta records various later Hindu stories: the myth of Parvatī cursing some gods to be reborn as trees; a Gadaba tribal story of five sisters (Mango, Tamarind, Fig, *Jamun,* and Plantain) who are reborn as trees when their husbands run away in fright at the great number of children that they bear; a post-Portuguese legend of an ugly princess who kills herself and produces a tobacco plant from her cremated ashes; and the myth of Tulasī who, in the wake of atrocities committed by her husband, becomes a *satī,* giving rise to the Vaiṣṇava-sacred Tulsī (basil) plant from her pyre.[62] Pandey notes the myth of Sūrya Bai, daughter of the sun, who, to escape persecution from a sorceress, becomes a golden lotus; when the flower is burnt to the ground by the sorceress, a mango tree emerges from the ashes, and from the ripe fruit Sūrya Bai emerges again.[63] And the Majupurias record the folk tale of a minister's daughter becoming a Campaka tree with golden flowers.[64]

The most "authentic evidence" of rebirth as a plant would be personal testimony in which one recalls one's own previous plant rebirths. We know that such recall is believed possible from texts like the Buddhist Dīgha Nikāya where rebirth recall is one of the fruits of life as a recluse:

> He recalls to mind his various temporary states in days gone by – one birth, or two or three or four or five births, or ten or twenty or thirty or forty or fifty or a hundred or a thousand or a hundred thousand births...(saying) "In such a place such was my name, such my family, such my caste, such my food, such my experience of discomfort or of ease, and such the limits of my life. When I passed away from that state, I took form again in such a place..."[65]

Thus, in the Jain Uttarādhyayana, an adept knows that in an "infinite number of...(rebirths) I suffered dreadful pains of body and mind, repeated misery and dangers," and in "every existence I have undergone suffering which was not interrupted by a moment's reprieve."[66] Here an adept identifies himself as a Śālmalī tree[67] and, again, reports that as "a tree I have been felled, slit, sawn into planks, and stripped of the bark by carpenters with axes, hatchets, etc., an infinite number of times."[68] Later the poet Kabir sings of a past life born as a tree: "Scorched by the forest fire, the wood still stands and wails: 'Don't let me fall to the smith! Don't let me burn again!'"[69] Thus, Indian folklore describes rebirth in tree form as full of both pleasure and pain.

5.2 How Plants Might Be *Karma* Beings

We move now to the question of whether plants can be mounts of *karma* and, if so, on what basis such an assertion can be made. In a general sense, plants might be included as *karma* mounts, simply because they are subject to birth, growth, and decay for, as the Ācārāṅga Sūtra says, the "condition of living beings arises from karman."[70] Simply "to live," then, or simply "to be born" may be all that's needed to be designated as "karmically-produced" – that is, to arise from and be reproduced by a "parent organism" and then to be able to give rise to another being dependent on the new parent for life. Because this might put plants in the same conditioned category of production as that of fire arising from fire, crystal arising from crystal, or breeze arising from breeze, however,[71] some other attributes are needed that are separately true of plant generations. Most helpful here would be attributes that fit plant generations and not the more mechanical generations of fires, crystals, or breezes, for example, and that fit also within traditional Indian models posited for the *karma* system. That plants are individual, but immensely diverse in variety, that plants produce offspring like unto themselves, but different from plants of divergent families and lineages, that plants can be injured and then cured and can experience pain and pleasure, that plants respond in manifold and complex ways to the sense stimuli (light, temperature, water, nutrition, and forces of motion) of their environment – all suggest some *karma* process at work. Such observations about "plant being" are clearly suggestive to Jain thinkers, for instance, who attribute life and *karma* to plants, and who are open to a host of rebirth possibilities that include those of plants. From the Sūtrakṛtāṅga come the following verses:

> ...there are...in the world four kinds of seed: seeds generated at the top (of the plant), at its root, at its knots, at its stem. According to the seed and place (of growth) of these plants some beings – born in earth, originated in earth, and grown in earth, having in it their birth, origin, and growth, being impelled by their Karman, and coming forth in it on account of their Karman, growing there in particles of earth, the origin of various things – come forth as trees *(vanaspati)*.
> ...some beings born in trees, originated by trees, sprung from trees...springing from trees that originated in earth, come forth as trees originated by trees. These beings feed on the sap of the trees originated in earth.
> ...some beings born in trees...growing in trees, that are originated by trees, come forth as their roots, bulb, stem, branches, twigs, leaves, flowers, fruits, and seeds. These beings feed on the sap of those trees originated by trees.[72]

The text goes on to attribute the same pattern of growth and reproduction to grass *(tṛṇa)*, herbs *(oṣadhi)*, and greens or vegetables *(hariya/harita)*, which like trees come out of the earth.

Sense-Faculties and Touch as the Basis of Rebirth

To think about plants in the system of *karma* is to think about them in terms of moral causality, in terms of acting in a certain way so as to bring about a certain kind of effect. To be *karma*-bound, then, is to be fruitful as an agent or actor, and to be the producer and the recipient of the fruits of one's work within a context of certain places and over spans of time.[73] This we can do by examining the characteristics attributed to plants beginning, first, with their sentience as one-facultied beings, having the sense of touch – and, in particular, having touch as a foundational sense present, and perhaps functional, at the point of passage of *karma* from one body to another.

In the Hindu tradition, we have noted that touch is often the first or last sense-faculty mentioned in the list of sense-faculties given in texts like the Upaniṣads,[74] suggesting the presence of touch at both the arising and passing on of the person during the process of rebirth. And the Caraka Saṁhitā is clear that sensations associated with touch like hot and cold, coarse and smooth, and hard and soft, are perceived lastly as a person is dying, and that treatment through touch is an especially helpful way both to know that a person is dying, and to help the dying person transit more smoothly on to the next mode of being.[75] Moreover, the Mahābhārata has a passage describing the way that volatile and uncontrolled senses operate through *karma* by "rolling" a being around through myriad rebirths:

> ...the man who is alert to them is seduced by his rapacious senses, as an unconscious driver by vicious, bolting horses. When the...senses each get hold of their objects, then the mind's plan, which has grown from a prior intention, becomes clear through them....Then, pierced by desire...with the arrows of sense objects, he falls into the fire of greed, as the moth falls because of its desire for light....in the runaround, he falls here into womb after womb, spun around like a wheel by ignorance, *karman*, and thirst. He rolls about in creatures, from Brahmā down to a blade of grass, born over and over again, in water, on land, or in the air.[76]

In this way, having senses, and allowing them to run wild, ties one to the karmic system – "from Brahmā down to a blade of grass"– and results in the continuation of *saṁsāra.*

In the Jain tradition, the Ācārāṅga Sūtra describes the process of dying as follows:

> ...the life of some mortals...is shortened. For when with the deterioration of the perceptions of the ear, eye, organs of smelling, tasting, touching, a man becomes aware of the decline of life, they (the sense-faculties) after a time produce dotage.[77]

Here touch is noted as the last of the sense-faculties to go into decline as the person moves through old age toward death. Moreover, when a questioner in the Tattvārtha tradition asks how the sense of touch originates at the beginning of life, the answer is given that the "manifestation of the first sense of touch...(is) due to many concurrent karmic causes,"[78] suggesting that the sense of touch appears immediately out of the contingencies of *karma* present as a new life takes shape. Again, the text notes that of all the senses "the sense of touch...(is the only one) pervasive of the whole body of the individual" and, as it is the "first sense, (it is found) in plants...(and) is pervasive in all the living beings."[79]

Akalaṅka's commentary on the Tattvārtha Sūtra goes on to state, first, that the very fine material particles or *karmas* that make up *karma*-bound bodies have four attributes of touch: temperature (hot and cold) and positive and negative qualities. Large numbers of touch-characterized *karmas* then aggregate together and form entities "capable of homolocation and mutual contact with the soul."[80] It notes, second, that because to be *karma*-bearing means to be alive, and because all of the five non-mobiles (including plants) have the four vitalities that indicate they are living (the sense-faculty of touch, bodily strength, respiration, and life-span), these vitalities demonstrate the "livingness" of the five non-mobiles who, possessing touch, are located at the beginning of the living scale of beings. And, "plants are placed in the (beginning) end because they grow with the help of all the earth, water," and so forth.[81] The characterization of *karmas* as having four 'touch' attributes, then, and the inclusion of touch as one of the four "livingness" attributes, provide support for the inclusion of touch-possessing plants in the Jain system of *karma*.

For early Buddhists, the role that "touch" might have in determining the *kamma* properties of plants is found, first, in the ways in which *kamma* is produced. Older texts in the Pali canon frequently give a formula for the three *kammantas,* activities or agents that describe three channels by which *kamma* is made: *kāyena vācāya uda cetasā,* that is, through body *(kāya)*, speech *(vācā)*, and mind *(ceto)*.[82] In this way, *kāya* is one of the three avenues through which beings are connected ethically with their surroundings,[83] and through which any assessment of their intentioned behavior is expressed in future fruits – e.g., beings can make *kamma* by using the body *(kāya).* Not only is the body an instrument of *kamma*, however, it is, in fact, "the first and most conspicuous agent" of the three for making *kamma*.[84] Especially to the point here is that although *kāya* is used as "body" with a generalized sense of agency,[85] it can also specifically refer to the "faculty of touch" *(kāyātana*[86] and *kāyindriya)*.[87] And, given that such dual usages are not ordinarily coincidental, it would seem that anything endowed with *kāya* (e.g., plants) would be *kamma*-producing and would have indisputable membership among *kamma*-qualified beings.[88]

The relation between touch and *kamma* properties can be suggested, second, by noting again the application of plant experience to the *paṭiccasamuppāda,* the cycle of dependent origination or conditioned genesis.[89] Here *phassa* or contact, stimulus, touch – the sixth element in the chain that gives rise to sensation *(vedanā),* desire *(taṇhā),* and attachment *(upādāna)* – cannot come into being unless it is conditioned by sense organs (skin and body) and the sequentially antecedent factors of rebirth, consciousness *(viññāṇa)*, forces of *kamma*/individual dispositional tendencies *(saṅkhārā)*,[90] and ignorance *(avijjā)*. Thus, from the Buddhist point of view, all *saṁsāra* existence is causes and conditions, and neither *kamma* nor touch/contact can exist independently, for in this scheme descriptive of moral causality – in this "explanation of the experience of 'dependently arisen phenomena'"[91] – each one depends upon the other until the causal chain is broken by insight.[92]

The *paṭiccasamuppāda,* moreover, is not only a description of causality, but also a description of rebirth and, concerning rebirth, a text from later Pali Buddhism supports touch-bearing plants as *kamma*-beings. In the Kathavathu, contact or touch *phassa* is thought to be, "alone among the sense-organs," congenital and continuing unbroken from one birth to another, while the other four sense-faculties – seeing, hearing, smelling, and tasting – scatter at the death of the previous body, taking seventy-seven days to regroup in a new one.[93] To accept this as a normative Buddhist doctrine would be, then, to entertain the *kamma* possibility of touch-only sentient beings, that is, of plants in Buddhism.

Pertaining to this but unsupportive of plants as *kamma*-bound beings, however, is the Visuddhimagga's description of the "kinds of resultant consciousness...(that) occur as *rebirth-linking,*" and that are involved with *kamma,* especially as it appears at the time of dying.[94] These rebirth-linking-consciousnesses are associated with the senses-faculties, which are described in order as seeing, hearing, smelling, tasting, and touching.[95] It happens, however, that these processes are descriptive only of the four types of birth found in traditional Pali texts: e.g., egg-birth, womb-birth, moisture-birth, and spontaneously arising.[96] Plants are excluded from this collection, perhaps because rebirth requires the arising one by one of all five (or six) senses[97] and plants, having only one, are thus separated (in this text) from the rebirth community.

Consciousness, Pleasure, and Pain: A Karmic Review

If we take our cues from the Buddhist twelve-fold cycle of dependent origination, to be fully *karma*-bound is be to able to entertain, as a being, first, the issues of knowledge, ignorance, and consciousness and, second, the issues of pleasure and pain, and of desire and aversion. We ask, then, whether plants can be wise or ignorant, whether they can experience pleasure, desire, and attachment, and whether our observations of their behavior – or whether the observations of Indian traditional texts of their behavior – are sufficient enough to impute any of these attributes to the sentient beings that are plants. While this constitutes, in part, a review of some previous material, it is also a suggestion of the degree to which these issues for plants can be specifically associated with *karma.*

For Hindus, the passages already noted are useful to work from. Manu, as we know, states that plants have mental processes *(saṁjñā)* but that they are only "interior" because of the demeritorious and unresolved deeds that they carry forth from previous lives. The very presence of *saṁjñā*, however, is associated with plants' ability to experience pleasure and pain. Parāśara's Vṛkṣāyurveda echoes this view but does not describe the mental process of *saṁjñā* as "interior:" *vṛkṣaḥ sajño bhavedantaḥ sukhaduḥkhasamanvitaḥ.*[98] In Ramachandra Rao's important summary of Indian medical texts on this issue, plants are

> possessed of internal consciousness *(antaḥ-saṁjñā)*, as distinguished from animals which although similarly constituted possess consciousness both internally and externally *(bhair-antaś-cetanā)*...being internally conscious, they [plants] are capable of experiencing pleasure and pain: having hidden consciousness *(avyakta-cetanā)*, they are sensitive to pressure or touch.[99]

The characterization of the *saṁjñā* of plants as "interior" is glossed here by the term *avyakta-cetanā,* which suggests either a) an undeveloped and thus unevolved, or b) an imperceptible and thus unmanifest, mental process. This distinction that may suggest important differences in understanding plant consciousness, or it may suggest, alternatively, a single view incorporating both: perhaps something like *the mental processes of plants are largely imperceptible because they are undeveloped.* Another clue as to how to read *antaḥ* is from the Sāṁkhya use of *antaḥ* in *antaḥkaraṇa* which suggests that "interior processes" can be of a very high order, given that the three such "internal organs here noted are intellect or reflective discerning *(buddhi),* egoity or self-awareness *(ahaṁākra),* and mind or purposive intellectual activity *(manas).* These are opposed to the "external organs" *(bāhyakaraṇa)* that include the five sense capacities and, in the context of *antaḥkaraṇavṛtti* or "awareness," suggest "the 'private' life of thc mind."[100]

Yet another clue might be to turn to the initial term in Roy's compound *bhair-antaś-cetanā* that probably refers to *bahirdhā,* suggesting outward or external. We are helped here by passages like the following from the Buddhist Dhammasaṅgaṇi:

> 1044. Which are the states that are personal *(ajjhatta;* Skt. *adhyātma)*? Those states that, for this or that being, are of the self, self-referable, one's own, individual...
>
> 1045. Which are the states that are external *(bahiddhā;* Skt. *bahirdhā)*? Those states that, for this or that other beings, for other individuals, are of the self, self-referable, their own, individual...[101]

Using this suggestion, interior mental processes might be said to be those that are self-referential only, while exterior mental processes might be said to be self- as well as other-referential.

However *antaḥ* is specifically understood, the attribution of *antaḥsaṁjñā* to plants in passages like Manu 1.49 as well, where plants are said to experience rebirth because of previous actions and, in this plant birth, to experience pleasure and pain,[102] may give canonical *dharmaśāstra* status to plants' full placement within the *karma* system. Likewise, the Caraka Saṁhitā indirectly includes plants in the *karma* system as touch-sensed beings when it says that "of all the senses, the tactile sense *(sparśa)* alone pervades all the sense organs and is also associated inherently with mind *(cetas),* so due to pervading of tactile sense, mind also pervades."[103]

As we have seen, the basic Jain position about consciousness and plants is given in the Tattvārtha commentarial tradition where plants, though *karma*-bound, belong to the group of beings who are non-mind-possessing. This category includes all one-to four-sensed beings and some five-sensed beings.[104] To be "mind-possessing," a being has to possess all five sense-faculties and to be able to discriminate between good and bad, that is, to have both the physical *(dravya-manas)* and the psychic *(bhāva-manas)* mind. Those who are non-mind-possessing, that is, who have only the psychic mind, "have only dormant mental functionings...(where) the senses themselves may perform these functions but (the beings)...have no capacity to think."[105] At the lowest level, however, "there will always be some residue of...perception (and) knowledge,"[106] for "consciousness in its living substratum (still) consummates in the lowest form...(and) it is inferred that whatsoever beings have it at the lowest level, they are the 1-sensed beings like the earth, etc."[107] These one-sensed beings are observed to "have functional consciousness because they have tendency for intakes (food) etc. like other living beings,"[108] that is, the "fading and growth of plants depends upon their intakes."[109] Plants, then, are attributed with at least the lowest level of consciousness by the Jains because they are seen to take in things equivalent to food that help them grow and maintain good health.

In the case of Buddhism, considering any possibility of *kamma* in connection with touch for plants means to consider as well the issue of consciousness, for it is consciousness shaped by *kamma* that takes mount in the new body as the old body subsides. The traditional Buddhist view is that plants are excluded from the modes of the occurrence of consciousness as given by the canon that is, the modes for the occurrence of consciousness are so described in the canon as to make no provisions for plants.[110] Any argument for consciousness in plants, then, must rest on implication, and we see this at work when we look, for example, at the five aggregates or *khandhas,* the doctrine where the complex dynamics of the experienced "self" are laid out. In the case of plants, we can observe contact between the sense organ and the object, that is, a stimulus, as well as a resulting response. For example, we can observe leaves in contact with the warmth and light of the sun and the resultant turning of the leaves toward the sun, e.g., heliotropism. Likewise, we observe a withered plant watered by rain and its resultant rejuvenation as roots orient themselves to new sources of water, e.g., hydrotropism. These examples suggest that the first *khandha, rūpa* or material form that is the body-cum-sense-organ, *may be* at work in plants. But, as Reat suggests, technically "speaking, *phassa* does not automatically result from the mere physical juxtaposition of organ and object...[for the] object must be present to consciousness"[111] in order for contact to occur. We can only really posit that *phassa* has taken place, then, when there is a response.

Because in both these examples, however, there is a response – leaves turn toward sun and roots turn toward water – we can suggest that responses like these fall under the fifth *khandha, viññāṇa,* that is, in these plant examples, there is *kāyaviññeyya* or discernment through the body or touch.[112] This would be true because in *viññāṇa*, according to early Buddhism, there are both "animating" and "discriminating or discerning" qualities as a result of the sensory process[113] – animating, because plants are caused to grow when they turn towards sun and water, and discriminating or discerning, because plants "choose" to turn towards these life-supporting sources and rather than away from them. If, further, we observe both the first and fifth of the *khandhas* as part of plant experience, then, perhaps we can posit the second *(vedanā,* sensation or taste of experience as pleasant or unpleasant), third *(saññā,* perception, identification, labeling, or interpretation of objects), and fourth *(sankhārā,* concrete mental syntheses or constructing activities) *khandhas* as being present as well.[114] Texts like the Visuddhimagga, however, offer cautionary words at this point in assessing stimulus and response, for in the same way that sweat coming from the pores of skin doesn't mean that the skin is conscious of the process, so water coming from broken openings in plants doesn't mean that plants are conscious of the process.[115]

Moreover, aggregates of the *khandha* system numbers four and five, *sankhārā* (concrete mental syntheses) and *viññāṇa* (discriminating consciousness), contribute to the linking of the *khandhas,* the experience of the body as "self," with the *paṭiccasamuppāda,* the understanding of body giving rise to body in the doctrine of rebirth. As numbers two and three, respectively, of the twelve-fold linkage of dependent origination, concrete mental syntheses and consciousness pass into the new body shaped by the attribute of *kamma,* whose continuation is the result of ignorance. Thus, as one billiard ball passes on speed, direction, and type of motion to the next one it comes in contact with, so one body passes on *kamma*-shaped consciousness to the next one it comes in contact with. In the course of development, then, as schematized by the *paṭiccasamuppāda*, consciousness takes mount in *nāmarūpa* or name and form (number four) that immediately gives rise to the sense spheres or organs *(āyatana)*. From these sense spheres then proceed contact, sensation, desire, and attachment – the operative building blocks of the *kamma*-endowed, *saṁsāra*-bound, individual. Thus, *phassa* or touch/contact implicates plants both in the layout of the experiencing individual, and in the cycle of rebirth.

In the early Buddhist case, however, the case for plants having *kamma* is, more or less, circumstantial for we do not have any clear attribution of *kamma* or of consciousness to them. The division of consciousness into interior and exterior, made in Manu and in some Hindu medical texts, is not a feature of early Buddhist discussion, although later Buddhist texts describe interior as indicating a process of self-referencing and exterior indicating a process of other-referencing.[116] While this may be helpful in some discussions, it is not necessarily helpful here, as the canon does not provide enough descriptive material about plants to distinguish the presence of self-referencing and the absence of other-referencing qualities. Moreover, discussions in the Visuddhimagga[117] undermine arguments for plant consciousness, and, therefore, plant involvement in the life of *saṁsāra*, and the Ājīvika view described in Buddhaghosa, that plants belong to the *asaññi-gabbha* or unconscious types of birth such as rice, barley, and wheat, may in fact be an amenable view to the Buddhist commentator himself.[118] It makes most sense, then, to argue for an agnostic position. That is, as in the case of the soul and god, our epistemological tools for an empirical observation of plant consciousness, i.e., our senses, do not give us the kind of direct information that would be conclusive, and therefore the question about plant consciousness must be bracketed as unanswerable and, consequently perhaps, as unedifying for the task of human perfection. The absence of such certain evidence leads Schmithausen to suggest that plants "lack higher cognitive faculties"[119] – leaving open the possibility for plants having "lower cognitive faculties" – a position consonant with that of Jainism, for example, that places plants at the lower end of the animate (and *karma*) scale.[120]

Karmic Activity: Accumulating and Expending

If to be fully *karma*-bound is to have, indisputably, higher cognitive faculties and to experience, indisputably, pleasure and pain, desire and aversion, then the materials reviewed here are less than wholly persuasive. On the one hand, Hindu and Jain materials indicate strong support in this direction, though most understand plants as sentient beings that are at the least complex end of possible development. On the other hand, Buddhist materials make it difficult to characterize plants as *kamma*-bound, though there are doctrines that would support this view, given a basic philosophical and psychological commitment to plant life. What, however, if we entertain the possibility that plants are not "fully" *karma*-bound but only "partially" so – in a way that would allow all the materials under discussion to fit in? Since this idea may prove to be a workable solution for understanding plant nature in relation to *karma*, we will begin with Buddhist material and an observation made by Schmithausen. He states the problem as follows:

> ...the question arises why the Buddhists, unlike the Jainas and most Hindus, have not also included plants into the karmically determined rebirth system...there is no reason why one should not — as the Jainas and many Hindus actually do — regard them [plants], too, as owing their state to former karma, and hence as another possible form of rebirth.[121]

Beginning with early Buddhists, we find that although they do not admit to *kamma* endowment in plants, they do observe two things in particular about plants that are *kamma*-like. In the canon, plants are described, first, as being in a constant state of changing, growing, ripening, and transforming, and as producing vegetation of great lushness and intricate variety within spaces and under conditions that give rise to myriad different plant forms.[122] These properties can easily be compared to processes of cause and effect that are moral *(kamma)* and not simply physical *(hetu)*. While laws of physical causation are for the most part predictable (e.g., water in a pot boils when subject to heat), laws of moral causation are generally not, producing more complicated and surprising variet-ies of results than do physical processes, comparable to the myriad different plant forms observed in Indian texts. Processes of *karma,* like the growth of plants, then, both undergo continuous change as seeds are deposited with each passing moment and ripen under the influence of constantly new and changing conditions.

Second, canonical observers frequently note the continuity of plant behavior: a seed grows into a plant, which produces a fruit, which has another seed, and so forth.[123] The Therīgāthā, for example, compares the succession of leaves, twigs, and grasses to that of fathers, both of which continue without beginning and without end.[124] The Milindapañha notes that inasmuch as there is a continuing lineage of father to child, father to child, and teacher to student, teacher to student, there is also the continuity of seed to sprout, seed to sprout.[125] And the Visuddhimagga says:

> ...a great tree is growing on the earth's surface supported by the essences of humus and water and, with that as condition, [it] increases its roots, trunks, branches, twigs, shoots, foliage, flowers, and fruit, till it fills the sky, and continues the tree's lineage through the succession of the seed up till the end of the aeon.[126]

Given that the canon makes two observations about plants (that they grow luxuriantly with constant variety and change, and that they have ongoing lineages like human families), one way of describing the possible *kamma*-nature participation of plants is suggested by Schmithausen. "It is here," he says, "that one may advance the argument that plants do not *perform* or accumulate good and bad karma," but rather only consume or expend it. This fits "the early rebirth pattern [where] it is only in *human* existence that karma...is accumulated," while "in the other world karma is only *consumed* but not accumulated."[127] Referring to the verse quoted in BĀU 4.4.6, he suggests that if plants are thought to be in a world where they can consume, but not accumulate *kamma* as they can in human existence – that is, their *karma* seeds can ripen and bear fruit, but no new seeds can be sown (because no action is performed that is governed by moral choice) – then, while plants may not be fully sentient, they are not necessarily "excluded...from the range of possible forms of rebirth."[128]

In the Jain tradition, the question of a being's accumulation of, and liberation from, bondage by *karma* is very clear. Commentaries on Tattvārtha Sūtra 8.2 say, first, that bondage "is associated with mattergic living beings;" second, that (only) "non-living entities" cannot bind *karmas;* and, third, that the "living entity and karma are beginning-lessly associated with each other like the seed and sprouts." That is, being a *jīva,* a worldly or "mattergic living being," means to be in the bondage of *karma,* being in the bondage of *karma* means to be in the process of attracting and binding fine particles of mattergy, and being in this relationship of being alive and being *karma*-bound "can be proved to be beginningless." Mattergies taken in "are transformed into eight different karmic species,"[129] which means that the two aspects of *karma*-bondage most discussed in terms of plants – the "body" aspect and the "life-span" aspect – are operative at all times of the living process. In Jainism, then, all *jīvas* (including plants) are associated with all the processes of *karma,*[130] a conclusion that makes sense in a system where plants have a full and clear accounting as to their place within the whole.

One caveat to this, however, has to do with the nature of the mind *(manas)* at work. We noted above that worldly or *saṁsāra* beings are either "with mind" *(samanaska)* or "without mind" *(amanaska),* the former including some five-sensed beings, and the latter including all one- to four-sensed beings and some five-sensed beings. It happens that a being without *(manas)* is really a being without *dravya-manas,* or the actual, external, physical mind, but having, nevertheless, *bhāva-manas,* the internal potential for mind that creates and supports the physical mind. Thus, those "with mind" have both types, and those "without mind" have only *bhāva-manas.* Now, Sukhlalji's commentary on the Tattvārtha Sūtra notes that there is a difference between the *dravya-manas* and *bhāva-manas* with regard to karmic bondage:

> Saṁsāra is but the bondage of the *dravya* and *bhāva* types – that is, of the physical and mental types. A specific associatedness with the karmic particles is the *dravya* or physical type of bondage, as associatedness with the cravings like attachment, aversion, etc. is the *bhāva* or mental type of bondage.[131]

Not to have the *dravya-manas* at work in plants, say, would mean that the association with *karma* particles would not be at work, though the *bhāva-manas's* association with cravings of various sorts would be. Could this mean that, in beings like plants that are "without mind," *karma* particles are not accruing, but that the information about them is, it being kept in some kind of storage? Since Sukhlalji's commentary also notes that *"bhāva-manas* cannot undertake clear reflection without assistant of *dravya-manas*," might it not also mean that those beings like plants who are "without mind" also lack the ability to clearly evaluate and make choices, and therefore the ability to "intend" in acting – a critical part of the *karma* process? Such a viewpoint might modify our earlier discussion of Jainism that all *jīvas* are full participants in the *karma* process, and might suggest a way that the Jain tradition could support Schmithausen's suggestion about plants, that, because they have only *bhāva-manas*, they only expend but don't accumulate *karma*. This might be further confirmed by Tattvārtha Sūtra 2.25/24 where those with *manas* are called *saṁjñin*. Here the commentary notes that "intelligent beings...[have] the capacity to remember the past and ponder the future," and have "thoughtful knowledge [that] is engaged in judging objects and situations that arise in the wake of specific enquiry,"[132] a capacity of choice needed to acquire *karma* available only to those with *dravya-manas*.

Two conclusions from Schmithausen's suggestion, and from our exploration of it in Buddhist and Jain materials, can be drawn. First, under this particular interpretation of the *karma* scheme, where a plant does not create (that is, acquire or accumulate) *karma* but only consumes or expends it, there is no way for a plant to behave well or to behave poorly – it just lives, neutrally and equanimously, as a plant. As a plant, then, a being cannot consciously choose to live a certain way, carrying out certain actions and refraining from other actions. And whatever its "behavior" might be, it is not a self-conscious choice regardless of how is it judged against the culturally acknowledged standards of moral behavior. Such a status in Indian social structure is normatively reflected in the Hindu *varṇāśramadharma* system, and is ordinarily assigned either to those who are very young, that is, who are not yet ready for traditional social duties, or to those who are much older, that is, to the spiritually advanced who have forsaken all occupational, family, and ritual ties, and ordinarily live lives as renunciants.

Second, since living or experiencing the world as a plant might consist only in the reaping (or consuming) of the fruit of previous rebirths, not in the depositing of more *karma* seeds to ripen, the ordinary view about the place in the schema plants are thought to occupy is clear as well. Because the normative traditional assumption is that the behavior of a plant in previous rebirths has been demeritorious, then the normative assumption would also be that that being – because of its consumption of *karma* as a plant – can, in time, only go on to a better rebirth. This conclusion is suggested in Hindu and Jain texts that 1.) place plants near the bottom of the rebirth heap, 2.) describe the eons that they must remain there, and 3.) offer the hope of eventually being born into higher stations as their *karma* properties as plants are transformed over time. We know, for instance, from the Jain tradition that plants are specifically involved in the process of dissociation from *karma* (that is, of expending rather than acquiring *karma)*, for the Yogaśāstra of Hemacandra notes that while there is a deliberate *(sakāma)* dissociation of *karmas* undertaken by mendicants, dissociation of *karmas* by other beings, including plants, is not deliberate but natural *(akāma)*.[133]

There is another alternative to putting plants at the bottom of the *karma* heap, however, and that is putting them at the top. We note again that in relation to *karma*, in Jainism, one-sensed beings are classed with two other groups, "the living ones under transmigratory motion" (in between rebirths?) and "the omniscients with activity under extrication" (those about to be fully liberated?).[134] This location of plants at points of "*karma*-in-extremis" has suggestive ties to Buddhism, for example. In the Buddhist tradition, the critical location where a sentient being does not acquire or accumulate *karma* (i.e., lives a *barren* life) but does consume it, is in the post-*nibbāna* and pre-*parinibbāna* stage when the adept is unable to generate new *karma*, but is still living out the residue of old *karma*.[135] For Gotama Buddha, this period covers the approximately forty-five years of his ministry up to and including his final death when all *karma* residues dissipate and the end of the *saṁsāra* experience occurs. Like the behaviorally amoral stations that are at the beginning and ending of an ideal life cycle, then, the stations barren of *karma* occur at the beginning and ending of *saṁsāra* experience. We suggest that while plants may be considered, under the Schmithausen *karma* scheme, to be at the young and beginning end of life and *saṁsāra*, it is just as possible (and as plausible) for them (also) to be at the old and waning end of life and *saṁsāra.* These new possibilities have implications, ultimately, for whatever we might say about the "spiritual lives" of plants.

5.3 The *Guṇas* Again

As noted, in those traditions in which plants do belong to the *karma* system, they are situated in the *karma* hierarchy at the low end. Manu, for example, notes that plants are on the bottom of the food scale, for those who are without motion are destined to be the food of those who have motion. Moreover, when he describes the "sacrifice" of the lives of ritual victims and their consequent rebirth in higher existences, he begins with herbs and trees and then moves on to cattle and other animals, suggesting a hierarchy in the order of beings auspicious for use in the sacred Vedic ritual.[136] In the Jain system, as well, plants fall into the lowest class, that of the immobile beings,[137] a category textually designated as beneath that of the mobile beings. And, as immobile beings, plants are placed by the Tattvārtha tradition in the non-mind possessing category – with a long duration to go in *saṁsāra* before experiencing salvation.[138] This low status is generally attributed to the fact that plants exhibit behavior indicative of the attribute of *tamas* or darkness; they are seen to be, thus, unmoving and unresponsive, full of slothfulness, lethargy, and inertia, and have minds that are dull, dim-witted, and ignorant. We arrive at this conclusion through the lead of several texts, including Manu, the Caraka Saṁhitā, and the Tattvārtha Sūtra, and certainly through even a generous reading of the early Buddhist material that at best can be seen as undergoing development in its ideas about plant life and sentience. A second look at the textual observations of plant behavior in all three traditions (and, especially surprisingly, in Buddhism) suggests, however, that we may be mistaken to trust fully the theoretical conclusions of the texts. Rather than being led too far astray in the *tamas* direction, then, we return to behavior observed of plants and reassess the possibilities of the *guṇas*, all the time remembering that, as the Śvetāśvatara Upaniṣads says, to be bound by *guṇas* is to be bound to *karma* and to its fruit: "he who has qualities and is the doer of deeds that are to bear fruit (i.e. bring recompense), he is the enjoyer, surely, of the consequence of whatever he has done."[139]

Sattva Revisited

In returning to the *guṇas,* we are reminded that *tamas* qualities (mass stuff)[140] include darkness, envelopment, and delusion; indifference, dullness, and ignorance; and passivity, lethargy, sleepiness, stagnation, and inactivity; heaviness, restraint, and indiscernible mass – said, in a few traditional texts, to describe the behavior observed of grasses, herbs, creepers, shrubs, and trees. And *rajas* qualities (energy stuff) include energy, motion, activation, external action, stimulation, spontaneity, and dynamism; passion, lust, desire, greediness, indulgence, and longing; hatred, envy, pride, blame, dishonesty, and disagreeableness; and aggression, pain, and frustration – a set of qualities not ever under discussion with respect to plants.

Sattva, however, is "the passive principle revealing itself…in receptivity…lightness, luminosity and transparency of things."[141] *Sattva* qualities (intelligence stuff) conventionally include intelligence, thought, reflection, discrimination, and knowledge; luminosity, purity, goodness, and agreeableness; freedom from attachment, stinginess, anger, malice, violence, and fear; freedom from egoism and expectations; control over organs, modesty, and propriety; and surrender, patience, tranquility, contentment, equability, steadfastness, constancy, resoluteness, and subtly.[142] Indian medical texts also describe *sattva* beings as being of "the true or the natural category...the innate reality, the pure," as having "strength or the stable mooring" being able to "stabilise himself" in the midst of others, as being "always patient...free from perturbation...(and) equanimous to all."[143]

Noting these qualities – and remembering both that plants are the immobile, stationary beings and that their one sense-faculty, that of touch, occurs alone both at the beginning of life (just as *karma* is taking mount in a new physical body) and at the end of life (just as *karma* is linking to a new body)[144] – we ask, if plants are "borderline beings," at what border are they found, or to what border do they belong?

Before noting qualities of plants that might render them *sattva*-like, there are two treatments of plants that tie them to renunciant life at the fulfilling end of the path: the centrality of renunciant dwelling at the root of trees, and the use of trees in metaphors for spiritual advancement. To begin the argument that plants may belong at the high and *sattva* border rather than (or as well as) at the low and *tamas* border, then, we turn to traditionally observed (and prescribed) behavior of renunciants and other religious adepts around plants and trees, and find that it is in the company of trees, especially, that the spiritual quest normatively matures and is realized. As Lutgendorf notes of traditional Indian literature, "*the forest is cherished by sages...the forest is a place of transcendence...the forest is a state of mind.*"[145]

This sentiment is, more or less, ubiquitous in Indian culture. According to Sensarma, most "of the Purāṇas treat the forests as holy places."[146] To Gupta, "trees are associated with the attainment of Omniscience,"[147] and to Banwari, as quoted in Ranchor Prime, "the Hindu idea is that this whole world is a forest...the forest symbolizes the divine attribute of 'totality,' combining all life forms together in a single interdependent whole."[148]

Moreover, Banwari notes that there are three basic categories of forest. The *mahāvana* is a dense, almost impenetrable, place, spreading over a large area and filled with a vast array of flora and fauna who live there without any interference. Thus, this "great natural forest (is) where all species of life find shelter,"[149] and where there is very little human habitation except for hunters and hermits. The *tapovana*, on the other hand, is a forest one can enter with ease, though it too abounds "in flora, plants, and trees," and monks, recluses, and sages are attracted to it "due to its easy accessibility and serenity" and as a place of contemplation and search for truth.

> They can meditate in the peaceful atmosphere provided by these forests. Being away from human habitation, they are saved from mundane problems and suffering. As these forests are easily accessible, even people leading ordinary worldly life, who wish to learn and discuss philosophical and spiritual problems with the *sādhu-s, saṁnyāsins-s* and *ṛṣi-s* living in these forests can reach them.

The *śrīvana*, finally, is the forest as provider of prosperity, for upon it the well being of the human community depends. It is near villages, towns, and cities, and includes those trees or groves of trees one might plant near homes to provide shelter and food for communities nearby. *Śrīvana*-located trees not only provide material resources, but beauty as well for one should be able to see green all around wherever one lives, and it is toward this category of "forests" that humans have the most immediate duties and responsibilities for maintenance and preservation.[150]

The Hindu *āśramas*, or life states, are where we first encounter systematic use of tree images in the description of individual or personal spiritual quests, and where the tradition acknowledges that the forest trees have heroic powers *(vīrya)*, helpful to human spiritual endeavors.[151] The traditional Vedic student or *brahmacārin*, for example, who is under tutelage of a teacher for a given length of time, begins that time by requesting teaching through the offer of a bundle of twigs to be used as firewood for the teacher's fire.[152] Having then undergone initiation *(upanayana)*, the student uses a staff *(daṇḍa)* made from various kinds of wood,[153] performs ritual venerations of sacred trees in each of the different directions,[154] and circumambulates sacred spots including places where special trees grow.[155] The third *āśrama*, that of the *vānapraṣṭha* or "forest hermit,"[156] involves the retiring of the husband and wife to the forest, there to perform rituals and penances; the husband is "to wear a deer-skin or a tattered garment (i.e. one of bark or kuśa grass)...[and] should gradually give up residing in a house, but should stay under a tree and subsist only on fruits and roots." Within the forest, he "should study...for the increase of his knowledge and ultimately for realising *brahma.*"[157] In the final stage of life after householdership, that of the *saṁnyāsin,* the renunciant uses a wooden *daṇḍa* of particular form,[158] wanders the countryside without attachment, and in some cases, such as that of the Paramahaṁsa, uses a tree as one of his abodes.[159] Throughout the Saṁnyāsa Upaniṣads, ascetics – who are not to live in one place[160] – are allowed to take up temporary residence in a number of places, one of which is at the foot of a tree.[161] "Let a yogin," one text says, "duly embark on his meditation always in a deserted place, in a forest, or in a cave,"[162] and another notes that the ascetic, though actually in a cemetery, "lives as if in a blissful grove,"[163] the preferred place of contemplation.

In Vedic literature, the Āraṇyakas and Upaniṣads are especially important as texts arising out of forest experiences of introspection, reflection, and spiritual realization. The Āraṇyakas or "Forest Books" belong to conversations at *araṇyas* or "peaceful resorts where sages like Yājñavalkya lived and maintained their *āśramas,* both for personal contemplation and for the instruction of students."[164] Some of the dialogues, debates, and teachings from encounters in the forest among teachers and students are preserved not only in the Āraṇyakas, but especially in the Upaniṣads, a collection of teachings representing the sitting *(sad)* down *(ni)* up close *(upa)* of students around teachers in the forest, as they speculate about the meaning of the older ritual and its implications for deeper, more personal and internal, spiritual development.

That trees are sites of holy power and spiritual maturation is evident also from the forest books *(araṇyakāṇḍa)* of the two Indian epics. In a passage from the Mahābhārata, for example, when the Pāṇḍavas are in forest exile, Yudhiṣṭhira requests help in finding a place of rest and insight: "Sir, tell us of another good wood...sought out by men of holy deeds."[165] Again, in the Rāmāyaṇa, where exile in the forest is exile to a place of knowledge and illumination, a place of meditation, refuge, and spiritual wisdom:

> Soon after entering the vast wilderness (of the forest), Rāma...saw a circle of ashrams where ascetics dwelt. *Kuśa* grass and bark garments were strewn about it...it was a place of refuge for all creatures...Tall forest trees encircled it, holy trees that bore sweet fruit...Wildflowers carpeted it...Ancient sages were present there, temperate men who ate only roots and fruit, wore bark garments...Supreme seers, holy men given to rigorous fasting...
> (In the forest were) plantain trees and *āḍhikas* growing densely, and coconut palms lending their beauty, along with *sālas, tālas, tamālas,* and other flowering trees. Supreme seers given to rigorous fasting graced it...
> And there he saw a banyan tree where seers were gathered.[166]

Again, the image of the ascetic hermitage deep in the forest is found throughout Indian literature. At the end of the Rāmāyaṇa, for example, the forest hermitage is the place where Sītā retires to to raise her two young sons and to live out her exile from Rāma's court, and, in Śakuntalā, King Duṣyanta describes the *vanapraṣṭha* state by saying:

> As world protectors they first choose
> palaces filled with sensuous pleasures,
> but later, their homes are under trees
> and one wife shares the ascetic vows.[167]

The Jain Rāmāyaṇa attests as well to the broadly based view that ascetics achieve states of wisdom under trees. One long passage names a number of sages who "attained supreme knowledge" under trees peculiar to their attainments, and another notes a forest area that "had the trees which relieved the sages of worldly bondages making them achieve salvation."[168] Again, there is mention of trees in a forest bowing to sages who have entered, in the hopes that their welcome of the sages will be gracious enough to entice the sages to stay and practice. And in another example, trees show gratitude to ascetics who practice under them and, in a process similar to sympathetic magic, the trees and ascetics here become one like another.

> There was an orchard known by the name of Jaiparvata. A group of ascetics arrived there. Each one of them selected a

> tree for his abode...The trees started sprouting with tender leaves. There was an increase in their leaves, flowers and fruits. The ascetics also occupied their respective places becoming stable and the tender leaves covered them. The ascetics also were facing the heat of the season like the trees. They had the flower beds like the trees and they also bestowed the fruit of salvation like the trees.[169]

Śaivite poems in Tamil often call upon Śiva as the wise teacher, Dakṣiṇāmūrti, who resides seated under a tree, by saying, "O Lord, seated under the ancient banyan tree...O Lord, you sat under the spreading banyan tree and taught the sacred Law." Of him, they say: "This is the wise teacher who sat in the shade of the sacred banyan tree, calmly teaching the sacred Law,"[170]

> The temple of the god
> who sat under the tall banyan tree,
> and graciously taught the four ancient sages
> the enlightened way
> by discoursing on the essence of the four true Vedas...[171]

Finally, we note that the forest as place of religious transformation is not always the place of transformation through quiet, contemplative renunciation, but also the place of transformation through ecstatic and erotic devotional fervor. In the Kṛṣṇa tradition, for example, the god entices the *gopīs* or cow-girls into the nighttime dark, deep in the forest where there will be sexual awakening as an allegory for spiritual awakening. The opening of the Gītāgovinda, for example, describes Rādhā taking Kṛṣṇa 'home,' as monsoon clouds cover the evening sky: "Tamāla trees darken the forest. The night frightens him...passing trees in thickets on the way, until secret passions...triumph on the...riverbank." Rādhā says, "I reach the lonely forest hut where he (god) secretly lies at night;" and the poet Jayadeva says "he dwells in dense forest wilds...frantically calling your name" and those of "adulterous women, lighting depths of Brindaban forest."[172] In the same tradition, the poet Vidyāpati describes the awakening of spring when nature foreshadows the love-making of the 'Kṛṣṇa community:' "Birds...(fly) in the air and cowherd-girls smile face to face...Krishna has entered the great forest" and "the trees grow again...Krishna has come...the forest is charged with a new flavour of love."[173]

The tradition of renunciants as tree-root-dwellers becomes especially common among the groups of religious wanderers present in the countryside at the time of early Buddhism.

> It was the general custom at the time in India for those who were seeking a spiritual way of life to leave household life and wander from village to village; thus forest dwelling became part of their way of life. The admonition to go to the forest, to the root of a tree and the empty places of nature *(sunnagara)* .... is found in the discourses of the Buddha.[174]

Thus, monks and nuns "for the sake of meditation and spiritual perfection, retire from the noisy bustle and allurements of the cities and inhabited places into solitude,"[175] and they find this solitude in the wilder places of trees and woodlands for, says Harvey, from "the beginning of Buddhism, the forest has represented the ideal place for meditation for monks."[176] Moreover, despite the Buddha's preference for urban scapes as places for ministry, and despite his fear of the dangers that forests represented, the great moments of his life take place around groves of trees: his birth in Lumbini Grove among Śāl trees, certain childhood experiences under the rose-apple and Jambu trees, his enlightenment at Bodh Gaya in the company of trees that include the fig and banyan, and his death in Kuśinara at the feet of two Śāl trees.[177]

The forest-dwelling renunciant is a staple of our view of the period of the emergence of Buddhism[178] and, by tradition, is known as *vanavāsin* or *āraṇyavāsin.* Jacques Maquet notes that these forest dwelling monks have a "life style (that) is most congenial to the practice of meditation" and that is clear in opposition to that of the village or town dwelling monk or *grāmavāsin* – a dichotomy that, though ancient, is still useful today in places like contemporary South and Southeast Asia. Moreover, this distinction may, as Maquet argues, parallel that between the renunciant who focuses on self, by practicing insight meditation, and the one who focuses on others, by developing scholarship and social action.[179] Tambiah describes this distinction as well – between the *āraññavāsin/*

vanavāsin or forest dweller and the *gāmavāsin/nagaravāsin* or village and town dweller – and the frequently made correspondence between this and the vocational distinction of meditation versus book learning. Though he continues by describing the complexities and ambiguities of making such a stark dichotomy, as well of making such a neat set of correspondences, we note it here simply to highlight the forest-dwelling mode and the activities accompanying it – including *dhūtaṅga* or ascetic practices that are to be followed by the *tapasvin* or ascetic renunciant.[18C]

Such meditational practices have their disciplinary origins in the Pali canon, where what is originally a habitual convention becomes a disciplinary prescription. Early dictates for the *nissayas,* for example – that is, for obtaining resources for maintaining a minimum level of comfort in the spiritual quest – include scrap cloth for robes, scrap food for food and medicine, and – tree roots for lodging.[181] Moreover, the code given in the Visuddhimagga for ascetic practices for the Buddhist renunciant include "the forest-dweller's practice," that requires that the renunciant "adopt the habit of dwelling in the forest" and "the tree-root-dweller's practice," that requires that the renunciant dwell "at the root of a tree."[182]

Again, Aśvaghoṣa's Buddhacarita encourages those seeking wisdom, in particular the future Buddha, to head for the forest: "go to the forests for liberation, overcoming in mind all doctrines...excellent bodhisattvas, they all went to the forest...dwelling just at the foot of trees, or somewhere in mountains or forests...in this way I wander, in search of the highest."[183] And, in a song by the Tamil poet Vairamuthu, we hear: "(man) do you want to become a human being?/ Come close to the tree / Every tree is a bodhi tree."[184]

The many passages in Hindu and Buddhist texts prescribing life beneath or in the company of trees propose not only that trees provide protection from the extremes of weather and climate for those who dwell at their roots, but that tree areas, and more particularly forests, provide solitary, secluded places for quiet meditation and spiritual transformation. They may also suggest a process of "contagious magic" – for the symbolism of the tree, as a vertical axis connecting the ordinary to the transcendent, hints that, in abiding under a tree for long and continuous times, a renunciant may partake of the special state that is the tree.

Trees as Metaphors for Spiritual Advancement

More than just being and marking places of special spiritual power and transformation, plants, and particularly trees, provide images that give pattern to renunciant life. On the one hand, plants may provide negative examples of how to behave as a noble being, as this verse from the Pañcatantra suggests:

> Do not act as does the grass-blade.
> Lacking honest pride,
> Drooping low in feeble meanness,
> Lightly brushed aside.[185]

Another verse, however, suggests that trees, unlike grasses, may be better models of upward-tending strength and endurance:

> The hurricane innocuous passes
> O'er feeble, lowly lending grasses,
> But tears at lofty trees: the great
> Their prowess greatly demonstrate.[186]

The lowly grass, however, gets a more positive turn in Surdas, where it exemplifies unyielding tenacity, beneficial to others, and self-sacrifice. Says Surdas:

> ...a dumb blade of grass: if someone swept down a river reaches out a hand and grasps, that grass holds as fast to its roots as it can and surrenders its tortured self as it must.[187]

Again, in a twist on the association of trees with truth, the Mahābhārata story of Damayantī and Nala narrates how the young beauty invokes the Aśoka tree in a truth act: citing the power of her own sorrow for the lost Nala, her devotion to her heroic king, and the tree's own association with suffering, Damayantī says:

> Rid me swiftly of my grief, beautiful *aśoka:* have you chanced to see the king, free from sorrow and fear and torment?...Make it come about, *aśoka* tree, that I find without sorrow my

> hero...make it come about that I find him come to this forest!
> Be true to your name, *aśoka*, by dispelling my sorrow![188]

And in Śakuntalā, ascetic conduct is exemplified in that of Mārīca who, like a tree, is undistracted by the confinement of the earth around his lower half, unbothered by the stings of ants in the hill touching his skin, and unphased by the laceration of thorns on the vines around his neck:

> ...the sage stands staring at the sun,
> as immobile as the trunk of a tree,
> his body half-buried in an anthill...
> His throat pricked by a necklace
> of withered thorny vines.[189]

The Jain Ācārāṅga Bhāṣyam reflects this same view of ascetic comportment, for the Jain monk is said to endure the constant presence of gnats during his practice, and Mahāvīra himself is said to have tolerated the touch of grass while meditating with great equanimity.[190]

In the Buddhist tradition, the Suttanipāta suggests that in removing marks of a householder as a tree does its leaves, a renunciant should wander in solitude throughout the countryside.[191] In the Theragāthā, the renunciant is asked to shake off unvirtuous characteristics as the wind shakes off the leaves on a tree, to dwell alone like a tree rejected in the woods, and to endure gnats and mosquitoes mindfully as a plant does in the forest.[192] In this text also, the development of a 'forest sentiment' is encouraged, in which the renunciant becomes as a tree on a mountain top that shoots up well-watered by fresh rain; and, in spaces where rain falls, grass grows high, and groves are full of flowers, the renunciant is to be among the mountains like a tree[193] – as a still, lofty, solitary sentinel undistracted by the beauty around it. We must add to these, then, all the extended imagery of carefully planting good seeds in fertile soil, watering with fresh rain, and nourishing with warm sun that, in many configurations, is a pattern for an efficacious Buddhist practice, as well as for the process of *kamma*.[194] Trees are excellent models for the contemplative meditator for, as Schmithausen notes, "life in the wilderness involves various hardships, like being pestered by gadflies and mosquitoes...(and) foregoing the comforts of civilization...what a hermit should learn...is precisely to endure such things without becoming displeased and to abandon all wants and desires,"[195] just like a tree.

In Aśvaghoṣa's Buddhacarita, the contemplative renunciant is urged to be unattached to the loss of pleasurable things around him like a tree who loses its flowers, fruits, and companions:

> For when a tree(is) abandoned...
> by its flowers and by its fruits,
> when it is cut or when it falls,
> then another tree does not grieve.[196]

In the Saddharmapuṇḍarīka's story of the rain falling on herbs, plants of all sizes, shapes, and varieties stand in for all sentient beings: "Though all these plants and trees grow in the same earth and are moistened by the same rain, each has its differences and particulars...each, depending upon its species and nature, receives its full share of moistening and is enabled to sprout and grow." With his teaching, that is, his rain, the Buddha

> showers moisture upon
> all the dry and withered living beings,
> so that all are able to escape suffering,
> gain the joy of peace and security,
> the joys of this world
> and the joy of nirvana.[197]

Not only do the various plants symbolize all the sentient beings in the diversity in which they receive the Buddha's teachings, but the large trees are like mature meditators:

> ...there are those who dwell in meditation,
> who have gained the strength of transcendental powers...
> and emit countless rays of light
> to save living beings —
> these we call large trees
> that have gained growth and maturity.[198]

This spiritual maturity in trees is recognized in the Vimalakīrti Nirdeśa Sūtra where Vimalakīrti is said to have uttered:

In the garden of full retention of the teachings
grow the trees of the Law free of outflows.
Their wonderful blossoms are the seven factors
of enlightenment,
their fruit, emancipation and wisdom.[199]

The tree, and in particular, the bodhi tree, is thought to be able to give instruction to human beings not only about about salvation, but also "about this earth and how it can and ought to be." Vasudha Narayanan cites a Tamil song by the Tamil poet Vairamuthu in which every tree is the bodhi tree and that coming close to it, as the Buddha did to the bodhi tree during his own enlightenment, will give insight into higher wisdom and also into the essential environmental connections our lives have with the living plants around us.[200] Finally, a contemporary verse from Ajahn Chah in the Theravāda tradition, entitled "A Tree in the Forest," makes clear that the image of the tree as a model for advanced religious practice by humans is a powerful one even in contemporary meditative practice:

People have asked me about my practice.
How do I prepare my mind for meditation?
There is nothing special. I just keep it
where it always is. They ask,
"Then are you an arahant?" Do I know?
I am like a tree in a forest, full of leaves,
blossoms and fruit. Birds come to eat
and nest, and animals seek rest
in its shade. Yet the tree does not
know itself. It follows its own nature.
It is as it is.[201]

Trees as Having Sattva Guṇa

We have seen that the space at the foot of trees, under widespread branches, is space that is traditionally conducive for contemplation and spiritual development, and that the steadfast, undistractible, and fully present bearing of trees is thought to provide a beneficial model for renunciants' own behavior – views that cross the spectrum of Indian religious traditions. As we move toward another kind of conclusion about exactly where, and at what border, plants and trees may stand in the continuum of sentient beings, we are inspired by materials from East Asian Buddhism.[202] Some of these studies inform a short article by LaFleur called "Sattva: Enlightenment for Plants and Trees,"[203] whose title suggests an important interpretation of vegetable life, given our discussions here. As noted above *sattva* qualities conventionally include intelligence, thought, reflection, discrimination, and knowledge; luminosity, purity, goodness, and agreeableness; freedom from attachment, stinginess, anger, malice, violence, and fear; freedom from egoism and expectations; control over organs, modesty, and propriety; and surrender, patience, tranquility, contentment, equability, steadfastness, constancy, resoluteness, and subtly.[204] Indian medical texts also describe *sattva* beings as being of "the true or the natural category...the innate reality, the pure," as having "strength or the stable mooring" being able to "stabilise himself" in the midst of others, as being "always patient...free from perturbation...(and) equanimous to all."[205] We suggest now that, just as there are ways to see "stationary" plants in early Buddhism as *tamas*-bound, there are also ways to see "stationary" plants in early Buddhism as *sattva*-bound.

Not only are renunciants to find pattern in certain characteristics of plants and trees (as they might also in the steadiness of a rock, or in the adaptability of water, for example), but plants and trees themselves have an attribute that can suggest the achievement of a certain state – their stationariness as living beings. This attribute can be understood in two ways. First, Schmithausen discusses an alternate etymology for *tasa* (moving) and a new ensuing interpretation of *thāvara* (stationary) that is found in Pali commentaries. This alternate etymology derives *tasa* from *tṛṣ* "to be thirsty" or from *tras* "to tremble with fear," thus connecting *tasa* to *tasiṇā/taṇhā* and suggesting that "the *tasa* are those animate beings who are still under the sway of Thirst or Desire...and of fear...i.e., ordinary beings." In the case, then, of the *thāvara* or "stationary" beings, they would be reinterpreted as those "of spiritual and emotional stability...those who are free from thirst and fear, i.e., the saints."[206] The Pali Text Society Dictionary describes the application of the alternate etymology of *tasa* as follows: "Metaphorically...(to) people who are in fear & trembling, as distinguished from a thāvara, (to) a self-possessed & firm being (=Arahant)."[207] This reversal of the normal application of terms identifies mobile beings with those still subject to hindrances of *saṁsāra*, and stationary beings with those free from them and, now, living out their final lives. This alternate description, moreover, fits the distinctions made between the energetic, passionate *rajas* beings and the tranquil, reflective *sattva* ones. Schmithausen, however, cautions against this exegesis on the grounds that it is not borne out in other contemporary contexts, such as Vedic, Jain, or Hindu sources, much less in later Buddhist texts, and could only be dreamed up when Pali commentators need to reinterpret plants (the original stationary beings) *out* of the category of those counted as living.[208]

The stationary nature of plants is resonant in one other way, so as to endow them with *sattva* nature. As so many discussions of plants in this period draw on Jain sources, this one does as well and assumes, at the very least, that there is some contact and exchange of ideas between early Buddhists and Jains. In this light, a striking parallel can be drawn between the notion of plants as stationary beings and the descriptive posture of the advanced Jain saint, who is to renounce activity, to attain to inactivity and, in resolving already acquired *karma*, to acquire no new *karma*.[209] This description of the Jain saint is clearly reminiscent of suggestions made here of possibilities for plants in early Buddhism, for not only are plants rooted to one spot and don't move, but they are in a class of beings who don't perform or accumulate *karma*, but only consume it. In this light, then, we note that the Jain adept is to take proper care of his body "being immovable like a beam;" to abide for a long time in the forest and, though "animals destroy the body...not stir from his position;" and to constantly check "all motions of the body," not stirring "from one's place."[210] Such a comparison between plants and Jain adepts points to the East Asian notion of plants as (already) enlightened beings and suggests that such an idea may be present originally in early forms of Buddhism, as well, perhaps, as in other early South Asian traditions.

Hindu medical texts descriptive of yoga support the attribution of *sattva* qualities to stationary plants, for the practice of yoga gives rise, for example, to (1) mastery over the fluctuations of the mind; (2) "a tranquil attitude of life in the transient events of the world;" (3) "a firm foundation or a *terra firma* (for mind control) when it is continued for a long time uninterruptedly;" and (4) "complete controlling of the thirst of...sensual desire."[211] Vidyāpati describes a god as "stalwart as a tree,"[212] and the Mahābhārata notes that trees stand in one place, unyielding with regard to the spot where they stand and that yogīs, in their practice, become fixed like a piece of wood.[213] Moreover, in examining the duality of the Sāṁkhya tradition, we note that the Mahābhārata reminds the reader that *prakṛti* or material nature is mobile *(cala)* while *puruṣa* or the spirit is unmoving *(niścala)*,[214] thus allying the immobile or stationary beings such as plants with the spirit side of creation.

In early Buddhism, the monk is urged to bear "heat, cold, hunger, thirst, contact of flies, mosquitoes, wind and sun and creeping things...abusive, pain-causing words of speech...painful bodily feelings, (and) grievous, sharp, racking, distracting and discomforting (experiences)."[215] In these ways, the monk perseveres – like the stalwart tree in the woods – by living unflinchingly in the face of even the most distracting and painful experiences. Moreover, Śāntideva points to an ethical or behavioral quality of trees that again suggests their *sattva* nature: that "among the trees...no dissension jars."[216] Here he compares trees in the forests to exemplary human communities, where anger, contrariness, and hostility no longer prevail.

Taking Śāntideva's idea, that tree groups act without dissension, we argue that this suggests an aspect of the ethical dimension of the nature of *sattva*, expressed in the *sat* ("being") notion of perfection in early Hinduism. The tension between *sat* and *asat* belongs to a traditional Vedic rendering of the difference between perfection and not-quite-perfection, and can be schematized as follows:

Deva: *sat* - being - fully actualized - possessing knowledge - ethically non-violent

Asura: *asat* - becoming - potentially actual - still possessing ignorance - ethically violent

Viewed from right to left, one can identify the degree of perfection of a being by the behavior it exhibits. Thus, a violent being is one who has not yet realized his or her full truth *(satya)* or potential, while a non-violent one is one who resides in truth, is stabilized in truth, and for whom this embodied life is a fully realized one. To place plants, as *sattva* beings, in the category of full *sat,* or actualized being, then, is to have noted first that their behavior can be described as non-violent. Returning to Śāntideva's comment, then – that among trees there is no dissension – we suggest that this later Indian Buddhist tradition has identified the non-violent ethic of plants' *sattva* nature.

Sattva nature can also be ethically expressed in compassion, resonant in the common attribution to plants of their "service" to human beings. Bruce Sullivan quotes the following from the Bhāgavata Purāṇa:

> Observing that the trees served as parasols by spreading their shade in the scorching heat of the sun, Krishna (said)... "Look at these great blessed souls who live only for the welfare of others, suffering stormy winds, heavy rains, heat and frost, saving us from these.
> The birth of trees is truly the most blessed in the world, for it contributes to the well-being of all creatures. Just as no one needy returns disappointed from generous persons, so also one who approaches trees for shelter.
> They meet the needs of others with their leaves, flowers, fruits, shade, roots, bark, wood, fragrance, sap, ashes, and coal.
> That one should offer life, wealth, intellect and speech to benefit others is the height of service of embodied beings for fellow creatures."[217]

This speech of Kṛṣṇa in praise of the service trees give to human beings places trees squarely within an ethic in which they – although perhaps unknowingly, as would be true for any perfected being – treat others with the utmost generosity and compassion. Other texts as well, many from the Kṛṣṇa tradition, describe trees as symbols of "tolerance and generosity" and as "models for all devotees of God to follow."[218] These traditional texts – as gathered in one collection by Balbir Mathur, founder of the Trees for Life movement in India, for example – focus on the great gifts trees give to people through their shade from sun and protection from rain, through the food and medicine they give as gathered from leaf to root, and through people's use of tree body parts for fuel. This service is often given at the cost of great sacrifice to the trees themselves, as they endure extreme weather events, and loss of fruit, leaves, bark, root – and even their lives – in acts of care, kindness, service, and self-surrender.[219]

The Jain tradition notes the service of plants as well, for the epic poem, the Ādipurāṇa, underscores the importance of forests. Forests, for example, "moderate the climate, check thunderstorms and floods, protect the neighboring areas from cold winds, and enable the constant flow of rivers. They provide shelter for wild-life and fodder for animals...and thousands of excellent medicines." Like "saints, or *munis,* who, overcoming all obstacles, create a better welfare for all," forests also "remove fatigue, and every type of life feels better off because of the unique type of ecosystem they create, consisting of trees, plantations, animals, air, and water. The forest is the basis for survival and a symbol of happiness."[220] Thus, as in the case of the Hindu examples, plants can be seen as having *sattva* nature because of the service they provide to other sentient beings, but as traditional material portrays this, it is not just that plants trees *are useful* for other sentient beings, but that plants and trees *give themselves up to use* by other sentient beings.

It is here, then, that we can entertain a comment made by McDermott about the Buddhist position in relation to plants, that "creatures in non-human form are not usually (considered) capable of doing meritorious deeds."[221] Given what we have argued about the *sattva* nature of plants and the possible ethical dimensions of it, this comment about plants *not doing meritorious deeds* is most appropriate. For if, as suggested, plants are beings who are expending but not accumulating *karma*, they are not then acquiring merit or demerit for any of their actions. Plants are simply acting spontaneously and naturally in a manner seen by others to be good – given the general cultural assumption that having full wisdom naturally gives rise to what is seen as good behavior. Thus, to be non-violent and compassionate is not necessarily to consciously perform actions that are non-violent and compassionate, but to exhibit a public presence consonant with an interior state that has this certain cultural cache.

We conclude, then, in the land of inconclusiveness. The attribution of a Buddha-nature, and even final Buddhahood, to grasses, plants, and trees, for example, might seem a positive development of the Buddhism originating in Indian-influenced cultures. But, in the end, it functions as a recapitulation of an idea present already in Vedic times, that of *ṛta.* According to the notion of *ṛta,* plants are part of a system in which all things are identified as having an essential truth (e.g., sun, water, fire, cow) that, if maintained by the proper performance of the ritual, successfully contributes to the ongoing life of the cosmos. The good news is that both the Vedic *ṛta* idea and the universal Buddhahood idea (of East Asia) give grasses, plants, and trees an equal status alongside humans in the process of moving towards (or being in possession of) Buddhahood. The bad news is that they also give plants an equal status alongside what we might consider non-animate things (e.g., stones and water) as well, thus undermining the distinction of including plants, as fully as possible, among those who are sentient, *karma*-bound, and spiritually transformable beings. And here, again, we are reminded of Jain hylozoism where souls or life *(jīva)* is thought to be located in all matter, including earth, air, fire, and water-bodies.

It is Schmithausen's conclusion that plants are "not sentient in the same way as men or so-called higher animals...(but that) they are certainly alive. We simply do not know what it means for a plant itself to live or to be injured or killed."[222] While it is true that we don't know what it means for a plant to live, these chapters have made some suggestions towards that end using materials available to the three traditions of Hinduism, Jainism, and Buddhism: specifically, that a plant can experience the world around it through its sense of touch, and that a plant's stability indicates either a lethargic and dull *(tamas)* karmic composition or a steady, unflappable, and compassionate *(sattva)* one. We argue that it's possible that traditional Indian religions are aware of both these two possibilities for plants, and that when Schmithausen calls plants a "borderline case," they can be considered "borderline" at the borders on either end of the continuum: either plants are so rudimentary that they can't move and accumulate *karma*, but only expend it, or plants are so advanced, like perfected saints, that they no longer move about and need only dissipate a few remains of *karma* before final enlightenment.[223] Whichever border a given Indian tradition understands plants to live on, it is clear that many traditions see plants as alive, sentient, and *karma*-bearing in some way. With this notion, then, we can move toward an understanding of the relationship between plants and people that makes ecology a medium of authentic interaction. Thus, "the idea that nonhuman beings have exactly the same *spiritual* potential as humans...is often cited as a move toward biocentrism."[224] And moving toward a more activist stance we, as a Jain commentator notes, "face environmental problems because we do not recognize our own interdependence with the physical world, nor take responsibility for the violence we inflict upon it."[225]

Endnotes :

1 Coward, "Ecological Implications of Karma Theory," pp. 41, 45.

2 Padmasiri de Silva, " Environmental Ethics: Buddhist Perspective," p. 176; Padmasiri de Silva, "Environmental Ethics in Buddhism," pp. 56-57; Lily de Silva, "Early Buddhist Attitudes Toward Nature," p. 94.

3 Deutsch, *Advaita Vedānta: A Philosophical Reconstruction*, p. 76.

4 See SK 1.2.3.18.

5 Potter, *Encyclopedia of Indian Philosophies* 2.233, 262, 330-331.

6 Padmasiri de Silva, "Environmental Ethics in Buddhism," p. 62.

7 Harvey, *Buddhist Ethics*, p. 174. He goes on, however, to discuss the numerous canonical passages where plants, as living beings, are the objects of an early Buddhist doctrine of *ahiṁsā;* Harvey, *Buddhist Ethics*, pp. Pp. 174-175.

8 M 1.73; D 3.230; Mil 128; see Vism 551-552.

9 D 3.234; M 1.73: S 5.474-477; A 4.459; see Harris, "Buddhist Environmental Ethics," pp. 203, 205; McDermott, "Animals and Humans in Early Buddhism," p. 269.

10 M 1.73; S 5.474-477.

11 Mil 271.

12 RV 10.16.3; O'Flaherty, *Rig Veda*, p. 49.

13 TS 3.1.4: *suvargaṁ yāhi pathibhir devayānair oṣadhīṣu prati tiṣṭhā śarīraiḥ*. Keith, *Taittirīya Saṁhitā* 1.226 .

14 Schmidt, "Origin of *Ahiṁsā*," p. 629.

15 Manu 5.55; Bühler, *Laws of Manu*, p. 177.

16 Schmidt, "Origin of *Ahiṁsā*," pp. 644-645.

17 Schmidt, "Origin of *Ahiṁsā*," pp. 644-645.

18 AU 3.1.3. The term *udbhijja* also appears for plant in CU 6.3.1.

19 Keith, *Religion and Philosophy* 2.526.

20 CS Śārīrasthānam 16.

21 Manu 1.40-42; Bühler, *Laws of Manu*, p. 15.

22 Manu 1.49; Bühler, *Laws of Manu*, p. 16.

23 Manu 1.55-57; Bühler, *Laws of Manu*, pp. 17-18.

24 Jain, *Biology in Jaina Treatise on Reals*, p. 31.

25 SK 2.7.11-12; Jacobi, *Jaina Sūtras* 2.424-425; see also the discussion in 2.431-433.

26 Jain, *Jaina Karmology*, p. 53; Jain, *Jaina World of Non-Living*, pp. 180-181.

27 Quarnström, *Yogaśāstra of Hemacandra*, p. 37 (2.34)

28 Jaini, *Jaina Path of Purification*, p. 108; Babb, "Giving and Giving Up," p. 72.

29 Jaini, *Jaina Path of Purification*, p. 108.

30 Tatia, *Tattvārtha Sūtra: That Which Is*, p. 159.

31 Jaini, *Jaina Path of Purification*, pp. 109-110.

32 TAS 2.32; Tatia, *Tattvārtha Sūtra: That Which Is*, p. 51.

33 TAS 2.36: *śeṣāṇāṁ sammūrchchanam;* "all other beings are born by agglutination;" Tatia, *Tattvārtha Sūtra: That Which Is*, p. 54; see also p. 51.

34 Included in this category are invertebrates, hermaphrodites, those without a physical mind, and all insects, worms, and animals not born of a womb. Tatia, *Tattvārtha Sūtra: That Which Is*, p. 54.

35 Tatia, *Tattvārtha Sūtra: That Which Is*, p. 55.

36 Tatia, *Tattvārtha Sūtra: That Which Is*, p. xxviii. Translator's italics. Says Tatia, as

> can be seen in the Tattvārtha Sūtra, no other Indian school has invested so much energy in describing the precise mecha-

nism of karmic bondage and release from that bondage nor has any other tradition conceived of the reward and retribution of karma as part of the unequivocal physical law of the universe.

37 B. Kumar, "Transmigration and *Karma,*" p. 28.

38 Jain, *Biology in Jaina Treatise on Reals*, pp. 166, 189.

39 Tatia, *Tattvārtha Sūtra: That Which Is*, pp. 55, 59, 56-58.

40 Tatia, *Tattvārtha Sūtra: That Which Is*, p. 56.

41 Jain, *Biology in Jaina Treatise on Reals*, pp. 44-45.

42 TAS 8.2: *sakaṣāyatvāj jīvaḥ karmaṇo yogyān pudgalān adatte;* Jain, *Jaina Karmology*, pp. 52-53.

43 TAS 6.3-4: *Śubhaḥ puṇyasya* (3); *aśubhaḥ pāpasya* (4). Tatia, *Tattvārtha Suūtra: That Which Is*, pp. 151-152. *Puṇya* (beneficial *karma*) and *pāpa* (non-beneficial *karma*) both occur in two types: a *dravya* (physical) type and a *bhāva* (mental) type. Dixit, *Sukhlalji's Commentary on Tattvārtha Sūtra*, p. 10.

44 Jain, *Jaina Karmology*, p. 71.

45 TAS 8.1: *mithyādarśanā-virati-pramāda-kaṣāya-yogā bandhahetavaḥ;* Tatia, *Tattvārtha Sūtra: That Which Is*, p. 189.

46 TAS 8.3/8.4: *prakṛti-sthity-anubhāva-pradeśās tadvidhayaḥ;* Tatia, *Tattvārtha Sūtra: That Which Is*, p. 191; see also Jain, *Jaina Ḳarmology*, p. 58.

47 TAS 8.4/8.5: *ādyo jñāna-darśanāvāraṇa-vedanīya-mohanīyā-yu ṣka-nāma-gotrāntarāyāḥ;* Tatia, *Tattvārtha Sūtra: That Which Is*, p. 191.

48 Tatia, *Tattvārtha Sūtra: That Which Is*, p. 213. In the Yogaśāstra of Hemachandra we find: "Since the activities of mind, speech and body, beget people's wholesome and unwholesome *karma,* [these] activities are called *[karma-]* "creators" *(āsrava).*" Quarnström, p. 89 (4.74).

49 Tatia, *Tattvārtha Sūtra: That Which Is*, p. xxvii.

50 TAS 5.21: *parasparopagraho jīvānām.* Tatia, *Tattvārtha Sūtra: That Which Is*, p. 131.

51 Tatia, *Tattvārtha Sūtra: That Which Is*, p. xxi.

52 See Jain, *Jaina Karmology*, p. 114.

53 Jain, *Jaina Karmology*, p. 120.

54 Jain, *Biology in Jaina Treatise on Reals*, pp. 31, 81.

55 Jain, *Biology in Jaina Treatise on Reals*, pp. 33, 98.

56 Jain, *Jaina World of Non-Living*, p. 175.

57 Tatia, *Tattvārtha Sūtra: That Which Is*, p. 87.

58 Jain, *Jaina World of Non-Living*, pp. 186, 187, 198.

59 See Jain, *Biology in Jaina Treatise on Reals,* p. 46 for a discussion on the processes for controlling the volitions. The psychological aspects of such control involve repression, regression, denial and projection, sublimation, displacement, rationalization, compensation, redirection, and dissolution.

60 See Tatia, *Tattvārtha Sūtra: That Which Is*, pp. 253-254.

61 AV 1.24.1.

62 Shakti Gupta, *Plant Myths and Traditions in India,* pp. 24, 57, 62, 67.

63 Shakti Gupta, *Plant Myths and Traditions in India,* pp. 24, 57, 62, 67.

64 Majupuria and Majupuria, *Sacred and Useful Plants & Trees of Nepal*, p. 161.

65 D 1.81; T. W. Rhys Davids, *Dialogues of the Buddha* 1.90-91; see also Vism 411-424; Ñāṇamoli, *Path of Purification*, pp. 406-418.

66 UD 19.45, 74; Jacobi, *Jaina Sūtras,* pp. 93, 95.

67 UD 20.36.

68 UD 19.66; Jacobi, *Jaina Sūtras* 2.96. The Tattvārtha Sūtra states that rebirth in the animal realm (and all sub-realms including plants) comes from behaving with deceit, crookedness, amorality, and treachery; Tatia, *Tattvārtha Sūtra: That Which Is,* p. 159.

69 Hawley and Juergensmeyer, *Songs of the Saints of India*, p. 59.

70 ĀS 1.3.1.4; Jacobi, *Jaina Sūtras* 1.29.

71 Other examples, magnet from magnet, cloud from cloud.

72 SK 2.3.1, 3, 5; Jacobi, *Jaina Sūtras,* pp. 388-390

73 Krishnamurthy, *Source Book of Indian Medicine*, p. 47.

74 BĀU 4.4.2; 4.5.12, 15; CU 3.13.8; 7.8.1; 7.9.1; AU 1.1.4; KU 2.1.3.

75 Sharma, *Caraka Saṁhitā* 1.498, 502.

76 Van Buitenan, *Mahābhārata* 2-3.226.

77 ĀS 1.1.2; Jacobi, *Jaina Sūtras* 1.15-16.

78 Jain, *Biology in Jaina Treatise on Reals*, pp. 122-123.

79 Jain, *Biology in Jaina Treatise on Reals*, p. 113.

80 Jain, *Biology in Jaina Treatise on Reals*, pp. 44-45.

81 Jain, *Biology in Jaina Treatise on Reals*, pp.100-101.

82 This is true in Jainism as well. TAS 6.1: *kāya-vaṅ-manaḥkarma yogaḥ;* "the operation of the body, speech and mind is action;" Tatia, *Tattvārtha Sūtra: That Which Is,* p. 151.

83 *Kāyakamma:* D 1.250; 3.191, 245, 279; M 1.415; A 1.104; 5.289; Therī 277.

84 T. W. Rhys Davids and Stede, *Pali Text Society's Pali-English Dictionary*, p. 208. The body is also a means through which there is

consciousness or discernment *(kāyaviññeyya)*, e. g., D 1.245; 2.281; 3.234; M 1.85.

85 On the production of the body by one's *karma*, see Potter, pp. 233, 262, 330-331.

86 *Kāyātana:* D 3.243, 280, 290; Dhs 613, 653, 678, 679, 783.

87 *Kāyindriya:* D 3.239; Dhs 613, 972.

88 For the controversies over whether the *material* of the sense organ is the results of *karma*, see KV 12.4. Note that in Jain texts, the body *(kāya)* — as a producer of *karma* in the triad, body, speech, and mind — is also of that triad, as of touch *(kāya)* among the five sense faculties, the last to cease functioning at death, after, first, mind, then, speech; UD 29.72.

89 See Yamada, "Premises and Implications of Interdependence," pp. 270-272.

90 Kalupahana, *Buddhist Psychology*, pp. 17-21, 33; Reichenbach, *Law of Karma*, p. 25:

> *Saṁskāras* are the invisible dispositions or tendencies to act, think, experience, or interpret experiences in way which are conducive to one's happiness or unhappiness, produced in the agent as a result of the action. They constitute, in effect, special modifications of the agent...every karmic act produces *saṁskāras* in the agent.

91 Kalupahana, *Principles of Buddhist Psychology*, p. 26.

92 Vism 517-586. The breaking of the twelve-fold chain most effectively happens between stages seven (sensation) and eight (desire). Moreover, as Steven Collins argues, the "creation of continued life in time" is the result of a "construction-consciousness" *(abhisaṅkhāra-viññāṇa)* "which continues throughout *saṁsāra*, both constructing future temporal existence, and itself constituting the medium for the temporal reality thus constructed...It does not refer to the elongation of a personalised consciousness through time, but to the creation of time by the accumulation of instances;" Collins, *Selfless Persons*, pp. 205, 208. Having touch *(phassa)*, then, brings plants into this system of conditioned continuity that is connected sequentially to *kamma* through *saṅkhāras* and also to consciousness.

93 KV 14.2; Aung and C. A. F. Rhys Davids, *Points of Controversy*, pp. 283-284.

94 Vism 457; Ñāṇamoli, *Path of Purification*, p. 459.

95 Vism 458; Ñāṇamoli, *Path of Purification*, pp. 459-460.

96 Vism 551-552; Ñāṇamoli, *Path of Purification*, pp. 564-565; following M 1.50, 73.

97 See Vism 457-460; Ñāṇamoli, *Path of Purification*, pp. 459-462.

[98] Parāśara, *Vṛkṣāyurveda*, pp. 2-4.

[99] Ramachandra Rao, *Encyclopedia of Indian Medicine* 2.151. My italics and emendations in the Sanskrit.

[100] Larson & Bhattacharya, *Sāṁkhya*, pp. 25, 52, 77.

[101] C. A. F. Rhys Davids, *Buddhist Manual of Psychological Ethics*, p. 250.

[102] Manu 1.49.

[103] CS Sūtrasthāna 38; Sharma, *Caraka Saṁhitā* 1.76.

[104] TAS 2.11; Tatia, *Tattvārtha Sūtra: That Which Is*, pp. 40-41; Jain, *Biology in Jaina Treatise on Reals*, p. 95.

[105] Jain, *Biology in Jaina Treatise on Reals*, pp. 96, 97.

[106] Jaini, *Jaina Path of Purification*, p. 111.

[107] This refers to the presence of the psychic mind in one-sensed beings, here, in plants; Tatia, *Tattvārtha Sūtra*, pp. 40-41.

[108] Jain, *Biology in Jaina Treatise on Reals*, p. 101.

[109] Jain, *Biology in Jaina Treatise on Reals*, p. 98.

[110] See, for example, Vism 457-460.

[111] Reat, p. 308.

[112] E. g., D 1.245; 2.281; 3.234; M 1.85.

[113] T. W. Rhys Davids and Stede, *Pali Text Society's Pali- English Dictionary*, pp. 618-619.

[114] For a good description of the *khandhas*, see Harvey, *Introduction to Buddhist Ethics*, p. 32.

[115] Vism 361. This is clearly distinct from the conclusion in the Mahābhārata passage where the authors, observing some of the behaviors of plants — e.g., filling open space with fruit and flowers and open surface with vines, withering in the cold, responding to sounds and smells, turning towards water and drinking it in for health — conclude that it is unimaginable that plants are not conscious *(acaitanya);* Mbh 12.177.10-18; see also Jacobi 1.10n.

[116] E. g., Vism 349. Says the Dhammasaṅgaṇi:

> 1044. Which are the states *(dhamma)* that are personal *(ajjhatta;* Skt. *adhyātma)*? Those states which, for this or that being, are of the self, self-referable, One's own, individual...
>
> 1045. Which are the states that are external *(bahiddhā;* Skt. *bahirdhā)*? Those states which, for this or that other beings, for other individuals, are of the self, self-referable, their own, individual...

C. A. F. Rhys Davids, *Buddhist Manual of Psychological Ethics*, p. 250.

[117] Vism 556-559.

118 Basham, *History and Doctrines of the Ājīvikas*, pp. 248-249.
119 Schmithausen, *Problem of the Sentience of Plants*, p. 82n.
120 Jain, *Biology in Jaina Treatise on Reals*, p. 31.
121 Schmithausen, *Problem of the Sentience of Plants*, p. 101.
122 Sn 239; D 1.87, 111; S 3.137; J 5.46; Vism 353.
123 Vin 4.34; S 5.46-47; A 1.184; Vism 555.
124 Therī 499.
125 Mil 269.
126 Vism 688.
127 Schmithausen, *Plants as Sentient Beings*, p. 29. Schmithausen's italics. He refers here to the verse in BĀU 4.4.6.
128 Schmithausen, *Problem of the Sentience of Plants*, p.101.
129 Jain, *Jaina Karmology*, pp. 54-57.
130 Jain, *Jaina Karmology*, pp. 53-54; Jain, *Jaina World of Non-Living*, pp. 180-181.
131 Dixit, *Sukhlalji's Commentary on Tattvārtha Sūtra*, p. 84.
132 Tatia, *Tattvārtha Sūtra: That Which Is*, p. 46.
133 Quarnström, *Yogaśāstra of Hemacandra*, p. 91 (4.87).
134 One of the reasons for classifying these three groups together is their co-participation in the destruction-cum-subsidence volition; Jain, *Biology in Jaina Treatise on Reals*, p. 76.
135 See Vism chapters 22 and 23..
136 Manu 5.29, 40; see Schmidt, "Origin of *Ahiṁsā*," p. 631.
137 While, in the Śvetāmbara canon, plants are thought to be of a more sophisticated nature than the equally immobiled earth-lived and the water-lived, in later texts, they are less sophisticated than the mobile fire-lived and wind-lived, and less sophisticated, certainly, than the organic mobile beings; UD 36.70-247.
138 Jain, *Biology in Jaina Treatise on Reals*, p. 31.
139 *Guṇānvayo yaḥ phala-karma-kartā kṛtasya tasyai va sa copabhoktā*; ŚU 5.7; Radhakrishnan, *Principal Upaniṣads*, p. 740.
140 These "stuff" allocations are given by Dasgupta, *History of Indian Philosophy*, p. 43.
141 Nahar and Ghosh, *Jainism* 1:195.
142 See Larson and Bhattacharya, *Encyclopedia of Indian Philosophies* 4.197-198; Larson, *Classical Sāṁkhya*, pp. 11-14; Gītā chs. 17 and 18; Manu ch. 12.
143 Krishnamurthy, *Source Book of Indian Medicine*, pp. 109, 111, 114, 115.

144 The list of senses losing power and dying out "when your body grows old and your hair turns white" occurs in this order in UD 10.21-25: ears, eyes, nose, tongue, touch; Jacobi, *Jaina Sūtras* 2.44.

145 Lutgendorf, "City, Forest, and Cosmos," pp. 279-280. Lutgendorf's italics.

146 Sensarma, *Plants in the Indian Purāṇas*, p. 107.

147 Shakti Gupta, *Plant Myths and Traditions in India*, p. 48.

148 Prime, *Hinduism and Ecology*, p. 10.

149 Prime, *Hinduism and Ecology*, p. 10.

150 Banwari, *Pañcavaṭī: Indian Approach to Environment*, pp. 31-38.

151 AV 1.35.3.

152 Kane 2.1.329.

153 Kane 2.1.279-280.

154 Kane 2.1.304-308.

155 Kane 2.1.346.

156 NpU 149; Olivelle, *Saṁnyāsa Upaniṣads*, pp. 181-182.

157 Kane 2.2.920, 921, 922;

158 Kane 2.2.937.

159 Kane 2.2.939, 941.

160 NpU 177; Olivelle, *Saṁnyāsa Upaniṣads*, p. 200.

161 JU 70-71; NpU 154; BhU 235; Olivelle, *Saṁnyāsa Upaniṣads*, pp. 146, 184, 237.

162 NpU 192; Olivelle, *Saṁnyāsa Upaniṣads*, p. 210.

163 NU 228; Olivelle, *Saṁnyāsa Upaniṣads*, p. 232.

164 Rukmani, "Literary Foundations for an Ecological Aesthetic," pp. 107-108.

165 Van Buitenan, *Mahābhārata* 2-3.399.

166 Pollock and Goldman, *Rāmāyaṇa of Vālmīki* 3.155, 156, 157; see Lee, "Natural History of the *Rāmāyaṇa,*" pp. 245-268.

167 Miller in Thapar, *Sakuntala*, p. 163.

168 Nagar, *Jain Rāmāyaṇa*, pp. 117, 88-89.

169 Nagar, *Jain Rāmāyaṇa*, p. 121.

170 Peterson, *Poems to Śiva*, pp. 128, 149, 140.

171 Peterson, *Poems to Śiva*, p. 129.

172 Miller, *Love Song of the Dark Lord*, pp. 69, 80, 91, 97.

173 Bhattacharya and Archer, *Love Songs of Vidyāpati*, pp. 89, 132.

174 Padmasiri de Silva, "Environmental Ethics in Buddhism," p. 61.

175 Schmithausen, "Ecological Ethics," p. 11.

176 Harvey, *Buddhist Ethics*, p. 174.

177 Ryan, *Buddhism and the Natural World*, pp. 52-55, 63-71.

178 Collins, *Selfless Persons*, p. 64; see the selections in Kaza and Kraft, *Dharma Rain*, pp. 14-20.

179 Maquet, "Bhāvanā in Contemporary Sri Lanka," pp. 143-145.

180 Tambiah, *Buddhist Saints of the Forest*, pp. 53-57.

181 Sn 708, 709, 712, 958; Vin 1.58, 96; D 1.71; A 1.183; 2.38; 3.353; 4.139, 231,392; 5.109, 207, 323; S 1.199; Thera 6, 18, 27, 31, 34, 55, 59, 62, 110, 119, 217, 466, 523, 602, 851, 852, 887, 925, 948, 962, 998, 1057, 1102, 1120, 1146-1149; Therī 24, 230, 362, 366; It 102; Vism 74, 182, 183, 269, 270.

182 Tambiah, *Buddhist Saints of the Forest*, p. 34.

183 Schotsman, *Buddhacarita*, pp. 8, 34, 80.

184 Narayanan, "One Tree Is Equal to Ten Sons," p. 311.

185 Pañcatantra, p. 40.

186 Pañcatantra, p. 45. See Kale, *Hitopadeśa*, pp. 52, 81.

187 Hawley and Jurgensmeyer, *Songs of the Saints*, p. 113.

188 Van Buitenan, *Mahābhārata* 2-3.340.

189 Miller in Thapar, *Sakuntala*, p. 159.

190 Tulsi, *Acharanga Bhasyam*, pp. 480, 527.

191 Sn 44.

192 Thera 2, 62, 243-244. It should be noted that there are many other objects used as metaphors for renunciant life in the Theragāthā, e.g., fire, the elephant, cotton, a rock, good seed, good field, sharp sword.

193 Thera 110, 1137.

194 Sn 77, 209; S 5.46; A 1.223, 229, 239; 3.39, 200, 360; 4.99, 336; 5.4ff. These images, and others like them, are, of course, reflective of the culture Buddhism is now flourishing in, where some forested land is left standing, but other land is cleared for broad agricultural use. See also, Collins, *Selfless Persons*, pp. 218-224.

195 Schmithausen, "Ecological Ethics," p. 11.

196 Schotsman, *Buddhacarita*, p. 64.

197 Watson, *Lotus Sutra*, pp. 98, 99, 102.

198 Watson, *Lotus Sutra*, p. 105.

199 Watson, *Vimalakīrti Nirdeśa Sūtra*, p. 97.

200 Narayanan, "One Tree is Equal to Ten Sons," p. 311.

201 Dhamma Garden, *A Tree in a Forest*, frontispiece quote.

202 Material from Buddhist traditions in East Asia, especially from those Buddhist traditions influenced by Daoism in China, and by Shinto in Japan are helpful here. It can be argued that there are threads in Chinese and Japanese Buddhism that suggest not only that plants are living, sentient beings, but also that plants do not belong (only) at

the lowest end of *saṁsāra* life but (also) near the most perfected end, characterizing them (using Hindu terms) not as *tamas*-bearing, but as *sattva*-bearing. Figures like Chi-t'sang, Chan-jan, Saichō, Kūkai, Ryōgen, and Dōgen, for example, see plants as not only of *sattva* nature but, moreover, as beings who are already enlightened; Dōgen, "Mountains and Waters Sutra," pp. 65-76; Groner, "Realization of Buddhahood by Grasses and Trees," pp. 1-23; LaFleur, "Enlightenment for Plants and Trees," pp. 109-116; LaFleur, "Sattva: Enlightenment for Plants and Trees," pp. 136-144; LaFleur, "Saigyō and the Buddhist Value of Nature," pp. 183-209; Parkes, "Voices of Mountains, Trees, and Rivers," pp.111-128),

William LaFleur notes that discussions among Chinese and Japanese Buddhists are "concerned explicitly with the problem of whether or not "plants and trees" *(sōmoku)* could "attain Buddhahood" *(jōbutsu)*." He cites Chi-t'sang (549-623) as "the first (Chinese Buddhist) to use the key phrase "Attainment of Buddhahood by Plants and Trees,"" though, as Harvey notes, Chi-t'sang's San-lun school believes that plants and trees lack a mind, and so cannot actually "actualize this potential by experiencing Buddhahood." Chan-jan (711-782) of the T'ien-t'ai school argues that nothing, not even soil and dust, can be excluded from Buddhahood because the Buddha-nature "is the immutable mind at the base of all phenomena;" LaFleur, "Saigyō and the Buddhist value of Nature," p. 184; Harvey, *Buddhist Ethics*, pp. 176-177.

In Japan, Saichō (766-822) is said to be the "the first Japanese to use the phrase "the Buddha-nature of Trees and Rocks."" And Kūkai (774-835), the founder of the tantric school of Shingon, is "the first one in Japan to elaborate the idea of the Buddhahood of all phenomena and make it central to his thought." He attributes Buddhahood to "insentient" trees and plants based on the notion that the *dharmakāya* consists of the five elements "within which space plants-and-trees *[sōmoku]* are included." Thus "Kūkai's argument differs...(from others) inasmuch as he is less interested in pursuing the logical consequence of a universalistic trend in Buddhism and more interested in the positing of an identity of the Buddhist Absolute, the dharmakaya or "body of the dharma," with all forms and things in the phenomenal, mundane world;" Parkes, "Voices of Mountains, Trees, and Rocks," p. 114; LaFleur, "Saigyō and the Buddhist Value of Nature," pp. 184, 186, 187; see Groner, "Realization of Buddhahood by Grasses and Trees," p. 2.

Continuing, a debate takes place between Ryōgen (912-985), of the Tendai school, and Chūzan (935-976), of the Hossō school, over whether plants and trees can desire enlightenment, discipline themselves, and attain Buddhahood (Ryōgen's view); while another member of the Tendai school, Chūjin (1065-1138), argues on behalf of the Buddhahood of plants, saying that "plants and trees...(are) already enlightened and in possession of Buddha-nature." In Saigyō (1118-1190), "Buddhism in Japan...(is) forced to accommodate itself to the longstanding and pre-Buddhist attribution of high religious value to the natural world," for in his work we see a "valorization of nature which...goes beyond that given to trees and plants by Chūjin." In his view nature is both already saved, that is, already realized in its Buddha-nature, and itself soteric, that is, having a salvational role for others. According to LaFleur, Saigyō experienced the "natural world as both a soteric reality and as the ultimate Buddhist absolute." Finally, Dōgen (1200-1253), founder of the Sōtō school, has much in common with Kūkai in his assertion of "the nonduality of Buddha-nature and the world of impermanence" and in his regard that nature is "sacred and a source of wisdom." For him, the whole phenomenal world does not *manifest* or *contain* the Buddha-nature, rather, it *is* it: the "whole changing flux of empty phenomena...(is) nothing but the Buddha-nature, within which it...(is) not possible to designate anything as "non-sentient;"" LaFleur, "Saigyō and the Buddhist Value of Nature:" pp. 188-193, 195, 202-208; LaFleur, "Enlightenment for Plants and Trees," pp. 109-116; Parkes, "Voices of Mountains, Trees, and Rivers," pp. 114-118; Groner, "Realization of Buddhahood by Grasses and Trees," pp. 22-23. Harvey, *Buddhist Ethics*, p. 177.

Donald Shively find these exchanges on the Buddhahood of plants and trees present as a theme in Nō plays in Japan, in which characters discuss "the doctrine of attainment of Buddhahood by grasses and trees." Much of the discussion draws upon the parable of the herbs from the Lotus Sūtra that convinces both lay characters and monks that "nonsentient grasses and trees can rely [on becoming Buddha]" and "reveals that grasses and trees and land, the sentient and the nonsentient, are all elements in their True State."

...the grasses and trees
In their own colors and fragrances,
Will become Buddha, the land will become Buddha,
And belong to the land of Buddhahood....
The nonsentient grasses and trees are, in truth,

The substance of Genuine Thusness without form...
The grasses and trees and the land, each of itself,
Has an affinity through adoring the Buddha and hearing the Law.

Important to remember here, as in the discussion above of other East Asian Buddhist sources, is that plants, grasses, and trees, while attributed with Buddha-nature and the possibility of Buddhahood are, nevertheless, described as "nonsentient." Their Buddha-nature is based on "the view that the grasses and trees contain the same basic nature as all things," and thus are like mountains and rocks in the availability of Buddhahood to them. This inclusivistic view is reminiscent of the hylozoistic view of Jainism where all matter has life and where souls *(jīvas)* are ubiquitous, even appearing in earth, air, fire, water, and plant bodies; Shively, "Buddhahood for the Nonsentient," pp. 137, 141-145; see also Grosnick, "Buddhahood of Trees and Grasses," pp. 200, 201, 207; Johnson, *Harmless Souls*, p. 1.

203 LaFleur, "Sattva: Enlightenment for Plants and Trees," pp. 136-144.

204 See Larson and Bhattacharya, *Encyclopedia of Indian Philosophies* 4.197-198; Larson, *Classical Sāṁkhya*, pp. 11-14; Gītā chs. 17 and 18; Manu ch. 12.

205 Krishnamurthy, *Source Book of Indian Medicine*, pp. 109, 111, 114, 115.

206 Schmithausen, *Problem of the Sentience of Plants*, pp. 61-62; *Plants as Sentience Beings*, p. 33.

207 T. W. Rhys Davids and Stede, *Pali Text Society's Pali-English Dictionary*, p. 298.

208 Schmithausen, *Problem of the Sentience of Plants*, pp. 61-64.

209 UD 29.37; SK 2.4.

210 UD 29.37; SK 2.4.

211 Krishnamurthy, *Source Book of Indian Medicine*, pp. 82-90.

212 Bhattacharya and Archer, *Vidyāpati*, p. 87.

213 Mbh 12.114.7; 12.294.24-27.

214 Mbh 12.306.42.

215 S 2.117-118, 143, 153; A 3.163; Woodward, *Gradual Sayings* 2.122, 146, 158; Hare, *Gradual Sayings* 3.123.

216 Shantideva, *Way of the Bodhisattva*, p. 113.

217 Sullivan, "Paradise Polluted: Religious Dimensions of the Vrindāvana Ecology Movement," p. 565; Prime, *Hinduism and Ecology*, p. 56. See also Banwari's remark that planting "a tree on the roadside can be a more worthy act than giving birth to unworthy children, because a tree can at least provide shade, flowers, fruits, and wood to

a common man;" *Pañcavaṭī: Indian Approach to Environment*, p. 161.

218 Prime, *Hinduism and Ecology*, p. 84.

219 Prime, *Hinduism and Ecology*, pp. 88-89.

220 Shilapi, "Environmental and Ecological Teachings of Tīrthaṅkara Mahāvīra," p. 162.

221 McDermott, *Early Buddhist Concept*, p. 41.

222 Schmithausen, *Buddhism and Nature*, p. 26.

223 Says Collins: "In general, enlightened men are said to be still affected by the results of their past bad *karma*, though they create no new *karma;* "Collins, *Selfless Persons*, p. 207; see p. 223.

224 Nelson, "Reading the *Bhagavadgītā* from an Ecological Perspective," p. 139. Nelson's italics.

225 Tatia, *Tattvārtha Sūtra: That Which Is*, p. xix.

B.
PLANTS AND HUMANS

6

Plants as Humans : Humans as Plants

The inquiry into plants as living, sentient, non-moving, *karma*-bound, and *guṇa*-bearing beings falls under discussions of biology, botany, philosophy, and ethics. These discussions aim to determine certain things about the nature of plants that have every appearance of pertaining to grasses, creepers, herbs, shrubs, and trees in and of themselves – but are, in truth, determined with the human, and to some extent the animal, kingdoms in mind. We now turn to areas where there is no pretense of their being just about the nature of plants alone, but where humans manifestly intertwine their lives with plants and plants, conversely, are understood to do the same with humans. Thus, in this first chapter, we examine the "deities" who take up residence in trees, often using that benign abode for human good or ill; the homologies that are made between plant and human bodies, plant and human behaviors, and plant and human social structures; stories about being transformed into a plant or tree; conversations with plants and trees; marriage with and conception through trees; and divination using trees. Much of this material falls into the realm of folklore and, here, represents some of the roles – usually supportive and enabling – that plants and trees have come to play in human life.

6.1 Tree Deities

We have seen how central plants and trees are in the lives of humans, and with that recognition comes a concern about how "to protect them and preserve them for posterity." Rajan argues that one of the best ways for doing this is already well-established in Indian culture, that of making plants and trees the objects of religious veneration: the "best way to protect the plants is to create a sense of fear and respect in...human mind[s] towards some plants as abodes of God." If we add to this an ethic of *ahiṁsā* that has plants and trees as its objects, there is every reasonable chance that vegetal beings will continue to thrive and flourish within the larger earthscape known to humans.

> The idea of divinity in plants and religious sanctions against destruction of these plants...[is] perhaps the most successful method of conserving and preserving those plants.[1]

As Dwivedi notes, moreover, it continues to be a popular belief in Hinduism that every tree has a *vṛkṣadevatā* or a deity dwelling in the tree,[2] and many domestic and holy spaces have a *caitya vṛkṣa,* or a large tree growing in a sacred spot.[3]

With this, an important distinction needs to be made. It is evident that stories about a tree deity are, in fact, stories about a "spirit as merely living in, and not having its life in, the tree."[4] That is, we can differentiate between issues concerning the tree itself and issues concerning the deity living in the tree. This is made clear, for example, in the narrative given for Pācittiya 11 in the Pali Vinaya where monks decide to cut down a tree to make repairs to a shrine. The *devatā* living in the tree asks the monk assigned to his tree not to fell the tree because he lives there, but the monk does so anyway injuring the *devatā's* son on the arm in the process. The *devatā* considers killing the monk but decides against it, and instead complains to the Buddha who agrees with deity's choice of actions and encourages him to go to live in a certain other tree in a more solitary place. With the resolution of this first part of the narrative a second crisis emerges, for the people *(manassa)* now rise up in complaint, not on behalf of the displaced *devatā,* but because the monks are depriving one-facultied beings, i.e., plants, of life. It is this offense, then, and not the displacement of the deity, that brings about the famous Pācittiya ruling against the destruction of vegetable growth.[5] Thus, M. S. Randhawa notes,

> The tree spirit is independent of the tree. The tree is merely its abode and when it is cut the spirit is requested to move elsewhere...the tree is the abode of a *vana devata* or a tree-god.[6]

Deities living in trees are not all the same, however, and reside there for different reasons and have ritual relations with humans for different purposes.

Tree Deities: Spirits of Fertility, Prosperity, and Protection

One early understanding of the nature of a deity inhabiting a plant is how the deity relates to the health of humans. That is, those plants with healing properties house deities of health and prosperity, while those that cause symptoms of disease house deities of wickedness and debilitation. Concerning the latter, the Atharva Veda has many examples of plants being used to protect humans from curses and witchcraft, and from sorcerers and black magic-inflicting enemies.[7] Atharvan hymns often ask plants outright to find the sorcerers, "by thee let me see all beings, O divine herb...Show me the sorcerers, show the sorcerers...with this intent I take hold of thee, O herb." But there is also evidence that the plants themselves may house or hide the afflicting sorcerers. In AV 4.20.7, for example, the poet calls on a plant by saying: "The eye of Kaśyapa art thou, and of the four-eyed bitch; conceal thou not the *piśāca*"[8] – thus, just as plants are used to reveal those of evil intent, they are also believed to conceal them. Again, an example in the Mahābhārata says that "the cowardly Kali quickly entered the *vibhītaka* tree," causing the Vibhītaka tree to now stand "in ill repute, because Kali took possession of it."[9]

More often, however, the deities that reside in trees are seen as patrons of fertility, prosperity, and protection. The forest goddess, Araṇyānī, for example – the spirit of a whole collection of trees – is called upon in RV 10.146 by those in fear, to protect them against whatever is making nighttime noises and whatever is hiding in the dark.[10] In the Atharva Veda, reference is made to a group of beings called upon to help ferret out enemies, and these include *those "of the forest-trees, herbs and plants,* Gandharvas-and-

Apsarases, serpents, gods, pure-folk *[yakṣas]*... Fathers." And, in the same text, "O thou of ten trees" is called upon as if there is a deity dwelling within, and trees are treated ritually as the equal of the deities: e.g., "O forest tree, sit on the strewn *barhis*, being commensurate with...the deities."[11] Moreover, the Bṛhat Saṁhitā, in a section on the use of trees for building, calls upon those spirits dwelling in the trees to take up residence in another place so that the tree body formerly occupied can be used for various constructions:

> Hail to all beings living in this tree! Salutations to you. May you change your abode after receiving this gift offered by me. O great tree, hail to thee! The kings elects thee for (making) the banner of the Lord of Gods. Kindly accept this worship (and leave the tree).[12]

Popular Hindu lore associates traditional gods and goddesses with certain trees, either as abodes for the deities or as plants sacred to the deities and thus the object of special ritual practice. The god Viṣṇu, for example, is associated with the Indian fig or Pīpal/Pippala /Aśvattha tree; Śiva with the wood apple or Bilvā/Bela tree; Brahmā with the flame/parrot or Palāśa/Kimṣuka tree; Brahmā and Viṣṇu with the Indian fig/banyan tree or Nyagrodha/Vaṭa tree; the sun (Sūrya) with the Nimba or Neem tree; the moon with the Uḍumbara/ Gular tree; Garuda with the mango or Amra tree; and the Buddha with several trees.[13]

Female deities are also thought to have special relations with plants and trees. The goddess Lakṣmī, for example, is associated with the basil or Tulasī/Tulsī plant (a plant sacred to Vaiṣṇavas); Śītalā with the Nimba or Neem tree;[14] and Kālī with the myrobalan or Vibhītaka tree.[15] Moreover, there are nine plant forms ritually associated with the goddess Durgā: Rambhā or the banana plant; Kachavī/Kacu or an edible root; Haridrā or tumeric; the Jayantī plant with medicinal leaves; the Bilvā/Bel or wood apple tree; the Dāḍima or pomegranate tree; the Aśoka tree; the Mānkacu or arum plant; and Dhān or paddy, unhusked, harvested rice.[16]

Perhaps the most well known early expression of tree goddesses are the *yakṣīs* or *yakṣiṇīs* (P. *yakhinīs)*[17] (or *vṛkṣakās)*, said by

Ananda Coomaraswamy to be "auspicious emblems of vegetative fertility." They often appear at Buddhist sites like Bharhut, Sanchi, Amaravati, and Mathura, and are known for their broad hips and firm, round breasts, suggesting "the fecundity of nature." *Yakṣīs* are often depicted in the *śālabhañjikā* pose, a term used for an image made from Śāl wood, but also describing a scantily-dressed and curvaceous woman holding on to a tree. One famous pose has the *yakṣī* grasping the overhead branches of a tree with her right hand and embracing the tree trunk with her left arm and her left leg.

> This is the famous *dohada* pose when a beautiful maiden awakens asoka flowers by the touch of her foot. The buds of the asoka suddenly open and this characteristic has possibly given rise to the poetic fancy of its flowering when kicked by a beautiful young woman.[18]

This image has an early rendering in the Buddha's mother, Mahāmāyā, who is depicted standing in the Lumbini garden stretching out her right arm to hold onto a Śāl tree while delivering Siddhārtha from her right side.[19]

Tree deities of both genders have a variety of relations with human beings. In addition to giving the blessing of children,[20] they offer food and drink to wayfaring travelers,[21] and express emotions to humans, such as grief at having limbs cut off or at the thought of being completely cut down.[22] In one Jain story, a man comes by a large banyan and eats his fill of the fruit, but in the process breaks off one of the branches. The spirit dwelling in the tree is outraged at the injury to such a magnificent tree and wonders what people would do if the tree stopped bearing fruit. The tree spirit then comes to Tīrthaṇkara Mahāvīra and complains that someone has cut off his child's arm, whereupon Mahāvīra rules against the mutilation of trees.[23]

Anxiety is another emotion expressed by tree *devatās*, as narrated in a story from the Majjhima Nikāya. Here a creeper threatens to encircle and choke a Śāl tree, and the resident deity becomes greatly agitated but "seems powerless to do anything about the danger." Ryan sees in this story the sharing of the tree's "passive nature" by its resident spirit who cannot act but also cannot be comforted by anyone who comes to visit. Such a visitor could "only urge him not to be afraid" as he imagines the tree's seeds being eaten, its trunk being chopped down, or its whole body being consumed by a forest fire.[24]

Another story, told by Buddhaghosa, is of a female tree spirit joining the community of renunciants. Given permission to build lodgings outside the walls of the monastery, a certain monk decides to cut down a tree that he wants to use in the building. The resident spirit, a mother with a child, appears before the monk to beg him not to destroy her home, saying she will never find another one like it. She puts her child on a branch of the tree hoping to further persuade the monk, but it's too late and the monk swings his axe cutting off the child's arm. The mother spirit is furious and vows to kill the monk, but then reconsiders for fear of setting a precedent for such actions by other tree-spirits. Ultimately she decides to tell the Buddha, and confesses to him her urge to kill the monk for his injury to her child and his destruction of her home, and then confesses her subsequent prudence. The Buddha congratulates her on the restraint of her anger, and the mother tree spirit is welcomed into the Buddhist community.[25]

Tree spirits are frequent players in the Buddhist Jātaka tales, often being the rebirth body of the Buddha-to-be, or Bodhisattva, himself.[26] In these stories, as in others noted above, the tree spirits are great conversationalists, and play active roles in solving human problems and in teaching moral lessons to other members of the forest community, including to other tree spirits resident in trees nearby. In Jātaka 98, for instance, a merchant has his father hide in the hollow of a tree and pretend to be a tree spirit so as to decide a case in his son's favor against another competing merchant. The Bodhisattva, reborn as the merchant who loses the falsely adjudicated case, decides to test the "spirit-judge" and sets fire to the tree, rousting (or roasting) out the father. The deceit unveiled, the two merchants agree to split the proceeds, but at their deaths each goes separately to their own rewards.

Another version of this story is found in the Kathāsaritsāgara where two brothers, Dharmabuddhi and Duṣṭabuddhi, bury their wealth at the foot of a tree. One day the extravagant brother, Duṣṭabuddhi, digs up the money and, in time, suggests to his brother that they go and retrieve their wealth. When it is not found, Duṣṭabuddhi accuses Dharmabuḍdhi of taking it and demands that he give him his share. In time, the case is to be decided by the tree himself, but Duṣṭabuddhi bribes their father to hide in the hollow of the tree and be his witness. This the father does, but the king's officers witnessing the adjudication are not fooled and smoke the father out of the tree who then dies on the ground. Both the hands and the tongue of Duṣṭabuddhi are cut off, and Dharmabuddhi is rewarded with all the money and a good reputation.[27]

Again, in Jātaka 121, the Buddha-to-be is born as a Kuśa grass spirit who saves a sacred tree from being cut down for use as a pillar in the king's palace. The grass spirit is impelled into action when the nearby tree spirit bursts into tears at not being able to save the tree herself and thus to protect the home of her children. So, the grass spirit turns into a chameleon, getting into the roots and branches of the tree, and making it look as if it is full of holes. The tree spirit, delighted, then says: "Sprites of the Trees, for all our mighty power we knew not what to do; while a humble Kusa-sprite had wit to save my home for me."[28]

Again, in Jātaka 414, a tree spirit speaks in riddles with the Buddha-to-be and, in Jātaka 392, a female tree spirit debates the Buddha-to-be over whether smelling a flower involves "stealing" its scent. The tree spirit contends that the Bodhisattva was never actually given the flower that he's smelling, so that by sniffing the scent he's committed a theft; he counters by saying that he has never taken or broken the flower and is smelling it only from afar.[29] Finally, in Jātaka 475, when a lion gets angry at a tree because a branch accidentally falls on him, he persuades a cartwright to cut the tree down to make a wheel. Discovering this, the tree spirit assumes the shape of a woodman in order to trick the wheelwright into flaying the lion's skin to make a cover for the new wheel, thus putting off the destruction of his home. In the end, however, both lion and tree meet their ends.[30] Thus, the Buddhist world of the Jātakas is a lively one, where the magnanimous and the malicious get their just desserts.

Tree Deities: Ghosts of the Dead

Trees can house spirits who bring sickness, who bestow fertility, prosperity, and protection, and who have sacred ties with particular plants. They can also house the spirits of the recently departed who, while still in states of transition, are unsatisfied and need human attending. The ritualist in AV 18.3.70, in fact, says to a tree: "Give back, O forest tree *(vanaspati),* him who is deposited here with thee, that in Yama's seat he may sit speaking counsels."[31] The tradition of the *preta* or *pretī* (P. *peta/petī)*[32] or the dead, but not-yet-reembodied, person appears early in the Vedic practices of cremation and reverence of the ancestors. Oldenberg notes the many times that plants and plant materials are used in the preparation of the cremation site, in the cremation itself, in the treatment of a dead person's relics, and in the offerings to and for the ancestors. Of the use of ŚB 13.8.1.20 in the building of the mound over the relics – i.e., "the fathers slip into the roots of the plants" – for example, he suggests this as a possible "instance of the belief in dead souls living in plants and trees."[33] Certainly, the later presence of ancestral spirits or ghosts in plants and trees is prefigured in the early Śrāddha rituals, and also in such verses as RV 10.16.3 where the dead person's limbs are sent to reside in plants *(oṣadhi).*[34]

Just prior to the Vedic rite of *sapiṇḍīkaraṇa,* for example – "the moment of entry of the deceased into the world of the ancestors" or *pitaraḥ,* and "the series of bodily constructions and dissolutions the deceased undergoes before becoming established in the world beyond"[35] – there can occur an important custom relating to the tradition of ghosts of the dead living in trees. This custom, one less expensive than the standard one, includes hanging two clay pots (with water and a lamp) in a Pippala tree for the dead. The water is for the dead "who lingers in or near the tree until the rite of sapiṇḍīkaraṇa," and the lamp is to provide light for the *preta* during his time in and around the tree. When, on the tenth day, "the subtle body disappears in favor of the newly ritualized intermediate body," the pots are destroyed.[36] For the full (and more expensive) ritual, during these ten days, the appropriate descendant of the deceased ritually pours water with sesame seeds over a ball of cooked white rice *(piṇḍa)*. This is repeated with a single ball of rice each day for the ten days, but with the number of cups of sesame water increasing each day by one.

> And each day of the rites results in a new portion of the preta's intermediate body, the head being created on the first day, then in succession the neck and shoulders, the heart and torso, the back, the stomach, the thighs and bowels, the lower legs and skin, the knees and hair, the genitals, and, on the tenth day of the offerings, the preta receives digestive powers so that the sufferings of hunger and thirst now experienced by the 'body of nourishment' duly created may be allayed by continued offerings of piṇḍas and water from the living.[37]

During this period, prior to receiving digestive powers, the *preta* is immensely hungry. Moreover, he or she can be even hungrier if the survivors are not properly providing food and water to create the intermediate body so that the *preta* can enter the world of the *pitaraḥ*. A hungry *preta*, then, is something to avoid – as the 'hungry ghost' stories so well known in Buddhist literature make clear.

In the Pali Petavatthu, or stories about the departed, the *petas* and *petīs* are living out the fruit of past wicked deeds in a purgatory where they are constantly hungry and thirsty. They can appear any time, day or night, in many places, and are often recognized by their friends and relatives; from these people the *petas* then seek relief from their suffering through the giving of gifts. The *petas*, however, do not profit directly from the gifts, but instead receive the merit transferred to them from the act of giving itself and can, thus, be "released from the peta purgatory by the devotion of friends and the concomitant transfer of merit."[38] In Pali mythology, the *petas* and *petīs* are non-humans who live in a world populated by other non-humans, in particular, the powerful and often corpulent *yakkhas* who "range in appearance immediately above the Petas" and who may indeed be happy or successful *petas*. The *yakkhas* "represent creatures of the wilds and forests"[39] and are "images of prosperity universally associated with agrarian cultures."[40] Thus, they have a connection with the *petas* who often live in trees. Life as a *peta* is considered a low one, a status reflected in lowness of their some-time abode, a tree: "at the moment of death his heart became impure, and he was reborn in a lower state and became a dryad in a large banyan tree of dense shade in the jungle."[41] Groups of *petas* can be reborn together in tree groves – "Reborn as petas in the Vindhya forest, their sufferings are here told" – and any tree home of a *peta* will be evident to viewers by the food and water offerings that have been placed at its roots.[42]

A slightly different vision of the *preta* issue is presented in Shively's discussion of the fourteenth and fifteenth century *nō* plays of Japan. While we have already noted the debates over the Buddha-nature and Buddhahood of grasses and trees that take place among Chinese and Japanese Buddhists and that form part of Shively's discussion, the main theme of these plays is, he notes, to pose such questions in a more popular setting. While a central focus of the *nō* plays is the attainment of Buddhahood by the ghosts of historical figures, Shively turns to what happens when the ghost *(preta)* under discussion is not of an historical figure but of "a plant or tree or flower, or some other nonsentient phenomenon,"[43] for there is, he argues, very little difference in the structure of the play when the protagonist is a plant spirit. It is important to remember, then, that at least in the *nō* plays, the discussion of the Buddha-nature or Buddhahood of plants comes up in the context not (1) of live plant bodies themselves, or (2) of the *pretas* of other beings who happen to live in plants, but (3) of the *pretas* of plants themselves whether living in plants or in some other place.[44] The implication of the discussions is that plants are sentient beings equal to humans in that they, too, can become *pretas* – spirits in the process of being re-membered on their way to rebirth. A sobering element in an otherwise hopeful scheme for plant enthusiasts, however, is that there also appear such spirits as that of the snow, a reminder that the doctrine that makes the *preta*-hood of plants and trees possible is one that also posits the Buddha-hood of grasses, trees, and land– that is of "earth and sand, mountains and rivers," as well.[45]

Rituals for Trees and Tree Deities

Deities present in grasses, plants, and trees are often the objects of worship, as are the trees that they inhabit. Beginning with the latter, the Bṛhat Saṁhitā describes the ritual preparations for planting a tree:

> After becoming pure (by taking bath) and having worshiped a tree by bathing it (ablutions) and smearing it (with fragrant paste), one is to plant (a tree).[46]

Planting a tree brings great merit and, depending on what kind of tree one plants, merit accrues accordingly: the Nyagrodha tree, for example, brings the blessing of children;[47] the Tulasī brings powerful life in heaven; the Bilvā brings sons and grandsons; the Aśvattha brings rebirth in Hari's land; the Nyagrodha/Vaṭa brings rebirth in Śiva's land; five mango trees brings rescue for many generations of ancestors; while the Kṣīriṇī, Dāḍimī, Rambhā, Piyāla and Paṅa all bring misery to the planter for seven rebirths.[48] Kane describes the festival of Vṛkṣotsavavidhi that is performed at the time a tree is planted. It includes the decoration of the tree with scented powders, flowers, cloth, and water and the offering to it of fruits and gold; offerings are also made to the gods Indra, Vanaspati, and the Lokapālas, as well as to the attendant priests and brāhmaṇas. In this way, the Matsya Purāṇa prescribes the following:

> Decorate trees with garlands, burn the guggula perfume in front of them, and place one pitcher filled with water by the side of each tree. Offer prayer and oblation and then sprinkle holy water on trees. Recite hymns from the Rigveda, Yajur and Sama and kindle fire. After such worship the actual plantation should be celebrated. *He who plants even one tree, goes directly to Heaven and obtains Moksha.*[49]

The Matsya Purāṇa expresses a key sentiment of this ritual: that "a son is equal to ten deep reservoirs of water and [that] *a tree planted is equal to ten sons.*" The Varāha Purāṇa, moreover, notes that while a good son saves his family, a tree that bears fruits and flowers saves its owner from hell – a sentiment echoed in the Viṣṇudharmottara Purāṇa.[50]

Ritual honoring of trees continues in contemporary times where the worship of Durgā, for example, is performed through the ceremonial bathing of nine plants: the Rambhā (banana) plant, the

Dāḍima (pomegranate) tree, Dhān (paddy or unhusked, harvested rice), the Haridrā (tumeric) root, the Kachavī/Kacu root, the Mānkacu (arum) plant, the Bilvā/Bel (wood apple) tree, the Aśoka tree, and the Jayantī plant. Each plant form of Durgā is worshipped for some particular blessing, such as peace, grace, boons, protection, and destruction of obstacles.[51]

Worship of trees is found in Buddhism as well. The most important tree rituals are directed toward the Pippala or bodhi tree, who is worshipped at the instruction of the Buddha himself. It is said that the Buddha asked Ānanda to get "a branch of the tree under which he...obtained Buddhahood, and to plant it in the court of the Vihara at Sravasti; adding that 'he who worships it will receive the same reward as if he worshipped me in person.'" As part of its worship, the roots of the bodhi tree are bathed every anniversary of the Buddha's *nirvāṇa*-day with scented water and perfumed milk, and the tree is honored with music, flowers, perfumes, and other gifts.[52] Moreover, of Jātaka 479, it is said that Ānanda planted a seed from the Buddha's bodhi tree at the gateway of the Jetavana grounds so that people would have a place to honor the Buddha in his absence. Notes the Buddha:

> This is not the first time, Brethren, that Ānanda led captive mankind in the four great continents, with all the surrounding throngs, and caused a vast quantity of scented wreaths to be brought, and made a bo-festival in the precinct of the great bo-tree.[53]

Many renunciants who heard of the tree shrine, Ānanda's Bo Tree, came to Jetavana to make offerings.[54]

In the Jātakas, rituals for other trees are mentioned often and that of a mango tree is as follows:

> Great was the worship paid to this tree; milk-water was poured about it; perfumed garlands with five sprays were hung upon it; wreaths were festooned about it; a lamp was kept burning, and fed with scented oil; and all round it was a screen of cloth.

This particular mango bore great and wonderful fruit as a result of such worship, but when bitter creepers became entangled in it – that is, when the gardener failed to take appropriate care – the fruit became sour and bitter.[55]

Other trees are venerated in Buddhism, but not ordinarily for the tree itself; instead, they are venerated for the presence of the deity living in the trees to whom the worship is actually directed. Randhawa notes that, ordinarily, the "tree is worshipped not for its own sake, but because it is the home of the spirit." Worship of tree deities is especially important when builders seek to chop down the deities' tree-homes, and the deities are asked to move elsewhere.[56] Rituals are then undertaken to ask for forgiveness from the soon-to-be-destroyed-tree for those about to take its life.

In Buddhist literature, rituals for tree deities are customary, and the most well known, perhaps, is that of Sujātā who promised the deity in the local banyan tree that she would offer him a gift of rice-milk if she bore a son. When she did, she sent her maid Puṇṇā to the tree to prepare a spot for the offering. Puṇṇā, however, found the newly enlightened Buddha sitting under the tree and, when told, Sujātā herself came with the offering thinking the Buddha to be the tree deity. In the Jātakas, many trees like the Nyagrodha, the Śāl, and the silk-cotton trees, are homes for tree deities, and each appears in rituals dedicated to their occupant:

> Long on this spot a famous tree has stood,
> Meet dwelling-place for spirits of the wood;
> With deepest awe such beings I revere,
> they guard, methinks, some sacred treasure here.[57]

In one such ritual, a wounded man-eating robber goes to the foot of a banyan tree, lies down in its shoots and says a prayer to the tree deity:

> My lady, nymph of the tree, if within seven days thou canst heal my wound, I will bathe thy trunk with blood from the throats of one hundred and one princes from all India, and will hang the tree all round with their innards and offer up a sacrifice of the five sweet kinds of flesh.[58]

Although the narrative of the tale proceeds with great complication, this short passage illustrates the power attributed to tree deities and the extent of the offerings a petitioner is willing to give for successful outcome of a request. Tree deities are not only the object of worship, but also the giver of gifts, most clearly depicted, for example, in sculpture at Bodhgaya, Bharhut, and Mathura where the tree deity is shown offering food and drink to a traveler. "Only the projecting hands of the tree-god can be seen, one holding a plate with a *chapatti* and another a vessel containing water."[59] Thus, tree deities are suggestive of the many ways service is offered by the trees themselves.

6.2 Plants and Human Homologies

To draw such a parallel – that the services offered by the deity living in a tree are much like the services offered by the tree itself – suggests that there may be even more ways that lives of plants are correspondent, that is, homologous, with the lives of humans. We have already seen the example of the fertilizing power of sesame (Tila). From the Vṛkṣāyurveda, for example, we know that sesame is important in preparing soils and seeds for healthy growth in the ground.

> A soft soil is favourable (for planting) trees of all kinds. Sesamum is to be sown in that (such a soil). After (sesamum plants) have blossomed they are to be crushed (to be mixed in the soil). This is the first work to be done for (the improvement of) the soil.[60]
> A seed, soaked in milk and besmeared with the ashes of Bṛhatī and sesamum *(tila)* and with ghee, rubbed with cowdung and fumigated with fat *(vasā)* and then sown, grows at once.[61]

We know, moreover, that, in the funerary rituals prior to the *sapiṇḍīkaraṇa,* sesame seeds in water are poured over the white rice balls *(piṇḍa),* representing the *preta,* for ten days: "the cups of [sesame] water offered...increase by one each day until there are ten on the final day. And each day of the rites results in a new portion of the preta's intermediate body" being created, beginning with the head, then moving down through the body, until finally on the tenth day the intermediate body is finished and is at last endowed with the powers of digestion – so that he will no longer be hungry and thirsty.[62] This suggests that what is known about the fertilizing powers of sesame for plant bodies is transferred to what is hoped to be the fertilizing powers of sesame for human bodies, here the specific body of the *preta* who is to be transformed, through sesame application, into a new being ultimately destined for rebirth. Moreover, the growth-support powers of sesame must have been known early on, given what we see of its homologic appearance in this portion of the Vedic Śrāddha rites.

The possibilities for homologies between plants and humans are many, for as the Jain Uttarādhyayana notes: "As the fallow leaf of the tree falls to the ground, when its days are gone, even so the life of men (will come to its close)."[63] Such possibilities are suggested early on in discussions of sacrificial causality, where Schmidt highlights the sentiment of Manu 5.54, for example, in his proclamation that the eater will be eaten in the next life by him whom he ate in this life. Schmidt develops this by examining materials in the Śatapatha Brāhmaṇa and finds, in ŚB 12.9.1.1, the notion that what "food a man consumes in this world, that consumes him, in return, in yonder world." There are, again, some examples in ŚB 11.6.1.1-13: of someone (a former tree) now cutting a tree who is the former woodcutter who cut him; of someone (a former animal) now slaughtering and eating an animal who is the former slaughterer and eater of him; and of someone (a former plant) now eating someone who is the former eater of him. He further cites H. Lommel's remark about the sacrificial system involving "the conception of yonder world as an inverted world where everything of this world is turned into its opposite."[64] Although Schmidt uses this idea to evoke early views about behavior and consequences *(karma),* it is considered here as a possibility of homologic inversion: first, this world and yonder world are homologies, but are in inverse relation one to the other; and, second, the players in this system are all living beings, humans, animals, and plants.

Plants in Sacrificial and Cosmic Homologies

The practice of understanding this world as patterned with respect to another world around plants and trees is perhaps first expressed in literature of the Vedic sacrifice. In RV 1.24.7, an inverted tree is correlated with the cosmos for, as sustained by the god Varuṇa, the cosmic tree is held aloft with its roots above and its branches below – an image echoed later in the Bhagavad Gītā.[65] An early example of ritual homologies using plants appears in the Aitareya Brāhmaṇa: "The sacrificial post is yonder sun, the altar the earth, *the strew the plants, the kindling wood the trees,* the sprinkling waters the waters, the enclosing sticks the quarters."[66] By identifying parts of the sacrifice with parts of the external world, the ritualist understands that, by properly setting up and manipulating the central items of the ritual, he is creating again, and continuing to properly maintain, the central order of the life-sustaining world without which humans cannot survive.

Ritual homology becomes cosmic at the beginning of the Bṛhadāraṇyaka Upaniṣad with the sacrificial horse as its base pattern:

dawn = horse's head	seasons = limbs
sun = eye	months, mid-months = joints
wind = breath	days and nights = feet
mouth = fire	stars = bones
year = body	clouds = flesh
sky = back	sand = food in stomach
atmosphere = belly	rivers = blood vessels
earth = hoof	mountains = liver and lungs
quarters = sides	*herbs and trees = hair*
mid-quarters = ribs[67]	

The homology of herbs and trees with the cosmic horse's hair here is reminiscent of other Upaniṣadic passages that describe plants' place in the cycle of life and death, where at death a person's hair is distributed among the plants.[68] Related to this image – of plants growing out of the earth being like hairs growing out of the head – is one of the metaphors used for the cosmos' relation to Brahman:

> As a spider sends forth and draws in (its thread), as herbs grown on the earth, as the hair (grows) on the head and the

> body of a living person, so from the Imperishable arises here the universe.[69]

Moreover, the fruit of the Nyagrodha tree becomes the homologous object of instruction when Śvetaketu's father wants him to understand the imperceptibility of the subtle essence that is the *ātman* or 'self' permeating the very fine seeds of the fruit as well as the whole world: and "that," he says to his son, that is in the very fine fig seed "you are" *(tat tvam asi)*.[70] Again, in the Chāndogya Upaniṣad, cereal grains become part of the paradoxical instruction on both the subtlety of the self within the heart and the concomitant expansiveness of the self in the cosmos. Thus, Śāṇḍilya says: "This is my self within the heart, smaller than a grain of rice, than a barley corn, than a mustard seed, than a grain of millet or than the kernel of a grain of millet. This is myself within the heart, greater than the earth, greater than the atmosphere, greater than the sky, greater than these worlds."[71]

Plant and Human Bodies

As Joel Brereton says of Upaniṣadic homologists, their "most frequent correlation is between the macrocosm and the human body."

> That is, they equate the parts of the body to the constituents of the visible world, so that the whole world becomes the image of the human form. In this way, instead of appearing external and alien, the world becomes a familiar place and a place in which humans occupy a central position.[72]

A well-known example of this is BĀU 3.9.28 in which a man is compared to a tree: "as is a mighty tree so, indeed is a man." Thus, a person's hairs are the tree's leaves and his skin the outer bark; and when blood flows from skin, it is as sap flowing from a tree's bark, for "when a man is wounded blood flows as sap from a tree that is struck." A person's flesh is the tree's inner bark, his nerves tough like the tree's inner fibers, his bones the wood inside, and his marrow the interior pith. The homology continues here with the proceeds from death, for when a tree is cut a new one normally springs up from the root – though this seems not to be true of a person unless the later doctrine of *karma* is applied where the roots giving rise to a new person are the roots of past karmic deeds. This passage, however, ends with the homology in place, for if "a tree is pulled up with the roots, it will not spring again" like a person who when "born...is not born" again.[73]

A correlation of the creation of a person with the creation of the cosmos appears in the Aitareya Upaniṣad where, as each body part is separated out, another aspect comes into being:

> mouth – speech, then fire
> nostrils – breath, then air
> eyes – sight, then sun
> ears – hearing, then quarters of space
> *skin – hair, then plants and trees*
> heart – mind, then moon
> navel – out breath, then death
> generative organ – semen, then water[74]

Note here, first, that plants and trees are again associated with the hairs on a person's or the cosmic body and, second, that they are associated with the skin – and therefore with touch – as is consonant with their assignment to the category of one-sense-facultied beings. In the Bṛhat Saṁhitā, the correlation continues: "just as there are veins in the human body," so there are rivers and water channels on earth,[75] and an alternate homology correlates tree roots with human mouths, as inlets where both take in water allowing growth. From a Śiva collection:

> The root is the mouth
> of the tree: pour water there
> at the bottom
> and, look, it sprouts green
> at the top.[76]

Other kinds of homologies have to do with classification systems related to the body. The Vṛkṣāyurveda passages in the Bṛhat Saṁhitā suggests a parallel between tree medicine and human medicine with the application of the three humoral classification types used in human medicine – wind, bile, and phlegm – to trees. Speaking about BS 55.15, Bhat notes the interpretation of a commentary "that trees get diseases by the vitiation of the three humours, *vāta, pitta* and *kapha* (wind, bile and phlegm),"[77] and should be treated, as humans are treated, according to the standard humoral diagnoses. In Surapāla, there is an assessment of plant diseases that notes they are of two kinds, those arising from the body, that are internal, and those arising from outside the body, that are external. Of those arising from inside the body, plant diseases "are caused by (disorders of) wind, phlegm and bile *(vāta, kapha, pitta)*."[78] And, finally, trees provide an analogy for the progress of human disease. As the Suśruta Saṁhitā notes:

> As a tree *(vanaspati),* full grown in due course of time, drives its roots, which derive their nourishment from the rain water, deeper and deeper into the successive strata of the soil, so this disease... first affecting and confining itself to the upper layers of the skin, in due course of time will invade the deeper tissues and organs...of the patient.[79]

A second kind of body homology uses plants and trees as they evoke the sensual and erotic life, especially in relation to women. In Aśvaghoṣa's Buddhacarita, for example, the Aśoka tree increases love's sorrow, as shown by the black bees humming around it "as if they are with fire burning." The Tilaka tree embraced by a mango branch is like a man dressed in white embraced by a woman covered with yellow balm. And the branches of the Kurubaka tree with their lac-red flowers are bent down like the hands of beautiful ladies with painted nails.[80]

Women's Bodies

One of the most powerful homologies is that specifically of a woman's body, and parts of a woman's body, with plants. Speaking of Sītā in the Rāmāyaṇa, for example, Rāma says,

> O my dear, thou delightest greatly in flowers. Covering thy own person with *Asoka* twigs thou art increasing my grief. Thy thighs are like unto the trunks of plantain trees and thou has hidden thyself behind the plantain grove.[81]

In the Jātaka tales, a queen-consort is described as "lithe as a shoot of fair moringa tree," and stories of female tree deities may serve, argues Ryan, as reminders of "the dangers of sensuality, represented by the 'young, soft, and downy arms' of female religious mendicants."[82] In Śakuntalā, a woman's body is likened to a plant with fluid and agile lines, empowered even more by its beauty in all seasons and by the service it offers during the year. Of Śakuntalā, the poet says

> She seems a flower whose fragrance none has tasted...
> A branch no desecrating hands have wasted...
> Your body, soft as siris-flowers.[83]

Moreover, a woman living among ascetics is said to be like a ripe bud among withered leaves,[84] and certainly the erotic lure of Śakuntalā is not diminished by her living close to nature in a grove of trees. Of separated lovers, Vidyāpati says of the woman that "the ache of parting has thinned her body," leaving it like a withered flower.[85] Bilhaṇa describes the object of his fantasy as "beautiful and fine-limbed...ready for the festival of love...looking like a champac flower in bloom...[and] gleeming in garlands of gold champac flowers," and the girl of Ciṟaikkuṭiyāntaiyār's dreams "is the new leaf in the rain."[86] Finally, Campantar describes Śiva's bride, the daughter of the mountains, as a "woman who glows with the loveliness of a young sprout."[87]

Body : Creeper. The most well known image is that of the woman's body compared to a creeper. This image is used often in Śakuntalā, as when Priyaṁvada says to her, "when I see you there, it looks as if a vine were clinging to the mango-tree," and "the jasmine-vine...has chosen the mango-tree as her husband."[88] Of Kṛṣṇa's love, Jayadeva says that "when spring came, tender-limbed Rādhā wandered like a flowering creeper in the forest wilderness."[89] Ūma, the bride of Śiva, is described as "slender as a creeper"[90] and, in Hemacandra, a girl is said to be "like a creeping plant, ready to flower, if only manured."[91] Finally, Surdas says of the young girls looking for their lover that the "trees dispatch their messenger girls – the vines – to find their loves."[92]

Face : Lotus. The beloved has, for Vidyāpati, a lotus-face, shining in the moonlight with new leaves all around that "caress the lotus bud" but, though like a lotus, the beloved's face "outshines the lotus."[93] With the dawn of love, for Bilhaṇa, the beloved's face is a "lotus face blossoming" or "a golden lotus in full bloom" or a "lotus face outshining the moon."[94] In Jayadeva's poem, Rādhā has a "sublime lotus face" and a cheek that "is a honey-colored flower," while Kṛṣṇa also has a lotus face, for he has "the lotus face of Madhu's killer...the lotus face of Mura's foe."[95] And in the Suśruta Saṁhitā, beautiful, young "lotused-faced" girls are healthy advertisements for the application of medicinal pastes to the body.[96]

Eyes : Lotus. Again, as it describes the application of these pastes, the Suśruta notes the "languid blue-lotus-like eyes" of young girls.[97] In the Rāmāyaṇa, Rāma asks of his lost Sītā, "having eyes resembling lotus-petals...[has she] gone to bring lotuses?"[98] and Vidyāpati describes the beloved's eyes as "rival lotuses," and together as lotuses that open wide with "widening smile."[99] A "lotus-eyed girl," says Bilhaṇa, has "long eyes, like petals of night-blooming lotus," and Jayadeva repeatedly calls Rādhā, the other gopīs, and even Kṛṣṇa, lovers with lotus-petaled eyes.[100] In Jayadeva, again, the young women who look for love under the cover of darkness have "night-lily eyes," and Rādhā has "dark lotus pupils" in eyes that are "angry...scarlet lilies," and eyes that "glower like gleaming dark lotuses."[101] Kapilar says of the young beloved that her eyes are "like flowers, gathering flowers from pools for her garlands," and Ciṟaikkuṭiyāntaiyār notes that

> Her eyes are cool, full-bodied
> buds of the dewy rain flower
> streaked with red,
> and she is the new leaf
> in the rain.[102]

Lips : Berries and Buds. Lips "like the ripe *Bimba* fruit in their luminous redness" are the sign of health in Suśruta's description of the application of body pastes and unguents.[103] In Śakuntalā, the king says that the heroine's "lips are blossoms red and warm,"[104] and Bilhaṇa describes the beloved's lips as being "the luscious red of balsam apples." Jayadeva says Rādhā has "luscious red berry lips," or "sweet berry lips," or moist lips that "glow like crimson autumn blossoms," while Kṛṣṇa's lips are "ruby-red buds."[105]

Mouth : Lotus. Again, the king describes Śakuntalā's "mouth as red as red karkandhu-fruit,"[106] and when Rādhā encounters Kṛṣṇa, Vidyāpati says that her mouth is a shut lotus that blooms when she smiles," while Bilhaṇa describes the beloved's mouth as a "fresh red lotus petal" or a "crimson date bloom."[107] Jayadeva notes that for her lover Rādhā is asked to "bring wine in your lotus mouth," and that during love-making she exudes a heady "fragrance from her lotus mouth."[108]

Teeth: Jasmine. Of the beloved, Bilhaṇa says, she has "teeth like lustrous jasmine blooms...exquisite gleaming teeth outshining jasmine buds,"[109] an image also found in Jayadeva where Rādhā has teeth of white jasmine.[110] In Okkūr Mācātti, we find

> Her teeth of jasmine
> strung on the rain-shadowed creeper
> this season of cool rains
> will laugh.[111]

Jayadeva also says of Rādhā that her "teeth glow like seeds of ripe pomegranate," and Catti Nātaṉār that the beloved has "teeth like sprouts of new rice."[112] Moreover, a woman's throat is a thing of beauty for, in the Rāmāyaṇa, Sītā now lost is remembered by Rāma as having a "soft, lovely throat, pale as the *campaka* flower."[113]

Breasts : Plums, Wood Apples, and Palm Fruits. Vidyāpati describes Rādhā's breasts as being like plums as they grow "large, harder and crisper, aching for love," and again as "crisp green plums that change to crimson red."[114] In Jayadeva, Rādhā's "swollen breasts are riper than palm fruits,"[115] that is, coconuts, like the wood apple fruit that is also used as a comparison for a woman's breast. And, Bilhaṇa says that the beloved's heart is like "a fresh bouquet of wild flowers gathered for me from the forest."[116] Moreover, other intimate areas are homologized with plants and plant parts as well. In the Jain Rāmāyaṇa, Lakṣmaṇa asks of a young girl, are "these the loins? No, these are the ripe wood apples... [and are these] the lines of jewels[? N]o these are the new bards of the jasmine flowers."[117]

Arms : Creepers and Bamboo. In the Rāmāyaṇa, Sītā's arms are remembered as being "soft as a spray of leaves," and in Śakuntalā her "arms are tender shoots."[118] For Bilhaṇa, a beloved's arms are like creepers "chained around my neck," for Jayadeva her arm is like a creeper, or a flower, or a vine, or a "cool pale supple stalk;" while the lover has "soft black sinuous lotus limbs."[119] And for Orēruṛavaṉār, the beloved's "arms have the beauty of a gently moving bamboo," as in Maturai Eṛuttāḷaṉ Cēntampūtaṉ, she says "my arms have the grace of the bamboo."[120]

Hands : Lotus. In the Jain Kalpa Sūtra, the goddess Śrī has "hands and feet...like the leaves of the lotus," and Bilhaṇa says of the beloved, that her hands are "painted red like young leaves of asoka," or that they are "lac-lined...like crimson lotuses." For Jayadeva, the beloved's hands are simply each like a lotus petal and those of the lover are lotuses as well, while for Surdas "her hands...[are] the tender leaves of blossom-bringing Spring."[121] Again, in the Jain Rāmāyaṇa, a young girl's hands are likened to sprouting leaves, and her red palms are "the tender leaves of the Aśoka tree."[122]

Thighs : Plantain. Using the traditional image, Vidyāpati says that the beloved's "curving thighs were like a plantain tree laden with lilies of the earth" and, in Jayadeva, Rādhā's "thighs are plantains in motion."[123] In the Jain Rāmāyaṇa, thighs are "like the trunk of a banana tree,"[124] and, in the love season, thighs are traditionally rubbed golden with sandalwood.[125]

Feet : Lotus. The beloved, says Vidyāpati, has "lotus-soft feet" and, whenever she walks, "her feet shower...lotuses."[126] In Jayadeva, Kṛṣṇa applies a shining coat of lac to Rādhā's feet so that they are "like tender shoots tipped with pearls to honor Lakṣmī's place inside." Later, when her foot is on his head, it becomes "a sublime flower destroying poison of love," and her "hibiscus-blossom foot colors my heart" as Kṛṣṇa takes in her beauty. He asks her, then, to let him "dye your feet with the rich liquid of gleaming red lac," and to "leave lotus footprints on my bed of tender shoots, loving Rādhā!"[127]

Love Setting : Nature. The homologies between body parts and plant matter often belong to the season of love, bursting out in spring and in the monsoon, as vines, flowers, and fruit fill the natural world with color, scent, and the density of lush, wet growth. For, as Vidyāpati says, "spring comes with the fragrant southern wind...trees grow again...flowers bloom...the river bank [is] adorned with groves, [and] new lovers are lost in love."[128] During the season of love, young leaves are tender and beautiful, the forest is wrapped in red, and southern breezes drench the air with the scent of new blossoms. Then, love unfolds, for "the forests and the gardens, the groves and the huts are filled with your presence" and, when lover and beloved touch, "the forest...burst open with white *kunda* blooms."[129] The springtime symbiosis of luxuriant blooming in nature and intense flowering among human lovers is mutually enhancing for, as Jayadeva says,

> When spring came, tender-limbed Rādhā wandered
> Like a flowering creeper in the forest wilderness,
> Seeking Krishna in his many haunts....
> Wind perfumes the forests with fine pollen
> Shaken loose from newly blossomed jasmine
> As it blows Love's cactus-fragrant breath
> To torture every heart it touches here.[130]

And just as the flowering of spring opens human hearts everywhere, so the undulation of human passion catalyzes the burgeoning bloom of nature. Of Kṛṣṇa, Jayadeva says,

> When he quickens all things
> To create bliss in the world,
> His soft black sinuous lotus limbs
> Begin the festival of love...
> Melodious voices of cuckoos
> Raise their joyful sound
> When they spy the buds
> On tips of smooth mango branches.[131]

This opening of natural and human florescence is not always pleasant for the beloved and the lover, for in the course of their relationship, much pain emerges. Thus,

Rādhā:
Wind from lakeside garden
Coaxing buds on new aśoka branches
Into clusters of scarlet flowers
Is only fanning the flames to burn me.
This mountain
Of new mango blossoms
Humming with roving bumblebees
Is no comfort to me now, friend.[132]
Kṛṣṇa:
Lotus stalks garland my heart,
Not a necklace of snakes!
Blue lily petals circle my neck,
Not a streak of poison!
Sandalwood powder, not ash,
Is smeared on my lovelorn body!
...Don't attack, mistaking me for Śiva!
Why do you rush at me in rage?[133]

Final union is blissful, however, and again it takes its image from the vegetation around.

> Revel in a thick bed of red petals plucked as offerings...
> Revel in a bright retreat heaped with flowers...
> Revel in tangles of new shoots growing on creeping vines...
> Paint a leaf on my breasts...
> Twine my heavy braid with flowers![134]

Thus, for Maturai Eṛuttāḷa<u>n</u> Cēntampūta<u>n</u>, as for Jayadeva, love-making fits perfectly with organic leafing images for, in the lover, it brings "slow waves beating on his wide shores and the palmyra bringing forth heron-like flowers near the waters" and, in the beloved for Bilhaṇa, it leaves her "wanton, like wild life-giving herbs."[135]

Finally, plant images are used to describe the love couple itself. In one image, the lover and the beloved are a bee and a flower, with the bee hovering over the flower drinking honey from its fragrant center. Of lover and beloved in Śakuntalā, the clown says: "Here is a bold, bad bee. He steals honey, and so he flies to her lotus-face" and, when Śakuntalā cries out that a "bee has left the jasmine-vine and is flying into my face," the king responds "as the bee about her flies...she is practising...coquetry...eager bee...whispering in her ear, you seek secrets to deliver." Again, Kalidasa says of the lover and beloved, "you who kissed the mango-flower, honey-loving bee."[136] And in Vidyāpati we find:

> How the black-bee ravishes the lotus-bud.
> For hours,
> He crushes my frail body
> Quivering like a drop of water
> On a lotus leaf...
> In the midst of thorns
> Blossom flowers.
> The foiled bee
> Is wild with rage...
> My white fragrant flower,
> Watching you,
> Over and over again,
> He longs to drink.
> The anxious bee
> Floats from spot to spot....
> Lost without [me]...
> He roams the earth.
> The bee is possessed.
> *Jātaki* and *ketaki,*
> There are so many flowers
> Yet their honey tastes the same.[137]

And Bilhaṇa says, as if he were the lover, "I'll crush her in my arms and drink her mouth like a madman, a bee insatiably drinking a lotus," a bee wild in his desire "for perfume from her lotus mouth."[138] Again, in Jayadeva, Kṛṣṇa arches over Rādhā's face that is "like a red lotus shadowed by a bee hovering above."[139]

A second image of the lover and beloved is a tree encircled by a creeper. Vidyāpati describes Kṛṣṇa entwined by Rādhā as "stalwart as a tree, his deep embrace squeezes the vine with branch-like arms,"[140] and Jayadeva notes that during the time of love trees "tremble from the embrace of rising vines."[141] The sturdy tree with a creeper entwined around it is featured in many traditional miniature paintings – often in forest scenes specific to love and often related to the Kṛṣṇa-Rādhā allegory. Wherever it appears, it is a known mark of the Hindu painted landscape.

Plants and Human Behavior

Just as plant and human bodies are mapped each on to the other, so their behaviors are mapped as well, and many of these homologies relate to themes of growth and flourishing. In Manu, the woman is said to be the soil while the man is the seed, and it is only through their union that production of beings can come about. The seed is said to be more important, however, than its receptacle, for the offspring of their union has the characteristics primarily of the seed; in fact, "the offspring of all created beings is marked by the characteristics of the seed."[142] Flourishing people are like flourishing plants, and thus contact with the latter may be especially fortuitous for the former for, in the Mahābhārata, Bhṛgu says to a husband:

> At the time of your season, when both of you have bathed for the son-bearing-rite, you must each embrace a tree, she an *aśvattha*, you an *udumbara*.[143]

Modeled on a plant in its fecundity, the Jain queen Yaśodharā, having satisfied her pregnancy longing, "grew ever more beautiful...like a creeper" and Śiva, married in his youth to some princesses, is, when surrounded by them, "as beautiful as a tree surrounded by creepers."[144] Moreover, Śakuntalā, "like the fire-pregnant tree, bears kingly seed that shall be born for earth's prosperity."[145] And in Surapāla's Vṛkṣāyurveda, human behavior can produce – and be expressed as – flourishing behavior in plants. Thus, when a young woman with red painted feet kicks an Aśoka tree it blooms profusely with flowers; when a beautiful woman playfully clasps a Kurabaka tree with her creeper, lotus stalk, arms it bursts forth in a glory of flowers; and when a Śyāmā creeper is about to blossom it looks like a young woman in marriage clothes, performing her marriage ceremony.[146]

When there is a lack of flourishing, however, the parallel still holds: "Dhāriṇī was childless. One day she thought, 'Like a barren tree, my childless life produces no fruit.'"[147] In a similar way, the flourishing that is a 'lack of flourishing' is a homology as well, for Buddhist enlightenment is like a barren tree: that is, just as a farmer who no longer wants his fruit tree to produce fruit applies poison to it to make it barren, so the Buddhist practitioner applies meditation to his or her own person to halt the seeding of *karma*.[148] Flourishing or not flourishing, however, all sentient beings come into existence and, inevitably, go out. Thus, in the Saṁyutta Nikāya,

> There are mighty trees...grown from tiny seeds, of mighty bulk, which overspread (other) trees. The trees thus overspread break up, break down, fall to the ground and so lie...Just in the same way...such and such a clansman, who, whatsoever lusts he abandons and goes forth from home to the homeless [life, nevertheless]... is broken up, broken down: down he falls and so lies.[149]

In this way, no matter how large and powerful, no matter how advanced in spiritual life, just as the great tree grows up, grows old, and dies, so the Buddhist practitioner does as well, regardless of whatever achievements he's made in his own cultivation.

Agricultural images using the life cycle of plants are especially helpful in describing cause and effect processes in human life. In the Āpastamba Dharma Sūtra, for example, a person's auspicious rebirth – marked by "a high birth, a beautiful body, a fine complexion, strength, intelligence, wisdom, wealth, and an inclination to follow the Law" – is "the residue of his merits" built up in times before this life, and "is similar to the way the seeds of plants and trees, when they are sown on a well-ploughed field, increase their fruit."[150] Likewise, in Manu, "as a good seed, springing up in good soil, turns out perfectly well, even so the son of an Aryan by an Aryan woman is worthy of all the sacraments," and more specifically

> Whatever (kind of) seed is sown in a field, prepared in due season, (a plant) of that same kind, marked with the peculiar qualities of the seed, springs up in it.[151]

The Caraka Saṁhitā, however, refines this notion, in a way helpful to the *karma* system, saying: "There is no growth of sprout without seed. Result is in consonance with action, no other (plant) grows from another seed."[152] This suggests that, just as an oak tree comes only from an acorn and an acorn gives rise only to an oak tree, so specific results come only from specific seeds of *karma*, and specific seeds of *karma* give rise only to specific results.

In early Buddhism, this agricultural imagery – *mūla* 'root,' *bīja* 'seed,' *phala* 'fruit' and *vipāka* 'ripening' – is used particularly well to describe the working of causality. Thus, a sower sows seeds in a field and, depending on the rockiness or fineness of the soil, the seeds will grow with difficulty or with ease. Good growth depends also on the amount of fertilizer used, the frequency of the rains, the quality of the seeds, and the attention and competence of the sower and, depending on all these factors, the fruit of the harvest will be scanty or bountiful. This image establishes, in general, as Collins notes, the paradigm of "like the seed that is sown, so is the fruit that is harvested. The doer of good (plants and reaps) good, the doer of bad, bad."[153] And it works well, for example, when applied (1) to teaching (sowing) the Dhamma (seed) to lay or monastic hearers (field), (2) to giving (sowing) donations (seeds) to renunciants (field) at the household door, and (3) to acting (doing, speaking, thinking) whereby *karma* seeds are deposited in one's *karma* field – for all of these processes yield a result or fruit consequent to the quality of the sowing process. On the image applied to giving, for example, is a passage from the Petavatthu: "Like unto fields are the Arhans; the givers are like unto farmers; resembling seed is the gift; from this is produced fruit."[154]

The planting image can also describe the development of virtuous behavior. Note this passage from the Saṁyutta Nikāya:

> Just as...whatsoever species of seed and vegetation come to growth, increase and maturity, all of them depend on the earth, are supported by the earth; even so...a monk who, depending on virtue, supported by virtue, cultivates and makes much of the Ariyan eightfold way, attains growth, increase and maturity of conditions.[155]

Likewise, in the Aṅguttara Nikāya, a teaching compares the growth of a tree to one's growth in the practice: just as the Śāl tree grows five-fold in branches, leaves and foliage, in bark, in shoots, in pith, and in heart, just so the practitioner grows five-fold in faith, virtue, learning, charity, and insight.[156] And in Śantideva,[157] just as trees produce fruit, so also do virtues for, in Aśvaghoṣa, trees model virtuous conduct for Buddhists: that is, just as trees lose their leaves and are not distressed at the separation, so practitioners should not be distressed when good friends go.[158] Such patterning is noted in Hindu texts as well, such as the Hitopadeśa that describes the specific compassion that trees show: thus, "while a tree withstands scorching heat above, it provides cool shade below, indicating that great men do only good to others even while they are suffering."[159] And again, when the Matsya Purāṇa says that "a single tree is equal to ten sons" it bespeaks the many good deeds a tree does for humans, one of which is protecting. Indeed, V. Narayan notes the contemporary use of the phrase *vṛkṣo rakṣati rakṣitaḥ,* "trees protect: let us protect them" or "trees, when protected, protect us" or "trees protect insofar as they are protected."[160] The idea that "trees protect as they are protected" is drawn from a passage in Manu (8.15) describing dharma: *dharmo rakṣati rakṣitaḥ*, *"dharma* protects as it is protected." Plants give service, then but, like *dharma*, only in conditions where they themselves are supported.

Plant to human homologies appear in the area of human emotions as well. In the Mahābhārata when Kirmīra battles Bhīma, each takes a tree as a weapon, and

> ...there began a tree fight that spared no tree...The trees that fell on their heads splintered in many pieces, as lotuses that are hurled at the heads of rutting elephants. Withered like reeds, the many trees there in the great forest looked like discarded tatters. The tree fight went on for a long while...[161]

Thus, the flying trees and their dying, tattered bodies reflect the results of the great anger between the two sides, as well as the inevitable results of hostile conflict. In the Rāmāyaṇa, when the cottage grounds are empty and the trees are moved by passing winds, their rustling makes them seem "almost...to weep."[162]

In the Gītagovinda, plants are again anthropomorphized in terms of their emotional life. As the relationship between Rādhā and Kṛṣṇa becomes ever more joyful and abandoned, "tender buds bloom into laughter," and "budding mango trees tremble from the embrace of rising vines." "Flowers bloom in profusion, tearing deserted lovers' hearts...a garland strikes at the heart of my fragile body...[and] a mass of vines with thickly clustered shoots quivering in the wind like a hand seems to be gesturing to your tapering thighs to quicken your pace."[163] Again, in Śakuntalā, plant homologies speak, but here to the pain and sadness of human relationships:

> Her cheeks grown thin; her breast and shoulders fail;
> Her waist is weary and her face is pale:
> She fades for love...
> As vine-leaves wither in the scorching heat....
> The mango branches are in bloom,
> Yet pollen does not form...
> The amaranth-bud is formed, and yet
> Its power of growth is gone;
> The love-god timidly puts by
> The arrow he has drawn.[164]

And, in a south Indian love poem,

> When love is ripe beyond bearing
> and goes to seed,
> men will ride even palmyra stems
> like horses; will wear on their heads
> the reeking cones of the *erukkam* bud
> like flowers...[165]

Moreover, Kaccipēṭṭu Naṉṉākaiyār notes that the beloved grows "lean in loneliness, like a water lily gnawed by a beetle;" Aḷḷūr Naṉmullaiyār tells of the lover who, if he loses his beloved "could proclaim my misery in the streets riding mock horses on palmyra stems in my wildness;" Auvaiyār's lover wants to sate his "passion till this flood of desire that once wet the branch of the tall tree would thin till I can bend and scoop a drink of water with my hands;" and Pālaipāṭiya Peruṅkaṭuṅkō's beloved responds to the despondent lover who bemoans the wide spaces now as vacant as *"ōmai* trees that stand like ghost towns once busy with living."[166]

Thus, Indian literature portrays a plant population whose members are able to replicate, at least in image form if not in real behavior, a variety of human behaviors. Patterns of plant growth express the processes of human growth and of moral and spiritual development; of the teaching of students by a teacher; of the giving of religious gifts to renunciants by donors; and especially of the dynamics of the increasingly important *karma* system. Trees can be reanimated back to life as humans can be (and vice versa), as the legend of Gosāla and the sesame plant shows; trees can make decisions; trees can dance, and can express love, eroticism, and delight; and, finally, trees can hear teaching and respond, as the Lotus Sūtra's Parable of the Herbs so aptly shows.

Plants and Human Social Structures

Homologies between plants and humans are fairly common in Indian literature, when we examine those images that focus on bodies or behaviors. Such homologies occur as well, though less often, between plants and humans as they belong to groups, and in particular groups as they exhibit social structure. In Śakuntalā, for example, the young girl feels like a "sister" to the trees, and forests are thought to be "families" of trees[167] and, in the Pañcatantra, plants when alone are thought to be too weak to survive but strong enough to go on when living together.

> The union of the weak
> A powerful bully stumps:
> The hostile blizzard spares
> the shrubs that grow in clumps.[168]

Thus, in isolation a single plant can be doomed, but with others around plants cannot be uprooted by the violent wind. Again, in Hemacandra, four merchants who "had grown up together" are said to live jointly "like trees in an orchard"[169] – in the company of similar, though not identical, individuals.

There are two themes, both arising in the Vedic period, where plants are specifically thought to have social structures like those of humans: (1) the identification of one plant or one tree as the chief or head of the others, such as the Soma plant or the Uḍumbara tree, and (2) the assignment of trees to different *varṇas* or castes. Regarding the first, in the early ritual, the lord of the herbs *(oṣadhi)* is said to be the intoxicating Soma, who generates all plants and who is styled the "king."[170] Of the herbs Soma is given the highest oblation,[171] and he is often the specially invited guest *(atithi)* at the ritual. Of Soma, the Śatapatha Brāhmaṇa says that he is "the nobility and the other plants [are] the common people," and Soma is so important that when it is not available the text prescribes other as substitutes[172] – though it is clear that none can ever replace this plant as its equal.

In the case of trees, it is the Uḍumbara who is "regarded as having within it the condensed essence of all the trees" and who serves as the symbol for all trees as well as for all food.[173] The Śatapatha Brāhmaṇa notes that "that Udumbara represents all the trees here (on earth),"[174] a status given it when, as the gods and the Asuras sprang from Prajāpati, all the trees sided with the Asuras except for the Uḍumbara who sided with the gods. Once in possession of *all* the trees, however, the gods then

> laid into the udumbara tree what pith and essence there was in those trees; and on account of that pith it matures (fruit) equal to all the (other) trees: hence that (tree) is always moist, always full of milky sap – that udumbara tree, indeed, (being) all the trees, is all food.[175]

As Smith then notes, because the Uḍumbara has the power of all trees, the sacrificer can now manipulate the Uḍumbara tree in such as way as to manipulate the power of all trees: "because the tree has the essence of all trees within its fruits, the eating of its fruits places this sylvan essence – the power of growth, vitality, and nourishment – in the sacrificer, regardless of his social class."[176]

Trees known to the Vedic world are also classified according to the *varṇa* or caste that they belong to. Smith has arranged the material on this 'social structure' homology in great detail, and we give the following selections:

> *Brahmin trees* are exemplified by the *Palāśa* (*Parṇa*) tree, who helps produce the heavenly world for the sacrificer, and who conquers demons and other dangers. The Palāśa tree is also associated with the power to acquire Soma and with Soma itself, as both are said to "share a common origin...[and] to spring from the same womb."[177] Trees with minor

> associations with the brahmin *varṇa* include the wood-apple tree and the Plakṣa tree.
>
> *Kṣatriya trees* are exemplified by the *Nyagrodha* or *banyan*, said to be the king of the trees who grows "with independence of will." The Nyagrodha "towers over his people" and "is supported by them" having "many roots among them," and the juice squeezed from its roots is thought to be "a kind of Kshatriya version of soma."[178] Trees with minor associations with the kṣatriya *varṇa* include the Kārṣmarya tree, a large tree whose wood is used for making sticks "to keep out...cosmic riff-raff," the Khadira or cutch tree, whose wood belongs with virility and war-like activities; and the Aśvattha or Pīpal (bodhi) tree, with powers of dominance and overlordship, who is associated with the strength of a horse *(aśva)*.
>
> *Vaiśya trees* are exemplified by the *Aśvattha* or *Pīpal* tree, whose leaves are often ritual "signifiers for the commoner class," who are known for attributions of "fecundity and prosperity" and "the ability to pass along that trait [fecundity] to those humans who are desirous of it."[179] The Uḍumbara tree is also a Vaiśya tree and is, again, known for its "properties of fecundity, productivity, and multiplicity," bearing juicy fruit three times a year that give rise to the idea that it contains the essence of all trees and that it is all trees and all food.[180]

Thus, the caste association of certain trees known to the Vedic world is based on specific properties of the trees useful to the religious practitioner, and their correlation with the common theme generally attributed to each caste.

6.3 Transformation into a Plant or Tree

The folk and religious narratives that intertwine the lives of plants and humans include stories about human beings turning into plants or trees. We have already seen some examples of the appeal of such transformational possibilities: the Atharvan demoness who takes the shape of a forest tree, Pārvatī's curse that some gods be reborn as trees, Sūrya Bai who becomes a lotus who is burnt and then emerges as a fruit from the mango tree who springs from the lotus ashes, and the Jain adept who remembers his previous rebirth as a Śālmali tree being cut down, stripped of its bark, [and sawn into

The Kathāsaritsāgara has a number of examples of human transformation into a tree including, for example, the story of a brahman who is cursed to be a dry tree. It happens that during a time of famine a brahman, wretchedly hungry and almost dead, receives five fruits and gives three to his son, saving two for himself. When he goes to bathe, the son eats all five and then, when his father returns, pretends to be asleep. The father guessing what has happened, curses his son to become a dry tree on the bank of a lake that bears flowers and fruit on moonlit nights – a curse that can be broken only when a guest lying under the tree eats of the fruit. When such a guest breaks the curse, the tree-now-brahman-son, says: "As soon as my father had pronounced this curse on me, I became a dry tree, but now that you have tasted my fruit I have been delivered from the curse after enduring it for a long time."[181]

Among other stories from the Kathāsaritsāgara are those about tree goddesses, including the well-known one of Somaprabhā, a tree goddess who lives in the Nyagrodha tree. Somaprabhā is reborn as the daughter of the merchant Dharmagupta, and at that time there is great illumination in the room causing her father to be afraid. She tells him that she can't be given away in marriage but he marries her anyway to Guhacandra. Her husband, however, is so miserable with her that he won't go near her. One night he follows her and sees

> before him a Nyagrodha tree of wide extent, beautiful with its shady stem, and under it he heard a heavenly sound of singing, sweet with strains floating on the air, accompanied with the music of the lyre and the flute. And on the trunk of the tree he saw a heavenly maiden, like his wife in appearance, seated on a splendid throne, eclipsing by her beauty the moonbeam, fanned with white chowries, like the goddess presiding over the treasure of all the moon's beauty. And then Guhachandra saw his wife ascend that very tree and sit down beside that lady, occupying half of her throne.[182]

At once, the story teaches the curse of breaking a prohibition, the reward for one so violated, and the resolving power manifest in the goddess of the tree.

Another story is of a certain Devadatta who is addicted to gambling and who is instructed by an ascetic, in order to escape his addiction, to worship at the foot of a certain tree. One day during his worship, the tree opens up and a nymph appears summoning Devadatta into the middle of the tree to meet her mistress Vidyutprabhā, the daughter of the *yakṣa* king Ratnavarṣa. Devadatta is to marry Vidyutprabhā but, when he does and she gets pregnant, he is frightened and returns to the ascetic. The ascetic tells him to cut the *yakṣī* open and to take out the child, but Vidyutprabhā beats him to it, cutting herself open and flinging the unborn child at Devadatta who brings it to the ascetic where it is immediately cut up. The story continues eventfully and ends with Durgā appearing to Devadatta and commending him for his courage.[183] Other stories tell of *yakṣīs* or *yakṣiṇīs* who transform themselves into trees, and of Dānava (demon) ladies who conceal themselves in trees by means of magic.[184]

In addition to such traditional textual references, are several published stories from the oral tradition of India. The following selections are summaries.

"A Flowering Tree"[185]

In a town, there is once a king with two daughters and a son, as well as a poor woman with two daughters. In order to help out their mother, the daughters of the poor woman decide that one of them will turn herself into a tree so that the two can sell the flowers that grow on it for money. To do this, the younger daughter sits down by the front of the house and the elder daughter pours water over her. When the first becomes a tree, the second plucks all the flowers off and then pours more water over the tree so that she will become human again. The two then sell the flowers – fortuitously, to the queen living in palace. The two daughters do this for five days, hiding the money they make from selling the flowers from their mother each time.

One day, the king's son sees the flowers, is amazed by them, and wants to find out where they come from. So, he follows the girls home, but sees no tree and, being intrigued, goes back early in the morning and watches as the one daughter becomes a tree, is plucked of her flowers, and then returns to human form again. The prince returns to his palace and, when his father comes to know of the girls, calls their poor old mother to come to court. Knowing nothing of this, the mother resists the king's questioning but is forced to take home a symbolic offering of betrothal for the prince's marriage to the younger daughter. There, she confronts the daughters and beats them, but the marriage arrangements go ahead.

For several nights after the marriage ceremony, the new husband does not speak to his wife until, finally, he says:

> You know how to turn into a flowering tree, don't you? Let me see you do it. We can then sleep on flowers and cover ourselves with them. That would be lovely.

She responds:

> My lord, I'm not a demon, I'm not a goddess. I'm an ordinary mortal like everyone else. Can a human being ever become a tree?

And he replies:

> I don't like all this lying and cheating. I saw you the other day becoming a beautiful tree. I saw you with my own eyes. If you don't become a tree for me, for whom will you do that?[186]

So, the new wife has two pitchers of water brought and instructs her husband who then gathers many blossoms for their nuptial bed.

In time, the prince's younger sister sees all the withered flowers the couple is throwing out and wants some of the new flowers for herself. Coming to know the secret of the flowering tree, she asks permission for the new bride to come with her and some friends to the orchard. Permission is reluctantly given by the family and, in the orchard, the girls ask the new bride to become a tree. Eventually she agrees, but the girls are coarse and indifferent about the ritual and, in time, all they are able to produce is half a tree. When it begins to thunder and lightning, the girls carelessly pour the second pitcher of water over the tree and the new bride becomes human again, but has no hands or feet and only half a body.

Crawling into a gutter, she is found the next morning by a cart driver who sees her beautiful face, wraps her in a turban, puts her in his cart, and brings her to an old pavilion. Back at the palace, the absence of the bride causes the queen-mother, suspecting foul play, to become angry at her younger daughter, and the groom to retreat into grief taking up ascetic's robes and wandering the countryside. The half-bride, by this time, has somehow reached the town where the prince's elder married sister lives, and her illuminated form attracts the attention of the queen's maids, who see the resemblance to the queen's brother's wife. They bring the half-bride to the palace and care for her with oils and medicines.

In time, the groom, now a crazed and haggard beggar, comes to sit at the gate of his elder sister's palace and the maids, again making the recognition, ask that he be brought in. Bathed, dressed, and fed, the groom now recognizes his elder sister but has no words for her. The maids see the solution and bring the "illumined lump" that is the half-bride into the groom's room; during the night the half-bride massages her husband with her stumps and he then recognizes her as his lost wife. Discovering what has happened, the husband brings two pitchers of water and the wife chants and instructs him as follows:

> Pour the water from this pitcher over me, I'll become a tree. Wherever there is a broken branch, set it right. Wherever a leaf is torn, put it together. Then pour the water of the second pitcher.... [When he did so] she became a tree. But the branches had been broken, the leaves had been torn. He carefully set each one right and bound them up and gently poured water from the second pitcher all over the tree.[187]

Back in full human form again, the wife and husband are reunited, return home, and are celebrated lavishly by the prince's family. A pit of burning lime, however, is made for the younger sister of the prince – into which she is thrown by her father, the king.

"The Pomegranate Queen"[188]

A man with two daughters has been successful in arranging a good marriage for the elder daughter, but not so for the younger.

An obstinate girl, the younger daughter refuses all possible suitors. The father is so angry that once, when his wife is gone, he cuts the daughter up, buries her in the backyard, and tells his wife that their daughter has gotten sick and died. In the place where the daughter is buried, however, a pomegranate tree grows tall and green, bearing a single large flower that opens up only at night. In this flower lives the younger daughter, who plays music on the vina that is heard by her father and mother. One day, the son of the god Indra is traveling through the heavens and hears the music as well, and he is greatly astonished by its beauty. Tracing the music to the pomegranate tree and its single flower, he hovers over it and in time sees the Pomegranate Queen playing the vina. He falls in love with her and she too with him and, though they want to marry, he must get permission from his parents in heaven.

When the parents find that the bride-to-be is earth-born, they insist on a more suitable choice from among the Apsara women. The son resists, and challenges them to hear the music of the Pomegranate Queen before they turn her down. As Indra and his wife watch the single flower on the pomegranate tree give rise to the young girl, they find that she is so beautiful that they allow their son to marry her at once and to bring her to the sky-kingdom to live. Without the daughter, however, the pomegranate tree on earth withers up and the Pomegranate Queen's parents fall into great distress. One day, when the daughter returns to the garden, the tree greens up again and sprouts a new single bloom. Seeing her daughter step out of the flower, the mother is surprised and happy, and hears the story of the father's anger, his disposal of the daughter, and the growth of the tree from the burial spot. Now the daughter says:

> I became this pomegranate tree and lived in this flower as the Pomegranate Queen all these months. But now I'm married to Indra's son and live with him in the heaven-world. When I left, this tree dried up. When I came back visiting to see how things were, it sprouted again and regained life.[189]

The story ends suggesting that the daughter's return, and the renewed life of the pomegranate tree, will occur with every new season.

"How a Girl Became a Sacred Plant"[190]

Tulsī, or Sailī, is the beautiful daughter of an untouchable cobbler. A brahman boy brings shoes by for mending but finds only Tulsī at home to take them in. He returns home and tells his parents of his desire to marry her – to the great consternation not only of them but of the whole village, who now want to banish the cobblers from their area. Seeing no difference between the brahmans and cobblers, however, Tulsī does not understand when she finds that her own cobbler caste is also unhappy and, when the men of the caste declare that they will not marry her themselves, she asks her father what to do. He tells her to go become a stone and to wait for Kṛṣṇa who will marry her when he takes on human form.

The girl becomes a stone and, when Kṛṣṇa comes along, she returns to human form and tells him she is going to marry him. Kṛṣṇa, however, is already married to Rukmiṇī, but Tulsī becomes a milkmaid and sells curds by their house. Kṛṣṇa urges Rukmiṇī to buy some curds and, when she does, he tells Tulsī to come by every day. In time, Tulsī becomes a housemaid and helper to Rukmiṇī who has a heavy workload and, with Tulsī's help, the two women are able to finish the domestic chores quickly. One day, one hundred and one brahmans are to be fed and, as Kṛṣṇa has caused her to forget, Rukmiṇī sleeps through the preparation of the food, leaving the whole job to Tulsī. Rukmiṇī awakens and is horrified at her forgetfulness, but Tulsī asks her what she would do if she were to find the food already prepared. Rukmiṇī answers, "I'd give you anything that you asked for,"[191] and consents when Tulsī asks to bathe with Kṛṣṇa for five days.

When a crow alerts Rukmiṇī to the intimacy of the bathing in the river, however, Rukmiṇī sees that Tulsī has become Kṛṣṇa's wife, even asking Tulsī not Rukmiṇī to bring his garments and water pot to wherever he is. Rukmiṇī now hides the garments and water pot and Tulsī, at Kṛṣṇa's request, goes searching for them but can't find them. She is so late in returning to Kṛṣṇa, that he calls to ask her whether she has sprouted and taken root inside. Since, the story takes place in the era of righteousness when speech becomes true, Tulsī becomes a shrub – the Tulsī or holy basil plant.

"The Man Who Grew Roots"[192]

The poet Chandrashekhara is jealous of trees because they have roots, while he, without roots, has no stable place of his own. In a poem he writes,

> Oh tree,
> You have roots.
> I, an outsider,
> Am aimlessly wandering.
> In one city
> In one home
> With one woman
> I did not live,
> Nor did I find my roots.
> I wandered from city to city
> Changed houses
> And women too.
> I am rootless now.
> Oh tree, you are happy
> I am unhappy.[193]

After composing the poem, he hears a voice say, "I [am] the tree behind you," and in response to the poet's questions about whether a tree can speak, the tree responds, "Why not? Trees also can speak in thousands of languages. When men don't understand each other, how can they comprehend the language of trees."[194] A long conversation ensues between the poet and the tree covering issues of regional language, caste, and rivalry among the trees in the vicinity. At some point, Chandru tells the banyan tree that he wants to become a tree himself and as the banyan replies, Chandru's transformation begins, that is, he starts to grow roots.

> Roots started sprouting from his feet. Those two roots entered the earth and became a taproot. From that taproot thousands of secondary roots penetrated into the bowels of the earth. Chandru started experiencing immense joy. His entire body felt a sort of bliss. As the chief root went deeper and smaller ones with root-hairs spread their tentacles, it was all one rich feeling of softness, warmth and happiness.[195]

As this happens, he feels tremendous joy and remembers those times in the past that were immensely happy and blissful. Suddenly, however, he thinks of his home, his children's need for shoes, his own lack of a job, the debt he owes the grocer, and the difficulties his wife has in getting food. He tries to go for shoes for his children, but finds that his rooted legs have become entangled in the roots of the banyan. Full of humility, he begs the banyan to let him go, but the banyan chides him, asking what kind of person he is for wanting one thing one moment and the opposite the next. Chandru now thinks he is transformed into a tree permanently and begins to wail. A gardener comes by and cannot believe such a thing – that a man can grow roots into the earth – but consents to help the poet by going to find the poet's friend. The friend finally arrives but he and the gardener are unable to pull Chandru's legs out of the earth. Chandru persuades them to cut off his legs – which they reluctantly do – and all go to the hospital where Chandru, in terrible pain, is sedated and bandaged. When he comes to, his wife berates him:

> Could you not have continued [as a tree]...for a few more days? Millions of people would have bought tickets in order to see your floral condition. That would have straightened our financial position and given us a livelihood. Look at yourself now. You have got into heavy debts, lost your legs and we have to starve.[196]

Distressed at his condition, Chandru now wishes that he had continued living as a tree.

"The Girl Who Was Loved by a Tree Spirit"[197]

In the village of Chungliyimti (in Nagaland), there lived a beautiful daughter of a rich family. Although she had many suitors, she loved only one, a handsome man who came to see her only at night. She could never find him during the day, however, and one day she tied a new *dao* belt around her lover's waist and the next day went out looking for him. When she found the *dao* belt, it was tied around a tree by the well near her house on the bank of a stream. On another night she put an indigo shawl around her lover's shoulders and the next morning, again, she found it around the tree by the stream. The girl's father became suspicious and kept watch one night, following the mysterious young man to the stream:

> There he stood at the side of the well and quickly transformed himself into an ordinary tree. His body turned into the trunk, his arms into branches, and his hair into leaves. And behold, there stood a big tree in the place of the youth.[198]

The father decided to cut the tree down, and asked his daughter to stay inside the house. As the men chopped a small piece of wood from the tree flew through the window into the house where the girl was watching. The chip hit her in the eye and killed her instantly. When the tree was fully cut down, the father rushed happily into the house to tell his daughter only to find that the "two lovers had died together."[199]

6.4 Conversations With Trees

The idea that one can talk with a plant or tree goes back to early ritual times when poets and priests beseech shrubs and herbs for blessings, cures, and relief from curses. Prayers and ritual chants to plants and trees are common in Vedic literature, especially in texts like the Atharva Veda, and actual conversations between people and the deities or *devatās* who live in trees appear in the literature of most Indian traditions.[200] In the Buddhist Kuruṅga Jātaka, for example, a deer comes to a tree and, seeing its fruit on the ground and suspecting that a hunter has hidden and thrown the food down for him, says:

> My worthy tree, hither to you have been in the habit of letting your fruit fall straight to the ground like a pendant creeper; but to-day you have ceased to act like a tree. And therefore, as you have ceased to behave as becomes a tree, I too must change, and look for food beneath another tree.[201]

The hunter steps out and throws his javelin at the deer and misses, whereupon the deer (the bodhisattva) tells the hunter (Devadatta) that his reward will be rebirth in hell.[202]

In the Milindapañha, one of the dilemmas posed to Nāgasena is that of the 'talking tree.' It seems that accounts are known of people asking a tree after its welfare and of a tree then addressing the petitioner. Milinda proposes, however, that since a tree is an "incognisant, unhearing...[thing] that does not know the knowable *(acetanaṁ...assuṇantaṁ...jānaṁ ajānantam),*"[203] it cannot engage in a conversation with a person. Nāgasena's response is that any story about conversations with trees are just popular tales, for any such conversation is in fact a conversation between a person and the *devatā* who lives in the tree, for "a tree does not converse, a tree is incognizant, but as 'tree' is a synonym for the devatā who inhabits that tree, so to say 'a tree converses' is the popular expression."[204] While the view that the conversation is actually with the *devatā* in the tree belongs to Buddhist theory of the time (as represented in the text by Nāgasena), the view that it is the tree itself who engages in conversation with people also represents a current view – that of people in the local areas.

S. Gupta's compendium records a number of human-tree conversations which the author says take place in "the olden days, [when] plants could speak like human beings."[205] One is taken from the Mahābhārata and occurs between a Śālmali tree growing in the Himalayan mountains and the wind, and between this tree and the sage Narada. Narada notes that the strong wind bends and breaks many large trees, but seems to spare the Śālmali tree, who then boasts of being stronger that the wind. Narada cautions the tree against such high-handed pronouncements and says to the tree:

> Your perception seems to be thoroughly perverse. There is no created being who is equal to the Wind in strength...You are worthless and of wicked understanding. O Salmali, I am angry with you for indulging in such talk.[206]

Another story involves Śiva and the betel vine upon whom he has pronounced a curse. The vine is unhappy with him and complains that she will receive no respect, but instead will have her leaves chewed, spat on, thrown in the mud, and squashed underfoot. While Śiva cannot take the curse away, he does respond to her complaint and relaxes the curse by having her honored through the use of her leaves in auspicious ceremonies.[207]

In the Rāmāyaṇa, when Rāma searches for Sītā after her capture, he asks a Badarī tree if he has seen his wife. The tree answers that he has and, moreover, that he tried to save Sītā by holding on to her clothes with his branches – so much so that some of the cloth is still entangled there and, by its configuration, can point Rāma in the right direction of Sītā's abduction.[208] In fact, often on Rāma's search he calls out to the trees of the forest and asks them if they have seen his beloved.

> ...He rushed from tree to tree...O *Kadamba,* hast thou seen where is the one fond of *Kadamba* groves? If knowest thou this do thou tell me of Sītā having an auspicious countenance. O *Bilva,* tell me pray, if thou has seen her...having breasts like unto *Bilva* fruits...This *Kakubha* knoweth for certain about Maithilee having thighs like unto *Kakubha*...O *Tala,* if thou hast any pity on me do thou tell me whether thou hast beheld that fair damsel having breasts resembling ripe *Tala* fruits... O *Karnikara,* thou appearest very beautiful with this blossoming flowers, tell me if thou hast seen my dear devoted wife who was fond of thee.[209]

Thus, the verbal requests made of the trees carry hope of knowledge through homology: the Kadamba and Karṇikāra trees, for example, will know of Sītā because she is fond of them; the Bilvā and Tāla trees will know of Sītā because her breasts are like their fruit, the rose-apple and the palm fruit; and the Kakubha tree will know of Sītā, Maithilī, because her velvety thighs are like the Kakubha itself.[210] In Śakuntalā, the heroine calls out to her friends, "Oh, girls, that mango-tree is trying to tell me something with his branches that move in the wind like fingers," and Śārṅgarava tells his father, as they bid farewell to Śakuntalā, "the trees are answering your prayer in cooing cuckoo-song."[211]

Practice of conversing with trees is widespread in Indian traditions and is expressed in two contemporary examples. In the first, Balbir Mathur, founder of the Trees for Life movement, tells of a lemon tree he had in his Allahabad yard as a boy. Each day, when he takes a lemon from the tree, he says to the tree: "You have provided me with so much nourishment and love, [that] one day when I am rich I will plant thousands of lemon trees for poor people so that they too can share your nourishment."[212] During a series of transformative experiences as an adult, the tree comes back to him and speaks with him often, urging him to keep his promise to plant trees in India wherever he can. Mathur decides to fulfill his earlier promise and the Trees for Life movement, through which contemporary villagers plant many millions of lemon, papaya, banana, drum-stick (Moringa), and falsa trees, is begun in the mid-1980s. By 1989, the movement has become a large network of volunteers, with an office in Delhi and, in that year, 700,000 trees are planted in Indian villages and 200,000 blessed saplings are distributed to pilgrims at the Kumbha Mela to plant in domestic plots. Mathur believes that caring for the planted tree is a sacred duty, and part of that care is listening and responding to their conversation: "Trees have a power and language of their own which is not easy to communicate,"[213] he says.

In a second example, Stephanie Kaza, a student of Buddhism and ecology, writes in *The Attentive Heart: Conversations with Trees* of her "practice of writing with trees" as based "in the Zen form of *shikantaza* – just sitting."

> I spent time in silence, close to trees, doing my best to be simply present with the tree as Other, aware of my thoughts, moods, and projections...The writing became an excuse to listen for a call from the trees, in whatever form it took. I did not go to the trees with an agenda or story in mind, but chose rather to see what would unfold by being completely present in the specific place and moment.[214]

The book, then, represents some of her explorations in "human-tree conversations" as they come out of her Buddhist training, where her hope is to see a tree not as a symbol, but as an 'other' in a one-on-one dynamic relationship. In this experience, she hopes "to watch for the habits of language and mind that block the flow of communication between person and tree" – but since the relationship between person and tree is "one subset of all human-non-human relationships," the former can help open up the later. *Conversations with Trees,* then, is an exploration of what it actually means "to be in a relationship with a tree," and takes as its touchstone the Zen text by Dōgen, the Mountains and Rivers Sutra.[215] Kaza's practice reflects the "cultivation of intimacy with nature [that] is a central aim for many Buddhist environmentalists,"[216] that itself reflects the early Buddhist doctrine of *ahiṁsā* where a reverence for the life force in all sentient beings is extended to plants and trees.

6.5 Marriage With a Tree

Marriage between two trees or plants is an example of understanding plant behavior to be comparable to human, as in this example from Surapāla's Vṛkṣāyurveda:

> A Śyāmā creeper nearing the blossoming of flowers, closely clinging to a tree looks like a damsel, clad in finery, wearing auspicious marital decorations...her marriage cermony [to] perform...[217]

In Śakuntalā, much is made of the jasmine vine who chooses a mango tree as her husband. Says Śakuntalā: "What a pretty pair they make. The jasmine shows her youth in her fresh flowers, and the mango-tree shows his strength in his ripening fruit." And, like these two plants, Śakuntalā herself is thinking of how the jasmine vine "has found a good tree, and hoping that she will meet a fine lover." When she does, her father says:

> My child, you found the lover who
> Had long been sought by me;
> No longer need I watch for you;
> I'll give the vine a lover true,
> This handsome mango-tree.[218]

Again, Gupta notes the great pain of those concerned with "the yet unfulfilled marriage of the two trees that the queen had brought up so lovingly in the hope of getting them married."[219]

Such tree-to-tree marriage is often associated with the Aśvattha tree, and Gupta records contemporary village practice of the Aśvattha tree (male) being married to the Neem tree (female), a nuptial reversed in Rajasthan and the Punjab where the Neem tree is thought to be male.[220] In Orissa, there is practice of marrying the Vaṭa tree (male) to the Aśvattha tree (female), when they have grown up side by side and their branches and foliage have mixed – "their growing together is [thus] regarded as marriage." Likewise, the "*Aswattha* tree is also sometimes married to the *Kadali* tree, the two trees...grown so close together that their trunks intertwine and look like one."[221]

The practice of humans marrying trees appears to be a custom associated primarily with certain tribal areas of India.[222] As Gupta reports, for example, if a boy's first marriage is predicted to fall apart, he will be married to a tree first so that his taking of a human bride will constitute a second marriage. Again, when an Orissan man has been widowed twice, he can be married to a certain kind of tree so that will absorb his bad luck. He then becomes free to marry a human bride the next time with hopes for a more auspicious union. Again, because a girl who dies unmarried cannot be cremated, her father's duty, while she is still alive, is to marry her as soon as possible. If he cannot find a groom from the right caste, the daughter can be married to a tree first and then informally be given to a groom of a lower caste. Similarly, among the Gujarati Kunbirs, when a father does not find a groom for his daughter, she can be married to a bunch of flowers that are then thrown into a well; she can now marry anyone, or can be given to who ever will take her. Again, among the Orissan Gauras, a girl failing to get married is taken to a forest and married to a tree, and she remains tied to it until she is informally married to the first man who comes along and rescues her. Finally, Hindu dancing girls known as Pātars "marry a *pīpal* tree and then commence their career of prostitution."[223] As Gupta notes, in "some cases a girl is first married to a tree with a belief that she will imbibe some of the fertility of the tree, before she is married...to a man."[224]

In Nepal, marriage of *both* bride and groom to a tree takes place in some tribal groups. Each is covered with tumeric, for example, and the bride

> ...is married to *mahua* i.e., *Bassia latydia* while the groom is married to mango tree, or sometimes both are married to mango tree. They sprinkle vermilion on the mango tree and clasp it, and then remain tied to it for sometime. A marriage-procession is taken out during such marriages, accompanied by priests and a party playing on musical instruments. A hand-spun thread is tied around the trunk of the tree, whose one end is held by the groom. This priest moves five times round a young tree. The priest makes a scratch in the tree, takes out a piece of bark and gives it to the groom to taste it.[225]

The Majupurias also note the custom in Nepal of marrying groups of young Newari girls to Bel or Bilvā fruits. Each fruit used in the ritual must be beautiful and undamaged, as ugly and damaged fruit will bring an ugly and insincere husband. Likewise, each girl participating in the marriage must be pre-menarche and, ordinarily, between the ages of five and twelve. The girls and the fruits are dressed in marriage garb and proper rituals are performed: fasting, washing, ornamenting, chanting, and thread tying.[226] The use of the Bel fruit is significant as Bel tree materials are used in the worship of Śiva, and rituals employing it are especially powerful in the realm of marriage, protection, and fertility.[227]

Nagarajan notes that, in the Tamil village of Ammangudi, rituals of marriage to trees are used to restore relationships, in particular, to restore "the earth by establishing relationships with the powerful, creative, and auspicious force of trees."[228] When an informant, for example, says that "We have to marry trees again," it signifies the need in the community to relieve some experience of suffering.

> We suffer. There are times when suffering comes at us suddenly and we do not know how to handle the enormity of the suffering. And then we marry trees. Usually it is when someone cannot get married; and there are lots of obstacles in their path...we know that there is something about the life path of the person that is preventing them from marrying a human person. So, we arrange the marriage of that person to a tree, and then we pray that the tree will take on the burdens of that human being and therefore release that person from their suffering. Then, the human person is free to marry someone else.[229]

Marrying trees is a response to a wide range of familial sufferings: infertility, illness, or unsuitability of any sort in marriage negotiations. "Since trees, like humans, are seen as male or female, the tree selected may be of the opposite gender from the afflicted individual."[230] Moreover, suffering in a family or in a larger community is often understood as a "deterioration or souring of relationships between the natural and cultural worlds," and the ceremony of the afflicted person marrying a tree is a ritual reminder that there is an essential kinship between the community and the natural world that must be maintained in order for there to be health and well-being in individual lives.[231]

Finally, we note the story of Tara Lata, the tree-bride, as told by Bharati Mukherjee in her novel *Desirable Daughters.* Tara Lata, a five-year old girl, is to marry into a wealthy land-owning family but, just before the wedding, the thirteen-year old groom dies of a snake bite and Tara Lata is blamed for his death. Now thought to be unlucky and cursed, she is taken to marry a tree, and her meeting with her new husband is described as a moment of grace and homecoming:

> The bridal gaze angles up his strong, slender torso as tall as a ship's mast, and scales up, up, to where the tip of his head disappears in the night-black of the winter skies. She feels his arms, as strong as tree branches, brush against her, enfold her, shield her from life's potential brutalities.... now she recognizes her bridegroom. He is the god of Shoondar Bon, the Beautiful Forest, come down to earth as a tree to save her from a lifetime of disgrace and misery.[232]

The generative powers represented by trees as marriage partners are specifically applicable to the bearing of children – in particular, in the bearing of sons. In the Mahābhārata, for example, Ṛcīka Bhārgava successfully woos the daughter of the king Gādhi and, in order to have a son, the priest says:

> At the time of your season, when both of you have bathed for the son-bearing-rite, you must each embrace a tree, she an *aśvattha,* you an *udumbara.*[233]

Moreover, as reflected in early Buddhist materials, the *yakṣī* – especially in connection with the *śālabhañjikā* pose – is often associated with fertility and receives petitions from women who want to bear children.[234]

Of contemporary culture, Randhawa reports a story of a husband and wife who are childless. One day, the husband wanders through the forest sad and disappointed and sits down to rest under an Uḍumbara tree. He looks up and sees the figs hanging down, ripe and abundant, and thinks: "If only my wife was like this tree, what happiness we would have." It happens that the tree has a hole in it at the height of the man's waist, and the man "goes" into this hole. "In due time a human child was born from one of the figs and he was the father of the Dumariya clan."[235] Again, in the Tariyaparabok clan, the toddy palm (Tāla) is the local god for, once, when a couple is childless, the husband brings home the palm fruit and gives it to his wife to eat. She becomes pregnant and bears a child, a gift duly attributed to the Tāla tree.[236] And, again, the Jandi tree, revered by local peoples of Rajasthan and the Punjab, is often beseeched for children. "I have come to the grand darbar of Jandi to solicit from her the gift of a child," a young wife might say, or "The darbar of Jandi is ever brilliant with lamps, Give me a baby to play in my lap."[237]

Finally, in a homology mentioned previously, plants and trees are thought to be "with child," and in that condition themselves to have "pregnancy longings" *(dohada).* In the Viṣṇudharmottara Purāṇa section on Vṛkṣāyurveda, for example, trees are thought to need special things, like the cold water washing of fish needed by the mango tree, when they are in especially fertile and maturing stages.[238] In addition, a young woman in a *dohada* pose awakens a flower simply by the "touch of her foot."[239]

6.6 Divination Through Trees and Plants

Plant lives intersect with human lives, finally, in the processes of divination, whereby humans can find – in trees' abundance and decline – predictions of coming events, both individual and communal. In the Bṛhat Saṁhitā, for example, there will be victory for the king if the tree falls unbroken, unbent, and unentangled, and towards the east or north; otherwise the felled tree should be abandoned. When the tree trunk is put on a cart and the spokes of the wheels break, the king's army will be shattered; if the rim breaks, then the army will be destroyed; if the axle breaks, then the king's wealth will be lost; and if the axle-pin breaks, then the carpenter will have bad luck. If tree branches fall down suddenly, then war preparations will happen soon; if the trees sound like they're laughing, then the country will come to ruin; and if the trees sound like they're weeping, then there'll be much disease. Fruit and flowers out of season indicate the disintegration of the country; if young plants bear flowers or fruit, many children will die; and if trees secrete milk, all substances will decline. The secretion of wine from trees means vehicles will break down; blood – war is coming; honey – diseases are coming; oil – famine is coming; and water – danger is coming. The sprouting of withered trees or the withering of healthy trees means life-forces will wane; if trees who have fallen get back up again, there will be divine visitations. Likewise, the king will be destroyed if a tree of worship bears flowers or fruit out of season, and the population will be destroyed if trees start walking or talking.[240]

Using crops to divine the future, for example, the Bṛhat Saṁhitā says the farmer will die if lotuses, barley or wheat have unusual stalks, or if a twin fruit or flower appears. Excessive crop growths or varieties of produce from a single tree signify the invasion of a foreign army. There is danger ahead if sesame seeds yield low amounts of oil, or when edible things lose their taste. Evil is ahead if strange flowers and fruits are seen and they are not thrown out of the village and sacrificial oblations are not made; and, again, evil is ahead if any unnatural aspects of a crop appear and the offending field is not given away to a brahman and rice oblations are not offered to the earth at the center of the field.[241] Moreover, trees can be used to find water. Many useable varieties of tree are given in the Bṛhat Saṁhitā and, if one uses the exact measurements given in the text, as well as the exact land marks (ant-hills, colored stones, colored or strongly smelling dirt, snakes, lizards, frogs, etc.), water – sweet and abundant – will be found in the vicinity of most trees.[242]

There is, moreover, a tradition of the Kalpa or wishing tree, who grants the wishes of all petitioners, and whose branches are said to make up the slopes of Mount Kailāsa, where Śiva dwells. The Kalpa tree, also known as a tree of Indra's paradise,[243] appears often in the Kathāsaritsāgara and, in the story of Jīmūtavāhana, for example, is approached successfully by a childless king for a son. The young son, Jīmūtavāhana (an incarnation of the compassionate bodhisattva), grows up and himself approaches the wishing tree in order to have its benefits reach all human beings and to rescue those with few resources from their poverty. The wishing tree agrees and showers gold on people – and comes to be known as the source who continually comes to the aid of the needy. The prince's relations become jealous of him, however, and decide to wage war to get the wishing tree, but Jīmūtavāhana doesn't want to fight so he retires to the mountains, where he spends his days taking care of his father.[244]

In one other way, finally, trees and plants are involved in 'supernaturally' attending to the fortunes of human, and that is through an "act of truth," or *satyakriyā.*[245] A transformative event that ordinarily brings about a literary resolution to problems of narrative and plot, the act of truth is defined by E. W. Burlingame as "a formal declaration of fact, accompanied by a command or resolution or prayer that the purpose of the agent shall be accomplished." The "basis of the Truth Act," continues W. N. Brown, is the "integrity with which one fulfills his [or her] personal function," his or her "personal duty,"[246] which, tapping into the power of truth, creates a harmony within the cosmos. To make an act of truth work, however, the narrative must have some conflict or irresolution that an act of truth successfully negotiates by the agent performing a formal verbal action based on his or her truth, that can be accompanied by some ritual or ceremonial action.[247]

Two examples are especially relevant to interweaving of human and plant lives around an act of truth. The first comes from a Buddhist legend in the Mahāvaṁsa describing the missionizing activities of the third century B.C.E. Mauryan King Aśoka.

Concern arises about how to acquire and bring a branch of the bodhi tree to Śrī Laṅkā, as part of the spreading of Buddhist to the island. When the daughter of Aśoka, now a nun *(therī)*, raises the question – because the "great Bodhi-trees must not be injured with a knife, how then can I have a branch"[248] – the response is a *saccakiriyā*, "truth act," performed by the king himself. Thus, before the tree, he says:

> So truly as the great Bodhi-tree shall go hence to the isle of Laṅkā, and so truly as I shall stand unalterably firm in the doctrine of the Buddha, shall this fair south branch of the great Bodhi-tree, severed of itself, take its place here in this golden vase.

The truth of Aśoka's commitment to Buddhism is so firm, and the movement of Buddhism to places like the island of Laṇkā is so authentically important, that "the great Bodhi-tree severed, of itself, at the place where the line was," and deposits itself in the vase.[249] It is then, according to legend, carried over the Vindhyā mountain range to a port at the mouth of the Ganges River where it is taken by ship and installed in a neighborhood of the Śrī Laṅkan city of Anurādhapura.[250]

The second example comes from the Mahābhārata story of Nala and Damayantī, where Damayantī has already performed a *satyakriyā* in order to know which of the five men before her at her self-choice marriage *(svayaṁvara)* is Nala. Now married, she is immensely distressed in her search for her husband, moving from region to region, over mountains, across rivers, and through forests, in order to find him. Coming upon an Aśoka tree bending low under the weight of its bows, she cries out to this beautiful tree, growing in the middle of the woods.

> Rid me swiftly of my grief, beautiful *aśoka:* have you chanced to see the king, free from sorrow and fear and torment? The enemy-tamer Nala is Damayantī's beloved husband – have you seen my darling, the sovereign of the Niṣadhas? Make it come about, *aśoka* tree, that I find without sorrow my hero...make it come about that I find him come to this forest! Be true to your name, *aśoka*, by dispelling my sorrow![251]

Damayantī then circumambulates the tree three times, and continues her journey, eventually with good results.

As an example of a *satyakriyā*, this act is slightly different from the Aśokan example described above. That the truth is to work by sympathy is normal – *that is, by my formal utterance of my truth, may the cosmos bring truthful consequences about* – but the sympathetic correspondence here is not between the *truth qualities* of the agent of the speech (e. g., authenticity of love, fidelity, or purity of heart) and the norms of cosmic truth, but between the *intensity of feelings* of the agent of speech (Damayantī feels sad), the feelings of the agent of truth (the Aśoka tree is named for sadness), and the feelings of the object of desire (Damayantī imagines Nala to be sad). Perhaps, because it does not strictly follow the standard formula, then, the effectiveness is not as immediately, or as magically, known here as it is in her *svayaṁvara* truth act.

Developing parallel to the more scholastic discussions about the nature of plant life, then, are some more imaginative propositions. First, as we have seen, deities and spirits are thought to find trees and herbs especially amenable places to live and, from these places, deities – as emissaries from a tree abode – can have immediate, intimate, and influential contact with humans. Second, the establishing of correspondences between plant and human bodies, emotions, and behaviors amounts to nothing more than an expansion of the available range of metaphors and images for the use of human beings. These metaphors and images function, first, to give greater and more accessible linguistic control over and, therefore, greater knowledge of, the world humans live in and, second, to create contexts for seeing the plant world and human world as closely knit. Finally, in a most daring set of propositions, there is thought to be a significant interweaving of human and plant lives through conversation, marriage, procreation, and mutual transmutation.

Insofar as the more popular material sets out to answer the same questions as the more scholastic material does – that is, if plants are living, how are they living, and what is it like to live as a plant – these popular materials argue that plants are, in fact, *not* different from us! These materials, and especially the last, verify that plants and humans are not irremediably separate beings but beings whose lives are dynamically interwoven. And in answer to the general questions raised, we can now answer – as we might not have able to before – that living as a plant is not too different from living as a human being! Thus, the propositions of this chapter render the differences between humans and plants smaller rather than larger, and provide cultural testimony from Indian traditions that what plant-positive conclusions there are in the first half of this study are true, insofar as they posit a deep and clear continuity between human and plant lives.

Endnotes :

1 Rajan, "Ancient Indian Approach Towards Plants," pp. 83-84.

2 Dwivedi, "Vedic Heritage for Environmental Stewardship, " p. 34.

3 Rajan, "Ancient Indian Approach Towards Plants," p. 82.

4 Keith, *Religion and Philosophy* 2.415.

5 Vin 4.34; Horner, *Book of the Discipline* 2.226-227; see the discussion in Harvey, *Buddhist Ethics,* p. 175. See also the passage in UD 11.27; Jacobi, *Jaina Sūtras* 2.48-49.

6 Randhawa, *Cult of Trees and Tree-Worship,* pp. 11, 23; see pp. 11-12 for the Kathāsaritsāgara story of a king's request for a mighty tree trunk to be cut for use as a pillar in his palace. His craftsmen find such a tree in the king's own garden and make "the customary offerings to the tree-god living there, and asking him to depart." The tree-god becomes anxious not only about losing his own home but also about his relatives living in the neighboring Śāl trees around him losing theirs. So one night the *devatā* visits the king in his palace to argue for preserving his home as it has been loved and worshipped for a very long time and never cut down. The king, however, perseveres in his desire to cut the tree down, but hears the *devatā's* wish to be cut down in pieces; the king argues that this is an even more painful way to die than to die all at once, but the deity persists by saying that piecemeal cutting will best save his relatives living in surrounding trees. The king is so overcome by the *devatā's* compassion for others that he finally decides to spare the tree's life.

7 See, for example, AV 2.7.1, 3; 2.8.2, 3, 4, 5; 2.9.1, 3; 4.18.5; 4.19.2,

4, 8; 4.37.1, 2, 10; 5.14.1, 2; 10.1.4, 11; 12.3.15.

8 AV 4.20.2, 6, 7: *Tisro divastisraḥ pṛthivīḥ ṣaṭ cemāḥ pradiśaḥ pṛthak / tvayāhaṁ sarvā bhūtāni paśyāni devyoṣadhe // (2) darśaya mā yātudhānāndarśaya yātudhānyaḥ piśācāntsarvāndarśayeti tvā rabha oṣadhe // (6) kaśyapasya cakṣurasi śunyāśca caturakṣyāḥ / vīdhre sūryamiva sarpantaṁ mā piśācaṁ tiraskaraḥ / udagrabhaṁ paripāṇādyātudhānaṁ kimīdinam // (7)* Whitney, *Atharva Veda* 1.185.

9 Van Buitenan, *Mahābhārata* 2-3.354.

10 See Jātaka 257, where a tree spirit is expected to protect people who are passing through the forest, and who will receive offerings when that protection is extended; and Jātaka 272, where a tree spirit drives away the protecting lion and tiger from the forest because of their stench and, without their protection, is then cut down by the foresters.

11 AV 11.9.24; Whitney, *Atharva Veda* 2.655 (my italics); AV 2.9.1; Whitney, *Atharva Veda* 1.50; and AV 12.3.33; Whitney, *Atharva Veda* 2.688.

12 Bhat, *Bṛhat Saṁhitā* 1.348.

13 Of the Buddhist site at Bharhut, Randhawa notes that seven Bodhi trees are identified by Alexander Cunningham: 1. Aśvattha/Pippala/Pīpal or an Indian fig tree is the Bodhi tree of Śākyamuni/Śākyasiṅha; 2. Nyagrodha/banyan or an Indian fig tree is the Bodhi tree of Kāśyapa; 3. Uḍumbara/Gular is the Bodhi tree of Kanakamuni; 4. Śirīṣa is the Bodhi tree of Krakucchanda; 5. Śāl is the Bodhi tree of Viśvabhū; 6. Pāṭalī is the Bodhi tree of Vipaśyin; and 7. Puṇḍarīka or lotus plant is the symbol of Śikhin. Randhawa notes, however, that while his "remaining identifications are correct what Cunningham identified as Patali tree is in fact the asoka tree;" Randhawa, *Cult of Trees and Tree-Worship,* p. 13; see also Naravane, *Sages, Nymphs and Deities,* pp. 158-166.

14 Sadhale, *Surapāla,* p. 73; Dwivedi, "Vedic Heritage for Environmental Stewardship," p. 34.

15 Van Buitenan, *Mahābhārata* 2-3.354.

16 Khanna, "Ritual Capsule of Durgā Pūjā," pp. 475-479.

17 See discussions in Fisher, *Buddhist Art and Architecture,* pp. 21-22, 38, 42-43; Harle, *Art and Architecture of the Indian Subcontinent,* pp. 29-31.

18 Randhawa, *Cult of Trees and Tree-Worship,* p. 19. See, for example, some of the *yakṣīs* with Aśoka and Nāgakesara trees at Bharhut.

19 Randhawa, *Cult of Trees and Tree-Worship*, p. 19. The *yakṣī* is also said to be simply "a woman...shown plucking flowers of [a] sal tree," and a traditional *śālabhañjikā* festival is celebrated when the Śāl trees flower and are worshipped for offspring. Thus, from "its association with the birth of the Buddha, the Vrikshaka motif became a symbol of fertility and women prayed to it for gifts of children." Another pose shows a *yakṣī* hanging from lintel corners with her right arm down around a tree branch and her left arm holding a branch overhead (see, for example, some of the *yakṣīs* with mango trees at Sanchi). Here, the designs of the "wood nymphs" are well suited to act "as supports to the projecting ends of the lowest architraves" on temple or *stūpa* gateways. "Swaying gracefully from the branch of the tree, the *vrikshaka* is singularly beautiful," and Randhawa quotes J. H. Marshall as saying:

> Holding with both hands to the arching bough of a mango-tree, the *salabhanjika* 'curves the woodbine of her body' in an attitude which brings out her breasts 'like urns of gold.' Her locks spread out over her back are brought up on the crown of her head into a curious topknot, which may be compared to the coiffure of the female servants and jungle-dwellers....The type presents a pleasing compromise between the court lady and the woman of the woods.

Another pose for *yakṣīs* is, like the other versions, bent-kneed and/or cross-ankled and against the backdrop of a tree, but in this case with both arms overhead holding the tree branches. Examples such as these are found in Kushan Mathura with depictions of Aśoka trees, while other classical *yakṣī* poses are found there with Kadamba and Nāgakesara trees; Randhawa, *Cult of Trees and Tree-Worship*, pp. 19, 23, 31-32.

20 J 50, 509.

21 Randhawa, *Cult of Trees and Tree-Worship*, p. 24.

22 S . Gupta, *Plant Myths and Traditions in India*, p. 88; they also experience dread at their own stupidity which causes trouble for themselves (J 370).

23 Shilapi, "Environmental and Ecological Teachings of Tīrthaṅkara Mahāvīra," p. 162; see A 3.366-374.

24 Ryan, *Buddhism and the Natural World*, p. 52.

25 Kaza and Kraft, *Dharma Rain*, pp. 21-22.

26 See J 38, 74, 105, 109, 113, 209, 272, 294, 295, 298, 307, 311, 361, 412, 520.

27 Penzer, *Kathāsaritsāgara* 5.59-61.

28 Cowell, *Jātakas* 1.268; see J 438 for the story of a tree spirit who

[25] Kaza and Kraft, *Dharma Rain*, pp. 21-22.

[26] See J 38, 74, 105, 109, 113, 209, 272, 294, 295, 298, 307, 311, 361, 412, 520.

[27] Penzer, *Kathāsaritsāgara* 5.59-61.

[28] Cowell, *Jātakas* 1.268; see J 438 for the story of a tree spirit who plots with a mother lizard to release her babies from the stomach of a wicked ascetic.

[29] Cowell, *Jātakas* 3.192.

[30] Cowell, *Jātakas* 4.129-131.

[31] AV 18.3.70; Whitney, *Atharva Veda* 2.868.

[32] From *pra* + *ita* (past passive participle of the verb *i* "to go"), meaning "having passed on," or in other words, "having passed from this world to the next;" hence "the departed one" or "a spirit of the dead." "In both Sanskrit and Pāli, the word is specialized to refer only to the spirits in torment or in a state of purgatory...The petas live in *paraloka* or yonder-world." Their life, however, is not that of the greater torment of hell, but of a temporary and lesser kind of suffering, which is still, nevertheless, quite painful; Gehman, *Stories of the Departed*, pp. x-xi.

[33] Oldenberg, *Religion of the Veda*, p. 329.

[34] See Knipe, "*Sapiṇḍīkaraṇa*," p. 113.

[35] Knipe, "*Sapiṇḍīkaraṇa*," p. 111.

[36] Knipe, "*Sapiṇḍīkaraṇa*," pp. 115-116.

[37] Knipe, "*Sapiṇḍīkaraṇa*," p. 115.

[38] *Pretas* are described as having worms devouring their mouths and being of terrible odor; naked and ugly, with terrible stenches issuing from body and mouth; emaciated, with prominent veins, and with saliva, mucus, phlegm, and blood drooling out; and with coarsened skin, reddened eyes, and yellow teeth. And in the collection of *preta* stories in book five of the "Hīnayāna" Avadānaśataka, the purgatorial departed have an equally gruesome appearance: a face "like the peak of a mountain, a belly like a mountain or the ocean, and a mouth like the eye of a needle." The *preta* is nude and covered with hair forming a whole that looks like a single flame, and uttering cries of distress, they arouse sympathy among humans; Pv 1.3, 6, 7; 2.2, 4, 7; 4.10; Gehman, *Stories of the Departed*, pp. xi, 5, 12, 13, 30, 36, 41, 103.

[39] T. W. Rhys Davids and Stede, *Pali-English Dictionary*, pp. 545.

[40] Fisher, *Buddhist Art and Architecture*, pp. 38-39; see also pp. 42, 43; see also Harle, *Art and Architecture of the Indian*

...A spirit that knows
The after-death secrets.
It will guide your suffering soul
Through the shadow world,
The world between death and resurrection....
The Spirit will give you
The courage to surrender
To the black phantoms waiting.
There are many. Many and many....
Now comes the Spirit to remind you again
Not to be distracted,
Not to wander about...
But to prepare for the moment
To be born again....
This will be the moment
You could be born
A horse, a fowl, a dog, or a man.
Hold fast, Dead One,
Hold fast.
Your life-cycle is about to begin.
And give thanks to the Spirit
Of the Coffin Tree.

43 Shively, "Buddhahood for the Nonsentient," p. 135.

44 See Shively, "Buddhahood for the Nonsentient," pp. 135, 136, 137, 138, 139, 147, 148, 149, 150, 151, 153, 159, 160.

45 Shively, "Buddhahood for the Nonsentient," pp. 140-156.

46 Gopal, *Vṛkṣāyurveda*, p. 97.

47 Randhawa, *Cult of Trees and Tree-Worship*, p. 10.

48 Surapla in Gopal, *Vṛkṣāyurveda*, pp. 119-123.

49 Dwivedi, "*Satyagraha* for Conservation," p. 156. My italics.

50 Kane 5.1.415-416. My italics.

51 Khanna, "Ritual Capsule of Durgā Pūjā," pp. 475-485.

52 Randhawa, *Cult of Trees and Tree-Worship*, pp. 14, 8-9. Early on, the bodhi tree becomes a symbol of the enlightened Buddha, standing in for him in early Buddhist sculpture and bas-relief, as many of the images in Randhawa's study illustrate. Worship of the bodhi tree continues as an important practice in contemporary Buddhism; see Batchelor and Brown, *Buddhism and Ecology*, p. 80.

53 Cowell, *Jātakas* 4.142-143.

54 J 261; Cowell, *Jātakas* 2.222-223. Three kinds of shrines for pilgrimage are possible in the Buddha's time: using a relic of the body, a relic of use or wear, and a relic of memorial. Because a body-shrine cannot be made while the person is still alive, Ānanda decides on a

pilgrimage site with an offspring of the original bodhi tree as its focus. This meets with the Buddha's approval; J 479; Cowell, *Jātakas* 4.142-143.

55 J 186; Cowell, *Jātakas* 2.72-73.

56 Randhawa, *Cult of Trees and Tree-Worship*, pp. 11-12.

57 J 307; Cowell, *Jātakas* 3.16.

58 J 537; Cowell, *Jātakas* 5. 257.

59 Randhawa, *Cult of Trees and Tree-Worship*, p. 24.

60 BS 54.2; Gopal, *Vṛkṣāyurveda*, p. 95; see also, pp. 97, 99, 101, 103, 107, 113, etc.

61 Sur 4.53; Gopal, *Vṛkṣāyurveda*, p. 135.

62 Knipe, *"Sapiṇḍīkaraṇa,"* p. 115.

63 UD 10.1; Jacobi, *Jaina Sūtras* 2.42.

64 Schmidt, "Origin of *Ahiṁsā*," pp. 629, 644, 645.

65 Gītā 15.1: *ūrdhva-mūlam adhaḥ-śākham aśvatthaṁ prāhur avyayam;* "With roots above and boughs beneath, they say, the undying fig-tree [stands];" Zaehner, *Bhagavad Gītā*, p. 359.

66 AB 5.28; Keith, *Rigveda Brahmanas*, p. 252. My italics.

67 BĀU 1.1.1; Radhakrishnan, *Principal Upaniṣads*, p. 149. My italics. See also CS Śārīrasthānam 1.13.

68 BĀU 3.2.13; see also AU 1.1.4; 1.2.4; MU 1.1.7; 2.1.5; SU 2.1.

69 MU 1.1.7; Radhakrishnan, *Principal Upaniṣads*, p. 673.

70 CU 6.12; for a similar image, see Śantideva's Bodhicharyāvatāra 9.74.

71 CU 3.14.3; Radhakrishnan, *Principal Upaniṣads*, pp. 391-392; see Brereton, "Upanishads," pp. 130-131.

72 Brereton, "Upanishads," p. 120.

73 BĀU 3.9.28; Radhakrishnan, *Principal Upaniṣads*, p. 244; see Chapple, *Nonviolence to Animals, Earth, and Self in Asian Traditions*, p. 51. Another passage (CU 6.11) of instruction about Brahman to Śvetaketu compares a tree to a human body in this way. A tree struck at the root, in the middle, or at the top would bleed at each place, but with each strike it would still live — "being pervaded by its living self, it stands firm, drinking in its moisture (which nourishes it) and rejoicing." Likewise, however, when life leaves a branch of the tree it dries up, as it does in the case of a second and a third branch, as well as of the whole of the tree, but, though, the body of the tree (or person) dies, the living self does not; Radhakrishnan, *Principal Upaniṣads*, p. 460.

74 AU 1.1.4; 1.2.4; Radhakrishnan, *Principal Upaniṣads*, p. 516. My italics. See also, Brereton, "Upanishads," pp. 120-121.

[75] Bhat, *Bṛhat Saṁhitā* 1.499.

[76] Ramanujan, *Speaking of Śiva,* p. 80.

[77] Bhat, *Bṛhat Saṁhitā* 1.531; the citation is "the *viśvavallabha* of Cakrapāṇimiśra in VIII."

[78] Sur 8.165-166; Gopal, *Vṛkṣāyurveda,* pp. 176-177.

[79] Bhishagratna, *Suśruta Saṁhitā* 2.46.

[80] Schotsman, *Buddhacarita,* p. 60.

[81] M.N. Dutt, *Rāmāyaṇa* 2.653.

[82] J 353; Cowell, *Jātaka* 3.107; Ryan, *Buddhism and the Natural World,* p. 52.

[83] Ryder, *Shakuntala,* pp. 21, 35.

[84] Miller in Thapar, *Sakuntala,* pp. 91, 103, 114, 115, 132.

[85] Archer, *Vidyāpati,* p. 83.

[86] Miller, *Phantasies of a Love-Thief,* pp.89, 15; Ramanujan, *Interior Landscape,* p. 69.

[87] Peterson, *Poems to Śiva,* p. 280.

[88] Ryder, *Shakuntala,* pp. 9, 10; Miller in Thapar, *Sakuntala,* pp. 90, 110, 113, 124.

[89] Miller, *Love Song of the Dark Lord,* p. 74. The plant and flower homology can be used of the lover's body as well, for Jayadeva notes of Kṛṣṇa's dark body that it is "like a dark lotus wrapped in veils of yellow pollen."

[90] Peterson, *Poems to Śiva,* p. 140.

[91] Hem 7.27; Fynes, *Hemacandra,* p. 146.

[92] Hawley and Juergensmeyer, *Songs of the Saints of India,* p. 108.

[93] Archer, *Vidyāpati,* pp. 83, 111.

[94] Miller, *Phantasies of a Love-Thief,* pp. 15, 61, 85. Additionally, for the beloved in Kaymaṉār, "her face [has] the color of the new mango leaf;" Ramanujan, *Interior Landscape*, p. 94.

[95] Miller, *Love Song of the Dark Lord,* pp. 86, 114, 76, 101, 120, 124.

[96] Bhishagratna, *Suśruta Saṁhitā* 3.371.

[97] Bhishagratna, *Suśruta Saṁhitā* 3.369.

[98] M. N. Dutt, *Rāmāyaṇa* 2.656.

[99] Archer, *Vidyāpati,* pp. 55, 118; see Ramanujan, *Interior Landscape*, p. 72.

[100] Miller, *Phantasies of a Love-Thief,* pp. 15, 53, 83, 87; Miller, *Love Song of the Dark Lord,* pp. 72, 81, 88.

[101] Miller, *Love Song of the Dark Lord,* pp. 104, 112, 114.

[102] Ramanujan, *Interior Landscape,* pp. 62, 69.

[103] Bhishagratna, *Suśruta Saṁhitā* 3.369.

[104] Ryder, *Shakuntala,* p. 10.

[105] Miller, *Phantasies of a Love-Thief*, p. 83; Miller, *Love Song of the Dark Lord*, pp. 78, 119, 114, 84, 85.

[106] Ryder, *Shakuntala*, p. 71.

[107] Archer, *Vidyāpati*, p. 108; Miller, *Phantasies of a Love-Thief*, p. 87.

[108] Miller, *Love Song of the Dark Lord*, pp. 112, 85.

[109] Miller, *Phantasies of a Love Thief*, pp. 53, 83.

[110] Miller, *Love Song of the Dark Lord*, p. 114.

[111] Ramanujan, *Interior Landscape*, p. 57.

[112] Miller, *Love Song of the Dark Lord*, p. 118; Ramanujan, *Interior Landscape*, p. 54.

[113] Pollock and Goldman, *Rāmāyaṇa of Vālmīki* 3.215.

[114] Archer, *Vidyāpati*, pp. 40, 106.

[115] Miller, *Love Song of the Dark Lord*, p. 109.

[116] Miller, *Phantasies of a Love-Thief*, p. 83.

[117] Nagar, *Jain Rāmāyaṇa*, p. 265.

[118] Pollock and Goldman, *Rāmāyaṇa of Vālmīki* 3.215; Ryder, *Shakuntala*, p. 10.

[119] Miller, *Phantasies of a Love-Thief*, p. 65; Miller, *Love Song of the Dark Lord*, pp. 113, 114, 123, 77, 101.

[120] Ramanujan, *Interior Landscape*, pp. 59, 72.

[121] KS 3.36; Jacobi, *Jaina Sūtras* 2.232; Miller, *Phantasies of a Love-Thief*, pp. 23, 83; Miller, *Love Song of the Dark Lord*, pp. 101, 122; Hawley and Juergensmeyer, *Songs of the Saints of India*, p. 107.

[122] Nagar, *Jain Rāmāyaṇa*, p. 265.

[123] Archer, *Vidyāpati*, p. 117; Miller, *Love Song of the Dark Lord*, p. 114.

[124] Nagar, *Jain, Rāmāyaṇa*, p. 265.

[125] Miller, *Phantasies of a Love-Thief*, p. 23.

[126] Archer, *Vidyāpati*, pp. 129, 118; see Surdas in Hawley and Juergensmeyer, *Songs of the Saints of India*, p. 107

[127] Miller, *Love Song of the Dark Lord*, pp. 102, 113, 112, 122.

[128] Archer, *Vidyāpati*, p. 132.

[129] Archer, *Vidyāpati*, pp. 136, 64, 87.

[130] Miller, *Love Song of the Dark Lord*, pp. 74-75.

[131] Miller, *Love Song of the Dark Lord*, p. 77.

[132] Miller, *Love Song of the Dark Lord*, p. 81.

[133] Miller, *Love Song of the Dark Lord*, p. 84.

[134] Miller, *Love Song of the Dark Lord*, p. 118.

[135] Ramanujan, *Interior Landscapes*, p. 72; Miller, *Phantasies of a Love-Thief*, p. 45.

[136] Ryder, *Shakuntala*, pp. 73, 11, 52.

[137] Archer, *Vidyāpati*, pp. 45, 59, 64; see also pp. 50-51, where Vidyāpati says of the lover that he is as eager as a bee to take the honey of his lover, and of the beloved that she will feel "the beautiful bee...seize my chin, suck honey from my lips, and loot my senses."

[138] Miller, *Phantasies of a Love-Thief*, pp. 15, 37.

[139] Miller, *Love Song of the Dark Lord*, p. 83.

[140] Archer, *Vidyāpati*, p. 87.

[141] Miller, *Love Song of the Dark Lord*, p. 75.

[142] Manu 9.33, 35; Bühler, *Laws of Manu*, p. 333. Manu himself, however, records that there is some controversy about the relative importance of the seed and the field, for:

70. Some sages declare the seed to be more important, and others the field; again others (assert that) the seed and the field (are equally important); but the legal decision on this point is as follows:
71. Seed, sown on barren ground, perishes in it; a (fertile) field also, in which no (good) seed (is sown), will remain barren.
72. [But] as through the power of the seed (sons) born of animals became sages who are honoured and praised, hence the seed is declared to be more important.

Manu 10.70-72; Bühler, *Laws of Manu*, p. 418.

[143] Van Buitenan, *Mahābhārata* 2-3.445.

[144] Hem 1.394, 423; Fynes, *Hemacandra*, pp. 32, 34.

[145] Ryder, *Shakuntala*, p. 42.

[146] Sur 7.149-151; Gopal, *Vṛkṣāyurveda*, p. 171.

[147] Hem 2.11; Fynes, *Hemacandra*, p. 40.

[148] Thus: MN 1.250; "Even as...a palm-tree whose crown is cut off cannot come to further growth... [likewise, a tree] got rid of, cut off at the root, made like a palm-tree stump, so...those cankers...can come to no further existence in the future;" Horner, *Middle Length Sayings* 1.304; see pp. 286-287.

And MN 1.435; "Just as this situation occurs...that having cut off the bark of a great, stable and pithy tree, [and] having cut out the softwood, there can be a cutting out of the pith...[there can also be a] course for getting rid of the five fetters binding to the lower (shore);" Horner, *Middle Length Sayings* 2.104; see p. 137.

And SN 3.27; "That desire and lust, brethren, which is in body, do ye renounce them. So will that body become rejected, cut down at the root, made like the stump of a palm-tree, made something that has ceased to be, so that it cannot grow up again in the future;" Woodward, *Kindred Sayings* 3.26-27; see also SN 1.69; C. A. F. Rhys Davids, *Kindred Sayings* 1.95, and SN 4.85; Woodward,

Kindred Sayings 4.51.

149 SN 5.96-97; Woodward, *Kindred Sayings* 5.80.

150 ĀD S2.2.2-4; Olivelle, *Dharmasūtras*, pp. 44-45.

151 Manu 10.69; 9.36; Bühler, *Laws of Manu*, pp. 418, 333-334.

152 CS Sūtrasthāna 32; Sharma, *Caraka Saṁhitā* 1.74.

153 Collins, *Selfless Persons*, p. 220; see also pp. 218-224.

154 Pv 1; Gehman, *Stories of the Departed*, p. 3. Aśvaghoṣa's Buddhacarita applies the plant homology to another Buddhist doctrine, that of the *pratītyasamutpāda:* "Leaf and stalk, they exist only when a shoot exists; and likewise the sense organs arise only when this name-and-form does exist;" Schotsman, *Buddhacarita*, p. 249. Thus, the conditioned nature of a shoot giving rise to a stalk and leaf in a plant is patterned in the doctrine of twelve-fold dependent origination, such that name-and-form is the natural and necessary condition of the sense organs.

155 SN 5.46-47; Woodward, *Kindred Sayings* 5.37; see also SN 3.54-55; Woodward, *Kindred Sayings* 3.46-47.

156 AN 3.44; Hare, *Gradual Sayings* 3.36; see also Mil 375-376.

157 Śantideva 1.12.

158 Śantideva 1.12.

159 Rajan, "Ancient Indian Approaches Towards Plants," p. 84.

160 Narayan, "One Tree is Equal to Ten Sons," pp. 300-301. See also Manu 9.255.

161 Van Buitenan, *Mahābhārata* 2-3.242.

162 Pollack and Goldman, *Rāmāyaṇa of Vālmīki* 3.213.

163 Miller, *Love Song of the Dark Lord*, pp. 75, 90, 98, 116.

164 Ryder, *Shakuntala*, pp. 29, 66.

165 Pēreyiṉ Muṟuvalār in Ramanujan, *Interior Landscape*, p. 27.

166 Ramanujan, *Interior Landscape*, pp. 32, 34, 52, 56.

167 Ryder, *Shakuntala*, pp. 8, 10, 45; Miller in Thapar, *Sakuntala*, p. 123.

168 Ryder, *Pañcatantra*, p. 299.

169 Hem 6.6; Fynes, *Hemacandra*, p. 126

170 RV 9.97.18-19; 9.114.2; 1.91.22; 9.86.10; 9.87.2; 9.89.2; 9.97.24, 58; 9.109.4; KB 7.10; see also ŚB 5.4.5.2; AB 1.8.

171 AV 6.15.3.

172 ŚB 3.3.2.8; 4.5.10.2-6; Eggeling, *Śatapatha Brāhmaṇa* 2.65, 421-422.

173 Smith, *Classifying the Universe*, p. 227.

174 ŚB 6.7.1.13; Eggeling, *Śatapatha Brāhmaṇa* 3.267.

175 ŚB 6.6.3.3; Eggeling, *Śatapatha Brāhmaṇa* 3.257.

176 Smith, *Classifying the Universe*, pp. 227-228.

[177] Smith, *Classifying the Universe*, p. 218.

[178] Smith, *Classifying the Universe*, p. 222.

[179] Smith, *Classifying the Universe*, pp. 224-226.

[180] Smith, *Classifying the Universe*, pp. 226-227.

[181] Penzer, *Kathāsaritsāgara* 6.25-26.

[182] As rendered in Randhawa, *Cult of Trees and Tree-Worship*, p. 18; see Penzer, *Kathāsaritsāgara* 2.42-44.

[183] Penzer, *Kathāsaritsāgara* 2.231-236.

[184] Penzer, *Kathāsaritsāgara* 3.25; 8.185.

[185] "A Flowering Tree," taken from Ramanujan, *A Flowering Tree and Other Oral Tales from India*, pp. 53-62. This is a collection of oral folk tales in Kannada, assembled by A. K. Ramanujan from family and friends between about 1950 and 1970 and translated into English.

[186] Ramanujan, "A Flowering Tree," p. 56.

[187] Ramanujan, "A Flowering Tree," p. 61.

[188] Ramanujan, "The Pomegranate Queen," pp. 135-137.

[189] Ramanujan, "The Pomegranate Queen," p. 137.

[190] K. Narayan, "How a Girl Became a Sacred Plant," pp. 487-494. This story comes from Kangra in the Himalayan foothills of Himachal Pradesh out of "a rich corpus of women's songs and stories cluster[ed] around the worship of Tulsī," or the sacred basil shrub.

[191] K. Narayan, "How a Girl Became a Sacred Plant," p. 492.

[192] Nadig, "The Man Who Grew Roots," pp. 116-123.

[193] Nadig, "The Man Who Grew Roots," p. 116.

[194] Nadig, "The Man Who Grew Roots," p. 117.

[195] Nadig, "The Man Who Grew Roots," p, 119. We note here the resonance with part of Martin's translation of a section of the Apollo and Daphne story from Ovid's *Metamorphoses* (p. 37):

> Her prayer was scarcely finished when she feels
> a torpor take possession of her limbs —
> her supple trunk is girdled with a thin
> layer of fine bark over her smooth skin;
> her hair turns into foliage, her arms
> grow into branches, sluggish roots adhere
> to feet that were so recently so swift,
> her head becomes the summit of a tree;
> all that remains of her is a warm glow.

[196] Nadig, "The Man Who Grew Roots," p. 123.

[197] Beck et al, *Folktales of India*, pp. 7-9.

[198] Beck et al, *Folktales of India*, p. 8.

[199] Beck et al, *Folktales of India*, p. 9.

[200] See, for example, the story in the Kathāsaritsāgara of a *devatā*, identified there as a *yakṣa*, in an Aśvattha tree who speaks to Somadatta, sleeping under him one night, and urges him to go on a mission of good fortune to the land of King Ādityaprabha; Penzer, *Kathāsaritsāgara* 2.97-98.

[201] Cowell, *Jātaka* 1.57-58.

[202] Cowell, *Jātaka* 1.57-58.

[203] Mil 172; Horner, *Milinda's Questions* 1.243.

[204] Horner, *Milinda's Questions* 1. 244.

[205] S. Gupta, *Plant Myths and Traditions in India*, p. 79.

[206] S. Gupta, *Plant Myths and Traditions in India*, p. 21; see Mbh 12.150.1-36.

[207] S. Gupta, *Plant Myths and Traditions in India*, p.79.

[208] S. Gupta, *Plant Myths and Traditions in India*, pp. 100-101.

[209] M. N. Dutt, *Rāmāyaṇa* 2.649-650.

[210] Pollock and Goldman, *Rāmāyaṇa* 3.213-214.

[211] Ryder, *Shakuntala*, pp. 9, 46.

[212] As quoted in Prime, *Hinduism and Ecology*, p. 84

[213] As quoted in Prime, *Hinduism and Ecology*, p. 87; see pp. 86-89.

[214] Kaza, *Attentive Heart*, p. 5.

[215] Kaza, *Attentive Heart*, pp. 9-11.

[216] Kraft, "Greening of Buddhist Practice," p. 486.

[217] Sur 7.151; Gopal, p. 171.

[218] Ryder, *Shakuntala*, pp. 10, 46.

[219] S. Gupta, *Plant Myths and Traditions in India*, p. ix.

[220] Randhawa, *Cult of Trees and Tree-Worship*, p. 61.

[221] S. Gupta, *Plant Myths and Traditions in India*, p. 45.

[222] See Keith, *Religion and Philosophy* 1.184, and Majupuria, *Sacred and Useful Plants & Trees of Nepal*, p. 15.

[223] Penzer, *Kathāsaritsāgara* 1.239.

[224] S. Gupta, *Plant Myths and Traditions in India*, p. 9.

[225] Majupuria, *Sacred and Useful Plants & Trees of Nepal*, pp. 94-95.

[226] Majupuria, *Sacred and Useful Plants & Trees of Nepal*, pp. 87-88.

[227] Majupuria, *Sacred and Useful Plants & Trees of Nepal*, p. 89.

[228] Nagarajan, "Marrying Trees," p. 454.

[229] Nagarajan, "Marrying Trees," p. 457.

[230] Nagarajan, "Marrying Trees," p. 458.

[231] Nagarajan, "Marrying Trees," p. 458-459.

[232] Mukherjee, *Desirable Daughters*, p. 16. Again, we note the resonance of this passage with one from the Apollo and Daphne story from Martin's translation of Ovid's *Metamorphoses* (p. 37):

Loving her still, the god puts his right hand
against the trunk, and even now can feel
her heart as it beats under the new bark;
he hugs her limbs as if they were still human,
and then he puts his lips against the wood,
which, even now, is adverse to his kiss.

[233] Van Buitenan, *Mahābhārata* 2-3.445.

[234] Randhawa, *Cult of Trees and Tree-Worship*, p. 23.

[235] Randhawa, *Cult of Trees and Tree-Worship*, p. 61.

[236] Randhawa, *Cult of Trees and Tree-Worship*, p. 62.

[237] Randhawa, *Cult of Trees and Tree-Worship*, p. 62.

[238] VP 2.300.23; Gopal, *Vṛkṣāyurveda* p. 109.

[239] Randhawa, *Cult of Trees and Tree-Worship*, p. 19.

[240] BS 43.20, 22; 46.25-30; Bhat, *Bṛhat Saṁhitā* 1.348-349; 380-381.

[241] BS 46.33-37; Bhat, *Bṛhat Saṁhitā* 1.381-382.

[242] See BS 54.6-105; Bhat, *Bṛhat Saṁhitā* 1.500-521.

[243] Penzer, *Kathāsaritsāgara* 1.8, 144; 9.87-88.

[244] Penzer, *Kathāsaritsāgara* 2.138-141; see also 8.124.

[245] Known primarily in the Pali phrase *saccakiriyā*, a Sanskrit equivalent, **satyakriyā*, is proposed, and supported by such terms as *satyādhiṣṭhāna, satyavādya, satyavacana*. It is found in various types of literature: e.g., Ṛgveda (4.33; 10.34), Mahābhārata, Rāmāyaṇa, Chandogya Upaniṣad (6.16), the Jātakas, and the Milindapañha; Burlingame, "The Act of Truth," pp. 433-434, 437-438; Brown, "The Basis for the Hindu Act of Truth," pp. 40-45; Brown, "The Metaphysics of the Truth Act," pp. 173-174; Brown, "Duty as Truth in the Rig Veda," pp. 57-67; Brown, "Duty as Truth in Ancient India," pp. 255ff.

[246] Burlingame, "The Act of Truth," p. 429; Brown, "The Basis for the Hindu Act of Truth," pp. 38, 40.

[247] This formulaic utterance often appears in various syntactic forms — the Sanskrit *yathā...tathā* and *tena satyena* being common examples—and usually, but not always, makes direct reference to *sacca/satya* "truth;" see Burlingame, "The Act of Truth," p. 434; Brown, "Duty as Truth in Ancient India," p. 252; Findly, "Speech as Performative in the Ṛgveda," pp. 15-47; Wayman, "The Hindu Buddhist Rite of Truth," p. 369.

[248] Geiger, *Mahāvaṁsa*, p. 123.

[249] Geiger, *Mahāvaṁsa*, p. 125.

[250] Geiger, *Mahāvaṁsa*, pp. 128-131.

[251] Van Buitenan, *Mahābhārata* 2-3.340-341.

7
Plant Rights and Human Duties

We now move from traditional understandings of *what is* to *what should be.* While it may seem fairly easy, after delineating some common threads about the nature of plants, to describe plant life at its optimum, deciding what language best *provides* for such a possibility is difficult. However carefully we may designate any sort of outlook with regard to language, it is determined, necessarily, by humans. Humans construct the vantage points that are used, and humans are the self-proclaimed agents for maintaining them. It need hardly be argued, then, that there cannot be any truly flora-centered system that is knowable by ordinary means – for our mental processes naturally and continually impose systems on the world that obscure rather than illuminate. Leaving the plant world alone might be a start, but the simple absence of human interference does not necessarily give humans any knowledge about what plants themselves may find to be ideal contexts for their lives.

The built-in human bias in any conventionally available material about plant life is especially apparent in the previous chapter, where the defining model of the question "what is it like to live as a plant" is none other than the human being. That is, narratives about tree deities, homologies between humans and plants, conversations and marriages with plants, and transmutations into plants all tell us much more about human desires and human imagination than they do about actual plant life. Indeed, the more scholastic materials treated earlier – that provide schemata arranging all living beings into certain categories, orders, and hierarchies, for example – also tell us much more about humans than they do about plants. In fact, it is the *primary goal* of these systems to present visions of the world which afford meaningful places to human beings, such that human identity is established only *in relation to* other beings and elements and, in particular, is established only through other-defined relationships that are understood to be of benefit to humans.

7.1 Taylor's "Biocentric Outlook"

One way to pursue what kinds of rights, if any, plants have – that is, one way to explore the promotion of optimal plant life – is to examine the work of someone like Paul Taylor who, in his book *Respect for Nature: A Theory of Environmental Ethics*, develops an accessible set of parameters that can be helpful in getting at the "what should be" dynamics of plant life as described in early Hinduism, Jainism, and Buddhism. Taylor frames a "biocentric outlook on nature" that proposes that plants, among other living beings, have an "inherent worth" that establishes the basis of an obligatory human "attitude of respect for nature." Taken in conjunction with his discussion of whether plants (and animals) have legal and moral rights, we find constructive categories for taking up the prescriptive questions of advocacy as given in Indian materials on plants. The summary of Taylor's argument below shapes the application of his biocentric outlook to our discussion.

Taylor: 1. Humans and Nonhumans Alike Belong to the "Earth's Community of Life."

This recognition is grounded in "five general empirical truths."[1] First, there are *physical requirements for survival*, such that for living beings "to live a long, healthy life at their fullest biological capacities and thus [to] realize their good at a high level of *biological flourishing*, it is necessary…[to] carry on their life functions in ways that allow successful ecological coexistence with other organisms."[2] Second, all members of this community, human and nonhuman alike, have *"a good of their own,"*[3] which means that a being does not necessarily *have an interest in* something (as a subjective category), but that for that being there is something that *is in its interest* (as an objective category). Thus, a being is benefited by the preservation of a condition that is favorable to it and, in that *"all plants are...beings that have a good of their own,"* for example, we

> can intentionally act with the aim of helping a plant to grow and thrive, and...because we have genuine concern for its well-being. As moral agents we might think of ourselves as under an obligation not to destroy or injure a plant. We can also take the standpoint of a plant and judge what happens to it as being good or bad from its standpoint...Nothing in the above ways of responding to and dealing with plants implies that they have interests in the sense of having conscious aims and desires. We can deny that subjective value concepts apply to vegetative life and yet hold that plants do have a good of their own, which can be furthered or damaged by our treatment of them.[4]

Third, the lives of humans and nonhumans share a notion of freedom. While humans alone exercise free will in making decisions and autonomy in governing themselves, they share with nonhumans a freedom to preserve their own existence and to further their own good, such that an "organism may be said to be free if it has the ability and opportunity to promote or protect its good according to the laws of *its nature*." This falls, for Taylor, under the possibility of experiencing an "absence of constraint."[5] In the case of a plant, an absence of constraint might mean something like not having its roots bound by a container, or not being deprived of sun, nutrient-rich soil, or water. *Free from* such constraints, a plant is *free to* "grow in a normal manner and cope successfully with the problems of survival.[6] Fourth, humans and nonhumans belong to the same community as well because they share a common origin, that is, "the same order of evolutionary processes, governed by the same laws of natural selection and genetic transmission, which gave rise to our existence and to the existence of every other species."[7] Fifth, and finally, belonging to the same evolutionary process means being equally vulnerable to specialization and extinction. With this in mind, notes Taylor, while nonhuman life forms can do without humans, human life forms cannot exist without nonhumans:

> Our demise would be no loss to other species, nor would it adversely affect the natural environment. On the contrary, other living things would be much benefited. The physical environment of the Earth would be greatly improved.

In short, he says, "our presence...is not needed."[8]

Taylor: 2. The Natural World is a System of Interdependence

The second core statement of the biocentric outlook posits that all human and nonhuman beings are essential constituent elements in a system of interdependence. Here, the survival and flourishing of each living being is a function not only of the conditions of the physical environment, but of its relationships with other living beings. "When one accepts the biocentric outlook, the whole realm of life is understood to exemplify a vast complex of relationships of interdependence similar to that found in each ecosystem."[9]

Taylor: 3. All Living Beings as Teleological Centers of Life

The third statement shifts from beings in relation to each other and interacting within the environment as a whole to an "attention on the lives of individual organisms." Here Taylor proposes not only that each unique living being is an "entity-having-a-good-of-its-own," but that it is pursuing "its good in its own way."[10]

> To say... [an individual being] is a teleological center of life is to say that its internal functioning as well as its external activities are all goal-oriented, having the constant tendency to maintain the organism's existence through time and to enable it successfully to perform those biological operations whereby it reproduces its kind and continually adapts to changing environmental events and conditions.

As Taylor notes, then, to propose that a particular tree is a teleological center of life is not to say that it *intentionally* aims at preserving its existence, but that like all "organisms, whether conscious or not," it is a teleological center of life "in the sense that each is a unified, coherently ordered system of goal-oriented activities that has a constant tendency to protect and maintain the organism's existence."[11]

Taylor: 4. A Rejection of the Idea of Human Superiority

Of all the core points of the biocentric outlook this last is the most crucial in setting an attitude of respect for nature, for it asks us to shift our point of view to that of all living beings: "All we need to do is to look at the capacities of animals and plants from the standpoint of *their* good to find a contrary judgment of superiority."[12] Of the biocentric outlook as a whole, Taylor says: "As moral agents we see ourselves under an ethical requirement to give equal consideration to the good of every [living] entity, human and non-human alike, that has a good of its own."[13]

Taylor: Do Animals and Plants Have Legal Rights?

To "have a right is to have a legitimate claim or entitlement to something" whose legitimacy is recognized by others and, in the case of legal rights, such rights are "imposed by a given system of law on all members of the legal community in question."[14] In this regard, animals and plants *do have legal rights* "in those societies whose legal systems contain laws that protect their good in various ways" – that is, in those societies where there is an attitude of respect for nature, and thus a view of animals and plants as beings possessing inherent worth.[15] This is increasingly true of the contemporary setting and, more to the point, *has been true*, as we shall see, of traditional Indian political and medical traditions for centuries, particularly under such rubrics as *rājadharma* and *vṛkṣāyurveda*.

Taylor: Do Animals and Plants Have Moral Rights?

On this question, Taylor finds that there are four aspects of moral rights "that make it *conceptually impossible for either animals or plants to be bearers of moral rights*." First, plants are not members of a community of moral agents; second, they are not capable of "having self-respect;" third, they cannot "choose to exercise or enjoy a right;" and fourth, they cannot exercise "certain second-order entitlements" that come with moral rights such as "the right to complain."[16] But there is a modified concept of moral rights that "makes it conceivable for (animals and) plants to have such rights," a view that requires a respect for nature based on regarding animals and plants as possessing "inherent worth.

Tandem to Taylor's concept of "the good of a being" is the concept of a being's having an "inherent worth," a "fundamental value-presupposition" that underlies the attitude of respect for nature. This notion is different from the "good of a being" in that one "can acknowledge that...[a] plant has a good of its own and yet...deny that moral agents have a duty to promote or protect its good or even to refrain from harming it." That is, just because a being is recognized as having a good of its own does not require that "moral agents ought or ought not to treat it in a certain way." To be of inherent worth, however, is "to be *worthy of respect* on the part of all moral agents,"[17] and is a valuation outside of an agent finding value in a being, but obliging an agent to regard the being in a respectful way.

> If it is true that a living thing has inherent worth, then it possesses such worth regardless of any instrumental or inherent *value* it may have and without reference to the good of any other being.[18]

That a being has inherent worth also means that it deserves moral consideration and that all moral agents have a duty to promote "the entity's good as an end in itself and for the sake of the entity whose good it is." In the case of plants, then, having inherent worth means, first, that they

> have the same status as...[any other] moral subject to which duties are owed by moral agents. Whatever its species may be, none is thought to be superior to another and all are held to be deserving of equal consideration. Second, each is never to be treated as a mere means to human ends...Third, the promotion or protection of each one's good is taken as an ultimate end, to be brought about for the sake of the being whose good it is.

And, fourth, moral agents owe each being "the duty of respect" whether they are drawn to that being or not, and whether they want to do their duty or not.[19]

Understanding animals and plants as having inherent worth then commits the holder of the view "to the moral principle that the good of wild living things is to be preserved and protected as an end in itself and for their sake." Committed to this view, then, the holder is committed to the consequent

> *duties* that are *owed to* the living beings in questions. To carry out such duties is not only understood as fulfilling moral requirements binding upon agents. It is also thought of as the appropriate or suitable way for agents to respond to the moral subjects to which duties are owed.[20]

Using Indian materials, then, plants (and animals) may now be thought of as being "bearers of rights." That is, because of their inherent worth, plants have claims that must be respected, and the duties that are obliged to all moral agents are understood as the way in which these very claims are met. In a "valid ethical system grounded on respect for nature," these duties, in Taylor's view, have a four-fold basis: the right not to be harmed,[21] not to be interfered with, not to have one's trust broken, and to have restitution when one has been wronged. In "the language of rights," then, plants, having inherent worth, "are 'entitled' to be treated in certain ways."[22]

For this entitlement, we look to concepts embedded in traditional materials that directly promote plant life at its most beneficial and most promising. Plant life at its optimum is marked by "flourishing,"[23] a word deriving from "flower" and suggesting growth and change that allow a living being to thrive and prosper, and to reach a level of fullest potential. Based on the notion of "flourishing," we argue for three areas of wellbeing that are extended to plants by Indian traditions. As given by the particularities of these traditions, we might say that plants flourish when they are seen as having three rights: (1) *the right to protection and care*, (2) *the right to progress towards salvation*, and (3) *the right to expression of own-truth*. And these rights signify corresponding duties. First, plants' rights to protection and care might be described as human duties *(dharma)* to promote the health and wellbeing of plants as they provide service to humans. Second, plants' rights to move towards salvation might be described as human duties to recognize *duḥkha* as the experience of the whole sentient condition and to respond to it with compassion as all the living, including plants, progress toward a perfected state. And, third, plants' rights to express their own-truths might be described as human duties to uphold something like *ṛta* and to maintain, in harmony, the integrity of every natural (that is, "living") thing in the cosmos.

7.2 Human Duty to Provide Protection and Care for Plants

We begin with the place of plants in systems of human responsibility where they are the objects of duties conferred upon humans within a broad cultural schema. These duties are primarily to protect and care for plants and, especially in Hinduism, they fall within writings on the more sociological aspects of *dharma* and *āyurveda*. Moreover, the duties of humans to protect and care for plants – and thus the rights of plants to this protection and care– derives from the dependence of human flourishing on plant flourishing and these, in turn, draw on the *sattva*-bearing nature of plants to provide service to others, in the form of protection, clothing, food/medicine, lumber, and fuel. In addition, the issue of plants as *sattva*-bearing has resonance with contemporary works such as Christopher D. Stone's *Should Trees Have Standing?* where the notion of human duty toward plants is based on plants as beneficial resources for present and future generations of humans.

Rājadharma: The Duty to Protect Plants

Human responsibilities in the Indian context fall under the category of *dharma*,[24] a term referring to the duties that, if perfected in ideal human conduct, and combined with the perfection of *artha* (material affairs) and *kāma* (sensuality/pleasure), will give rise to *mokṣa* or liberation from the round of rebirth.[25] Dharmic duties, moreover, are prescribed in traditional manuals *(dharmasūtra/śāsana/śāstra)* that outline the consequences of violating the laws described within them. These consequences are often religious, tied to the workings of *karma* but can, in traditional settings, bear civic and legal penalties as well. Because the full practice of *dharma* signifies a *sattva* context,[26] a context of goodness – or better here, of truth – Manu declares that *dharma,* when violated, destroys but, when protected, protects[27] and, thus, to follow duty is to bring about "flourishing," an individual's experience of full potential. In the contemporary context, *dharma* is applied to human treatment of the natural world and the Manu 8.15 passage on *dharma* is then applied to trees: thus, *"trees* protect as they are protected" *(vṛkṣo rakṣati rakṣataḥ).*[28]

The work of scholars like Mary McGee makes clear that the traditional Indian locus of *dharma* with regard to the environment is the ruler, who has the primary task of environmental stewardship. Provision for the "legal" protection of plants and trees is given by the authors of the *dharmaśāstras* and *nītiśāstras*, she argues, as based on four views:

> 1) a recognition of plants as sentient beings with consciousness, which therefore should be protected from harm (advocacy of *ahiṁsā)*; 2) a designation of certain trees as sacred objects, due to their religious value, identification with certain deities, or resident *bhūtas;* 3) a respect for the economic value of trees; [and] 4) a legal interpretation that recognized certain trees as personal property.[29]

Based on these views, and especially on the economic value, of plants, the king has "the right and responsibility to develop the land and [to] manage its resources in the pursuit of the economic and social welfare of the kingdom."[30] This suggests, first, that the king has "a moral responsibility to protect and maintain the...resources of his kingdom" and, second, that this maintenance involves not only the conservation and preservation, but also the development, of the kingdom's resources. Benefits from these resources devolve not only upon the general populace but also upon the ruler himself, for quite "a substantial income may be supposed to come to the state from its forest wealth."[31] The view that the king is specifically entrusted with the well-being of his land, as well as with the living beings on his land, is put forward in a number of early texts: the Yajur Veda, for example, the Mahābhārata,[32]

Śākuntalā,[33] the Purāṇas,[34] and the Śukranīti, a later authority on political administration.[35]

Central in importance to the Hindu texts that prescribe sovereign duties on behalf of plants is the Manusmṛti, which requires a king to employ companies of soldiers, "both stationary and patrolling, and spies" in order to protect old gardens, forests, and natural and artificial groves from the onslaught of thieves.[36] Kauṭilya's Arthaśāstra also prescribes such protection of vegetation, and has as its premise

> that the livelihood of humans depends on material wealth *(artha)*, that land *(bhūmi)* provides that wealth...[for] the earth is a source of wealth and enjoyment for humankind, and the king has the responsibility to protect and maintain this source of wealth, as well as to distribute its bounty.[37]

In order to ensure that these goals are carried out, the Arthaśāstra calls for the appointment of a superintendent of forest produce whose job is, first, to oversee the collection of timber used in the running of the kingdom, second, to provide for guards to secure those forests designated as productive, third, to exact fines from anyone causing damage, or unlawfully felling trees, in productive forests, and, fourth, to manufacture from forest produce whatever articles are needed for the defense of military forts.[38] The Arthaśāstra chapter on forest produce, however, while it provides for the protection and conservation of trees, does not address the question of the ethics of "injury" to trees, or the nature and treatment of "unproductive" forests.[39] Moreover, it is clear that these administrative policies are set out specifically for present and future benefit to humans, and that benefit to humans is the basis of the Arthaśāstra's environmental policy and, thus, of the granting of any place to plants in the arena of human responsibilities.

Vasudha Narayanan's essay, inspired by the Matsya Purāṇa's famous slogan attributed to the goddess Pārvatī that "one tree is equal to ten sons" *(daśa putra samo druma)*,[40] begins her discussion by recounting epic texts that tie the decline of *dharma* to the despoilation of nature. Plants, among other things, will reflect the unrighteousness of the human behavior for, according to the Mahābhārata, with the loss of *dharma*, trees will be filled with crows and will give forth few flowers and fruits; in their natural cruelty, people will destroy trees and parks; and as the end of the world approaches, the crops will not grow. As Narayanan points out, the text argues that as humans move increasingly away from *dharma*, they will wreak havoc on nature: we "notice a close correlation between [the violation of] *dharma*...and the ravaging of the earth. When *dharma* declines, human beings take it out on nature."[41] Especially in texts like the epics, the particular behavior of a people is the particular charge of their ruler, so that *a-dharma* among the citizens signifies the lack of *rājadharma*, and the lack of *rājadharma* results in a decline in the protection and care of plants.

Kings can be persuaded to follow their *rājadharma,* however, for there is a story in the Kathāsaritsāgara of a king who, out of greed, learns about the tree protection duties of his office. Brahmadatta, king of Banaras, it seems, calls for tree trunks to be procured to make pillars for his palace. One particular tree chosen to be a pillar is a Śāl tree in the king's own park and the tree cutters make the appropriate propitiations to the tree and its *devatā* in order to cut it down. The *devatā* is outraged that so many of his relatives will lose their homes, however, and goes to see King Brahmadatta at night. Compassion eventually arises in the king and he is persuaded not to cut the tree down. Thus, the "tree-god gave the king good counsel and went his way; and the king next day gave generous alms, and ruled as became a king." He ruled according to *rājadharma,* that is, following the sovereign duties that require him to protect, as fully as possible, the tree life around him.[42]

The central importance of the king in the protection and care of the natural world and especially of plants and trees, is a common theme in Indian history and is reflected is this passage from the Tamil Parananuru.

> Even kings with vast domains
> strive in vain when the land is dry,
> when fields sown with seed
> must look to the sky for rain.

So Pandyan king, who makes dreadful war,
do not disdain my words: expand quickly those watery places
built where water moves across the land!
For those who harness water
harness rewards for themselves,
and those who fail cannot endure.[43]

In the social process in Tamil culture, Ludden argues, "a central axis of power ran from farmers, through local leaders, to kings and gods." And various rituals "enabled the kings to empower cultivators...[and] brought gods to bear on the prosperity of kings, and kings and cultivators together in pursuit of power over prosperity.[44]

This connection between Hindu kings and the prosperity of growing vegetation is found in the contemporary period in the example of Vansh Pradip Singh, a north Indian ruler of the twenty seven village kingdom of Sawar from 1914 to 1947. Singh presents an unusual model of kingship in that he cares extraordinarily about the trees in his kingdom, and goes so far as to proclaim "his own physical identification with them."[45] During his reign, he not only promotes the care of wild life on his lands, the protection and expansion of existing forests, and the prosecution of persons who cut reserved trees, but also holds the view that "trees...[are] extensions of his [own] royal body."[46] If anyone cuts a tree, for example, he says "it is just as if my finger were cut," or "if you cut the smallest branch of a tree it is just as if you cut my finger."[47] After Vansh Pradip Singh dies, many of the trees he planted are cut down on the orders of succeeding rulers and sold. These acts are understood as sins that are "ascribed to the rulers who had the trees cut and sold," and are thought to be the reasons why the rain in the region – attracted by the presence of trees – becomes less."[48]

The duty of Hindu rulers to protect trees extends to the very local level as well, for each village is responsible "through its *pancayat,* or committee of five elders, for maintaining the forests in its own locality." This is based on the belief that village life is most prosperous when wooded lands are in close vicinity of individual houses and village compounds. As Prime quotes Banwari:

> The village has many things – it is not significant only because of its human population. It is significant because of its water, because of its animals and because of its trees. According to tradition, a village will be a full entity only when there are certain categories of forest or trees in and around it. This is called shrivan, the forest of prosperity.[49]

In early Buddhism, a *khattiya* tradition prescribes the protection of the earth as one of the duties of the Buddhist king. Although the *khattiya* is normally associated with combative activities, the epithet *khettānaṁ pati* or "lord of the fields" suggests another side of overlordship, that of the preservation and safekeeping of the ongoing natural bounty that can come from lands under his purview. P. D. Ryan argues that this phrase "comprises the meaning of 'husband of the fields,' and so the title may have overtones of a sacred marriage between the ruler and the land," a relationship that arises not from "dominance, possessiveness, or acquisitiveness...[but] from love." The *khettānaṁ pati*, then, Ryan continues, is "the husband of the land and the consort of the earth, who...[is] called upon to administer the rule of righteousness."[50]

Protection "of the fields" for Buddhist kings does not necessarily mean, however, the practice of non-violence towards plants. On the one hand, we have the example of early kings who became Buddhist lay followers. King Seniya Bimbisāra of Magadha, a contemporary of Gotama Buddha, for instance, stands out for "having seen *dhamma,* attained *dhamma*, known *dhamma*, plunged into *dhamma*, having crossed over doubt, put away uncertainty, [and] having attained without another's help to full confidence in the teacher's instructions." He eventually became a lay disciple *(upāsaka)* – "gone for refuge from this day forth for as long as life lasts."[51] This *upāsaka* status for King Bimbisāra may well have included the practice of non-violence, for there is evidence that, among the governing norms for rulers, was the practice of *avihiṁsā* or "non injury."[52] Furthermore, the practice of non-violence was a proposed component of the lay householder life, as evident from the Sigālovāda Sutta. In speaking to the young householder Sigāla, for example, the Buddha says that the Aryan disciple *(ariya-sāvaka)* has gotten rid of four impurities *(kilesa)*, the first of which is the destruction of life *(pāṇātipāta)*.[53]

On the other hand, the *pāṇa* or living, "breathing" being that is the object of non-violence in both of the Dīgha Nikāya passages has no specific gloss in the either of them. In fact, it is a term of some ambivalence with regards to plants as the tradition develops, for, in time, it becomes important for the Buddhist community to understand plants as *outside* the category of "breathing."[54] Early on, however, in passages like Sutta Nipāta 146-147, plants are the "still beings" of the passage below but clearly fall as well into the category of living/breathing beings.

> Whatever living creatures *(pāṇabhūt)* there are,
> Moving or still, without exception...
> May all those creatures live happily.[55]

While the Sutta Nipāṭa verses above decidedly include plants *(thāvara)* among the breathing *(pāṇa)*, they are verses probably meant primarily for the practice of renunciants, for it would be hard for regular laypeople to maintain a non-violent livelihood if plants were one of the objects of that practice. Since the same word is used in both texts, we may assume that the Sutta Nipāta passage (which specifically mentions plants as among the *pāṇa)* is an early one and is for renunciants, and the *mahāpurisa* and Sigāla passages in the Dīgha (which do not specifically mention anything in particular for *pāṇa)* are later ones and are for lay. Thus, in the case of the Pali material, kings care for and protect plants, but do not necessary have practices of non-violence directed towards them – that is, plants are not normally named as explicit objects of the sovereign practice of non-violence.

A good traditional example of Buddhist kingship coupled with a king's duty towards plants is King Aśoka.[56] Aśoka's calls for the application of *ahiṁsā* to all living beings *(sarva bhūta)*. While this may seem to open new ground in a ruler's practice of non-violence as *bhūta* is the term normally used for plants in Pali materials – note our earlier discussion of the use of the term *bhūtagāma* for trees, shrubs, grass, etc. – *bhūta* here, however, may only carry the more narrow reference of animals and humans, because the prescriptions are particularly for the practice of *ahiṁsā* by lay people.

As prefigured in the canonical declaration of King Bimbisāra who "plunged into *dhamma*," moreover, a theme of many of Aśoka's rock and pillar edicts is his understanding of himself as a king devoted to the love, study, and inculcation of *dharma*. As Pillar Edict seven and Rock Edict thirteen note, for example, moral conquest *(dharma-vijaya)* is the most important kind of conquest there is and, to that end, Aśoka appoints *dharma-mahāmātras* or officers who are charged with the spread of *dharma*.[57] The particular *dharma* activity he prescribes for plants is found in Rock Edict two where he calls for the importation and planting of medicinal herbs *(oṣadhi)* and, as needed, roots and fruits – all to be used against illness in humans and animals.[58] And in Pillar Edict seven, Aśoka notes that he has ordered banyan trees to be planted along the side of roads to provide shade for humans and animals, and mango trees to provide refreshment. In addition, he has ordered wells to be dug about every half mile, and rest houses to be built "for the convenience of men and animals." Of these conveniences, he goes on to say:

> These are trifling comforts. For the people have received various facilities from previous kings as well as from me. But I have done what I have primarily in order that the people may follow the path of Dharma with faith and devotion.[59]

The kingly tradition in Buddhism to protect and care for plants–arising from the benefit to other beings of plant health and abundance – was not always so for Aśoka, however. Randhawa tells the story of Aśoka's original antagonism to Buddhism as reflected in public aboricide. Prior to his conversion, King Aśoka desired to destroy all traces of the Buddha, and expressed this impulse by destroying a bodhi tree. "He cut through the roots; the trunk, branches and leaves were all divided into small bits and heaped up in a pile a few tens of paces to the west of the place." He ordered the pile of sticks to be burned but, from the ashes, sprang "a double tree...and because the leaves and branches were shining like feathers, it was called ashes bodhi tree.'" Eventually repenting of his crime, Aśoka bathed the roots of the old tree with scented milk to nourish them and in the morning the tree sprang up as before. When the queen, a "heretic," heard what had happened, she ordered the tree to be cut down again but, again, with the same ministrations by Aśoka it sprang up as before.[60]

Vṛkṣāyurveda: The Duty to Care for Plants

Stewardship duties of protection for the environment appear early as part of the *rājadharma* of the traditional Indian king, but – as we see in the story above – these duties soon become part of the responsibilities assumed by an individual, insofar as he or she not only protects, but cares for, the plants in his or her domestic environment. The ancient Indian king, in modeling such behavior for an individual, provides in his government for a "superintendent of agriculture" who, according to the Arthaśāstra, is to be trained in sciences relating to the planting of trees and vegetation. This officer's duties are to collect seeds "of all kinds of grains, flowers, fruits, vegetables, bulbous roots, roots...fibre-producing plants, and cotton," and to employ all those who are needed to sow the seeds on the king's land after it has been properly plowed. The text also allows for supplementing the work of these sowers with a supply of personal provisions, all necessary tools, and any extra help that may be required.[61]

It is very important, moreover, that these agricultural workers be properly trained in the sciences of Vṛkṣāyurveda, for if the king is to make best use of the resources under his protection, his workers must have precise knowledge of plants, soils, fertilizers, plant diseases and medicines, and climate. And in this way, the Indian tradition of Vṛkṣāyurveda provides plants with what we might call "medical rights" to available health care. In fact, the Vṛkṣāyurveda worldview as expressed in Surapāla begins with a discussion of the duties of the king whom he calls the *pṛthvīpati* or "lord of the earth:"

> He is the (real) king, in whose residence there are big gardens, with large lakes which are the sole instrument for the fruits of all the pleasures for people...and (which lakes) are beautiful

> because of the swelling of the weight of lotus awakened by the humming bees.[62]
>
> The movement from king and communal responsibility to person and individual responsibility is reflected in Vṛkṣāyurveda texts that... show that trees not only have the right to be well-cared for, but "looked after in much the same way as humans" are.
>
> The texts of the *Vṛkṣa-āyurveda* place vegetation in the category of living beings. The religious implication of according such a treatment to trees is that our *papa-s* and *puṇya-s* depend on the way we treat trees.[63]

The text continues by prescribing plans for planting trees when laying out a house, the cultivation of plants in various areas and climates, and the treatment of plant diseases. In all sections of Vṛkṣāyurveda texts, it seems assumed that the audience is normally the householder, by whom plant science is to be used for individual projects. In this way Surapāla, for example, questions the use of having many trees growing in a forest when there are sons who will not take up their duty to ensure the trees' prosperity. It is better, he argues, to have fewer trees that are well-used and well-taken care of than many that are left alone, not providing any service to humans or animals and not being given the nourishing attention they need. Thus, for individuals, as well as for kings,

> Having acquired well (the knowledge of) this truth, one should start planting trees. Because the means for (the realisation of) duty, material welfare, pleasure and emancipation are through trees.[64] A man, learned in *dharma,* who has duly planted three Neem trees, having reached the world of sun resides there for three *ayute* (ten thousand) years.[65]

Such views are reflected earlier in the Dharmśāstras, as in this passage from the Āpastamba:

> Let him not follow the Laws for the sake of worldly benefits, for then the Laws produce no fruit at harvest time. It is like this. A man plants a mango tree to get fruits, but in addition he obtains also shade and fragrance. In like manner, when a man follows the Law, he obtains, in addition, other benefits.[66]

Also in the Āpastamba is the requirement for the *brahmacārin* student that he not cut anything off a plant or tree if he's just going to smell it.[67]

Moreover, rules for the *gṛhastha* householder continue this strictness with regard to seeds and grains, and include that the householder must, at all times, properly cultivate his land and properly distribute his harvest. In addition, he must grow a variety of plants (like fruit trees and cereal grains) from seeds, bulbs, and roots; he must gather such grain seeds as he may find and protect live seeds; and, when he exhausts the householder life either through sickness or old age, he must make use of the resources of the forest by obtaining the produce of fruit-bearing trees, vines, and creepers, and from wild cereal plants.[68]

As we have seen, the ethical precepts of the Jain tradition are thoroughly centered in non-violent behavior toward all sentient beings, beginning with the one-sense-facultied beings –earth-beings, water-beings, plants, fire-beings, and air-beings–and moving up to those with five senses, and thus to those closest to the prospect of liberation.[69] Plants appear especially often in the instructions for renunciants, where duties to protect plants of all sizes and types are a constant presence:

> I shall not do (acts relating to plants) after having entered the order...for one destroys this (body of a plant) by bad and injurious doings...
> I say thus: all beings, those with two, three, four senses, plants, those with five senses, and the rest of creation, (experience) individually pleasure or displeasure, pain, great terror, and unhappiness....
> ...all breathing, existing, living, sentient creations should not be slain, nor treated with violence, or abused, nor tormented, nor driven away...
> When a male or female mendicant...recognizes food...as affected by, or mixed up with living beings, mildew, seeds or sprouts...they should not...accept...such food, thinking that it is impure and unacceptable.
> A monk or nun on a begging-tour should not accept such raw fruits which are not yet modified by instruments...
> A monk or nun on a begging-tour should not accept such like

> raw substances as seeds or sprouts, growing on the top of the root or the stem or the knots (of a plant).[70]

Thus, while the *rationale* for the wide-ranging rules of *ahiṁsā* for renunciants are given in the schemata of living beings as outlined in the Uttarādhyayana, the details of the *ahiṁsā application* suggested above are given in the charges to monks and nuns as outlined in the Ācārāṅga. These passages contain (1) a prohibition on killing living beings, (2) an acknowledgement that the category of "living beings" includes plants, and (3) a view that all in this category experience pain. They can then prohibit male and female renunciants from accepting plant materials that may still be living as food.

For early Buddhism, as for Jainism, Schmithausen points out that the ethic of *ahiṁsā* is on the whole directed toward the sentient *individual*

> *not [towards] species* or ecosystems, nor even individuals *as representatives* of species. The value at stake in *this* spiritual context is the life (and happiness) of the *individual,* not the transindividual continuity of the species or of life as such, or of nature as a whole.[71]

Moreover, primary individual human responsibilities towards plants are exemplified, in the ideal, in the monastic code for renunciants around the idea of non-violence. The Vinaya prescribes non-violence towards *human beings* in Pārājika three, in which the intentional deprivation of human life – or the intentional verbal or physical support for such action – results in expulsion from the Saṅgha.[72] The Vinaya prescribes non-violence towards *animals* in Pācittiya sixty-one, where the deprivation of life for a living being constitutes an expiation.[73] Here the word for living being is *pāṇa* (breathing being), a term ordinarily referring to an animal or human being. The most significant material with regard to human responsibilities towards *plants* in the Vinaya is a rule of expiation, Pācittiya eleven, which declares that the destruction of vegetable growth *(bhūtagāma)* is an offence of expiation.[74] Important here is that, first, vegetable growth is described, in the narrative just previous to the ruling, as beings who have one sense faculty[75] and, second, the offence of destroying vegetable growth is the same as that for destroying animals – a Pācittya, or expiation.

Strong support for the inclusion of vegetable growth in the community of beings towards whom the renunciant duty of *ahiṁsā* is directed, and towards whom the practice of loving-kindness *(mettā)* is directed, is the Sutta Nipāta passage: "Whatever living creatures there are, moving or still, without exception...let all creatures be happy-minded." Although the term for living creature is *pāṇa,* a term normative for humans and animals, the gloss "moving" *(tasā)* and "still" *(thāvarā)* makes clear that, in this instance, *pāṇa* refers to non-moving plants.[76]

While the tree-protection duties of the king are individual duties, they are specific to the one particular individual who has *dharma* obligations to a mass of people whom he must protect and provide for, in part, by protecting and properly using the resources of the natural environment that include plants and trees. Using the king as a model, individuals in his protected population also take up duties with regard to the vegetal life around them, duties to propagate, care for, and nurse to health those plants and trees immediately involved in their daily affairs. These two contexts of obligations to the plant world relate particularly to providing benefit for human beings and have, as their immediate sources, social and civic rationales.

We have seen another such context for the protection of plants, however, and that is the context of the renunciant who has responsibilities towards plants based on religious vows of *ahiṁsā,* vows that aim to focus more specifically on *the life in the plant* than on *the benefit of the plant to human beings.* Padmasiri de Silva reminds us, for example, of the rules for Buddhist monks and nuns against such things as cutting down trees or branches, destroying vegetation, and digging around in the soil where there may be seeds and roots of plants.[77] The religious responsibilities of renunciants towards plants, however, also have implications for the social and civic responsibilities of laypeople. As in the case of the king – who attaches "great importance to the planting of trees, the construction of parks, reforestation, etc."[78] – renunciant conduct can provide a model for ordinary citizens, a behavior to strive for and to use as a guide in everyday life. On the one hand, renunciant conduct represents ethical prescriptions that a lay might actually follow some day, if and when renunciation becomes a life choice in this life or in a life to come. And, on the other, while non-violence towards plants in the absolute is an ethical standard that is not amenable to current everyday householder practices of farming, cooking, traveling, and making clothing, renunciant ideals for *ahiṁsā* towards plants can *guide and inspire* the behavior of householders in the present as they feed, treat, and protect the plants in their surrounds.

Sattva: The Service Basis for Human Duties Toward Plant Flourishing

Taylor notes above that animals and plants can have legal rights in those societies where there are laws that protect their good. Christopher Stone, in his *Should Trees Have Standing?*, suggests a way such legal rights might come about. He refers to Darwin's observation that, in the history of human moral development, there "has been a continual extension in the objects" receiving human "'social instincts and sympathies.'"[79] The law has followed suit, Stone argues, so that there has been a continual extension of those objects who possess legal rights: men, women, children, corporate bodies (such as trusts), corporations, joint ventures, municipalities, nation states, and ships, for example. Each time the circle moves out a ripple, "there is a movement to confer rights onto some new 'entity,'" and some of those most newly conferred with rights are natural objects:

> I am quite seriously proposing that we give legal rights to forests, oceans, rivers and other so-called "natural objects" in the environment – indeed, to the natural environment as a whole.[80]

Stone proceeds to outline what, in this "moral extensionism,"[81] it would mean to be a holder of a legal right: e.g., that *"some public authoritative body"* be prepared to review actions that are inconsistent with the right, that the conferred could "institute legal actions *at its behest,"* that the court would take *injury to it* into account in the discussion of legal rights, and that legal relief to the conferred "must run to the *benefit of it*."[82]

Stone then proposes a "guardianship" approach whereby natural objects, animate and inanimate, would be handled as legal incompetents and have, thereby, someone speak for them. A "friend" of the natural object would apply for guardianship and that friend would provide continuous supervision over a period of time.[83] The main question would be how to recognize "injury" and, for Stone, injury would not be to the natural object in and of itself, but in reference to *long-term injury to human beings* – that is, injury to natural objects would be interpreted in terms of *economic hardship to humans*. Injury to natural object X, then, would be calculated in terms of the cost to the environment as a whole, and hence to human beings as they are affected by that environment.

> Indeed, one way – the homocentric way – to view what I am proposing so far, is to view the guardian of the natural object as the guardian of unborn generations, as well as of the otherwise unrepresented, but distantly injured, contemporary humans.[84]

Stone argues that understanding injury to natural objects in terms of economic hardship for contemporary and future human beings is to recognize injury to natural objects as "the invasion of a property interest." And to have a property interest is to have an economically measurable interest; that is, to violate a natural object's "rights" is to create a monetary loss for humans. Thus, the cost to an injurer of a natural object, is the cost to humans plus the cost to the environment, that is, the cost of making the environment whole again.[85]

This kind of interpretation, unfriendly though it may seem to the view of plants as sentient, experiencing, and *karma*-bearing beings that we know to be found in Indian traditions, is in fact a view that is consonant with ideas about *rājadharma.* As McGee points out, the concern for forests and crown lands, and for the success of sylvan and agricultural technologies, in the Arthaśāstra is not just about the beauty of the natural surroundings in a king's domain and not just about the absolute value of plant health and wellbeing, but rather (and primarily) about what monies could come into the king's treasury. As she notes,

> The revenue from the produce of crown lands was a significant part of the king's treasury...Agriculture was serious business and those who did not cultivate arable lands leased to them were charged a fine to reimburse the state for loss of production...Another great source of revenue for the state came from resources found within the forests.

In fact, the knowledge of Vṛkṣāyurveda that was put toward the care of trees, shrubs, and grass was, in part, about making sure that the vegetation under the overall care of the king was in optimal health so that it could be of optimal value to him as a monetary resource. This does not mean that financial benefit was the only basis for care and protection of plants – Kauṭilya mentions the role of forests and thickets in state defense systems, and the importance of beautiful shade trees, flowering plants, and open forests for the pleasure and enjoyment of the king and his subjects[86] – but it does mean that the primary impetus for caring for and protecting vegetation was for the resources (monetary and material) it provided for human beings on the land. In fact, in the Āpastamba Dharma Sūtra plant materials are specifically noted as *property*: "If someone unknowingly takes the property of another, such as fuel...roots, flowers, fruits...fodder, or vegetables, he should be verbally reprimanded."[87]

Moreover, another example of government protection and care of plants is noted in King Aśoka's edicts. Here he prescribes the procuring – by planting locally or importing from outside sources – of medicinal herbs, roots, and fruits for use against sickness in humans and animals. He also orders trees to be planted alongside roadways to shade animal and human passers by and the fruit of mango trees to be available for eating. Although these are not ordered specifically for the embellishment of the royal treasury, it does show the kind of view Stone is arguing: that is, that protecting and caring for plants is a good thing to do precisely because there is direct benefit to humans of this generation and the next.

The argument that humans need to protect and care for plants because plants provide humans with things that sustain their lives and livelihood is essential not only to the *rājadharma* and *vṛkṣāyurveda* prescriptions of human duties and responsibilities, but is also an essential part of our argument about the place of plants in the matrix of the *guṇas.* As noted above, the traditional view of plants and *guṇas* is that, found particularly in Hindu and Jain sources, which ascribes the *guṇa* of *tamas* to plant life. This is based on the division of living things into moving and still, with all sentient beings placed in the category of moving except plants who, bounded by their roots in the soil, are characterized by an inability to change locations, that is, by stability. This is seen to coincide with the tamas qualities of lethargy, sluggishness, and passivity, while their apparent obscuration in consciousness is seen to coincide with the indifference, dull-mindedness and dim-wittedness also associated with *tamas.*

We argued in addition, however, that within the *guṇa* system, plants might also be located at the other end, at the end marked by *sattva.* Given that plants, and especially trees, are used as models for ascetic behavior (behavior at the perfected end of the human career) by citing their stillness, rest, repose, ease, and contentment as marks of a being moving towards the culmination of the *saṁsāra* enterprise, plants might instead be exemplars of the *sattva* thread – in that their stability might represent the serenity, tranquility, and distractlessness of the contemplative place in the world. In arguing for the placement of plants at the *sattva* end, we also attribute another of *sattva's* characteristics, that of compassion, to plants. This fits well with the "great service" plants are said to provide for humans.

One of the categories of forest in Indian tradition is the *śrīvana,* "the forest which provides your prosperity,"[88] that is, the prosperity of shade, lodging, and protection, as well as the prosperity of resources like leaves, bark, wood, flowers, fruit, and roots. Religious rituals rely on plant materials to please the gods and to enact the homologies that make the liturgical action effective; medical practices cannot proceed without the health producing aids that herbs provide; and houses, vehicles, clothing, and food all depend on the use of vast amounts and varieties of vegetal materials for the very survival and prosperity of human life. The fact that plants provide so much of what humans need to live and that their provision of these materials is ongoing and continuous is reflected in how often texts, like the early Buddhist suttas,[89] encourage, and prescribe, that gratitude be given to a tree who provides shade and timber or vegetable plants who provide food. Moreover, it is a mark of the realization of the greatness of the service of plants to humans, that prayers are offered before cutting plants, and rituals are performed for all parts of the growing, harvesting, and preparation of plants for human use. This service of plants to others fits fully with the idea of *sattva*-bearing nature, for, in that plants "give fully of themselves," they can be said to "show compassion for humans," and in this way their service to humans is the rationale for human responsibilities towards them, specifically as they provide for present and future benefit from generation to generation.

7.3 Human Duty to Provide Plants a Place in the Salvific Process

If we return to Taylor's biocentric outlook, we find substantial support for obliging humans to provide a place for plants in the salvational process. This outlook – that plants belong, with humans, to the earth's common community of life, that plants along with humans are integral elements of a system of interdependence, that each organism is a teleological center of life pursuing its own good in its own way, and that humans are not innately superior to other living things – is well suited to a comparison with the idea of *saṁsāra*. Each of the three traditions we've looked at understand plants against the background of rebirth and *karma*, though some, like Jainism, have more perseverance in this than others, like Buddhism. Moreover, we can say that the biocentric ideas of common community and interdependence fit neatly with the Indian view of myriad interrelated births across a great span of time and space, and that the ideas of teleological pursuit of an individual goal and a level playing field fit neatly with the parameters of unique *karma*-bearing histories interweaving the full range of possibilities for living beings across any boundaries that may be thought to demarcate separate species. While some things are not so natural a fit – such as the Indian view that it is normally in human birth that salvation takes place – we can argue with reason that there is an attitude of respect for nature in Indian thought as well as a view that animals and plants possess inherent worth. And it is on this basis that we argue above for the appropriateness of imposing on humans, through the *dharma* and *āyurveda* traditions, certain duties and obligations for the care and protection of plants.

We turn now to another marker that binds plants (and animals) together with humans in a common, interdependent community, and that is that, in India, this community is salvific. Here we have the recognition that the common experience of all sentient beings in the cycle of *saṁsāra* is one of "suffering." To be recognized as suffering beings – as plants are at some points in Indian tradition – is to be recognized as interwoven in the system of *karma* whereby the constantly changing quality of one's *karma* is reflected in continuous rebirths until an ultimate goal of liberation is experienced.

The idea of highlighting the experience of suffering by plants to get at what might be due them by way of rights is supported by the work of Peter Singer, whose *Animal Liberation* first appeared in 1975, as "a demand for a complete change in our attitudes to nonhumans."[90] Responding to the use of animals in such things as medical and cosmetic testing, Singer is among those who argue for the equal consideration of all animals in terms of how they are treated. He supports his view with an earlier argument of Jeremy Bentham who incorporated moral equality into his system of ethics in this way:

> "Each to count for one and none for more than one." In other words, [says Singer] the interests of every being affected by an action are to be taken into account and given the same weight as the like interests of any other being.[91]

Within the context of the scientific testing of animals by humans, this "taking into account" is compromised by what Singer sees as a problem of "speciesism."

> Speciesism – the word is not an attractive one, but I can think of no better term – is a prejudice or attitude of bias in favor of the interests of members of one's own species and against those of members of other species.[92]

Taking up the critique of speciesism, Singer argues that this view separates human from nonhuman animals and allows humans into the circle of moral protection while excluding nonhumans from it. Singer proposes a non-anthropocentric view "which provides moral protection to a larger group of living beings, a group of beings he identifies as having 'interests' to be protected because they have the capacity for suffering and enjoyment."[93]

While it does not seem useful to develop the various discussions in support of or against speciesism here,[94] it does seem important to follow the thread in the discussion that helps us elicit an argument from the Indian traditions. To this end, we return to Bentham who proposes a classic reason for why "all animals are equal:"[95]

> The day *may* come when the rest of the animal creation may acquire those rights which never could have been withholden from them but by the hand of tyranny...The question is not, Can they reason? nor Can they talk? but, Can they suffer?[96]

Singer notes that Bentham here "points to the capacity for suffering as the vital characteristic that gives a being the right to equal consideration...The capacity for suffering and enjoyment is a prerequisite for having interests at all." And Singer continues by proposing that it is "sentience" – "a convenient if not strictly accurate shorthand for the capacity to suffer and/or experience enjoyment) – [that] is the only defensible boundary of concern for the interests of others." He notes that a "stone does not have interests because it cannot suffer," and reaffirms that the capacity for suffering and enjoyment is both the necessary and sufficient condition for saying that a being has interests and "at an absolute minimum, an interest in not suffering."[97]

In proposing that plants in Indian traditions come by rights in this way, we remember that they are considered to be sentient (e.g., by virtue of having the sense of touch) and that they are thought to share in common with other sentient beings an experience of suffering. In support of this, some traditions observe that plants experience the world as too sunny or too dark, too hot or too cold, too wet or too dry, and too windy or too still, and that this experience of suffering places plants in a schema where humans are responsible for allowing them movement towards salvific perfection, that is, a condition of "not suffering." It happens that Singer himself addresses the question of plants, but not favorably. He says, at "this point someone is bound to ask: 'How do we know that *plants* do not suffer?'" To which he answers, there "is no reliable evidence that plants are capable of feeling pleasure or pain." Singer believes that there are

> three distinct grounds for believing that nonhuman animals can feel pain: behavior, the nature of their nervous systems, and the evolutionary usefulness of pain. None of these gives us any reason to believe that plants feel pain. In the absence of scientifically credible experimental findings, there is no observable behavior that suggests pain; nothing resembling a central nervous system has been found in plants; and it is difficult to imagine why species that are incapable of moving away from a source of pain or using that perception of pain to avoid death in any other way should have evolved to capacity to feel pain. Therefore the belief that plants feel pain appears to be quite unjustified.[98]

In direct response to Singer, we cite just a few examples from Indian beliefs and observations that respond to each of these three objections. With regard to plant behavior that exhibits pain, we note the canonical Buddhist injunction against wearing palmyra leaf sandals due to the withering and bleeding of the leaves after being cut, which suggests to Buddhist observers that the plant feels pain. With regard to a plant nervous system, we note the canonical Jain memory of rebirth as a tree in which a current human remembers being cut up for planks and the ensuing pain he felt while a tree. And, finally, we note Singer's description of plants as being "incapable of moving away," a description exactly at the core of some Indian texts' description of plants as *sthāvara/thāvara*, stationary, still, and unmoving. This agreement is misleading, however, for that plants have roots instead of legs does not actually prevent them from moving to avoid pain or death. Note, for example, the many instances in Hindu, Jain, and Buddhist discussions of plants' sense of touch where humans observe plants moving towards the sun and away from darkness, moving toward water and away from dryness, moving around obstruction to find open space to grow, and, in particular, "moving" (i.e., growing) to offer flowers and fruit to other beings in order to ensure their being kept around – by advertently or inadvertently dropping plant seeds on the ground.

Moreover, the following two passages, chosen from the Jain Ācārāṅga Sūtra, are examples of one tradition's routine attribution of suffering to plants:

> I say thus: all beings, those with two, three, four senses, plants, those with five senses, and the rest of creation, (experience) individually pleasure or displeasure, pain, great terror, and unhappiness.[99]

Given that senses two through five are explicitly mentioned but that one-sensed beings are not, and that plants are included in this list and elsewhere explicitly mentioned as one-sensed, we conclude that they are included here to designate the one-sensed beings. Again,

> All beings are fond of life, like pleasure, hate pain, shun destruction, like life, long to live. To all life is dear.[100]

Although plants are not explicitly mentioned here, the Jain tradition clearly includes them among all beings in their vast schema, in which plants occupy, along with earth-, water-, fire- and wind-beings, the beginning place in the movement of beings toward liberation. We add to this the following passage from the Hindu Caraka Saṁhitā:

> The contact with the tactile sense organ and that with mind – this twofold contact gives rise to pleasant and painful sensations.[101]

In this regard, we remember that plants in the Caraka are thought to have one sense faculty, that of touch, and that they are also thought to have some form of "interior mental capacity."

In drawing on the view of plants as both sentient and suffering, we identify, among the many responsibilities of humans in Indian thought, one that recognizes the experience of suffering in all sentient beings, as well as the attendant movement of all beings across species boundaries towards a perfected state. We might call this the "soteriological right" of sentient beings, including plants, through which they are allowed, and encouraged, to become free from suffering. This "due" is central to Indian religious systems where there is the shared view that beings are trapped in the experience of *saṁsāra* and rebirth and, through religious means, are able to experience freedom from this rebirth. To make such an argument, however, we note that suffering is often identified as the core experience addressed by paths of spiritual transformation.

In the case of Hinduism, we use two examples, the emergent Vedic view as described by F.B.J. Kuiper and Sāṁkhya philosophy. Kuiper's understanding of the *deva* and *asura* myth is that, in its development, it lays out a dualistic structure of the nature of the cosmos that moves away from a Manichean style good versus evil dichotomy and proposes one based instead on sát and ásat. These sets of pairs can be diagramed as follows:

> good : *deva* : *sát* : being : fully actualized : knowledge : non-violence
> evil : *asura* : *ásat* : becoming : potentially actualized : ignorance : violence[102]

In the Vedic or early Hindu understanding of these pairings, beings are divided into those who are fully actualized (very few of us) and those who are only potentially actualized (all of us still in *saṁsāra)*. We become fully actualized by "acquiring knowledge," and the ethical or behavioral expression of our full knowledge or wisdom is full non-violence. There are two implications of this schema important to our discussion here. First, it suggests that we don't do bad things not because we consciously choose not to do them, but because we are ignorant of how and why to make the right choices. While we receive the consequences of our ignorant behavior in the future, our tendencies toward such behavior can be ameliorated only by the acquisition of knowledge in the present. Second, because in this schema it is *committing of violence* that expresses our distance from human perfection, it is the *presence of suffering* by which we experience this distance, and this interpretation then places suffering at base of a being's saṁsāric condition.

Our second example is Sāṁkhya, which posits a "dualism of two all-pervasive ultimate principles, namely, pure consciousness *(puruṣa)*, construed pluralistically, and one primordial materiality *(mūlaprakṛti)*."[103] From contact between a *puruṣa* (a pure onsciousness) and *prakṛti* (matter), evolution takes place, resulting in the presence of sentient beings living as we know them in the context of *saṁsāra*. The experience of *saṁsāra* in Sāṁkhya is one of *duḥkha*, suffering or, as translated by Larson and Bhattacharya, "frustration," and it has three aspects: internal or personal, whether mental or physical; external, from some agent in the outside world; and celestial, from supernatural beings, cosmic forces, and so forth.[104] Sāṁkhya posits that *duḥkha* "is inescapable in ordinary experience" and in order to overcome it "it is necessary to transcend the transformations and combinations of primordial materiality altogether,"[105] that is, to separate *puruṣa* from *prakṛti*.

In the Jain tradition, the primary cause of *saṁsāra* is "longing," which produces suffering, which produces carelessness, and which then produces violent behavior.

> He who longs for the qualities, is overcome by great pain, and he is careless...Longing for these objects, people are careless, suffer day and night...[and] commit injuries and violent acts...A man who carelessly conducts himself...[engages in] killing, cutting, striking, [and] destroying...

but someone who takes control of his carelessness, of his violent behavior, and of his suffering, "will be liberated in the proper time."[106] Likewise, in Buddhism, the notion that suffering *(dukkha)* is caused by attachment *(taṅha)* to things that change *(anicca)* is experienced as the through line of the sentient condition. And the goal in Buddhism is to overcome attachment to the changing world, including to the self, and, having undermined the power of attachment, to thereby undermine the experience of suffering. In these ways, then, a normative evaluation of the sentient condition in Indian traditions is one based in suffering (as well as in an ignorance of the nature of suffering), with its alleviation giving rise to liberation.

For Indian traditions, the alleviation of suffering ordinarily takes place within the context of *karma* and rebirth. As we discussed in earlier sections, the possibility that plants belong to the *karma* system, and with this are then part of the cycle of rebirth, appears sometimes but not always in the traditions. The early Jain tradition is especially positive about plants as *karma*-bearing, and views them as life forms that humans can move in and out of in the normal course of rebirth. To the degree that there is a pan-Indian conclusion about plants as *karma*-bearing beings, it may be that beings as plants cannot accumulate *karma,* but that they can spend it (i.e., *karma* cannot build up in plant lives, but it can bear fruit in plant lives). To belong to a moral schema such as *karma*, then, where present suffering is the result of past demerit, life in a plant body must be the result of some serious wickedness in the past – given that plants are traditionally situated, when they are situated at all, at the beginning of the salvific line as *tamas*-bearing beings. The terrible suffering then endured while being a plant can be illustrated in the Jain verse in which an adept remembers the pain of life as a tree being cut up for planks. Moreover, the Jain Ācārāṅga Sūtra expresses great worry about the suffering endured by plants, as the rules for alms-touring routinely caution male and female renunciants against accepting food in their bowls that in any way could still contain life – the examples given for such foods being things like seeds, grains, sprouts, molds, and mildews "which are not yet modified by instruments."[107] Plants, then, at least in Jainism and Hinduism are seen to participate in salvific schemas where pain and suffering is the mark of being bound in *saṁsāra*, and where the hope is to progress beyond the experience of suffering in the movement toward liberation.

The Indian Buddhist tradition is more ambiguous, early on suggesting support for the belief in a moral status for plants, but later on not – based, as we have argued, on the changing needs of donors in terms of their practice of *ahiṁsā*. This shift, moreover, causes problems in contemporary assessments of Buddhist ethics on the issue of plants. As we have seen, early texts routinely note that plants are one-sensed stationary beings to whom good wishes are sent, and who are to be protected from suffering harm by restrictions on renunciants' walking habits during the rainy season, habits of agriculture and of lumbering, and of wearing such things as palmyra leaves as sandals. In later texts, however, like the Milindapañha – where Buddhism moves away from its more Jain influenced roots – plants are clearly excluded from the category of objects of *ahiṁsā*, in that they are specifically excluded from the category of those "born of karma."[108] This shift comes about because donors increasingly want to practice non-violence and can't if plants are to be included in *ahiṁsā*. And because donors' wishes must be honored, the moral status of plants is then rendered uncertain, if not nonexistent. As Keown specifically notes:

> Due to its belief in cross-species rebirth, respect for animal life is a prominent feature of Buddhist ethics. Respect for plant life is also in evidence, but there is considerable variation from school to school concerning the moral status of vegetation.[109]

Here, he recognizes Buddhism's anti-speciesism[110] as well as the borderline quality of the moral status of plants. But when he goes on to say of early Buddhism that an "important implication of karma is that forms of life are interchangeable" – e.g., "it is held...that over the course of time humans can be reborn as animals and vice versa" – plants are clearly not included.[111] Moreover, Keown's discussion of plants in Buddhist ethics is to take the *later* view (of texts like the Milindapañha) as what is normative for Buddhism.

For example, those *earlier* passages admonishing monks and nuns from harming plants when they walk in the rain are described as referring to vegetation, but Keown argues that the rules given concerning vegetation are not about establishing standards of *ethics*, but about establishing standards of *etiquette*.

> It will be seen that the passage above makes reference not just to organic life but also vegetation, and monks are elsewhere cautioned not to cause damage to seeds and plants....this is best seen as an issue which concerns monastic etiquette and deportment, and has more to do with the public image of Buddhism than its ethics.

This is a surprising assessment, and we quarrel not only with Keown's view that vegetation is different from organic life, but also with his conclusions about Buddhism. This passage is both preceded and followed by a recognition that the Buddhist tradition varies over time, and that single final conclusions ought not be made concerning whether "the Buddhist respect for life extends to vegetation," because there is significant *"absence of any clear guidance* in Buddhist sources as to where exactly to 'draw the line.'" In spite of this, however, Keown goes on to argue that the line should be drawn at "sentiency," because "it would exclude both vegetation and biological organisms such as amoebas and the like in which the capacity for pain is presumably absent."[112] While we agree that drawing the line at sentiency is what Indian traditions tend to do, in doing so plants are included, not excluded as Keown has done here. The one-sided, mono-tonal nature of Keown's conclusion is problematic, given even a cursory reading of the Pali texts, and is certainly a conclusion that violates his own words of caution in the face of variant evidence. His argument would be better served with a stronger overall assessment that insists on recognizing that Buddhism has a rich, varied, and often inconsistent, diversity of views on plants that reflects the changing contexts of its Indian tradition.

The difficulty in evaluating just what the Buddhist view on plants is – a difficulty we certainly acknowledge – continues in Keown's discussion of Buddhist views on life, life's worth, *karma*-bound life, and the possibility of experiencing *nirvāṇa*. He notes that, although the norm would be to include plants, along with cells, tissues, organs, and organisms in the category of life, this is not possible in Buddhism. Moving backwards, he argues that *nirvāṇa*, as the end of *saṁsāra*, can only be experienced by life forms that are subject to rebirth, and declares that "none" of the above category "undergo rebirth." "A lettuce," for example, "will not be reborn, and it is difficult to conceive of it having an end or *telos* beyond its present existence." In direct contrast to Taylor, he argues that

> What is being suggested is that life has intrinsic value only when it possesses the capacity to attain nirvana. According to Buddhist doctrine only karmic life has this potential. To say that life has 'intrinsic' value is to say that it is affirmatively valued for its own sake rather than as a means to something else....Karmic life can be contrasted with other forms of 'life' which do not undergo rebirth; since these have no moral past or present it is hard to see how they can have nirvana as their future goal or *telos*....[This] means that what Buddhism values is not merely life itself...seen, for example, in vegetation...but life which has a spiritual *telos*."[113]

To be karmic, Keown argues, is, first, to be sentient and, second, to be individual. Because he agrees that "a lettuce is an ontological individual" but disagrees that it can have "a karmic past or future,"[114] the issue for Keown, then, must be with lettuce's sentience – something we have shown to be true of plants in early Buddhism. Again, the issue is not that this view is not found in Buddhism, but that it isn't the only view found in Buddhism. In presenting traditional materials for use in modern ethical discussions, it seems that perhaps a more fulsome and authentic range of a tradition's views might be more appropriate. P. De Silva's assessment of this, for example, is to argue against early Buddhism espousing "a biotic egalitarianism" (here separating all animal life from plant life), and at the same time continuing to consider plants as living.

> Although the Buddha preached the doctrine of the concern for human and animal life, the concern for the physical world and trees is somewhat different. The Buddha did not preach a

> biotic egalitarianism in which plants have an equal status with animals.

Or, drawing the line differently a few pages later (between humans and other forms of life),

> While the Buddha attached great importance to the planting of trees, the construction of parks, reforestation, preservation of water, etc. he does not espouse a "biotic egalitarianism," in which plants and animals are considered ethically on an equal footing with humans.[115]

Even given all the complications of Buddhism, we can argue in conclusion, nevertheless, that many segments of Indian tradition are non-speciesist or, in fact, anti-speciesist with regard to plants. In that a particular understanding holds that there is movement of sentient beings into and out of various rebirths, and that these various rebirths can include any manner of human, animal, or plant form, then there cannot be an absolute divide between any of these life forms as boundary crossing is happening all the time, from life to life to life. The boundary crossing of the rebirth system certainly underscores the interdependent nature of the Indian system, and to the degree that *bios* really does only refer to what has "life," and does not make specific reference to stones and rivers, then the Indian systems may be said, in Taylorian fashion, to be "biocentric" as well.[116] To push Ryder and Singer's original motivation for arguing against the biomedical testing of animals forward, then, we could argue that one should not injure an animal not only because the animal suffers as a result of the testing, but also because the animal, according to Indian traditions, most likely has already had, or will have, a human rebirth at some time. When a human system such as *saṁsāra* – a system that affords its participants what may seem to be endless crossings over species boundaries – includes plants in it, then plants are "due" the chance (or have the right) to make whatever crossings are necessary to reach a perfected state.

7.4 Human Duty to Maintain the Truth of Plants

A third human duty towards plants places them within a structure where they can express their "own-truth," and where they can be affirmed in, and maintained in, their own place. A consequence of this duty is that humans must uphold this system of "own-truth" – a system like *ṛta* – and thereby preserve the integrity of all things as parts of the harmonious whole. This notion finds resonance in Taylor's claims that, in a biocentric outlook, each living thing can be described as an entity-that-has-a-good-of-its-own. Each living thing, moreover, has "inherent worth," obliging humans not only to respect it,[117] but to assume their duties pursuant to its flourishing as well. Because in the biocentric outlook each individual organism is considered a teleological center of life, humans must recognize "the reality of...[a being's] existence as a unique individual, [and as] pursuing its own good in its own way,"[118] by taking on as their duty the active promotion of this teleology.

Helpful here is James A. Nash's *Loving Nature: Ecological Integrity and Christian Responsibility* where he says that traditionally,

> ...moral rights have been discussed only in the context of human interactions. Ethics has been understood generally as a strictly interhuman concern. But the situation is changing dramatically. A serious debate has emerged over the last couple of decades about the rights of nature.

In raising the idea of "nonhuman (or biotic) rights,"[119] he proposes that there be a "rights boundary," like Singer's boundary of sentience demarcated by animal (and plant) abilities to suffer. Nash proposes, however, that the criterion of his "rights boundary" be "conation," "a striving to be and to do," that supposes living beings "to have 'interests' in their biological roles *for their own sakes* – a characteristic that is not evident in inanimate objects."

> The diverse species of plants and animals...may be good for systemic wholes, like ecosystems. They may be good instrumentally for one another. They may also be good for human interests...Yet whether they are good or bad for others' inter-

> ests, *they are good for themselves* – and this claim is the basis for whatever rights ought to be respected by moral agents.[120]

Nonhuman beings are not machines, Nash contends, but beings who beget their own kind, who interact with their environments in unfixed ways, who are able to "adapt more fittingly to their niches and even to evolve into new and more complex life forms," and who can be defined "by a vitality that struggles to fulfill their 'reasons for being.'" Again, nonhuman beings

> ...are good for themselves because they possess... conation – that is, drives or aims, urges or goals, purposes or impulses – whether conscious or unconscious – to be and to do. They are characterized by a...striving to live in order to realize their possibilities, [by]... the "will to live." They are [quoting Taylor] "teleological centers of life" that pursue their own good in their own unique ways.[121]

For Nash, as for Taylor, then, "nonhuman organisms – animals and plants – are more than means to others' ends; they are ends for themselves."[122]

Nash's argument, that plants "are ends for themselves," takes us beyond the first human duty toward plants, where plants are due protection and care from humans because they provide benefits and services. And it gives support to the second, where "plant" is one of the bodies that *karma*-bearing aggregates can take in their evolving history towards liberation. Regarding the third, Nash's view, like Taylor's, seems to stake out ground beyond the first two duties by focusing on what might be due to plants without any reference to humans. But this, in fact, turns out not to be the case. Nash's view is not a "flora-originated" view but, like the other two, it relates plants to the human process, for the "whole" within which the "own-truth" and integrity of a plant is expressed includes humans as well, and involves plant relationships with humans inso-far as each element of the whole is related to each of the others.

Specifically, it is through the old Vedic idea of *ṛta* that Nash's view of conation as "a striving to be and to do," in which all living beings have interests in their biological roles for their own sakes, might be powerfully important in contemporary Indian environmentalism. Mahony notes, following Julius Pokorny, that *ṛta* is ordinarily thought to be derived from Indo-European *ar – to "fit together, unite" in its transitive form, and to "be fit, be proper" in its intransitive form – and thus related to such words as the Sanskrit adverb *aram*, "suitably, properly, fitting."[123] The Sanskrit root *ṛ*, to "move (upwards), to meet with, to place in or on, to fix or fasten," suggests to "'go in a fitting manner' or to 'move smoothly'" and, thus, notes Mahony, *ṛta* is "a principle of harmony in which all things move together smoothly and support each other in a fitting manner."[124]

> ...it connotes a universal quality in which different elements fit together in a balanced and structured yet dynamic way....It thus suggests both a correctness or smooth compatibility of things as well as the principle of balance and integrity that gives foundation to that compatibility.[125]

As an adjective, *ṛta* suggests what is suitable, right, proper, fitting; as a noun, it suggests rule, order, law, truth; and as an adverb, it suggests regularly, properly, rightly, duly.

> If *ṛta* is the normative principle of order that organizes and supports reality as a whole, then *anṛta* characterizes the chaos that fractures or destroys that universal order.[126]

In this way, the most useful understanding of *ṛta* in the Ṛgveda is something like the "essence" or "truth" of a thing, a view suggested by Heinrich Luders' translation of *ṛta* as *Wahrheit*, in recognition of the Vedic use of *anṛta* ("falsehood") "almost interchangeably with *asatya*, 'untrue.'"[127] The *ṛta* of a thing is that which in some way points to the contribution that thing makes to the cosmic whole: e.g., the sun's *ṛta* is to give warmth, light, and, in its movement, the basis for time; water's *ṛta* is to flow and to support life; a cow's *ṛta* is to give milk; and the gods' *ṛta* is to provide blessings to humans. All elements of the cosmos have a *ṛta* and unlike the later concept of *dharma*, which more or less replaces *ṛta* as a way of prescribing place (and therefore of staving off the fearful powers of chaos) in the Hindu world, the *ṛta* of a thing is less complicated than the *dharma* of a thing and is not subject to the kind of changes that *dharma* is in the movement of beings from life to life in rebirth. The Ṛgvedic hymns, moreover, are not about giving the explicit *ṛta*-details for each element of the cosmos, but rather about highlighting the general principle of *ṛta* as an idea – which can then, in practice, mark each individual thing in the cosmos as distinct, and as contributing to the life of the cosmos as a whole. What is of importance in Ṛgvedic *ṛta*, then, is the notion that all things have a place and that, when occupying that place in right relation to all other places around it, they support the harmony of the whole – "a place for everything and everything in its place."

Ṛta, as Mahony suggests, then, is a "beginningless principle of cosmic harmony...an underlying yet transcendent, timeless yet dynamic, cosmic integrity that girds, directs, coordinates, and ordains the movements of the universe as a whole."[128] As this primordial, universal, and unifying principle that gives "structure and movement to the universe as a whole,"[129] *ṛta* is identified with the eternal Word, with the truth that is envisioned by the speaker, and is expressed in the proper recitation of his sacrificial performance and associated, then, with the powerful ritual speech formulation known as *brahman*.[130] Because it is from *ṛta* that the power of the poetry which emerges from Vedic seers emanates – "How have you, adhering to ṛta by means of ṛta, come to know our newest song, O Agni?"[131] – then it is for the creative reassertion of cosmic truth and order that is *ṛta*, that the ritual itself is undertaken. And it is thus that we come to know what the *ṛta* of the human being is: to maintain, through ritual, the *ṛtas* of all other things in the cosmos.

The major aspect of *ṛta* that deviates from Nash and Taylor, however, and from the argument that might ascribe Vedic authority (through *ṛta)* to contemporary Indian environmentalism, is that *ṛta* (unlike *dharma)* includes *all* elements of the cosmos, animate (e.g., cows and humans) and inanimate (e.g., sun and rivers). While the inclusion of inanimate elements is consonant with parts of such traditions as Jainism (e.g., earth-, water-, fire-, and wind-bodies) and East Asian Buddhism (the Buddhahood of mountains and rivers), it is the inclusion of plants along with other beings *that are animate* that is significant as we discuss rights and duties. Animate things, like inanimate things, says Nash, as above,

> may be good instrumentally for one another. They may be good for human interests... Yet, whether they are good or bad for others' interests... *[only animate things] are good for themselves* – and this claim is the basis for whatever rights ought to be respected by moral agents.[132]

Furthermore, that plants have a "place" or "truth" in a cosmos that includes *all* things, such as stones and water, undermines the power of ascribing life, sentience, suffering, consciousness, and the attribute of *karma* to plants with the thought that such things obligate humans to treat plants in certain ways that promote their flourishing.

Given the "place for everything and everything in its place" prescription provided by the concept of *ṛta*, there is a more significant aspect of *ṛta* that ties it to the arguments of Nash and Taylor. The clear thrust of the doctrine of *ṛta* in the Ṛgveda is, as we noted, that it is the human being's *ṛta* to make sure that all other *ṛtas* are properly expressed. Thus, it is through the proper performance of the *śrauta* ritual by human beings that ensures the maintenance of the *ṛta* of all things and, in practicing precise ritual behavior, human priests are able to make sure that the rite, as performed, efficaciously maintains the cosmos. The Vedic assumption is that the cosmos has the right to (is entitled to) be maintained by the ritual, for otherwise the integrity of cosmic place-holding would not cohere and its natural entropic tendency would result in chaos and disorder. Where this all-inclusive treatment is helpful is in the fact that plants *are* seen to have a place in a cosmo-ritual schema, and thus to make their own unique contribution to cosmic harmony. Of all the Indian systems, a *ṛta*-like one in which, in their places, plants express their "own-truth," preserves the notion of human duty towards plants without compromising a vision of full flourishing for each and every being.

It is interesting, finally, to note that there may be a linkage between *ṛta*, rite (ritual), and right. Mahony reminds us that "the

Sanskrit word *ṛta* is distantly related, not only to the English words *art* and *harmony* as well as to *order, coordinate*, and *ordain*, but also to *rite* and thus to *ritual.*"[133] With this in mind, we might say that the world is right when each thing in it is in its right place, continually maintained there by rightly performing the rite or ritual. And each thing rightly put in its right place by the rite, has a right to the rights of its place because of its maintenance there by the rightly performed rite.

7.5 Plants, the Food Cycle, and Eating Habits

Taylor has said that, in the biocentric outlook, there "is a common relationship to the Earth that we share with wild animals and plants." The first "reality" of our "membership in that universal Community of Life," however, is that all beings, including humans, "face certain biological and physical requirements for...survival and well-being," such that beings pursue life functions in coexistence with others.[134] This reality suggests that the most obvious context in which the rights of plants, and animals, are compromised is in their use as human food. In Indian traditions, the case of animals can be managed by the practice of *ahiṁsā* in eating habits, that is, simply by a person's being vegetarian. With plants, however, there is no such easy answer for, short of our not eating at all, plant rights to live are violated routinely in our harvesting, preparing, and ingesting them as food. *Hiṁsā* towards plants, then, is commonplace, given that all beings "face...biological and physical requirements for...survival and well-being."

Indian traditions can respond to this dilemma out of an old widely accepted view that elements in the cosmos are interrelated one with the other, and that this interrelation involves a positioning of beings within a system of eating patterns. Thus, for example, humans and animals "consume" plants and other animals, as well as nutrients from water, minerals, and sunlight. Plants, on the other hand, do not normally "consume" humans and animals, but do "consume" nutrients from water, minerals in the soil, and the beneficial effects of sunlight and air. In terms of plant rights and human duties, then, the parameters of non-violence are not absolute but come to be highlighted insofar as a proper and harmonious balance can be maintained in the *process* of consuming. The Purāṇas, for example, caution against excess – the felling of trees on a *massive scale* and the "*irresponsible grabbing*...of trees" that can upset the ecological balance – but at the same time suggest that natural culling through seasonal events[135] or the moderate gathering of wood from the forest floor can work with rather than against the larger processes of the cosmos. The world of interrelated living beings in India, then, is not one where *ahiṁsā* reigns supreme but where pervasive connection is recognized, and the use of one living being by another for purposes of survival and well-being is undertaken in moderation, attentiveness, and with great care.

Plants as Food: The Interconnection of Cosmic Life

It is in the Upaniṣads where the interconnective material of the world is fully celebrated as food. Along with water and heat, food is the material and agent of the cyclical movement of life – of the transformation of elements from one form to another[136] – as the world turns impelled first by the powerful machine of the *śrauta* ritual and then by the more internal disciplines of yoga. In the Maitrī Upaniṣad, for example, the eating "of food is represented as a sacrifice offered by the self to the self,"[137] in the Bṛhadāraṇyaka, Prajāpati produces the world as food *(anna)* for himself,[138] in the Aitareya, food is the first need of the cosmic person *(puruṣa)* and of those who follow him,[139] and in the Taittirīya the importance of food is established as follows:

> Do not speak ill of food. That shall be the rule. Life, verily is food. The body is the eater of food. In life is the body established; life is established in the body. So is food established in food. He who knows that food is established in food, becomes established. He becomes an eater of food, possessing food.[140]

In the Mahābhārata, the cosmic cycle that begins with hunger and ends with food draws heavily on the earlier Vedic vision.

> When the creatures were first created, they suffered great hunger, and in his compassion for them the Sun acted like a father. Going his northern course he absorbed with his rays the saps of heat; then, on returning to his southern course, the Sun impregnated the earth. Thereupon, when he had become the fields, the Lord of the Herbs collected the heat from heaven, and, with the water, engendered the herbs. Thus the sun, having gone unto earth, and ejaculated by the fervors of the moon, is born as the herbs of the six flowers...and thus is he born as the food of the living ones on earth. In this fashion, the food that sustains the life of the creatures is made of the Sun.[141]

Note here that it is plants, and not animals, who are the essential components of the cycle that alleviates hunger with food. We might say then that, with authoritative passages like these, when food is considered it is "food as plants" and not "food as animals" that is thought to be the norm, making "vegetarianism" the common rather than the uncommon choice in eating habits. This is especially evident in the eating habits of Indian ascetics, for whom rules are strictly enjoined about the eating of plants and animals.[142] Thus, while plants are living, and are part of the cycle of life, *they, as the common, normative food, are that very thing which gives life to the living.* This is echoed in Tamil literature where the Parananuru counsels the king:

> Those who give food give life to
> all living beings,
> who cannot life without water.
> Food is first for all bodies made of food,
> and food is but the soil and water mixed.
> So those who unite water and soil
> create living bodies and life in this world.[143]

While animals are not excluded from this description of food, the immediate suggestion of mixing soil and water is that the food made here is plant material, grown directly out of the soil and watered directly by the rain. We find the same kind of cyclic vision of the cosmos with plant material as food in the Buddhist Saṁyutta Nikāya:

Again, again is seed in furrow sown,
„ „ the cloud-king sends down rain,
„ „ the ploughmen plough the fields,
„ „ comes corn into the realm,
„ „ do beggars go their round,
„ „ do generous donors give,
„ „ when many gifts are given,
„ „ the donors find their heaven...
„ „ we tire and toil anew,
„ „ the slow wits seek rebirth,
„ „ comes birth and dying comes,
„ „ men bear us to the grave.[144]

Plants as Food: The Cycle of Water

In Chapter III, we discussed the "livingness" of plants as based on three things: their participation in the circulation of sap *(rasa)* or fluid, the attribution of growth to them, and the possibility that they may be animated by breath. It is in the first, belonging to and invigorating the cycle of water, where the livingness of plants is most associated with food. In RV 5.83.4, for example, when the wind blows and lightning flies out during a thunderstorm, plants of all form surge up and bloom, as the sap of life animates all living things. In AV 4.27.1-3, the watery storm gods, the Maruts, give sap to the plants. In Taittirīya Saṁhitā, plants are often said to spring from the waters and the rains, *to be filled with sap, and to be the food of humans.*[145] Moreover, we often find plants as food in conjunction not only with water but also with fire.

> In the waters, O Agni, is thy seat,
> Thou enterest the plants;
> Being in the germ thou art born again.
> Thou art the germ of plants,
> The germ of trees,
> The germ of all things,
> O agni, thou art the germ of the waters.[146]

Again, in the Kauṣītaki Brāhmaṇa, water invigorates plants which then become food for humans.

> [The gods] pushed upward the sap of the waters; it became the plants and the trees. They pushed upwards the sap of the

> plants and the trees; it became fruit. They pushed upwards the sap of fruit; it became food. They pushed upwards the sap of food; it became seed. They pushed upwards the sap of seed; it became man.[147]

Not only are plants a part of the food chain, but they are the guint-essential form that human food takes, for when sap moves up from water through the food chain it specifically enters plants in order to become *the* food that is on the human table.[148] Moreover, in the Śatapatha Brāhmaṇa, the ritual process depends on the association of water and plants with food, for waters mingle with plants as water is put into the ground rice. "All herbs means all food," says this text, and "that which consists of all plants is all food." Trees are filled with life-giving sap, and the rains produce plants which when eaten allow the cycle to continue.[149] But the cycle, however, contains a paradox.

Plants as Food: Living and Inviolable?

The role of hierarchy in rebirth becomes important as we now address the eating of plants and the question of a nonviolent ethic. David Kinsley notes that in the Hindu understanding of rebirth there is "a general tendency for life to evolve into higher forms...[such that] life naturally becomes more complex with the passage of time." In this way, plant and animal life is followed by human life. There is also, he notes, a movement into and out of the various types of birth, thus relativizing "one's notion of a chain of being in which higher forms dominate lower forms."

When *ahiṁsā* is considered in the system of rebirth, eating habits change, in particular with a preference for vegetarianism among more observant practitioners. As Kinsley says,

> the aim is to keep to a minimum the amount of violence one performs in the course of daily life. Restricting one's diet to vegetables minimizes the amount of violence one inflicts on sentient creatures. (A presupposition of vegetarianism is that higher life forms suffer more when injured or killed than do lower life forms.)[150]

Rightly, these remarks suggest, first, that within the traditions, "absolute" nonviolence is not possible, for any group practicing nonviolence would absolutely die out. Consequently, some kind of view that advocates a "compromised" or "proximate" nonviolence is necessary, at least in terms of eating habits. They also suggest, second, that views about vegetarian habits may have developed along side the need for clarification about the nature of plants. From earlier chapters, we've seen that, when attention turns specifically to plants, questions arise about their participation in "livingness," e.g., are plants among the "breathing?" do plants have senses, and if so, do they have one or more than one? can plants feel pleasure or pain, and do they suffer? are plants conscious, and what is interior consciousness? are plants karmic, and can a being spend karma but not accumulate it?

Answers to these questions, though far from definitive, often support the traditional placement of plants at the bottom of the hierarchy of the living. This placement, we might argue, constitutes recognition that what we eat as food is organic, and therefore living; that plants are food and therefore living; and that there is a problem with an item being both food and a living object of a nonviolent ethic. In other words, we can handle not harming most living things that are objects of *ahiṁsā*, but we cannot handle not harming plants, because we need to eat them to survive. Plants, then, are placed at the bottom of the hierarchy precisely because they need to remain "borderline," that is, marginalized among living things. In this way, as the normative foodstuff, plants can continue to serve as food. They can also continue to serve as objects of nonviolent vows, but only when these vows are made by renunciants who can foreswear killing plants themselves so to eat what others have killed (but only killed especially for these others). Those under such vows, then, might say: "I can eat it if it's not killed especially for me, since someone else's taking the demerit for the *ahiṁsā*."

Kinsley's remarks suggest, finally, that the hierarchy of the living may be a hierarchy of consumption, insofar as all beings in the hierarchy benefit from the initial consumption happening at the bottom of the pile. Vegetarianism is not just a *proscription against* eating meat, but a *prescription for* eating plants: under such an eating habit, we are enjoined to eat plants so that earth, water, fire, and air can enter the organic world – the cycle of the living – and can move upward in the chain to benefit those higher in the living hierarchy. Plants at the bottom of the hierarchy, then, are "borderline" in yet another way: they become the machines that transform, the catalyzing engine, the very agent by which nutrients are transmuted from a "raw" form into a "cooked" form, and in that cooked form pass benefits upwards to other living beings.

This notion of a food chain, through which nutrition, energy, and strength move up through various living forms, is found in traditional texts. In the Taittirīya Saṁhitā, for example, by eating cattle, and plants, humans get vitality and strength.[151] In the Aitareya Brāhmaṇa, certain people get certain powers by eating certain kinds of foods, that in their origins reach back to plants and backwards still to waters.[152] And in the Śatapatha, the ritual sacrificer eats what grows in the forest and, in particular, forest plants and the fruits of the trees.[153]

The views about plants in the food chain that are part of the Vedic-Hindu worldview are not necessarily found in Buddhism and Jainism. Speaking about ecological ethics as it pertains to Buddhism, Schmithausen says:

> I for one do not remember any canonical text [in Buddhism] that affirms the food chain universe in the same was as Vedic and Hindu sources sometimes do. Eating may have to be accepted as inevitable for survival, but this does not exclude that it is at the same time detested, and that the natural situation of killing and eating the weaker and of the domination of the strongest is deeply abhorred, not only in society but also in nature. Therefore, I do not think that it is correct to derive, from the necessity of body and food for human existence... an *ultimately positive* evaluation of nature characterized by the food chain.[154]

Schmithausen does note, however, that the Buddhist view of *ahiṁsā* towards living beings includes a similar hierarchy "or gradation in terms of the intensity of sufferance caused by killing or injuring" and suggests that plants fall at the bottom of this hierarchy in the application of the *ahiṁsā* ethic, perhaps because of this. He says, for example, about lay Buddhists, that "their life is kept practicable by confining non-injury, by and large, to *animals*, whereas plants may be utilized more or less freely," given that "there is a tendency to ignore and, later on, even deny their sentience."[155] In comparison with the kind of materials we have seen in the Hindu tradition that celebrate the beauty and sensuality of nature, Schmithausen describes early Buddhism as being in stark contrast.

> My impression is that early Buddhism, at least its primarily monastic tradition as we know it from the canonical texts, was, on the whole impressed not so much by the – undeniable – beauty of nature as by its – equally undeniable – somber aspects: the struggle for life, killing and being killed, devouring and being devoured, greed, suffering, and especially by the ubiquity of decay and impermanence.[156]

This view of nature as a location of devouring and being devoured does not lead, he continues, to special efforts in Buddhism to transform or subjugate nature, but rather to transcend it.[157]

The Jain tradition has a slightly different view of the livingness, inviolability, and edibility of beings at the lower reaches of the life scale. Plants for Jains are not alone in their location at the beginning of the life chain, but rather reside there, in the one-sensed category, with four other types of bodies: earth-bodies, water-bodies, fire-bodies, and air-bodies. According to commentaries on the Tattvārtha Sūtra, members of each of the five categories can be rendered "non-living," and therefore edible, by several processes. Earth-bodies, for example, can be rendered non-living by digging, heating, mixing, adding liquids, ploughing, and adding woods and grasses, faeces and urine, or poultices. Water-bodies can be rendered non-living by filtering, drawing from a well, using to wash, carrying, heating, and adding soil, chemicals, sugar, salt, and poultices. Fire-bodies can be rendered non-living by covering with earth, sand, blankets, water/liquids, wet vegetables, husks, and mobile beings, and by mixing with other fires. Wind-bodies can be rendered non-living by heating, mixing with other airs, blowing through fans, applying water or fire, and cooling. Finally, plants can be rendered non-living by heating, ripening, cutting, mixing, drying, permeating, and drowning. Thus, "non-violent Jainas have a principle of eating only those things which have been rendered non-living by any of the above processes."[158]

That plants are both living and edible, then, presents Indian traditions with a paradox, especially in those pathways where *ahiṁsā* is practiced. One must eat, and food was once living. Whenever and whatever one eats, violence will happen in getting the food to the dinner table. To solve this paradox, the first step is to restrict all but the lowest lives, e.g., plants, from being in the food category, and this is done by designating plants (and not plants and animals) as the food that moves through the cosmic cycle, and vegetarianism as the eating habit of norm. The second step is to acknowledge that the killing of plants will still take place but that, because plants are (normally) hierarchically low, they will now be understood as those who suffer the least when killed. The third step, then, is to mediate the very processes through which plants are killed, and this happens as ritual practices develop by which to treat plants compassionately.

7.6 Living Compassionately with Plants

Agreeing that, even within a comprehensive practice of non-violence, injury to plants will necessarily take place, we now review some of the traditional ways humans can treat plants with moderation, attentiveness, and empathy.

Creating and Maintaining Tree-filled Areas

We begin by reiterating the importance of simply planting trees. Surapāla's Vṛkṣāyurveda makes clear that the planting of trees, done with the detailed, scientific techniques that are outlined in his text, will provide the basis of fulfilling the four aims of a Hindu life:

> Having acquired well (the knowledge of) this truth, one should start planting trees...the means for (the realization of) duty, material welfare, pleasure and emancipation...[is] through trees.[159]

The encouragement to plant trees for both worldly prosperity and spiritual fulfillment is found in texts like the Matsya Purāṇa, and the planting of trees is often associated special celebrations and rituals.[160] Moreover, prayers must be used when moving trees from one location to another, as noted in Surapāla:

> O tree, I shall transfer thee from this place to a better place and shall provide thee watering so that thou shall obtain satisfaction.
> Thou shall grow there free from the danger of lightning and other (calamities). There I shall nourish thee like my dear son that cannot move.[161]

Planting trees in appropriate places is of special concern, not only in relation to the best soils, proper sunlight, appropriate water supplies, and proximity to other beneficial living things, but also in relation to human grids of meaning. When landscaping a house, only trees deemed auspicious to each of the four directions can be planted there. The Nyagrodha, for example, is best planted to the east, the Uḍumbara to the south, the Pippala to the west and the Plakṣa to the north. And trees deemed inauspicious to certain directions should not be planted in them, , e.g., Aśvatha to the east, Plakṣa to the south, Nyagrodha to the west, and Uḍumbara to the north.[162]

Moreover, the concept of a "sacred grove" has great power, and people have traditionally set them aside as places of physical and spiritual benefit to humans and nonhumans alike.[163] They are "one of the finest instances of traditional conservation practices,"[164] and throughout India, there is a network of sacred groves that

> since time immemorial [have] been the locus and symbol of a way of life...in which the highest levels of biological diversity are found where humans interact with nature....Far from being a mini nature preserve, the sacred grove is both the locus and sign of the regeneration of body, land, and community. It stands for the integration of the human community in nature.[165]

Wherever they are, sacred groves are places where "every tree and bush, every branch and twig is sacred." They are thought to be the property of the gods of the villages in which they are found, and the trees of a grove cannot be cut down without express permission from the village headman who is also the priest of the temple to the village god.[166] The great respect given to the trees in a sacred grove is most famously expressed in the actions of the Bishnois of Rajasthan who would never kill any *khejadi* tree. About four centuries ago, it is reported, the prince of Jodhpur needed fuel for kilns involved in building a new palace, and so tried to cut down a grove of *khejadi* trees in a local village. Several of the Bishnois began hugging the trees in order to save them, but were killed by soldiers. The prince was so overcome by his men's action that he ordered them back and "granted Bishnois religion, founded by Guru Jambaji in 1451, state sanction."[167]

Ordinarily, the divinity associated with a sacred grove is a goddess whose local embodiment is a shrine that serves as "the permanent material sign of these periodic processes of regeneration...[which follow] the rhythms of the seasons and of women's bodies."[168] According to a contemporary informant at an annual festival for the goddess Haracandi in Orissa, "no one owns the sacred grove; it belongs to every one; it is common land, the land of the Goddess."[169] Another says:

> This festival is almost like our menstruation; in this festival we do not bleed but we follow the same rules as during our menses. We sleep apart from our husbands. We do no work, no cooking, no cutting of anything, no grinding of grains or spices. In this festival the Goddess is at her menses and we follow all these rules of menstruation as we are of the same kind as Her.[170]

The whole community – men and women – is involved in regeneration, and the festival highlights cooperation, solidarity, and reciprocation.

> Just as the Goddess, and women too, must be undisturbed and pleased during their menses, the sacred grove as the material embodiment of this state is the locus where all the male villagers live in common. In this communal state, this unified household, they treat each other as brothers, undisturbed by quarrels and dissension.[171]

Thus, the sacred grove is of immense importance to human culture, both material and spiritual. The multi-layered contributions of the forest can be seen in the traditional division of forests into three types: the *śrīvana* that provides prosperity, the *tapovana* where sages go to contemplate, and the *mahāvana* or great natural forest where all manner of life find shelter and flourish.[172]

Ritual Prayers to Plants

Gratitude towards trees and plants for the many things they give human beings, such as shelter, food, clothing, and building materials, is often given in prayers made directly to the tree or plant itself. Many of these are part of rituals accompanying the cutting of trees and plants for religious or secular purposes.[173] When trees are used for firewood or as utensils in Vedic rituals, for example, rites must be performed in order to prevent karmic retribution "at the hands of trees in the next world."[174] The historical Bodhi tree was washed annually on the *nirvāṇa* day of the Buddha as "scented water and perfumed milk" was poured over its roots,[175] and such ritual pouring of washing of the Śrī Laṅkan Bodhi tree continues today.[176]

Prayers to plants to minimize the effect on humans of their injuring plants go back to early Vedic times. In Ṛgveda 10.97.20, for example, in cutting an herb to be used in medicine, the practitioner says "May he not come to harm who digs you, nor he, for whom I dig you."[177] In the Maitrāyaṇīya Saṁhitā, the cutting down of the tree that will serve as ritual post for the animal sacrifice is done by protecting it with a blade of grass put between the blade edge and the tree trunk:

> 'O plant, protect it,' he (the adhvaryu) says in order to protect it. 'O axe, do not injure it' – with these words he puts this (blade of darbha-grass) between it (the tree) and the thunderbolt – the axe is, in truth, a thunderbolt – so that there be no injury.[178]

In the Taittirīya Saṁhitā, the plants are asked to give up their king, Soma, to be used in the Soma ritual: "May the divine plants in accord with Indra grant us the Soma for the pressing."[179] In the

Bṛhat Saṁhitā, a tree that is to be cut for by the King is greeted in this way before its felling to the ground: "O great tree, hail to thee! The king elects thee for (making) the banner of the Lord of Gods. Kindly accept this worship."[180] And, finally, in Kauṭilya's Arthaśāstra, instructions are given for how to begin sowing seeds: bath a handful of seeds in water with a piece of gold and sow them first, accompanied by the following verse, "Salutation to the God Prajāpathi Kaśyapa. Agriculture may always flourish and the goddess (may reside) in seeds and wealth."[181]

Conversing and Identifying With Trees

Ritual prayers and practices that ease the injury of killing of plants often coincides with views that humans and plants can actually engage in conversation with trees and plants for, says Gupta, in "the olden days, plants could speak like human beings.[182] These conversations are not between humans and the tree-spirits who live in trees, such as early Buddhist *pretas/petas*, but between humans and the very trees themselves. Such conversations can be found in the well-known interchanges between Rāma and the trees of the forest, where he is living exile, as he races through them looking for Sītā after her abduction. Having just found her absent from their forest home, he runs out, crying "Where is Sītā?" to each tree he passes. The trees there, being ever-present and ever watchful, would have felt her as she rushed by, he hopes, and would tell him truly of her fate.[183] Likewise, in the Mahābhārata, a heated conversation takes place between the Śālmali tree and the sage Narada over whether the prosperity of the silk-cotton tree is due to the powerful wind or not. Again, Śiva is charged with convincing the plants to come to earth and has to argue with the betel vine to do so, as she is afraid she will get no respect from humans and will be trampled under their feet. [184]

The traditional Indian notion that one can converse with trees to experience their experience and to learn from them may be part of the background of contemporary (Buddhist) practices, like that of Stephanie Kaza, of listening to trees. She encounters each tree "as Other, as one party in an I-Thou relationship," and listens to each with an "attentive heart," responding to the revelatory experience in mutual conversation that is full of sensual detail. Her conversations are grounded in a respect and gratitude for each tree, for its life through the vagaries of history:

> I am here to see the bristlecone pines, the world's oldest living trees. I want to ask their blessing; I want their help in remembering the wild source... I want to see the ultimate tree elders, the ones who have withstood the test of millennia. A journey to the elders tests the journeyer, keeping the conversation focused on life and death.[185]

Other contemporary Buddhist practices include invitations to plants to grant forgiveness and understanding to humans for previous harm and abuse they have inflicted on the plant world. From the Zen-based Green Gulch Farm in Marin County, California comes the following selection from the 1990 Earth Day text:

> Plants and Animals in the Garden, We welcome you – we invite you in – we ask your forgiveness and understanding. Listen as we invoke your names, as we also listen for you... [We call up] all plants we have shunned: poison hemlock, pigweed, bindweed, stinging nettle, bull thistle; We call up plants we have removed by dividing you and separating you, and be deciding you no longer grow well here. We invoke you and thank you and continue to learn from you. We dedicate this ceremony to you. We will continue to practice with you and for you.[186]

Contemporary Buddhist practices also focus on "identification" with the living plant – much like the traditional meditation on the corpse, where the sentiment is "so you are, that am I." A typical response during Joanna Macy's Council of All Beings, for example, is the paraphrased remark, "I, lichen, work slowly, very slowly. Time is my friend. This is what I give you: patience for the long haul and perseverance."[187] Or,

> I am that part of the rainforest recently emerged into thinking... I am Rainforest. Counted in your human years I am over a hundred thirty million years old. If I were one of your buildings, you would take precious care of me. But instead you destroy me... You destroy me so carelessly,

> tearing down so many of my trees for a few planks, leaving the rest to rot or burn...[188]

In the Gaia Meditation of Macy's *Coming Back to Life*, practitioners are asked to imagine themselves as making a long planetary journey through the elements of water, earth, air and fire as they die to old forms and pass into new: "Each worn-out cell consumed, recycled...through mosses, leeches...Be conscious of that give-and-take when you move among trees."[189] Again, the Vietnamese Zen teacher Thich Nhat Hanh uses a series of verses for seated meditation that begin with, "Breathing in, I know that I am breathing in. Breathing out, I know that I am breathing out." The verses immediately following this develop identification with aspects of nature, animate and inanimate, beginning with this one for plants: "Breathing in, I see myself as a flower. Breathing out, I feel fresh."[190] These practices, says Gary Snyder, are "'a kind of ultimate democracy,' in which 'plants and animals...are given a place and a voice in the political discussions of the humans.'"[191]

And these practices are in the lineage of the early Buddhist Aṅguttara Nikāya passage 2.72-73,[192] a passage so often quoted, but here in a different translation:

> My love to the footless [plants], my love to the two footed, my love to the four footed, my love to the many footed. Let not the footless harm me, let not the two footed harm me, let not the four footed harm me, let not the many footed harm me.[193]

To practice *mettā* for plants through something like the Mettā Sutta – "For footless beings may I have friendly feelings"[194] – is indeed to generate a compassionate view towards them, in spite of an argument made by Schmithausen to the contrary. He understands that historically *maitrī* or *mettā* was "an alliance or a peace-or friendship-contract with" those, including wild animals or nature, who were hostile or who posed a danger. It did not, he argues, entail an appreciation or protection of a species, tribe, or group of individuals who were "deserving to be *valued*."[195] Let us say, first, that older Vedic concepts are routinely rethought and interpreted as they are incorporated into Buddhist culture. With that in mind, we note that the Aṅguttara passage is immediately preceded by the Buddha asking the monks to guard and protecting themselves by filling four royal families of snakes[196] with thoughts of *mettā (mettena cittena)*. This charge from the Buddha is a kind of preemptive diplomacy,[197] and what follows is structurally identical: *Virūpakkehi me mettaṁ* is followed in the next section by *apādakehi me mettaṁ*, so that "my love to the Virūpakkhas" or "for the Virūpakhas may I have friendly feelings," is exactly parallel to "my love to the footless" or "for footless beings may I have friendly feelings." Clearly in the case of the model, that is, in the case of the snakes, the monks are concerned about protecting themselves from danger. This need for protection might also be true in the case of the plants, humans, animals, and many-footed insects, but chances are good that the preemptive diplomacy of the snake *mettā* passage is in the process of reinvention into a "self-other" process in which both parties are transformed: in the two passages that follow the snake passage, the self becomes more peaceful towards the other (in the practice, a positive, neutral, or negative figure for the self) and, in response to that change, the other is transformed him/her/itself. In fact the Aṅguttara passage is quite clear about the change taking place: looking at the three verses pertaining to *mettā,* and using yet another translation, this by F. L. Woodward, we have the following:

> *Older model:*
> Passage: 1. "May I have kindness with Virūpakkhas (the snakes)" (I change)
> Missing: 1a. (Let not the Virūpakkhas do me harm.) (they change)
> *Newer model:*
> Passage: 2. "May I have kindness with the footless (the plants)" (I change)
> Passage: 3. "Let not the footless do me harm."[198] (they change)

Thus, reciprocity is clearly built into this early version of the Mettā Sutta, and clear as well is that protection from danger is not the only issue in using *mettā* with the footless, two-footed, four-footed, and many-footed – for how hostile can a plant be anyway? Reciprocal transformation is the key to *mettā* in post-Vedic Buddhism, a view we seen hinted at already: returning to the modern environmental version of Manu 8.15 about *dharma,* we have: *vṛkṣo rakṣati rakṣataḥ,* that is, "trees (or plants) protect *insofar* as they are protected."

Endnotes :

1 Taylor, pp. 99, 101, 115.

2 Taylor, pp. 101-103. My italics. This description is of particular interest because it brackets the belief of East Asian Buddhists in the Buddhahood of grasses and trees as being outside our discussion, because the belief, though part of the Buddhist tradition, also includes such things as mountains and trees which are not by Indian standards "alive." As Taitetsu Unno notes, the Hua-yen belief that, quoting D. T. Suzuki, "each individual reality...reflects in it something of the universal" provides the basis "for affirming the universality of Buddha-nature, found in both sentient and insentient existence." Unno, "Personal Rights and Contemporary Buddhism," pp. 137-138. See also the discussions of particular East Asian thinkers like Kūkai and Dōgen in Parkes, "Voices of Mountains, Trees, and Rivers: Kūkai, Dōgen, and a Deeper Ecology," pp.111-128, and Malcolm David Eckel, "Is There a Buddhist Philosophy of Nature," pp. 331-332. Taylor's discussion, which is of special significance here, speaks only to those entities who are considered to have life.

3 Taylor, pp. 101-102, 104.

4 Taylor, pp. 104, 60-71.

5 A constraint can be positive, as in experiencing "restrictions, obstacles, or forces [which] frustrate one's attempt" to pursue one's ends, or negative, as in lacking "the necessary abilities, opportunities, and means to gain one's ends;" Taylor, pp. 107-108.

6 Taylor, pp. 105-111. My italics.

7 Taylor, p. 111.

8 Taylor, pp. 113-114.

9 Taylor, pp. 117, 100.

10 Taylor, pp. 104, 100. Again: "Our conceiving of each organism as a teleological center of life is our recognition of the reality of its exist-

ence as a unique individual, pursuing its own good in its own way;" Taylor, p. 128.

11 Taylor, pp. 119-122.

12 Taylor, p. 130. See especially the arguments of Louis G. Lombardi on behalf of the view of human superiority, as summarized in Taylor, p. 147.

13 Taylor, p. 158.

14 Taylor, p. 219.

15 Taylor, p. 224.

16 Taylor, pp. 246-251. My italics.

17 Taylor, pp. 71-72. Taylor's italics.

18 More specifically, inherent worth differs from two other concepts: first, it differs from "intrinsic value" a notion that describes the value of an event or condition, the experience of which satisfies — and is enjoyed — by the agent; and, second, it differs from "inherent value" a notion that describes an object or place prized for its "beauty, or historical importance, or cultural significance." Taylor, pp. 71-75. Taylor's italics.

19 Taylor, pp. 75-79.

20 Taylor, p. 252. My and Taylor's italics.

21 Damien Keown asserts "that non-injury, and the respect for life it presupposes, lie at the very heart of Buddhist teachings," but he understands Buddhism as placing plants outside of this "livingness" insofar as they are "without a karmic past or future" and therefore lack "the capacity to attain nirvana;" Keown, *Buddhism and Bioethics*, pp. 44-47.

22 Taylor, pp. 252-254.

23 See, for example, Taylor pp. 64, 102.

24 As Kane notes "the rule of *dharma*" is nothing other than "the duties common to all," as quoted in Carman, "Duties and Rights in Hindu Society," p. 119.

25 Note John Carman's discussion of the modern Indian constitution, whose language and structure reflect the process in the western world where "the language of duties was rather quickly replaced by the language of rights." He goes on to say that "this process was perhaps even speeded up by Indians themselves during the struggle for independence;" Carman, "Duties and Rights in Hindu Society," p. 117. He notes that the contemporary "shift from outlining duties to listing rights has been done by lawyers, most of whom are Hindu," and that this "shift from *duties* to *rights*" came about "so easily and apparently unconsciously" (p. 120). Carman's italics.

26 Manu 12.50.

27 *Dharma eva hato hanti dharmo rakṣati rakṣataḥ;* Manu 8.15.

28 Narayanan, "One Tree is Equal to Ten Sons," p. 301.

29 McGee, "State Responsibility for Environmental Management," p. 93.

30 McGee, "State Responsibility for Environmental Management," p. 60. See also Carman, "Duties and Rights in Hindu Society," pp. 121-122.

31 Kangle, *Arthaśāstra*, p. 174.

32 See Narayanan, "One Tree is Equal to Ten Sons," pp. 291-292.

33 See, for example, Ryder, *Shakuntala*, p. 11.

34 See Narayanan, "One Tree is Equal to Ten Sons," pp. 300-301; and Sensarma, *Plants in Indian Purāṇas*, pp. 29, 41, 56, 71 on prohibitions on the felling of trees, and pp. 10, 30, 43, 56, 98 on the particular duties about donating plants as given in the Purāṇas.

35 See McGee, "State Responsibility for Environmental Management," pp. 61-64; Kane, *History of Dharmaśāstra* 2:895.

36 *Jīrṇodyānānyaraṇyāni...vanānyupavanānica*; Manu 9.265-266; Bühler, *Laws of Manu*, p. 388.

37 McGee, "State Responsibility for Environmental Management," p. 63.

38 Artha 3.19.197; Shamasastry, *Arthaśāstra* ch. 17.

39 Two kinds of forests belong to the state: the *dravyavana* that holds various kinds of forest produce, and the *hastivana* that provides a sanctuary for elephants, held primarily for purposes of war; Kangle, *Arthaśāstra*, p. 174. See Sensarma, *Plants in the Indian Purāṇas*, pp. 11-12.

40 Narayanan, "One Tree Is Equal to Ten Sons," p. 300; *Mastya Purāṇa* 154:506-512.

41 Narayanan, "One Tree Is Equal to Ten Sons," pp. 291-292.

42 Randhawa, *Cult of Trees and Tree-Worship in Buddhist-Hindu Sculpture*, pp. 11-12.

43 Ludden, "Archaic Formations of Agricultural Knowledge in South India," p. 41.

44 Ludden, "Archaic Formations of Agricultural Knowledge in South India," p. 41.

45 Gold, "If You Cut a Branch You Cut My Finger," p. 318.

46 Gold, "If You Cut a Branch You Cut My Finger," p. 321.

47 Gold, "If You Cut a Branch You Cut My Finger," p. 323.

48 Gold, "Sin and Rain," pp. 168-176.

49 Prime, *Hinduism and Ecology*, pp. 11, 16, 87.

50 Ryan, *Buddhism and the Natural World*, pp. 88-90.

[51] *Ajjatage pāṇupetaṁ saraṇaṁ gatan;* Horner, *Book of the Discipline* 4.49.

[52] See J 1.260, 399; 2.400; 3.274, 320; 5.119, 378. Jātaka no. 385 (J 3.273-274) sets the recitation of these ten rules of kingship within the narrative of a king refraining from killing a deer, having taken a vow of non-violence towards animals, birds, and fish.

[53] D 3.181-182. In another passage, the Dīgha Nikāya describes the objects of the "great person's" *(mahāpurisa)* restraint from the taking of life, and of his great compassion, as *pāṇa* and *pāṇabhūta* or "living (that is 'breathing') beings." See D 3.149: *pāṇātipātaṁ pahāya pāṇātipātā paṭivirato ahosi...sabba-pāṇabhūta-hitānukampī vihāsi.*

[54] In early Buddhist times, donors, it seems, wanted to give to Buddhist renunciants who were seen to follow donors' ideas of ascetic behavior. One of these markers was *ahiṁsā*, which in this period had humans, animals, *and plants* as its objects. In time, however, when laypeople themselves wanted to practice *ahiṁsā* (and donation, or *dāna)*, they needed to exclude plants from the collection of the objects of *ahiṁsā*, as they needed to be able to use plants for food, shelter, clothing, tools, and vehicles — both as part of, and outside of, their practice of Buddhist "laypersonship."

[55] *Ye keci pāṇabhūt atthi / tasā vā thāvarā vā anavasesā... / sabbesattā bhavantu sukhitattā.*

[56] Schmithausen, "Ecological Ethics," p. 8.

[57] Nikam and McKeon, *Edicts of Asoka*, pp. 27-30, 33-34; Woolner, *Asoka: Text and Glossary*, pp. 24-31, 50.

[58] Nikam and McKeon, *Edicts of Asoka*, p. 64; Woolner, *Asoka: Text and Glossary*, p. 4.

[59] Nikam and McKeon, *Edicts of Asoka*, pp. 64-65; Woolner, *Aśoka: Text and Glossary*, p. 50.

[60] Randhawa, *Cult of Trees and Tree-Worship in Buddhist-Hindu Sculpture*, p. 9. This account is apparently taken from Chinese accounts.

[61] Shamasastry, *Arthaśāstra*, ch. 24.

[62] Sur 1.1; Gopal, *Vṛkṣāyurveda*, pp. 116-117.

[63] Banwari, *Pañcavatī: Indian Approach to Environment*, p. 178.

[64] Sur 1.4, 8; Gopal, *Vṛkṣāyurveda*, pp. 118-119.

[65] Sur 1.14; Gopal, *Vṛkṣāyurveda*, pp. 120-121; see pp. 120-123.

[66] ĀDS 1.20.1-4; Olivelle, *Dharmasūtras*, p. 31.

[67] ĀDS 1.7.4-5; Olivelle, *Dharmasūtras*, p. 15.

[68] BDS 3.2.1-19; Olivelle, *Dharmasūtras*, pp. 211-213.

[69] UD 36.70-126.

70 AS 1.1.5.1; 1.1.6.2; 1.3.2.3; 1.4.1.1; 1.4.2.5; 2.1.1.1; 2.1.8.4, 11; Jacobi, *Jaina Sūtras,* pp. 9, 11, 31, 36, 39, 88, 109, 110.

71 Schmithausen, "Ecological Ethics," p. 9. This is a view, he argues, that is true of the Aśokan edicts as well. "From a typically Buddhist ethical point of view, protection would rather refer to the totality of *individuals* constituting the social group and the animal population."

Likewise, Aśoka's 5th Pillar Edict stating that he in fact put various *species* of wild animals under protection may, to be sure, suggest some kind of conservationist intention....Aśoka's prohibition of killing these species...[may well have been] motivated by the *Buddhist* attitude towards animals which had first led him to recommend *unrestricted* abstention from killing animals. But from *this* point of view it may well be that even in the 5th Pillar Edict he aims not so much at conservation of *species* as at minimizing the killing (and injuring) of *individual* animals, by prohibiting at least unnecessary, useless and disproportionate killing.

Schmithausen, "Ecological Ethics," p. 8.

72 *Yo pana bhikkhu sañcicca manussaviggahaṁ jīvitā voropeyya satthahārakaṁ vāssa pariyeseyya, ayaṁ pi pārājiko hoti asaṁvāso 'ti*; Vin 3.71; see 3.73.

73 *Yo pana bhikkhu sañcicca pāṇaṁ jīvitā voropeyya, pācittiyan ti;* Vin 4.124.

74 *Bhūtagāmapātabyatāya pācittiyan ti;* Vin 4.34.

75 *Ekindriyaṁ samaṇā Sakyaputtiyā jīvaṁ viheṭhentīti;* Vin 4. 34.

76 Sn 146-147; Norman, *Group of Discourses,* p. 24. See the discussion in Schmithause *Problem of the Sentience of Plants,* pp. 17-22; P. De Silva, "Environmental Ethics," p. 182. Let me note here how unfortunate it is for modern translators of the Sutta Nipāta's Metta Sutta to take *tasā vā thāvarā* as "strong or weak" rather than "moving or still," as, most obviously, such a translation ignores the actual meaning of the words and thus disenfranchises the plant world from any part of this powerful practice.

77 P. De Silva, "Environmental Ethics," pp. 179, 182.

78 P. De Silva, "Environmental Ethics," p. 182.

79 Stone, *Should Trees Have Standing?*, p. 1. For Stone, having a "right," or a "standing," is to have a legal right, to have a right in court and a right to have a case brought to court on one's behalf.

80 Stone, *Should Trees Have Standing?*, pp. 5-6. See also the discussion of "nonanthropocentric extension of ethics" in Des

Jardins, *Environmental Ethics*, pp. 109-11; and Christopher Stone, "Should Trees Have Standing? — Toward Legal Rights for Natural Objects," in Van DeVeer and Pierce, *Environmental Ethics and Policy Book*, pp. 189-201.

81 On moral extensionism, see Des Jardins, *Environmental Ethics*, pp. 115-118, 191-195.

82 Stone, *Should Trees Have Standing?*, pp. 7-8.

83 Stone, *Should Trees Have Standing?*, pp. 12-20.

84 Stone, *Should Trees Have Standing?*, pp. 21-22.

85 Stone, *Should Trees Have Standing?*, p. 22. Another interesting result of this discussion is that if natural objects have rights, as Stone has proposed, then they also have liabilities: rivers drown people and destroy crops; forests burn things, cost lives, and destroy sproperty, etc. In this way, a trust fund would have to be created in order to satisfy judgments brought against the environment. Stone, pp. 26-27.

86 McGee, "State Responsibility for Environmental Management," pp. 66-67, 69.

87 Olivelle, *Dharmasūtras*, pp. 71-72.

88 Prime, *Hinduism and Ecology*, p. 10. The two other types of forests are the *tapovana*, "where you can contemplate as the sages did and seek after the truth," and the *mahāvana*, "the great natural forest where all species of life find shelter."

89 De Silva, "Environmental Ethics: A Buddhist Perspective, " p. 182.

90 Peter Singer, "Animal Liberation," in Van DeVeer and Pierce, *Environmental Ethics and Policy Book*, p. 135.

91 Singer, *Animal Liberation*, p. 5.

92 Singer, *Animal Liberation*, p. 6. Paul Waldau, in his *The Specter of Speciesism: Buddhist and Christian Views of Animals*, gives as his working definition of speciesism, "the inclusion of all human...animals within, and the exclusion of all other animals from, the moral circle," Waldau, *Specter of Speciesism*, p. 38. And, again, Steven M. Wise describes it as "the historical gulf between human and nonhuman animals," Wise, *Rattling the Cage*, p. 35.

93 The anti-speciesism critique takes its vantage point from Darwin's argument that biologically speaking no essential threshold exists that marks the difference between humans and other animals. In an early usage, the philosopher Richard D. Ryder employs the term "speciesism" in a pamphlet published privately in 1970 in Oxford, with the intent, specifically, to respond to views behind biomedical

experiments that allow for the use of animals as "experimentees" and, in general, to respond to attempts to justify benefits gained for the "human species" at the expense of the "nonhuman species" of animals. He is particularly concerned that the morality-based protections that are offered to those of human status should not exclude those of other animal status. Findly, Review of *Specter of Speciesism*, pp. 685-687; See Wise, *Drawing the Line*, p. 24.

94 See, for example, Steinbock "Speciesism and the Idea of Equality," pp. 247-256; and LaFollette and Shanks, "The Origin of Speciesism," pp. 41-60.

95 Singer, *Animal Liberation*, p. 1.

96 Bentham as quoted by Singer, *Animal Liberation*, p. 7. The quantification of experience which marks the British utilitarian movement can be seen in "Bentham's hedonic calculus:" "intensity of pleasure or pain, duration of pleasure or pain, certainty or uncertainty of pleasure or pain, purity or impurity of pleasure or pain, etc.;" Inada, "Buddhist Response to the Nature of Human Rights," p. 95.

97 Singer, *Animal Liberation*, pp. 7-9. Wise argues against the sufficiency of "being able to suffer" in the designation of "dignity rights" to a thing. He says:

If I were Chief Justice of the Universe, I might make the simpler capacity to suffer, rather than practical autonomy, sufficient for personhood and dignity-rights. For why should even a nonautonomous being be forced to suffer? But the capacity to suffer appears irrelevant to common-law judges in their consideration of who is entitled to basic rights. What is at least sufficient is practical autonomy. This may be anathema to disciples of Bentham and Singer. I may not like it much myself. But philosophers argue moral rights; judges decide legal rights. And so I present a legal, and not a philosophical, argument for the dignity-rights of nonhuman animals.

Wise, *Drawing the Line*, p. 34. By "practical autonomy," Wise suggests a criterion "that is sufficient to entitle any being of any species to liberty rights," a notion that includes volition and self-determination — though not purposefulness, as in a mule, which "comes from instinct." Practical autonomy involves, first, being able to desire, second, being able to intentionally fulfill a desire, and, third, being self-sufficient enough to understand that "it is she who wants something and it is she who is trying to get it." And, thus, consciousness "is the bedrock of practical autonomy" (*Drawing the*

Line, pp. 24, 30, 32, 37), a conclusion that, drawing on *most* of our traditional Indian data, would rule plants out. On the other hand, Wise does address practical autonomy later in the book in this way: Can we imagine what it would be like to be a bat, for example, or in our case, a plant? (pp. 46-47). If we can't, then the thing doesn't have practical autonomy. From Indian literatures, however, we have numerous examples of such "imagining" experiences: a Jain adept remembering what it is like to be a tree being cut into planks, Hindu stories about being changed into a tree and back, and Buddhist admonitions to be like a tree in developing deep meditation.

98 Singer, *Animal Liberation*, p. 235. My italics.

99 Jacobi, *Jaina Sūtras* 1.11.

100 Jacobi, *Jaina Sūtras* 1.19.

101 Sharma, *Caraka-Saṁhitā* 1.409.

102 Kuiper, "Basic Concept of Vedic Religion," pp. 111-118.

103 Larson & Bhattacharya, *Encyclopedia of Indian Philosophies*, Vol. IV *Sāṁkhya*, p. 23.

104 Larson & Bhattacharya, *Encyclopedia of Indian Philosophies*, Vol. IV *Sāṁkhya*, p. 26.

105 Larson & Bhattacharya, *Encyclopedia of Indian Philosophies*, Vol. IV. *Sāṁkhya*, pp. 26-27.

106 Jacobi, *Jaina Sūtras* 1.15-17.

107 Jacobi, *Jaina Sūtras* 1. 109.

108 MP 127-129.

109 Keown, *Buddhism and Bioethics*, p. 22.

110 Note here Schmithausen's remark about interconnectedness in the present as opposed to interconnectedness over time: "the idea of *mutual* dependence, inter-connectedness or interrelatedness, *here and now*, of *all* things and beings does not seem to be expressed in the canonical texts of early Buddhism...What seems to come closest...is the idea that in the course of beginningless *saṁsāra*, all *living* beings have already been one another's relatives." Schmithausen, "Early Buddhist Tradition and Ecological Ethics," p. 6. Schmithausen's italics.

111 Keown, *Buddhism and Bioethics*, p. 32. See McDermott who notes "there is no permanent or ultimate distinction between beings within these two courses of existence *(gati)*...[therefore] it becomes incumbent upon humans to relate to animals on the basis of the same ethical principles that govern their relationships with other people;" "Animals and Humans in Early Buddhism," p. 270.

[112] Keown, *Buddhism and Bioethics*, pp. 34-35. My italics.

[113] Keown, *Buddhism and Bioethics*, pp. 45-46.

[114] Keown, *Buddhism and Bioethics*, p. 47.

[115] P. De Silva, "Environmental Ethics," pp. 178, 181-182.

[116] See Eckel's discussion on this in "Is There a Buddhist Philosophy of Nature?" p. 343.

[117] Taylor, pp. 61, 71-72, 79.

[118] Taylor, p. 128; and, again, this outlook posits: "The belief that all organisms are teleological centers of life in the sense that each is a unique individual pursuing its own good in its own way;" Taylor, p. 100.

[119] Nash, *Loving Nature*, pp. 173-175.

[120] Nash, *Loving Nature*, p. 178. Other discussions of "conation" or "conative" life can be found in Des Jardins, *Environmental Ethics*, p. 114.

[121] Nash, *Loving Nature*, pp. 178-179; quoting Taylor, *Respect for Nature*, p. 100.

[122] Nash, *Loving Nature*, p. 179.

[123] Mahony, *Artful Universe*, p. 234.

[124] Mahony, *Artful Universe*, p. 235.

[125] Mahony, *Artful Universe*, p. 3.

[126] Mahony, *Artful Universe*, p. 235.

[127] Mahony, *Artful Universe*, p. 235.

[128] Mahony, *Artful Universe*, pp. 46, 59, 210.

[129] Mahony, *Artful Universe*, p. 59.

[130] Mahony, *Artful Universe*, pp. 54, 71, 115.

[131] Mahony, *Artful Universe*, p. 102

[132] Nash, *Loving Nature*, p. 178. My and Nash's italics.

[133] Mahony, *Artful Universe*, pp. 3, 261.

[134] Taylor, *Respect for Nature*, p. 101.

[135] Sensarma, *Plants in the Indian Purāṇas*, p. 21. My italics.

[136] See the discussion in Brereton, "The Upanishads," pp. 122-124.

[137] MU 6.9; Radhakrishnan, *Principal Upaniṣads*, p. 823.

[138] BĀU 1.5.1-13.

[139] AU 1.2.1-1.3.10.

[140] TU 3.7.1; Radhakrishnan, *Principal Upaniṣads*, p. 558.

[141] Van Buitenan, *Mahābhārata* 2-3.227.

[142] In the Hindu tradition, food rules (e.g., what can be eaten and what not, and with whom eating can take place and with whom not) traditionally govern, among other things, the makeup of sacrificial offerings, caste behavior, and the behavior of students, forest hermits,

and wandering ascetics. The *vānaprasthas*, the forest hermits, for example, are divided along distinct food lines: (1) eaters who cook or eat ripe food, comprising five groups, a. eaters of whatever the forest can offer (divided into those who cook creepers and shrubs, and those who cook animal flesh from the kill of animal predators), b. eaters of husked grain alone, c. eaters of fruits, roots, and bulbous roots alone, d. eaters of fruits alone, and e. eaters of vegetables alone; and (2) eaters who do not cook, again comprising five groups, those who do not eat from iron or stone implements, those who do not eat from any implement except from the hand, those who do not use the hand but only the mouth, those who drink only water, and those who eat or drink nothing, observing a total fast. See Bühler, *Laws of Manu*, pp. 170-177; 200-203; 478; Olivelle, *Dharmasūtras*, pp. 28-31; 108-113; 122-123; 193; 212-215; 261; 285-288; Kane, *History of Dharmaśāstra* 2.2.922; Olivelle, "From Feast to Fast; Food and the Indian Ascetic," pp. 17-36.

Eating rules for Jain ascetics are less varied. Regarding plants as food, the Jain ascetic can eat "only such vegetables, fruits, &c. as have no trace of life left." Rules for applying the "eat no living plant" ideal are fulsome and laid out in great detail in the Ācārāṅga Sūtra, and there are traditional rules for how to render all members of the one-sense-facultied group (earth-, water-, fire-, air-, and plant-bodies) "non-living" and thus edible. See Jacobi, *Jaina Sūtras*, pp. xxvi-xxvii. Moreover, "the taboo against eating animal flesh is enforced more strongly in the Jaina community than in any other," and if "there is a single practice which can be called the hallmark of the Jaina, it must be this strict adherence to vegetarianism; his refusal to eat meat constitutes the most basic expression of his commitment to ahiṁsā." Jaini, *Jaina Path of Purification*, p. 108.

The Buddhist Vinaya, taking some pattern after Vedic rules for students, forest hermits, and renunciants, and after Jain rules for renunciants, prescribes equivalently detailed rules for early monks and nuns. In general, however, Buddhist renunciants can eat anything that has been made "allowable" by donors — from a mango fallen from a tree to the flesh of animals. While exceptions are made (e.g., fallen fruit can be eaten off the ground if there is no one around to make it allowable, and eating flesh from humans is forbidden even if it has been made allowable), the general guidelines are (1) *ahiṁsā* — as for the Jains, a non-renunciant needs to render the foodstuff "non-living," and it has to be so rendered for someone other than the monk or nun who has come to eat — and, unlike for

Jains, (2) keeping the good will of the donors is critical. For a discussion of vegetarianism in Mahāyāna Buddhism, see Reugg, "Ahiṁsā and Vegetarianism in the History of Buddhism," pp. 236-238.

143 Ludden, "Archaic Formations of Agricultural Knowledge in South India," p. 41.

144 SN 1.74; C.A.F. Rhys Davids, *Kindred Sayings* 1.220-221.

145 TS 1.1.8; 1.2.8; 2.4.9; 3.3.6; 3.3.9; Keith, *Taittiriya Sanhita*, pp. 7, 27, 182, 259, 262. My italics.

146 TS 4.2.3; Keith, *Taittiriya Sanhita*, p. 311.

147 KB 2.7; Keith, *Rigveda Brahmanas*, p. 354.

148 See Smith, *Classifying the Universe*, p. 211.

149 ŚB 1.2.2.2; 3.6.1.7; 7.2.4.14; 9.3.4.4; 6.6.3.3; 7.5.1.15; 2.3.1.16; 3.7.4.4; 4.2.2.15; Eggeling, *Śatapatha Brāhmaṇa* 1.42; 2.142; 3.337; 4.224; 3.256-257; 3.390; 1.331; 2.182; 2.292. See also Manu 3.76 on the role of plants and the water cycle in ritual: "An oblation duly thrown into the fire, reaches the sun; from the sun comes rain, from rain food, therefrom the living creatures (derive their subsistence);" Bühler, *Laws of Manu*, p. 89.

150 Kinsley, *Ecology and Religion*, pp. 64-65.

151 TS 4.2.7; Keith, *Taittiriya Sanhita*, p. 319.

152 AB 7.30, 32. Keith, *Rigveda Brahmanas*, pp. 315, 316.

153 ŚB 1.1.1.10; Eggeling, *Śatapatha Brāhmaṇa* 1.5-6.

154 Schmithausen, "Early Buddhist Tradition and Ecological Ethics," p. 4. Schmithausen's italics.

155 Schmithausen, "Early Buddhist Tradition and Ecological Ethics," p. 9.

156 Schmithausen, "Early Buddhist Tradition and Ecological Ethics," p. 14.

157 On this, I understand that early Buddhism does not seek to transcend a Darwinian nature twilled with "devouring and being devoured," but to see this simply as a view, a *ditthi*, to be noted without judgment.

158 N. L. Jain, *Biology in Jaina Treatise on Reals*, pp. 102-103. Perhaps another way of interpreting the inclusion of earth-, water-, fire-, and air-bodies in the cycle of the living, is by was of recognizing that they are constituent "foodstuffs" at the base of the cosmic food cycle.

159 Sur 1.8; Gopal, *Vṛkṣāyurveda*, pp. 118-119.

160 Narayanan, "One Tree is Equal to Ten Sons," pp. 300-301.

161 Sur 5.85-86; Gopal, *Vṛkṣāyurveda*, pp. 146-147.

162 Sur 2.24-26; Gopal, *Vṛkṣāyurveda*, pp. 124-125.

[163] E.g., Sivaramakrishana, "Colonialism and Forestry in India," p. 13.

[164] Gadgil and Chandran, "Sacred Groves," p. 183. Sacred groves, report Gadgil and Chandran, "are a legacy of shifting cultivators." Because humid tropical regions have their "nutrient capital" in vegetation rather than in soil, that is, vegetation is luxurious while the soil is impoverished, the declaration of forests as sacred groves has kept "the vegetation unchanged...[and] preserved the biological diversity" in certain regions (p. 185).

[165] Marglin and Mishra, "Sacred Groves: Regenerating the Body, the Land, the Community," p. 198.

[166] Gadgil and Chandran, "Sacred Groves," pp. 184, 186.

[167] Gadgil and Chandran, "Sacred Groves," p. 184.

[168] Marglin and Mishra, "Sacred Groves: Regenerating the Body, the Land, the Community," pp. 198.

[169] Marglin and Mishra, "Sacred Groves: Regenerating the Body, the Land, the Community," p. 205.

[170] Marglin and Mishra, "Sacred Groves: Regenerating the Body, the Land, the Community," p. 199.

[171] Marglin and Mishra, "Sacred Groves: Regenerating the Body, the Land, the Community," p. 205.

[172] Prime, *Hinduism and Ecology*, pp. 10-12.

[173] Rajan, "Ancient Indian Approach Towards Plants," p. 82-83.

[174] Smith, *Classifying the Universe*, p. 213.

[175] Randhawa, *Cult of Trees and Tree-Worship*, pp. 8-9.

[176] Ariyaratne and Macy, "Island of Temple and Tank," p. 80.

[177] Zimmer, *Hindu Medicine*, p. 25.

[178] Schmidt, "Origin of *Ahiṁsā*," p. 647.

[179] TS 3.1.8; Keith, *Taittiriya Sanhita* 1.230.

[180] Bhat, *Bṛhat Saṁhitā* 1.348.

[181] Shamasastry, *Kautilya's Arthaśāstra*, p.130. Or better, "May agriculture always flourish and (may) the goddess (reside);" *prajāpataye kaśyapāya devāya namaḥ sadā /sītā me ṛdhyatām devī bījeṣu ca dhaneṣu ca.*

[182] Gupta, *Plant Myths and Traditions in India*, p. 79.

[183] Dutt, *Rāmāyaṇa* 2.649-650.

[184] Gupta, *Plant Myths and Traditions in India*, pp. 20-23, 79, 100-101.

[185] Kaza, *Attentive Heart*, p. 223.

[186] Kraft, "Greening of Buddhist Practice," pp. 488-489.

[187] Kraft, "Greening of Buddhist Practice," p. 490.

[188] Seed, *Thinking Like a Mountain*, pp. 36, 85-86.

[189] Macy, *Coming Back to Life*, pp. 185-187.

[190] Kraft, "Greening of Buddhist Practice," pp. 435-486.

[191] Kraft, "Greening of Buddhist Practice," p. 490.

[192] Or see SN 146-147: *ye keci pāṇabhūt atthi / tasā vā thāvarā vā anavasesā... / sabbesattā bhavantu sukhitattā;* "Whatever living creatures there are, moving or still, without exception... May all those creatures live happily."

[193] Kraft, "Greening of Buddhist Practice," p. 496. AN 2.72-73: *Apādakehi me mettaṁ mettaṁ dipādakehi me / Catuppadehi me mettaṁ mettaṁ bahuppadehi me / Mā maṁ apādako hiṁsi mā maṁ hiṁsi dipādako / Mā maṁ catuppado hiṁsi mā maṁ hiṁsi bahupado.*

[194] From the Aṅguttara Nikāya, as translated by Ryan, *Buddhism and the Natural World,* p. 38. The word for "friendly feelings" is *mettā* and is, in this and other versions of this Sutta, directed towards all beings from footless to many-footed, and covers all types of beings *(sattā, bhūtā),* including *pāṇā,* thus taking plants into the world of "beings who breath."

[195] Schmithausen, "Ecological Ethics," p. 8. Schmithausen's italics.

[196] The Virūpakkhas, the Erāpathas, the Chabyāputtas, and the Kaṇhā-gotamakas.

[197] My thanks to Fred Pfeil for this phrase as it applies to the early *maitrī.*

[198] Woodward, *Gradual Sayings* 2.82.

C.
VIEWS ON PLANTS AMONG CONTEMPORARY ENVIRONMENTALISTS

Having charted some common, though not always consistent, threads in traditional Indian materials about the nature of plant life, and about the ways plants are thought of in human terms, we now turn to views of plants in contemporary times. The focus of this section is the degree to which people, currently active in environmental areas that pay specific attention to plants, come to their work grounded in some of the traditional views we have discussed above – and, if so, whether these views inspire their work on behalf of grasses, plants, and trees. Do, for example, contemporary Hindu environmentalists think of plants as sentient, as feeling pain and pleasure, as having an internal consciousness, as being *karma*-bearing, or as being able to carry on conversations, and marry, with humans? Do contemporary Jains working in the reforestation of religious spaces and in the promotion of broad scale nonviolence do so using the traditional hierarchy of living beings, who are categorized by the number of senses they have and by their ability to move? And do contemporary Buddhists (here in Thailand) using, for example, the Milindapañha view of plants, think of them as living yet not *karma*-bearing, but nevertheless use forests as transformative places in which to meditate and the trees therein as models of the practice?

We have proceeded, following Schmithausen, by thinking of plants as being "borderline cases." This, we have usually understood, suggests that plants are at one end or the other of a continuum of living beings, participating and not participating in those aspects normally associated with life in Indian traditions because they represent life at the edge. Being a "borderline case" suggests, as well, that in each of the traditions, especially in Hinduism, there are a variety of views about plants and that, while we have focused on those texts and passages that we might call "plant-positive," many texts, thinkers, and movements pay no attention to plants at all – or may hold dismissive views. Borderline, then, here suggests that the case on behalf of plants is highly selective and may not represent a whole tradition's view – except, perhaps, in the case of Jainism. Knowing that, we now turn to another selective process. In each of the traditions we have examined, there is considerable work related to the environment being done today, but not all of it involves plants. What we present here is a small selection of people and movements for whom there are clear "plant-positive" views and whose testimony is, in some form, available to us. These short reports, then, represent samples of some of the pro-life views on plants as found among those today who are actively working in the field of flora.

8
Hinduism: New Blooms from Old Roots

There is much written about the ecological history of India, and about the state of India's environment today. Part of this literature includes broad assessments of the "use and abuse of nature in contemporary India," especially in such studies as the eloquent *Ecology and Equity* by Madhav Gadgil and Ramachandra Guha. One of the questions they raise is reminiscent of the "service" issue discussed above on the *sattva* nature of plants, and that is "what are forests for?" Gadgil and Guha note that

> ...all segments of Indian society – peasants, tribals, pastoralists, slum dwellers and industry – have a heavy dependence on the produce of the forests, as the source of fuel, fodder, construction timber or industrial raw material.

Given this, a "forestry debate" has emerged in which the program of commercial timber harvesting, sponsored by Indian Forest Department, has been criticized for undermining "local subsistence economies" – a charge levied as part of a view "that state control over woodland (as opposed to local community control) is illegitimate."[1] Gadgil and Guha review the question of the *raison d'etre* of forests, and in consulting various groups – wilderness conservationists, timber harvesters, rural social activists, and scientific foresters – they conclude that forests fill three functions, ecological, subsistence, and developmental, with the latter assuming "overwhelming importance for forest management."[2] India, they continue, "has a great diversity of environmental regimes" and "qualifies as one of the top twelve countries in the world in terms of biodiversity because of its tropical and subtropical climate."

Conserving this diversity is imperative, but efforts have thus far focused primarily on large nature reserves. Attention now needs to move outside of these nature reserves, so that "a biologically richer overall matrix in which the species-rich fragments of nature reserves will be embedded." To address how such a rich matrix is to be developed, Gadgil and Guha note that the state apparatus is an inadequate agent to entrust this to, and argue instead that a

> ...decentralized system of biodiversity conservation, which might come to cover all of rural India, provides a great opportunity for developing a symbiotic relationship between systems of folk knowledge, traditional knowledge systems such as Ayurveda, Siddha or Unani medicine and modern scientific knowledge.

Gadgil and Guha propose, finally, that the rewards for effectively undertaking issues of biodiversity go directly to the geographical defined communities (or to the individuals, caste/tribal groups, or village clusters) involved. These rewards should assert community rights over public lands and waters, and should include rights "to exclude outsiders...to regulate the harvests...[and to receive] assurance of long-term returns from restrained use."[3]

Emphasizing the distinctness of ecological pockets and of cultural practices in India, environmental efforts are now taking place on small, local scales peculiar to the history and environmental degradation of the site in question. There are many such efforts, and we note only a few. Ashok Chowdhury, for example, is convener of the National Forum for Forest People and Forest Workers and, on the national level, undertakes to restore the rights of forest-dependent people.

> As various forest movements gather momentum in the quietness of Indian forests, a debate is about to take shape at the national level. The forest-dependent people now have a platform to voice their stories and consolidate their hope to fight a democratic battle for survival and dignity.

Founding his group NFFPFW on September 3, 1998 in Ranchi, Jharkhand, Chowdhury believes that restoring the rights of forest-dependent people is essential to making sure that the forests themselves survive. He says, the "collective cultural identity of forest people and the traditional economic systems must be maintained for forests to survive, because forest dwellers are as important to the forest biosphere as its biomass and wildlife."[4]

Again, in her article "One Tree Is Equal to Ten Sons," Narayanan highlights the work of the Tirumala Tirupati Initiative, in Andra Pradesh, in south India. Responding to the contemporary ecological crisis, the Venkateswara temple in Tirumala-Tirupati initiated a program known as Vriksha Prasada (or the blessed offering of trees). The Venkateswara temple is at an elevation of 3,000 and has established a tree nursery on surrounding hills; pilgrims who come to the temple are encouraged to take home a sapling as *prasāda.* The reach of this effort is broad, as this temple "is the richest shrine in India" and carries with it a great deal of religious and financial clout with Hindus both in India and abroad.[5]

Again, following in the historic footsteps of the Chipko Movement, Hindu women, on the festival day of Rakti in 2001, "marched through monsoon rains to the Advani forest" to protect the trees slated for removal in order to build a dam. These were some of the same trees protected by "tree-hugging" thirty years before, and the group was led by Bachchni Devi, an organizer of the earlier movement.[6] And, again, on September 1, 2002, an international center for sustainable development, called Amrita Bhoomi, "The Eternal Planet," was founded

> as an alternative to the efforts of privatization of Genetic Resources in Food and Agriculture...This resolve...was [first] announced in 1993 when the Indian farmers started the 'Seed Satyagraha' in a meeting attended by 500,000 farmers in Bangalore.

The center, to have over one hundred acres of land, is to host a national seed bank

> to collect and conserve all available indigenous varieties of seeds, plants, trees, and medicinal plants, will also have a Gene Bank, a Green School, teaching informally environmental issues, and a school of Civil Disobedience.

Moreover, the school for civil disobedience promises to teach techniques to work against "the global powers attempting to create monopolies over food and agriculture."[7]

Efforts today to create a culture that promotes ecological wellbeing in India rest upon contributions of scholars like O. P. Dwivedi. Dwivedi outlines a perspective based in India's Vedic and Hindu heritage in which stewardship of the environment "requires that one consider the entire universe as one's extended-family with all living beings in this universe as the members of the household." This family includes not only human beings but also all the "other creatures living on earth." The challenge for India, he argues, is to create conditions "for *environmental Sarvodaya and Abhyudaya* – welfare of all without harming others and destroying the environment."[8] That which makes Hinduism especially open to whole-earth ecological wellbeing, he notes, is the "Hindu belief in the cycle of birth and rebirth, wherein a person may come back as...birds, fish, animals, and humans." Although plants are not mentioned here, he notes later that the main environmental feature of the Ṛg Veda is the worship of plants and trees from which later religion "provides moral guidelines for environmental preservation and conservation."[9] Plants, then, for Dwivedi, are included in his notion of the earth's extended family.

Dwivedi is one of the strongest contemporary advocates of the application of *dharma* to environmental concerns, and interprets Hindu *dharma* as having two foci: on the one hand *dharma* "enables us to express ourselves in acts of service," and, on the other, it "impels us to avoid exploiting other human beings as well as other living organisms." Thus, *dharma* maintains order in society and gives rise to harmony and understanding in our relationships with all...creation."[10] If part of the concept of human duty is the promotion of the condition of "flourishing," then it is well found in Dwivedi's understanding of a contemporary Indian environmental ethic. He extends the notion of *abhyudaya,* or the elevation and increase of prosperity and happiness, to the practice of "global dharma," whereby "one considers the entire universe [not just India] as his/her extended family with all living beings in this universe as the members of the household."[11] Such personal engagement in the struggle to protect and care for the nonhuman beings around us (here plants) is what inspires a number of contemporary movements in India.

8.1 The Chipko Movement: Saving the Forest or Developing Judicious Use?

The modern Chipko Andolan or Movement began in the Uttarakhand region of north India, in Mandal in the upper Alakananda Valley of Himalayan Uttar Pradesh, close to the Nepal and Tibetan borders. This was then an area of thick monsoon forest with limited human inhabitation in the upper regions and small princely states in the lower.[12] This area has pilgrimage routes running through it that allow Hindus to reach shrines at Kedarnath, Gangotri, and Badrinath. From the late nineteenth century on, encouraged by the British who were intent on getting more timber for an expanding railway system, logging increased in the region. To better facilitate this, clear state control over forests was needed and

> through the Indian Forest Act of 1878, the state reasserted its rights of ownership and control over one-fifth of India's land area. In succeeding decades this vast forest estate was managed with the help of a sophisticated legal and bureaucratic infrastructure that closely monitored its use.[13]

This extension of state control, however, was in obvious conflict with the use of forests by rural villagers all over India, amounting as it did to an "exclusion of agrarian society from the fruits of colonial forest management."[14] In the twentieth century, followers of Mahatma Gandhi were well aware of their leader's goal to have labor "intensive small-scale farming where manure was returned to the soil as fertilizer, [and] where a proper balance of animal, human and plant life was achieved"[15] and, thus, during his Civil Disobedience campaigns, they openly protested the prevailing forest laws in favor of a village-centered economic order.[16] As a part of Gandhi's promotion of *sarvodaya*, "the uplift or good of all," attention focused on forest and vegetation cover and, emanating from this general movement, a protest took place against forest policies by villagers in Tilari, in the Tehri Garhwal district, on May 30, 1930 – during which a number of forest-dwelling protesters were killed by troops under state command.[17]

Need for timber products greatly increased with World War II, as well as with the efforts of post-war nation building,[18] but, in the wake of a brief border war between India and China in the early 1960s, the Indian government made efforts to secure its borders even more tightly. This led to rapid economic development in Uttarakhand, which involved expanding road-building programs for commercial forestry operations.[19] Among the early activists against such large-scale lumbering were Sundarlal Bahuguna and Chandri Prasad Bhatt.

Sundarlal Bahuguna was a young local in the Gandhian movement in Uttarkhand who entered politics in 1947 where he worked on behalf of Harijan uplift and founded the Navjeevan ("new life") Ashram, later to house the Chipko Information Center. In 1958, a local legislative committee investigated the "grievances of the people of Uttarakhand concerning forest management" and reported a deplorable situation in the hill tracts where, even after Independence, there is "not only great discontent against the Forest Department...but it is also looked upon with extreme suspicion and distrust."[20] In 1960, encouraged by Vinoba Bhave, Bahuguna began going from village to village on the border between Nepal and India preaching a message of self-sufficiency. In 1963, he wrote an article for the *Hindustan* arguing that the deforested condition of the Himalayan mountainsides, resulting from, among other things, the Indian government's border concerns, could cause erosion and flooding on the plains. Increasingly, Bahuguna became associated with questions of forest use. Soon, a memorial was put up commemorating those killed, thought of now as "martyrs," in the 1930 Tehri Garhwal district protest and, in 1968, the day "May 30" was declared Forest Day. On the next Forest Day, a manifesto was issued and read in village after village. It included the following:

> Protection of trees is our main duty and we solicit our birthright to get our basic needs and employment in forests and forest products. To maintain a loving relationship with forests, the basis of our happiness, it is essential that the treasure of the forests be used primarily for the needs of the inhabitants of this region.[21]

During the late 1960s, Bahuguna turned his attention to work with women on alcohol abuse among hill peoples and, along with other *sarvodaya* activists, "opposed the widespread sale and distillation of liquor." The movement sponsored large demonstrations, and Bahuguna himself undertook several fasts.[22] Inspired in part by Bahuguna, Chandri Prasad Bhatt, from Gopeshwar (the district town of Chamoli), pursued *sarvodaya* activities in villages that focused on forest issues in the hill areas. During these years, concern arose as outsiders began working the forests and, in areas "in which organized village self-sufficiency was being attempted," discriminatory policies increasingly led to "widespread dissatisfaction among the local population."[23] Then, in 1970, an unusually heavy monsoon gave rise to devastating floods in the Alakananda Valley, with landslides coming off deforested and eroded hillsides affecting most those villages just below the most tree ravaged areas.[24] In October 1971, in Gopeshwar, villagers protested demanding" an end to the contractor system, restoration of their ancient forest rights, and an equitable supply" of the sap from the *chir*-pine.[25] In the next two years, Bahuguna and Bhatt responded to the grievances of the villagers in the countryside, and began to use mass media to spread the word against "vested commercial interests and a discriminatory forest policy." "A campaign of demonstrations was launched," and in these ways

> The organization base of the future Chipko movement had been established...and its rapid spread was ensured by the grass-roots efforts of the *sarvodaya* activists and the public awareness that developed as a consequence.[26]

Centering on economic issues, the Chipko movement was born in 1973,[27] in Chamoli district in the Alakananada Valley, one of the eight hill districts of Uttarakhand. It came about as the people of the villages began to realize that it was their responsibility to protect the forests that were so important a base for "a viable economy in the hills." The Uttar Pradesh Forest Department had denied the usual supply of ash wood to the woodworking unit of the Dashauli Gram Swarajya Sangh (later to be named the Dashauli Gram Swarajya Mandal) – a cooperative founded by Chandri Prasad Bhatt to keep young men from being forced outside their villages for employment.[28] The ash wood, slated in part to make agricultural implements, was offered instead to the Symonds Company, a maker of sporting goods in Allahabad. When agents of the Symonds Company arrived in March of 1973 to oversee the cutting of trees, members of the DGSS, now in full battle mode against the outside contract system, met to plan actions. At one such meeting, according to tradition, Bhatt declared, "Let them know that we will not allow the felling of ash trees. When they aim their axes upon them, we will embrace the trees." In another version, an elderly villager proclaimed, "When a leopard attacks a child the mother takes his onslaughts on her own body," and another said "Yes, that is it, we'll hug the trees when Symonds' agent comes to axe them."[29] And at another meeting three days later, Bhatt said

> Our aim is not to destroy the trees but to save them. And we will not accomplish this by burning them or felling them ourselves. And what purpose will it serve to block the truck's path once the trees are felled? Is it not possible that when these people go to cut them, we cling to the trees and dare them to let their axes fall on our backs?[30]

And thus, the Chipko or "tree-hugging" (to cling to, stick to, adhere to)[31] Movement came into being. Following these meetings, Bhatt went for consultations on the issue and returned to find that ten ash trees and twenty-two others in the Mandal Forest had been branded and were to be cut by loggers imminently. Negotiations proceeded, now involving not only Bahuguna, the chief *sarvodaya* worker in Uttarkhand, but also the folk singer Ghanshyam Sailani, whose poem became famous in the movement.

> Embrace our trees
> Save them from being felled.
> The property of our hills
> Save it from being looted.[32]

Both sides of the battle took off on *padayātrās*, or foot marches, to spread their version of the conflict among the villagers: the Symonds Company arguing that it had already paid for the trees, and Bahuguna arguing for the need to save the trees through direct non-violent action. In December, during an evening public meeting, and when no one was guarding, loggers cut down five trees, but with renewed activity the villagers were able to protect the rest until the company's permit expired.[33] The Chipko Movement spread to other forested areas with Bahuguna undertaking *padayātrās* into many of the hill districts.

One of the most significant early developments took place at the Reni Forest near Joshimath in the Alakananda Valley when women, who themselves had "to trudge ever further for fuel and fodder as the trees vanished," became "the front line" soldiers in the movement.[34] In March of 1974, knowing that the men for the local villages were absent, the loggers moved into the forest to cut down the trees. They were spotted by a young girl who ran to tell Gaura Devi, head of the village Mahila Mandal, or women's union.

> Gaura Devi, a child widow, now in her fifties, quickly gathered some others, and twenty-seven women and little girls rushed after the labourers. Some of the men [perhaps drunk][35] were rude to the women. One, armed with a gun, tried to frighten them. The matronly Gaura Devi pushed herself forward, in front of the gun, and challenged the man to shoot her instead of cutting the trees. She compared the forest with her mother's home. Most of the labourers were also from the hill regions and their shame at having to fight with women and their instinctive understanding of the problems...helped them to decide to withdraw.[36]

The women stood guard – "hundreds of them – [and] tied themselves to the trees."

> They sang songs and chanted mantras to honour the forest. There was neither hatred, nor anger, nor abuse. The women simply said, 'Trees are our bodies, if you wish to cut down the trees, your chainsaws have to go through our bodies. We will live or die with our trees. We are born in the forest, we live with the forest and we will die for the forest.

The next morning, the women were joined by the men and the group stayed there for four days. The loggers "waited for days in the hope that the women's patience would run out...[but w]omen organized a rota for being in the embrace of the trees. Men organized a support system to cook and feed the women as well as the children and themselves." [37] A huge demonstration took place on March 31, and the forest was saved.[38] The action at the Reni Forest was important in two ways. First, it was the first time that women were the major participants – here because of the absence of men and of DGSM workers. Gaura Devi said: "Our men were out of the village so we had to come forward and protect the trees. We have no quarrel with anybody, but only wanted to make the people understand that our existence is tied with the forests." Second, Chipko could now no longer be treated as a "reaction of local industry deprived of raw materials...Chipko was to emerge as a peasant movement in defense of traditional fc rest rights."[39] The fight to save the hill forests continued for years and, though there has been periodic abatement, the Chipko Movement has become a standard bearer for local efforts to save the environment and is, among other things, celebrated in such children's books as Jeannine Atkins' *Aani and the Tree Huggers* and Deborah Lee Rose's *The People Who Hugged the Trees*.[40]

Chipko's message to followers has taken many forms. One is scientific. Guha notes that, in his field work, he found "almost everyone I interviewed was aware of the importance of forest cover in regulating soil and water regimes."[41] And Dr. T. M. Dass, explaining why the Chipko movement is important, argues that "the real value of a tree is in oxygen production, purifying the atmosphere, holding humidity in the atmosphere, controlling soil erosion, offering shelter to animals and birds," and providing fodder.[42]

Another form of Chipko's message drew on to traditional Hindu folklore, and it often moved from hill village to hill village through folk songs sung by women and children. One example records what happens at a confrontation between a forest officer, sent to persuade the people to give up their struggle, and those left defending the trees.

> The forest officer:
> What does the forest bear?
> Resin, timber and foreign exchange.
> The chorus of village women:
> What does the forest bear?
> Soil, water and pure air.
> Soil, water and pure air
> Are the basis of our life.[43]

Bahuguna felt early on that the impetus for Chipko grew out of ancient Hindu philosophies and cultural traditions. He says: "One of the main gifts of Indian culture is to see God in Nature – in rivers, mountains, forests and in all forms of life. It is a sacred duty to protect these."[44] Here he describes not only a Vedic vision of *ṛta* in which each element of nature has a place, but also the Vedic view that it is the responsibility of humans to make sure all natural elements are rightly in that place. Again, he sets out a *ṛta*-like view, but for all those things that are alive: "every living being has a birthright to fulfill his basic need from the Mother Earth. Every one needs oxygen first, then water, food, clothing, and shelter."[45] Turning specifically to trees, and the focus of the Chipko movement, he makes clear that the very objects of the villagers' attention are alive: "Some see nature as a commodity. They see a tree not as a living being, but as timber! But Hindu culture teaches us life."[46]

Two themes in Chipko material provide the basis for human responsibility towards plants and trees. The first is a kind of identification between trees and plants of the kind found in some Chipko folksongs. Most folksongs are from Ghanshyam Shailani, who was active in the Chipko Movement almost from the beginning. One of his best-known is "The Appeal by a Tree," in which trees are portrayed as speaking like humans, and which "calls for the establishment of a harmonious relationship between man and nature."

> I have been standing for ages,
> I wish to live for you.
> Do not chop me. I am yours.
> I wish to give you something in future.
> I am milk and water for you.
> I am thick shade and showers.
> I manufacture soil and manure.
> I wish to give you food grains.
> Some of my kind bear fruits.
> They ripen for you.
> I wish to ripen with sweetness.
> I wish to bow down for you.
> I am the pleasant season.
> I am spring. I am rains.
> I am with Earth and life.
> I am everything for you.
> Do not cut me. I have life.
> I feel pain, so my name is tree.
> Rolling of logs will create landslides.
> Remember: I stand on slopes and below in the village.
> Where we were destroyed,
> Dust is flying there.
> The hilltops have become barren.
> All the water sources have been dried up.
> Do not cut us. Save us.
> Plant us. Decorate the Earth.
> What is ours, everything is yours.
> Leave something for posterity.
> Such is the Chipko movement.[47]

This song links the hearer to the Jain adept remembering his birth as a tree and his pain at being cut up into planks, to Rāma conversing with trees as he runs through the forest looking for Sītā, and to traditional Hindu stories of people being transformed into trees, then back into humans again. Another song from Ghanshyam Shailani, this from the 1980s, goes as follows:

> A fight for truth has begun
> At Sinsyaru Khala

> A fight for rights has begun
> In Malkot Thano
> Sister, it is a fight to protect
> Our mountains and forests
> They give us life
> Embrace the life of the living trees
> And streams to your hearts
> Resist the digging of mountains
> Which kills our forests and streams
> A fight for life has begun at
> Sinsyaru Khala.[48]

The second is a gratitude towards trees for what they give to humans – a view reflecting the "*sattva*" nature of trees and plants who give of themselves – and the corresponding duty of humans to protect these living immobiles for their service. In promoting Chipko, Bhatt describes trees as "life-giving" and the forest as "chiefly catering for the needs of fuel, foods, and fodder of the local people."[49] Bahuguna notes that

> Protection of trees is our main duty and we solicit our birth-right to get our basic needs and employment in forests and forest products. To maintain a loving relation with forests, the basis of our happiness, it is essential that the treasure of the forests be used primarily for the needs of the inhabitants of this region.[50]

Again, he asks "Does nature have the right to live?" And, since the answer is a definitive "yes," he asks, "to whom should she appeal...[to alleviate] the miseries inflicted on her?...Today human beings have become managers of all living and non-living things."[51] And it is in this vein that Chipko followers adhere to the medical directives of the Vṛkṣāyurveda, for they see themselves as the people who "care for nature's wounds and nurse it back to health."[52] The founders of Chipko make clear, however, that plants are part of a larger cycle of life, onto which humans project some hierarchy and in which there are observed to be the "devourers" and the "devoured." Thus, as in the discussion around vegetarianism, it is not that one should not eat meat or not eat vegetables because they too are alive, but to "consume" them with great mindfulness, care, and gratitude. Such a position is found, as well, in Bhatt's view of the Chipko mission: "The main goal of our movement is not *saving* trees, but the *judicious use* of trees."[53]

Some of the language surrounding the Chipko mission as a whole casts its practice as one of *bhakti* or devotion. Bahuguna believes that the Bhagavad Gītā provides a holistic view of life: "The combination of these three – head, hands, and heart – make a balanced personality. These three represent the basic elements of the *Gītā* – Knowledge, Action, and Devotion,"[54] and it is with these, but especially with the heart, that Chipko followers take to their task of blocking corporate loggers. Moreover, Bahuguna often uses the story of Krishna in his talks to local villagers as a way of depicting the forest as the context for the most beneficial of all lives, and as a way of thinking about the forest as a sacred grove.[55] Says Bhatt,

> *Chipko* has germinated a devotional attitude among them towards trees that stand sentinel over troubled Nature. Today, *Chipko* has ceased to be a movement and become the very incarnation of bliss and benediction that affords respectability and prosperity to the woodlands and the woodlanders of the region.[56]

8.2 Vandana Shiva: *Navdānya*, Seed *Satyāgraha*, and Living Democracies

Trained as a physicist, Vandana Shiva is now one of the world's leading environmental, human rights, and anti-globalization activists.[57] In India, she is closely associated 1) with maintaining agricultural polycultures, through organizations like her "seed-savers" movement, *Navdānya* or "nine seeds," 2) with working against the colonization (i.e., biopiracy) of India's plant resources by big companies looking to patent indigenous medicinal plants, through movements like *bīja* or Seed *Satyāgraha*, and 3) with encouraging local villagers to protect the biodiversity of their local cultures through such processes as the living democracies movement of *Jaiva Panchayats*. Shiva's training as a quantum physicist prepared her for the complex issues she would later face in the company of "forest species and crop varieties and with the farmers who have conserved the amazing diversity of plants and animals." Instead of seeing the world in the mode of Descartes and Newton -- made up of "atomized, isolated, immutable entities" – she saw, through quantum theory, "the world as constantly changing and inseparable systems in dynamic interactions."[58] For her work, she was awarded the 1993 Right Livelihood Award, otherwise known as the Alternative Nobel Peace Prize.

Shiva was born in Dehra Dun, on the banks of the Ganges in the Himalayas. Her father was a forest conservator and her mother a school inspector, turned farmer, and she grew up, as she says, "in a family of India, a Hindu family," in that "I learned the sense that you cannot take more than you basically need; you cannot be a grabbing individual. That spirit of service has...informed everything else in my life." For her, "Hinduism is a thoroughly ecological religion concerned with the daily practice of living: how you practice agriculture, how you eat your food, how you care for others." [59] While she was at university, Shiva worked with the women of Garhwal as an activist in the Chipko movement. As a volunteer for several years, she lived in the community and drew on her family roots in forestry and agriculture.

> I have personally been inspired by my interaction with...the exceptionally courageous women...of Chipko...and...I feel that it is unjust that the real pillars of the movement are still largely unknown. The experience of these powerful women also needs to be shared to remind us that we are not alone, and that we do not take the first steps: others have walked before us.[60]

In 1982, she opened "an independent research institute to support grass roots movements, primarily in ecological research" and, while among the women who lived in the forest, she saw the great respect they had for the trees who supported their lives.[61]

> Every day, every year, every generation, they would go out among the trees, apologize to the goddess of the forest, and say, "I'm sorry for hurting you, but I know you understand that I need to take this much firewood and this much fodder to look after my family. I promise I will never take more than I absolutely need."[62]

In time, Shiva focused on several issues that are of immediate importance to the environment in India: the erosion of biodiversity, genetic manipulation of plant materials, and the patenting of indigenous plants by international companies. Biodiversity celebrates the rich diversity of life, and Shiva maintains that it is especially important to preserve, as, among plants, it provides the conditions for "life's emergence and maintenance, and [for] the many different ways in which that life is expressed." Moreover, biodiversity is intimately related to cultural diversity as "humans have co-evolved with other species in the diverse ecosystems of the world."[63] Shiva's work focuses on demonstrating that what industrial economy calls "growth" is nothing more than "a form of theft from nature and people." The cutting down of forests, or the conversion of "forests into monocultures of pine and eucalyptus," to generate raw materials for industry depletes the forest of its biodiversity. This growth, she says, "is based on robbing forest communities of their sources of food, fodder, fuel, fiber, medicine, and security from floods and drought."[64] Issues of biodiversity are especially consequential in the area of agriculture. For all people, "food security is in the seed," but for Indian farmers, the seed "is not merely the source of future plants and food; it is the storage place of culture and history." Thus, the "free exchange of seed among farmers has been the basis of maintaining biodiversity as well as food security"[65] and, while the maintenance of a diverse biosphere is at risk because of the intrusion of multinational forces, the battle can only be won by those who *themselves* live and work at the grassroots level. "Those who depend on biodiversity for survival know they must keep that diversity alive... This is evident from the fact that in sustainable indigenous cultures, the species on whom humans depend most is a sacred species [i.e., plants], held in reverence and conserved, even while being utilized for sustenance."[66]

Shiva also works to oppose the introduction of genetically manipulated plant materials – an undesirable project, she believes, on two grounds: first, on principle, because life forms should not be created by humans, and, second, on practical grounds, because such creations are eminently dangerous to humans and the environment.

On the first, she says that the genetic "engineering paradigm of biotechnology is based on the assumption that life can be made...[and] that life can be owned because it has been constructed"[67] – a proposition she disagrees with fervently. And, on the second, she says that genetically "engineered crops manufactured by corporations pose serious ecological risks. Crops such as Monsanto's Roundup Ready soybeans, designed to be resistant to herbicides, lead to the destruction of biodiversity and increased use of agrochemicals."[68]

> The new hybrid seeds, being vulnerable to pests, required more pesticides. Extremely poor farmers bought both seeds and chemicals on credit from the same company. When the crops failed due to heavy pest incidence or large-scale seed failure, many peasants committed suicide by consuming the same pesticides that had gotten them into debt in the first place.[69]

Leaving such genetic intervention out and letting local human experimentation flourish is imperative, for while "genetic engineering is modeled on determinism and predictability, indeterminism and unpredictability are characteristic of the human manipulation of living organisms."[70]

Tied to Shiva's work against the introduction of genetically manipulated seeds and plants is her denunciation of patenting plants and plant materials, for to "secure patents on life forms and living resources, corporations must claim seeds and plants to be their 'inventions' and hence their property."[71]

> Seed patent laws, forced upon countries by WTO rules, are...[one] way in which the resources of the Third World poor are being stolen to generate profits for giant corporations.[72]

This is known as "biopiracy," the piracy of the knowledge and resources of the poor by the rich.[73] Biopiracy is promoted, most notoriously, by U.S. laws and by World Trade Organization (WTO) agreements that globalize Western-style "intellectual property rights."[74] "These thefts have only stepped up since the advent of the globalized economy" for, along with other international institutions and agreements,

> the establishment of the World Trade Organization...[has] institutionalized and legalized corporate growth based on harvests stolen from nature and people. The WTO's Trade Related Intellectual Property Rights Agreement criminalizes seed saving and seed sharing. The Agreement on Agriculture legalizes the dumping of genetically engineered foods on countries and criminalizes actions to protect the biological and cultural diversity on which diverse food systems are based.[75]

Examples of "biopiracy" in India include neem and basmati rice. Neem, or *Azarichdita indica,* derives its name from Persian meaning "Free Tree."[76] It is a tree native to India that is worshiped as sacred and that, for centuries, has been used as a biopesticide and a medicine with anti-bacterial properties. In particular, the neem *datun* (toothbrush) is used daily by people to protect their teeth. Since 1985, however, "over a dozen U.S. patents have been taken out by U.S. and Japanese firms on formulas for stable neem-based solutions and emulsions – and even for neem-based toothpaste." These products are deemed patentable because "they were considered sufficiently novel and different from the original product of nature and the traditional method of use to be patentable."[77] Others would disagree. "My work...has been to fight against the patenting of neem...In Hindus stories, neem is a sacred tree that came to the earth from a drop of divine nectar, and this has been the inspiration for my promoting organic, non-violent agriculture."[78]

The case of basmati rice produces similar outrage. Over the centuries, basmati has become "one of the distinct 200,000 varieties of rice evolved by Indian peasants," and in India there "are 27 distinct documented varieties of basmati grown in India."On September 2, 1997,

> the Texas-based RiceTec Inc. was granted Patent No. 5663484 on basmati rice lines and grains...This patent will allow RiceTec Inc. to sell a 'new' variety of basmati, which the company claims to have developed under the name of Basmati, in the United States of America and abroad.

In the case of basmati, RiceTec defends the taking of a patent by saying that it has invented "novel rice lines," but Shiva notes that the "aroma of basmati rice is not novel. It has existed for centuries. It is a gift of nature which has been developed by the farmers of India and Pakistan."[79] Moreover, the

> development of the 'new' variety (Basmati 867) by RiceTec has been derived from Indian basmati through conventional breeding techniques. The claims of 'novelty' and 'invention' are therefore questionable.[80]

Arguing against the genetic manipulation and patenting of new plant materials, Shiva believes that preserving biodiversity is, at the most fundamental level, "*the ethical recognition that other species and cultures have rights*, that they do not merely derive value from economic exploitation by a few privileged humans." The establishing of ownership over life forms through patenting, then, "is ethically a statement of the opposite belief."[81] Echoing Taylor and Nash, she says: "*All life forms have an intrinsic worth and a right to evolve freely on their own terms.*"[82] Resisting genetic engineering and patenting is also resisting colonization for, through these new forms, "new colonies are being carved out."

> The land, the forests, the rivers, the oceans, and the atmosphere have all been colonized, eroded, and polluted...These new colonies are, in my view, the interior spaces of the bodies of women, plants, and animals. Resistance to biopiracy is a resistance to the ultimate colonization of life itself.[83]

In response to the above, Shiva has developed and supported some important "local" initiatives. Inspired by the Garhwal women of the Chipko movement, Shiva began collecting and saving seeds, as the "culture of the seed is really a culture of seeing the sacred in a seed. Vedic culture sees divinity in all creation, even the seed."[84] Out of this early practice, Shiva began perhaps her most famous initiative, *Navdānya* ("nine seeds"), a movement to save seeds, to protect India's biodiversity, and to keep seeds and agriculture, out from under international, monopoly control. In the face of the WTO's outlawing of seed saving, seed hoarding, and seed sharing, the idea of local, indigenously run seed banks returns Indian activism back to the days of Gandhi's civil disobedience. *Navdānya* began with almost twenty

> community seed banks in...[a number of] states in India...and today has thousands of members who conserve biodiversity, practice chemical-free agriculture, and have taken a pledge to continue to save and share the seeds... they have received as gifts from nature and their ancestors. *Navdānya*'s commitment to saving seed means we cannot cooperate with patent laws, which made seed-saving a crime.[85]

The seed banks begun by *Navdānya*, a "native seed conservation" initiative,[86] are "spreading seeds of hope, helping farmers off the chemical treadmill and out of a vicious circle of despair."[87] Through *Navdānya*, and its network for organizing community seed banks nationally, there is the hope of protecting seed diversity in India: "we have tried to build an alternative to the engineering view of life."[88]

As part of the *Navdānya* Movement for saving seeds, followers participate in what is known Seed *Satyāgraha*. Seed *Satyāgraha* is one of a number of attempts "to reclaim food democracy...[by] reclaiming the seed from the destructive control of corporations." On the anniversary of Gandhi's call for a *satyāgraha* around the issue of salt, March 5, 1998, "a coalition of more than 2,000 groups started the *bija satyāgraha*, a non-cooperation movement against patents on seeds and plants." Just as Gandhi's salt *satyāgraha* had reflected "India's refusal to cooperate with the unjust salt laws," the "*bija satyāgraha* is our refusal to accept the colonization of life through patents and perverse technologies."[89] As a part of Seed *Satyāgraha,* participants want "to declare the common intellectual rights of Third World communities"[90] and, in India, they want to realize the goal of *Navdānya* which is to cover the whole country with seed banks and organic farming initiatives, and to build "a food and agriculture system that is patent-free, chemical-free and free of genetic engineering."[91]

Shiva's attention is not only on the seeds, plants, and trees themselves, but also on those whose livelihood depends upon the continued wellbeing and diversity of vegetable materials, and to this end she has been fully supportive of what is known as the living democracy movement, or *Jaiva Panchayat*. These local communities draw on the idea that agricultural biodiversity will be "conserved only when farmers have total control over their seeds,"[92] and their commitments draw on Mahatma Gandhi's political philosophy.

> Non-violence or *ahimsā* combines justice and sustainability at a deep level. 'Not taking more than you need' ensures that enough resources are left in the ecosystem for other species and that sustainability is maintained by preserving essential ecological processes.[93]

These communities working for similar goals are involved in exchanges of ideas, knowledge, culture, and heritage – all of which is based on knowledge of how to work the seed. It is essential, as it always has been, that farmers learn about the plants they intend to grow by watching these plants as they are grown in other farmers' fields.

The *Jaiva Panchayats* movement began on June 5, 1999 when two hundred villages in the Himalayas organized themselves into communities as living democracies – *Jaiva Panchayats*– "reasserting their duty to defend biodiversity as a commons and their right to generate livelihoods in creative partnership with diverse species." This "grassroots movement of village communities – the movement for living – asserts the sovereign duties and rights of local communities to protect biodiversity and use it sustainably in accordance with local culture and conservation values." From the statement that launched the movement that day is the following:

> So that in our communities and country we can truly establish a living people's democracy wherein each and every individual can associate herself/himself with the conservation sustainable and just use of these biological resources in her/his everyday practical living. This tradition of sharing shall be kept alive through the *Jaiva Panchayat* – the living democracy.[94]

The basis of Shiva's commitment as an environmental activist can be found in traditional Hindu sources. She often quotes from authoritative texts in India's rich religious history as a way of aligning her views and her work with mainline Hinduism. For example, she quotes Taittirīya Upaniṣad 2.2.1 on food as "the very stuff of life."

> All that is born is born of *anna* [food]. Whatever exists on earth is born of *anna*, lives on *anna*, and in the end merges into *anna*. *Anna* indeed is the first born amongst all beings.[95]

In developing her arguments for biodiversity, Shiva returns to the Ṛg Veda and quotes 10.97.2-3 from a hymn to the healing plants.

> Mothers, you have a hundred forms
> and a thousand growths.
> You who have a hundred ways of
> working, make this person
> whole for me.
> Be joyful, you plants that bear
> flowers and those that bear fruit.[96]

Her view that the world is meant for the benefit of all creatures and that each individual in the world "must learn to enjoy its benefits by farming a part of the system in close relation with other species." "Let not," she argues, "any one species encroach upon others' rights" and, for support, quotes from the Īśa Upaniṣad.

> A selfish man over-utilizing the resources of nature to satisfy his own ever-increasing needs is nothing but a thief, because using resources beyond one's needs would result in the utilization of resources over which others have a right."[97]

And on biopiracy, Shiva, cautions against exploiting traditional folk knowledge for profit by quoting some advice, given to indigenous medical practitioners, from the Caraka Saṁhitā, a standard Āyurvedic text.

> By knowing from cowherds, tapasvis, forest dwellers, hunters, gardeners, and by knowing about their form and properties, learn about herbs and medicinal plants."[98]

And, again,

> Indian forests are a treasure house of food and medicine. Rural people knew how to use the abundantly available nutrients of the forest plants, and the knowledge was handed down to them from generation to generation, but now that knowledge is fast disappearing under the influence of mono-crops and factory made-synthetic medicine. I call it a monoculture of the mind.[99]

In an interview with Prime, Shiva notes three Vedic teachings she believes contemporary women and men should live by. The first is to think of the whole earth as one family. Hindus have never asked that their clan or their race be happy, but have always said, "let all beings be happy" *(sarve bhavantu sukhinaḥ)*. If "you accept the whole earth as your family, you have to think about every species whose life you impact." From this comes "a globalization of compassion, rather than the globalization of greed we see today." The second is to limit what we consume to what we need. Shiva notes that from "a timeless period the Vedas have taught us not to take more than we need," and quotes an Īśa Upaniṣad passage that says, "Take only what you need that is set aside for you." She notes further that this idea is reflected in Gandhi for whom "the earth...[has] enough for every one's need, but not [enough] for a few people's greed." Again interpreting Gandhi for modern times, she says,

> I believe that Gandhi recognized the core of non-sustainable, immoral, unethical values at the heart of industrial civilization. He understood that it lived at the cost of the future, of other people and other species. He tried to build a political philosophy based on the ethics of sharing.[100]

With Gandhi in mind, in fact, Shiva notes that ecological "and organic agriculture is often referred to in India as *ahimsic kṛṣi*, or 'non-violent agriculture,' because it is based on compassion for all species and hence the protection of biodiversity in agriculture."[101] And the third is that Hinduism "encourages everyone to be a teacher and a leader. It gives everyone a self-defined responsibility...by looking within the self to find the divine." Today people "are losing their sense of direction, of meaning and purpose for life on earth" working on behalf of the Earth Family imbues the "values...to serve humanity as a whole, to heal the wounds we have inflicted upon the earth and upon one another."[102] Thus, Shiva, who works at the forefront of scientific, political, and cultural circles, finds many of the values out of which her work springs in the traditional Indian philosophies that link human wellbeing to that of plants.

8.3 Vrindavan Forest Revival Project: Replanting the Sacred Grove

The town of Vrindavan is, in devotional practice, the place of the great love story of Rādhā and Kṛṣṇa, and "a profoundly sacred environment in India."[103] The story allegorizes the path of human perfection in relation to god, as it oscillates between separation and union, and as it moves through the tumultuous experiences of the sentiments *(rasa)* on the way to final spiritual consummation. The expansive *(adharma)* forests of Vrindavan, standing in opposition to constrained realm of *(dharma)* town life, offer a paradoxical combination of modes: on the one hand is the dark, secretive, antinomian, and dangerous aspect of being in and moving through the forest at night, and often in the monsoon rains, and, on the other, is the illumined, private, internal, and liberating aspect of being free from ordinary bounds to experience the joy of communion with the lord. As a pilgrimage town, then, Vrindavan is everywhere imbued with the Kṛṣṇa experience: images of him alone or with Rādhā, places from the stories of his life, symbolic foods, decorations, and body marks, pilgrimage paths in and around the town and forest, and the music and chanting of his worship.[104]

In contemporary times, the forest of Kṛṣṇa has suffered a great decline. The

> groves of sacred kadamba, pipal, tamal, amalaki and sacred fig...[are] now almost bare. Most of the groves and forests in the surrounding landscape have been removed for farming. Around the town itself the few remaining trees are rapidly disappearing at the hands of unscrupulous developers.[105]

But the tide has turned, for the "pilgrimage town of Vrindavan is [now] the focus for a unique experiment in conservation, in which environmental and religious leaders are working side by side to reverse the dramatic decline of its forests, wildlife and river." In the 1980s, a local retired engineer, Sevak Sharan, heard men cutting down the only large tree remaining in the area. Requests for help made to the head of the loggers and to the local police were to no avail, and the next day the tree was gone, propelling Sharan into action. "What was the use of my chanting and worship in the temples and bathing daily in the Yamuna... [if] I couldn't protect these trees and animals which were part of my devotion?" he said.[106] For some time, Sharan "studied Vrindavan's difficulties and had many ideas to improve the situation." Although he "had been trying alone for several years to enlist help... [it was] without much success"[107] until Ranchor Prime, or Ranchor Dasa, an English member of ISKCON, visited Vrindavan in 1975 as a pilgrim. Together they gathered community support and approached the World Wide Fund for Nature International for help. Using funds that Sharan had gathered, Prime's international contacts, and the support of WWF, the Vrindavan Forest Revival Project was founded.[108] In part, the project was about education. The original idea

> was to draw the attention of all Hindus to the destruction of Vrindavan, enlisting their help to save it. In the process we would educate them about India's environmental problems and how the traditional ecological values of Hinduism could be promoted as a solution to these problems.[109]

The immediate, practical side of the project, however, was to begin with the eleven-kilometer *parikrama*, the sacred path that encircles Vrindavan. Used by "some two million pilgrims per year" to circumambulate the sacred town, "the path is no longer the sylvan and pastoral setting for envisioning Kṛṣṇa's *līlā* which it once apparently was. Now the path is highly urbanized and suffers from the problems of deforestation and pollution."[110] Devotees, pilgrims and local residents helped to remove rubbish from the path and its surrounds, and then began a project to restore the path by planting and maintaining trees along the *parikrama*. "Tree nurseries were set up, and thousands of trees of local origin were raised along with a variety of flowering bushes and medicinal and religious plants of local origin." Ever-wider circles of people became involved, including students in schools who developed "their own commitments to environmental education following the programs introduced to them through WWF."[111]

Following the entrance of the WWF into the forest restoration project at Vrindavan was the establishment of the Friends of Vrindavan, locally known as Vraja Bandhu, but with strong original ties in Great Britain. This group, drawing on local support and support in Britain and America, raises money to restore and protect a number of sacred groves in the Vrindavan area, and to keep the town of Vrindavan itself clean and respectable. In addition, the Food for Life Vrindavan group continues the humanitarian work of the WWF in protecting sacred groves and encouraging rainwater harvesting in traditional ways.[112]

When the Vrindavan Forest Revival Project was formally initiated on November 21, 1991, all those present took the following pledge:

> The forest of Vrindāvana is the sacred playground of Rādhā and Krishna. However, we, the people of this region, have cut its trees, polluted its Yamunā River, and spoilt its sacred dust with our rubbish and sewage. I pledge that from now on I will do all within my power to protect Vrindāvana from further destruction and to restore it to its original beauty.[113]

Devotees understand the earthly Vrindavan to be the same as Kṛṣṇa's heavenly paradise – a place where the "trees spoke to Krishna." Thus, the effort to repair its deforestation and polluted water is "an undertaking that is essentially religious in inspiration and intent...[and] is based on the hope that people will love the Earth just as they love Krishna." In this way, the beautification of the environment is "an aid to devotional practice" and a way to serve Kṛṣṇa and to care for his creation, the earth.[114] Central to the work to reforest the area is the notion that trees provide service to other beings, in particular to humans. To illustrate this, Sullivan quotes the following from the Bhāgavata Purāṇa:

> Look at these great blessed souls who live only for the welfare of others, suffering stormy winds, heavy rains, heat and frost, saving us from these.
> The birth of trees is truly the most blessed in the world, for it contributes to the wellbeing of all creatures. Just as no one needy returns disappointed from generous persons, so also one who approaches trees for shelter.
> They meet the needs of others with their leaves, flowers, fruits, shade, roots, bark, wood, fragrance, sap, ashes, and coal.
> That one should offer life, wealth, intellect and speech to benefit others is the height of service of embodied beings for fellow creatures.[115]

The recognition that it is their human duty to work on behalf of the trees of these sacred groves prompted the Friends of Vrindavan to have as the first of the aims for their group, to "preserve and enhance the sacred forests and ecology of Vrindavan in order to protect its culture and traditional way of life for the general good of the community."[116]

8.4 Trees for Life: Planting Domestic Food Trees

In time, Friends of Vrindavan partnered its Food For Life program with another program just beginning in India, the Trees For Life initiative. Trees For Life is a non-profit movement[117] founded in the mid-1980s and based in Wichita, Kansas. Its main field of operation, however, is in India, and sister projects have been set up in other tree-needy places like Guatemala and Haiti. The goal of Trees For Life is to empower people by teaching them to plant fruit-bearing trees, such as coconut, papaya, mango, guava, and drumstick (Moringa) trees, near their homes in order to enhance nutrition and, having planted them, to care for them over the long term. In this way, teaching people that trees can provide them years of life-giving service – *if* the trees themselves are taken care of by their beneficiaries – is an important reflection of the "tree" twist on the *dharma* verse, Manu 8.15: *vṛkṣo rakṣati rakṣataḥ*, "trees protect insofar as they are protected." The particular philosophy of Trees For Life founder, Balbir Mathur, is an affirmation of human responsibility for the flourishing of nature: while by giving someone an apple, you feed that person for a day, if you give someone the knowledge by which to grow an apple tree, you then feed that person for a lifetime.

The goal of Trees For Life is to contribute to the relief of world hunger, and this movement has planted millions of fruit trees in underdeveloped countries, and provided material to teach people in those countries how to use the trees for food, building and clothing materials and income. On May 4, 1988, for example, villagers from Mulbar, Orissa met with Mathur and Trees For Life to implement the planting of two thousand mango, coconut, jackfruit, guava, papaya, and lemon saplings. Trees For Life provided training on how to plant the trees, and on how to care for the saplings to ensure their survival. In the third year, fruit tree planting had spread to about three hundred villages in Orissa, with trees like lime, guava and the Moringa, planted in family backyards. By 2000, people were

> harvesting two crops of rice per year, plus sugarcane, bananas, oil seeds and vegetables. In places that were dry, barren land only a few years, ago, large stretches of sugarcane and rice fields appear. The planting of fruit and forest trees has become a credo with the villagers. Lemon, mango, jackfruit, moringa and other trees provide nourishment and income for the farmers.[118]

By 1989, Trees for Life had grown to include a large number of volunteers with a full time office in Delhi and, during that year, over 700,000 trees were planted by the movement in villages throughout India. Also in that year, Mathur returned to the Kumbha Mela, the world's largest religious festival, and distributed 200,000 saplings to visitors at the gathering. He believes that "ninety-nine percent of these trees have now been planted and are being cared for."[119]

Trees for Life has also worked with leper colonies in Orissa. In collaboration with Father John Maliekal, the director of a charity hospital, an elementary school, and a home for physically handicapped children, Mathur and his volunteers have worked at the Ruhunia and Jamurda leper colonies to keep the lepers from begging on the street and to develop their self-sufficiency on farm land. Efforts have focused on planting lemon and banana trees, rice and other grains, and vegetables, and on developing wells for water to irritate the fields.

Trees For Life has also been able to move quickly in response to natural disasters. When a cyclone destroyed forty-five lakh coconut palms in fourteen districts of Orissa, undermining life-sustaining income for many, Mathur was able to move swiftly with the hope of planting one million coconut saplings on the coastal belt. And, in April 2005, representatives from Trees For life, including Mathur, traveled to the Andaman Nicobar Islands, "to investigate how Trees For Life may be able to serve the tsunami-affected people of those islands." This area was chosen because "in our initial contacts we learned that the tribal people there were interested in helping themselves" and because, among the things the islanders requested were "fruit trees such as coconut, banana, papaya, betel-nut trees...and vegetable seeds for their kitchen gardens," and "forest and mangrove trees [to plant] on the islands."[120]

Balbir Mathur was born and raised in a Hindu environment in Allahabad. He graduated from the University of Allahabad with a master's degree in political science, and moved successfully into business management in the United States. There are two stories about his transformative return to his Hindu roots. In the first, on a trip to India once in 1976 to visit his mother, Mathur found that preparations were being made for the Kumbha Mela, the world's largest religious festival that takes places in the winter at the convergence of the Ganges and the Yamuna rivers. As part of the festival, millions of Hindus bathe in the icy waters at the time of the full moon, and it "is said that anyone who bathes there at this time is released from their karma and freed from the cycle of birth and death." Mathur was amazed by this large gathering and raced back to Washington D.C. to get National Geographic to cover the story. Returning with two photographers, Mathur waded into the crowd and met a barber who, when asked how he felt about the effect of the rain on his business, replied: "Rain is an act of God. It's neutral. How can I decide whether it's good or bad? Who am I to judge an act of God?"[121] Mathur was impressed by this answer and, in the wake of the festival, became increasingly interested in religious matters, practicing yoga and regular fasting. In time "his business began to fail...[and in] 1980, after a six-day fast, Mathur vowed to dedicate the rest of his life to fighting world hunger by planting fruit trees."[122] In the second, in 1982, after doing some consulting on joint ventures for international businesses, he was flying home and, over Cyprus, "he had what he describes as a visionary experience, a sort of epiphany."

> I was flying over Cyprus when it happened...I looked down, and it looked so small. And suddenly I could see how small the earth would like from a divine eye. And I was going round and round that little speck of dust...One side of this speck of dust was so different from the others...[it had plenty, but] on the other, one child dies of malnutrition every few second and another is blinded or retarded...I decided to dedicate my life to fighting world hunger.[123]

Mathur's decision came out of his Hindu roots. He tells visitors that he has always loved trees, not as a scientist, "but in a mysterious and personal way. He felt drawn into deep empathy with them. Influenced by his mother and his Hindu upbringing, he had imbibed a natural sense of the dignity of trees."[124] Moreover, he grew up with stories about trees conversing with human beings, stories about trees and humans transforming one into the other and back again, and stories about young women marrying trees if no match was found for her among eligible young men in the area.[125] From his childhood, Mathur remembers his mother reciting prayers from the Krishna tradition that compare a tree to a humble devotee and, more especially, that focus on the "service" trees give to other living beings. Prime tells of Mathur's memory of the service of trees as follows:

> The tree lives to a great age standing upright in scorching heat, freezing cold, wind and rain, and is always prepared to give shelter to passers-by. It freely gives its fruits and flowers. Healing herbs grow among its roots. A host of creatures live in its branches. If someone cuts its limbs, it remains silent and does not complain. The tree is the very symbol of tolerance and generosity.[126]

Banana Tree – Orissa
Photo Courtesy : "Trees for Life"

Boy Planting – Orissa

Photo Courtesy : "Trees for Life"

Farmers – Orissa
Photo Courtesy : "Trees for Life"

Garden – Orissa
Photo Courtesy : "Trees for Life"

Girls with Seedlings – Orissa
Photo Courtesy : "Trees for Life"

Harvest – Orissa

Photo Courtesy : "Trees for Life"

Kids with Seedlings – Orissa
Photo Courtesy : "Trees for Life"

Moringa Tree – Orissa
Photo Courtesy : "Trees for Life"

Planting Trees – Orissa
Photo Courtesy : "Trees for Life"

Perhaps most important for his later work with Trees For Life, Mathur, as a child, had a special, and very close, relationship with a particular tree. This lemon tree grew in the garden by his house and each day Mathur would get a lemon for his tea. Taking the lemon, Mathur remembers saying to the tree: "You have provided me with so much nourishment and love. One day when I am rich, I will plant thousands of lemon trees for poor people so that they too can share your nourishment."[127] All his life, in fact, Mathur has "had conversations with the [lemon] tree on an ongoing basis," and continued to do so as the decisions about his life change were underway.[128]

Later, while in the United States, Mathur sometimes felt that the lemon tree came back to him "to remind me of my promise: 'When are you going to do it?'" Finally, he decided to act by planting 144 lemon trees in India. Unfortunately, all those he asked about planting trees by their houses declined, and Mathur realized with this that his real hope was "to plant unlimited trees." To make this happen, he decided to ask a local holy man to bless the lemon saplings and to make them available to all those who visited him each day. Sc,

> Mathur arranged for the man to bless 2,500 trees. Suddenly everyone wanted one because the trees were blessed. Some people stood in line all day to get one. Not only did they take the trees to plant at home, but some promised to plant many more as well.[129]

From this start, Mathur began going into villages and discovered that the choice of the tree sapling he offered the villagers was essential. Through trial and error, Mathur found that he needed to offer trees with nutritious fruit, which grew quickly and gave fruit within one year, that were easy to look after, that grew in poor soil, and that could grow in a confined space. Five trees best fit these conditions: the lemon, the papaya, the banana, the falsa, and the drumstick (Moringa) trees. The Moringa tree, native to India and known as the "miracle tree," has been an especially significant tree for Trees For Life. Not only does it grow quickly and easily in poor soil, but also every part of the tree is edible, the bark, the leaves, the roots, and the seeds. The leaves have been shown to provide nutrients – like vitamins A and C, calcium, protein, and potassium – with special focus on using Moringa leaves in food to save eyesight from disease. According to the May 31, 2000 edition of *The Wichita Eagle*,

> Trees For Life made it a project to try to communicate [the] value [of the Moringa tree] to 40,000 people in 20 remote villages in India in 1995. A year later, a study revealed that 84 percent of the people were eating the leaves at least three times a week, compared with 30 percent before the program started.

Mathur also discovered that it was best to work with the women of the household than with the men.

> Give a fruit tree to the woman of the family, for her to plant outside her back door, and she will guard it carefully. She has to feed her family and the fruit from the tree will help her...[Moreover], the women of the villages naturally wanted to care for the trees he gave them.[130]

The basis of Mathur's work is clearly set within the Hindu view "that to care for a tree...[is] a sacred duty." He says: "Wherever possible, we distribute trees as *prasadam* (spiritual blessing), whether from temples, gurdwaras or mosques – it doesn't matter...Trees have a power and a language of their own that is not easy to communicate." Moreover, he often passes out a leaflet with quotes from Hindu scriptures that emphasize that "the whole life of these trees is to serve," and that "trees are like good people who care for others."[131]

In the larger context, Mathur believes that plants are indeed part of the system of rebirth because they are a part of the "continuum of life...The same energy taking different shape." Moreover (reflecting the old idea of *ṛta*), he posits that stones, mountains, and the sea, plants "have consciousness...We may not understand their language, we may not understand their consciousness," but it is there. Among those things in this continuum, plants are rated much higher than humans: if one were to ask, says Mathur, who "in the genetic game is liable to survive, plants or humans, I would vote for the plants...and who has more genetic resiliency, the humans or plants, I would say the plants." Regardless of this greater resilience on the part of plants, human owe plants special care.

> All things try to survive...so [humans] perform duties towards plants to help them survive...for example, if carrots help us survive and you plant carrots, take very good care of them, we "protect" them from the rabbits and protect them from the bugs, and then we eat them ourselves or destroy them ourselves. So duty is for human beings...[as for] all of the plants, simply for the reproduction of their own genetic materials.

Thus, it is in the interest of the humans "to make sure that the vegetation lasts." There is, he says, "a symbiotic relationship, symbiotic dance between" plants and humans, and when humans "destroy plants [they do so] at their own personal risk."[132]

A comparison of two members of Trees For Life is especially interesting. Both are male workers from India, both in their mid-20's, both trained in India in computer science, and both working at Trees For Life in their capacity as computer specialists. While of seemingly equivalent background and training, they had opposite views on the nature of plants. While Praveen,[133] a Lingayat, had remarkably fulsome answers to interview questions that reflected, positively, the wealth of traditional Hindu views on plants, Satish C.,[134] of the Mudaliar caste and Thuluvavellalar subcaste, answered "no" to every question on plants, beginning with "do you believe that plants are alive?" The following are selected quotes from the Praveen interview taken from a longer written version of his answers.

1. **Are plants living?** It is obvious that plants have life. Scientifically, we classify beings that can breathe, eat, grow, and reproduce as living things. All of these have been established in plants and trees and so they are known to be living things. Even to this day, in certain parts of Indian forests, the locals pray to the trees to forgive them for cutting them off. And for every tree they cut, they plant a new one. They believe that in this way, the tree will not be offended and will forgive them for killing it.

2. **Are plants sentient? And how do we know?** Sentience is a state of being alert, conscious, and having feelings. A being is said to be conscious whenever it responds or is responsive to any stimulus in the surroundings. If we closely observe the plants and their nature, it can be easily established that they are sentient. When they are exposed to extreme heat, the plants wither or lose their vitality and the leaves and flowers droop and once they are watered, they spring back in vitality. Having been brought up in a rural environment, during younger days I was told by my grandparents that plants and trees could respond to us and they had feelings too. And so, I used to spend some time with my grandparents in the village each day and learn how to speak to trees. I started to talk to trees and plants! Every time I used to visit the trees and plants in the farm, I used to feel that they were welcoming my presence. I used to ask them how their day went and tell them what I did the whole day.
3. **Do plants have stability?** Stability is often a characteristic attributed to a quality that signifies resistance to change, immovability, and strength. One of the qualities that a human being must possess is this stability to stick to his virtues. And people always quote trees as an example for this. If a good human being is being told to stick to his principles and virtues, he would obviously be steadfastly rooted to his values no matter what comes, such as the trees do.
4. **Do plants have consciousness?** Consciousness is a state of being aware of our selves. And plants are aware of their state and being. In ancient India the trees were believed to have consciousness. They knew the difference between good and bad. Personally this is a tough question to answer.
5. **Can plants feel pleasure and pain?** Can plants suffer? Just because plants do not express pleasure and pain in forms such as ours, we cannot conclude that they do not have such feelings at all! They have their own methods of showing it. When we look at a withered plant, can we feel that it is happy? If we were to study the reactions of the plants and trees to various conditions of discomfort or pleasure, we can easily make out that they too respond to it, albeit in a manner unique to them.
6. **Do plants have *karma*?** *Karma* is a rather controversial topic that I haven't personally got much insight into. For a being to obtain the karmic fruits, he must indulge in *karma* or activities. The activities a plant is involved in is just growing, bearing fruits and flowers, and giving shade, etc. None of these can result in it acquiring any bad fruits of *karma*. The

tree is just being itself. It can be concluded that the tree does not acquire any karmic fruits by itself or by its actions. And in fact if there is such thing as rebirth, after having been born as a tree the being can truly be reborn as a more noble being.

7. **Do plants have *sattva* or *tamas* in their nature?** If we closely observe we can easily realize that the plants have attributes applicable to both sattvic and tamasic. They are selfless in the sense of sattvic and because of their inertia they imbibe the tamasic tendency. The whole issue of attributing the tamasic nature to trees is baseless. Trees aren't concerned about any of these attributes. They are what they are.
8. **Do humans have duties regarding plants?** Yes! If man has to survive he must realize his duties towards plants and stand up to them and execute them.
9. **Do plants have rights?** Again, yes! Every being that is living has rights. And if plants and trees must be conserved, we must give those rights. Practically speaking this is necessary for the survival of man.[135]

On the whole, the views of Praveen mirror the common views of the Hindu tradition on plants. Plants are alive because they breathe and grow. They are sentient because we humans observe them to respond to stimuli from the outside world – although, even when asked, Praveen had no thoughts about which of the five senses are found in plant life. Plants are obviously stable, and Praveen proceeded (without prompting) to talk about homologies between plants and humans on the issue of stability – in particular, that the steadiness and constancy of plants is a good thing for humans to model themselves after. Though Praveen had a tough time with plants and consciousness, as the Hindu tradition does, he did suggest an awareness of their state and being on the part of plants (note the *antaḥsaṁjñā* "interior consciousness" with regard to plants found in a few early texts). Plants can indeed feel pain and pleasure, he believes, and we know this because we can see their reactions to what we would imagine to be painful and pleasurable stimuli. On *karma*, Praveen says plants cannot acquire *karma,* but he is open to the idea of plants being involved in rebirth – in both cases, more or less following tradition. On the question of plants being *tamas*- and or *sattva*-bearing, he is in perfect accord with the tradition; on the one hand, one could see the *tamas* qualities of lethargy, indifference, and dullness in plants but, on the other, the *sattva* qualities of calmness, harmoniousness, and tranquility. His repetition of "they are what they are" several times suggests a belief in the achievement of perfect fullness and "own truth" by plants, and that "trees aren't too concerned about any of these attributes" suggests, likewise, a shift by plants into a higher spiritual plane. Finally, as in the case of Mathur, and following some Hindu folk tradition, Praveen believes that one can talk to trees and, in return, can experience them as responding.

On the surface Praveen shared a similar professional trajectory with his colleague, Satish C. Not only were both trained in computer science, but also both came to Trees For Life to work on the computer side of TFL education. Moreover, both chose TFL because it was an environmental organization working with trees. Their answers to the questions posed, however, couldn't have been more different. While Praveen had full and detailed answers to the questions, reflecting a thorough grounding and fulsome assimilation of "plant-positive" traditional Hindu views, Satish C. did not. His "no" answers to all the questions above could represent a decidedly anti-tradition view, or an assimilation of more modern, secular views. In any case, the whole suggests a gamut of views about plants among Indians working in plant-oriented environmental activism – not just views reflective of plant-positive traditional Hinduism.

8.5 Auroville: Flower Power in Contemporary Devotionalism

In Pondicherry, Tamil Nadu, is the city of Auroville. This "City of New Life" or "City of Dawn" was officially announced as a project of the Sri Aurobindo Society on All India Radio on November 11, 1967, with the full approval of the Mother, President of the Society.

> Auroville wants to be a universal town where men and women of all countries are able to live in peace and progressive harmony, above all creeds, all politics and all nationalities... The purpose of Auroville is to realize human unity.[136]

Auroville is in the area of Sri Aurobindo Ghose's ashram in French India. After an early career with the nationalist independence movement, Aurobindo moved to Pondicherry in 1910 as his interests were turning away from political issues towards yoga and religious concerns. There he spent the next forty years, until he died in 1950, developing his system of "spiritual evolution" and "integral yoga." Aurobindo's view of spiritual evolution holds that consciousness is present in all things, in inert matter as well as in plants, animals, humans, and suprahuman life. Consciousness is involved in all levels of being and in various ways: the absolute is *saccidānanda* or the highest level of "being, consciousness, and bliss;" just below, the super mind mediates *saccidānanda* to the manifold world; and, further below, other levels of mind – the over mind, the intuitive mind, the illumined mind, the higher mind, and just mind – each participate in distinct ways in human mental experience. The hierarchical structure of spirit or consciousness allows for spiritual evolution, a series of ascents arising up from physical, material existence to a state beyond all mental existence, and it is an evolutionary process that moves towards the divine through nature and transcending nature. Yoga is the discipline by which this movement takes place, and integral yoga seeks to combine all other forms of yoga into a system beneficial not only to all humans but to the entire cosmos as well.

Aurobindo developed this system over the course of forty years while in residence at his ashram in Pondicherry. In his first year there, 1910, he met Paul Richard who, when he returned to France, told his wife Mirra Alfassa Richard (1878-1973), a talented artist, pianist, and writer,[137] about Aurobindo. Her response – coming as it did out of a lifetime of psychic and spiritual experiences, and out of intensive readings of Indian religious classics – was to move to India. Mirra and Paul Richard met Aurobindo on March 29, 1914 and when Mirra (soon to be known as the Mother) saw Aurobindo she saw him fully manifest in his highest mental form. She stayed there for eleven months, returned to France, and then went to Japan for a period of four years. In 1920 she returned to Pondicherry, and from this point on, the two entered into an intense and fruitful collaboration that involved, among other things, the publication of

Aurobindo's teachings in a journal called "Arya," published in both French and English. Increasingly, the Mother took charge over all the disciples and over the details of the growth of the ashram, while Aurobindo retreated into seclusion to follow his spiritual practice. After Aurobindo's death in 1950, the ashram continued to grow and expand under the Mother's care "into a large, many-faceted community," and she in her turn reached the highest spiritual experience of the super mind on February 29, 1956. In 1952, the Mother created the Sri Aurobindo International Centre of Education; in 1954, Pondicherry became, politically, a part of India; in 1960 the Mother started the Sri Aurobindo Society; and in 1968 she founded the city of Auroville. Having retired to her room in 1962, she continued to guide the activities of the Ashram, and in 1973, the Mother died.[138]

The project of Auroville, begun in 1964, was intended to give material realization to Sri Aurobindo's ideal of unity in diversity, as part of his goal of progressive universal harmony. The site includes areas of Pondicherry and Madras, and early models proposed four zones, residential, cultural, international, and industrial, with a projected 50,000 residents. The vision called for no employment; work that was both an expression of the worker and a gift of service to others; basic needs supplied to all; and as few rules as possible so that individuals could develop self-discipline within a culture of freedom. Specific buildings proposed included cultural pavilions, a university, an institute of integrated health sciences, a seaside resort, a world trade and information center, and a film studio. The foundation of Auroville was laid on February 28, 1968, and UNESCO provided initial support; in 1988, the Government of India took over and the city came under the administration of the Auroville Foundation.[139]

At the center of Auroville is the Matrimandir, a meditation chamber surrounded by gardens around which the four zones are planned and beyond which is a Green Belt or ring of forest area. Work on the gardens and on the forest areas has been, for some long time, under the guidance of Richard (Narad) Eggenberger who first came to Auroville in 1961 as an aspirant to the integral yoga practice of Sri Aurobindo. When Narad met the Mother, she said he could stay as long as he liked, and in 1969 she asked him "to design and build the gardens of the Matrimandir."[140] In 2004, he says:

> The Matrimandir is an extraordinary structure with an inner room that is meant only for one to find one's soul, no meditation, no music, just concentration. And it is absolutely one of the greatest force fields one could enter into. Surrounding the Matrimandir will be twelve gardens, and each of those gardens will be symbolical, but a living symbolism.

The symbolism of these twelve gardens is as follows: existence *(sat)*, consciousness *(cit)*, bliss *(ānanda)*, life, light, power, wealth, utility, progress, youth, harmony, and perfection. The Mother told Narad, as head gardener and nurseryman at Auroville, that the garden must be a thing of great beauty, such that in each one people will experience the symbol as it is: "in the garden of youth, they will know youth, in the garden of bliss, they will know bliss, and so on." She also said "one must know how to move from consciousness to consciousness," reflecting the spiritual pathway as it was set out by Aurobindo.

Narad worked on the gardens of the Matrimandir from 1969 to 1981 planting flowerbeds and trees, introducing new seeds, developing hybrids, and writing books. Narad notes that one of the greatest experiences of his life is "to have been able to grow flowers to send to [the Mother]...from 1969-73...and to have more than 65 flowers from the Matrimandir gardens of Auroville named by her:" the significance of the Myrtle, for example, is "To live only for the Divine."[141] Although the Matrimandir itself is almost finished, the gardens have not yet been started. Originally, Narad "felt that the way ahead would be revealed by the plants themselves, through my communication with them, rather than through my drawing up garden designs." Since this has not happened yet, Narad says, the gardens will be a collaborative effort and will arise out of a vision that comes "with the harmony of our labor and our shared aspirations for the realization of the Gardens...My faith is that it will eventually be done exactly according to the Divine Will."[142]

> The vision has to come; I feel the vision is the most important thing because of Mother's words to me. It just can't be another garden, it has to be a physical living experience of the significance of each garden.

Patience is necessary, Narad believes, for "sufficient harmony and...true collaboration" to emerge. In working with plants for fifty years, as he's done, a great intimacy is allowed to develop between gardener and flower: "great gardeners through all the history of the world...simply understand what a plant needs, and there are many of them around today. I think that one has to be open to the nature of the plant." As an example of this, Narad notes that the climate of Auroville is very hot and tropical, and many of the plants might ordinarily find it inhospitable. Because of this,

> it has to get into the plant's consciousness that it can blossom there...and, so, I planted plants time and time and time again, talking to them and praying for them that they could make it there, and now things from climates that are not tropical are growing there.

Most of Narad's views about plants have been shaped, and are taken from, the views of the Mother and, of these views of plants, two are most important: first, their relation to the psychic and, second, their particular role in communication. Because Sri Aurbindo's philosophy is based on "spiritual evolution" whose stages are of increasingly advanced consciousness, views about the nature of flowers and how they work in Aurovillian practice take up their relation to consciousness. If one should ask whether plants have consciousness the first answer would be "yes." The Mother says:

> Those who have studied the vegetable kingdom in detail are well aware that there is a consciousness there. For instance, plants need sunlight to live – the sun represents the active energy which makes them grow – so, if you put a plant in a place where there is no sunlight, you see it always growing up and up and up, trying, making an *effort* to reach the sunlight.

Applying this image of growing upwards and making an effort to reach the sunlight to other plants and trees, she continues by saying, "Therefore there is a consciousness, a will to live which is already manifesting."[143] Narad noted that plants "are conscious, but they are unable to express it in words;" there is, then, no mental process in plants. "Not in the flower, no," he continues, but "there is the psychic presence, and aspiration, obviously for light, but there is not yet the beginning of the mental consciousness."[144] *Aspiration* is, then, "the urge, the movement, the push towards light," and the word used to describe "the call of the being for higher things...for all that belongs to the higher or divine consciousness."[145] Thus, says Narad, flowers "don't have the mental development, but their aspiration for light is very obvious."[146]

It is "the psychic" rather than "consciousness" that is the focal point for the discussion of flowers in Auroville. "Since flowers are the manifestations of the psychic in the vegetal kingdom," says the Mother, "love of flowers would mean that one is drawn by the psychic vibration and consequently by the psychic in one's own self."[147] According to Narad, plants do not have senses "because the mental has not formed in them. It's a much more spontaneous aspiration even than human beings have because our minds get in the way."[148] Instead, says the Mother, "Directly there is organic life, the vital element comes in, and it is this vital element which gives to flowers the sense of beauty." This vital element is not individualized in flowers, for the "psychic is individualized only in man, but it was there before him;" in flowers, "it manifests as a force, as consciousness rather than as individuality."[149] In this way, then, for flowers there are no mental processes per se, no experience that is sentient per se, only aspiration that is spontaneous and non-individualized.

Viewing the place of plants on a scale, the Mother notes that "pure psychic consciousness is instinctive to flowers,"[150] and that flowers and plants are "one of the most beautiful forms of psychic consciousness in the world."

> But the higher one rises in the scale of mental activity, the rarer it becomes. For with intelligence come all the skill and cleverness, and corruption, calculation...when a rose blossoms it does so spontaneously...it does not calculate, it has nothing to gain out of it...[but] for a human being...the mo-

> ment his mind is active he tries to get some advantage out of his beauty and cleverness.

"Consequently," she continues, "from the psychic point of view, the rose is better than human beings."[151] We might see this hierarchy, then, from the point of view of the *guṇas*: on the one hand, flowers are thought to be without mental powers and so are *tamas*-bearing beings; but this state is consonant with having pure psychic consciousness which, at the same time, signifies the presence of *sattva*. Thus again, in another context, we find an argument that flowers/plants are at both extremes, at both borders of the living experience.

The psychic quality of flowers is expressed in two ways, in their silence and in their beauty.[152] The language of flowers is a language of silence, a language of "our inner communication:"

> Here is a process of transmutation, of stimulation... The flower is the active agent which accomplishes the aim... The mute message of the flower is neat, precise, often as sharp as a razor's edge.[153]

If it is through silence that flowers speak, it is through their visual beauty and fragrance that they attract us humans to the psychic: "Perhaps the beauty of flowers," says the Mother, "is a means used by Nature to awaken in human beings the attraction for the psychic."[154] And it is through both of these, the silence and the beauty of flowers, that we come to know the *sattva* quality of plants, for it "is through flowers that Nature expresses herself most harmoniously."[155]

The second important thing about plants for the Mother is their role in communication. "Flowers are the prayers of the vegetal kingdom,"[156] and flowers "speak to us when we know how to listen to them – it is a subtle and fragrant language."[157] Central to this view is that flowers are especially receptive, and they are especially receptive to the positive affection of human beings: "Flowers... are happy when they are loved."[158] The Mother says,

> I can transmit a state of consciousness more easily to a flower than to a man: it is very receptive, though it does not know how to formulate its experience to itself because it lacks a mind. But the pure psychic consciousness is instinctive to it. When, therefore, you offer flowers to me their condition is almost always an index to yours.[159]

The Mother understood flowers to be "mediums of transmission," and she "gave significances to almost nine hundred flowers," so that each flower is associated with a psychic prayer. As noted above, when some one gave her a flower the particular flower chosen was "almost always an index to" the condition of the giver, and when she gave a flower it was filled with an energy especially appropriate to the receiver.[160] The significances the Mother gave flowers are encapsulated in the spiritual names of the flowers. Each flower, she thought, has "a certain essence of a character,"[161] a very special vibration, "neither sensation nor a feeling, but something of both," and that "is how I have given a meaning to flowers and plants – there is a kind of identification with the vibration, a perception of the quality it represents."[162] "Through her interaction with them," the Mother gave names to flowers, "for instance, the marigold to her is the essence of plasticity, the rose is love," and calendulas are endurance.[163] In giving flowers, the Mother, says Narad, would match the flower to the person, "she would put the vibration into the flower that the person needed."[164] Other examples include the gladiolus which is known as "receptivity," the geranium as "spiritual happiness," and the sunflower as "consciousness turned towards the light;" the solitary pink rose brings "loving surrender," honeysuckle "constant remembrance of the divine," and sweet basil "the joy of union with the divine."

In my interviews with both Narad and June, an aroma therapist who works with flower oil distillations, and a follower of the teachings of Sri Aurobindo and the Mother, I asked questions that are raised about plants in traditional Hindu materials. Here are selections from their answers:

1. **Are plants living?** "Yes! In Auroville, that's just a given, that plants are living creatures. The members of the Auroville

community know that plants are living, first, from their experiences with plants in growing them and, second, based on the beliefs of Sri Aurobindo and the Mother" (June).

2. **Do plants have senses?** "I think they do, but in a different way than we think of them for ourselves" (June). They do not, according to Narad, "because the mental has not formed in them. It's a much more spontaneous aspiration even than human beings have because our minds get in the way."
3. **Do plants have consciousness?** "I do believe that plants are conscious and respond, and that there is a growing interaction between plants and human beings – here I'm going into my own view. I think there is a co-evolution, and increasingly a sort of interaction, between plants and humans. I think the people in Auroville who want to work with distilling the essences of plants or to do flower essences based on what Mother said about each flower, I think those people in Auroville do accept that," that plants have consciousness (June).
4. **Do plants feel pleasure and pain?** "Definitely. Definitely. They're transmitters also. Hundreds and hundreds of people a day would come to [the Mother]... and she would give them a flower, and she would say that she could more easily put the force that a person needed through the flower than through the mind, because the flower was such a medium" (Narad). "I think...[plants] do [feel pleasure and pain]. I think they react to thoughts or energy; they feel it and it shows, because they don't thrive, they die. Under normal conditions of living, if there's something in the environment that they experience negatively [they don't flourish]" (June).
5. **Can humans be reborn as a plant?** "No. The cycle of evolution always tends upwards. It's a spiral" (Narad). "I personally don't believe [in such rebirth]. Because I think of evolution...[People in the Auroville community] would probably say 'no.' I don't think that they would feel that you could be reborn as a plant. No" (June). Can a plant be reborn as an animal or human? "Not to my understanding because the form is more 'primitive,' if you don't mind my saying that. The capacity is not there in the flower for rebirth, but it is a symbol for aspiration" (Narad).
6. **Can there be conversations with plants?** "Yes! I have been in my garden and been told 'I don't like it here,' 'I want to be moved.' Or why am I not getting water,' 'I need food,' 'I need more attention.' Then I've also personally had this experience...where plant will exceed themselves... beyond what they're supposed to be. For example, plants are

> supposed to have this much sun, this much shade, in order to grow, but if you have a personal connection with them, they will exceed themselves...Being in aroma therapy...I find that they will teach you...the oils will say 'yes, this can be used for that' – and none of my books tell me that (June).[165]

Narad has also done substantial work on the trees in Auroville, growing them from seeds, nurturing them, and taking care of them as they have gotten mature. "I planted trees in the outer area of the gardens, which would be a kind of buffer zone between the city and the gardens in the Matrimandir and those trees, many of them, were the result of seed exchanges with more than 30 countries."[166] The Green Belt is now flourishing with tree after tree received from the Matrimandir Gardens nursery – and many of the trees are now towering giants: massive, kingly trees, full of flowers and fragrances. Current generations of gardeners have become very knowledgeable because of their work at Auroville, and their work is so good that bird and animal species counts are way up in the forested areas. "The planting of indigenous species and the return of the natural forest has been the aspiration and aim of those who have worked in the Green Belt since its inception." Many of the species collected from 1970 on are grown in the Matrimandir Garden Nursery specifically for the Green Belt, and "many of the species we planted were indigenous to South India, collected on visits to forest and jungles with some of the finest Conservators of Forests in the Indian Government." Some trees, however, come from other areas of the world with the same climactic condition.[167]

Narad believes that the two most sacred trees in the world today are The Service Tree over the Samadhi of Sri Aurobindo and the Mother, and the Banyan Tree at the center of Auroville.[168] "There's a large banyan tree which I just finished pruning with some other Aurovilians, and that's the geographic center of the city. Around the banyan tree will be the garden of unity, as the banyan represents unity."[169] Narad has special relationships with both trees. "Mother gave me the work of caring for the Service Tree for the rest of my life. It is an inestimable blessing carrying with it a great responsibility, and it is in this light and with the same sense of devotion that I speak of the Banyan Tree." Care for trees at Auroville is based on not using power tools, and coming to decisions out of much communal discussion before anything like pruning can start.[170]

For gardeners and flower workers at Auroville, then, flowers are part of a hierarchy, with plants at the bottom (for the most part), animals following, and humans beyond; and because this hierarchy is a spiral plants cannot be part of a system of rebirth. Since evolution tends upwards, humans cannot go "down" to a plant rebirth, and plants don't have the capability to be reborn "upwards" into human form. In this way, there is a species barrier between plants and humans. Plants and flowers are conscious, however, and can have feelings of pleasure and pain. Because plants and flowers do not have any mental powers, but have "aspiration" instead, they can be seen to be both *tamas*-bearing, that is, dull and dimwitted, and also *sattva*-bearing, that is, beyond thought, in accord with having pure psychic consciousness as might be found in an advanced spiritual state of humans. And, thus, Aurovillians support the view that flowers/plants are at both borders of the living experience. In addition, plants are natural communicators – as whole plants they let their caretakers know what they need, and as flowers they transmit messages that can heal and transform.

8.6 Karunamayi: Giving *Darśan* in the Forest

The final two examples of contemporary Hindu "plant-positive" activists are in fact not activists in the ordinary sense of the word. They are *gurvīs*, or female *gurus*, who are known internationally, and whose teachings imbibe traditional Hindu values about plants and encourage followers to be active agents in protecting and promoting plant culture. The first figure is Karunamayi Sri Sri Sri Vajayeswari Devi who is thought to be a manifestation of the goddess,[171] and is called by various combinations of Devi "goddess," Amma "mother" in Tamil, and Karunamayi "compassionate mother." She was born to a traditional family in south Indian in 1958, and her father followed the teachings of Ramakrishna Paramahansa, while her mother followed those of

Ramana Maharshi. Naturally drawn to doing good deeds for the impoverished and the needy as a child, she increasingly spent time in meditation and, in 1980, at the age of 21, she left home and traveled by foot to remote Penusila, "a sacred rural and tribal forest area in the South Indian state of Āndra Pradesh where many *rishis* have done *tapas* and a famed Narasimha temple is located."[172] In Penusila, she "would go to one of the forest's many sacred groves and remain there, absorbed in meditation for hours, days, or even weeks at a time." She sat so still and for so long a time that many of her devotees thought she was a statue.[173] Karunamayi stayed there in contemplation "for twelve years and then founded a holy āshram where countless devotees come to meditate."[174] Sometimes hard to find in the forest, Karunamayi sits in concentration there, receiving devotees who have searched her out in order to get *darśan*. A devotee is known to have said, "At last, we spotted Her on the other side of Shivalinga amidst the tender leaves."[175]

Karunamayi is open to the approach of all who come to her, as if they are on pilgrimage to Mt. Kailasha, and welcomes all to her regardless of caste or creed.[176] Many of her followers are farmers who live in rural areas and who make their livelihood planting seedlings in fields, so her teachings on compassion towards all living beings in nature are well suited to her audience.[177] Although her teachings are often given beneath a tree in the forest areas of Penusila, her programs might also include Vedic rituals around the sacrificial fire and recitations of mantras.[178]

Coming out of her decade long seclusion in the forest, Karunamayi was invited by a devotee to stay in Bangalore where she began giving teachings. These teachings attracted increasingly large numbers of people and, in time, she was able to bring medical care to the villagers of Penusila through free medical camps and a free hospital. In 1995, she was invited to come to the United States to give public teachings and has returned there ever since. She now divides her time among communities in India, the United States and Europe, though her home base remains the forest ashram in Penusila.

Karunamayi's own particular message is a compassion for all living things of the world, including plants. When asked how she could be here "for the entire world," and not just for human beings, she replied: "The sun is in the sky, but the rays of the sunlight is not for a single person. It is for the whole world that he shines. Similarly Karnunamayi is for every one." Karunamayi makes clear in her talks that she has come to this world out of compassion, in order to relieve the sufferings of those in need. That is, "She has descended *to console the suffering of the downtrodden and the needy as also these trees*," and other things in nature.[179]

> The richness of forest wealth of this Bharath (vana sampada) is enhanced by the wonderful medicinal herbs that are derived from the combination of sweetness of the particles of this earth and the effulgent energy of thousand of golden rays of...the Sun god. The trees on this land of Bharath are not ordinary trees – they are "Kalpa Vriksha" – wish fulfilling trees/divine trees. The sweetness beyond imagination and the Truth are reflected in all the trees, forests, animals and birds and in the entire Nature of Bharath.[180]

Her compassion towards plants in particular is reminiscent of the attitude of nonviolence shown to flora of all kind by Jain renunciants, and the care she takes not to harm even the smallest evidence of plant life marks the far boundary of the *karuṇā* of her name.

> Amma never plucks flowers because she feels the plants would be hurt by doing so. Once Amma stepped on a strand of grass without noticing. She could hear the strand crying of pain. Since then, She has never walked on the grass in Her life. This is the direct relationship. She shares with every living thing in the nature, which is impartial.[181]

Woven through her teachings are the kinds of plant-human homologies found, in particular, in early Buddhist texts, and that understand the tree the best model for ascetic behavior. For example, devotees say, "In this forest, whenever we see Karunamayi, she has been sitting unshaken, similar to [the] Goddess in the sanctum of the temple...She has been sitting undisturbed, day and night with closed eyes" – following the model of the stability of tree. Again, "the tall trees are standing still, undisturbed, like the rishis."[182] The text also homologies Karunamayi to a flower, especially the lotus, for in every way she is connected with the *lotus flower* – she is born in it, is seated in it, looks like it (her complexion, face, eyes, and feet), is fragrant like it, wanders wearing them, holds one in each hand, and is worshipped by means of them.[183] Probably the most pronounced aspect of her homology with the flower is her fragrance, which we understand to be the fragrance of the spiritually achieved.

> Karunamayi resembled that divine flower of Himalayan forests, which blossoms during the midnight...The entire atmosphere is filled with enchanting fragrance emanating from Karunamayi'ș body...The enchanting fragrance emanating from Karunamayi with sandal perfume, purified us and the air. A unique energy flowering from Karunamayi Devi, entered all our bodies.[184]

Very often, devotees notice something like the following, "we are getting the fragrance of sandal, tumeric and kumkum from Her, though She is far away from us,"[185] and this very experience of Karunamayi as one of extraordinarily wonderful fragrance is reflected in the spiritual life story of the devotee Mr. Durga Prasad Rao. Mr. Rao's original teacher was a great mendicant, who told him "Parabrahmamayi [Karunamayi Amma] will take you closer to Her by herself and bestow liberation to you." Just before his guru died, he told Mr. Rao that

> Brahmanamayi (Divine Mother) is taking incarnation. She will give you darshan, amidst dense forest, as Dakshinamurthi, under a peepal tree. The Goddess is coming down to earth on Vijayadashami day. She shall bestow the Motherly love and the Liberation to the mankind.

After his guru died, Mr. Rao went on a long tour of India, ending up in Madras. There he remembered the words of his guru to go to Tiruvannamalai where he would have a vision. And there, indeed, he did – a vision of Śiva's son – a vision marked by a fragrance: "What a fragrance?! No flower in this world has this fragrance." He continued seeking *darśan* of the Divine Mother, of Brahmamayi, of Amma, however, in forests and on mountain peaks, and came to think of her silence as "her language." Wanting *darśan* of the Mother when she wouldn't appear to him, he would say, "the Mother is playing hide and seek with us."[186] Eventually, he smelled a strange, soothing fragrance, and his spiritual friends "suddenly became silent without our knowledge. There was a large banyan tree. The Mother is seated under the tree!!"[187]

> My body is enjoying the vibration of real divinity acquired in Mother's presence...The "SELF" fragrance is flowering as the sun rays from the Ether...What a fragrance! This is not present in any of the flowers like lotus, rose, jasmine or in any of Her creation...She will give you darshan in the middle of the forest, under a banyan tree, as Dakshinamurthi personified.[188]

The focus on the flowery fragrance of the spiritual achievement of Karunamayi, on her giving *darśan* primarily in the forest among trees, and on her special compassion for even the smallest plants highlights the attention to plants common among her devotees. I interviewed three of them living in Fishkill, New York. The first two disciples, a couple, I interviewed together; they have been followers of Karunamayi for years, and she has been coming to their Fishkill community for at least nine years. "She is like a mother to all of us, and teaches us meditation and how to lead a good life. She is very fond of nature."[189] The wife is Shyama and the husband Satish B,[190] and below is a selection from their responses.

1. **Are plants living?** Yes, plants are living. Because when you see the plants or trees in full bloom – with flowers and fresh green leaves – then you know they have life. Seeing any dead plant, you will not find all those things: they are not green, they are brown, their lives are dying and falling (Shyama). They [also] have life [because] they can feel good and bad conditions. [They know] whatever you are doing, whatever you are not doing for them, the weather, and their surroundings, everything. So they have feelings. And they are living also because they can breathe (Shyama).
2. **What about the breathing of plants?** [We know plants breathe] because of the [response they have to] fresh air. You bring a plant in and close the room, where there's no air or light, then they die. When they're outside with fresh air, they are happy and in full bloom (Shyama).
3. **Do plants have senses, and which one(s)?** Yes they have senses. Otherwise, how will they feel all these things if they

don't have senses? If you see a dull or dying plant, sometimes if you go and talk to them, you *touch* them, care for them and gradually as days pass, you will see the change that they are coming back to life. Plants have some kind of sense, like the sunflower, which has the sense to follow the direction of the sun (Shyama). And also, with the varying seasons, they are changing, the plants take care of themselves. At night [the flowers] close [which tells us] that they are living, and that they have feelings (Satish).

4. **What feelings do plants have?** If we think that we, and they, are the same, then they are the same kind of feelings (Shyama). They feel in their own way *as we do* (Satish). Yes, Yes. Oh, yes! [Plants can feel pleasure and pain] (Shyama).
5. **Are plants conscious of what they feel?** I'll give you a very good instance. Sri Karunamayi, 'Amma,' got a plant from the mountains and planted it in her Ashram. And it was a flowering plant. Now that plant, somehow it flowered only once in the year, on a particular day, which is when we celebrate and honor our teacher (Guru). So, just on that day, it would flower and not any time else. So it must have feelings or some senses to know when to flower (Satish).
6. **Do plants have consciousness?** You can see the plants and leaves moving from the wind and, if you are happy, you say, "Oh, they are moving with happiness, they are dancing with happiness"...Because any time in the morning, you see the plants and all the flowers moving happily, and they are looking at the sun, you imagine "Oh, they are looking with happiness." Maybe it's like if we are happy, we see everything happy. If we are sad, then we say even the trees are crying (Shyama). [That's what we are projecting on to the trees?] Yes, Yes. Amma always says that nature and we, we are the same (Shyama).
7. **Are plants aware of their environment?** Oh, yes! Definitely, you can see plants outside and inside. In a closed room, in a dark room, they won't do well. Once they are out they grow fast and start to bloom. So they can sense and imagine anything (Shyama).
8. **Can we hear plants speaking?** Amma will never walk on the grass, because once she was walking and she said she heard grass crying. So, when you think of living persons – that you will hear them when they cry – same thing with plants or anything. So Amma will never pluck a flower. Some people will talk to the vegetable and flower plants every morning, and we have seen at a friend's house that those plants are blooming beautifully (Shyama). The plants really

don't talk back. Probably they respond in their own way by doing better, growing better (Satish).

9. **Amma's view of nature.** She loves nature. She goes out, and she will sit in a garden, or on a bench under some tree. She finds it peaceful, and enabling to calm her mind. There she can meditate for hours. Watching someone burn or cut a tree, she feels sad and cries (Shyama).
10. **Do plants participate in *karma*?** *Karma*. I will think, that if the plants are in a nice place, like in some ashram or some secret place, we think, "Oh, these plants are lucky." Because like the plants that grew for Amma once a year, we think "Oh, that plant is a lucky plant." If you believe in *karma*, it has good *karma* in a past life. And if it's like in the old days, in the jungle or any place that is not so good, we think "Oh what a place," [it is from] bad *karma*. We say, "It's a good plant, but what it's doing here when all the surroundings are so bad?" We don't know, we cannot say for sure that we can be reborn as an ant or a dog or a cat. It's a story, but we don't know [if humans can be reborn as plants]. We don't know about any of our rebirths. No one can say about our previous births, as some tree or as anything. What we can say is that, "plant is plant, stone is stone" (Shyama).[191]

In summary, this couple believes that plants are alive because they grow and breathe. Plants are aware of and respond to their environment, and have senses, but it's unclear which distinct senses they have. And plants feel pleasure and pain. The two are unclear about whether the *karma* system is at work at all and, if at work, whether it includes plants, though they are quite willing to thing of a plant's circumstances as lucky or unlucky. And following the story of Karunamayi, the two believe humans can hear plants speak.

The third "informant," Kameshwar, is not himself a disciple of Amma Karunamayi's, but runs in her "circle." He is a retired professor of botany and plant diseases in India, also now living in Fishkill, New York. Kameshwar believes that plants are living insofar as they show the characteristics of living beings, i.e., movement, growth, reproduction, and respiration. Plants are made of cells "which have got protoplasm which is a living entity" and, in that the protoplasm can be damaged or destroyed (through heat or an agent entering the cell), then so can the tissue, and then so can the plant. (Thus, plants can be affected by violence.) He understands plants to have "a sense of perception," insofar as, though

> fixed in the ground...they show movements by their roots in the ground and by their upward growth in the atmosphere. And then in certain plants there are tendrils...[which] try to reach such places where they can get a support and, when they get a support, they die down those supports and the plant is able to stand up and live and prosper.

With regard to the senses, he believes that it is through "their perception of taste that...[plants] are able to take up water from their roots, and then the water gets evaporated from the stem or the leaves." Plants "are also sensitive to experience pain, for when a plant is cut or is starved – no water is given – it wilts. But as soon as you give it water, it is upright."[192] While it is not altogether clear what particular senses plants have, "they can perceive. They have tendrils (and, though) they can't see, just by perception there is something in that plant that these tendrils always try to reach their goal." This would be like Aurovillians saying plants have "aspiration"–to reach up for the light, to reach out to establish themselves in space, and through their roots "to reach and grow for that in search of water." Concerning the word "perception," Kameshwar says "perception is the sense that they try to reach their objects, if they feel the necessity of that." Plants have "perception" in that "we can say they react to the environment and that reaction is due to some perception or feeling which they have." On the question of *karma*, he notes, "I can't tell you about it; this is a difficult question...I'm not against anything that is believed, but somehow I have not paid any attention to these things."

8.7 Ammachi: Restoring the Lost Harmony of Humans and Nature

Mata Amritanandamayi, or as she is more affectionately known, Ammachi (the Malayalam version of Sanskrit/Hindi Mataji), was born as Sudhamani "into a poor, low-caste family in a rural fishing village," Parayakadavu in the Quilon district of Kerala in 1953.[193]

She attended school up through the fourth grade, but soon had to remain at home full time to care for her ailing mother.[194] During this early time, she was absorbed in Krishna worship, often breaking out in devotional songs and manifesting the presence of Krishna himself in her body. She could also become withdrawn and absorbed by meditation, "slipping into God-intoxicated states."[195] A shift took place in her spiritual career, however, when, still young, she followed "the inner call to manifest the Devi *bhava*...the mood of the divine Mother."

> In the months following the inner call...Ammachi adopted the Devi *bhava* in addition to the Krishna *bhava*. The devotees...believed that "she had now merely become possessed by Devi as well as Krishna." Since then Ammachi has only been manifesting the Devi *bhava*.[196]

As her spiritual fame spread, so also did the stories of her miraculous powers, but the center of her ministry became her power to "directly induce God-realization." In 1979, two westerners joined her and her circle of devotees began to grow. In May 1981, she established her formal ashram as Amritapuri in Kerala, and it often has over a thousand people in residence, including *sannyāsīs* and *sannyāsiṇīs* (male and female renunciants), *brahmacārīs* and *brahmacāriṇīs* (male and female aspirants), and many short-term visitors. In 1987, her disciples from the United States invited her to visit and, in 1989, she established her first U.S. ashram in San Ramon, California, called Mata Amritanandamayi Center or MA Center. From here, her movement became a worldwide phenomenon with a network of charitable organizations and a spiritual community that is broad and diverse, with ashrams in North and South America, Europe, Australia, and Africa.[197]

Like Karunamayi, Ammachi was never herself initiated by a guru, but her own followers revere her as a *satguru,* "a true and perfect spiritual master." She describes herself "as a compassionate guru guiding her devotees to god-realization," the gradual awakening of one's own inherent divinity that comes about by cultivating attachment to the *satguru* – that attachment being "both the means and ends to the spiritual quest."[198] She describes her teaching and disciplining role to her disciples using the metaphor of a garden.

> I am like a gardener. The garden is full of colorful flowers. I was not asked to look after the beautiful flowers...but I have been asked to remove the insects and worms from pest-ridden flowers and plants. To remove the insects I may have to pinch the petals and leaves which is painful, but it is only to save the plants and flowers from destruction.[199]

Ammachi is not only a *satguru*, but also a self-recognized and self-professed embodiment of the goddess and, "in her weekly Devi *bhava* where she assumes the goddess mood or form," one of the most unusual forms of *ḍarśan* is the "spiritual hug," something Ammachi does, on average, "to over a thousand devotees a day."[200]

> She speaks through her eyes, reaching out to embrace each astonished American or Australian or Swede who shuffles forward, rubbing our backs and slipping us chocolate Kissess.[201]

This communication between Ammachi and her devotees is a "language of the heart" just as a child and mother communicate with each other; nothing need be said between them for in "this ritual idiom, the message, the medium, and the messenger and her charisma are rolled into one."[202] And like Karunamayi, part of Ammachi's charisma is her "holy fragrance," attested to by Linda Johnsen who noticed it while she herself was sleeping and who found that it permeated "every room in the house" where they stayed.[203]

Some of Ammachi's teachings focus on nature and, in particular, on reclaiming the lost balance and harmony that had originally been between humans and the natural world. This idea comes naturally to Ammachi who, in her early years, might have been described as an *avadhūta*, "someone totally beyond this world...crazy."

> You used to find Mother lying in the backwaters in Kerala, in the water and mud, or dancing under the trees at night. She would eat off the ground, whatever anyone would give her...Many times she'd be sitting out in the sun in *samadhi*

> and it would start raining – you know the tremendous monsoon rain – and she wouldn't move.[204]

Of her philosophy, Sam La Budde notes that Ammachi believes that nature is God in visible form: "Nature is nothing but God's visible form which we can behold and experience through our senses."[205]

> Although many people believe that man was meant to conquer Nature, in attempting to do so we have become our own worst enemy. We are a part of Nature. Her continued capacity to protect and nurture depends on our ability to re-establish a balance in our relation to the Earth and all its creatures.[206]

In this way, human beings and nature are not separate or different. Humans are a part of nature, and they depend on nature for their very existence.[207] When there are problems, then, the "destruction of Nature is the same things as the destruction of humanity. Trees, animals, birds, plants, forests, mountains, lakes and rivers– everything that exists in nature."[208]

Although Ammachi here cites many parts of nature, most often nature is symbolized by reference to trees and plants. The centrality of trees is found often in her text *Man and Nature*. For example, "Trees and plants...are absolutely necessary for the purification of vital energy (the life force)," necessary for the purification of the atmosphere, without which human life span would decrease, there would be more disease, poor eyesight, blindness.[209] Moreover, as in traditional Hindu materials, the tree is the part of nature most singled out as giving service to humans: "Look at a tree. It gives shade even to the person who cuts it down. It gives its sweet, delicious fruits to the person who harms it."[210]

The situation today is alarming, however, for "Nature's calamities are greatly increasing. Nature has commenced Her dance of final dissolution. She has lost her balance owing to the unrighteous actions perpetrated against Her by humans."[211] Human beings no longer care about nature and, having turned against her, are more interested in exploiting and polluting her than in caring for her. And the reason humans are estranged from nature is their selfishness.[212]

> our [contemporary] attitude is completely different. When we plant a tree...we are only concerned about the profit we will make from it...If a tree stops yielding fruit, we will cut it down and make furniture or something else from it. Selfishness reigns supreme.[213]

For Ammachi, the solution is compassion along with the use of religious rituals: "compassion will arise, and we will sincerely wish to help and protect all. In that state, we won't feel like plucking even a leaf unnecessarily. We will pick a flower only on the last day of its existence, before it falls from the stem,"[214] rather than on the first day when we act out of greed. Religious rites are important, Ammachi says, because they help bring the balance of humans and nature back into harmony.

> The Ancients loved and worshipped trees and plants, such as the banyan tree, bilva and tulasi, not because the trees bore fruit and helped them to make a profit, but because the ancients knew that they themselves in truth were one with all of Nature...[they] knew that trees, plants...were absolutely necessary for the benefit and good of humans. They foresaw that man, in his selfish moments, would forget Nature...They also knew that future generations would suffer, due to man's disassociation from Nature. They therefore linked each religious rite with Nature.[215]

Because religious practices establish a caring attitude between humans and nature, a harmonious balance is then ensured. Religious rites for nature, that is, for trees, might include watering the plant every day, bowing down with reverence in front of it, and "worshipping it as an embodiment of the Goddess."[216] Ammachi notes that there are five daily rituals for the Hindu householder: worship of God, adoration of the sages, showing respect to parents and departed ancestors, giving service to mankind, especially those in need, and service to all living beings *(bhūta yajña),* in particular, animals and plants – through this last there arises a consciousness of the unity of life.[217] What Ammachi urges, then, is to use nature judiciously: use only what you need and no more.

Endnotes :

1 Gadgil and Guha, *Ecology and Equity*, p. 148.
2 Gadgil and Guha, *Ecology and Equity*, p. 155.
3 Gadgil and Guha, *Ecology and Equity*, pp. 155-161.
4 http://www.teriin.org/terragreen/issue27/feature.htm
5 Narayanan, "One Tree Is Equal to Ten Sons," pp. 301-302.
6 Vartan, "Half the World is Women," p. 36.
7 http://amritabhoomi-sep-1.8m.net/index.html
8 Dwivedi, "Vedic Heritage for Environmental Stewardship, " pp. 34-36. Dwivedi's italics.
9 Dwivedi, "Environmental Stewardship," pp. 177-179.
10 Dwivedi, "Our Karma and Dharma to the Environment," p. 63.
11 Dwivedi, "Our Karma and Dharma to the Environment," pp. 63, 64.
12 The Chipko Movement has historical precedent among the Bishnoi community of Rajasthan. "Three hundred years ago more than 300 members of the Bishnoi community in Rajasthan, led by a woman named Amrita Devi, sacrificed their lives to save their sacred *khejri* trees by clinging to them. With that event begins the recorded history of Chipko;" Shiva, *Staying Alive*, p. 67; Rangan, *Of Myths and Movements*, p. 33; Weber, *Hugging the Trees*, pp. 91-94; Agarwal, "Can Hindu Beliefs and Values Help India Meet Its Ecological Crisis,?" p. 170-171.
13 Guha, "The Malign Encounter: The Chipko Movement," p. 83.
14 Guha, "The Malign Encounter: The Chipko Movement," p. 83. For further discussion of Guha and Gadgil's work see Sivaramakrishnan, "Colonialism and Forestry in India," pp. 20-28.
15 Weber, *Hugging the Trees*, p. 31.
16 See Guha, "The Malign Encounter: The Chipko Movement," pp. 90-91.
17 For a full description of this event, see Guha, *The Unquiet Woods*, pp. 72-79.
18 Weber, *Hugging the Trees*, pp. 17-32.
19 Shepard, *Gandhi Today*, p. 66.
20 Guha, "The Malign Encounter: The Chipko Movement," p. 97; Guha, *The Unquiet Woods*, pp. 153-154.
21 Weber, *Hugging the Trees*, p. 34; see pp. 33-34.

22 Guha, "The Malign Encounter: The Chipko Movement," p. 98.

23 Weber, *Hugging the Trees*, pp. 35-37.

24 Guha, *The Unquiet Woods*, pp. 155-156.

25 Weber, *Hugging the Trees*, pp. 35-37.

26 Weber, *Hugging the Trees*, p. 38.

27 Guha, "The Malign Encounter: The Chipko Movement," p. 98.

28 Rangan, *Of Myths and Movements*, pp. 22-26. Chandri Prasad Bhatt and Sundarlal Bahuguna have different approaches. While "Bahaguna sought a total ban on green felling and the preservation of the forest for traditional subsistence use such as gathering of fuel and fodder," Bhatt's "'appropriate technology' group...sought [simply] a less destructive use of the forest based on local sawmill cooperatives;" Akula, "Grassroots Environmental Resistance in India," p. 133. Guha notes that for Bahuguna, operating in a "prophetic mode" and active in the Bhageerathi Valley, the problem is "the anthropocentric view of nature intrinsic to modern industrial civilization," with the cure being to revert back from a contemporary materialistic culture that "makes man the butcher of Earth." Bhatt, operating in a "reconstruction mode" and active in the Alakananda Valley, however, "does not deny the villagers' role in deforestation" but stresses the importance of overcoming the separation of "the local population from the management of the forest wealth;" "The Malign Encounter: the Chipko Movement," pp. 90-91 102; Guha, *The Unquiet Woods*, pp. 179-184.

29 Weber, *Hugging the Trees*, pp. 39-40.

30 Weber, *Hugging the Trees*, pp. 40-41.

31 Rangan, *Of Myths and Movements*, pp. 5, 20. The word *chipko* is a verb in both Hindi and Garhwali "used by village communities living near forested areas of Chamoli district in Garhwal in 1973 for a particular set of actions that involved people hugging trees."

32 Shiva, *Staying Alive*, p. 73.

33 Weber, *Hugging the Trees*, pp. 42-43. See also, Guha, *The Unquiet Woods*, pp. 157-158.

34 The argument can be made that the platform for the organization of women in Chipko had already been provided by the earlier fight against the consumption of alcohol among women spearheaded, by among others, Sundarlal Bahuguna. See http://www.unu.edu/unupress/unupbooks/80a03e/80A03E08.htm

35 Shepard, *Gandhi Today*, p. 75.

36 Weber, *Hugging the Trees*, pp. 45-46.

37 Kumar, *You Are, Therefore I Am*, p. 167.

[38] Weber, *Hugging the Trees*, pp. 45-46. Says Guha:

The widespread participation of women in Chipko has been frequently commented upon. Women have always played an important role in local economic life, and their involvement in Chipko has clearly been influenced by the impact of recent economic changes in intensifying their dependence on the natural environment.

"The Malign Encounter: The Chipko Movement," p. 101. See, especially, Shiva, *Staying Alive*, pp. 67-77; and Agarwal, "Can Hindu Beliefs and Values Help Meet Its Ecological Crisis,?" pp. 165-166.

[39] http://spot.colorado.edu/wehr/49R10.TXT

[40] See also Barbara Bash's *In the Heart of the Village: The World of the Indian Banyan Tree.*

[41] Guha, *The Unquiet Woods*, p. 168.

[42] Weber, *Hugging the Trees*, p. 86.

[43] http://www.fov.org.uk/hinduism/11.html

[44] Rangan, *Of Myths and Movements*, p. 28.

[45] Rangan, *Of Myths and Movements*, pp. 31.

[46] http://www.fov.org.uk/hinduism/11.html

[47] Weber, *Hugging the Trees*, pp. 89-90.

[48] Shiva, "The Chipko Women's Concept of Freedom," p. 247.

[49] Rangan, *Of Myths and Movements*, pp. 24, 25.

[50] Rangan, *Of Myths and Movements*, p. 27.

[51] http://www.mtnforum.org/resources/library/pirtr00b.htm

[52] Rangan, *Of Myths and Movements*, p. 26.

[53] Shepard, *Gandhi Today*, p. 79.

[543] 0 Prime, *Vedic Ecology*, p. 122. A good discussion of the religious aspects of the Chipko Movement can be found in James, "Ethical and Religious Dimensions of Chipko Resistance," pp. 499-530.

[55] Prime, *Vedic Ecology*, pp. 124-125.

[56] Rangan, *Of Myths and Movements*, p. 26.

[57] Rangan, *Of Myths and Movements*, p. 32.

[58] Shiva, *Tomorrow's Biodiversity*, p. 6.

[59] Prime, *Vedic Ecology*, pp. 128-129.

[60] Shiva, *Staying Alive*, p. 67.

[61] Rangan notes that, based on the "feminine principle," Shiva draws a connection among women, nature, and the earth. He quotes her as saying, women "in India are an intimate part of nature both in imagination and in practice. At one level nature is symbolized as the embodiment of the feminine principle, and at another, she is

nurtured by the feminine to produce life and provide sustenance;" *Of Myths and Movements*, p. 32.

[62] Prime, *Vedic Ecology*, pp. 129-130.

[63] Shiva, *Tomorrow's Biodiversity*, p. 8.

[64] Shiva, *Stolen Harvest*, p. 1.

[65] Shiva, *Stolen Harvest*, p. 8.

[66] Shiva, *Tomorrow's Biodiversity*, p. 28.

[67] Shiva, *Biopiracy*, p. 24.

[68] Shiva, *Stolen Harvest*, p. 16.

[69] Shiva, *Stolen Harvest*, p. 10.

[70] Shiva, *Biopiracy*, p. 22.

[71] Shiva, *Stolen Harvest*, p. 8.

[72] Shiva, *Stolen Harvest*, p. 3.

[73] Shiva, *Tomorrow's Biodiversity*, p. 132.

[74] Shiva, *Stolen Harvest*, p. 89. The revolution in biotechnology applied to plants supplanted, in India, the Green Revolution. In which the "crossbreeding of different varieties to make them more resistant to chemicals was a departure from the earlier centuries of plant breeding based on farmers' knowledge;" Shiva, *Tomorrow's Biodiversity*, p. 54. "While the Green Revolution was based on the assumption that the earth is inert," however, "the biotechnology revolution robs the seed of its fertility and self-regenerative capabilities;" Shiva, *Biopiracy*, p. 49; see p. 107.

[75] Shiva, *Stolen Harvest*, pp. 102.

[76] Shiva, *Tomorrow's Biodiversity*, p. 40.

[77] Shiva, *Biopiracy*, p. 70. For a selected list of plant products and patents taken out on them, see also http://www.vshiva.net/biodiversity/pirate.htm

[78] Prime, *Vedic Ecology*, p. 130.

[79] Shiva, *Tomorrow's Biodiversity*, p. 43; *Stolen Harvest*, p. 79. On the fight against the biopiracy of basmati rice, see http://search.netscape.com nscp_results.adp?start=11&first=9&nav=next&

[80] Shiva, *Tomorrow's Biodiversity*, p. 44.

[81] Shiva, *Biopiracy*, p. 123. My italics.

[82] Shiva, *Tomorrow's Biodiversity*, p. 10.

[83] Shiva, *Biopiracy*, p. 5.

[84] Prime, *Vedic Ecology*, p. 130.

[85] Shiva, *Stolen Harvest*, p. 3; see *Biopiracy*, pp. 124-126.

[86] Shiva, *Biopiracy*, p. 57.

[87] Shiva, *Tomorrow's Biodiversity*, p. 137.

[88] Shiva, *Biopiracy*, p. 39.

[89] Shiva, *Stolen Harvest*, pp. 120-121.

[90] Shiva, *Biopiracy*, p. 126.

[91] Shiva, *Stolen Harvest*, pp. 120-121.

[92] Shiva, *Biopiracy*, p. 99. Mark Shepard describes an earlier initiative known as Agrindus (short for "agroindustrial") in the south-eastern tip of Uttar Pradesh. The region is hilly and forested, with about four hundred villages, and with a population of mostly *adivasis* ("a native tribal people found in many parts of India and making up about 7 percent of India's population") who lived off the wild produce of the forests. As modernization — e.g., government presence and imported workers — infiltrated on *adivasi* life, the forests became depleted and the local people had to turn to farming. With poor farm land and few farming skills, however, the *adivasis* experienced recurrent famine. The Gandhian based Agrindus then began programs of training in farm, seed, and water management — but, in hindsight, leaders say that the "achievement of Agrindus and similar development projects was to bring the Green Revolution to the village poor...perhaps this was a mixed blessing." Shepard, *Gandhi Today*, pp. 105-109.

[93] Shiva, *Tomorrow's Biodiversity*, p. 131.

[94] Shiva, *Tomorrow's Biodiversity*, pp. 133-134. One of the ways that Jaiv Panchayats work to protect their local biodiversity is to send petitions of protest to companies involved in patents of plants like neem. For examples of the letters, or "notices served to biopirates," that have been sent, see http://www.ratical.org/co-globalize/BPandWTO.html

[95] Shiva, *Stolen Harvest*, pp. 5, 12.

[96] Shiva, *Biopiracy*, p. 43.

[97] Shiva, *Stolen Harvest*, p. 17.

[98] Shiva, *Biopiracy*, p. 68.

[99] Kumar, *You Are, Therefore I Am*, p. 169.

[100] Prime, *Vedic Ecology*, p. 133.

[101] Shiva, *Stolen Harvest*, p. 119.

[102] Prime, *Vedic Ecology*, pp. 132-134.

[103] Prime, *Vedic Ecology*, p. 142.

[104] Prime, *Vedic Ecology*, pp. 142-145.

[105] Prime, *Vedic Ecology*, p. 146; see Agarwal, "Can Hindu Beliefs and Values Help India Meet Its Ecological Crisis,?" pp. 169-170.

[106] http://www.fov.org.uk/contact/contact.html

[107] Prime, *Vedic Ecology*, p. 150.

[108] http://www.fov.org.uk/contact/contact.html

[109] Prime, *Vedic Ecology*, p. 151.

[110] Sullivan, "Paradise Polluted: Religious Dimensions of the *Vrindāvana* Ecology Movement," p. 568.

[111] Prime, *Vedic Ecology*, pp. 151-152.

[112] Prime, *Vedic Ecology*, p. 152. See below for a discussion of the efforts by Trees for Life, a program promoted in India by Friends of Vrindavan in partnership with Food for Life.

[113] Sullivan, "Paradise Polluted: Religious Dimensions of the *Vrindāvana* Ecology Movement," p. 568.

[114] Sullivan, "Paradise Polluted: Religious Dimensions of the *Vrindāvana* Ecology Movement," p. 569.

[115] Sullivan, "Paradise Polluted: Religious Dimensions of the *Vrindāvana* Ecology Movement," p. 565.

[116] http://www.fov.org.uk/contact/contact.html

[117] Balbir Mathur, the founder of Trees For Life, routinely reminds people that this initiative is "not an organization but a movement," an open-ended process that will spread one person at a time, one tree at a time, until everyone has enough to eat.

[118] Sahu, *Dancing with a Dusty Angel*, p. 16.

[119] Prime, *Vedic Ecology*, p. 116.

[120] Email correspondence with Balbir Mathur, April 28, 2005.

[121] Prime, *Vedic Ecology, pp*. 109-111.

[122] Prime, *Vedic Ecology*, pp. 109-111.

[123] Robbins, "Kansas Man Sows Seeds of Dream."

[124] Prime, *Vedic Ecology*, p. 111.

[125] Mathur personal interviews, Trees For Life, taped June 27-28, 2003.

[126] Prime, *Vedic Ecology*, p. 111.

[127] Prime, *Vedic Ecology*, p. 112.

[128] Mathur personal interviews, Trees For Life, taped June 27-28-2003.

[129] Prime, *Vedic Ecology*, p. 113. The holy man agreed to bless the trees only on the condition that Mathur was doing this not with the thought of other people's benefit or of his own benefit, but, as in the Bhagavad Gita, as an act without any consequences. "Only such as act can be free of karma, and consequently completely selfless."

[130] Prime, *Vedic Ecology*, p. 115.

[131] Prime, *Vedic Ecology*, pp. 114-117.

[132] Mathur personal interviews, Trees For Life, taped June 27-28, 2003.

[133] I omit last names for privacy.

[134] Satish C., to distinguish him from Satish B., below.

[135] Praveen personal interview, Trees For Life, taped June 28, 2003.

[136] http://www.sriaurobindosociety.org.in/subnav/aurovil.htm

[137] Johnsen, *Daughters of the Goddess*, p. 22; The Mother, *Flowers and Their Messages*, p. 309.

[138] The Mother, *Flowers and Their Messages*, p. 309; see also the website http://www.sriaurobindosociety.org.in/subnav/aurovil.htm

[139] http://www.sriaurobindosociety.org.in/subnav/aurovil.htm

[140] Narad phone interview, Auroville, taped March 21, 2004.

[141] Narad phone interview, Auroville, taped March 21, 2004.

[142] Narad, *Auroville, Today*, March 2004.

[143] The Mother, *Flowers and Their Messages*, pp. i-ii.

[144] Narad phone interview, Auroville, taped March 21, 2004.

[145] The Mother, *Flowers and Their Messages*, pp. 1, 301. Aspiration, as the "push towards light," moves from a material image to a spiritual one in this way:

Plants have more of...[this push towards light] in their physical being than men. Their whole life is a worship of light. Light is of course the material symbol of the Divine, and the sun represents, under material conditions, the Supreme Consciousness. The plants have felt it quite distinctly in their own simple, blind way. Their aspiration is intense, if you know how to become aware of it.

[146] Narad phone interview, Auroville, taped March 21. 2004. Says the Mother: "Flowers lift towards the sky their fragrant prayer and aspiration...By communing with flowers we can see that the vegetal kingdom has her own way of aspiring towards the Divine;" *Flowers and Their Messages*, p. 146.

[147] The Mother, *Flowers and Their Messages*, p. vii.

[148] Narad phone interview, Auroville, taped March 21, 2004.

[149] The Mother, *Flowers and Their Messages*, p. vii.

[150] Vijay, *Flowers — Their Spiritual Significance*, p. 79.

[151] Vijay, *Flowers — Their Spiritual Significance*, p. 8.

[152] The Mother, *Flowers and Their Messages*, p. 154.

[153] Vijay, *Flowers — Their Spiritual Significance*, p. 18.

[154] The Mother, *Flowers and Their Messages*, p. vii.

[155] The Mother, *Flowers and Their Messages*, p. 55.

[156] The Mother, *Flowers and Their Messages*, p. 252.

[157] The Mother, *Flowers and Their Messages*, p. 197.

[158] The Mother, *Flowers and Their Messages*, p. 104.

[159] The Mother, *Flowers and Their Messages*, p. ix.

[160] Narad phone interview, Auroville, taped March 21, 2004.

[161] June phone interview, Auroville, taped February 16, 2004.
[162] Vijay, *Flowers — Their Spiritual Significance*, p. 11.
[163] June phone interview, Auroville, taped February 16, 2004.
[164] Narad phone interview, Auroville, taped March 21, 2004.
[165] June phone interview, Auroville, taped February 16, 2004; Narad phone interview, Auroville, taped March 21, 2004.
[166] Narad phone interview, Auroville, taped March 21, 2004.
[167] Narad, *Auroville Today*, March 2004.
[168] Narad, *Auroville Today*, March 2004.
[169] Narad phone interview, Auroville, taped March 21, 2004.
[170] Narad, *Auroville Today*, March 2004.
[171] Swami Vijayeswarananda, *Karunasāgari: The Ocean of Compassion*, p. 4. The only diacritical used in this text is *ā*.
[172] Swami Vijayeswarananda, *Karunasāgari: The Ocean of Compassion*, pp. 184-185.
[173] www.karunamayi.org
[174] Swami Vijayeswarananda, *Karunasāgari: The Ocean of Compassion*, pp. 184-185.
[175] Swami Vijayeswarananda, *Karunasāgari: The Ocean of Compassion*, pp. 3, 21, 25.
[176] Swami Vijayeswarananda, *Karunasāgari: The Ocean of Compassion*, pp. 6, 9, 36-37.
[177] Swami Vijayeswarananda, *Karunasāgari: The Ocean of Compassion*, p. 81.
[178] Swami Vijayeswarananda, *Karunasāgari: The Ocean of Compassion*, pp. 10, 8.
[179] Swami Vijayeswarananda, *Karunasāgari: The Ocean of Compassion*, p. 23. My italics.
[180] Swami Vijayeswarananda, *Karunasāgari: The Ocean of Compassion*, p. 136.
[181] Swami Vijayeswarananda, *Karunasāgari: The Ocean of Compassion*, p. 59.
[182] Swami Vijayeswarananda, *Karunasāgari: The Ocean of Compassion*. p. 23.
[183] Swami Vijayeswarananda, *Karunasāgari: The Ocean of Compassion*, p. 17.
[184] Swami Vijayeswarananda, *Karunasāgari: The Ocean of Compassion*, p. 25.
[185] Swami Vijayeswarananda, *Karunasāgari: The Ocean of Compassion*, p. 24.

[186] In an article in *Hinduism Today*, "Personal Peace Leads to Universal Peace," Karunamayi states that: "Language is for sharing feelings with each other in this world. But in absolute silence is the connection with the entire universe without any disturbance...holy people...transmit their feelings in silence. Silence is the language of Divinity. I like silence very much;" *Hinduism Today*, January 1997. And in "The Language of Silence," from *Yoga International*, Karunamayi says,

[Silence, the absence of sound, gives you divine energy and refreshes you. Silence gives immortality, peace, divine strength. There is great power in our silence. In silence we hear the inner voice of the soul...When we have absolute silence inside, no force coming from the external environment will ever affect us, because we will be surrounded by the spiritual power of our meditation.]

[187] Swami Vijayeswarananda, *Karunasāgari: The Ocean of Compassion*, pp. 87-114.

[188] Swami Vijayeswarananda, *Karunasāgari: The Ocean of Compassion*, pp. 113–115.

[189] Shyama and Satish B. phone interview, Karunamayi community, taped February 16, 2004.

[190] Satish B. is to distinguish him from Satish C., who was interviewed from Trees For Life.

[191] Shyama and Satish B. phone interview, Karunamayi community, taped February 16, 2004. My italics.

[192] Kameshwar phone interview, Karunamayi community, taped February 22, 2004. From contemporary scientific studies, Kameshwar knows of certain experiments testing plants on their reception of vibrations from various kinds of music. The studies show, in general, that plants prospered and flourished with music. Kameshwar agreed: "Yes! They became better and the production was also up/higher." On the implications for senses, he believes that in addition to the sense of taste, plants might have the senses of touch and of hearing, but perhaps not sight and smell.

[193] Raj, "Ammachi, the Mother of Compassion," pp. 206-207.

[194] Johnsen, *Daughters of the Goddess*, p. 95. Unlike Karunamayi, then, who completed high school and one year of college, Ammachi had little formal schooling.

[195] See www.amma.org

[196] Raj, "Ammachi, the Mother of Compassion," pp. 206-207. ["On Devi *bhava* nights, Ammachi is believed to reveal her identity as the divine Mother, according to her devotees, in certain visible physical changes in her person,

most notable among these being the change in her facial hue; her face is believed to turn bluish."]

197 Raj, "Ammachi, the Mother of Compassion," pp. 205-209.

198 Raj, "Ammachi, the Mother cf Compassion," pp. 210-211.

199 Raj, "Ammachi, the Mother of Compassion," p. 211.

200 Raj, "Ammachi, the Mother of Compassion," p. 212.

Devotees are...instructed to wipe their face with a tissue and/or remove facial make-up. After these instructions, devotees are individually ushered before Ammachi...[who] receives the devotee into her bosom in loving spiritual embrace, applies sandal paste on the devotee's forehead, hugs and kisses the devotee, frequently stroking the devotee's head, neck, chest, spine, or back and whispering the words "Amma, Amma" and "my darling son" or "my darling daughter." As the devotee rises to leave, Ammachi looks directly into the eyes and pulls him/her unto herself once more and lavishes another round of kisses.

201 Johnsen, *Daughters of the Goddess*, pp. 97-98.

202 Raj, "Ammachi, the Mother of Compassion," p. 213.

203 Johnsen, *Daughters of the Goddess*, p. 107.

204 Johnsen, *Daughters of the Goddess*, pp. 103-104.

205 Sri Sri Mata, *Man and Nature*, p. 23.

206 La Budde is Director of the Endangered Species Project, Earth Island Institute, San Francisco; Sri Sri Mata, *Man and Nature*, p. 6.

207 Sri Sri Mata, *Man and Nature*, p. 10.

208 Sri Sri Mata, *Man and Nature*, p. 20.

209 Sri Sri Mata, *Man and Nature*, p. 10.

210 Sri Sri Mata, *Man and Nature*, p. 12.

211 Sri Sri Mata, *Man and Nature*, p. 25.

212 Sri Sri Mata, *Man and Nature*, pp. 27, 11.

213 Sri Sri Mata, *Man and Nature*, pp. 12-13.

214 Sri Sri Mata, *Man and Nature*, pp. 21-22.

215 Sri Sri Mata, *Man and Nature*, p. 13.

216 Sri Sri Mata, *Man and Nature*, pp. 12, 14.

217 Sri Sri Mata, *Man and Nature*, pp. 15-16.

9
Jainism: Minding the Continuum of Life

There is a plethora of contemporary environmental work tied to Hinduism that highlights plants as living and sentient, and due the care of human beings because of the service they provide. In contrast, however, there seems to be less in contemporary Indian Jainism, reflected perhaps in this observation of John Cort: "To put it boldly," he says, "as of the early 2000s there is no Jain environmental ethic per se."

> Statements that Jainism is an inherently environmental religious tradition or that Jainism has always 'enthroned the philosophy of ecological harmony' are largely untrue as statements about history, and I would argue that such misstatements will hinder more than help in the development of a Jain environmental ethic.[1]

It is not only that environmentalism is just "one of several new epistemes to which the world's religious traditions have had to respond in recent centuries,"[2] but also that, as Paul Dundas says, "the recent equation of Jainism and environmentalism is not always so comfortable as its advocates would suggest."[3] Our goal here is, first, to note the "discomfort" between environmental work and traditional Jain views; second, to note any new directions for such work that might fit "comfortably" with Jain views and, finally, to turn to Satish Kumar as someone actively working out of the Jain tradition today with a heightened sensibility to the ecological whole. Kumar's training in, and affirmation of, a life of restraint within the context of *padayātrās* or walking tours allows for ongoing mindfulness of the diverse ecospheres around him that include, as he notes, the living world of plants.

9.1 The Jain Declaration on Nature (1990)

There are no shortage of voices making the claim that Jainism has something to say about the connection between ecology and spirituality. The most well known recent voice is L. M. Singhvi, a jurist and Member of Parliament, who published his "Jain Declaration on Nature" in London in 1990. Singhvi believes that the "ecological philosophy...[of Jainism] has always been central to its ethics, aesthetics, art, literature, economics and politics...[One of] the message and motifs of the Jain perspective...[is] its commitment...to the preservation of the natural environment."[4] The Singhvi document identifies five teachings, all of which might bear on the particular treatment of plants.[5] The first is *ahiṁsā*. The "Jain ecological philosophy is virtually synonymous with the principle of *ahimsa* (non-violence) which runs through the Jain tradition like a golden thread." *Ahiṁsā* is a practice, says Singhvi, to be used not only towards human beings but also for all of nature.[6] The second teaching is "*parasparopagraho jivinam* (interdependence)" through which "Jain cosmology recognizes the...symbiosis or mutual dependence, which forms the basis of modern-day science of ecology." The third is "*anekantavada* (the doctrine of multiple aspects)" in which "the world is a multifaceted, ever changing reality with an infinity of viewpoints," one of which would be the viewpoint of nonhuman living beings like plants.[7] The fourth is "*samyaktva* (equanimity)," which

> inspires the personal quest of every Jain...towards both *jiva* (animate beings) and *ajiva* (inanimate substances and objects). It encourages an attitude of give and take and of live and let live.[8]

Finally, the fifth is "*jiva-daya* (compassion, empathy and charity)," which "means caring for and sharing with all living beings, tending, protecting and serving them. It entails universal friendliness *(maitri)*, universal forgiveness *(kshama)* and universal fearlessness *(abhaya)*."[9]

Moreover, the Declaration recognizes that all souls are bound in *karma*, and that Jain evolutionary theory "is based on a grading of the physical bodies containing souls according to the degree of sensory perception." While "trees and vegetation have the sense of touch and are therefore able to experience pleasure and pain," and have souls, Singhvi does not say *what this means* in terms of plants in the evolutionary process. That is, he does not say that plants are at the least developed end of the process, having arrived in these bodies through the accumulation of great demerit, and have less-than-human resources to work with towards liberation. Instead, he returns to the issue of *ahiṁsā* (or lack of *ahiṁsā* as practiced by humans), and says there is grave demerit "caused by the destruction of plants and trees," and that the assigning of demerit for their destruction means that the tradition "understood the meaning and merit of reverence for nature."[10] Finally, the Declaration turns to Jain codes of conduct, only one aspect of which deals directly with plants, e.g., vegetarianism. About this, Singhvi says "Except for allowing themselves a judicious use of one-sensed life in the form of vegetables, Jains would not consciously take any life for food or sport."[11]

9.2 Jainism and the Environment: The "Discomfort" Zone

In Christopher Chapple's fine collection, *Jainism and Ecology*, the article that most clearly identifies the "discomfort" between (plant-oriented) environmental work and the traditional Jain viewpoint is the one by Dundas.

> At first blush, there would appear to be a remarkable fit between environmentalism and Jainism's teachings about the ubiquity of embodied souls in the natural world and the desirability of adopting a nonviolent stance toward them... Yet there may be some grounds for suspecting that the recent equation of Jainism and environmentalism is not always so comfortable as its advocates would suggest.[12]

Dundas notes, first, that Jainism accepts "a plurality of real entities," but one in which spiritual advancement is related to various gradations ("codifications and taxonomies") of epistemology. Nature does not have "autonomous value," but is related to humans only within these gradations of epistemology. Given that, in the view of one important Jain scripture, plants "fall into the negative soteriological category of 'having false belief,'" and given that increasingly developed knowledge belongs with increasingly advanced spirituality,

> Nature *qua* flora and fauna has no meaning in its own right. Instead, it is consistently envisaged in Jain literature as representing a type of diminished or inadequate humanity, with proximity to or distance from human birth being in the last resort the most significant determinant of the value of its constituent elements.[13]

Second, Jainism historically provides its followers with a structure of time in which decline is followed by renewal, and followed again by decline and renewal, and so on. As each period comes to an end, "it is necessary and inevitable that both humankind and the natural world socially and ecologically decay," and thus "the destruction of the environment, whether brought about by humans or spontaneously engendered, is an essential fact of existence within the Jain universe." Throughout Jainism, Dundas continues, there is a danger to human beings from interaction with nature and from the resulting propensity to violence – a person "cannot engage with this world without injuring living creatures," for example.[14] Nature is not

> a source of comfort or succor, but...a potentially menacing force that by its mere existence has the capacity to threaten the embodied soul at all times...[taming] the passions...through disengagement from nature is thus the sole means of gaining the ultimate goal of deliverance.[15]

Chapple reiterates Dundas' concern about making a "natural" connection between historical Jainism and environmental activism, saying that such activism "at best could earn a secondary place in the practice of Jain faith." Thus, the practice of *ahiṁsā* is ancillary to that of increasing isolation *(kevala)* as the adept moves toward final liberation. "Although the resultant lifestyle for monks and nuns resembles or approximates an environmentally friendly ideal, its pursuit focuses on personal, spiritual advancement, not on a holistic vision of the interrelatedness of life."[16] It seems, then, that with the same material but different emphases, one could say either that "all Jains are environmentalists," or that "no Jain is an environmentalist."

9.3 Jainism and the Environment: Possible "Comfort" Zone

Chapple does believe, however, that a "shift in consciousness," authentic to the Jain tradition, can occur "that places greater value on life in its myriad forms," resulting in "the development and enhancement of an earth-friendly way of life."[17] This shift could begin, Cort suggests, with an historical investigation of how particular Jain groups have understood the place of human beings in nature and how these understandings have shaped their lived experience – both as ideal visions and as real actualities. In exploring what kinds of environmentally and plant friendly behavior a Jain might undertake, Cort goes on to outline what he calls "local and regional" areas of ecology that might be the focus of mental and physical endeavor among renunciants and laypeople. For example, when monks and nuns stop wandering for four months of the rainy season, this practice "could be reinterpreted as a call for them to develop greater connections with specific bioregions" in which they have halted. Again, two of the twelve vows specifically suggested for the lay *(anuvrata)* "involve the individual vowing not to go beyond a certain geographical limit," and thus these areas "could be reinterpreted in a bioregional light." Again, some "of the Jain mindfulness techniques could be reinterpreted as calling for greater attention to bioregions," such that precise and detailed awareness of one's voluntary and involuntary actions, cultivated "with an eye toward reducing occasions of causing harm to other bodies," could be reoriented to "a form of environmental mindfulness."[18] Finally, Cort notes that there are five rules of conduct *(samitis)* that supplement the great vows *(mahāvratas)* of the renunciant and that "could be fruitfully applied to environmental awareness." They are care in walking *(īryā),* care in speech (*bhāṣā*), care in accepting things *(eṣaṇā),* care in picking up and putting down things *(ādāna-nikṣepaṇa)*, and care in performance of excretory functions *(utsarga-samiti).*[19]

Vegetarianism

Two traditional issues are natural practices for the development of care and attention toward nature within Jain doctrine : vegetarianism as a way of remembering that plants are living and are providing essential service to human beings, and tree planting as a way of maintaining beneficial bioregions and of noting that trees and forests are both models and spaces of practice for the Jain ascetic life. Given the authority with which the vow of *ahiṁsā* is practiced,[20] the need to practice vegetarianism seems obvious. "Jains have almost universally understood *ahiṁsā* to entail being vegetarian, and the unique ways in which *ahiṁsā* has informed Jain diet are well known."[21] As we have seen, texts on Jain biology make clear that the practice of *ahiṁsā* normally has as its objects: humans and other five-sensed animals, all two- through four-sensed animals, and all one-sensed beings in the categories of air, water, earth, fire, and plants, for these are all body forms that are available to the countless souls of the world.

It is often pointed out, however, that in practice, at least, and in spite of all good intention such as this from the Sūtrakṛtāṅga,

> As our body is born, plants are born. As we grow, so plants grow. As we have consciousness, so plants have consciousness. As our body is damaged when cut, so a plant is damaged when cut.[22]

"vegetarian ascetics such as the Jains still destroy life-forms in plants, and the mere act of mendicant wandering inevitably leads to the destruction of life."[23] Attendant on the practice of *ahiṁsā*, then, is the realization that, no matter how strong the vow, whether taken by lay or renunciant, there must be an inherent acceptance of doing at least some harm, if *only to one-sensed beings*, and if only because they are "*only one-sensed beings*"[24] – that is, there must be some "judicious use of one-sensed life in the form of vegetables"[25] in order for survival. Given that all life forms in the world are classified according to the number of senses they have, and given that the lowest life forms are those with only one sense (the sense of touch), and given that this is the category where plants are located, then it is most reasonable that plant bodies would be among those with some exclusion as objects from the doctrine of *ahiṁsā*. In this way, we might say not only that the sole living matter considered allowable for human consumption is the one-sense kind,[26] but also that one-sense beings can be objects of *hiṁsā* when it is a matter of judicious consumption by humans. It would seem in line with traditional texts, as well, that greater leeway on harming plants for judicious use by humans would be granted to laypeople than to renunciants.[27]

"Vegetarianism is not what is on your plate, it is a holistic lifestyle,"[28] and with this we note that Jain vegetarianism for lay includes periodic fasting, and a prohibition on snacking between meals and on eating after sunset. Jain vegetarianism, as practiced in contemporary times, is predicated on knowledge of what is edible among plant-based foods. What is considered "allowable" are fruits and vegetables that have been taken only when they are ripe and ready to fall off the plant (or have dried on the stalk), and grains that have been taken only when the plants or the pods are dead and dry – thus grains, cannot be taken from a green plant but only from plants that have dried standing in the field. Drinking water must be filtered through three layers of homespun cotton cloth, though many contemporary Jains do drink pre-boiled water.[29] Since Jains are not ordinarily vegans,[30] dairy products are allowable (as taking milk out of the body of a goat or cow does not do the animal any harm), but cheese and yoghurt can only be used if they have been made fresh that day. Since these foods involve "starters," they are considered "stale" and not edible if kept over night.

The list of "forbidden" things is considerable. Eggs, of course, are prohibited as they are the offspring of five-sensed beings.

Vegetables and fruits that grow underground are prohibited as they are "roots" and, in pulling the root out, the whole plant dies, as do the microorganisms around the root in the soil.[31] Five fruits from the fig family (the Five Udambars) are prohibited. Some of these figs are pollinated by wasps and, because certain wasps specific to them inhabit the figs for most if not all of their life cycles, eating these figs involves some harm, if not killing, to the wasps. Again, orthodox Jains don't eat multi-seeded fruits (like apples or guava) or vegetables (like tomatoes and eggplant), because this would mean killing multiple lives *and* because such foods often contain worms.[32] Again, orthodox Jains don't eat cauliflower and broccoli, because the textured surfaces of each of these may have caught little insects that might still be stuck on their surfaces. Mushrooms and fungi are also prohibited because they are said to grow in unclean conditions, as among parasites; and, likewise, honey (as the excrement of bees), vinegar, molasses and wine are not allowable – wine, because the process of fermentation, it is believed, engenders minute forms of life. Finally, leaf plants must be peeled leaf by leaf, and inspected in order to extract worms and insects still living between them. Most Jains still don't eat garlic and onions as they bear too much *tamas* a foodstuff, and orthodox Jains do not eat food prepared in shops, but only what is cooked hygienically at home.

Tree Planting

Those who write about tree planting and protection among contemporary Jain workers make reference to Jain texts in support of this work.[33] Chapple, for example, has quoted the Ācārāṅga Sūtra in which "Mahavira addresses his monks and nuns on the topic of forest preservation...Mahavira tells the monks and nuns to 'change their minds' about looking at big trees" and "to turn their thoughts [away] from materiality by reflecting on the greater beauty of sparing a tree from the woodsman's ax."[34] In like manner, Sadhvi Shilapi, a Jain nun and an academic, and main assistant to her mentor, Acharya Chandanaji, describes the foundational teachings of Jainism by referring to scripture. In particular, she notes the Ādipurāṇa, an epic poem about the first Tīrthaṅkara, which highlights the importance of forests and the benefits they have for the ecosystem: "forests moderate the climate, check thunderstorms and floods, protect the neighboring areas from cold winds...enable the constant flow of rivers...[and] regulate the underground water levels." Moreover, forests provide services for other living beings: they "provide shelter for wildlife and fodder for animals, innumerable industrial raw materials...thousands of excellent medicines...[and] panoramic beauty." Because of the inestimable benefits of trees and forests, Shilapi notes that the Ādipurāṇa "suggests the planting of a tree. It is said that one who plants a tree remains steadfastly close to God."[35]

The experiences of tree planting and reforestation by Jains in India are reflected in the following two examples: first, the planting of trees at Veerayatan, begun first in Bihar, by Jain nuns and, second, the efforts at reforesting the sacred Mūrtipūjaka Jain mountain of Śatruñjaya in Gujarat.

Veerayatan was established some thirty years ago as a Jain institution where monks and nuns not only taught the concept of service, but practiced it as well. This humanitarian group was founded in Rajgir, Bihar by Acharya Sri Chandanaji, said to be the first woman in the 2,500-year tradition of Jainism to be promoted to the monastic rank of *darśan-ācārya,* a recognition of her spiritual progress as well as her high status as a teacher, received in 1986 at the age of 49. Acharya Chandanaji is a different kind of contemporary Jain, choosing to follow a particular aspect of Mahāvīra's life: "She was impressed by the fact that Mahavira did not confine himself to personal spiritual perfection, but dedicated his life to the cause of social reconstruction through *ahimsa, aparigraha* and *anekantavada.*" She was convinced "that Mahavira's central message of *ahimsa* is in reality a call for the service to humanity and all living beings,"[36] and quickly recognized "the seriousness of the lack of direct involvement by the Jain ascetics. She was aware of the globally evolving new concept of spirituality in terms of social justice, human rights and the rights of all the living beings," and in 1973 she was asked to go to Bihar to help the poor. And from these efforts, undertaken with great difficulty, the humanitarian mission known as Veerayatan emerged.[37]

Veerayatan is personally managed and supervised by Chandanaji and, in that it uniquely combines service and spirituality, she encourages "her nun disciples to get professionally trained in such fields as medicine, philosophy and business management." Ordained nuns are sent overseas to study at universities, and her message "of humanitarian service, social justice, education, and spiritual fulfillment" goes with her followers to Africa, Europe, and the Americas.[38] Veerayatan's success is partly due to such nun disciples as Sadhvi Shilapi herself, who in January 2001 led the Veerayatan delegation to Gujarat to respond to the earthquake in Kutch. There, Shilapi oversaw the education of thousands of children, and now runs a facility for hundreds of the children orphaned in the earthquake, as well as a vocational training program for older students.[39] Veerayatan in Bihar includes an ophthalmology hospital, where sight-restoring surgeries are performed free of charge to poor patients, as well as orthopedic clinics, prosthetic-fitting clinics, dispensaries, and mobile health units to serve the poor. The work has been so successful that two other sites have been opened – in Pune and Bhuj – and a fourth is being opened in Jahkania, also in Kutch.[40]

Another project at Veerayatan is the tree planting effort, undertaken "as a preventative measure...to save the environment." Shilapi stresses the need to plant trees in rural India, much like the initiative at her own community through which thousands "of trees have been planted in the area where Tīrthaṅkara Mahāvīra spent fourteen rainy seasons." Part of the effort is to give local people the incentive to plant trees, and this includes provisions of drinking water, food, shelter, and employment. As Shilapi describes the success of the Veerayatan community's work, she compares its motivation to the compassion of Mahāvīra – in both eras, she argues, there has been "the concern of the religious community and the active involvement of its saintly people in the betterment of our surroundings."[41]

The second example is a reforestation project known as the Greening of Palitana Project, undertaken to reforest the sacred Jain mountain of Śatruñjaya in Gujarat. Śatruñjaya is a pilgrimage center for Mūrtipūjaka Jains, and the project involves planting trees on the hills, in and around the approaches to the center, and at the pilgrim facilities.[42] Cort reports that medieval accounts of the mountain area describe it as forested, but in contemporary times it has become a "denuded mountain," caused by local, lower caste herders grazing their cattle and goats on the hilly areas. The project to reforest the mountain area to its former condition was funded by upper caste Jains, with "significant contributions from overseas Jains,"[43] but the project was not a success. The project leaders had fences of thorn bushes put up, restricting livestock movement and, in this way, deprived "the herders of their grazing lands, rights which have existed for centuries."[44] This effort to reforest a particular Jain pilgrimage site is an example of an older model running headlong into more current concerns – dealing both with human wellbeing and economic survival. While the goal was laudable, the process of consultation and negotiation was flawed.

9.4 Satish Kumar: Walking to Engage the World

Like Acharya Chandanaji and Sadhvi Shilapi, Satish Kumar sees the performing of service as one of the great strengths of Jainism. This view, that service is at the center of Jainism, was often reflected in the verses recited to Kumar by his mother when he was young. In one example, "Souls render service to one another, and thus find salvation," and in another, the seed

> serves the earth, and the earth serves the seed. A tree sheds its leaves to the earth, and the earth gives nourishment to the roots of the tree. Thus souls are serving each other and being fulfilled.[45]

As a contemporary Jain working for ecological wellbeing, Satish Kumar is expressive and accessible. Once a Śvetāmbara Jain monk, Kumar has his base in a traditional Jain heritage, but adapts that heritage to engage the modern world with compassionate activity. Following the examples of his teacher Acharya Tulsi and his mentor Vinoba Bhave, he uses walking tours *(padayātrā)* to raise awareness and to bring about change in individuals, change marked by restraint (through vows) in relation to the world and, in particular, *in relation to the natural world* – now in great need of benefit.

Satish Kumar was born in Sri Dungagarh, a small village in Rajasthan, in 1936.[46] His experience of village life was one of hard work, simple living, vegetarian meals ("no meat, no fish, no eggs")[47] and time spent in nature, where "wealth was the well-being of the family, the community and the temple," not materialism.[48] Kumar's father died when he was four, and he spent a lot of growing-up time with his mother, Anchi Devi, and she spent a lot of time in the presence of Jain monks. In particular, she felt drawn to the idea of having just a few possessions, of "reducing her need from the outside world and seeing that what we need is something inner."[49] When he was eight, "the head of our branch of the Jain order, the 'guru' Acharya Tulsi, with his entourage of monks and nuns, spent the monsoon months in our town."[50] And, when he was nine (in 1945), Kumar became a Jain monk under Tulsi:[51]

> The guru declared in a loud voice, 'My disciple, I accept you. The first thing you have to practice is *ahimsa* [total non-violence]. Respect all that is living and all creation. Do not hurt any person – neither plants, nor water, nor fire, nor air.[52]

The first vow was followed by the next four, and Kumar remained in the community of Jain monks until he was eighteen (1954). During these nine years, he studied Sanskrit and Prakrit languages and read Jain texts, meditated morning and evening, and went out once a day to beg food.

Kumar was, of course, critically shaped by his experience under Tulsi's guidance, for this guru was immensely active, and two prongs of his work are reflected in Kumar's own later life. In reforming the Śvetāmbara Terāpanthī movement, Tulsi was interested in retaining "an ascetic's code of behavior" and increasing "his sect's involvement in the social activities." Realizing that Mahāvīra had recommended two sets of vows – introductory vows *anuvrata* for laypersons and *mahāvratas* for renunciants – Tulsi "decided to create a new class of laity – *samans* and *samanis* – who would actually take anuvrata vows and thus be bound by these vows, but not being ordained...not have to follow the very demanding strictures of an ascetics life." Moreover, unlike "ordained ascetics, these *samans* and *samanis* can travel out of the country in order to provide spiritual guidance to the laity abroad...and participate in social activities designed for...moral and ethical reform." [53] The first aspect of Tulsi's influence on Kumar, then, was the Anuvrat Movement emerging in the late 1940s, which Tulsi began hoping to build individual character through social reform and moral regeneration. The movement was open "to people of all religions, color, creed, nationality and language," and he believed that people could develop new directions when they were introduced to spiritual life as "restraint," for not only does life based on vows of restraint build human character, but from such lives society itself can be rebuilt as well. According to Kumar, Tulsi taught that

> By living a life of compassion (dharma) we prevent the inflow of karma. We need not engage in any action in order to live in accordance with dharma. We only need to restrain from damaging action. Dharma is to *be* good rather than *do* good.[54]

There are many categories of vows in the Anuvrat Movement, some for all people (such as "I will not kill any innocent creature," and "I will practice religious toleration") and some for various categories of occupation, such as student, teacher, businessman, worker, and peasant (e.g., "I will not be cruel to the animals dependent on me.")

Second, Tulsi wanted to take his Anuvrat Movement to the people, and the best way to do that was through *padayātrās* or walking tours. By the 1960s and 1970s, Acharya Tulsi's walking tours had become a massive movement. Logging thousands and thousands of miles throughout India (and eventually in other parts of the world), Tulsi led increasingly popular *padayātrās* to administer the vows of Anuvrat. In the process, however, he began to see that people couldn't keep their vows so, in the mid-1970s, he asked his main assistant and heir apparent, Acharya Mahaprajna, to develop a method of inner purification that, when practiced, could give the vow-takers strength. This special kind of meditation was called *prekṣadhyāna*, much like Buddhist *vipaśyanā,* designed to "engage the mind fully in the perception of subtle, internal and innate phenomenon of consciousness."[55]

When he was eighteen, Kumar left the Jain order of monks because he felt that, while he was following the development of his inner life, he was doing so at the expense of the rest of himself and of the rest of the world. Two encounters were influential. Around 1954, he made a connection with the life and work of Gandhi (1889-1948) who taught that the pursuit of the inner journey should be deeply connected with the pursuit of an outer and social journey.

> Gandhi's ideas were in contradiction with my guru's teaching that as monks we should keep our back to society and our faces toward God. According to the guru, people like Gandhi who involved themselves in the world and in politics were 'living in darkness.' Gandhi's words raised doubts in me about the monk's life.[56]

His second encounter was with Vinoba Bhave (1895-1982) whom he had already met while a monk, and "was touched," [57] Leaving the monk's life, Kumar was encouraged to go to Bhave's ashram, where there were many dedicated to following Gandhi's directive of intertwining social/political work with spiritual work. Vinoba Bhave had been walking the whole of India for years, passing on the "message that just as air, sunshine, and water are nature's gifts which you cannot own or possess, similarly the land, the earth, is our mother...and no one should claim ownership on it."[58] His walks were part of the Land for the People (Bhoodan) Movement,[59] during which millions of acres of land were collected and donated to the poor. Inspired by the writings of Gandhi and by Bhave's movement, Kumar joined the land distribution effort where, walking throughout India, Kumar helped persuade landlords to donate some of their land to those without.

During this time, Kumar often talked with Bhave who, like Tulsi, drew deeply from Indian religious classics and who helped form the young activist's views. One subject often at the center was nature and activism. Once Vinoba told Kumar,

> We are engaged in a People's Revolution. We must be supported by the people...A handful of grain should be taken by a child of the household and put into this pot once every day. The grain collected in this way will provide our livelihood.[60]

Again, he suggested to Kumar that,

> A gardener, while gardening with love, identifies with the vegetable kingdom. Through gardening he or she attains oneness with the universe. That way gardening becomes a noble act, a spiritual act, a prayer and a play...Gardening comes to the gardener as naturally as eating, drinking or sleeping.[61]

And, on tree planting,

> Vinoba also spoke of the Buddhist practice of nourishing nature by planting trees. He told me about...Ashoka, who proclaimed that all citizens should plant a minimum of five trees in their lifetime and look after them. He asked the citizens to include one medicinal tree, one fruiting tree, one tree for firewood, one hardwood tree for house building, and one for flowers. He called it the grove of five trees *(panchavati)*."[62]

In 1962, Kumar was inspired to walk on a Peace Pilgrimage[63] beyond the borders of India[64] and so, at age 26, he left on this *padayātrā* from Gandhi's grave. With no money and relying on the kindness of friends and strangers, Kumar walked from India, through Pakistan, Afghanistan, Iran, the former Soviet Union, Poland, Germany, Belgium, France, England, and the United States where, in 1964, he ended his walk at John F. Kennedy's grave. On his way, he had an experience:

> In wandering I felt a sense of union with the whole sky, the infinite earth and sea. I felt myself a part of the cosmic existence. It was as if by walking I was making love to the earth itself. Wandering was my path, my true self, my true being...My dreams are of wandering. From birth I was wandering – as a monk, with Vinoba, and on the walk – whatever I learnt came through wandering.[65]

Following his Peace Pilgrimage, Kumar lived for a year in a forest in the Vindhaya Mountains near Jumudi village. He and his friend Anant built their own hut and lived among the tribal people of the forest, where they worked on the land, growing vegetables and rice. Gardening "became a real joy – looking at each plant growing every day, seeing the leaves coming, then the flowers, and after a few days the fruit, which then became bigger and bigger." There he had another experience: "I came to a tall tree with large overhanging branches, sat down cross-legged under the tree and closed my eyes. I looked into my body," encountered struggles, and emerged with "a sense of divinity. This newness brought a surrender, a surrender where nothing mattered, where everything was accepted."[66]

Eventually returning to England in 1973, Kumar was asked to become the editor of *Resurgence*, a Britain-based magazine that focused on ecology, new economics, and spiritual values. He became close friends with E. F. Schumacher with whom he worked on *Resurgence* and, after Schumacher's death, Kumar helped found Schumacher College in 1991 for study informed by ecological and spiritual values.[67] There, Kumar developed a curriculum where students could mix social activism with a commitment to nonviolence stemming directly out of Kumar's Jain background. Many organizations were founded through the help, or inspiration, of Schumacher, and these belong to what is known as "The Schumacher Circle:" Green Books, Intermediate Technology, The New Economics Foundation, Resurgence Magazine, Schumacher College, The Schumacher Society, Schumacher Book Service, and The Soil Association. Partnered with Dr. Atul K. Shah, Kumar founded, and produces, *Jain Spirit: Advancing Jainism into the Future,* a publication that comes out six times a year and is distributed internationally. It is designed to educate Jains about current trends in ecology.

In 1985, Kumar again went on pilgrimage, this time around the holy places of Britain. "It is an Indian tradition," he says, "that when you are fifty you should go on a pilgrimage," so when a number of *Resurgence* readers volunteered places for him to stay, Kumar set off from Stoke near Hartland. He walked through much of England, took the Pilgrims Way from Winchester to Canterbury, traveled through the pine forests of Scotland into the land of the lochs, through Mull, and finally to Iona. Of this pilgrimage, he said,

> Walking was my birthright. From the age of five I walked every day with my mother...Then from the age of nine to eighteen I had walked from village to village as a monk of the Jain order. When I left the Jain order and joined Vinoba Bhave I was again a part of a walking way of life. And then I had walked almost around the world! Walking was not solely a means to get somewhere. Walking in itself was an end, a form of meditation, a way of being."[68]

Remembering Cort's suggestion to use Jain meditation as a way to be fully attentive to the details of "bioregionalism,"[69] we note Kumar's experience on the Britain *padayātrā*. Walking through England and Scotland, he says, "My pilgrimage is in every moment in every place," and he observes that, on the way, "Breathing in I inhaled the warmth of the air, the smell of the wet grasses, the coolness of the water, the purity of Nature."[70]

While Kumar is primarily an activist and educator rather than a philosopher, he works out of a Jain and Hindu background in which he can make sense of a life of restraint through vows, a noble orientation towards the land, and the walking tour as a method of education and of meditation on ecological interdependence. In *No Destination*, he describes "eleven points of reference" – "aspirations and inspirations" – that are taken from a list composed by Gandhi and that act as guidelines for his, Kumar's, conduct. The first five are the five traditional vows: (1) *ahiṁsā*, nonviolence of the mind as well as of the body that includes overcoming violence against nature:

> At the ecological level, humanity has been at war with nature. Our desire to conque nature has led to destruction of wilderness, reduction of biodiversity...This has resulted in...depleted foods and eroded land.

In the new story Kumar wants to tell, "all relationships are embedded in the spirit of mutuality and reciprocity, the spirit of reverence for all life – human life, animal life, plant life, the life of rock, soil, and water."[71] This mutuality reflects all of the "living" elements recognized by traditional Jainism. *Ahiṁsā* is followed by (2) *satya* "truth," and then by (3) *asteya* "non-stealing," about which Kumar says,

> *Asteya* is more than illegal theft: when family farms are destroyed by agribusiness, it is theft of the countryside...to follow the way of *Asteya* is to use and consume only what nature can replenish. It is a way to consume only to meet our vital needs.[72]

Asteya is followed by (4) *brahmacarya* or "appropriate sexuality," (5) *asaṁgraha* (or *aparigraha)* or "non-acquisition/consumption/ accumulation," (6) *śarīrāśrama* or "daily manual labor," and (7) *asvāda* or "not eating bad food," which is to eat only *sattva* food:

> *Satvik* food is associated with true food. It is simple, natural, seasonal and local. Fruit, vegetables, grains, pulses, nuts and herbs come in this category...Those who eat *satvik* food need no other medicine. This is the diet of gods and angels, sages and sadhus, mothers and babies.[73]

Asvāda is followed by (8) *sarvatra bhaya varjana* or "fearlessness always and everywhere," (9) *sarvā dharmā samānatva* or "respect for all religions, and (10) *svadeśī* or "local economy," which for Kumar means, among other things, "local apples, local vegetables...[and] eating home-grown food." Finally, (11) *sparśa bhavana* or respect (empathy/contact with) for all beings, leads Kumar to note the following with regard to the current speciesism about non-human life, including plant life:

> We are even further from looking at speciesism. To some extent the concept of human rights has been brought into public discourse, but animal rights and the rights of wildlife, including the whole animate and inanimate world, have hardly been expressed...If we are to cultivate respect for all beings, then we need a radical change in our own attitudes.[74]

Kumar notes three principles of Hinduism that are important to the human community, each of which is related in some way to taking vows of restraint. The first is sacrifice *(yajña)*[75] through which a person takes only what he or she needs. Noting "the great virtue of restraint,"[76] Kumar says, "Mahāvīra's goal was to take as little as possible from the natural world and to live in harmony with nature."[77] If the "principle of limiting one's consumption is the bedrock of Jain ecology,"[78] nature can teach us how to do it:

> mother would say...Look at the honeybee: she goes from flower to flower taking only small amounts of nectar from each flower; a flower has never complained that a honeybee came and took all of its nectar away.[79]

Not only does one limit one's consumption, but one also gives back manifold what one takes, e.g., "If you take a tree to build your house, you must plant five trees for the future"[80] in return.

> The worker bee labors diligently and dedicatedly to show us that, not only should we take little from nature, but what we take should be transformed into something greater than what has been taken – into something that is replenishing, nourishing, and nurturing to life.[81]

The second principle is giving *(dāna)* and, much like the first, it is about replenishment. When human beings no longer live only as consumers, but give something back, the resulting society, emerging out of *dāna*, will have banished poverty, exploitation, and deprivation. Finally, the third principle is self-control *(tapas)* in which there is a replenishment of one's own internal spiritual environment, through such practices as fasting, taking a vow of silence, or sexual self-restraint. One might argue that the combining of inner and outer restraint, leading to inner and outer peace, can be found in the *padayātrā* or walking tour, for like the pilgrimage, *padayātrā* nourishes both.

Turning to the *padayātrās*, Kumar's own view is best expressed in his bee and pollination metaphor:

> Mahāvīra was like the bee, a great pollinator of wisdom. He went alone, always walking barefoot, carrying no possessions...Walking the earth was a most sacred act – a form of continuous pilgrimage...The Tīrthaṅkaras, communing with

> and meditating upon nature, roamed through the wilderness with a deep sense of wonder about the mystery of life.

Nature images again are most helpful as he remembers the description of how Tīrthaṅkaras became enlightened. My mother, he says, said that they "lived in the wilderness, sat under trees, and communed with nature." And why are there none such great ones today? "Because we have cut ourselves off from nature."[82]

Although Kumar's interests center around ecology and spirituality, and although he uses a lot of plant images to clarify his views, the nature and place of plants *qua* plants are not especially significant to him. In an email correspondence, I asked him about plants and he said that the questions were too factual. He responded with a narrative of his own, and I have divided its content as follows.

1. **Everything in the world is alive and sacred.** The basic point is that the whole earth is alive. Everything moving and unmoving is a divine gift and that includes plants, grasses, herbs, trees, rocks, water, all the elements. Everything is imbued with the divine. All life is sacred. Therefore, it is essential to develop a sense of the sacred and a sense of reverence for all life.
2. **All life (all the world) is interconnected and is in mutually symbiotic relationship.** All life is interconnected. There are no exceptions. All life flourishes in symbiotic relationships. When we show disrespect to plants or animals we are damaging ourselves as much as damaging other forms of life.
3. **There will be some injury and taking of life.** Life gives life and sometimes it is essential to take life.
4. **If there is killing, then it is done to those "other forms of life," like plants.** Although human beings are no more important than other forms of life, when there is the need to kill (as in eating), it will happen to those "other forms of life." Whatever life is harmed, that life will certainly be low on the sensory scale – perhaps among the lowest, like plants.
5. **Necessary killing should be done with great attention and with the minimum harm possible.** If there must be the taking of life, it should be done in humility, and we must disturb or damage other life as little as we can. We always need to be on guard and to minimize harming other forms of life.

> 6. **Life is intrinsically valuable in and of itself, not because it is of benefit to humans.** If environmentalists protect the environment only because it is useful to humans then it is a shallow kind of environmentalism. Deep and profound and comprehensive environmentalism regards life as intrinsically sacred. Because all life forms have intrinsic value, they have rights to live and to flourish and to be self-realized.[83]

Kumar reflects traditional Jainism in that his views don't lend themselves to a clear environmental program or to clear environmental action. Viewing plants as "sacred and divine" makes them stand out in no particular way from other parts of the whole, for everything, along with humans, is also, for him, sacred and divine. Moreover, unlike in Hinduism, where there is the Vṛkṣāyurveda to provide guidelines for the special care of plants, plants are not to be separated out from the whole as a special focus of study, for Kumar (and Jainism) are not especially interested in the particular health and wellbeing of plants as plants. Kumar does, however, highlight one aspect of Jainism (and of Mahāvīra's view) that is very contemporary – the presence of compassion which gives rise to social, political, and economic service. Environmental activism among Jains, however, is not supported by Kumar if it is undertaken only, and precisely, because plants give service to humans.[84] For Kumar does not hold to the "plant rights are the same as human duty" view that we find so often in Hinduism, but holds views more like Nash and Taylor, where plants are "good for themselves," and have "inherent worth." Nevertheless, taking from nature needs to be accompanied by great care, attentiveness and empathy for the living being under disturbance. While we have, he says,

> to take wood for the house, food for the body...cotton for our clothing...we must take these things not as a right but as a gift and feel gratitude toward nature. If we have that kind of attitude, then we will take with care and restraint because we will think that if we cut down a tree, we are not only taking the life of that tree, but also taking away a whole environment...for all kinds of creatures.

The judicious use of nature, then – or as Singhivi says, the "judicious use of one-sensed life"[85] – is accompanied by sensitivity to the life being taken in that use, and to use it means to replenish it multi-fold: "So if we are taking one tree away," says Kumar, "we should plant five trees in its place."[86]

Calling this chapter "minding the continuum of life" allows us to highlight some themes important in contemporary Jain approaches to things in nature. With "minding," we highlight meditation and the development of attentiveness in the context of the taking and practicing of vows, and of going on walking tours. We are especially grateful here for Cort's suggestions about seeing and paying attention to various bioregions during specific parts of Jain practice. At one end of the continuum is the "the far," where we highlight the ultimate goal of Jain practice of "liberation," as well as the agents of the cultivation of practice to reach liberation who are "humans." And at the other end is "the near," where we highlight the "everyday" experience at the beginning of the quest for liberation, as well as those beings who most often inhabit everyday experience with humans, that is, the "plants, trees, herbs, and grasses." We note also that for modern Jains, plants can be borderline – on the lower end they can be *that class of living* who can be eaten, and on the upper end they can be *that class of living* who are models for human perfection for, as in Buddhism, forest trees can be looked upon as saints, or more specifically, trees can be interpreted as *sattva* beings. In this way, Shilapi believes that "forests are like saints, or *munis*, who, overcoming all obstacles, create a better welfare for all."[87] Even in contemporary Jainism, then, the views are various on how eco-friendly Jainism is, but perhaps in no other way except friendly chaos can "a self-conscious and...effective Jain environmental ethic"[88] emerge.

Endnotes :

1. Cort, "Green Jainism?," p. 65. Cort is quoting from Singhvi, "The Jain Declaration on Nature," p. 217.
2. Cort, "Green Jainism?," p. 66. "Others include the scientific method, Copernican astronomy, nationalism, industrial capitalism, globalization, feminism, social justice, human rights, nuclear weapons,

and cultural and religious pluralism, to name a few." As Anne Vallely notes, "Cort rejects as artificial efforts to graft environmental principles only Jainism or Jain principles onto environmental practice, and argues instead that a Jain environmental ethic must develop out of a 'creative investigation and reinterpretation' of Jain thought and practice;" Vallely, "From Liberation to Ecology," p. 205.

3 Dundas, "Limits of a Jain Environmental Ethic," p. 95.

4 Singhvi, "The Jain Declaration on Nature," p. 217.

5 These five teachings are different from the five basic Jain vows *(anuvratas)*: *ahiṁsā* or non-violence, *satya* or truth, *asteya* or not stealing, *brahmacarya* or total celibacy for monks and fidelity in marriage for laypeople, and *aparigraha* or "nonaccumulation and nonpossessiveness;" Bhaskar, "Ecology and Spirituality in the Jain Tradition," pp. 176-178. Kumar give as an example of *asteya*, " clearing an entire forest would be seen as a violation of nature's rights and as theft;" Kumar, "Jain Ecology," p. 188.

6 Singhvi, "The Jain Declaration on Nature," p. 218.

7 Singhvi, "The Jain Declaration on Nature," p. 219-220.

8 Singhvi, "The Jain Declaration on Nature," p. 220.

9 Singhvi, "The Jain Declaration on Nature," pp. 220-221.

10 Singhvi, "The Jain Declaration on Nature," pp. 221-222.

11 Singhvi, "The Jain Declaration on Nature," p. 223.

12 Dundas, "The Limits of a Jain Environmental Ethic," p. 95.

13 Dundas, "The Limits of a Jain Environmental Ethic," p. 96.

14 Dundas, "The Limits of a Jain Environmental Ethic," pp. 96-99.

15 Dundas, "The Limits of a Jain Environmental Ethic," p. 98. Dundas turns to *anekāntavāda,* "usually interpreted as endowing opposing intellectual standpoints with a limited and provisional validity," as a Jain doctrine that could allow alternative views on environmentalism. He argues against this use of the term, however, for there "is no scope for invoking *anekāntavāda* as providing a relativistic underpinning for non-Jain versions of environmentalism or a justification for some sort of even handedness toward non-Jain perspectives;" "The Limits of a Jain Environmental Ethic," p. 101.

16 Chapple, "The Living Earth of Jainism and the New Story," pp. 137-138.

17 Chapple, "The Living Earth of Jainism and the New Story," p. 138.

18 Cort, "Green Jainism?," pp. 82-83.

19 Cort, "Green Jainism?," p. 83.

20 *Ahiṁsā* is part of the *mahāvrata* code of Jain renunciants and of the *anuvrata* code of Jain lay.

[21] Cort, "Green Jainism?," pp.74-75. Chapple says, "Jainism has campaigned for the 'vegetarianization' of Hindus and Muslims throughout Indian history, successfully convincing high caste Hindus to spurn consumption of meat and very nearly converting the Muslim Mughal emperor Akbar to a meatless diet;" "Contemporary Jaina and Hindu Responses to the Ecological Crisis," p. 211. Satish Kumar records that his teacher Acharya Tulsi said: "Nonviolence is common to all four great religions which originated in India: Hindu, Buddhist, Sikh and Jain. However, the Jains pay much greater attention to compassion for animals. Being a Jain is synonymous with being vegetarian;" Kumar, *You Are, Therefore I Am*, p. 46

[22] Titze, *Jainism*, p. 17.

[23] Dundas, "The Limits of a Jain Environmental Ethic," p. 100,

[24] Chapple, "The Living Earth of Jainism and the New Story," p. 138. My italics.

[25] Titze, *Jainism*, p. 227.

[26] "No Jaina is allowed to eat nonvegetarian food or engage in professions that promotes violent activity;" Chapple, " Contemporary Jaina and Hindu Responses to the Ecological Crisis," p. 211.

[27] "In order to extirpate these harmful influences *[karma]*, Jaina society advocates a quasi-ascetic lifestyle for its lay adherents and a rigorously ascetic lifestyle for its monks and nuns;" Chapple, "Contemporary Jaina and Hindu Responses to the Ecological Crisis," p. 211.

[28] Dr. Pushpendra K. Jain, "Dietary Code of Practice Amongst Jains," *Toronto Vegetarian Association*, 34th World Vegetarian Congress, Toronto, Canada, July 10th to 16th, 2000; see Titze, *Jainism*, p. 262.

[29] Parikh notes that boiling water or rendering it pure through chemical means may seem "like a paradox since...[the Jain] code of nonviolence forbids active destruction of any life form." Storing water with bacteria remaining in it, however, would allow the bacteria to grow, and drinking it subsequently would be even more harmful for the drinker as well as for the greater number of new bacteria killed; *Jainism and the New Spirituality*, p. 41.

[30] "In response to the cruelty to cattle in today's dairy industry, some modern Jains are abandoning milk and milk products also [i.e., becoming a vegan]...Jains obtain their protein from lentils and legumes;" Parikh, *Jainism and the New Spirituality*, pp. 40-41.

[31] Currently, however, most Jains (except the orthodox) eat "underground vegetables" such as potatoes and carrots in the context of

prevailing social circumstances. Satish Kumar notes that Mahāvīra "asked his followers not to eat root vegetables because, in order to eat a root, one has to dig up the whole plant: thus, grains, beans, peas, pulses, and fruit are suitable foods, whereas onions, garlic, potatoes, carrots, and other root vegetables are not," e.g., radishes, beets; Kumar, "Jain Ecology," p. 183.

32 Says Kumar: "Mahāvīra instructed his followers that when they prepared fruit and vegetables containing multiple seeds, such as melon, they should remove all the seeds carefully for resowing and regeneration." Reflecting Vandana Shiva's concern for seed saving and seed sharing as practices that should be encouraged among Indian farmers, Kumar notes this of early Jain teachings: "when peas, pulses, and grains are harvested, farmers should keep enough seed for sowing the following year and should also leave seed on the ground for wildlife:" Kumar, "Jain Ecology," p. 183; see also Kumar, *You Are, Therefore I Am*, p. 51.

33 Dundas notes that deforestation "has probably been the most significant ecological problem in South Asia throughout its history," and sends the reader to the Jain text, the Niśītha Sūtra, where there is "extensive discussion of the desirability of not harming trees;" "The Limits of a Jain Environmental Ethic," p. 116.

34 Chapple, "The Living Cosmos of Jainism," at footnote 14.

35 Shilapi, "The Environmental and Ecological Teachings of Tīrthaṅkara Mahāvīra," p. 162.

36 Parikh, *Jainism and the New Spirituality*, p. 195.

37 Parikh, *Jainism and the New Spirituality*, p. 197. Chandanaji believes that throughout history humans have adjusted easily to their changing social and natural circumstances for, normally, people are not bound by inertia and resistance to change, but instead evolve, adapt, and remain open to new ideas. This applies to her view of Jainism, and to her commitment to Jain renunciants themselves getting involved in the activity of service.

38 Parikh, *Jainism and the New Spirituality*, pp 197-198.

39 Sadhvi Shilapiji, on www.charityfocus.org

40 www.veerayatan.org

41 Shilapi, "The Environmental and Ecological Teachings of Tīrthaṅkara Mahāvīra," p. 166.

42 Jaini, "Ecology, Economics, and Development in Jainism," p. 150.

43 Cort, "Green Jainism?," pp. 78-79; see Jaini, "Ecology, Economics, and Development in Jainism," p. 150, who notes that

the project was "being underwritten by several prominent Jain Trusts."

[44] Cort, "Green Jainism?," pp. 78-79.

[45] Kumar, *You Are, Therefore I Am*, p. 19.

[46] Prime, *Vedic Ecology*, p. 94.

[47] Kumar, *No Destination*, p. 9.

[48] Prime, *Vedic Ecology*, p. 99.

[49] http://www.context.org/ICLIB/IC17/Kumar.htm

[50] Kumar, *No Destination*, p. 14.

[51] Around 1970, Acarya Tulsi (1913–1997) reformed the Śvetāmbara Terāpanthī movement. The Terāpanthīs, a "third order" associated with both the Śvetāmbaras and the Digambaras, "worship no idols and build no temples;" Kumar, *No Destination*, p. 288. Tulsi's community was established in Ladnun, Rajasthan, and it included the Jain Vishva Bharati, which was deemed a university in 1991, offering courses in language, Jain scriptures and doctrine, and peace and nonviolence studies. See Chapple, *Nonviolence to Animals, Earth, and Self in Asian Traditions*, pp. 61-64.

[52] Kumar, *No Destination*, p. 19.

[53] Parikh, *Jainism and the New Spirituality*, pp. 188-189.

[54] Kumar, *You Are, Therefore I Am*, p. 44. Kumar's italics.

[55] Parikh, *Jainism and the New Spirituality*, p. 189.

[56] Kumar, *No Destination*, p. 34. For a good discussion of Gandhi who drew upon the existing tradition as learned primarily from Jainas...[and who said] the very word non-violence, a negative word, means that it is an effort to abandon the violence that is inevitable in life. Therefore, whoever believes in Ahiṁsā will engage himself in occupations that involve the least possible violence.

Chapple, *Nonviolence to Animals, Earth, and Self in Asian Traditions*, pp. 53-62. Chapple goes on to note that, "the best and most cutting-edge solutions seem to follow the model proposed by Acharya Tulsi in India. It is only when each individual makes a change in his or her lifestyle that a societal leap forward can occur;" p. 63. Another important discussion of Gandhi and ecology is Lal, "Too Deep for Deep Ecology: Gandhi and the Ecological Vision of Life," pp. 183-212.

[57] Kumar, *No Destination*, p. 32.

[58] http://www.context.org/ICLIB/IC17/Kumar.htm

[59] Kumar, *No Destination*, p. 47.

[60] Kumer, *No Destination*, p. 59.

61 Kumar, *You Are, Therefore I Am*, p. 85.

62 Kumar, *You Are, Therefore I Am*, pp. 77-78.

63 Kumar, *No Destination*, p. 80.

64 The decision to make the peace walk was inspired by Lord Bertrand Russell who went to prison at age ninety for civil disobedience. http://www.context.org/ICLIB/IC17/Kumar.htm

65 Kumar, *No Destination*, p. 110.

66 Kumar, *No Destination*, p. 137.

67 Kumar, *No Destination*, p. 285.

68 Kumar, *No Destination*, p. 176.

69 Cort, "Green Jainism?," pp. 81-83.

70 Kumar, *No Destination*, pp. 183, 196.

71 Kumar, *No Destination*, pp. 298-299.

72 Kumar, *No Destination*, p. 301.

73 Kumar goes on to include in *sattva* food: "natural spring water; fresh and untreated milk and yoghurt; pure boiled rice; potatoes baked in their skins; beans and peas; salads of all kinds; thyme, rosemary, sage, cardamom, cumin, tumeric, basil, coriander, chives and other herbs;" *No Destination*, pp. 306-307.

74 Kumar, *No Destination*, pp. 297-317.

75 Prime, *Vedic Ecology*, p. 96.

76 Kumar, "Jain Ecology," p. 182.

77 Kumar, "Jain Ecology," p.184.

78 Kumar, "Jain Ecology," p. 183.

79 Kumar, "Jain Ecology," p. 181. My italics.

80 Prime, *Vedic Ecology*, p. 96.

81 Kumar, "Jain Ecology," pp. 181-182.

82 Kumar, "Jain Ecology, " p. 182.

83 Email correspondence from Satish Kumar, August 11, 2003.

84 Although this is the precise view of Shilapi: "As in the relationship between bride and bridegroom, it is the duty of all of us to protect and preserve the forest;" "The Environmental and Ecological Teachings of Tīrthaṅkara Mahāvīra," p. 162.

85 Singhvi, "The Jain Declaration on Nature," p. 223.

86 Kumar, *No Destination*, p. 316.

87 Shilapi, "The Environmental and Ecological Teachings of Tīrthaṅkara Mahāvīra," p. 162.

88 Cort, "Green Jainism?," p. 85.

10
Buddhism: Nature as Dhamma, Dhamma as Nature

As in the case of Jainism, Buddhism comes into the contemporary environmental arena with some critics who question its grounding in canonical sources. The most well known voice, perhaps, is Ian Harris who believes that "EcoBuddhism...[is] an ecologically engaged form of recent *American* Buddhism"[1] engaged, as others are, in "terminological revisionism."[2] He does argue, however, that "it is unhelpful to characterize...[it] as a deviation from traditional norms...[and] far closer to the truth to see...[it] as an example of a vigorous tradition engaged in a healthy process of reflexive apologetics."[3] Harris's critique insists, first, on "the primacy of the spiritual quest" in Buddhism over engagement with concerns of the natural world. While humans may be intertwined with animals and other non-human beings in the cycle of rebirth, only humans can study and cultivate *dhamma* and *vinaya* and only in human birth can there be liberation. Thus, he argues, beings "have no intrinsic value in their animal form" and, along with other parts of the natural world, are considered only as things to be cultivated or improved upon, or encountered therapeutically.

Second, he contends that the "contemporary American attempt to articulate an authentically Buddhist response to present environmental problems" represents a "teleological transformation" of traditional Buddhist views on causality and conditionality.[4] In its traditional forms, Harris notes, Buddhism "cannot account for purposive change...[because] conditionality so understood implies the full equality and mutuality of interpenetrating entities. Under such conditions it is impossible to envisage any...cumulative or incremental change in the structure of reality" – and thus at the heart of Buddhism is a dysteleological or anti-evolutionary principle that holds that all "is in a state of flux yet all is quiescent for all forward movement lacks a sense of purpose."[5]

Swearer's response is, first, that a wider reading of the Pali Canon would reveal a substantially more affirmative view of the natural world, its value to humans (and in and of itself), and the proper responsibility humans should show towards it. And, second, he suggests, a fuller reading of contemporary Buddhist "environmentalists," say in the Thai forest tradition, would reveal less reliance on American teleological visions and more reliance on strict interpretations of canonical views of causality.[6]

That there is significant environmental writing and activism among Theravada Buddhists in Asia leads us to undertake this short discussion with some confidence – confidence that there are environmental workers and movements dealing with plants and trees among Pali Buddhists, and confidence that they must work out of some views about plants, whether traditionally Buddhist or not. So why choose Thailand? First, there are few if any contemporary Buddhist environmental activities in India whose work is immediately accessible. Second, Thailand is "the only Theravadin nation to have avoided the 'disestablishment' influences of colonialism in the nineteenth century."[7] Third, about 95% of Thais identify themselves as Theravada Buddhists, though some of their Buddhist practices intermingle with animistic and Hindu elements.[8] And, finally, there are significant activist movements in the contemporary Theravada world, and many of those in Thailand take grounding in "a Buddhist focus on the environment" and, in particular, on plants and trees.[9] Thailand then presents a fortuitous case in which to test our question: to what degree do contemporary environmental activists and movements, working in areas of plants and trees, do so with traditional views of plants and trees in mind?

10.1 The State of Trees and Forests in Modern Thailand

> In recent decades...selfishness aided by modern technology has destroyed whole forests merely to extract certain marketable kinds of wood, while leaving much of the vegeta-

> tion to rot or be burned. The folly of this has become only too apparent in the...polluting...of much of Southeast Asia.[10]

The origin of the environmental problems in contemporary Thailand goes back to mid-nineteenth century changes in forest policies made by the Thai government, in part, advised by various colonial enterprises. Deforestation in Thailand owes much to the Bowring treaties of 1855 when Siam "was forced to open up the country for foreign exploitation of natural resources and for agricultural production destined for overseas markets." Thus during the reigns of Kings Mongkut (r. 1851-1868) and Chulalongkorn (r. 1868-1910), "British, French and Danish concessionaires began logging teak and other timber in Thailand."[11] In 1896, Chulalongkorn, under British advice, established the Royal Forest Department in order to manage timber cutting and its revenue, marking the initiation of government involvement in forestry, and the move of control over northern teak forests from the local princely states to Bangkok.[12] From this point on, forest reduction proceeded as follows: by 1936, about 70% of the country was still forested; by 1961, 53%; and in the 1990s, following the 1989 logging ban, 25%, "unevenly distributed among the country's four regions with more than half of the forest areas situated in Northern Thailand."[13] In fact, the "rate of deforestation in Thailand is higher than in any Asian country except Nepal and possibly Borneo."[14]

Various government acts responded to the issue. While the Forest Act of 1941 raised conservation as an issue, it was the National Park Act of 1961 that resulted in active conservation, by prohibiting the exploitation of natural resources in "ecologically interesting areas." With the National Forest Reverse Act of 1964, 40% of "the land area in Thailand was allocated for conservation and economic forests," even though in most cases the land was "ridden of trees" and "used for agricultural purposes." It is interesting to note that: *"Forest reserve land is today still legally defined by its Crown status rather than by the vegetation that does or does not cover it."*[15] Recognizing the great reduction in the forest cover in Thailand, the government passed, in 1985, the National Forest Policy that set a goal of 40% actual permanent forest cover, with 15% completely protected, and 25% as productive forest; this changed a few years later to 25% completely protected and 15% as commercial forest. In the government's commercial forest plans for the forest programs of the 1980s, the goal was to focus primarily on eucalyptus plantations that would supply the pulp and paper industries. Increasingly, the private sector became involved and increasingly there were protests by local peoples against these efforts – despite military intervention. As landslides caused by heavy rains and denuded hillsides increased, "popular demonstrations forced the government to declare an end to further logging in Thai forests." As awareness of environmental problems increased in the 1990s, so did public campaigns – against such things as "eucalyptus plantations, water pollution, [and] new electricity generating dams."[16]

In 1993, a new effort was presented by the Royal Forest Department, the "Thai Forestry Sector Master Plan," drawn up with the World Bank's Tropical Forestry Action Plan. This plan outlined a new collaboration that would be between local people and the RFD, reducing drastically the role of feudal chiefs and outside concessionaires. The plan was interesting in two ways: first, in admitting some of its own mistakes of the past, and by blaming the country's deforestation on "population increase and agricultural intensification in the country since the 1950s" and, second, in including public participation.

> The Master Plan acknowledges that forest protection or conservation need not necessarily preclude people from inhabiting the forest. It suggests that an amount of land and the rights to this land should be given over to local people and management.[17]

Although implementation of the plan was precarious – as there were issues of trust on both sides (and groups of local forest-dwelling peoples were evicted from some areas) – Isager says "the RFD appears to thread its way along a new path by expressing self-criticism and openness towards the ideal of people-managed forest" signifying that alternative positions have more voice "not just within the RFD but within Thai environmental discourse in general."[18]

10.2 Thai Orientation to Trees and the Environment

In Thai culture, the political organization of the state *(meuang)* forms the basis of the understanding of nature, and in this way "religion is intimately linked to geography." Religious merit *(bun)* moves from the center of the state outward, such that at the center of the *meuang*, the "civilized world," is the capital city that houses the most important Buddhist temple and the royal palaces. Outside the capital city are rice fields *(naa),* the economic support for the city, and then farther out are other towns and villages. In the most distant areas from the city, falling outside the "umbrella of merit" are the forests and the forested wildernesses. "Such forest areas are perceived by people within the *meuang* as being filled with spirits, wild animals and non-Thai people who are uncivilized, undisciplined and immoral" – the opposite of civilized and cultured. Words used to signify nature include *paa* or forest and *paa theuan* or wilderness; these mean "nature as space not human" and have "negative and even pejorative overtones." Another word *thammachaat* (P. *dhammajāti)* "was created under European influence during this century," and suggests, according to Buddhadasa Bhikkhu, "something which exists within itself" or, as Isager suggests, a "principle [that] embraces both physical and human nature."[19]

A new view of the relationship between the *paa* and the *meuang* has arisen around the issue of environmentalism. The *paa* is no longer an uncivilized and dangerous place but a place that is in need of protecting and conserving because its very existence in is jeopardy. Forest monks have been increasingly involved in re-visioning these two spheres: first, the *paa* has been brought into the merit-making sphere of the modern state and, second, the *paa* has been "transformed into *thammachaat,* the civilized or 'tamed' kind of nature."[20] These monks have also played an important role in the conservation of forests and wilderness areas. Monks such as Phra Pongsak, for example, who walked the hills of northern Thailand for years and who, upon arriving in Chom Thong District, was deeply troubled by the deforestation he saw there, have been intensely involved in conservation efforts, along with other like-minded monks, for some long time.

Along with these changes, there has been renewed recognition of the importance of trees in traditional folk culture, and views about the sacredness of trees, in particular, have received more public attention. A tree is recognized as sacred, for example, because it has power, and that power is, in part, because it gives food, shelter, fuel, materials for boats, houses, and medicine, as well as beauty, hope, comfort, and inspiration[21] – i.e., because it provides "service" to humans, a component of the "*sattva*-bearing nature" of trees. Moreover, trees and groups of trees can be thought of as sacred because a spirits resides in them, or because a particular tree is unusually "extraordinary in age, size, shape, or other attributes."[22] As markers of such public celebration of trees as sacred, one can see throughout Thailand a

> colorful cloth wrapped around the lower trunk of a tree. A small spirit house with offerings such as candles, incense, and fruit may be located at the base of the tree. Local people believe that the tree is the residence of a spirit, usually from a deceased person. Generally such sacred trees are respected to the extent that they are protected. Anyone who harms such a tree might experience misfortune, sickness, or even death as the spirit takes revenge.[23]

Sulak Sivaraksa, an energetic and long time activist in Thailand, believes that, through current efforts based on both reconceptualizing forest areas and celebrating the sacredness of trees, "development will arrange the rhythm of one's life...while maintaining an awareness that man is but a part of the universe, and that ways must be found to integrate mankind with the laws of nature."[24]

Buddhist Models for Responding to Forest Degradation

> In the past several years the media in Thailand has devoted considerable attention to the conflicts between the goals of national and commercial development, the wellbeing of the majority of Thai people (especially the rural, farming populations), and the health of the environment.[25]

The recognition of serious problems involving forest conservation and management in Thailand has engaged many people and groups. Clearly important, in both the recognition and response to these problems, is the Buddhist dimension of Thai life, where there is broad response by monks, laypeople, and concerned non-Thais both in the country and internationally. We would like to highlight four of these responses: the responsibility of the traditional Buddhist king to be a model for environmental engagement; the contemporary development of "Buddhist policies" towards the environment; the use of the ordination of trees as a way to protest, and to protect trees against loggers and others; and the affirmation of the Thai forest tradition, whereby there is preservation of forest space for use by Buddhist practitioners, and preservation of individual trees as models for spiritual maturation.

The King as Model for Engagement

While the Theravada canon details the principles of moral governance by the ruler, it was not until Aśoka (272-232 BCE) that "Buddhism first acquired the role of a state religion."Under him the Buddhist monarch had responsibility for ensuring the adherence of monks to the monastic code of conduct or *vinaya,* but did not have authority over *dhamma* – that is, orthopraxy but not orthodoxy.[26] This Aśokan model – which included providing, preserving, and caring for plants, trees, and forests for the wellbeing of those living under his charge – "provided the pattern for church-state relations in the early Thai kingdom of Sukhothai, and the association of the Buddhist Sangha with the Thai state has been significant since that time."[27] The view, then, that "the King was of course the leader, but he was also the teacher in righteousness,"[28] is one strongly present in the historical evidence. According to a Thai inscription of 1292 of King Rama Kamhaeng (Raam Khamhaeng), when the Thai successfully separated themselves "from the Khmer Empire of Angkor and set... themselves up as an independent state at Sukhothai around 1250," they were already devout Buddhists. "It was through Theravada inspiration regarding the behavior of the righteous ruler as a father to his people *(dhammarājā)*, unlike the authoritarian god-kind *(devarājā)* of Brahministic Cambodia" that brought the Thais into Buddhism. In the inscription is the notice that

> west of this city of Sukhothai is the forest monastery *(āraññika)*, built by King Rama Kamhaeng as a gift to the Supreme Patriarch *(Sangharājā)*, the sage who has studied the Three Baskets of the Buddhist canon form beginning to end.[29]

These views about the king derived from Buddhism were also intertwined with "animistic beliefs, inherited from or mingled with Khmer culture." The inscription continues, for example, by saying the

> divine sprite of that mountain is more powerful than any other sprite in this Kingdom. Whatever lord may rule this Kingdom of Sukhothai, if he makes obeisance to him properly, with the right offerings, this Kingdom will thrive, but if obeisance is not made properly or the offerings are not right, the sprite of the hill will no longer protect it and the Kingdom will be lost.[30]

Not only was the king of a Buddhist region to refrain from exploiting those he ruled, but also to refrain from exploiting "other beings, namely animals, spiritual beings like gods and ghosts, as well as mountains, trees, lands, air and water."[31]

The modern king most important to developments in the Thai forest tradition is Mongkut (1804-1868). Prior to coming to throne as Rama IV in 1851, Mongkut was a Buddhist monk for twenty-six years and, during that time, he studied the tradition critically and was a serious practitioner of meditation. Acquainted with all aspects of Buddhism in Thailand, he "could perceive the essential and pure teaching of the Buddha; and distinguish between what was mythological and popular Buddhism, magical beliefs and

Brahministic rites." From this study, Mongkut was encouraged to reform the *sangha,* and began by founding the Thammayutika (P. Dhammayutika) Order "which claims to be in strict adherence to the *dhamma* (teaching) and *vinaya* (disciplines) laid down by the Buddha" and practiced by traditional elders through an unbroken lineage.[32] For Mongkut, strengthening the classical Buddhist tradition among Thai practitioners meant to "survive Western imperialism," and he did this in part by depicting "the king as a just and moral ruler *(dhammarājā)* rather than a divine king *(devarājā)*...Mongkut said that the king had the right to rule as long as he was righteous, and if the people did not want him on the throne they had the right to remove him."[33]

In early Indian thought, the figure of the king provides the model for the development of the idea of the individual, for it was the king who, though he performed the rituals, did so for the benefit of his citizens. As the tradition moved from corporate religious agency to individual religious agency, it was the person of the king to whom religious turned for instruction. This very same process has been at work in Thailand for, of Buddhadasa's teaching, Ken Jones notes:

> The *dhammaraja* and the elite *(ksatriya)* were Buddhist political forms appropriate to a specific historical era, and no more than that. Truly rooted in Dhamma, and much more enduring, is the Buddhist tradition of egalitarian respect for the individual person. Each must light his or her own way.[34]

As Peter Jackson notes, part of Buddhadasa's reform is that he reinterprets Buddhist doctrines of salvation by laying the foundation for a world-involved, and socially involved, Buddhism; he proposes the abolition of the monk-lay distinction; and he moves away from the Theravada Buddhist ideal of a renunciate *arahant* monk and instead supports "a world-involved *bodhisattva*-like layperson who simultaneously works for personal salvation and social welfare." These re-visions give grounding to Buddhadasa's above concern that "each must light his or her own way," a view consonant with the early Buddhist idea of "being an island unto oneself, a refuge unto oneself." While the traditional Buddhist king has in the past provided the model for social and worldly welfare, it is now also an individual responsibility. As Buddhadasa says:

> Nature wants there to be peace. If there isn't peace there will be destruction and ruin...The nature spoken of here is the cosmic-moral order of dhamma, and the destruction and ruin is consequent upon the factionalism and conflict which arise from self-centered attachment and greed.[35]

Development of Buddhist "Policies" Towards the Environment

In recent decades, several documents have been published from meetings of Buddhist practitioners and scholars, focusing on more formal Buddhist responses to environmental degradation. Among the participants of some of these meetings have been speakers on behalf of the Theravada tradition and we include them here, as these broadly based, international initiatives can have influence on what happens at national or local levels. At the very least, these documents begin the process of developing something like a collection of "Buddhist policies" toward ecological issues that could give guidance and support to local environmental efforts.

The Green Buddhist Declaration (1984). Developed by members of the international Buddhist community in 1984 at the Fourteenth General Conference of the World Fellowship of Buddhist in Columbo, Sri Lanka, this short document opens by stating that the members are called to "compassionate action" in "a growing empathy with other beings' sufferings." While much of the document takes up larger issues of "engagement and the Sangha," the relation between "church and state" as they respond to social issues of flourishing, and attitudes and structures reflecting "gender equity," some mention are made of Buddhist involvement in environmental activism. Statement 2.8, for example, notes:

> Many Buddhists have shown an attraction to the ecology...movements and greater theoretical and practical work is necessary to explicate our common, underlying perception, and what unique contribution Buddhists can make to these causes.

And Statement 3.10 says:

> We believe that since world resources and the ecosystem cannot support all peoples at the level of consumption of the advantaged nations, efforts [must be made] towards global equity... We must become mindful of our interdependence on the welfare of other beings and the ecosystem, and gear our awareness towards a global Middle Way.[36]

These statements from a meeting of Buddhists in Sri Lanka serve to affirm efforts already being made worldwide, and give encouragement to those to be made in the future.

The Buddhist "Declaration of Interdependence" (1995). This declaration was produced at the end of the Online Conference on "Buddhism and Human Rights," sponsored by the *Journal of Buddhist Ethics*, from October 1-13, 1995. In the Preamble, the participants state that since humans are fortunate to have such a "rare and precious" birth, they have the "duty to not abuse the rights of others to partake of the possibilities of moral and spiritual flourishing offered by human existence." As in the views of James Nash (plants "are ends for themselves") and Paul Taylor (plants have "inherent worth"),[37] humans, according to this declaration, have "an obligation to treat other forms of life with the respect commensurate to their natures."[38]

Moreover, the document proposes that contemporary Buddhists affirm that "in its teachings Buddhism recognizes," first, the "interdependency of all forms of life and the reciprocal obligations which arise from it," second, the "need for universal compassion for sentient beings who are all alike in that they dislike pain and wish for happiness" – as in the argument of Singer as founded on Bentham ("The question is not, Can they *reason*? nor Can they *talk*? but, Can they *suffer*?"[39]) – and, third, the "inalienable dignity which living creatures possess by virtue of their capacity to achieve enlightenment in this life or in the future."[40] These proposals or proclamations are significant because (1) they focus on the human responsibilities that emerge from the fact that all living beings arise, one like the other, as part of the contingent conditions of existence, (2) they recognize that living sentient beings feel pleasure and pain and that the experience of suffering (by plants, say) must be addressed by a teaching like Buddhism in its hope to afford living beings a chance to live without suffering, and (3) they suggest that because, living creatures have the "capacity to achieve enlightenment," noninterference in, and encouragement of, that process of flourishing should be promoted to the degree that it is possible.

Voices from the Buddhist Perspectives on the Earth Charter (1997). In 1972, the Stockholm Conference on the Human Environment successfully added "ecological security" to peace, human rights, and equitable socioeconomic development as the fourth major concern of the United Nations. Since that time there "have been numerous Earth Charter consultations and efforts to draft a Charter," and in the late 1990s a Benchmark Draft Earth Charter was readied for circulation in 1998.[41] One of the responses to this draft was to call upon scholars in Buddhist studies to write short essays discussing the charter from some aspect of their fields. The Benchmark Draft of the Earth Charter opens with the position that "Earth, each life form, and all living beings possess intrinsic value and warrant respect independently of their utilitarian value to humanity," and continues with the call to protect and restore "the diversity, integrity, and beauty of the planet's ecosystems," to practice nonviolence...with oneself, other persons, other life forms and Earth," and to treat "all creatures with compassion and protect them from cruelty and wanton destruction."[42] The charter does not, however, specifically mention plants, grasses, and trees, but this issue is addressed, if obliquely, in a short essay in the pamphlet by Susan Darlington focusing on the work of "ecology monks" in Thailand who perform tree ordinations.

Darlington assesses some of the principles in the Earth Charter that are reflected in the work of one of these monks, Phrakhru Pitak Nanthakhun, from northern Thailand, Nan Province. Born in the mountains, Phrakhru Pitak watched as the forests around him disappeared, and continually worked at making connections between human action and the state of the environment. As a monk, he often preached to villagers about the problems, but that this proved too abstract and he soon put his preaching into practice by undertaking local projects. According to Darlington, Phrakhru Pitak's environmentally focused projects tie into several of the principles of the Earth Charter:

> **Concerning Statement #1** – that emphasizes the *intrinsic value of all things* – Phrakhru Pitak promotes projects for the benefit of "all beings within the environment," including trees.
> **Concerning Statement #3** – that emphasizes *sustainable living* – Phrakhru Pitak promotes Theravada values that eschew becoming "too dependent on material goods," that discourage using products that contribute "to the destruction of the natural environment," and that encourage restraint from "desire for things which a consumer-driven cash economy promotes." Instead, villagers should work for integrated agriculture and biodiversity, and raise their own domesticated animals, with the aim of producing only what they need.
> **Concerning #6** – that focuses on promoting the *social and financial structures needed to support sustainable living* – Phrakhru Pitak's work in this area aims at building local communities, and ensuring that "the villagers themselves...implement and maintain" the projects that are initiated. For example, "after establishing a sanctified community forest through a tree ordination ceremony, a local committee takes on the responsibility for monitoring and protecting the forest." In another example of direct involvement,

Phrakhru Pitak himself leads a "dhamma walk" summer ordination program for up to fifty boys every year. The novices walk through the district, living with people in various villages and witnessing the struggles with the environmental destruction and poverty they face daily...Another monk regularly accompanies children from his village on walks through the forest, teaching them the values of the natural environment and how they can peacefully live in and protect it.

> **Concerning # 13 and 14** – that focus on *integrated agriculture and new technologies* – Phrakhru Pitak, like other ecology monks, "works closely with environmental NGOs to bring new techniques and knowledge to the rural villagers," processes that are initiated only when "existing systems of agriculture and financing which contribute to environmental destruction...[have been] challenged" first.
> **Concerning #18** – that focuses on *sharing responsibility for*

> *the well being of the earth community* – Phrakhru Pitak, in his work, "stresses compassion and co-dependence between humans and other living beings."[43]

The importance of these documents is that they were put together by students and followers of the Buddhist tradition, based on contemporary interpretations of canonical and traditional materials that include Theravada perspectives. The documents are important also because they affirm the inclusion of ecology and environmental activism in the contemporary period, under the umbrella of modern Buddhist activities.

The Ordination of Trees

At the core of the Buddhist ecology movement in Thailand are several "ecology monks" *(phra nak anuraksa)* who come from both the Mahanikaai (P. Mahānikāya) and Thammayut sects. They engage in actions to preserve the vanishing forests, watersheds, and wildlife of Thailand, and to ameliorate the affect that this diminishment may have on peoples' lives. "Their efforts provide the motivation for re-examining the scriptures in light of environmentalism" and thus for "reinterpreting and rearticulating religious concepts, the role of the Sangha, and the function of Buddhist rituals in the process." The ecology monks see their work, both as Buddhists and as monks, "as promoting human responsibility toward the natural (and inherently social) environment"[44] and, for this, have become involved in a particular practice known as the tree ordination ceremony *(buat ton mai)*.

One of the most well known, and successful, monks who has sponsored tree ordinations is Phrakhru Pitak, who "began campaigning for forest preservation in Nan in 1975 as a seventeen-year-old novice monk,"[45] having grown frustrated as the destruction of trees and forests by loggers continued despite the teaching and activism of the ecology monks. In early 1990, he visited Phrakhur Manas Natheepital, the abbot of Wat Bodharma in Phayao Province in northern Thailand, who is said to have performed the first symbolic ordination of a tree in 1988 with the hope of making people aware of their environmental responsibili-

Monks walking to the tree ordination

Tree ordination in Chiang Mai, Thailand, July 2005

Photo Courtesy : "Susan Stein"

Lay people carrying ordination robes for the trees
Tree ordination in Chiang Mai, Thailand, July 2005
Photo Courtesy : "Susan Stein"

Monk tying ordination robes on a tree

Tree ordination in Chiang Mai, Thailand, July 2005

Photo Courtesy : "Susan Stein"

Monk tying ordination robes on a tree
Tree ordination in Chiang Mai, Thailand, July 2005
Photo Courtesy : "Susan Stein"

Head Monk by ordained Tree

Tree ordination in Chiang Mai, Thailand, July 2005

Photo Courtesy : "Susan Stein"

Monk tying ordination robes on a Tree

Tree ordination in Chiang Mai, Thailand, July 2005

Photo Courtesy : "Susan Stein"

Monk's at Lunch

Tree ordination in Chiang Mai, Thailand, July 2005

Photo Courtesy : "Susan Stein"

ties. "According to Phrakhru Manas, he invented the tradition of tree ordination as part of a local movement to bring an end to logging that was taking place in a watershed forest close to Wat Bodharma."[46] Of his "invention," Phrakhru Manas said in 1992:

> If a tree is wrapped in saffron robes, no one would dare cut it down. So I thought that perhaps this idea could be used to discourage logging, and I began performing ceremonies on trees in the forest near the temple. I called the ritual an "ordination" to give it more weight. The term "tree ordination" sounds weird to Thai people since an ordination is a ritual applied only to men. This weirdness has helped spread the news by word of mouth.[47]

Phrakhru Pitak performed *his* first tree ordination in the forest belonging to the community of his home village, in Nan Province at Ban Khiew Muang, in June of 1990.

> Letters were sent to the surrounding communities announcing the creation of the protected area, and that it was forbidden to cut trees or hunt in the community forest. The villagers still maintain their protected forest, and it is now seen as a model project and is visited frequently by visitors from across Thailand.[48]

Phrakhru Pitak realized that in order to make ecosystem management successful, he needed to spread the idea of forest ordination to more areas and so, in July of 1991, he performed his second in the forest around ten of the neighboring villages. These and subsequent tree ordinations are "the symbolic center of Phrakhru Pitak's conservation program," and "the emotional and spiritual commitment created by the ceremony"[49] stresses the interconnection of the people with their natural environment and the importance of themselves getting involved in its preservation.

The tree ordination ceremony is adapted from a traditional Buddhist ritual whereby a person is ordained into the Buddhist monkhood, and is performed for a number of reasons, but in part "to build villagers' commitment to...ecology projects."[50] Before the monks arrive, offerings are made by laypeople and the local deities are notified that "the forest will be sanctified through the ritual...[moreover,] they are called upon to help protect the forest." After the monks arrive, they are connected to each other, and to the Buddha statue, by white thread, as the "Buddha statue represents the guardian of the forest and through this statue the power of the holy chanting is dispersed to the forest as a whole." Laypeople then take an oath not to cut down trees in the forest, and the monks then symbolically ordain one of the giant trees of the forest by wrapping saffron robes around it.[51] Attending the tree ordination of July 1991, Darlington notes that nurseries from the area donated 12,000 carefully chosen seedlings to the monks. Once Phrakhru Pitak has ritually accepted the forest robes, he and the highest-ranking monk there "accepted the seedlings, thus sanctifying them and conferring merit on the donors and participants." A few of the seedlings were planted on the temple grounds but most were given to the villagers to plant in denuded areas. The officiants and participants then went to the site of the chosen tree, newly prepared with an image of the Buddha and a tent for the monks. At the appropriate moment of the ceremony, two monks wrapped saffron robes around the tree's trunk, thus marking its sanctification.[52]

The purpose of tree ordination is several-fold. *First*, as Darlington points out, the ceremony is "to raise the awareness of the rate of environmental destruction in Thailand and to build a spiritual commitment among local people to conserving the forests and watersheds."[53] As Santikaro Bhikkhu says, the

> ...whole point is to get the villagers involved so that peer pressure will protect the forest, or in some cases the villagers will work together to protect the forest against outsiders, in some cases against the military.[54]

Before the ceremony, a plaque is nailed to the tree to be ordained, saying *tham laay paa khee tham laay chaat*, or "to destroy the forest is to destroy life," suggesting that the ordained tree is emblematic of the forest as a whole.[55] It also raises the question of what is the life that would be destroyed by destroying the forest: the lives of the trees, and/or the lives of the animals, insects, and birds, for example, living in the forest. The answer is – all of the above.

With regard to tree ordination, many point out that a single tree is "part of a hierarchy of progressively larger ecological systems...if a single tree can have some importance, then...a community of trees such as a grove or forest can be appreciated even more."[56] Focusing on a number of single sacred trees promotes recognition of the need for biodiversity,[57] and for the importance of many trees in an ecological area. Trees can host many living beings – micro organisms, mosses and fungi, monkeys and birds – and trees can create microclimates, for fallen leaves yield nutrients for living beings below. In these ways, a single "tree is an integral part of its ecosystem and wider ecological contexts."[58] The idea that a tree can host many living beings is reflected in the rationale for a tree ordination performed in June 1989 by Phra Prajak and four other monks. At the ceremony, the chief monk declared the ordained tree to be a *ton phraya* (great tree)

> which had been sheltering all living things around and underneath its spreading branches from way back in time. Every villager and the villagers' children and grandchildren were requested "not to cut down this Phraya tree and not to harm the animals and all other living things in the 10,000-rai forest, for they are all under the protection of this tree.[59]

Darlington thinks about the plaque in another way as well. Regardless of what body is considered "living" in the forest habitat, destroying it is demeritorious and this act of destruction affects one's next rebirth.[60] Tree ordination, then, *second*, recognizes life somewhere in the tree or in its vicinity and calls attention to the violation of Buddhist *ahiṁsā* that would be the destruction of the tree. Moreover, it "is believed among the villagers that such ordained trees will be protected by spirits or supernatural powers. If somebody goes to cut them down, he will meet with misfortunes or death."[61]

Concerning spirits who are connected to trees, Santikaro Bhikkhu notes that tree ordination is also about "veneration," given that there's "a not-always-expressed assumption that the tree will be the home of a spirit." In popular culture in Thailand (and in India), tutelary deities were associated with things like villages, forests, and rivers, "and so in a patch of forest, it's assumed that a particularly large tree is the most likely spot where the tutelary deity lives. And people will talk about feeling an energy around a tree – you feel some presence or power." In putting a saffron robe around the tree one is venerating not only the tree "but the spirit in that part of the forest" as well.

Another, *third*, reason behind tree ordination is to protect the tree, and the forest it stands in, from loggers,[62] or as Santikaro Bhikkhu noted above, from the military.

> Nowadays...the forest monks' worst threat comes not from wild animals but from loggers, poachers, and soldiers. When they encountered soldiers or illegal loggers in the forest, the monks had difficulty communicating with them. No amount of loving-kindness seemed to affect these men with their guns...Fighting for the survival of the remaining forests has become the most difficult test of a monk's spiritual training.[63]

Difficult as these encounters are, the robes and the plaque are intended to warn intruders off, announcing that local people object to their destructive efforts. As Phra Paisal Visalo notes,

> For me, tree ordination is an attempt to restore the sense of sacredness toward the tree among the people. In the past, people feel that trees and forests are sacred, partly because of the traditional belief that some divine beings live in trees and forests. Another reason is that trees nourish peoples' lives and wellbeing. But after the flood of modernization and capitalism, trees become commodity in people's mind. This is one main reason for deforestation in Thailand. By covering or tying yellow robes to the trees, tree ordination is telling people that trees are worthy of respect, and should not be treated as object for profit.[64]

It is precisely that it *is* robes the trees are wrapped in that is especially significant, some say, because, *fourth*, the ordination of the tree has, in effect, rendered the tree a surrogate monk, a being of complete "*sattva* qualities," whose killing would be the worst crime in Buddhism.[65] In connection with a tree ordination in the area of Chiang Rai, for example, it has been said that an "ordained tree is acknowledged to be a member of the Buddhist Order and effectively becomes a monk, making it a grave offence to fell it."[66] And again, in a tree ordination performed by Khru Ba Wisit Winyakorn and his monks, it is said that the monks "essentially ordained the trees as monks and officially consecrated the forest. Now whoever cuts a tree in this forest in effect kills a monk – a mortal sin."[67] Darlington would, however, caution against this view, however, for it

> is important to note that in this ceremony, like all tree ordinations, the monk did not claim to be fully ordaining the tree, as that status is reserved for humans only. The ceremony was used symbolically to remind people that nature should be treated as equal with humans, deserving of respect and vital for human as well as all life.[68]

With tree ordination really being about veneration, Santikaro Bhikkhu notes that some who have done tree "ordinations" have also done ordinations for rivers, like the Nan River in northern Thailand. Furthermore, the ceremony of "ordaining a river" has been done for rivers and streams in southern Thailand and, in fact, "theoretically, you can ordain anything" – since it's done for something you want to protect by giving it "cultural, spiritual meaning." With such ordinations, the thing being ordained is recognized differently: it's "not like the tree [or river has] changed internally...[but] it's being recognized differently," because ordination is, as it were, a social convention.[69]

The meaning of tree ordination is thus complex, Darlington notes, *fifth*, and one of its aspects has to do with the new role of Buddhist monks: "Through the ordination...Phrakhru Pitak extended his traditional role as a spiritual and moral leader of lay villagers to embrace an activism which necessitates political involvement.[70] Moreover, although the ordination is of only one tree, it is in fact the sanctification of a whole area. "By mere association, the surrounding trees may also be protected...during the ritual, strings may be attached from the sacred tree to others, which makes them sacred as well." What is clear is that tree ordination is successful "as a conservation technique...[for it] involves the creation of a new sacred place. Such actions by environmentalist monks in Thailand have led some naturalists to recognize them as 'custodians of nature'."[71] It helps as well to have the endorsement of some of the most influential monks in Thailand, such as Buddhadasa Bhikkhu, who himself calls for "ordaining trees" as a part of the practice of "right ecology."[72]

Since the early 1990s, the practice of tree ordination has spread through Thailand. In the north, for example, villagers from the Thai lowlands and hill tribes of Karen and Hmong background banded together to form the Northern Farmers' Network with the aim of ordaining 50 million trees in their community forests, a project to mark the fiftieth anniversary of the Thai king's accession to the throne. "The Project aims to cover one million rai in 100 community forests spanning eight northern provinces, namely Mae Hong Son, Chiang Mai, Chiang Rai, Phayao, Lampang, Lamphun, Phrae, and Nan provinces." The network encourages many types of participation: attending the ordination, and/or giving labor, financial support, or ordination robes. It also has the support of the Thai king who speaks out primarily for the preservation of the forests as they are: "The forests flourish naturally in the wild and not a single tree is planted by man...It is important to let the trees thrive naturally. Don't disturb them. It suffices to give the trees some protection. Just don't hurt them."[73]

In a study of this particular example of mass tree ordination, Lotte Isager and Soqoqoren Ivarsson propose yet another, *sixth*, set of reasons behind the ceremony: that local communities often use it as a way to "counter the territorialization of the Thai state by reasserting local identities and environmental responsibilities." These rural communities invoke Buddhist symbols and the honor of the king in order to identify themselves positively with contemporary Thai society and to combat the depiction of them as "enemies of the nation."[74]

> Performance of the ritual might...constitute an act of resistance against government territorialization or it might be part

> of a pragmatic process of land-use change; it might also serve as a strikingly visible symbolic mark of new social or political ties between groups hitherto not connected with one another.

Just as tree ordination may be seen as a sacralization of forest space by monks, Isager and Ivarsson argue that by "ordaining trees people culturally construct a landscape both in the material sense of 'making' or 'protecting' it and in the more symbolical sense of conferring particular meaning(s) upon it."[75]

Among the "meanings" of the tree ordination given to them by the participating villagers, *seventh*, is a particularly interesting one: that the ceremony is to honor the king. While they are aware of the intertwined Buddhist symbolism, "the villagers...barely mentioned the Buddhist aspects of the tree ordination ritual, whereas they eagerly stressed that they ordained the forest as a gift to the king...*they clearly perceived themselves to be local caretakers of the forest in behalf of the king.*" Moreover, disturbing or cutting down trees in an ordained forest was "not only a crime against the environment but an insult to the king."[76] This brings us full circle back to the idea of the king as the model for environmental engagement, which is an old Buddhist ideal in India and one well established in early modern times in Thailand with the activities of King Mongkut as *dhammarājā.*

Tree ordination carries forward other ideas from early Indian traditions as well. In the use of this ceremony, there is recognition, first, that trees are alive and are part of a living ecosystem. The desire to prevent loggers from destroying the trees suggests that, in some of present-day Thai Buddhist thought, trees (if not all plants) come under the vow of *ahiṁsā* and, if this is the case, there is concurrence with the older, and earliest, Buddhist views about objects of the ethic of nonviolence: that they include humans, animals, *and plants*. Second, human action to perform tree ordinations suggest ties to old Indian views, present in such works as the Vṛkṣāyurveda, that humans have a duty to care for trees and to protect trees from harm. And the reasons for protecting trees are noted as at least two. (1) Trees, when felled by loggers, are suffering and need efforts by humans to protect them from harm.

Concerning this, Darlington suggests that the actions of the ecology monks "are based on interpretations of the *dhamma* calling for the *sangha* to make concerted efforts to relieve the sufferings of all sentient beings while also following their own spiritual practice."[77] And (2) trees provide services such as food, medicine, clothing, lodging, and fuel – that is, they are imbued with the *sattva*-bearing quality of compassion. Third, if we see the ordination of the tree as ordination in its fullest possible form – that is, of a monk – then tree ordination follows in the tradition both of plant/human homologies, and of the tree as model of ascetic behavior: the tree is stable, grounded, enduring, erect in posture, calm, serene, undistractible, even-minded, neutral in its judgment, without desire, aversion, or delusion, that is, the tree *is just as it is.*

10.3 The Thai Forest Tradition

The final model for responding to forest degradation examined here is the preservation, maintenance, and revitalization of a tradition that has been practiced in Thailand for some time, that of *renunciant life and practice in the forest* by Buddhist religious. To examine the history of the Thai forest tradition, and then to note its decay, is to call for efforts to safeguard it with care, for the sake of those who find living in the forest useful in their spiritual practice and of the forest systems themselves, large and small, that house the myriad matrices of life on which so many other lives depend.

Leaving the town or city and going into the forest to seek liberation was a tradition long before the Buddha. While the civilized life of the city was spiritually "dulling" with the safety and security of material wellbeing and the company of family and friends, forest life was spiritually "enlivening" with the freedom from civic and domestic distractions and greater access to possibilities for the mind to quiet and rest. For the Buddha, the forest was the space where his great moments of transition took place. Says Ajahn Chah, the "Buddha was born in the forest...he practiced in the forest. He was enlightened in the forest, he taught in the forest, and he died in the forest."[78]

Santikaro Bhikkhu notes that there are four strands of forest practice in Thai Buddhism: shamanistic, northeast, development (later, environmental or ecology), and the forest style of Buddhadasa Bhikkhu. For the older, shamanistic Buddhist monks, strict adherence to the monastic discipline is less important and, while there is some meditation practice, it is "not necessarily what mainstream Theravada would consider meditation... They've been in the woods for centuries and are as much descendents of pre-Buddhist stuff as they are Buddhist."[79]

As Buddhism developed in Thai history, forests continued to be important places for Buddhist practice, and in the early Sukhothai, there was the replication of the Sinhalese custom of dividing the Sangha into town dwellers *(gāmavāsin/nagaravāsin)* and forest dwellers *(araññavāsin)*, each with heads appointed by the king. In all four quarters of the city, there were temple buildings and monks, but "the most important was the forest monastery, where the spiritual head of the realm resided." An inscription tells us that, at the end of the rainy season,

> They present robes to the monks *(kathin* ceremonies)... Everyone goes to the forest monastery... When they are ready to return to the city they walk together, forming a line all the way from the forest monastery to the parade ground. They repeatedly do homage together, accompanied by music.[80]

The second strand of forest tradition in Thai Buddhism, then, is the *northeast* strand. "The old tradition of wandering in the forest was also shared by the Laotians, and northeast Thailand is ethnically Laotian... so this particular forest tradition is more ethnically Laotian than it is central or Bangkok Thai."[81] The monks of Thai forest practice of the northeast are known as *phra thudong* (ascetic wandering monk) or *phra thudong kammathaan* (wandering ascetic meditating monk), and their practice emphasizes strict adherence to monastic discipline, meditation, and forest wandering.

The forest-dwelling monks have, for centuries in Thailand, been the bridge between the *meuang* (state and its civilized center, the capital city) and the *paa* (the forest). In the forest tradition, some monks lived together in forest monasteries, some were hermits in huts, some were permanently settled in the forest, and others spent only a season (hot or cool) there.[82] Historically, the various *meuangs*, states or kingdoms in Thailand, had different religious customs and practices and these included the various *nikaais (nikāyas)* or communities of "monks adhering to common beliefs and disciplinary practices." In the Lan Na kingdom, for example, "there were as many as eighteen nikais or lineages of Buddhist monks in Chiang Mai."[83] The separate *nikaais* had assorted practices, and were "permitted some laterality of personal expression as [they]...were not homogeneous and monolithic entities."[84] These traditions, in fact, were regional Buddhist traditions, bound by the "common feature...that monastics would remain engaged in village life. Regional monks organized festivals, worked on construction projects in the wat, tilled the fields, kept cattle or horses, carved boats, played musical instruments...taught martial arts – and were still considered to be respectable *bhikkhu* (monks) all the while."

> The wat was in fact the center of lay Buddhism. In regional traditions, the monastery served many functions necessary to community life. It was a town hall for meetings, a school, a hospital...a social and recreation center, a playground for children, an inn for visitors and travelers, a warehouse for keeping boats and other communal objects, and a wildlife refuge.[85]

Thai Government and the Forest Tradition

The story of the emergence of the modern forest tradition, with its connections to the "northeast" and the "development or environmental/ecology" strands of forest practice, begins with King Mongkut. Before he became king[86] Mongkut, in 1824, ordained as a monk and attained great spiritual maturity[87] in studying the Pali Canon with precision, and in practicing mindfulness meditation and the austere disciplines of *thudong)*. After he had been a monk for six years, in 1830, "Mongkut met the abbot of a Mon monastery located across the river from Bangkok." He was impressed by the strict discipline he saw there and was equally dissatisfied with the practices of the forest dwelling *(araññavāsin)* order, "proclaiming that meditation and ascetic practices...that are not based on a study of the texts...are of insignificant value."[88] He subsequently founded the Thammayutika Order, a new *nikaai*, adhering or "yoked" to the *dhamma* and emphasizing Pali studies, "especially the mastery of the vinaya."[89] Most of his monks came from middle-and upper-class families, and they were distinguished from other monks by a new style of robes that fell over both shoulders, new ritual and religious routines, and new chanting pronunciation – all considered to be more authentic.

It is quite possible that, given the resentment the new sect caused, it would not have survived without help,[90] for after Mongkut ascended the throne, the new Thammayut Order prospered only due to its having royal patronage. "The germinal *sangha* reforms of Mongkut were nurtured in the capital and part of the intent [was] to control the national *sangha* and improve the level of textual knowledge and monastic practice."[91] Those who followed other Buddhist traditions were referred to by Mongkut as "Mahanikaai," that is, those monks and laypeople of customary (and therefore "lower") habits who "blindly followed the Buddhism of their fathers and grandfathers," and whose practices often included aspects of local or traditional culture imbued with folklore.[92]

> ...the monastic forest dweller, largely because of his regular habitat (co-existing with the anomalous wilderness, decay, and death), informal network of pupils and movement within the fringe of established order, has long been a cause of concern, ambivalence, and mistrust to the establishment.[93]

Although Mongkut intended the new order to be a reform movement, it quickly became "integrated with the newly centralized bureaucratic government...[and] became the model for the modern state Buddhism."[94] According to Santikaro Bhikkhu,

> ...it became in the end a somewhat elitist, royally sponsored, subgroup within Thai Buddhism which, because of its royal sponsorship, tended to lord it over the other monks...King Mongkut, Rama IV, was quite arrogant towards other monks and put himself in a position of being "the one who knew."[95]

The reform Thammayut order was presented as being "rational and anti-superstition" and as aiming "to eliminate practices that he [Mongkut] felt were too ritualistic, metaphysic, or overly influenced by local or regional culture"[96] but, while it appealed to those with modernized western-oriented sensibilities, it was not amenable to all Buddhists.

> ...in the views of some, like myself, [the order] had pushed any notion of the transcendent aside in order to make Buddhism "practical," basically to serve worldly ends. I'm not opposed to that, but you don't chuck out the transcendent to do it, and he more or less did.[97]

The Sangha Act of 1902. Three acts formally brought the *sangha* under the government's control, and each "of these Acts created a state-imposed organizational structure for the *Sangha* that paralleled the current forms of government." The Sangha Act of 1902, passed under Mongkut's successor, King Chulalongkorn, Rama V, while Thailand was still a monarchy, integrated "monks of all traditions into a national sangha hierarchy,"[98] and centralized the *sangha* in Bangkok under a Supreme Patriarch.[99] Local monks were discouraged from continuing regional practices, and the Mon tradition (favored by Mongkut) "became known as the Thammayut order, while the Lao and the Siamese traditions were lumped together" into what was now "the other order,." the Mahanikaai. In separate camps, the Thammayut saw themselves as superior, with a clear de-emphasis on meditation, and *did not* allow non-Thammayut to participate in their rituals, while the Mahanikaai emphasized meditation practice, and *did* allow Thammayuts to participate in theirs."[100] And the tradition of dividing the monkhood into two categories – town and forest – was maintained: "Town dwellers *(gāmavāsin)* concentrated on *gathadhura* – the task of learning the scriptures. Forest dwellers *(araññavāsin)* concentrated on *vipassanādhura* – the task of meditation practice."[101]

The dominance of the Thammayut at this time is illustrated in the history of the monk most important to the emergent modern forest tradition, Phra Ajahn Mun Phurithatto (1870-1949), who led a revival of *thudong* practices and of forest meditation.[102] Ajahn

Mun was trained in a Lao tradition and practiced forest disciplines in the northeast but was, in time, re-ordained in the Thammayut order. Ajahn Mun's career crystallized "the formation of a distinctive forest-dwelling monastic tradition in the wake of national reforms."

> The charismatic and idiosyncratic Ajaan Man and his widely revered forest-dwelling disciples remained on the rim of the establishment for much of their lives – yet constituted the mystical core of orthodoxy, eventually recognized at the centre.

Mun was seen as the expression of convergence for indigenous and universal Buddhist ideals, and was deeply influenced by teachings on discipline and practice of the new Thammayut order.[103]

Of this "domestication" of the forest tradition, one disciple has said: at "first the movement was disparaging of these meditation monks living in the woods, but later...found it expedient to incorporate them." These forest monks "were 'used,' and continue to be used, to legitimize certain elements of the state, the royal family and, what to me is most insidious, the military."[104] From Bangkok's vantage, however, the emphasis was on the positive continuity of forest practice, for it is said that even though Mongkut had left the monkhood for the monarchy, he practiced mindfulness all his life.

> In the Sangha he set up a strong *araññavāsī* tradition concentrating on the task of deep meditation practice. The Dhammayutika Order of the Northeast, in particular, carries on this spiritual heritage until today, especially through charismatic meditation masters like the Venerable Phra Acariya Mun.[105]

The acceptance of Mun and his disciples by the Thammayut elders,[106] that is, the approval of Thammayut *thudong* monks, was based on a changed attitude toward the wandering monks. Their acceptance was seen to help shore up the Thammayut order when its prestige was in decline, for example, and to help ease conflict between the Thammayut and Mahanikaai orders. But, in time, the tide began to shift publicly in favor of the Mahanikaai, as when a

Mahanikaai elder was appointed supreme patriarch by the government, the first time such a thing had happened in eighty-four years.[107]

The Sangha Act of 1941. In 1941, a new Sangha Act was passed to replace the act of 1902, with the intention of decentralizing and democratizing *sangha* governance, parallel to "the democratic, constitutional monarch in place at the time."[108] "The new Sangha Act undermined the authority of the pro-monarchist Thammayut order and transferred administrative control of the sangha in Thailand to the Mahanikai order."[109] Following this, there was increasing acknowledgment that "the wandering meditation monks [were]...worthy of respect and emulation by book-learning monks"[110] and worthy, as well, of continued allegiance by local villagers.

> It is not hard to see why the thudong tradition found acceptance in the countryside. The monks were tolerant of the belief in local spirits and ghosts, accepting it as an integral part of the villagers' world...Indeed, the idea that different kinds of spirits abided everywhere (in forests, trees, rivers, mountains, caves, fields, earth, sky, and animals) was convincing to the wandering monks, who had experienced meetings with some of these spirits in their visions.[111]

The lineage of Ajahn Mun, then, "although embedded in the primitive tradition of forest dwelling" and, recharged by "recognition from the ecclesiastical establishment, was due to a combination of personal charisma and informal associations with influential northeastern monks," who were situated in the capital and connected with elite laity.[112]

The Sangha Act of 1962. In 1962 a third Sangha act was enacted in which a "top-down structure" was reintroduced "to match the autocratic government of Field Marshall Sarit Thanarat."[113] One of the objectives of the government was to legitimize and promote its development agenda. The concept of development "was first formulated in the mid-1800s when King Mongkut brought his kingdom into the global economy and restructured the Buddhist *Sangha* to legitimize the central government." The third strand of forest tradition, then, are the "development monks" in the 1970s, or the "environmental/ecology monks" in the 1980s, who "challenged the government's concept of development, Buddhism's legitimation of it, and the suffering that they believed it caused the Thai people."[114] According to Santikaro Bhikkhu, the development monks "were not as strict in terms of discipline and didn't get caught up in royalist politics. Rather they consciously wanted to do something about the poverty they saw around them." Despite the global social consciousness of their times, this movement "grew more out of indigenous sources rather than the western ecology movement or Bangkok,"[115] and local cultural resources show how "development monks" could easily morph into "ecology monks." According to Santikaro, there is an

> aspect of Thai culture where rivers, forests, fields, and home and temple or *wat* are all intertwined. The Thai word for village is *ban* and it's the same word for home... When people say "going home" it's not so much the house, but where you grew up and where your family is. The word *ban* includes the *wat* or temple, that is never separate from the rice fields, the rivers and streams where people fished, and the forest where people got a lot of their food. So all these are intertwined.[116]

As concern grew about the rate of environmental degradation stemming from policies of the government, many of the NGOs involved in development issues turned to environmental issues and with them many Buddhist monks and laypeople.[117] Caught up in the debate about how best to manage forest reserves and parks, monks are involved in many projects. Beginning in 1985, with their "first case in which [they]...took an environmental position *as monks,*" the environmentalist monks opposed the building of a cable car up Doi Suthep mountain, traditionally an important pilgrimage site for Buddhist followers.[118] Since then ecology monks have worked to protect forests just by living there or, more vigorous, by directly approaching loggers and trying to convince them not to cut the trees.[119] A number have engaged in tree ordination and have encouraged tree planting[120] and, in some cases where forested areas slated to be national forests or a forest preserves, they are given instead to a monastery or to its abbot, so that the monks there could protect the forest in situ. In fact, one argument for working to save the forests is so that the forest monks have a place to practice. As Ajahn Pasanno has said,

> If we don't have forests we're not forest monks. We're definitely protecting areas where monks can practice within a forest setting, because you need to have a stable and quiet environment for practice...So, definitely, I'm looking out for myself. Our tradition has always been connected to the forest."[121]

Finally, the forth strand in the modern forest tradition is that of *Buddhadasa Bhikkhu* whose project was to reframe Theravada themes away from the promotions of the Thai state and more towards apolitical perspectives. Buddhadasa believed that "monks had a moral responsibility to act, teach, and live in ways such that Buddhist teachings and moralities were more important than what the state wants." On the one hand, the state was involved in shaping the varieties of Thai Buddhism into a single mold to be subsumed under "the Bangkok state-dominated Buddhism that...[was to be] the standard." This process, of course, played an important role in nation building" and, in this, mainstream Thai Buddhism "had basically been bought by the state through perks and through titles, and this was part of the centralizing process." Buddhadasa Bhikkhu's view was that if monks and laypeople felt "the government is doing something immoral," they should point it out because their social role was to "encourage the government to follow Buddhist ethics and values." The greatest issue on which Buddhadasa disagreed with the government was what was development was really about. For Bangkok, it was about economic development according to the capitalist model, but for Buddhadasa it was about development as a human being: "to blindly follow western models is not wise, nor should the Thais reject these models, but that they should look more deeply."[122]

In terms of development and the environment, particularly the forest, Santikaro notes, "the forest became seen more and more in the modern way," as a resource and, while there was creation of national forests and forest preserves, there was no "commitment to preserving the environment or even natural resources." Instead, these national forests and forest preserves were to be opened up "for logging by companies owned by generals...[and others] including foreign corporations." This started "impinging more and more on the monks, who had been free, traditionally, to wander wherever they wanted....And later, in the 80s when deforestation had reached such a serious level, the government decided they had to preserve the forest but this was done in an autocratic way:...they started banning monks from going into areas where they previously could wander freely."[123]

Thai Forest Practice and the Forest

The first thing to note about this practice is that it takes place in the forest and that the forest and the natural world are important to the efficacy of the practice for followers. It is said that Ajahn Mun once told some Thammayut book-learning monks that, "nature was his teacher...After ordination my ajan took me wandering in the forests and on the mountains. I learned the dhamma from the trees, the grass, rivers, streams, caves, and rocks. I listened to the sounds of birds and other animals."[124] Ajahn Mun's forest practice was based on the idea that the "soteriology of the forest tradition...is the most direct spiritual route to 'liberation' from the world of psycho-social mundanity...Those who have reached the end are few and far between," and most have been forest monks in the lineage of Ajahn Mun.[125] The forests are important because, first, they "are seen as sources of life;" second, they represent "the wilderness...this is the wild part where you go as a wandering monk, to test yourself, to challenge your fears, to be away from your comforts;" and, third, through them one comes to know the truth, that "dharma is nature, nature is dharma...Nature is truth in itself, and we can learn by living close to nature, meditating in nature."[126]

The spiritual practice of the forest tradition centers around *thudong* (P. *dhutanga)* or ascetic practices, the foremost of which is the practice of living in the forest either in a forest monastery or in a solitary forest hut, and walking through the forest for short or long periods of time, accompanied by the practice of concentration meditation *(kammathaan*; P. *kammaṭṭhāna)*.[127] This practice goes back to the time of the Buddha when monks walked long distances as part of their alms rounds, and as part of their ministry to teach the *dhamma*. The walking of the Thai forest tradition uses the traditional patterns of "walking meditation," and it encourages open attention and awareness of one's surroundings, and encourages awareness of plant life and the inter-workings of biosystems. In addition, the forest practice highlights vows of *ahiṁsā,* for as one of Ajahn Mun's disciples notes: "I ate only once a day...I refrained from digging the ground and cutting greenery."[128] Another noted that nature responded to acts of violence, for on certain mountains, "if anyone went to cut any of the trees, they would either die a violent death, become seriously ill, or suffer misfortune of one sort or another."[129]

Living in the forest as part of one's practice encourages special sensitivity to the transitoriness of life processes. "When you're out in the woods," says Santikaro, "and your windows are just holes with shutters, no glass, and whatever's going on around you is immediately touching you, you are not insulated from the constant change, and ebb and flow, of life in the forest." Moreover, in the forest, so many of the tensions of life among people simply aren't there:

> So, in hanging out with trees, just being around trees a lot...trees don't have egos the way other people do, so for me it's an ongoing reflection. When I interact with people, the whole ego business – fears and worries – is constantly provoked...But with trees it just doesn't happen, and for me that's always been helpful.[130]

Not only is forest life stripped of some of the "ego business" of life in the city, for instance, but it's a place that's especially helpful in facing one's fears. Living a *thudong kammathaan* life in which one works towards liberation, involves rooting out fear of ghosts and fear of wandering in the forest alone. In this way, being deep in the forest or at the forest cemetery "were thus training grounds for the thudong monk."[131]

Moreover, much can be learned from living in the forest. Santikaro, for example, notes,

> Around our huts in the woods, the ground is bare and we keep it swept. Most monks would do this once a day and leave it, but I'm a little bit of an anal-retentive type. So, in the course of sweeping the area of about forty by forty feet, leaves would fall. And there's this urge in me to run over and pick up these leaves, which means that I could sweep all day long. So, I learn to notice this one little thing that my mind does that's a slight obsessive quality, and then I learn to relax: OK, the leaves are going to fall, get them tomorrow.

Breathing meditation is also enhanced in the forest, for like the practitioner, "trees breathe, and, when you're breathing among trees, you have really fresh air. So, I feel here I am breathing, and the trees are breathing, and I feel a lot more connection [with them] than I do with a rock."[132] What can be learned from living in the forest differs according to the individual and especially according to the teacher, for the teacher's lineage will pass on views about plants and trees to followers not only in Thailand, but in Buddhist communities around the world. Below are some views of three of the most important contemporary Thai teachers who take the "forest" part of the Thai forest tradition very seriously: Ajahn Chah, Buddhadasa Bhikkhu, and Phra Prayudh Payutto.

10.4 Ajahn Chah (1918-1992)

Ajahn Chah Suphattho was born to a family of subsistence farmers in a rural village, near the town of Ubon Rajathani, in the Lao area of northeast Thailand. Leaving home of his own accord, he ordained as a novice monk at age nine, and took higher ordination *(upasampada)* as a *bhikkhu* at age twenty. Ajahn Chah had formal education through the fourth grade level, but continued studying *dhamma, vinaya,* and basic scriptures in the monastery. In 1946, "dissatisfied with slack standard of discipline in his village temple and yearning for guidance in meditation,"[133] he left the monastery and undertook the life of a wandering ascetic monk *(thudong)*, practicing meditation and staying in caves, forests, and cremation grounds.

> Previously I lived together with a lot of monks, but I didn't feel right. I ran away to the forests and mountains, fleeing the crowd, the monks and novices...I was a Dhutanga monk, I went travelling, but things still things weren't right.[134]

He practiced under the guidance of local forest teachers and spent some time with Ajahn Mun. Of this tradition he says: "The way of the Forest Masters is the way of renunciation. On this Path there's only abandoning. We uproot views stemming from self-importance. We uproot the very essence of our sense of self."[135]

> If we talk about understanding Dhamma then both study monks and practice monks use the same words. But the actual understanding that comes from practicing dhamma is not quite the same. It may seem to be the same, but one is more profound...deeper than the other. The kind of understanding that comes from practice leads to surrender, to giving up.[136]

In 1954, he moved back to his home village and settled nearby in the thick and dangerous forest of Pah Pong, "a place of cobras, tigers, and ghosts." A large monastery known as Wat Pah Pong formed around him, made up of monks, nuns, and laypeople and, in time, Wat Pah Nanachat was formed for foreigners. Although Ajahn Chah

> does not belong to the Reformed Sect [Thammayut], he was a close disciple of the late venerable Phra Acariya Mun and has spread his lifestyle, his method of meditation practice and his strict adherence to the Buddha's disciplines to the majority of monks in the Mahānikāya Order.[137]

Known also as Luang Por ("venerable father"), Ajahn Chah has attracted Thai and foreign monks to his teachings, and there are now many forest branch temples of Ajahn Chah's monastery in northeast Thailand.[138] Moreover, he has also set up monastic orders in Britain, the United States, Sri Lanka, New Zealand, and Australia.

Ajahn Chah's overall style is that "each person has his own natural pace," that one should "simply stick to the present moment," and that "eventually the mind will reach its natural balance where practice is automatic." He does not emphasize any special meditation techniques, but does demand discipline, strict training in virtue, the precepts, renunciation, concentration, and bearing in mind the dignity of the monastery's high standards. He often taught by anecdote, example, story, and koan-like questioning, and in his teaching he used humor, close-knit relationships, and honest self-examination to its best advantage. To a newcomer, practice at Wat Pah Pong often seemed difficult, especially "the seeming arbitrary rules of conduct" one had to follow but, though life with Ajahn Chah often appeared inconsistent and contradictory, it was simply the constant adjustment for individual practitioners with a mind to keeping overall balance.[139]

At Wat Pah Pong,

> there is usually group meditation twice a day and sometimes a talk by the senior teacher, but the heart of the meditation is the way of life. The monastics do manual work, dye and sew their own robes, make most of their own requisites and keep the monastery buildings and grounds in immaculate condition...Scattered throughout the forest are individual huts *[kuti]* where bhikkhus and nuns live and meditate in solitude, and where they practice walking meditation on cleared paths under the trees.[140]

In addition to the monastic life as lived within the boundaries of a fix location, monks and nuns could undertake, as part of their spiritual training, the practice of *thudong*, the wandering on foot throughout the countryside, either as a pilgrimage or in search of a quiet spot for solitary retreat. "Even thought the forests have been disappearing rapidly throughout Thailand...it has still been possible for this way of life and practice to continue."[141] As reflection of the *dhutanga* practices used to uproot defilements when basic practices were not enough, Ajahn Chah would say of *thudong*: "Living at the foot of a tree...try it out."[142] For Ajahn Chah, living at the foot of a tree was beneficial in several ways:

> Good meditation temples are increasingly hard to find. For most monks, Buddhism is a lot of study without real practice. Everywhere, there is more interest in cutting down forests and building new temples than in developing the mind.[143]

Ajahn Chah's teachings are filled with references to natural images, and perhaps the most famous of them is given in the title of his book, *A Still Forest Pool*:

> Be mindful and let things take their natural course, then your mind will become quiet in any surroundings. It will become still like a clear forest pool and all kinds of wonderful and rare animals will come to drink from it. Then you will clearly see the nature of all things in the world. You will see many wonderful and strange things come and go. But you will be still. This is the happiness of the Buddha.[144]

A practitioner in the Thai forest tradition, Ajahn Chah felt that the most beneficial spiritual pursuit took place in a forest under a tree. "To practice effectively we should find a suitably quiet place, free from distractions. Suitable environments are a garden in the shade of a tree in our backyard, or anywhere we can be alone."[145] Venerable Santacitto, a disciple of Ajahn Chah, notes that there's "an emphasis in this tradition which says that if one really wishes to practice under ideal conditions, then the forests provide these conditions."[146] And in the quietude of the forest, practitioners can "develop subtle feelings and prepare the ground for cultivating wisdom."[147] Caution needs to be taken, however, from getting attached to the peace of mind the forest gives.

> ...people who come and live in the forest become attached to living in it...The Buddha praised living in the forest because the physical and mental solitude that it gives us is conducive to the practice for liberation. However, he didn't want us to become dependent upon living in the forest or get stuck in its peace and tranquility.[148]

Part of Ajahn Chah's teaching style is to use images to impart the *dhamma*, and some of the most powerful are of trees and forests. These images convey his ideas with great effectiveness and are often like homologies, using the formula: some aspect of a person is like some aspect of a tree, and it is dhammic, therefore, to use the tree as a guide for human life. To say that what we know about trees can act as Buddhist teaching assumes, however, that tree and plant life has *sattva* quality, and is, therefore, exemplary, and this is an assumption that Ajahn Chah seems to make. Because we are like trees, then, and, moreover, because we can aspire to be like trees, trees can be excellent teachers of *dhamma.* The following are quotes from Ajahn Chah's teachings.

Trees and people are as they are:

"In the forest there are beautiful trees and ugly trees. Some are bent and gnarled, some straight and tall. There are trees with pith and those without. Just like people. There are bad and good people, crooked and straight people. This is also nature."[149]

"The whole world is already just fine as it is. All the trees in the forest are already just fine as they are: there are tall ones, short ones, hollow ones...all kinds. They are simply the way they are. Through ignorance of their true nature we go and enforce our opinions onto them. 'Oh, this tree is too short! This tree is hollow!' Those trees are simply trees, they're better off than we are...Let the trees teach you. There are so many trees, all with something to teach you. Dhamma is everywhere, in everything in Nature."[150]

Planting a tree is like practicing the dhamma:

"In meditation you must continually be attentive, like when planting a tree. If you plant a tree in one place and after three days you pull it up and plant it in another place, and after a further three days you pull it up again, then go and plant it in yet a different place, it will just die without producing anything. Meditation is the same, it won't bear any fruit,"[151]

"When planting a tree, if you want to do it the right way and get fruit from it, how should you go about it in order to have a relaxed mind? You do that which is your responsibility. Getting hold of the sapling is your job; digging the hole is your job; planting it, fertilizing and watering it...is your job. That's it. Stop there. How fast or slow it grows isn't your job. Let go of this part."[152]

"As with fruit trees, it's possible to get fruit quickly by taking a cutting and planting it, but the tree won't be long-lasting or resilient. Another way is to take a seed and cultivate the tree right from the seed, and thereby it will be truly strong and enduring. Practice follows in accordance with this truth."[153]

"The Buddha taught that this [spiritual] process matures at its own rate...Whether the progress is swift or slow is out of our control. It's just like planting a tree. The tree knows how fast it should grow...If we do the work, the results will be forthcoming – just like planting a tree. For example, say we wanted to plant a chili bush. Our responsibility is to dig a hole, plant the seedling, water it, fertilize, it, and protect it from insects. This is our job, our end of the bargain...Whether the chili plant grows or not is up to it. It's not our business. We can't go tugging on the plant, trying to stretch it and make it grow faster. That's not how nature works."[154]

"Does anyone order the trees to grow the way they do? They can't talk nor can they move around, and yet they grow away from obstacles. Wherever it's cramped and growing will be difficult, they bend outwards. They act on natural laws, yet they do know enough to grow away from danger, to incline toward a suitable place. People are like this. We want to transcend suffering."[155]

Trees and the Mind

"Right now we are sitting in a peaceful forest. Here, if there's no wind, a leaf remains still. When a wind blows, it *flaps* and *flutters*. The mind is similar to that leaf. When it contacts a mental impression, it, too, flaps and flutters according to the nature of that mental impression."[156]

"It can be likened to a tree. A tree has roots, a base, a trunk, branches and leaves. Every single leaf and branch, including the trunk, depends on the roots to absorb nutriment and sent it up to those other parts. A tree is dependent on the roots to sustain it. We are the same. Our actions and our speech are the "branches," "twigs" and "trunk." The "mind" is the root which absorbs nutriment and sends it out to sustain the "trunk," "branches" and "leaves" which in turn bear fruit,"[157]

"A tree has bark, softwood and heartwood. These three parts are inter-dependent. There is heartwood due to the presence of the bark. There is bark because of the soft wood. There is softwood due to the heartwood. They come together just like the Three Teachings of *sīla, samādhi*, and *paññā.*"[158]

Trees are teachers:

"Do the trees in the forest teach us something? Sometimes we like some of the trees. We may feel they look beautiful and have a nice smell and so forth. The trees are just growing according to their nature, and on our own side, we develop these good feelings about them... We don't need to go teaching people, trying to impress something on them. We only need to develop ourselves through our own practice."[159]

"When the tree gives fruit, we gather and eat it indifferently without any real investigation or consideration. The sweet and sour tastes of fruit are their nature; these characteristics are Dharma and the fruits are teaching us something, but we don't understand that... The leaves of the tree fall, then the new buds appear. We see this cycle but don't really think much about it, so we don't learn anything of significance from it. If we were to turn it inward, we would see that our own birth and death are not so very different from that of trees... The natural phenomena of trees, vines, and shrubs are continuously and unceasingly in a state of flux, and if we turn this inward, we will understand birth, aging, and death."[160]

"The forest is peaceful, why aren't you? You hold onto things causing your confusion. Let Nature teach you. Hear the bird's song and then let go. If you know nature, you'll know Dhamma. If you know Dhamma, you'll know nature."[161]

"We will come to understand that everything in the world is a teacher. Trees and vines, for example, can all reveal the true nature of reality... We can learn from Nature enough to be enlightened... Take trees, for example; all trees upon the earth are equal, are one, when see through the reality of 'anicca-dukkha-anatta.' First they come into being, then grow and mature, constantly changing, until they finally die as every tree must."[162]

"We can learn Dhamma from nature, from trees for example. A tree is born due to a cause and it grows following the course of nature. Right here the tree is discoursing Dhamma to us, but we don't understand this."[163]

"This body of ours is born and exists dependent on conditions, on the elements of earth, water, wind and fire. It has its food, it grows and grows. Every part of the body changes and flows according to its nature. It's no different from the tree; hair, nails, teeth and skin – all change. If we know the things of nature, then we will know ourselves."[164]

While any good teacher can use what's around him or her as a means of teaching with great ease, it is the power of solitude from other humans coupled with the fullness of life present in the forest that makes it such an ideal place to *teach in*, and to *teach with.* Coupling the commitment to live in the forest with Ajahn Chah's clear sense that understanding the patterns in tree and plant life is paradigmatic for spiritual development makes evident how Ajahn Chah can hold up the tree as a model of sattvic life. Hence the following well known passage:

> People have asked about my practice. How do I prepare my mind for meditation? There is nothing special. I just keep it where it always it. They ask, "Then are you an arahant?" Do I know? *I am like a tree in a forest, full of leaves, blossoms and fruit. Birds come to eat and next, animals seek rest in its shade. Yet the tree does not know itself. It follows its own nature. It is as it is.*[165]

Ajahn Chah also liked to use mango images in his teaching, and they were especially helpful in giving him access to ideas of seeding, ripening, fruiting or lack of fruiting – that is, change with all its benefits and frustrations.

Mango tree and the cycle of life

"The world revolves like this. It's something like a mango tree. The tree matures, puts forth blossoms, and fruits appear and ripen. These become rotten, and the seed goes back into the ground to become a new mango tree. The cycle starts again."[166]

Mangoes and change

"It's like a mango. When it's a flower we call it a flower. When it becomes a fruit we call it a mango. When it ripens we call it a ripe mango. It's always one mango but it continually changes."[167]

"All the stages and characteristics of mangoes, such as sourness and sweetness, being small and growing large, can be found in a single mango. Studying one, it is possible to know about all mangoes."[168]

Mangoes and lack of fruit

"Many of the mangoes fall and rot before they are ripe. Others never ripen well, so what's the use? Well, it's like this: some fall and some you will have to throw away, but you plant and take care of the trees [anyway]...If you think, Who wants to plant fruit trees when the mangoes just fall off prematurely? You won't be eating any mangoes."[169]

"If a tree has not fruit, nobody disturbs it, so its leaves and branches are not damaged."[170] This realization caused the king who realized it to spiritual awakening.

"Sometimes, when a fruit tree is in bloom, a breeze stirs and scatters some of its blossoms. Some buds remain and grow into small green fruit. A wind blows and some of these fall to the ground. Other fruits ripen, and then they too fall. And so it is with people. Like flowers and fruit in the wind, they fall at different stages of life."[171]

We argue, then, that Ajahn Chah follows the early Pali tradition in at least three ways. First, he believed that *practice in the forest* was the most appropriate for spiritual progress, and in this he took example from the Buddha's life. Second, his teaching draws on plants and trees to make *generous use of homologies*.

> (1) Plants and trees are like and correspondent to humans in the variety of their appearance, e.g., ugly-beautiful, bent-straight, short-tall. (2) Plants and trees are models for humans in their self-evolution, e.g., you plant the tree properly, but then let it grow on its own – you cultivate the spiritual process properly, but then let it mature on its own; or "I am like a tree in a forest, full of leaves, blossoms and fruit. Birds come to eat and next, animals seek rest in its shade. Yet the tree does not know itself. It follows its own nature." And (3) by observing trees attentively, practitioners can learn something, especially about the *dhamma:* e.g., all things as dependent on conditions and as impermanent.

Finally, Ajahn Chah, in using plants and trees as models and paradigms appears to work out of the assumption that *tree life is exemplary*: plants and trees are stable and calm, undistractible and even-minded, and content with abiding in their own nature that is marked by conditionality and impermanence. And in this way, he attributes sattvic quality to them.

10.5 Buddhdasa Bhikkhu (1906-1993)

One of best-known *dhamma* teachers in Thailand, Buddhadasa Bhikkhu was a great interpreter of Buddhist scriptures and tradition. He is known as a promoter of modernist reform based on an "integration of the spiritual and mundane," and was involved in a reconstruction of Theravada thought "in accord with reinterpreted doctrinal principles,"[172] in areas of both theoretical interpretation and social application.

> In reinterpreting the totality of Theravada doctrine, Buddhadāsa is fundamentally concerned to shift the focus of Thai Buddhism from the transcendent to this world, and to incorporate the hopes and aspirations of contemporary Thai laymen and laywomen into Buddhism by conferring religious value on action in the social world.[173]

This "innovative work" had a number of historical precedents in the Theravada world, including the Buddhist reforms instituted by King Mongkut who "sought to remove inconsistencies between monastic practices and the clerical code of conduct or *vinaya,* and between a doctrinal interpretation of Buddhism and popular views."[174]

Buddhadasa was born to a merchant family in Chaiya, in the province of Surat Thani in southern Thailand in 1906. He was not ordained as a novice as Ajahn Chah had been, but entered the Sangha at age twenty-one. After much study and some teaching, he returned to Chaiya and, in time, moved several miles outside of the village to the forest hermitage he had established earlier.[175] Here, inspired by "his sense of the liberating power of nature-as-*dhamma,*" he founded Wat Suan Mokkh[176] or the Garden of Liberation in 1932, as a center for teaching and practice,[177] and here began his systematic reappraisal and reinterpretation of Theravada Buddhist teachings. At the center of Suan Mokkh, he

> forbade all statues of the Buddha and all the popular forms of worship and merit-making. Instead of building a large temple for the monks to meet for ceremonies, he placed great stones in a circle under the trees to create a holy place as it was in the forests of India over 2,500 years ago.[178]

A variety of methods for practice were allowed at Wat Suan Mokkh, as Buddhadasa had the ability "to synthesize traditional formulations of doctrine with fresh insights derived from personal experience."[179]

> The synthetic genius of Buddhadāsa is...illustrated by the nature of his forest hermitage. It combines the traditional with the modern...The monks...live in small, relatively isolated dwellings spread throughout a wooded hillside...The focus of the hermitage, however, is a modern building that has an auditorium for lectures, and audio-visual capability.[180]

As a young Thai monk, Buddhadasa had been "dissatisfied with the division of the Sangha into meditation *(vipassanādhura)* and textual learning *(ganthadhura)*"[181] and, as he developed, his teaching was based on a combination of personal experience and meditation, drawing freely from Theravāda as well as from Mahāyāna. Out of many sources, then, including an understanding of the Pali Tipitaka, Buddhadasa developed his views on social reform and, in particular, his proposals for Dhammic Socialism.[182] By official standing, Buddhadasa was a Mahanikaai monk, having ordained in that order in 1926, though he could well have been influenced to become a monk by the "monks of the Thammayut Order from Wat Racchathiwat in Bangkok" a year or so before his ordination.[183]

Swearer argues that the "core of Buddhadāsa's ecological hermeneutic is found in his identification of the *dhamma* with nature."[184] In Buddhadasa, nature can be understood in two ways:

first, nature refers to the natural world and, in this sense, the natural world (e.g., the forest) is considered a good place to practice in, and the natural world is a good teacher. Second, nature refers to the nature of things, that is that they are caused, conditioned, and impermanent and, with humans, are tied up with attachment and suffering. In both of these ways, *dhamma* is nature, and nature is *dhamma*.

In the *first sense of nature*, as *"the natural world,"* Buddhadasa, like Ajahn Chah, believes that nature, rather than a business office, is a more effective context for pursuing spiritual liberation. He says,

> Trees, rocks, sand, even dirt and insects can speak...if we reside in nature near trees and rocks we'll discover feelings and thoughts arising that are truly out of the ordinary. At first we'll feel a sense of peace and quiet...that may eventually move beyond that feeling to a transcendence of self. The deep sense of calm that nature provides through separation...from the troubles and anxieties that plague us in the day-to-day world functions to protect heart and mind...Trees and rocks, then, can talk to us. They help us understand what it means to cool down from the heat of our confusion, despair, anxiety, and suffering.[185]

Not only is nature, and especially the forest, a felicitous and beneficial place for practicing meditation, but Buddhadasa's identification of nature with *dhamma* allows one to read nature as if it were a text. Spending time at places like Wat Suan Mokkh among the trees, rocks, birds, and insects, for example, can teach humans about forgetting the self. Or better, in the presence of all the life of the forest, one experiences being as caused, conditioned, and impermanent, and infused with attachment and suffering. Thus, "in Buddhadāsa's spiritual biocentric view, being attuned to the lessons of nature is tantamount to at-one-ment with the *dhamma*."[186]

Buddhadasa also understands the natural world as teaching human practitioners about the process of cultivation. In inquiring about how best to behave, the practitioner sees that the "condition of normalcy all around us" is that "stones, sand, trees, and insects simply *are;* no artificial theory or social system directs their interrelationships. They exist in a pure, natural state of balance." And this then provides a model for how to behave, a morality of nature *(sīla-dhamma)*,[187] that is to let things be as they are and to follow that prescription as a model for oneself.

Trees teach as well in that they exemplify the "service" quality of the realized being. Phra Pongsak tells a story of his time at Wat Suan Mokkh:

> A newly ordained monk cut down a large tree to build a kuti. Buddhadasa went for a walk and saw the stump one afternoon. The next day after the meal he demanded of the assembled monks. Who cut down the tree? The monk who was building the kuti owned up. That day Buddhadasa lectures us on how trees had a value for our lives. He talked for an hour and I summed up that trees are an unlimited resource for human beings. It is from trees and other plants that man finds the four basic needs: food, shelter, clothing, and medicine. Trees are also the creator and protector of the natural balance...How can a monk who is not grateful to the trees for the benefits they provide, be successful in practicing dhamma?[188]

As "the creators and protectors of the balance of nature," forests are the basic element of the teaching of morality. "The survival of forests is essential to the survival of the sila-tham, and ensures human well-being and harmony in society. It is," says Phra Pongsak, "a direct responsibility of monks to teach people to protect the forest and environment."[189]

Again, Buddhadasa suggests that the mind best understood as a kind of ecological system that is flourishing when it is fully expressing *dhamma*. He says of this view that "Dhamma is the ecology of the mind:" when the mind is "fresh, beautiful, quiet, and joyful" it is at its most natural and reflects "a natural spiritual ecology" which is a mind with *dhamma*. This mind is marked by "a deep spiritual solitude, so that nothing can disturb or trouble it;" it has cool joyfulness rather than hot happiness, and it is fresh and not dried up or parched.[190]

Finally, Buddhadasa's view, that nature and the natural world can teach us something, is tied in some measure to his vision of Dhammic Socialism. Buddhadasa believes "that in unjust societies where the rich selfishly hoard social wealth the poor have no opportunity for spiritual attainment because of the unbearable nature of their worldly existence."[191] As a social design, Dhammic Socialism highlights "an egalitarian commonwealth, democratic and decentralized, wherein the modest wealth and power of each obliges them to learn to be sisters and brothers of one another."[192] It also allows for the citizens of a country like Thailand to remain independent, and to experience social and cultural growth such that "loving kindness and compassion...replace competition and violence against oneself, one's own society and the environment."[193] Thus, "the welfare-minded practice of aiding those in need, while lessening personal self-centeredness, also concretely helps the victims of injustice and poverty overcome the social barriers which prevent them from following the path to end suffering."[194] On a larger scale, Buddhadasa's Dhammic Socialism proposes that,

> We must honor and worship the cooperative system. Take a good look. The entire cosmos is a cooperative system. The sun, the moon, the planets, and the stars are a giant cooperative. They are all inter-connected and inter-related in order to exist. In the same world, everything co-exists as a cooperative. Humans and animals and trees and the earth are integrated as a cooperative...These birds and trees all around us form a cooperative. I watch each day as the birds eat the caterpillars that feed off the leaves of the trees...Without the birds these trees wouldn't last.[195]

With the world a cooperative, whatever problems are present anywhere are necessarily intertwined with the environment:

> This mental, emotional, and spiritual alienation then has given rise to the vast number of the environmental problems, such as pollution, climate change, the absence of wild and untouched places...the disappearance of species, and the loss of biodiversity...a forest (for example) is seen only as board feet or dollars.[196]

This last, he imagines – the consumer relationship of humans to the forest – can, like all things, be resolved by Dhammic Socialism, based as it is on the identification of nature and *dhamma*. Says Ajahn Pongsak,

> The forest does not simply mean valuable resources, goods or money. It has its own life, and is useful to all mankind. The forest stands for the world's life and land. It is the source of food for the world, feeding man and animals since the beginning of time...Forests and its benefit are a boundless source of wealth, not just money and wood. They are the foundation for maintaining the natural cycles of the air we breathe; they help to regulate the rainfall upon which our lives depend; they form a giant "sponge" with their extensive roots in the soil from which the rivers emerge...Every tree and its leaves are useful to the world. They give freely of their produces and ask for nothing in return. They are common property belonging to the whole nation. Cutting trees or making charcoal is no compensation for the death of the forest that used to sustain us.[197]

Buddhadasa's position is that if human beings used the earth's resources "according to the laws of Nature...we would not need to use as much as we do now. There would be plenty for everyone for years to come."[198] And what are the laws of nature?

> By living with only what we really need, we are living according to the way of Nature whether we are aware of it or not...Notice that among all the many non-humans forms of life in the Natural world, no one kind takes more than its share...In all these various levels of living things, none ever consumed more than it needed....plant life evolved, each plant consuming only what it needed to maintain itself.[199]

For Buddhadasa, humans can live according to the laws of nature by not consuming goods beyond their simple needs, and by sharing everything that is not essential with others.

> Nature did not provide any of its various forms with the means of hoarding more resources than were necessary for survival and development. Birds, insects, trees – all consume only as much as Nature has given them the means to take in, a level of consumption perfectly adequate for their needs.[200]

By using only what is needed, humans are in accord both with the laws of nature and with the basic principle of socialism: "Socialism...is based on this one simple principle in accord with the way of Nature, that none of us should take more than we really need. We should share whatever extra we have with those with less."[201] Nature, then, "is the embodiment of socialism...[for] nothing in nature exists independently."[202]

Beyond nature as the natural world, Swearer suggests that Buddhadasa understands a *second sense of nature*, whereby *nature is the nature of things*. Buddhadasa could be criticized, argues Swearer, both for promoting escape from (rather than engagement with) the world, and for valuing nature and the forest for human benefit alone (in this case for spiritual practice) rather than for its inherent value. Swearer challenges these criticisms by investigating two terms: "care" (Thai, *anurak*; Pali, *anurakkhā)* and "nature" (Thai, *thamachaat*; Pali, *dhammajāti*).

For Buddhadasa, *anurak* is more than just "conservation," says Swearer, it is "imbued with the quality of protecting, sheltering, or caring for...a pervasive feeling of human empathy (Pali, *anukampā*) for all of our surroundings...caring is the active expression of empathy." In this way, one practices *anurak* by actively expressing empathy in all one does: "One cares for the forest because one empathizes with the forest just as one cares for people."[203] Moreover, the term for nature is *thamachaat* and, for Buddhadasa, "nature" is other than the natural world for it "includes all things in their true, natural state," the way that "things are in the true, dhammic condition."

> To conserve *(anurak)* nature *(thamachāt)*, therefore, translates as having at the core of one's very being the quality of empathetic caring for all things in the world in their natural conditions.[204]

That is, *anurak* signifies having empathy for all things in their caused and conditioned contexts *(thamachaat)*. Because this view implies "that the 'I' is not over against nature but interactively co-dependent with it," Swearer can propose "that Buddhadasa's identification of nature and *dhamma* makes his view inherently biocentric. That is, listening to nature and caring for nature are both forms of dhammic self-forgetting, not merely instrumental to human flourishing."[205]

In his talk, "Forest Wat Wild Monk," Buddhadasa speaks of what was envisioned for Wat Suan Mokkh. "Forest Wat" means that to live in the forest is to live in the simplest way. "Wild Monk" means that to live as a wild person is to live in the simplest way. When we live stripped down in this way, he says, "we live like 'forest wat wild monks,' and we do this to understand voidness fully. Practicing voidness as fully as possible, we will get results: "a heart that is void and cool, that is clean, clear, and calm."[206] Being hot is being lustful or greedy, angry or hateful, deluded or ignorant, and such people lack *dhamma.* Being cool is being simple, humble, fresh, peaceful, not troubled or anxious or agitated or disturbed, and such people have *dhamma.* In this way, Buddhadasa says,

> we study Dhamma from within, by living in the midst of Nature which reveals and demonstrates the Dhamma all the time. Uphold a form of life that doesn't sound very good at all: live like a forest wat wild monk,

here or as a householder. "Please don't forget this short phrase: 'forest wat wild monks' is the way of living for the person who wants to reach the Buddha quickly."[207]

10.6 Phra Prayudh Payutto (1930-)

While Buddhadasa was "a philosopher oriented more to an oral rather than a written medium," Phra Prayudh Payutto is primarily a textual scholar who is most comfortable writing systematic interpretations of the *dhamma.*[208] Known by the monastic title Dhammapitaka beginning in 1993, Phra Prayudh is an outstanding scholar, and "the Thai *saṅgha's* most highly regarded interpreter of the *buddhadhamma.*"[209] Prayudh was born in 1939 to a merchant family in the village of Ban Krang, Siprachan, Suphanburi, in central Thailand. A sickly child, he was ordained as a novice monk at age seven, but lasted only one week; he then reentered the novicehood at age eleven. He was "a very adept and resourceful student...keeping his own meticulous notebooks of canonical references," and developing excellent powers of memory. His higher ordination was sponsored by King Bhumibol Adulyadej, and in 1962 he received an M.A. from Mahachulalongkorn Buddhist University.[210] Following his degree, he set about a career of teaching and scholarship and, in 1993, based on his "masterpiece of modern Thai Buddhist scholarship" *Buddhadhamma*, he received the rank of Phra Dhammapitaka for his firm grounding in the Pali Buddhist Canon.[211]

Like Buddhadasa, Phra Prayudh addresses environmental issues, but does so with greater reference to the Pali Canon and with greater systematic development. The problem of environmental degradation, he argues, comes from the influence of a western worldview that sees humans as separate from nature, humans as masters of nature, and happiness arising from the acquisition of material things.[212] These, he argues, are wrong views *(micchadiṭṭhi)*, to be rectified by cultivation of Buddhist ethical values. A positive and beneficial attitude toward the environment, including plants, animals, and fellow humans, comes from promoting the values of gratitude *(kataññū)*, loving-kindness or empathy *(mettā)*, and happiness *(sukha)*. As an example of *katannū*, or gratitude, Phra Prayudh says:

> ...the shade of a tree we enjoy is enjoyed by others as well. A tree is like a friend which we have no reason to injure. To injure a tree is like hurting a friend. Such a virtuous inner attitude toward nature will prevent us from destructive behavior, on the one hand, and will prompt helpful actions, on the other.[213]

In discussing the second value, *mettā*, loving-kindness, Phra Prayudh is less intuitive (like Buddhadasa) and more rationally doctrinal in his encouragement to consider "the karmic side of the mutual interdependence of all life forms." In this way, humans need to be aware of the consequences of their actions so that they do not "willingly," or perhaps unnecessarily, "increase the suffering of sentient and nonsentient beings." Thus, the human "use of plants and animals must be thought out carefully and rationally and not carelessly without contemplating the consequences of our actions."[214] This argument is reminiscent of the "judicious use" view of treating plants proposed above in some of the Hindu and Jain discussions.

The "third ecologically relevant moral value" is *sukha* or happiness that for Phra Prayudh is found, first, by living and practicing in a natural setting "which engenders a greater sense of happiness and well-being." As emphasized by the Thai forest tradition, and by the Buddhism from the beginning, living in a forest is a good practice for training body and mind to overcome the barriers to mental freedom: "Wild nature – the forests, mountains, caves – is the best context in which to overcome the defilements that hinder the attainment of *nibbāna*." Again, "the forest is the most appropriate place to pursue the religious life. Because of its quiet solitude, meditation *(bhāvanā)* or training the mind, is best pursued in a tranquil environment."[215]

On the grounds of its importance to Buddhist practice, Phra Prayudh makes the case for the preservation of the forest, relating to, first, the life and teachings of the Buddha, second, early Buddhist monastic practice, and, third, the development of Buddhism in Thai history. To practice Buddhism, he argues, the practitioner needs to follow the example of the Buddha, whose birth, enlightenment, teaching, and death took place in the forest, and for whom "the forest was the preferred environment for finding the solitude required for achieving this state of mind" – i.e., overcoming mental defilement, and separation from confusion, anxiety, and stress.

Early Buddhist monastic practice is important because the original requisite *(paccaya)* for a monk's lodging was at the foot of a tree, and eventually early monasteries were established in the forest.[216] Although the Buddha saw limitations to living in the forest – that is, that there had to be special instructions for where to build a lodging in relation to lay communities and to hermits (i.e., removed from lay life but not fully isolated from it; living on the fringe, in the liminal space or ecotone between full participation in, and full separation, from lay life) – the Buddha fully acknowledged forest life as wholesome for monks "who live in the forest striving for simplicity and solitude in order to train themselves."[217]

In addition, the practitioner should be able to follow Thai tradition for, from the Sukhothai and Ayutthaya periods on, Thai Buddhism has encouraged the Sinhalese idea of the distinction between forest *(araññavāsin)* and town *(gāmavāsin)* monasteries, "so that for the state not to support forest monasteries would fly in the face of a practice that has defined Thai Buddhism from its early beginnings." For Phra Prayudh, then, arguing for preservation of the forest is based on forests and nature being an "ideal venue for the pursuit of Buddhist spiritual goals and moral values."[218] These goals and values fall in part under the Thai *dhutanga* practices, undertaken voluntarily and meant for disciplining the self and removing defilements *(kilesa). Dhutanga* observance is relative to individual temperaments and environmental factors, and is assessed as to the perceived benefit to the surrounding community. Included in these practices are going for alms, eating only alms food, refusing invitations to eat in the homes of laity, and often gathering old cloth for robes, washing it, dyeing it, cutting it and sewing it.[219]

It's important to note a distinction Swearer makes about Phra Prayudh's position on forest dwelling.

> The *principle* behind the Buddha's advocacy of a forest as a monastic retreat was its appropriateness as a place for the pursuit of monastic training, not that forest dwelling was a necessary and sufficient condition of monastic life.

Because monks have responsibilities not only to their own enlightenment, he argues, but also to other *saṅgha* members and to lay practitioners, they must not be so far from towns as to make their work difficult.[220] This issue is important to Phra Prayudh's response to the activities of the activist monk Phra Prajak Kuttajitto who has now returned to lay life.[221] Phra Prajak, an activist monk from northeast Thailand, was arrested twice in 1991 for activities related to his promotion of forest conservation. Phra Prajak was accused of trespassing on National Forest Reserves land and setting up a meditation center there, and of organizing villagers in Korat Province. In both of these cases, he moved against the government's effort to remove villagers from the National Forest Reserves by questioning the action's legality, and by objecting to replacing natural and diverse forest growth with trees grown for commercial use, primarily eucalyptus.[222] Phra Prayudh's response to the case was to return to the Pali Canon and note, first, that forested, or planted, lands used by Buddhist monks were lands that were given specifically to them for their use – "many of the major monasteries donated to the *saṅgha* were in forest groves" – and, second, that monastic life was about cultivation leading to liberation wherever it might take place.

> The Buddha shouldn't be revered because he lived near trees...Rather, he should be respected as one who realized the *dhamma* and then taught it. The Buddha advocated a life of simplicity and sufficiency not as an end in itself but as the context for the development of knowledge of the cause and effect of all actions. The Buddha praised monks who lived in the forest...[but he] said that whether or not one lived in the forest was a matter of individual intent.[223]

Emphasizing again his view on the diversity of pathways in the Buddhist tradition, especially on the forest dwelling issue, Phra Prayudh says that the "path a person chooses to take...depends upon his expertise, character, and personal preferences. Some people may feel compelled to go to the forest, and others, while they may want to live in the forest, are not able to do so."[224]

The second aspect of *sukha* or happiness (the third ecologically relevant moral value) is that nature is an important teacher of both moral behavior and mental concentration. And, here again, Phra Prayudh uses the Buddha's life in the forest and the discipline of the time as illustration that "the forest [was seen] as a place to practice the *dhamma* and to achieve a feeling of well-being, a happy state of mind, and eventually higher states of mental consciousness."[225] Significant here is that one not only practiced the *dhamma* in the forest, but also learned *dhamma* from the forest by way of experience. While the truth of Buddhist teaching, *dhamma*, can be learned anywhere, Phra Prayudh makes clear that nature is an especially good teacher. First, nature is all we have. "There is nothing higher than nature, or nothing besides nature,"[226] and humans are only equally affective with "other causal factors" on what happens in nature."[227] Moreover, nature teaches many things consonant with Buddhist teaching: dependent origination, the conditioned nature of elements ("every component part comes into being due to the break up or disintegration of other component parts"), impermanence, attachment, and suffering.[228]

Phra Prayudh does, however, believe that people can bring about change in the world, and thus sees environmental activism as consonant with Buddhism.

> Because natural laws are usually neutral, the outcome of a given situation depends on the causal factors that brought it into beings. It is possible, then, for people to alter their circumstances, to bring about improvements in the world.[229]

The principle of impermanence, he argues "offers hope for increased progress," and with the effects of human deeds *(kamma)*, it is possible to emphasize "the importance of education and training in order to bring about wisdom that is able to change things for the better."[230] Because of this, he argues, *"we have an obligation to conserve the forest."*

> If the maintenance of forests is for well-being of the people and the peace of society, then monks have the responsibility to teach people the value of forests and how to protect them. Buddhist laypersons should help conserve forests and encourage monks to practice the religious life in the peace and solitude of the forest.[231]

And in that preservation of the forest, practitioners are reminded to "abstain from taking life *(pāṇātipāta)*... not harm others...have...loving-kindness towards all beings [and] assist in the sustenance of all life."[232]

****

Given "the rapid expansion of cash-cropping and corresponding deforestation in the 1960s, many of the traditional *dhutanga* sites in the northeast have disappeared,"[233] raising the call for this trend to be reversed, and for forest areas to be preserved and replanted. Among the many reasons given are that forests are places of practice for Buddhist seeking liberation and, in fact, some like Phra Pongsak have argued that one of the best ways to preserve and protect the Thai forests is to designate the forest area as a Buddhist park, "because it was the only way that the forest could possibly be protected. As a Buddhist Park, the trees and every kind of wild animal would belong to sasana (religion or Buddhism)."[234]

Besides the theme that forests are beneficial places to practice Buddhism, we have seen other themes as well. Among the most frequent is that nature (and especially forests and trees), acts as a teacher for practitioners. Depending on the character of a person's practice, forests and trees can teach any number of things – Buddhist views about natural laws and of things as conditioned and interdependent; the qualities of the mature ascetic; acute mindfulness of one's surroundings including bioregions; and the various models nature provides for social communities.

It is intriguing, moreover, that among the views presented here, there are two, not necessarily opposed, views of *why* we should be concerned about forests and trees at all. First is the "*sattva* behavior" argument, that trees provide great benefit to humans, animals, and ecosystems and that, given this "service" quality, they should be protected and preserved. Second is the view that a thing in nature, like a plant, should be considered solely for its value in and of itself, rather than for the value it may have in relation to any human being. Buddhadasa, for example, holds the latter view and says, "trees...simply *are;* no artificial theory or social system directs their interrelationships. They exist in a pure, natural state of balance."

Another intriguing difference is that while some clearly distinguish between the "animate" parts of the forest world and the "inanimate" parts, others explicitly combine "living" and "nonliving" elements under the single category of nature. It is especially noteworthy that, in the latter case, animate and inanimate things are both then the objects of an ethic of compassion, caring, and conservation – reminiscent of an East Asian theme of Buddhahood for grasses and trees, *and also* Buddhahood for rocks and rivers as well. Buddhadasa hints at support for the latter view when he says: "trees and rocks...can talk to us," and "stones, sand, trees and insects simply *are.*"

We end with Santikaro Bhikkhu, and with a colleague, Phra Paisal Visalo, and their responses to our interview questions about the nature of plants, and the ways they understand how contemporary Thai Buddhism picks up on early Indian Buddhist themes. On whether plants are living, Santikaro notes that the forest at Wat Suan Mokkh is not only full of plants and trees but of rocks and other such things – things the disciples there use in their mindfulness practice. However, breaking ranks with Buddhadasa, he says:

> But trees are alive and rocks aren't. Rocks are acted on passively by the forces of nature, whereas trees, being alive, may not be consciously intending the way we do, but the trees in the forest kind of grow around each other in a way that rocks don't...Plants...are sort of adapting to each other and...they grow together and give each other a little space, and this is something people could learn to do.

Here, then, he sees the beneficial possibilities of practitioners modeling themselves on the adaptive growth of trees. Asked about the "livingness" of plants, Phra Paisal notes,

> In my opinion plants are alive in the sense that they can grow, respond to environments, reproduce, and die. But I don't think that they are sentient beings. As you may know, according to Buddhism, plants are not included in any of the three planes of existence. Human beings are not supposed to be reborn as plants.[235]

On the nature of plants, Santikaro said that there was a sense that plants are living and may have the sense of touch. By way of getting at the latter, he remembered a talk by Buddhadasa about a "touch sensitive" plant was used as an example of "plants having a level of consciousness." Moreover, Santikaro noted that "many people, especially monks and Buddhists, believe 'yes' that plants experience pleasure and pain," but that "plants don't exactly experience suffering" because, according to Buddhadasa, "they [plants] don't conceive of themselves in an egoistic way," but plants are conscious in some way as they "have some level of primitive form of awareness and sensitivity." Phra Paisal's view here is that "I don't think that plants experience pleasure, pain, or have consciousness. I don't think plants have karma nor participate in the round of rebirth."[236] Thus these two contemporary monks reflect the ambiguous "borderline" view of plants represented especially in the Buddhist tradition.

Finally, says Santikaro, there is a Thai Buddhist tradition of thinking of all sentient beings as *friends* "in birth, aging, and death. Not everyone applies that to a tree, however. But those who have an especially ecological bent, or those who are doing tree ordination, see trees as '*dhamma*-friends,' see trees as different in important ways; they are a source of life, [and] they're friends."[237]

Endnotes :

1 Harris, "Buddhist Environmental Ethics and Detraditionalization: The Case of EcoBuddhism," p. 200. My italics.

2 Harris, "Buddhist Environmental Ethics and Detraditionalization: The Case of EcoBuddhism," p. 201.

3 Harris, "Buddhist Environmental Ethics and Detraditionalization: The Case of EcoBuddhism," p. 207.

4 Swearer, "The Hermeneutics of Buddhist Ecology in Contemporary Thailand," p. 38-39.

5 Harris, "Buddhist Environmental Ethics and Detraditionalization: The Case of EcoBuddhism," p. 206; Harris, "Causation and *Telos:* The Problem of Buddhist Environmental Ethics," p. 4. Again, Harris says, "the dysteleological character of Buddhist thought militates against anything that could be construed as injecting the concept of an 'end' or 'purpose' into the world;" "Causation and *Telos,*" p. 5.

6 Swearer, "The Hermeneutics of Buddhist Ecology in Contemporary Thailand," p. 39.

7 Taylor, *Forest Monks and the Nation-State*, p. 5.

8 Sponsel and Natadecha-Sponsel, "Why a Tree is More than a Tree," p. 365.

9 When Harris outlines a five-fold typology of "the contemporary

Buddhist discourse of environmental concern," the discourse involving Buddhism on the ground in Asia is focused on Thailand — "accounts of environmentally engaged activity in Asian Buddhist heartlands, most notably in Thailand;" Harris, "Getting to Grips With Buddhist Environmentalism," p. 3.

10 Editor's note on Buddhadasa Bhikkhu, "Conserving the Inner Ecology," p. 5.

11 Isager, "Forest and People in Thai Environmental Discourse," p. 17.

12 Isager, "Forest and People in Thai Environmental Discourse," pp. 17-18.

13 Isager, "Forest and People in Thai Environmental Discourse," p. 18.

14 Darlington, "The Ordination of a Tree: The Buddhist Ecology Movement in Thailand," p. 2.

15 Isager, "Forest and People in Thai Environmental Discourse," pp. 18-19. My italics.

16 Isager, "Forest and People in Thai Environmental Discourse," pp. 19-20.

17 Isager, "Forest and People in Thai Environmental Discourse," pp. 21-22.

18 Isager, "Forest and People in Thai Environmental Discourse," pp. 21-22.

19 Isager, "Forest and People in Thai Environmental Discourse," pp. 24-26.

20 Isager, "Forest and People in Thai Environmental Discourse," pp. 26-28.

21 Sponsel and Natadecha-Sponsel, "Why a Tree is More than a Tree," p. 364.

22 Sponsel and Natadecha-Sponsel, "Why a Tree is More than a Tree," p. 365.

23 Sponsel and Natadecha-Sponsel, "Why a Tree is More than a Tree," p. 364.

24 Sivaraksa, *A Socially Engaged Buddhism*, p. 6. Born in Thailand in 1933, Sulak Sivaraksa was educated in England but returned to Thailand in 1961 to take up teaching. In 1963 he founded the *Social Science Review*, which he edited for six years, and increasingly took part in education about and work on behalf of "democracy, human rights, and accountable government." Moreover, he "has been committed in all his endeavors to a rejection of Western consumerist models of development and an emphasis on the importance of the spiritual and religious dimension of human life;" Sivaraksa,

"Buddhism and a Culture of Peace," p. 39n.

[25] Swearer, "The Hermeneutics of Buddhist Ecology in Contemporary Thailand," p. 23.

[26] Jackson, *Buddhadāsa: Theravada Buddhism and Modernist Reform,* p. 25.

[27] Jackson, *Buddhadāsa: Theravada Buddhism and Modernist Reform,* p. 26.

[28] Sivaraksa, *A Socially Engaged Buddhism,* p. 24.

[29] Sivaraksa, *A Socially Engaged Buddhism,* p. 23.

[30] Sivaraksa, *A Socially Engaged Buddhism,* p. 25.

[31] Sivaraksa, *A Socially Engaged Buddhism,* p. 43.

[32] Sivaraksa, *A Socially Engaged Buddhism,* p. 29.

[33] Sivaraksa, *A Socially Engaged Buddhism,* p. 30.

[34] Jones, *The Social Face of Buddhism,* p. 259. It is reported recently by one of the abbots of a Chiang Mai monastery that government officials did not want monks, in this case like Phra Pongsak Techadhammo, to participate in forest protection movements. Said the deputy district officer: "Forest protection was the duty of the government officials not that of monks or villagers. If the monks continue to support the project, they will be placing themselves in an illegal situation. They are liable to being disrobed or arrested;" Payulpitack, "Social Impact of the Buddhadasa Movement: A Case Study," p. 229.

[35] Jackson, *Buddhadāsa: Theravada Buddhism and Modernist Reform,* pp. 201, 129-153, 232, 205.

[36] Hughes, *Green Buddhist Declaration,* pp. 1, 6, 10.

[37] Nash, *Loving Nature,* p. 179; Paul Taylor, *Respect for Nature,* pp. 71-80.

[38] "Declaration of Interdependence," *Buddhism and Human Rights,* pp. 221-222.

[39] As quoted in Singer, *Animal Liberation,* p. 7. Singer's italics.

[40] "Declaration of Interdependence," *Buddhism and Human Rights,* pp. 221-222.

[41] *Buddhist Perspectives on the Earth Charter,* "Overview" by Steven Rockefeller, pp. 17-18

[42] *Buddhist Perspectives on the Earth Charter,* pp. 13-15.

[43] Darlington, "The Earth Charter and Ecology Monks in Thailand," pp. 47-52.

[44] Darlington, "The Ordination of a Tree: The Buddhist Ecology Movement in Thailand," pp. 3, 4. Isager and Ivarsson note the following: that the important place that Buddhism has gained in the past three decades in environmental debate and action in Thailand is expressed

in two trends:

First, several NGOs are lacing a strong emphasis on Buddhism and spiritual development as they see an environmental and developmental ethic derived from Buddhism as the solution to environmental problems. Second, several Buddhist monks have been praised or criticized for their active use of Buddhist symbols in order to protect trees from being felled and to support locally initiated programs of forest protection.

"Contesting Landscapes in Thailand," p. 402.

45 Udomittipong, "Thailand's Ecology Monks," p. 195.

46 Isager and Ivarsson, "Contesting Landscapes in Thailand," pp. 404-405. Phrakhru Manas tells the story of the event that inspired him to first sanctify a forest. A highway was being constructed in front of Wat Bodharma, and

> A group of workers from the highway Department had been ordered to cut down a holy Bodhi tree in front of the temple to make way for the road. Subsequently, the workers experienced "bad luck," which was believed to have been caused by spirits as a consequence of the workers' misdeed — cutting down a tree considered holy.
>
> In wrapping monks' saffron robes around trees, Phrakhru Manas intends to transfer ordinary trees to the realm of the sacred and, as well, to call upon local guardian spirits to help protect the forest by the loggers who fell the trees.

47 Udomittipong, "Thailand's Ecology Monks," p. 195.

48 Ewers, et al, "Institutions and Natural Resources Management," p. 13.

49 Darlington, "The Ordination of a Tree: The Buddhist Ecology Movement in Thailand," p. 6.

50 Darlington, "The Ordination of a Tree: The Buddhist Ecology Movement in Thailand," p. 1.

51 A full description can be found in Isager and Ivarsson, "Contesting Landscapes in Thailand," pp. 405-407.

52 Darlington notes that bodhi trees are often found with sacred cloth wrapped around them, but that this serves to honor a tree that is already sanctified. This is different from the tree ordination which sanctifies a tree not already sacred; "The Ordination of a Tree: The Buddhist Ecology Movement in Thailand," pp. 6-9.

53 Darlington, "The Ordination of a Tree: The Buddhist Ecology

Movement in Thailand," pp. 6-7.

54 Phone interview with Santikaro Bhikkhu, Wat Suan Mokkh, taped on January 31, 2004.

55 Santikaro Bhikkhu notes that large trees are thought to be sacred, to be centers of power, so the largest tree in the vicinity is often used for the tree ordination, and in this way it stands in for the whole forest. It is not the biggest or tallest tree that is used, but more often the one with the largest perimeter; phone interview with Santikaro Bhikkhu, Wat Suan Mokkh, taped on January 31, 2004.

56 Sponsel and Natadecha-Sponsel, "Why a Tree is More than a Tree," pp. 366-367. Authors' italics.

57 See V. Shiva and Sponsel and Natadecha Sponsel, "Why a Tree is More than a Tree," pp. 368-370.

58 Sponsel and Natadecha-Sponsel, "Why a Tree is More than a Tree," p. 367.

59 Tiyavanich, *Forest Recollections*, pp. 246-247.

60 Darlington, "The Ordination of a Tree: The Buddhist Ecology Movement in Thailand," p. 9.

61 Wallapa Thanoo, abstract for M.A. thesis, "The Application of Buddhist Concepts on Tree Ordination for Forest Conservation: A Case Study of Tambon Srithoi, Amphoe Mae Chai, Changwat Phayao," (http://www.grad.cmu.ac.th/abstract/2000/gs/abstract/gs02088.html)

62 Tree ordination, in this case in the area of Chiang Rai, is "a response to unsustainable logging without regard for the environment or local people." (http://www.ozpositive.net/issues/ed_4/story_5/)

63 Tiyavanich, *Forest Recollections*, p. 248.

64 Email interview, Phra Paisal Visalo, southern Thailand, March 4, 2004.

65 Sponsel and Natadecha-Sponsel, "Why a Tree is More than a Tree," p. 366.

66 http://www.ozpositive.net/issues/ed_4/story_5/

67 Samantha Burman, "An Environmental Monk," *Good Morning Chiangmai News*, August 2002. (http://search.netscape.com/nscap_results.adp?start=31&first=30&nav=next&)

Explaining why the tree ordination ceremony was important, Khru Ba said: "When ordinary people see the bright orange strips of robe around the trees they know the forest has been ordained, so they must show the same respect for the forest that they would ascribe to a monk. It is therefore a powerful reminder to conserve nature and reduce the threat of deforestation."

68 Darlington, "The Ordination of a Tree: The Buddhist Ecology Movement in Thailand," p. 8.

69 Phone interview with Santikaro Bhikkhu, Wat Suan Mokkh, taped on January 31, 2004.

70 Darlington, "The Ordination of a Tree: The Buddhist Ecology Movement in Thailand," p. 10.

71 Sponsel and Natadecha-Sponsel, "Why a Tree is More than a Tree," p. 366.

72 Santikaro Bhikkhu, "The Four Noble Truths of Dhammic Socialism," pp. 146-147.

73 Tansubhapol, "Protecting the Forests" (http://www.geocities.com/RainForest/7813/tl-ordan.htm)

74 Isager and Ivarsson, "Contesting Landscapes in Thailand," p. 395.

75 Isager and Ivarsson, "Contesting Landscapes in Thailand," p. 396.

76 Isager and Ivarsson, "Contesting Landscapes in Thailand," p. 413. My italics.

77 Darlington, "Networking and Ecology Monk Seminars in Thailand," abstract for conference session on "Socially Engaged Buddhism in Southeast Asian Contexts" (http://www.aasianst.org/absts/1998abst/seasia/se14.htm)

78 Breiter, *Venerable Father*, p. 7.

79 Phone interview with Santikaro Bhikkhu, Wat Suan Mokkh, taped January 31, 2004.

80 Sivaraksa, *A Socially Engaged Buddhism*, pp. 24-25.

81 Phone interview with Santikaro Bhikkhu, Wat Suan Mokkh, taped January 31, 2004.

82 Isager, "Forest and People in Thai Environmental Discourse," p. 27.

83 Tiyavanich, *Forest Recollections*, p. 5.

84 Taylor, *Forest Monks and the Nation-State*, p. 12.

85 Tiyavanich, *Forest Recollections*, p. 23.

86 King Monkut Rama IV was the king of "The King and I."

87 Sivaraksa, *A Socially Engaged Buddhism*, p. 29.

88 "The Rise of the Thammayut Order: Reform: the Guise of Control?" (http://www.thaibuddhism.net/maha_tham.htm).

89 Tiyavanich, *Forest Recollections*, p. 6.

90 Tiyavanich, *Forest Recollections*, p. 6.

91 Taylor, *Forest Monks and the Nation-State*, p. 41.

92 Tiyavanich, *Forest Recollections*, pp. 6-7. Mahanikaai (Mahānikāya) can refer to a broad range of non-Thammayut monks and communities.

93 Taylor, *Forest Monks and the Nation-State*, pp. 154-155.

94 Tiyavanich, *Forest Recollections*, p. 8.
95 Phone interview with Santikaro Bhikkhu, Wat Suan Mokkh, taped January 31, 2004.
96 Darlington, "Rethinking Buddhism and Development," p. 2.
97 Phone interview with Santikaro Bhikkhu, Wat Suan Mokkh, taped January 31, 2004.
98 Tiyavanich, *Forest Recollections*, p. 40.
99 Darlington, "Rethinking Buddhism and Development," p. 2.
100 Tiyavanich, *Forest Recollections*, p. 63.
101 Sivaraksa, *A Socially Engaged Buddhism*, p. 31.
102 For more on Phra Ajahn Mun, see Tambiah, *The Buddhist Saints of the Forest and the Cult of Amulets.*
103 Taylor, *Forest Monks and the Nation-State*. p. 1.
104 Phone interview with Santikaro Bhikkhu, Wat Suan Mokkh, taped January 31, 2004.
105 Sivaraksa, *A Socially Engaged Buddhism*, p. 34.
106 Tiyavanich, *Forest Recollections*, p. 173.
107 Tiyavanich, *Forest Recollections*, pp. 187-188.
108 Darlington, "Rethinking Buddhism and Development," p. 2.
109 Tiyavanich, *Forest Recollections*, p. 189.
110 Tiyavanich, *Forest Recollections*, p. 195.
111 Tiyavanich, *Forest Recollections*, p. 209.
112 Taylor, *Forest Monks and the Nation-State*, p. 41.
113 Darlington, "Rethinking Buddhism and Development," p. 2.
114 Darlington, "Rethinking Buddhism and Development," p. 2.
115 Phone interview with Santikaro Bhikkhu, Wat Suan Mokkh, taped January 31, 2004.
116 Phone interview with Santikaro Bhikkhu, Wat Suan Mokkh, taped January 31, 2004.
117 Darlington, "Rethinking Buddhism and Development," p. 4.
118 Darlington, "Rethinking Buddhism and Development," p. 5. Darlington's italics.
119 Phone interview with Santikaro Bhikkhu, Wat Suan Mokkh, taped January 31, 2004.
120 Taylor, *Forest Monks and the Nation-State*, p. 239.
121 http://www.abm.ndirect.co.uk/fsn/35/forests.html
122 Phone interview with Santikaro Bhikkhu, Wat Suan Mokkh, taped January 31, 2004.
123 Phone interview with Santikaro Bhikkhu, Wat Suan Mokkh, taped January 31, 2004.
124 Tiyavanich, *Forest Recollections*, p. 257.

125 Taylor, *Forest Monks and the Nation-State*, p. 11.
126 Phone interview with Santikaro Bhikkhu, Wat Suan Mokkh, taped January 31, 2004.
127 For more on this, see Tambiah, *The Buddhist Saints of the Forest and the Cult of Amulets*, pp. 33-37, 53-61, 66-72.
128 Tiyavanich, *Forest Recollections*, p. 59.
129 Tiyavanich, *Forest Recollections*, p. 157.
130 Phone interview with Santikaro Bhikkhu, Wat Suan Mokkh, taped January 31, 2004.
131 Tiyavanich, *Forest Recollections*, p. 79.
132 Phone interview with Santikaro Bhikkhu, Wat Suan Mokkh, taped January 31, 2004.
133 Ajahn Chah, *Food for the Heart*, p. 17.
134 Ajahn Chah, *A Taste of Freedom*, p. 94. Note here the dissatisfaction with both options: living with other monks and wandering alone.
135 Ajahn Chah, *Food for the Heart*, p. 214.
136 As quoted in Taylor, *Forest Monks and the Nation-State*, p. 16.
137 Sivaraksa, *A Socially Engaged Buddhism*, p. 34.
138 Kornfield, *Living Buddhist Masters*, pp. 33-34.
139 Kornfield, *Living Buddhist Masters*, pp. 34-35.
140 Ajahn Chah, *Food for the Heart*, pp. 20-21; see Kornfield and Breiter, *A Still Forest Pool*, pp. 106-107.
141 Ajahn Chah, *Food for the Heart*, pp. 20-21.
142 Ajahn Chah, *Food for the Heart*, p. 267.
143 Kornfield and Breiter, *A Still Forest Pool*, pp. 121-122. Note here that one of the drains on living forest growth came from monastics themselves, who needed to used forest lumber to build their forest lodgings.
144 Ajahn Chah, *A Tree in a Forest*, p. 62; Kornfield, *Living Buddhist Masters*, p. 40.
145 Ajahn Chah, *Food for the Heart*, p. 47.
146 *Seeing the Way*, p. 43.
147 Ajahn Chah, *Food for the Heart*, p. 128.
148 Ajahn Chah, *Bodhinyana*, pp. 45-46.
149 Ajahn Chah, *Being Dharma*, p. 49.
150 Ajahn Chah, *Living Dhamma*, p. 6.
151 Ajahn Chah, *Meditation*, p. 21.
152 Ajahn Chah, *Being Dharma*, p. 118.
153 Ajahn Chah, *Meditation*, p. 2; see Dhamma Garden, *A Tree in a Forest*, p. 168.
154 Ajahn Chah, *Food for the Heart*, pp. 195-196; see Kornfield and

Breiter, *A Still Forest Pool*, p. 47.

[155] Dhamma Garden, *A Tree in a Forest*, p. 190.

[156] Dhamma Garden, *A Tree in a Forest*, p. 49. Editors' italics.

[157] Acharn Chah, *"Tuccho Pothila,"* p. 1; see *Living Dhamma*, p. 66.

[158] Acharn Chah, *"Tuccho Pothila,"* p. 23; see *Living Dhamma*, p. 78; see Dhamma Garden, *A Tree in a Forest*, p. 189.

[159] Ajahn Chah, *Being Dharma*, p. 147.

[160] Ajahn, Chah, *Being Dharma*, p. 152.

[161] Dhamma Garden, *No Ajahn Chah*, p. 115.

[162] Ajahn Chah, *Bodhinyana*, pp. 28-29.

[163] Ajahn Chah, *A Taste of Freedom*, p. 53; see Dhamma Garden, *A Tree in a Forest*, p. 81.

[164] Ajahn Chah, *A Taste of Freedom*, p. 54; see Dhamma Garden, *A Tree in a Forest*, p. 81.

[165] Dhamma Garden, *A Tree in a Forest*, frontispiece; my italics; see Kornfield and Breiter, *A Still Forest Pool*, p. 182. Another version is:

Once a visitor asked Ajahn Chah if he was an arahant. He said, "I am like a tree in a forest. Birds come to the tree, they sit on its branches and eat its fruit. To the birds the fruit may be sweet or sour or whatever. But the tree doesn't know anything about it. The birds say sweet or they say sour, but from the tree's point of view, this is just the chattering of the birds."

Dhamma Garden, *No Ajahn Chah*, p. 183.

[166] Ajahn Chah, *Food for the Heart*, p. 59; see *Living Dhamma*, p. 64; see Dhamma Garden, *A Tree in a Forest*, p. 123.

[167] Ajahn Chah, *Food for the Heart*, p. 304; see Ajahn Chah, *A Taste of Freedom*, p. 48.

[168] Ajahn Chah, *Being Dharma*, p. 5.

[169] Ajahn Chah, *Being Dharma*, p. 120.

[170] Ajahn Chah, *Food for the Heart*, p. 280; see *Bodhinyana*, pp. 26-27.

[171] Ajahn Chah, *Food for the Heart*, p. 279; see Dhamma Garden, *A Tree in a Forest*, p. 34; see *Bodhinyana*, p. 25.

[172] Jackson, *Buddhadāsa: Theravada Buddhism and Modernist Reform*, p. 261.

[173] Jackson, *Buddhadāsa: Theravada Buddhism and Modernist Reform*, p. 3.

[174] Jackson, *Buddhadāsa: Theravada Buddhism and Modernist Reform*, p. 37.

[175] Santikaro Bhikkhu, a disciple of Buddhadasa Bhikkhu's, notes concerning the question of whether Buddhadasa was in a strand of

the forest tradition:

> He went and lived in the forest, but he didn't do it in reference to the northeast forest tradition. He did it more on the basis of his scriptural reading and his awareness that this is something monks had always done. At that time, there wasn't much of it in southern Thailand. On the other hand, back then, there was a lot of forest, so being in a forest monastery wasn't a big deal because there was forest all over.

Phone interview with Santikaro Bhikkhu, Wat Suan Mokkh, taped on January 31, 2004.

176 Swearer, *Toward the Truth*, pp. 14-15.

177 Swearer, "The Hermeneutics of Buddhist Ecology in Contemporary Thailand," p. 24.

178 Buddhadāsa Bhikkhu, *Heartwood of the Bodhi Tree*, p. x.

179 Swearer, *Toward the Truth*, p. 16.

180 Swearer, *Toward the Truth*, pp. 18-19.

181 Sivaraksa, *Siam in Crisis*, p. 224.

182 Sivaraksa, *A Socially Engaged Buddhism*, p. 38.

183 Jackson, *Buddhadāsa: Theravada Buddhism and Modernist Reform*, pp. 10-11.

184 Swearer, "The Hermeneutics of Buddhist Ecology in Contemporary Thailand," pp. 24-25.

185 Swearer, "The Hermeneutics of Buddhist Ecology in Contemporary Thailand," pp. 24-25.

186 Swearer, "The Hermeneutics of Buddhist Ecology in Contemporary Thailand," p. 25.

187 Buddhadasa, *Dhammic Socialism*, p. 87.

188 "Social Impact of the Buddhadasa Movement: A Case Study," chapter 7, p. 217.

189 "Social Impact of the Buddhadasa Movement: A Case Study," chapter 7, p. 217.

190 Buddhadasa Bhikkhu, "Conserving the Inner Ecology," p. 7.

191 Jackson, *Buddhadāsa: Theravada Buddhism and Modernist Reform*, p. 207.

192 Jones, *The Social Face of Buddhism*, p. 259.

193 Sivaraksa, *A Socially Engaged Buddhism*, p. 106.

194 Jackson, *Buddhadāsa: Theravada Buddhism and Modernist Reform*, p. 231.

195 Buddhadasa Bhikkhu, "Conserving the Inner Ecology," p. 14;

Swearer, "The Hermeneutics of Buddhist Ecology in Contemporary Thailand," p. 29.

196 Santikaro Bhikkhu, "The Four Noble Truths of Dhammic Socialism," p. 96.

197 Payulpitack, "Social Impact of the Buddhadasa Movement: A Case Study," p. 227.

198 Buddhadasa, *Dhammic Socialism*, p. 51.

199 Buddhadasa, *Dhammic Socialism*, p. 59.

200 Buddhadasa, *Dhammic Socialism*, pp. 72, 86.

201 Buddhadasa, *Dhammic Socialism*, pp. 61, 62.

202 Buddhadasa, *Dhammic Socialism*, p. 118.

203 Swearer, "The Hermeneutics of Buddhist Ecology in Contemporary Thailand," pp. 25-27.

204 Swearer, "The Hermeneutics of Buddhist Ecology in Contemporary Thailand," p. 27.

205 Swearer, "The Hermeneutics of Buddhist Ecology in Contemporary Thailand," pp. 27-28.

206 Buddhadasa Bhikkhu, "Forest Wat Wild Monks," p. 10.

207 Buddhadasa Bhikkhu, "Forest Wat Wild Monks," p. 14.

208 Swearer, "The Hermeneutics of Buddhist Ecology in Contemporary Thailand," p. 31. When asked about the difference between himself and Phra Prayudh, Buddhadasa said, referring to Phra Prayudh by his royal title, Chaokhun Prayudh:

> [These [comparisons] should not be made in terms of which one is better or worse or more correct...Chaokhun Prayudh has put together Pali statements...that are beautiful...easy to study and listen to...In this current age, he has done very well. We [at Suan Mokkh] may not have done as well by mainly focusing on certain concepts or ideas...speaking directly to these concepts. But as to whether people now can accept this or not...we speak directly, so this is different.]

Olson in Phra Prayudh, *Buddhadhamma*, p. 18.

209 Swearer, "The Hermeneutics of Buddhist Ecology in Contemporary Thailand," p. 21.

210 Olson in Phra Prayudh, *Buddhadhamma*, pp. 1-2.

211 Olson in Phra Prayudh, *Buddhadhamma*, pp. 3-4, 6. The *Buddhadhamma: Natural Laws and Values for Life* is "Phra Prayudh distillation of the major principles of the Pali canon into one book" and is often referred to "as the most 'scientific' presentation of Buddhism in Thai history," and although somewhat controversial has often been the one book students of Buddhism (including "monk-students studying for higher degrees in Buddhist studies") read when they can't read the whole of the Pali

Canon; Olson in Phra Prayudh, *Buddhadhamma*, p. 25.

212 Swearer, "The Hermeneutics of Buddhist Ecology in Contemporary Thailand," p. 31.

213 Swearer, "The Hermeneutics of Buddhist Ecology in Contemporary Thailand," p. 32.

214 Swearer, "The Hermeneutics of Buddhist Ecology in Contemporary Thailand," pp. 32-33.

215 Swearer, "Dhammapitaka on Monks and the Forest," p. 464.

216 Swearer, "Dhammapitaka on Monks and the Forest," pp. 459-461.

217 Swearer, "Dhammapitaka on Monks and the Forest," pp. 462-463.

218 Swearer, "Dhammapitaka on the Monks and the Forest," p. 459.

219 Swearer, "Dhammapitaka on Monks and the Forest," p. 463.

220 Swearer, "The Hermeneutics of Buddhist Ecology in Contemporary Thailand," p. 36. Swearer's italics.

221 See Isager and Ivarsson, "Contesting Landscapes in Thailand," pp. 403-404.

222 Swearer, "The Hermeneutics of Buddhist Ecology in Contemporary Thailand," pp. 34-35.

223 Swearer, "The Hermeneutics of Buddhist Ecology in Contemporary Thailand," pp. 36-37.

224 Phra Prayudh, *Buddhadhamma*, p. 277.

225 Swearer, "The Hermeneutics of Buddhist Ecology in Contemporary Thailand," p. 33.

226 Phra Prayudh, *Buddhadhamma*, p. 95.

227 Phra Prayudh, *Buddhadhamma*, p. 96.

228 Phra Prayudh, *Buddhadhamma*, p. 61.

229 Phra Prayudh, *Buddhadhamma*, p. 66.

230 Phra Prayudh, *Buddhadhamma*, p. 67.

231 Swearer, "Dhammapitaka on Monks and the Forest," p. 467. My italics.

232 Phra Prayudh, *Buddhadhamma*, p. 242, taken one of the three principles of bodily cleanliness.

233 Taylor, *Forest Monks and the Nation-State*, p.169.

234 Payulpitack, "Social Impact of the Buddhadasa Movement: A Case Study," p. 222.

235 Email interview with Phra Paisal Visalo, southern Thailand, March 4, 2004.

236 Email interview with Phra Paisal Visalo, southern Thailand, March 4, 2004.

237 Phone interview with Santikaro Bhikkhu, Wat Suan Mokkh, taped on January 31, 2004.

Bibliography

Traditional Primary Sources : Texts and Translations

Ācārya Satyavrata Sāmaśrāmī, ed. *The Śatapatha Brāhmaṇa of the White Yajurveda with the Commentary of Sāyaṇa Āchārya.* Calcutta: Asiatic Society of Bengal, 1906 (vol./khanda II), 1910 (vol./khanda VII).

Acharya Mahaprajna, com. *Acharanga-Bhasyam: English Translation of the Original Text of Ayaro.* Synod chief: Ganadhipati Tulsi; English rendering: Dr. Nathmal Tatia, Muni Dulaharaj, Muni Mahendra Kumar. Ladnun, India: Jain Vishwa Bharati, 2001.

Aufrecht, Theodor, ed. *Das Aitareya Brāhmaṇa.* Hildesheim: Georg Olms Verlag, 1975.

Aufrecht, Theodor, ed. *Die Hymnen des Ṛgveda.* 2 vols. Bonn: Adolph Marcus, 1877.

Beck, Brenda E. F., Peter J. Claus, Praphulladatta Goswami, and Jawaharlal Handoo, eds. *Folktales of India.* Chicago: University of Chicago Press, 1987.

Belvalkar, Shripad Krishna, crit. ed. *The Śāntiparvan, Being the Twelfth Book of the Mahābhārata, the Great Epic of India.* Pts. 1, 2, 3a, 3b. Poona: Bhandarkar Oriental Research Institute, 1961, 1954.

Bhat, M. Ramakrishna, trans. Varāhamihira's Bṛhat Saṁhitā. 2 pts. Delhi: Motilal Banarsidass, pt. 1, 1981, rpt. 1992; pt. 2, 1982, 2nd rev. ed., 1987.

Bhattacharya, Deben, trans. and W. G. Archer, ed. *Love Songs of Vidyāpati.* London, 1963, 1969; rpt. New York: Grove Press, Inc., 1970.

Bhishagratna, Kaviraj Kunjalal, trans. and Dr. Laxmidhar Dwivedi, ed. *Suśruta Saṁhitā; Text With English Translation.* 3 vols. Varanasi: Chowkhamba Sanskrit Series Office, vols. 1 & 2, 2nd ed., 2002; vol. 3, 3rd ed., 2003.

Bühler, Georg, trans. *The Laws of Manu.* Oxford: Clarendon Press, 1886; rpt., New York: Dover Publications, 1969.

Carter, John Ross and Mahinda Palihawadana, trans. *Buddhism: the Dhammapada.* Oxford University Press, 1987; rpt. New York: Book of the Month Club, 1992.

Charpentier, Jarl, ed. *The Uttarādhayanasūtra, being the first Mūlasūtra of the Śvetāmbara Jains.* Uppsala: Appelbergs Boktryckeri Aktiebolag, 1914.

Dixit, K. K., trans. *Pt. Sukhlalji's Commentary on Tattvārtha Sātra of Vacaka Umāsvatī.* 1974; 2nd ed., Ahmedabad: L. D. Institute of Indology, 2000.

Dhupakara, Anantasarma Yajñesvara. *Kṛṣṇa-Yajurvedīyā Taittirīya Saṁhitā.* Bahālagaḍha, Sonīpata, Harayāṛā: Yudhiṣṭhira Mīmāṁsaka: Vitarakaḥ Rāmalāla Kapūra Traṣṭa, 1982.

Doniger, Wendy and Brian K. Smith, trans. *The Laws of Manu.* New York: Penguin Books, 1991.

Dutt, M. N., trans. and Drs. Ishvar Chandra Sharma and O. N. Bimali, eds. *Mahābhārata; Sanskrit Text With English Translation.* 9 vols. 1st ed., Delhi: Parimal Publications, 2001.

Dutt, Manamatha Nath, trans. *The Rāmāyāṇa: Translated into English Prose From the Original Sanskrit of Vālmīki.* 4. vols. Patna: Eastern Book House, 1987.

Eggeling, Julius, trans. *The Śatapatha Brāhmaṇa.* 5 vols. Clarendon Press, 1882, 1885, 1894, 1897. 1900; rpt. Delhi: Motilal Banarsidass, 1972.

Fynes, R. C. C., trans. *Hemacandra: The Lives of the Jain Elders (Sthavirāvalīcaritra).* New York: Oxford University Press, 1998.

Ganguli, Kisari Mohan, trans. *The Mahabharata of Krishna-Dwaipayanavyasa. Translated into English Prose from the Original Sanskrit Text.* 12 vols. new ed. Delhi: Munshiram Manoharlal Publishers, Pvt. Ltds., vol. 11, 1991; vols. 1, 4, 6, 1998; vol. 9, 1999; vols. 2, 3, 5, 7, 2001; vols. 8, 10, 12, 2003.

Gehman, Henry Snyder, trans. *Stories of the Departed (Peta-Vatthu)*. 1942; rpt. London: Pali Text Society, 1974.

Geiger, Wilhelm, trans. *The Mahāvaṁsa, or The Great Chronicle of Ceylon*. 1912; rpt. London: Pali Text Society, 1980.

Geldner, Karl Friedrich, trans. *Der Rig-Veda*. 3 vols. Cambridge, MA: Harvard University Press, 1951.

Gopal, Lallanji. *Vṛkṣāyurveda in Ancient India (With Original Texts and Translations)*. New Delhi: Sundeep Prakashan, 2000.

Granoff, Phyllis, trans. *The Forest of Thieves and the Magic Garden: An Anthology of Medieval Jain Stories*. New Delhi: Penguin Books. 1998.

Hawley, John Stratton and Mark Juergensmeyer, ed. and trans. *Songs of the Saints of India*. New York: Oxford University Press, 1988.

Hirakawa, Akira, trans. *Monastic Discipline for the Buddhist Nuns: An English Translation of the Chinese Text of the Mahāsāṁghika-Bhikṣuṇī Vinaya*. Patna: K. P. Jayaswal Research Institute, 1982.

Haughton, Graves Chamney. *Mānava-Dharma-Śāstra; or The Institutes of Manu*. London: Cox and Baylis, 1825.

Jacobi, Hermann, ed. *The Āyāraṁga Sutta (Ācharāṅga) of the Śvetambara Jains*. London: Pali Text Society, 1882.

Jacobi, Hermann, trans. *Jaina Sūtras*. 2 vols. Vol. 1 *Ācārāṅga Sūtra, Kalpa Sūtra;* vol. 2 *Uttarādhyayana Sūtra, Sūtrakṛtāṅga Sūtra*. Oxford University Press, 1884, 1895; rpt. Delhi: Motilal Banarsidass, 1973.

Jain, Mahendra Kumar, ed. and trans. *Tatvārtha-Vṛtti of Śrī Śrutasāgara Sūri; the Commentary on Tatvārtha-Sūtra of Umāsvāmi with Hindi Translation*. 3rd ed. New Delhi: Bharatiya Jnanpith, 2002.

Jain, N. L. trans. *Biology in Jaina Treatise on Reals. English Translation with Notes on Chapter Two of Tattvārtha-Rājavārtika of Alaṅkara on Tattvārtha Sūtra (Treatise on Reals) by Ācārya Umāsvāmi*. Varanasi, India: Pārśvanātha Vidyāpīṭha, 1999.

Jain, N. L. trans. *Jaina Karmology, English Translation with Notes on Chapter Eight of Tattvārtha-Rāja-Vārtika of*

Akalaṅka, on Tattvārtha-Sūtra by Ācārya Umāsvāmi. Varanasi: Pārśwanātha Vidyāpīṭha, 1998.

Jain, N. L. trans. *The Jain World of Non-Living, English Translation with Notes on Chapter Five of Tattvārtha Rājavārtika of Akalaṅka, on Tattvārtha Sūtra, by Ācārya Umāsvāmi.* Varanasi: Pārśwanātha Vidyāpīṭha, 2000.

Kāle, M. R. *The Hitopadeśa of Nārāyaṇa.* 6th ed. Delhi: Motilal Banarsidass, 1967.

Kangle, R. P. *The Kauṭilīya Arthaśāstra.* Pts. 1, & 3. Bombay: University Press, 1965, 1969.

Keith, Arthur Berriedale, trans. *The Aitareya Āraṇyaka.* Oxford: Clarendon Press, 1909, 1969.

Keith, Arthur Berriedale, trans. *Ṛgveda Brāhmaṇas: The Aitareya and Kauṣītaki Brāhmaṇas of the Ṛgveda.* Harvard University Press, 1920; rpt. Delhi: Motilal Banarsidass, 1971.

Keith, Arthur Berriedale, trans. *The Śāṅkhāyana Āraṇyaka.* London: 1908; rpt. New Delhi: Oriental Books, 1975.

Keith, Arthur Berriedale, trans. *The Veda of the Black Yajus School, entitled Taittiriya Saṃhita.* 2 vols. Harvard University Press, 1914; rpt. Delhi: Motilal Banarsidass, 1967.

Kornfield, Jack, ed. *Teachings of the Buddha.* Boston: Shambala, 1996.

Kulkarni, Prof. V. M., ed. and trans., *A Treasury of Jain Tales.* Ahmedabad: Sharadaben Chimanbhai Education Research Centre, 1994.

Martin, Charles, trans. *Ovid: Metamorphoses.* New York: W. W. Norton, 2004.

Miller, Barbara Stoler, trans. *The Bhagavad-Gita.* New York: Bantam Books, 1986.

Miller, Barbara Stoler, ed. and trans. *Love Song of the Dark Lord: Jayadeva's Gītāgovinda.* Full version. New York: Columbia University Press, 1977.

Miller, Barbara Stoler, trans. *Phantasies of a Love- Thief: The Caurapañcāśikā, Attributed to Bilhaṇa.* New York: Columbia University Press, 1971.

Müller, F. Max, ed., *Hymns of the Rig-Veda in the Samhita and Pada Texts.* 1873, 1877; 2 vols., rpt.: Varanasi: Chowkhamba Sanskrit Series Office, 1965.

Nadig, Sumatheendra. "The Man Who Grew Roots," in Kadambi Hayagrivachar, trans. *Masumatti and Other Stories*. Bangalore: Premasai Prakashana, 1992, pp. 116-123.

Nagar, Shantilal, trans. *Jain Rāmāyaṇa-Paumacaryu; Rendering into English from Apabhraṁśa*. Delhi: B. R. Publishing Corporation, 2002.

Ñāṇamoli, Bhikkhu, trans. *The Path of Purification (Viṣuddhimagga), by Bhadantācariya Buddhaghoṣa.* 5th ed. Kandy, Śrī Laṅka: Buddhist Publication Society. 1991.

Narayan, Kirin. "How a Girl Became a Sacred Plant," in Donald S. Lopez, Jr., ed. *Religions of India in Practice*. Princeton: University Press, 1995, pp. 487-494.

Nikam, N. A. and Richard McKeon, ed. and trans. *The Edicts of Asoka*. Chicago: University of Chicago Press, 1959.

O'Flaherty, Wendy Doniger, trans. *The Rig Veda: An Anthology*. New York: Penguin Books, 1981.

Oldenberg, Hermann and F. Max Müller, trans. *The Gṛhya-Sūtras; Rules of Vedic Domestic Ceremonies.* 2 vols. Oxford University Press: 1886, 1892; rpt. Delhi: Motilal Banarsidass, 1967.

Olivelle, Patrick, trans. *Dharmasūtras: The Law Codes of Ancient India.* Oxford: University Press, 1999.

Olivelle, Patrick, annot. and trans. *The Early Upaniṣads*. New York: Oxford University Press, 1998.

Olivelle, Patrick, trans. *Saṁnyāsa Upaniṣads: Hindu Scriptures on Asceticism and Renunciation.* New York: Oxford University Press, 1992.

Olivelle, Patrick, trans. *Upaniṣads*. New York: Oxford University Press, 1996.

Penzer, N. M., ed. and C. H. Tawney, trans. *The Ocean of Story; Somadeva's Kathā Sarit Sāgara.* Vols. 1-9. London: Chas. J. Sawyer Ltd., 1924-1928.

Peterson, Indira Viswanathan, trans. *Poems to Śiva.* Princeton: Princeton University Press, 1989.

Pollock, Sheldon I., trans. and Robert P. Goldman, ed. *The Rāmāyaṇa of Vālmīki: An Epic of Ancient India.* Vol. 3. *Araṇyakāṇḍa.* Princeton: Princeton University Press, 1991.

Quarnström, Olle, trans. *The Yogaśāstra of Hemacandra; A Twelfth Century Handbook on Śvetāmbara Jainism.* Harvard Oriental Series, vol. 60. Cambridge, MA: Harvard University Press, 2002.

Radhakrishnan, S., ed. and trans. *The Principal Upaniṣads.* London: George Allen & Unwin, Ltd. 1953.

Ramanujan, A. K., trans. *A Flowering Tree and Other Oral Tales From India.* Berkeley: University of California Press, 1997.

Ramanujan, A. K. "A Flowering Tree," in A. K. Ramanujan, trans., *A Flowering Tree and Other Oral Tales From India.* Berkeley: University of California Press, 1997, pp. 53-62.

Ramanujan, A. K. trans. *The Interior Landscape: Love Poems From a Classical Tamil Anthology.* 1967; rpt.: Bloomington: Indiana University Press, 1975.

Ramanujan, A. K. "The Pomegranate Queen," in A. K. Ramanujan, trans. *A Flowering Tree and Other Oral Tales From India.* Berkeley: University of California Press, 1997, pp. 135-137.

Ramanujan, A. K., trans. *Speaking of Śiva.* Baltimore: Penguin Books, 1973.

Rhys Davids, T. W., trans. *Dialogues of the Buddha*, Vol. 1. London: 1899; rpt. London: Pali Text Society, 1977.

Roth, R. and W. D. Whitney, eds. *Atharva Veda Sanhita.* Vol. 1: text. Berlin: Ferd. Dümmler's Verlagsbuchhandlung, 1856.

Roy, Pratap Chandra, trans. *The Mahabharata of Krishna-Dwaipayana Vyasa.* Vol. 9 (*Santi Parva*, pt. 2). Calcutta: D. Bose, 1925(?); rpt., Calcutta: Oriental Publishing Co., 1962-62 (?).

Ryder, Arthur W. *Shakuntala and Other Writings by Kalidasa.* New York: E. P. Dutton & Co., Inc., 1959.

Sadhale, Nalini. *Surapala's Vrikshayurveda (The Science of Plant Life by Surapala).* Secunderabad, Andhra Pradesh, India: Asian Agri-History Foundation, 1996.

Sastri, A. Mahadeva and K. Rangacharya, eds. *The Taittirīya Saṁhitā, With the Commentary of Bhaṭṭa Bhāskara Miśra.* Mysore: 1894; rpt., 5 vols.; Delhi: Motilal Banarsidass, 1986.

Sāstrī, T. Gaṇapati, ed. and comm. *The Arthaśāstra of Kautilya.* 3 vols. rpt.: Delhi: Bharatiya Vidya Prakashan, 1984.

Schotsman, Irma, trans. *Aśvagoṣa's Buddhacarita: The Life of the Buddha*. Sarnath, Varanasi: Central Institute of Higher Tibetan Studies, 1995.

Shamasastry, Dr. R., trans. *Kauṭilya's Arthaśāstra*. Mysore: Wesleyan Mission Press, 1929.

Shantideva. *The Way of the Bodhisattva*. Trans. by the Padmakara Translation Group. Boston: Shambala, 1997.

Sharma, Prof. Priyavrat, ed. and trans. *Caraka-Saṁhitā*. 3 vols. Varanasi: Chaukhambha Orientalia, vol. 1, 1st ed, 1981; vols. 2-3, 2nd ed., 1992.

Sircar, D. C. *Inscriptions of Asoka*. 1957. 4th ed.: New Delhi: Ministry of Information and Broadcasting, Government of India, Patiala House, 1998.

Sircar, N. N. and Roma Sarkar, eds. and trans. *Vṛkṣāyurveda of Parāśara*. Delhi: Sri Satguru Publications of Indian Books Centre, 1996.

Śrautakośa *(Encyclopedia of Vedic Sacrificial Ritual)*. Vol. 1 in 2 pts. Poona: Vaidika Saṁśodhana Maṇḍala, 1958 (1.1), 1963 (1.2).

Tatia, Nathmal, trans. *Tattvārtha Sūtra: That Which Is; Umāsvāti/ Umāsvāmī, With the Combined Commentaries of Umāsvāti/ Umāsvāmī, Pūjyapāda and Siddhasenagaṇi*. The Institute of Jainology. New York: Harper Collins Publishers, 1994.

Thanissaro, Bhikkhu, trans. *The Buddhist Monastic Code: The Patimokkha Training Rules*. Valley Center, CA: Metta Forest Monastery, 1994.

Thapar, Romila. *Sakuntala: Texts, Readings, Histories*. London: Anthem Press, 1999.

Tuck, Richard, ed. *Thomas Hobbes' Leviathan*. Cambridge: Cambridge University Press, 1991.

Vālmīki *Rāmāyaṇa: Text as Constituted in its Critical Edition*. Vadodara, India: Oriental Institute, 1992.

Van Buitenan, J. A. B., trans. *The Mahābhārata: 2. The Book of the Assembly Hall; 3. The Book of the Forest*. Chicago: University of Chicago Press, 1975.

Watson, Burton, trans. *The Lotus Sutra*. New York: Columbia University Press, 1993.

Watson, Burton, trans. *The Vimalakirti Sutra*. New York: Columbia University Press, 1997.

Woolner, Alfred C. *Asoka Text and Glossary*. 1924. Rpt.: Delhi: Low Price Publications, 1993.

Zaehner, R. C. trans. *The Bhagavad Gītā*. London: Oxford University Press, 1966.

All Pali Canon texts consulted are from the Pali Text Society series.

Contemporary and Secondary Sources

Ācarya Mahā Boowa Ñāṇasampanno. *Venerable Ācarya Mun Bhūridatta Thera: A Spiritual Biography*. Udorn Thani, Thailand: Wat Pa Baan Taad, Forest Dhamma Books, 2003.

Acharn Chah. *"Tucco Pothila" & "Our Real Home;" Nurturing Buddhism Through Contemplation of Mind.* Ubon Rajathani, Thailand: The Sangha, Bung Wai Forest Monastery, 1987.

Ackerman, Diane. *A Natural History of the Senses.* New York: Random House, 1990.

Agarwal, Anil. "Can Hindu Beliefs and Values Help India Meet Its Ecological Crisis?" in Christopher Key Chapple and Mary Evelyn Tuckers, eds. *Hinduism and Ecology: The Intersection of Earth, Sky, and Water.* Cambridge: Harvard University Press, 2000, pp. 165-179.

Ajahn Chah. *Being Dharma: The Essence of the Buddha's Teachings*. Trans. Paul Breiter. Boston: Shambala, 2001.

Ajahn Chah (Phra Bodhinyana Thera). *Bodhinyana: A Collection of Dhamma Talks.* 1979; rpt., rev. ed., Redwood Valley, CA: The Sangha, Abhayagiri Monastery, 2000.

Ajahn Chah. *Food for the Heart: The Collected Teachings of Ajahn Chah.* Boston: Wisdom Press, 2002.

Ajahn Chah. *Living Dhamma.* Ubolrachatani, Thailand: Wat Pah Nanachat, Bahn Bung Wai, 1993.

Ajahn Chah. *Meditation (Samādhi Bhāvanā).* Ubon Rajathani, Thailand: The Sangha, Bung Wai Forest Monastery, 1991.

Ajahn Chah. *A Taste of Freedom.* Ubon Rajathani, Thailand: The Sangha, Bung Wai Forest Monastery, 1980.

Akula, Vikram K. "Grassroots Environmental Resistance in India," in Bron Raymond Taylor, ed., *Ecological Resistance Movements: The Global Emergence of Radical and Popular*

Environmentalism. Albany: The State University of New York Press, 1995, pp. 127-145.

Alcorn, Janis B. and Augusta Molnar. "Deforestation and Human-Forest Relationships: What Can We Learn from India?" in Leslie E. Sponsel, Thomas N. Headland, and Robert C. Baily, *Tropical Deforestation: The Human Dimensions*. New York: Columbia University Press, 1996, pp. 99-121.

Ariyaratne, Dr. A. T. and Joanna Macy. "The Island of Temple and Tank, Sarvodaya: Self-help in Sri Lanka," in Martine Batchelor and Kerry Brown, eds., *Buddhism and Ecology*. London: Cassell Publishers Limited, 1992, pp. 78-86.

Atkins, Jeannine. *Aani and the Tree Huggers*. Illus. Venantius J. Pinto. New York: Lee & Low Books, Inc., 1995.

Babb, Lawrence A. "Giving and Giving Up: The 8-Fold Worship Among Svetambar Murtipujak Jains." *Journal of Anthropological Research* XLIV.1 (Spring 1998).

Badiner, Allan Hunt, ed. *Dharma Gaia: A Harvest of Essays in Buddhism and Ecology*. Berkeley: Parallax Press, 1990.

Bajracharya, Vd. Mana Bajra. *Ayurvedic Medicinal Plants and General Treatment*. Mahaboudha, Kathmandu, Nepal: Piyusavarsi Ausadhalaya, 1979.

Balasooriya, Somaratna et al., eds. *Buddhist Studies in Honour of Walpola Rahula*. London: Gordon Fraser, 1980.

Banwari, *Pañcavaṭī: Indian Approach to Environment*. Delhi: Shri Vinayaka Publications, 1992.

Bash, Barbara. *In the Heart of the Village: The World of the Indian Banyan Tree*. San Francisco: Sierra Club Books for Children, 1996.

Basham, A. L. "The Practice of Medicine in Ancient and Medieval India," in Charles Leslie, ed., *Asian Medical Systems: A Comparative Study*. Berkeley: University of California Press, 1976, pp. 18-43.

Batchelor, Martine and Kerry Brown, eds. *Buddhism and Ecology*. London: Cassell, 1992.

Beals, Allan R. "Strategies of Resort to Curers in South India," in Charles Leslie, *Asian Medical Systems: A Comparative Study*. Berkeley: University of California Press, 1976, pp. 184-200.

Bernhardt, Garry. "Dreading Those Pearly Gates," *Pacific Horticulture* 61.4 (Oct/Nov/Dec 2000): 46-47.

'Bhaskar,' Bhagchandra Jain. "Ecology and Spirituality in the Jain Tradition," in Christopher Key Chapple, ed., *Jainism and Ecology: Nonviolence in the Web of Life.* Cambridge, MA: Center for the Study of World Religions, Harvard Divinity School, 2002, pp. 169-180.

Bidwell, R. G. S. *Plant Physiology.* 2nd ed. New York: Macmillan, 1979.

Brereton, Joel. "The Upanishads," in *Approaches to the Asian Classics*, eds. Wm. Theodore de Bary and Irene Bloom. New York: Columbia University Press, 1990.

Brown, W. Norman. "The Basis for the Hindu Act of Truth." *The Review of Religion* 5(1940):36-45.

Brown, W. Norman. "Duty as Truth in Ancient India." *Proceedings, American Philosophical Society* 116(1972):252-268.

Brown, W. Norman. "Duty as Truth in the Rig Veda," in J. Ensink and P. Gaeffke, eds. *India Maior.* Leiden: E. J. Brill, 1972, pp. 57-67.

Brown, W. Norman. "The Metaphysics of the Truth Act (*Satyakriyā)." *Melanges D'Indianisme, a la Memoire de Louis Renou.* 1968:171-177.

Breiter, Paul. *Venerable Father: A Life With Ajahn Chah.* Bangkok: Mrs. Thiwasree Piyaphan, 1993.

Buddhadasa, Bhikkhu. "Conserving the Inner Ecology," in *Buddha-Dhamma Buddhadasa Archives.*(http://www.suanmokkh.org/archive/ecology1.htm)

Buddhadasa, Bhikkhu. *Dhammic Socialism.* Trans. and ed., Donald K. Swearer. 1986; 2nd ed, Bangkok: Thai-Inter-Religious Commission for Development, 1993.

Buddhadasa, Bhikkhu. "Forest Wat Wild Monks," in *Buddha-Dhamma Buddhadasa Archives.* (http://www.suanmokkh.org/archive/wildmnk2.htm)

Buddhadāsa, Bhikkhu. *Heartwood of the Bodhi Tree: The Buddha's Teaching on Voidness.* Boston: Wisdom Publications, 1994.

***Buddhist** Perspectives on the Earth Charter.* Cambridge, MA: Boston Research Center for the 21st Century, 1997.

Burlingame, Eugene Watson. "The Act of Truth (Saccakiriyā): A Hindu Spell and Its Employment as a Psychic Motif in Hindu Fiction." *Journal of the Royal Asiatic Society*. 1917:429-467.

Callicott, J. Baird and Roger T. Ames, eds. *Nature in Asian Traditions of Thought: Essays in Environmental Philosophy.* Albany: State University of New York Press, 1989.

Carman, John B. "Duties and Rights in Hindu Society," in Leroy S. Rouner, ed., *Human Rights and the World's Religions*. Notre Dame, Indiana: University of Notre Dame Press, 1988, pp. 113-128.

Chapple, Christopher. "Contemporary Jaina and Hindu Responses to the Ecological Crisis," in Michael Barnes, ed., *An Ecology of the Spirit.* University Press of America, 1993.

Chapple, Christopher Key, ed. *Jainism and Ecology: Nonviolence in the Web of Life.* Cambridge: Harvard University Press, 2002.

Chapple, Christopher Key. "The Living Cosmos of Jainism: A Traditional Science Grounded in Environmental Ethics." *Daedalus*, The American Academy of Arts and Sciences, 130.4 (Fall 2001).

Chapple, Christopher Key. "The Living Earth of Jainism and the New Story: Rediscovering and Reclaiming a Functional Cosmology," in Christopher Key Chapple, ed., *Jainism and Ecology: Nonviolence in the Web of Life.* Cambridge, MA: Center for the Study of World Religions, Harvard Divinity School, 2002, pp. 119-139.

Chapple, Christopher Key. *Nonviolence to Animals, Earth, and Self in Asian Traditions.* Albany: State University of New York Press, 1993.

Collins, Steven. *Selfless Persons: Imagery and Thought in* Theravāda *Buddhism.* 1982; rpt., Cambridge: University Press, 1992.

Cort, John. "Green Jainism? Notes and Queries Toward a Possible Jain Environmental Ethics," in Christopher Key Chapple, ed., *Jainism and Ecology: Nonviolence in the Web of Life.* Cambridge, MA: Center for the Study of World Religions, Harvard Divinity School, 2002, pp. 63-94.

Coward, Harold. "The Ecological Implications of Karma Theory," in Lance E. Nelson, *Purifying the Earthly Body of God: Reli-*

gion and Ecology in Hindu India. Albany: State University of New York Press, 1998.

Darlington, Susan. "The Earth Charter and Ecology Monks in Thailand," in *Buddhist Perspectives on the Earth Charter*. Cambridge, MA: Boston Research Center for the 21st Century, 1997, pp. 47-52.

Darlington, Susan. "Not Only Preaching – The Work of the Ecology Monk Phrakhru Pitak Nantakhun of Thailand." *Forests, Trees and People Newsletter* 34 (September 1997).

Darlington, Susan M. "The Ordination of a Tree: The Buddhist Ecology Movement in Thailand." *Ethnology* 37.1 (1998):1-15.

Darlington, Susan M. "Rethinking Buddhism and Development: The Emergence of Environmental Monks in Thailand." *Journal of Buddhist Ethics* 7 (2000) (http://jbe.gold.ac.uk/7/darlington001.html)

Darlington, Susan M. "Tree Ordination in Thailand," in Stephanie Kaza and Kenneth Kraft, eds. *Dharma Rain: Sources of Buddhist Environmentalism.* Boston: Shambala, 2000, pp. 198-205.

Dasgupta, Surendranath. *History of Indian Philosophy*. Vol. 1. Cambridge: Cambridge University Press, 1969.

"**Declaration** of Interdependence." Epilogue in Keown, Damien V., Charles S. Prebish, and Wayne R. Husted, eds., *Buddhism and Human Rights*. Surrey, UK: Curzon Press, 1998, pp. 221-222.

De Nicolás, Antonio T. *Meditations Through the Ṛg Veda: Four-Dimensional Man.* Boulder: Shambala, 1978.

De Silva, Lily. "Early Buddhist Attitudes Toward Nature," in Stephanie Kaza and Kenneth Kraft, eds., *Dharma Rain: Sources of Buddhist Environmentalism.* Boston: Shambala, 2000, pp. 91-103. See Lily de Silva, "The Buddhist Attitude Toward Nature," in Klas Sandell, ed., *Buddhist Perspectives on the Ecocrisis*. Wheel Pub. No. 346/348. Kandy: Buddhist Publication Society, 1987, pp. 9-29.

De Silva, Padmal. "Buddhist Psychology: Some Basic Concepts and Applications," in John Pickering, ed., *The Authority of Experience: Essays on Buddhism and Psychology* (Surrey, U.K.: Curzon Press, 1997), pp. 60-61.

De Silva, Padmasiri. "Environmental Ethics: A Buddhist Perspective," in *Buddhist Ethics and Modern Society*, eds. Charles Wei-hsun Fu and Sandra A. Wawrytko. New York: Greenwood Press, 1991, pp. 173-184.

De Silva, Padmasiri. "Environmental Ethics in Buddhism." *Religious Studies and Theology* 13-14 (December 1995):55-65.

Des Jardins, Joseph R. *Environmental Ethics: An Introduction to Environmental Philosophy.* Belmont, CA: Wadsworth Publishing Co., 1993.

Deutsch, Eliot. *Advaita Vedānta: A Philosophical Reconstruction.* Honolulu: University Press of Hawaii, 1973.

Dhamma Garden, comp. & ed. *No Ajahn Chah: Reflections.* Chungli, Taiwan: Yuan Kuang Publishing House, 1994.

Dhamma Garden Translation Group, ed., *A Tree in a Forest: A Collection of Ajahn Chah's Similies.* Chungli, Taiwan: Yuan Kuang Publishing House, 1994.

Dogen, "Mountains and Waters Sutra," in Stephanie Kaza and Kenneth Kraft, eds. *Dharma Rain: Sources of Buddhist Environmentalism.* Boston: Shambala, 2000, pp. 65-76.

Dundas, Paul. *The Jains.* London: Routledge, 1992.

Dundas, Paul. "The Limits of a Jain Environmental Ethic," in Christopher Key Chapple, ed., *Jainism and Ecology: Nonviolence in the Web of Life.* Cambridge, MA: Center for the Study of World Religions, Harvard Divinity School, 2002, pp. 95-117.

Dwivedi, O. P. "Our Karma and Dharma to the Environment: An Eastern Perspective," in Mary Ann Beavis, ed., *Environmental Stewardship: History, Theory and Practice – Workshop Proceedings* (March 11-12, 1994). Winnipeg, Manitoba: University of Winnipeg, 1994, pp. 59-74.

Dwivedi, O. P. "*Satyagraha* for Conservation: Awakening the Spirit of Hinduism," in Roger S. Gottlieb, ed., *This Sacred Earth: Religion, Nature, Environment.* New York: Routledge, 1996.

Dwivedi, O. P. "Vedic Heritage for Environmental Stewardship." *Worldviews: Environment, Culture, Religion* 1.1(April 1997) 25-36.

Dwivedi, O. P. and B.N. Tiwari. *Environmental Crisis and Hindu Religion.* New Delhi: Gitanjali Publishing House, 1987.

Eckel, Malcolm David. "Is There a Buddhist Philosophy of Nature," in Mary Evelyn Tucker and Duncan Ryūken Williams, eds. *Buddhism and Ecology: The Interconnection of Dharma and Deeds*. Cambridge: Harvard University Press, 1997, pp. 327-349.

Eppsteiner, Fred. "In the Crucible: the Precepts of the Order of Interbeing," in Fred Eppsteiner, ed., *The Path of Compassion: Writings on Socially Engaged Buddhism*. 1985; rev. ed., Berkeley: Parallax Press, 1988, pp. 150-154.

Ewers, Kirsten, et al. "Institutions and Natural Resources Management: Background, Approach and Working Hypotheses." Working Paper, Tjele, Denmark: Research Centre on Forest and People in Thailand, 2001.

Filliozat, J. *The Classical Doctrine of Indian Medicine: Its Origins and its Greek Parallels*. Trans. from French by Dev Raj Chanana. 1st Eng. ed., Delhi: Munshiram Manoharlal, 1964.

Findly, Ellison Banks. "Borderline Beings: Plant Possibilities in Early Buddhism." *Journal of the American Oriental Society* 122.2 (2002):252-263.

Findly, Ellison Banks. *Dāna: Giving and Getting in Pali Buddhism*. Delhi: Motilal Banarsidass, 2003.

Findly, Ellison Banks. "Mantra kaviśasta: Speech as Performative in the Ṛgveda," in Harvey P. Alper, ed. *Understanding Mantras* (hardcover) and *Mantra* (paper). Albany: State University of New York Press, 1989, pp. 15-47.

Findly, Ellison Banks. Review of *The Specter of Speciesism: Buddhist and Christian Views of Animals*, by Paul Waldau. *Journal of the American Oriental Society* 123.3(2003): 685-687.

Finnis, J. M. *Natural Law and Natural Rights*. Clarendon Law Series, ed. by H. L. A. Hart. Oxford: Clarendon Press, 1980.

Fisher, Robert E. *Buddhist Art and Architecture*. 1993; rpt. New York: Thames and Hudson, 1995.

Gadgil, Madhav and M. D. Subash Chandran. "Sacred Groves." *India International Centre Quarterly* 19.1-2(1992):183-187.

Gadgil, Madhav and Ramachandra Guha. *Ecology and Equity: The Use and Abuse of Nature in Contemporary India*. London: Routledge, 1995.

Garfield, Jay. "Human Rights and Compassion: Towards a Unified Moral Framework," in Damien V. Keown, Charles S. Prebish, and Wayne R. Husted, eds. *Buddhism and Human Rights.* Surrey, UK: Curzon Press, 1998, pp. 111-140.
Gold, Ann Grodzins. 'If You Cut a Branch You Cut My Finger:' Court, Forest, and Environmental Ethics in Rajasthan," in Christopher Key Chapple and Mary Evelyn Tucker, eds., *Hinduism and Ecology: The Intersection of Earth, Sky, and Water.* Cambridge: Harvard University Press, 2000, pp. 317-336.
Gold, Ann Grodzins. "Sin and Rain: Moral Ecology in Rural North India," in Lance E. Nelson, *Purifying the Earthly Body of God.* Albany: State University of New York Press, 1998, pp. 165-195.
Gombrich, Richard. *Theravada Buddhism: A Social History from Ancient Benares to Modern Colombo.* London: Routledge, 1988.
Groner, Paul. "Early Japanese Tendai Views on the Realization of Buddhahood by Grasses and Trees: Determinations from China." Unpublished manuscript.
Grosnick, William. "The Buddhahood of the Grasses and the Trees: Ecological Sensitivity or Scriptural Misunderstanding?" in Michael Barnes, ed., *An Ecology of Spirit,* pp. 197-208.
Gross, Rita M. "Toward a Buddhist Environmental Ethic." *Journal of the American Academy of Religion* 65.2 (Summer 1997):333-353.
Guenther, Herbert. "Basic Features of Buddhist Psychology," in John Pickering, ed., *The Authority of Experience: Essays on Buddhism and Psychology.* Surrey, UK: Curzon Press, 1997, pp. 72-96.
Guha Ramachandra. "The Malign Encounter: The Chipko Movement and Competing Visions of Nature," in Tariq Banuri and Frédérique Apffel Marglin, *Who Will Save the Forests?: Knowledge, Power and Environmental Destruction.* London: Zed Books, 1993.
Guha, Ramachandra. *The Unquiet Woods: Ecological Change and Peasant Resistance in the Himalaya.* Oxford, 1989; rpt. Berkeley: University of California Press, 1990.
Gupta, Kaviraj. R. L. *Hindu Practice of Medicine.* 2nd ed., Delhi: Sri Satguru Publications, 1986.

Gupta, Shakti M. *Plant Myths and Traditions in India.* Leiden: 1971; rpt. New Delhi: Munshiram Manoharlal, 1991.

Harle, J. C. *The Art and Architecture of the Indian Subcontinent.* 1986; rpt., New Haven: Yale University Press, 1994.

Harris, Ian. "Buddhist Environmental Ethics and Detraditionalization: The Case of EcoBuddhism." *Religion* 25(1995):199-211.

Harris, Ian. "Causation and *Telos:* The Problem of Buddhist Environmental Ethics." *Journal of Buddhist Ethics* (http://jbe.gold.ac.uk/1/harris1.html/).

Harris, Ian. "Getting to Grips With Buddhist Environmentalism: A Provisional Typology." *Journal of Buddhist Ethics* (http://jbe.la.psu.edu/2/harris2.html).

Harvey, Peter. *An Introduction to Buddhist Ethics.* Cambridge: University Press, 2000.

Hughes, James. *Green Buddhist Declaration.* Prepared by members of the International Buddhist community on the occasion of the 14th General Conference of the World Fellowship of Buddhists (Colombo, August 1984). Moratuwa: Sarvodaya Press, 1984.

Hunt-Perry, Patricia and Lyn Fine. "All Buddhism is Engaged: Thich Nhat Hanh and the Order of Interbeing," in Christopher S. Queen, ed., *Engaged Buddhism in the West.* Boston: Wisdom Publication, 2000, pp. 35-66.

Ihara, Craig K. "Why There are no Rights in Buddhism: A Reply to Damien Keown," in Damien V. Keown, Charles S. Prebish, Wayne R. Husted., eds., *Buddhism and Human Rights.* Surrey, UK: Curzon Press, 1998, pp. 43-51.

Inanda, Kenneth. "A Buddhist Response to the Nature of Human Rights," in Claude E. Welch, Jr. and Virginia A. Leary, eds., *Asian Perspectives on Human Rights.* Boulder: Westview Press, 1990, pp. 91-103.

Isager, Lotte. "Forest and People in Thai Environmental Discourse." Working Paper, Tjele Denmark: Research Centre on Forest and People in Thailand, Danish Institute of Agricultural Sciences, Research Centre Fonlum, International Unity, 2000.

Isager, Lotte and Soren Ivarsson. "Contesting Landscapes in Thailand: Tree Ordination as Counter-Territorialization." *Critical Asian Studies* 34.3(2002):395-417.

Jackson, Peter. *Buddhadāsa: Theravada Buddhism and Modernist Reform in Thailand.* 1987; rpt., Chiang Mai, Thailand: Silkworm Books, 2003.

Jaini, Padmanabh S. "Ecology, Economics, and Development in Jainism," in Christopher Key Chapple, ed., *Jainism and Ecology: Nonviolence in the Web of Life.* Cambridge, MA: Center for the Study of World Religions, Harvard Divinity School. 2002, pp. 141-156.

Jaini, Padmanabh S. *The Jaina Path of Purification.* Berkeley: University of California Press, 1979.

James, George. "Ethical and Religious Dimensions of Chipko Resistance," in Christopher Key Chapple and Mary Evelyn Tucker, eds. *Hinduism and Ecology: the Intersection of Earth, Sky, and Water.* Cambridge: Harvard University Press, 2000, pp. 499-530.

Jamieson, Dale. "Animal Liberation in an Environmental Ethic," *Environmental Values* 7 (February 1998):41-57.

Jensen, Derrick. "The Plants Respond: An Interview With Clive Backster." *The Sun* July 1997:4-9.

Jessell, Thomas M. and Dennis D. Kelly. "Pain and Analgesia," in Frank S. Salisbury and Cleon W. Ross, *Plant Physiology.* 4th ed., Belmont CA: Wadsworth Publishing Company, 1991.

Johnsen, Linda. *Daughters of the Goddess: The Women Saints of India.* St. Paul, Minnesota: Yes International Publishers, 1994.

Johnson, W. J. *Harmless Souls: Karmic Bondage and Religious Change in Early Jainism with Special Reference to Umāsvāti and Kundakunda.* Delhi: Motilal Banarsidass, 1995.

Jones, Ken. *Beyond Optimism: A Buddhist Political Ecology.* Oxford: Jon Carpenter, 1993.

Jones, Ken. *The Social Face of Buddhism: An Approach to Political and Social Activism.* London: Wisdom Publications, 1989.

Kabilsingh, Chatsumarn. "Early Buddhist Views on Nature," in Allan Hunt Badiner, ed., *Dharma Gaia: A Harvest of Essays in Buddhism and Ecology.* Berkeley: Parallax Press, 1990, pp. 8-13.

Kalupahana, David J. "Toward a Middle Path of Survival," in J. Baird Callicott and Roger T. Ames, eds., *Nature in Asian Traditions of Thought: Essays in Environmental Philosophy.* Albany: State University of New York, 1989, pp. 247-256.

Kalupahana, David J. *The Principles of Buddhist Psychology.* Albany: State University of New York Press, 1987.
Kandel, Eric R. and Thomas M. Jessell. "Touch," in *Principles of Neural Science*, by Eric Kandel, James H. Schwartz, and Thomas M. Jessell. New York: Elsevier, 1991, pp. 367-384.
Kane, Pandurang Vaman, *History of Dharmaśāstra.* Vols. 1-5. Poona: Bhandarkar Oriental Research Institute, rev. and enlarg, vol.1.1, 1990; vol. 1.2, 1975; 2nd ed, vol. 2.1, 2.2, 1974; 3rd ed., vol. 3, 1993; vol. 4, 1991; 2nd ed. vol. 5.1, 1974; 2nd ed. vol. 5.2, 1977.
Kaza, Stephanie. *The Attentive Heart: Conversations With Trees.* New York: Fawcett Columbine, 1993.
Kaza, Stephanie and Kenneth Kraft, eds. *Dharma Rain: Sources of Buddhist Environmentalism.* Boston: Shambala, 2000.
Keith, Arthur Berriedale. *The Religion and Philosophy of the Veda and Upanishads.* 2 vols. Cambridge: Harvard University Press, 1925; rpt. Delhi: Motilal Banarsidass, 1970.
Keown, Damien. V. "Are There Human Rights in Buddhism?" in Damien V. Keown, Charles S. Prebish, and Wayne R. Husted, eds., *Buddhism and Human Rights.* Surrey UK: Curzon Press, 1998, pp. 15-41.
Keown, Damien. *Buddhism and Bioethics.* 1995; rpt. New York: Palgrave, St. Martin's Press, 2001.
Keown, Damien. *The Nature of Buddhist Ethics.* 1992; rpt. New York: Palgrave. St. Martin's Press, 2001.
Keown, Damien V., Charles S. Prebish, and Wayne R. Husted, eds. *Buddhism and Human Rights.* Surrey, UK: Curzon Press, 1998.
Khanna, Madhu. "The Ritual Capsule of Durgā Pūjā: An Ecological Perspective," in Christopher Key Chapple and Mary Evelyn Tucker, *Hinduism and Ecology: The Intersection of Earth, Sky, and Water.* Cambridge: Harvard University Press, Center for the Study of World Religions, Harvard Divinity School, 2000, pp. 469-498.
Kinsley, David. *Ecology and Religion: Ecological Spirituality in Cross-Cultural Perspective.* Upper Saddle River, NJ: Prentice-Hall, Inc., 1995.

Knipe, David M. "Sapiṇḍīkaraṇa: The Hindu Rite of Entry into Heaven," in Frank E. Reynolds and Earle H. Waugh, eds., *Religious Encounters With Death*. University Park: The Pennsylvania State University Press, 1977, pp. 111-124.

Kornfield, Jack. *Living Buddhist Masters*. Santa Cruz: Unity Press, 1977.

Kornfield, Jack and Paul Breiter, comps. & eds. *A Still Forest Pool: The Insight Meditation of Achaan Chah.* 1985; 5th Quest printing: Wheaton, Ill: The Theosophical Publishing House, 1994.

Kraft, Kenneth. "The Greening of Buddhist Practice." *Cross Currents* Summer 1994:163-179, rpt. in Roger S. Gottlieb, ed., *This Sacred Earth: Religion, Nature, Environment*. New York: Routledge, 1996, pp. 484-498.

Krishnamurthy, K. H. *A Sourcebook of Indian Medicine: An Anthology*. Delhi: B. R. Publishing Corporation, 1991.

Kuiper, F. B. J. "The Basic Concept of Vedic Religion." *History of Religions* 15.2(November 1975):107-120.

Kumar, Bhuvanendra. "The *Astikāyas: Ajiva* Substances." *Jinamañjari: International Journal of Contemporary Jaina Reflections* 26.2(October 2002):14-26.

Kumar, Bhuvanendra. "Transmigration and *Karma*." *Jinamañjari: International Journal of Contemporary Jaina Reflections* 26.2(October 2002):27-34.

Kumar, Satish. "Jain Ecology," in Christopher Key Chapple, ed., *Jainism and Ecology: Nonviolence in the Web of Life*. Cambridge: Center for the Study of World Religions, Harvard Divinity School, 2002, pp. 181-190.

Kumar, Satish. *No Destination, An Autobiography*. Devon: Green Books, A Resurgence Book, 1992.

Kumar, Satish. *You Are, Therefore I Am: A Declaration of Dependence*. Devon: Green Books, 2002.

Kunwar, S. S., ed. *Hugging the Himalayas: The Chipko Experience*. Gopeshwar, Uttar Pradesh, India: Dasholi Gram Swarajya Mandala, 1982.

La Fleur, William. "Enlightenment for Plants and Trees," in Stephanie Kaza and Kenneth Kraft, eds. *Dharma Rain: Sources of Buddhist Enlightenment*. Boston: Shambala, 2002, pp. 109-116.

La Fleur, William R. "Saigyō and the Buddhist Value of Nature," in J. Baird Callicott and Roger T. Ames, *Nature in Asian Traditions of Thought: Essays in Environmental Philosophy.* Albany: State University of New York Press, 1989, pp. 183-209.

La Fleur, William. "Sattva – Enlightenment for Plants & Trees," in Allan Hunt Badiner, ed., *Dharma Gaia: A Harvest of Essays in Buddhism and Ecology*. Berkeley: Parallax Press, 1990, pp. 136-144.

La Follette, Hugh and Niall Shanks. "The Origin of Speciesism." *Philosophy* 1996:41-60.

Lal, Vinay. "Too Deep for Deep Ecology: Gandhi and the Ecological Vision of Life," in Christopher Key Chapple and Mary Evelyn Tucker, eds. *Hinduism and Ecology: The Intersection of Earth, Sky, and Water.* Cambridge: Harvard University Press, 2000, pp. 183-212.

Larson, Gerald James. *Classical Samkhya: An Interpretation of Its History and Meaning.* Delhi: Motilal Banarsidass, 1969.

Larson, Gerald James and Ram Shankar Bhattacharya, eds. *Encyclopedia of Indian Philosophies*, vol. 4, *Sāṁkhya*. Copyright, Princeton University Press. Delhi: Motilal Banarsidass, 1987.

Law-Yone, Wendy. *The Coffin Tree.* 1983; rpt., Boston: Beacon Press, 1987.

Lee, David. "The Natural History of the *Rāmāyaṇa*," in Christopher Key Chapple, and Mary Evelyn Tucker, *Hinduism and Ecology: The Intersection of Earth, Sky, and Water.* Cambridge: Harvard University Press, 2000, pp. 245-268.

Ludden, David. "Archaic Formations of Agricultural Knowledge in South India," in Peter Robb, ed., *Meanings of Agriculture: Essays in South Asian History and Economics.* Delhi: Oxford University Press, pp. 35-70.

Lutgendorf, Philip. "City, Forest, and Cosmos: Ecological Perspectives from the Sanskrit Epics," in Christopher Key Chapple and Mary Evelyn Tucker, eds. *Hinduism and Ecology: The Intersection of Earth, Sky, and Water.* Cambridge, MA: Center for the Study of World Religion, Harvard Divinity School, 2000, pp. 269-289.

McDermott, James P. "Animals and Humans in Early Buddhism." *Indo-Iranian Journal* 32 (October 1989):269-280.

McDermott, James Paul. *Development in the Early Buddhist Concept of Kamma/Karma.* Delhi: Munshiram Manoharlal, 1984.

McGee, Mary. "State Responsibility for Environmental Management: Perspectives from Hindu Texts on Polity," in Christopher Key Chapple and Mary Evelyn Tucker, eds., *Hinduism and Ecology: The Intersection of Earth, Sky and Water.* Cambridge: Harvard University Press, 2000, pp. 59-100.

Macdonell, A. A. *Vedic Mythology.* Strassburg: Karl J. Truxuuxbner, 1897; rpt., Delhi: Indological Book House, 1971.

Macy, Joanna. *World As Lover, World As Self.* Berkeley: Parallax Press, 1991.

Macy, Joanna and Molly Young Brown. *Coming Back to Life: Practices to Reconnect Our Lives, Our World.* Stony Creek CT: New Society Publishers, 1998.

Mahoney, William K. *The Artful Universe: An Introduction to the Vedic Religious Imagination.* Albany: State University of New York Press, 1998.

Majupuria, Trilok Chandra and Indra Majupuria. *Sacred and Useful Plants and Trees of Nepal.* Kathmandu: Sahayogi Prakashan, 1978.

Maquet, Jacques. "Bhāvanā in Contemporary Sri Lanka: The Idea and Practice," in Somaratna Balasooriya et al., eds. *Buddhist Studies in Honour of Walpola Rahula.* London: Gordon Fraser, 1980, p. 139-153.

Marglin, Frederique Apffel with Purna Chandra Mishra, "Sacred Groves: Regenerating the Body, the Land, the Community," in Wolfgang Sacks, ed., *Global Ecology: A New Arena of Political Conflict.* London: Zed Books, 1993.

Martin, John H. "Coding and Processing of Sensory Information," Ch. 23, in Frank B. Salisbury and Cleon W. Ross, *Plant Physiology.* 4th ed., Belmont CA: Wadsworth Publishing Company, 1991.

Martin, John H. and Thomas M. Jessell, "Modality Coding in the Somatic Sensory System," Ch. 24, in Frank B. Salisbury and Cleon

W. Ross, *Plant Physiology.* 4th ed., Belmont CA: Wadsworth Publishing Company, 1991.

Meulenbeld, G. Jan. "The Constraints of Theory in the Evolution of Nosological Classifications: A Study on the Position of Blood in Indian Medicine (Āyurveda)," in G. Jan Meulenbeld, ed., *Medical Literature From India, Sri Lanka and Tibet.* Leiden: E. J. Brill, 1991, pp. 91-106.

Mishra, Anupam and Satyendra Tripathi. *The Chipko Movement.* New Delhi: People's Action/Gandhi Peace Foundation, 1978.

Mishra, Prafulla K., ed. *New Dimensions In The Atharvaveda (Prof. K. C. Acharya Commemoration Volume).* Delhi: Pratibha Prakashan, 2003.

Misra, Arunkumar. "Consciousness in Plants." *Indian Journal of History of Science* 9.2(November 1974):178-184.

Montgomery, Edward. "Systems and the Medical Practitioners of a Tamil Town," in Charles Leslie, ed., *Asian Medical Systems: A Comparative Study.* Berkeley: University of California Press, 1976. pp. 272-299.

The Mother. *Flowers and Their Messages.* 1973; 4th rev. ed., Pondicherry: Sri Aurobindo Ashram, 1992.

Mukherjee, Bharati. *Desirable Daughters.* New York: Theia, 2002.

Mukherjee, Bharati. *The Tree Bride.* New York: Hyperion, 2004.

Murthy, S. R. N. *Ancient Indian Theories of the Earth.* Pune: University of Poona, Centre of Advanced Study in Sanskrit, 1992.

Nagarajan, Vijaya. "Rituals of Embedded Ecologies: Drawing *Kōlams*, MarryingTrees, and Generating Auspiciousness," in Christopher Key Chapple and Mary Evelyn Tucker, eds., *Hinduism and Ecology: The Intersection of Earth, Sky, and Water.* Cambridge: Harvard University Press, 2000, pp. 453-468.

Nahar, Puran Chand and Krishnachandra Ghosh. *Jainism: Precepts and Practice.* 2 vols. Calcutta, 1917; rpt., Delhi: Caxton Publications, 1988.

Naravane, V. S. *Sages, Nymphs and Deities: Excursions in Indian Mythology.* Allahabad: private publication, V. S. Naravane, 1997.

Narayanan, Vasudha. "'One Tree Is Equal to Ten Sons:' Hindu Response to the Problems of Ecology, Population, and Consumption." *Journal of the American Academy of Religion* 65.2 (Summer 1997):291-332.

Nash, James A. *Loving Nature: Ecological Integrity and Christian Responsibility.* Nashville: Abingdon Press, 1991.

Nelson, Lance E. "The Dualism of Nondualism: Advaita Vedānta and the Irrelevance of Nature," in Lance E. Nelson, *Purifying the Earthly Body of God: Religion and Ecology in Hindu India.* Albany: State University of New York Press, 1998, pp. 61-88.

Nelson, Lance E., ed. *Purifying the Earthly Body of God: Religion and Ecology in Hindu India.* Albany: State University of New York Press, 1998.

Nelson, Lance E. "Reading the *Bhagavadgītā* from an Ecological Perspective," in Christopher Key Chapple and Mary Evelyn Tucker, eds. *Hinduism and Ecology, The Intersection of Earth, Sky and Water*. Cambridge: Harvard University Press, 2000, pp. 127-164.

Neufeldt, Ronald W. *Karma and Rebirth: Post-Classical Developments*. Albany: State University of New York Press, 1986.

Noggle, G. Ray and George J. Fritz. *Introductory Plant Physiology*. Englewood Cliffs, New Jersey: Prentice-Hall, Inc. 1976.

Obeyesekere, Gananath. "The Impact of Āyurvedic Ideas on the Culture and the Individual in Sri Lanka," in Charles Leslie, ed., *Asian Medical Systems: A Comparative Study.* Berkeley: University of California Press, 1976, pp. 201-226.

Oldenberg, Hermann. *The Religion of the Veda*. Trans. by Shridhar B. Shrotri. 1894; new ed., Delhi: Motilal Banarsidass, 1988.

Olivelle, Patrick. "From Feast to Fast: Food and the Indian Ascetic," in Julia Leslie, ed., *Rules and Remedies in Classical Indian Law*. Leiden: E. J. Brill, 1991, pp. 17-36. "Open to Plunder." *Down to Earth* 9.17 (January 31, 2001).

Pandey, Brahma Prakash. *Plants for Human Kind: Sacred Plants of India*. New Delhi: Shree Publishing House, 1989.

Parikh, Vastupal. *Jainism and the New Spirituality*. Toronto: Peace Publications, 2002.

Parkes, Graham. "Voices of Mountains, Trees, and Rivers: Kūkai, Dōgen, and a Deeper Ecology," in Mary Evelyn Tucker and Duncan Ryūken Williams, eds. *Buddhism and Ecology: The Interconnections of Dharma and Deeds*. Cambridge: Harvard University Press, 1997, pp. 111-128.

Parpola, Asko. *Deciphering the Indus Script*. Cambridge: Cambridge University Press, 1994.

Payulpitack, Suchira. "Social Impact of the Buddhadasa Movement: A Case Study," in *Buddhadasa's Movement: An Analysis of Its Origins, Development, and Social Impact*. Dissertation, Universitat Bielefeld, 1991, pp. 201-247.

Phra Prayudh Payutto. *Buddhadhamma: Natural Laws and Values for Life*. Trans. by Grant A. Olson. Albany: State University of New York Press, 1995.

Pickering, John. *The Authority of Experience: Essays on Buddhism and Psychology*. Surrey, UK: Curzon Press, 1997.

Pickering, John. "Selfhood is a Process," in John Pickering, ed., *The Authority of Experience: Essays on Buddhism and Psychology*. Surrey, UK: Curzon Press, 1997, pp. 149-169.

Pieris, Aloysius. "The Notions of Citta, Attā and Attabhāva in the Pāli Exegetical Writings," in Somaratna Balasooriya et al., eds. *Buddhist Studies in Honour of Walpola Rahula*. London: Gordon Fraser, 1980, pp. 213-222.

Pollan, Michael. "An Animal's Place," *New York Times*, November 10, 2002.

Prime, Ranchor. *Hinduism and Ecology: Seeds of Truth*. London: Cassell Publishers Ltd., 1992.

Prime, Ranchor. *Vedic Ecology: Practical Wisdom for Surviving the 21st Century*. Novato, CA: Mandala Publishing, 2002.

"**Protecting** the Pirates: Biopiracy and the WTO Dispute," (http://www.vshiva.net/biodiversity/pirate.htm).

Queen, Christopher S., ed. *Engaged Buddhism in the West*. Boston: Wisdom Publications, 2000.

Raj, Selva J. "Ammachi, the Mother of Compassion," in Karen Pechilis, ed., *The Graceful Guru: Hindu Female Gurus in India and the United States*. New York: Oxford University Press, 2004.

Rajan, S. Sundara. "Ancient Indian Approach Towards Plants."

The Quarterly Journal of the Mythic Society (Bangalore) 85.2(April-June 1994):80-87.

Randhawa, M. S. *The Cult of Trees and Tree-Worship in Buddhist-Hindu Sculpture*. New Delhi: All India Fine Arts & Crafts Society, 1964.

Rangan, Haripriya. *Of Myths and Movements: Rewriting Chipko into Himalayan History*. London: Verso, 2000.

Rao, K. L. Seshagiri. "The Five Great Elements *(Pañcamahābhūtas):* An Ecological Perspective," in Christopher Key Chapple and Mary Evelyn Tucker, eds., *Hinduism and Ecology: The Intersection of Earth, Sky, and Water.* Cambridge: Harvard University Press, 2000, pp. 23-38.

Rao, Vidyalankara Prof. S. K. Ramachandra. *Encyclopedia of Indian Medicine*. 3 vols. Bombay: Popular Prakashan, vol. 1 1985; vol. 2 1987; vol. 3 1987.

Reat, N. Ross. *Origins of Indian Psychology*. Berkeley: Asian Humanities Press, 1990.

Reichenbach, Bruce R. *The Law of Karma: A Philosophical Study*. Honolulu: University of Hawaii Press, 1990.

Rhys Davids, C. A. F. *Buddhist Psychology: An Inquiry into the Analysis and Theory of Mind in Pali Literature.* London: Luzac & Co., 1924.

Robbins, William. "Kansas Man Sows Seeds of Dream." *The New York Times*, Monday, October 17, 1988.

Rocher, Ludo. "Karma and Rebirth in the Dharmaśāstras," in Wendy Doniger O'Flaherty, ed., *Karma and Rebirth in Classical Indian Traditions*. Berkeley: University of California Press, 1980, pp. 61-89.

Rose, Deborah Lee, adap. *The People Who Hugged Trees*. Illus. Birgitta Suxauxflund. Lanham, MD: Roberts Rinehart Publications, 1990.

Ruegg, D. Seyfort. "Ahiṁsā and Vegetarianism in the History of Buddhism," in Somaratna Balasooriya et al., eds. *Buddhist Studies in Honour of Walpola Rahula*. London: Gordon Fraser, 1980, pp. 234-241.

Rukmani, T. S. "Literary Foundations for an Ecological Aesthetic: *Dharma*, Ayurveda, the Arts, and *Abhijñānaśākuntalam*," in Christopher Key Chapple and Mary Evelyn Tucker, eds. *Hinduism* *and Ecology: The Intersection of Earth, Sky, and Water.* Cambridge: Harvard University Press, 2000, pp. 101-125.

Ryan, P. D. *Buddhism and The Natural World: Towards a Meaningful Myth.* Birmingham: Windhorse Publications, 1998.

Sahu, Manaswi. *Dancing with a Dusty Angel.* Wichita: Trees for Life, 2000.

Salisbury, Frank B. and Cleon W. Ross, "The Power of Movement in Plants," in *Plant Physiology*, 4th ed. Belmont, CA: Wadsworth Publishing Company, 1991

Sandell, Klas, ed. *Buddhist Perspectives on the Ecocrisis.* Wheel Publication no. 346/348. Kandy: Buddhist Publication Society, 1987.

Santikaro Bhikkhu. "Buddhadasa Bhikkhu: Life and Society Through the Natural Eyes of Voidness," in Christopher S. Queen and Sallie B. King, *Engaged Buddhism: Buddhist Liberation Movements in Asia.* Albany: State University of New York Press, 1996, pp. 147-193.

Santikaro Bhikkhu, "The Four Noble Truths of Dhammic Socialism," in Jonathan Watts, Alan Senauke, Santikaro Bhikkhu, eds. *Entering the Realm of Reality: Towards Dhammic Societies.* Bangkok: Suksit Sian, 1997, pp. 89-159.

Schmidt, Hanns Peter. "The Origin of Ahiṁsā," in *Mélanges D'Indianisme à la Mémoire de Louis Renou.* Paris: Editions E. de Boccard, 1968, pp. 625-655.

Schmithausen, Lambert. *Buddhism and Nature.* Tokyo: The International Institute for Buddhist Studies, 1991.

Schmithausen, Lambert. "The Early Buddhist Tradition and Ecological Ethics." *Journal of Buddhist Ethics* (http://jbe.la.psu.edu/4schm1.html).

Schmithausen, Lambert. *Plants as Sentient Beings in Earliest Buddhism.* Australia: Australian National University, 1991.

Schmithausen, Lambert. *The Problem of the Sentience of Plants in Earliest Buddhism.* Tokyo: The International Institute for Buddhist Studies, 1991.

Sensarma, P. *Plants in the Indian Purāṇas: An Ethnobotanical Investigation.* Calcutta: Naya Prakash, 1989.

Seed, John, Joanna Macy, Pat Fleming, Arne Naess. *Thinking Like a Mountain.* Stony Creek, CT: New Society Publishers, 1988.

Seeing *the Way: Buddhist Reflections on the Spiritual Life, An Anthology of Teachings of English-Speaking Disciples of Ajahn Chah.* Hertfordshire, England: Amaravati Publications, 1989.

Shepard, Mark. *Gandhi Today: The Story of Mahatma Gandhi's Successors*. Arcata, CA: Simple Productions, 1987. Rpt; Washington, D. C.: Seven Locks Press, 1987.

Shilapi, Sadhvi. "The Environmental and Ecological Teachings of Tīrthaṅkara Mahāvīra," in Christopher Key Chapple, ed. *Jainism and Ecology: Nonviolence in the Web of Life*. Cambridge, MA: Center for the Study of World Religions, Harvard Divinity School, 2002, pp. 159-167.

Shiva, Vandana. *Biopiracy: The Plunder of Nature and Knowledge.* Cambridge, MA: South End Press, 1997.

Shiva, Vandana. "The Chipko Women's Concept of Freedom," in Maria Mies & Vandana Shiva, eds. *Ecofeminism.* London: Zed Books, 1993, pp. 246-250.

Shiva, Vandana. *Staying Alive: Women, Ecology and Development.* London: Zed Books, 1989.

Shiva, Vandana. *Stolen Harvest: The Hijacking of the Global Food Supply.* Cambridge, MA, South End Press, 2000.

Shiva, Vandana. *Tomorrow's Biodiversity*. New York: Thames & Hudson, Inc., 2000.

Shively, Donald H. "Buddhahood for the Nonsentient: A Theme in *Nō* Plays." *Harvard Journal of Asian Studies* 20.1-2 (June 1957):135-161.

Singer, Peter. *Animal Liberation*. 1975; 2nd ed., New York: Ecco, Harper Collins Publishers, Inc. 1990.

Singer, Peter. "Navigating the Ethics of Globalization." *Chronicle for Higher Education* October 11, 2002.

Singhvi, L. M. *The Jain Declaration on Nature.* London: The Jain Sacred Literature Trust, 1990; rpt. Christopher Key Chapple, ed., *Jainism and Ecology: Nonviolence in the Web of Life.* Cambridge, MA: Center for the Study of World Religions, Harvard Divinity School, 2002, pp. 217-224.

Sivaraksa, Acharn Sulak. "Buddhism and a Culture of Peace," in David W. Chappell, ed., *Buddhist Peacework: Creating Cultures of Peace*. Boston: Wisdom Publications, 1999, pp. 39-46.

Sivaraksa, Sulak. *Siam in Crisis*, 1980; rev. 2nd ed.; Bangkok: Thai Inter-Religious Commission for Development, 1990.
Sivaraksa, Sulak. *A Socially Engaged Buddhism*. Bangkok: Thai Inter-Religious Commission for Development, 1988.
Sivaramakrishnan, R. "Colonialism and Forestry in India: Imagining the Past in Present Politics," in *Comparative Studies in Society and History* 37.1(January 1995):3-40.
Smith, Brian K. *Classifying the Universe: The Ancient Indian* Varṇa *System and the Origins of Caste*. New York: Oxford University Press, 1994.
Sponsel, Lee and Poranee Natadecha-Sponsel, "Why a Tree is More Than a Tree: Reflections on the Spiritual Ecology of Sacred Trees in Thailand," in Sulak Sivaraksa, ed., *Santi Pracha Dhamma: Essays in Honor of the Late Puey Ungphakorn*. Bangkok: Santi Pracha Dhamma Institute, dist. Suksit Siam, 2001, pp. 364-373.
Sri Sri Mata Amritanandamayi Devi. *Man and Nature*. 1994; 2nd ed.; Amṛtapuri, P. O. Kollam dist., Keralam, India: Mata Amritanandamayi Mission Trust, 1996.
Steinbock, Bonnie. "Speciesism and the Idea of Equality." *Philosophy* 53.204 (April 1978):247-256.
Stone, Christopher D. "Should Trees Have Standing? Towards Legal Rights For Natural Objects." 1972; rpt. in Christopher D. Stone, *Should Trees Have Standing and Other Essays on Law, Morals and the Environment*. Dobbs Ferry, NY: Oceana Publications, 1996.
Strauss, Virginia, ed. *Buddhist Perspectives on the Earth Charter*. Boston Research Center for the 21st Century: November 1997.
Sullivan, Bruce M. "Paradise Polluted: Religious Dimensions of the Vrindāvana Ecology Movement," in Roger S. Gottlieb, ed., *This Sacred Earth: Religion, Nature, Environment*. New York: Routledge, 1996, pp. 565-571.
Swami Vijayeswarananda. *Karunasāgari: The Ocean of Compassion*. 2nd rev. ed. Penusilakshetram, Nellore Dt., Andhra Pradesh 524 414: Sri Matrudevi Viswashanti Ashram Trust, 1999.
Swearer, Donald K. "Buddhism and Ecology: Challenge and Promise." *Earth First*, 10.1(Fall 1998). Center for Respect of Life

and Environment (http://search.harvard.edu:8765/custom/query.html?qt=vrindavana+forest+revival+project&)

Swearer, Donald K., trans. "Dhammapitaka on Monks and the Forest," in Sulak Sivaraksa, ed., *Socially Engaged Buddhism for the New Millennium: Essays in Honor of the Ven. Phra Dhammapitaka (Bhikkhu P. A. Payutto) On his 60th Birthday Anniversary.* Bangkok: The Sathirakoses-Nagapradipa Foundation / distr., Suksit Siam, 1999, pp. 459-469.

Swearer, Donald K. "The Hermeneutics of Buddhist Ecology in Contemporary Thailand: Buddhadāsa and Dhammapiṭaka," in Mary Evelyn Tucker and Duncan Ryūken Williams, eds., *Buddhism and Ecology: The Interconnection of Dharma and Deeds.* Cambridge: Harvard University Press, 1997, pp. 21-44.

Swearer, Donald K. *Toward the Truth, by Buddhadāsa.* Philadelphia: The Westminster Press, 1971.

Tambiah, Stanley Jeyaraja. *The Buddhist Saints of the Forest and the Cult of Amulets: A Study in Charisma, Hagiography, Sectarianism, and Millennial Buddhism.* Cambridge: University Press, 1984.

Taylor, J. L. *Forest Monks and the Nation-State: An Anthropological and Historical Study in Northeastern Thailand.* Singapore: Institute of Southeast Asian Studies, 1993.

Taylor, Paul W. *Respect for Nature: A Theory of Environmental Ethics.* Princeton: University Press, 1986.

Titmuss, Christopher. *The Green Buddha.* Totnes, Devon: Insight Books, 1995.

Titze, Kurt. *Jainism: A Pictorial Guide to the Religion of Non-Violence.* Delhi: Motilal Banarsidass, 1998.

Tiwari, Shashi. "Element of Life-breath *(Prāṇa-tattva)* in the *Atharvaveda,*" in Prafulla K. Mishra, ed., *New Dimensions in the Atharvaveda.* Delhi: Pratibha Prakashan, 2003.

Tiyavanich, Kamala. *Forest Recollections: Wandering Monks in Twentieth-Century Thailand.* Honolulu: University of Hawai'i Press, 1997.

Tobias, Michael. *Life Force: The World of Jainism.* Fremont, CA: Jain Publishing Company, 1991.

Tompkins, Peter and Christopher Bird. *The Secret Life of Plants*. New York: Harper and Row, 1973.

Udomittipong, Pipob. "Thailand's Ecology Monks," in Stephanie Kaza and Kenneth Kraft, eds., *Dharma Rain: Sources of Buddhist Environmentalism*. Boston: Shambala, 2000, pp. 191-197.

Unno Taitetsu. "Personal Rights and Contemporary Buddhism," in Leroy S. Rouner, ed., *Human Rights and the World's Religions*. Notre Dame, Indiana: University of Notre Dame Press, 1988, pp. 129-147.

Vallely, Anne. "From Liberation to Ecology: Ethical Discourses Among Orthodox and Diaspora Jains," in Christopher Key Chapple, ed., *Jainism and Ecology: Nonviolence in the Web of Life*. Cambridge, MA: Center for the Study of World Religions, Harvard Divinity School, 2002, pp. 193-216.

VanDeVeer, Donald and Christine Pierce. *The Environmental Ethics and Policy Book: Philosophy, Ecology and Economics*. 3rd ed. Belmont, CA: Wadsworth/Thomson Learning, 2003.

Vannucci, M. *Ecological Readings in the Veda*. 1993; New Delhi: D. K. Printworld, 1994.

Vartan, Starre. "Half the World is Women: But Empowerment – and Environmental Progress – Are Lagging." *E—The Environmental Magazine* 15.5 (September/October 2004):36-39.

Vijay, ed. *Flowers – Their Spiritual Significance*. 1st ed., 1988; 4th impress, Pondicherry: Sri Aurobindo Society, 1998.

Waldau, Paul. *The Specter of Speciesism: Buddhist and Christian Views of Animals*. Oxford: Oxford University Press, 2002.

Watts, Jonathan, Alan Senauke, and Santikaro Bhikkhu, eds. *Entering the Realm of Reality: Towards Dhammic Societies*. Bangkok: Suksit Siam, 1997.

Wayman, Alex. "The Hindu-Buddhist Rite of Truth – An Interpretation," in Bhadriraj Krishnamurti, ed., *Studies in Indian Linguistics, Professor M. B. Emeneau Ṣāṣṭipūrti Volume*. Poona: Centre of Advanced Study in Linguistics, 1968.

Weber, Thomas. *Hugging the Trees: The Story of the Chipko Movement*. 1987; New Delhi: Penguin Books, 1989.

Wheeler, Sir Mortimer. *Civilizations of the Indus Valley and Beyond.* New York: McGraw-Hill Book Company, 1966.

Wilhelm, Friedrich. "Hunting and the Concept of Dharma," in Julia Leslie, ed., *Rules and Remedies in Classical Indian Law.* Leiden: E. J. Brill, 1991, pp. 7-16.

Wise, Steven M. *Drawing the Line: Science and the Case for Animal Rights.* Cambridge: Perseus Books, 2002.

Wise, Steven M. *Rattling the Cage: Toward Legal Rights for Animals.* Cambridge, MA: Perseus Books, 2000.

Yamada, Isshi. "Premises and Implications of Interdependence," in Somaratana Balasooriya et al., eds. *Buddhist Studies in Honour of Walpola Rahula.* London: Gordon Fraser, 1980, pp. 267-293.

Zimmerman, Francis. *The Jungle and the Aroma of Meats.* Editions du Seuil, 1982; rpt. Berkeley: University of California Press, 1987.

Zysk, Kenneth. *Asceticism and Healing in Ancient India: Medicine in the Buddhist Monastery.* New York: Oxford University Press, 1991.

Zysk, Kenneth G. *Religious Medicine: The History and Evolution of Indian Medicine.* American Philosophic Society, 1985; rpt. New Brunswick, NJ, and London: Transaction Publishers, 1993.

Interviews

June, phone interview, Auroville, taped February 16, 2004.

Kameshwar, phone interview, Karunamayi community, taped February 22, 2004.

Kumar, Satish, email correspondence, Resurgence, August 11, 2003.

Mathur, Balbir, personal interviews, Trees For Life, taped June 27-28, 2003

Mathur, Balbir, email correspondence, Trees For Life, April 28, 2005.

Narad, phone interview, Auroville, taped March 21, 2004.

Phra Paisal Visalo, email correspondence, southern Thailand, March 2, 2004.

Praveen, personal interview, Trees For Life, taped June 28, 2003.

Praveen, email correspondence, Trees For Life, July 2003.

Santikharo Bhikkhu, phone interview, Wat Suan Mokkh, taped on January 31, 2004.

Satish C., personal interview, Trees For Life, taped June 28, 2003.

Shyama and Satish B., phone interview, Karunamayi community, taped February 16, 2004.

Index

A

K

L

M

N

O

P

T

U

V

W

Y

Z

*Terms are often given in Sanskrit/Pali, followed by the meaning used most often in this text.

**Titles are often affixed at the beginning of the name.